EUROPE'S WONDERFUL LITTLE HOTELS AND INNS

GREAT BRITAIN & IRELAND

****

Dear Reader,

Your reports are vital to the well-being of the *Guide*. Please write to us whenever you have visited a hotel. Even the briefest of endorsements is useful, but lengthier reports are of greater value, as they enable us to add new life to the entries. You may use the report forms at the back of the book, though this is not essential. Each year 24 correspondents (12 per volume) are awarded a bottle of champagne, for the literary style or generous number of their reports, or both.

How to contact the *Guide*:
By mail: From anywhere in the UK write to: Freepost, PAM 2931, London W11 4BR (no stamp is needed)
From outside the UK: *The Good Hotel Guide*, 50 Addison Avenue, London W11 4QP, England
By telephone or fax: (020) 7602 4182
By email: Goodhotel@aol.com
Via our website: www.goodhotelguide.org

ADAM AND CAROLINE RAPHAEL

****

EUROPE'S WONDERFUL LITTLE HOTELS AND INNS

2002

GREAT BRITAIN & IRELAND

25TH ANNIVERSARY EDITION

Editors
Caroline Raphael and Desmond Balmer

Consulting Editor
Adam Raphael

Founding Editor
Hilary Rubinstein

Editor for Wales, Channel Isles, and Ireland
John Ardagh

Editor for Scotland
Sarah Mitchell

Shortlist Editor
Tamara Moluch

STEERFORTH PRESS
SOUTH ROYALTON, VERMONT

This edition was first published under the title
The Good Hotel Guide to Great Britain and Ireland 2002
in 2002 by Ebury Press, Random House,
20 Vauxhall Bridge Road, London SW1V 2SA.

ISSN 1537-582X
ISBN 1-58642-034-8

FIRST U.S. EDITION

PRINTED IN CANADA

Contents

A note for new readers

The best way to find a good hotel is by personal recommendation. This guide is just that. It has fairly been described as word-of-mouth in print. Every hotel has been recommended to us by correspondents who have spent at least one night there, and have taken the trouble to write to us about it. Our entries are updated each year, using fresh reports from readers. We depend on your generous support. We verify and collate the reports, making an anonymous overnight inspection where necessary, and select those hotels which we consider make the grade. Hotels are dropped if critical reports outweigh those in favour, or if we have had no reports for some time. They are also dropped following a change of ownership, unless we are sure that standards have been maintained.

The *Guide*, which is updated annually, is truly independent. Contributors are not paid for writing to us; hotels do not pay for their entry; the editors and their staff accept no free hospitality, and no payments from anyone.

There are two volumes of the *Guide* – this volume covers Britain and Ireland, and a volume covering Continental Europe will be published early in 2002. Both volumes include inns, guest houses and B&Bs that are of unusual character and quality, usually owner-managed. There are three types of entry. The full entries describe hotels that we feel confident about; italicised entries are provisional, due to mixed or ambivalent reports, inadequate information or lack of recent feedback. The Shortlist recommends hotels which, while we are unable positively to recommend them, help to plug gaps, particularly in cities; we must emphasise, however, that these are not necessarily true *Guide* entries, though some might eventually receive an italicised entry or a full entry.

We do not attempt to be comprehensive, because we feel that would involve lowering our standards. As a result, there are many blank areas on our maps. We are particularly glad to receive nominations for hotels in a city, a town or a region that is poorly represented. Most of our entries, especially in rural areas, are for small establishments (though never with fewer than three rooms) in the hands of resident owners. We don't object in principle to large hotels and those run by managers, but in our experience they often fail to provide the welcome and care for guests' comfort that can be found in the best of the small, individually owned hotels. And this is particularly evident in the case of hotels owned by a chain, which explains why there are so few chain hotels in these pages.

The entries in this book cover a wide range. People want different things from a hotel, depending on whether they are making a single-night stop or spending a holiday in one place, whether they have young children with them, whether they are visiting a city or staying in the remote countryside, and also on their age and means. Despite the *Guide*'s title, many establishments included in it are distinctly unhotel-like. Please read the entries carefully. You should not expect of a simple B&B or pub the same type of facilities that are offered by a larger, more expensive hotel, and when staying in a restaurant-with-rooms, you will not necessarily find lounges and gardens. We try to convey the flavour of each place, with a description that will help you to find somewhere that suits your tastes, needs and purse.

The book's aim is to reflect the discriminating taste of its readers. Both positive and negative reports are vital to us. Do please write – an entry is often dropped if we get no positive feedback. You may use one of the report forms at the back of the book, but this is not essential. Any scrap of paper will do, or a fax or email. We appreciate even the briefest endorsement or comment; but it is, of course, the stylish, witty, perceptive reports that help to give the *Guide* its special character. If an entry has misled you, please tell us, so that we can do better next time. We are always grateful, too, for suggestions as to how we can improve the *Guide*.

This is a thoroughly personal work. The *Guide* was started 25 years ago by Hilary Rubinstein because he wanted a book that would tell readers honestly what to expect when making a reservation. His definition of a good hotel is: 'Where the guest comes first.' Brochures help, but they are often deceptive. Travel agents can be useful if they specialise in a particular locality, but they often know only a fraction of the hotels on their books, and usually only recommend hotels which pay them commission.

Inevitably, the book is full of personal prejudices and preferences, including the editors'. We loathe big, anonymous hotels where we might as well be in Los Angeles or Lisbon as in London. We try to avoid boring establishments which lack individuality in their decor and warmth in their welcome. We care about good food, but dislike pretentious menus. We cherish the dedicated hotelier who has a vocation for his work. It is to such rare people that this guide is dedicated.

Introduction

'The perfect hotel may be an idyllic fantasy, but many of us go on looking for it year in and year out. This guide is to help those engaged on the quest.' The opening sentences of founding editor Hilary Rubinstein's introduction to the first edition of this work in 1978 captures the crusading spirit that has sustained it for a quarter of a century. This spirit is at the heart of a creative partnership between the *Guide* and its readers. The reports from regular correspondents who take the trouble to report on their experiences, good and bad, are crucial to our continuing success. With their help, the *Guide* has grown in 25 years from one slender volume containing around 300 hotels to the current two-volume, 1,600-hotel edition.

We are proud to be the longest-running British guide to hotels of character and quality, and truly independent. We do not accept free hospitality from the hotels listed here. Unlike many guides, we do not take payment from hotels for their entry. Our inspections are anonymous. You can therefore be certain that the judgments we make are impartial.

The magnificent seven

Only seven hotels, five in England, two in Ireland, have had an entry in every edition of the *Guide*. They are:

Rothay Manor, Ambleside
Lastingham Grange, Lastingham
The Connaught, London
Chewton Glen, New Milton
Sharrow Bay, Ullswater
Currarevagh House Oughterard
Ballymaloe House, Shanagarry

Five of the hotels are *César* winners. We are delighted to share our celebrations with them (see pages 555–7).

What has changed?

The prices quoted in the 1978 edition of the *Guide* belong to another age. At *Rothay Manor*, bed and (full Cumberland) breakfast cost just £11 – and that included morning and afternoon tea, and a newspaper. A five-course dinner with coffee came to £6.25. A 'pampered night' at *Sharrow Bay* cost £19.50 D,B&B. At *Chewton Glen*, B&B was £15.25; dinner cost from £5.

Guests' expectations have changed too: Robert Deville marked his 25th anniversary at *Heddon's Gate*, Heddon's Mouth (*qv*) in 1993 with an article for us recalling hotel life in the decade before the *Guide* was founded. The building cost him £12,500 in 1967. His first visitors, in 1968, received 'a warm reception and a jolly atmosphere but few creature comforts'. A gong at 7 pm summoned guests to 'a most spartan dining room' where they dined on 'soup, a roast with one vegetable, generally peas, cabbage or carrots, and about a pound of potatoes each, followed by fruit pie with custard and, because it was Devon, clotted cream'. The most popular wines were Sauternes, Mateus Rosé and Liebfraumilch. Up to 20 guests had the use of one WC and one bathroom, leading to what one loyal guest called 'the white-knee, sponge-bag, 7 am shuffle'. 1969 marked the installation of the first private bathroom, the last one was completed in 1982. The meals are more sophisticated now at *Heddon's Mouth*, but a gong still signals dinner at 8 pm. We reprint Mr Deville's article in full as an appendix this year, with a 21st-century postscript (see pages 551–4).

How do we define a good hotel?

Selecting a good hotel is an art, not a science. We do not take a clipboard on our inspections, to tick off details like trouser presses and 24-hour room service. We resist the notion that hotels should be given stars or a score. A regular reader put her finger on the elusive qualities that we seek when she wrote this year: 'Sometimes a hotel can apparently meet all needs, and be perfectly located, but we just don't want to revisit. Conversely, a hotel may not conform to spec, but we will go again because it was a delightful experience. This is usually due to the style of management or ownership. It boils down to feeling welcome.' We couldn't put it better.

The introduction 25 years ago sought to answer this question thus: 'If we were to put all the entries through a computer, the results would show the frequency with which certain words and phrases recur – words like "relaxed", "unstuffy", "personal"; phrases like "made to feel welcome", "treated as an individual".' These definitions still hold good. The 600-odd places listed here range from the grandest of country house hotels to the homeliest of guest houses, but the common factor is warmth of welcome and value for money. More often than not, the tone is set by a resident owner, but we do not rule out well-managed hotels in some of the smaller chains.

How do we choose the hotels?

One person's 'idyllic hotel' can be another's nightmare. Some readers love dining with strangers in house-party style; for others this is anathema. Some feel uncomfortable in the new breed of designer hotels, with Armani-dressed waiters and a laid-back style; others love the buzz. We try, with our descriptions, to convey the spirit of each place. The more voices we can bring to a report, the more balanced our entry will be. We do not hesitate to include negative comments, provided that they do not outweigh the enthusiastic ones; if there are too many criticisms, the hotel will be dropped. We also drop a hotel when the ownership or management changes, unless we have sufficient evidence that previous standards have been maintained. And we omit a hotel if, after several years, we have had no feedback from readers. This may seem unfair, and regular visitors are quick to complain; to which we say: 'Please keep the reports coming in.' This year, 99 hotels have been omitted, and there are 103 new entries.

Each entry is rewritten every year, using up-to-date reports from readers and inspectors. Every hotel is sent a questionnaire, and we ask it for brochures, tariffs, specimen menus, etc. These tell us about changes that may affect the way it is run: the departure of a manager, the arrival of a new chef, perhaps an increase in size. The pitch of the brochure, and the tone of the menu, carry a host of clues.

We have 25 years of records, but every year we start with an open mind. We are keen to find new hotels, especially in areas that are under-represented: For existing entries, we use reports from correspondents, regular and new, to update us on how a hotel has been caring for its guests. We have built up a close relationship with many readers, and our knowledge of their likes and dislikes helps us to make a balanced judgment. We are well aware that some would-be *Guide* hotels persuade departing guests to send us 'unsolicited' recommendations, but we are confident that we can recognise the collusive reports, while making the best use of genuinely fresh information.

When in doubt about an existing entry or the suitability of a new nomination, we ask an inspector to make an overnight visit. This is the only way you can discover details that a visit with a clipboard will never reveal: thin walls, noisy plumbing, the quality of breakfast, the comfort of beds, and so on. Our budget is limited but it goes far, thanks to a team of experienced inspectors who work not for a fee, but for the (sometimes doubtful) pleasure of the visit, the cost of which we reimburse.

Why do we focus so much on the meals?

One reader, who has bought every edition of the *Guide,* complains this year about our 'increasing tendency to emphasise the food in the hotels as against their bedrooms and other facilities'. While not denying the importance of the accommodation, public rooms, etc, we believe that food is a vital part of a hotel stay, and we therefore list a number of restaurants-with-rooms. We do not seek to be food critics but, by quoting from menus, we try to give some idea of what is to be expected.

A frequent complaint is of inflexibility at mealtimes. At one hotel, a reader with an upset stomach had only a starter of asparagus, while his colleague ate only a main course. Both were charged the full *table d'hôte* price of £27.50, though after protests this was reduced to £15. A mother visiting an expensive Cornish hotel was amazed to be charged the full *à la carte* rate of £33 for her 11-year-old daughter's food: a bowl of soup and a chocolate dessert on the first evening, a small plate of ravioli on the second. Not a way to encourage repeat business.

Another regular complaint is: 'Too much.' 'I felt guilty that I could never finish all the food,' one correspondent wrote. 'Asking for a small helping has little effect,' said another. 'We never travel without a copious supply of indigestion remedies.' Conversely, we get comments like: 'Stingy servings'; 'we disliked the portion control'. Too many hotels seem incapable of recognising that appetites vary. We like the sensible approach of *The Pier*, Harwich (*qv*), where many dishes can be ordered in a smaller or a larger portion, and you pay accordingly.

Why breakfast is the most important meal

Again we make no apologies for devoting space in our entries to how breakfast is served. It is a meal that many of us eat properly only when away from home. Last year we commented on how hotels, especially those which charge extra for the meal, let themselves down at breakfast. Peter Herbert, the owner of *Gravetye Manor*, East Grinstead (*qv*), responded: 'I endorse your thoughts on breakfast. We always have a manager on duty for that most important meal when both the client and the staff are at their worst.' Another hotelier told us he had to take a member of staff off breakfast because 'she was not a morning person'.

We are sometimes teased about our desire for freshly squeezed orange juice – but why not? It seems a minimum requirement when you are paying a decent amount for bed and breakfast. We like fresh bread, crisp, warm toast made from proper bread, with home-made preserves, and a wide selection of cereals, fruit and yogurt for those who can't face cooked dishes before noon. We loathe packaged butter, jams and marmalades. We expect hot food to be cooked to order, not left congealing on a hot-plate. We expect breakfast to be served in an environment free of piped music. When done well, it can be the highlight of a stay, and as it is the guest's final impression, it is worth the hotelier's while to get it right.

A dressing down for dressing up

We don't mind dressing up on occasion, and we expect people to be decently dressed at dinner, but we dislike a draconian dress code. One inspector wrote of the *Painswick Hotel*, Painswick, a *César*-winner this year: 'It was a pleasure to see plenty of young couples dining in casual wear, instead of ranks of old farts so often found in the heavier kind of country house establishment.' Even the august *Connaught,* London (*qv*), has relaxed its code to allow 'jeans and plimsolls' in reception, and 'smart casual' dress in its lounges during the day. But this year, we stayed at one holiday hotel that displays a huge notice at the entrance to its restaurant insisting that men wear a jacket and tie at dinner. An Italian, who turned up in his best open-necked designer outfit was forced to wear a tie supplied by the manager. He checked out next day. Hotels like this should move into the 21st century before they put off more guests.

Lost deposits can mean lost customers

The vexed question of deposits was raised again this year by several correspondents. We accept that consumers have responsibilities as well as rights, and we understand why many hoteliers ask for a guarantee of a booking: the cost of a lost night cannot be recouped if a guest fails to turn up. It's the random nature of these deposits that we find alarming. An inspector planning a trip to the West Country was asked for deposits of between £20 and £30 which were deducted from her credit card well in advance of the visit. She much preferred the approach of the hotel whose receptionist said: 'We never debit the card, and only ask for a number for security.' Another inspector was asked for a deposit of £220 by a hotel whose rate was over £400 a night. When she asked what would happen if, through fate, she was unable to honour the booking, she was told they would hold the money for a future visit or 'try to arrange something'.

Two expensive London hotels illustrate good practice and bad practice. One inspector received an emailed confirmation warning that the full cost of the booking would be taken from the credit card if it was cancelled within 48 hours of the visit. Fair enough, and rather better practice than that of the hotel that deducted the entire cost (£250) when a reader had to cancel through illness. It may have been within its rights but she will not go back. Remember to take out insurance if you have any doubts about whether you can honour a booking. Many hotels send a leaflet about this with their confirmation.

The neglect of tourism

Tourism continues to be shamefully neglected by this government. Five days after Mr Blair's second landslide election victory, we telephoned the Prime Minister's press office and asked who the new Minister of Tourism was. 'It has not yet been announced,' came the reply. We then asked which department the new minister would come under. There was an even longer pause to allow for consultation before the answer came back: the Department of Culture, Media and Sport. We rang DCMS, and were told that Kim Howells was our man. When we pointed out that it might be helpful if they told No 10 about the appointment, there was an embarrassed silence.

Tourism's lack of political clout, as evidenced by this sorry tale, is a disgrace. Here is an industry which has created 20% of all new jobs over the past decade and generated £500 billion in revenues. It employs more people than agriculture, coal mining, steel, car manufacturing, aircraft manufacture, food production and textiles put together. Yet it has been almost totally ignored by successive governments. Over the past 15 years, there have been at least a dozen junior tourism ministers, all with little influence and no power. In the 2001 parliament, tourism doesn't even rate a mention in the title of its sponsoring department, and whereas sports and arts have a minister of state, tourism gets a mere parliamentary secretary, the lowest form of ministerial life. Compare the support given to agriculture with that given to tourism. Farmers get subsidies of around £3 billion a year; the British Tourist Authority gets £36m. No wonder it took months before it dawned on anyone in Whitehall that terrible damage was being done to hotels by the foot-and-mouth epidemic. The failure of Britain's tourist industry to live up to its potential has already cost this country billions of pounds and many thousands of jobs. When will the government wake up?

And finally

We wish to thank our publisher and our editor at Ebury Press, Amelia Thorpe and Hannah MacDonald, for their support and encouragement. This year they have given us colour maps with a grid system, and also much better paper. A great beginning to the *Guide*'s next quarter-century.

ADAM AND CAROLINE RAPHAEL AND DESMOND BALMER
JULY 2001

The 2002 César awards

For the past 16 years, as a way of celebrating different kinds of excellence among hotels in England, Wales, Scotland and Ireland, we have given annual awards called *Césars*, named after the most celebrated of all hoteliers, César Ritz. Hotels of the grandest sort, like the finest restaurants, rarely lack public attention, but there are also many more modest establishments that are supremely good at what they do. Their owners are dedicated and often work round the clock. Their contribution to innkeeping deserves to be honoured along with that of the professionals at the top of the ladder.

This year, as before, we have awarded ten laurel wreaths to a mixed selection of establishments, each of which we think outstanding in its own class. Previous *César* winners, provided that they are still in the same hands and as good as ever, are indicated in the text by the symbol of a small laurel wreath.

AWARD — WINNER

London hotel of the year

Hazlitt's
London

Peter McKay's quirky little Soho hotel has had a *Guide* entry for many years. Its charming decor, helpful staff and good breakfasts have brought it a well-deserved *César* this year.

Traditional hotel of the year

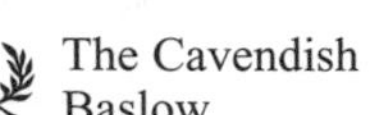

Like the *Guide*, Eric Marsh is celebrating a quarter-century this year. But he has moved with the times, at this former inn on the edge of the Chatsworth estate, and his new restaurant, with its informal style, has won much praise.

Country house hotel of the year

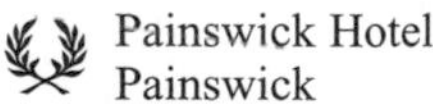

Helen and Gareth Pugh run the *Painswick Hotel* without stuffy rules (no dress code). They welcome all comers, including children, providing a delightful decor and excellent food of an unpretentious nature.

Yorkshire hotel of the year

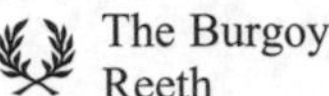
The Burgoyne
Reeth

The combination of the Dales setting, the impeccable bedrooms, the excellent food and happy atmosphere, make Derek Hickson and Peter Carwardine's small hotel one of our most praised Yorkshire entries.

Scottish B&B of the year

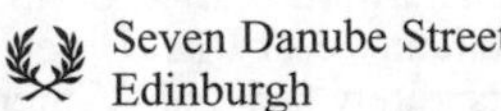
Seven Danube Street
Edinburgh

There are many appealing B&Bs in lovely Edinburgh New Town houses, but Fiona and Colin Mitchell-Rose and their pug, George, have received the warmest praise from *Guide* readers this year for their hospitality and good breakfasts.

Irish inn of the year

Buggys Glencairn Inn
Glencairn

Ken and Kathleen Buggy's old inn, with its quirky decor, good meals, comfortable bedrooms and relaxed style, drew high praise from visitors and an inspector this year.

Welsh country house of the year

Llanwenarth House
Abergavenny

Bruce and Amanda Weatherill welcome guests to their home in the Brecon Beacons National Park as if they were private visitors. *Llanwenarth House*'s country atmosphere, good food and informal style are all greatly admired.

Restaurant-with-rooms of the year

Little Barwick House
Barwick

Emma and Tim Ford have been at *Little Barwick House* for just two years but their restaurant-with-rooms, with its excellent cooking and relaxed style, has attracted more praise this year than any other entry in the *Guide*.

Designer hotel of the year

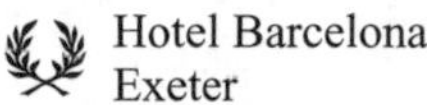

Hotel Barcelona
Exeter

Nigel Chapman and Nicholas Dickinson have succeeded resoundingly with their family-friendly hotels. Now they have opened two designer hotels, one in Cheltenham and this one in Exeter. *The Barcelona*, with its brilliant decor, is a welcome addition to the West Country hotel scene.

Utterly enjoyable mild eccentricity

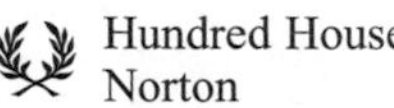

Hundred House
Norton

No other *Guide* hotel has swings in its bedrooms and patchwork on its staircase. The exotic decor, combined with the welcoming style of the Phillips family, makes *Hundred House* an eminently suitable winner of the most covetable of the *César* awards.

Special hotels

An at-a-glance guide to choosing a hotel

CITY HOTELS
Old-fashioned luxury

England
Bath Priory, Bath
Queensberry, Bath
Royal Crescent, Bath
Chester Grosvenor, Chester
Cadogan, London
Capital, London
Connaught, London
Dukes, London
Goring, London
22 Jermyn Street, London

Scotland
One Devonshire Gardens, Glasgow

CITY HOTELS
With designer style

England
Du Vin, Birmingham
Du Vin, Bristol
Kandinsky, Cheltenham
Hotel Barcelona, Exeter
42 The Calls, Leeds
Malmaison, Leeds
One Aldwych, London
Eleven Didsbury Park, Manchester
Malmaison, Newcastle-upon-Tyne
Lace Market, Nottingham
Old Bank, Oxford
Du Vin, Tunbridge Wells
Du Vin, Winchester

Scotland
Malmaison, Glasgow

Ireland
McCausland, Belfast

TOWN AND CITY HOTELS
Value for money

England
Homelands, Barnard Castle
Bridge House, Beaminster
On the Park, Cheltenham
Casterbridge, Dorchester
Evesham, Evesham
Haley's, Leeds
D'Isney Place, Lincoln
Portobello, London
Burgoyne, Reeth
Jeake's House, Rye
George, Stamford
Caterham House, Stratford-upon-Avon
Castle, Taunton
Wykeham Arms, Winchester
Mount Royale, York

Scotland
Clifton, Nairn

Ireland
Ash-Rowan, Belfast
Quay House, Clifden
Belcamp Hutchinson, Dublin
Simmonstown House, Dublin
Norman Villa, Galway

HOTELS WITH RURAL CHARM
Luxury

England
Farlam Hall, Brampton
Gidleigh Park, Chagford
Gravetye Manor, East Grinstead
Summer Lodge, Evershot
Manoir aux Quat'Saisons, Great Milton
Congham Hall, Grimston
Hambleton Hall, Hambleton
Chewton Glen, New Milton
Sharrow Bay, Ullswater

Scotland
Arisaig House, Arisaig
Glenapp Castle, Ballantrae
Kinnaird, Dunkeld
Inverlochy Castle, Fort William

Wales
Bodysgallen Hall, Llandudno

Channel Islands
Château La Chaire, Rozel Bay
Longueville Manor, St Saviour

Ireland
Marlfield House, Gorey
Park, Kenmare

HOTELS WITH RURAL CHARM
Medium price

England
Rothay Manor, Ambleside
Amerdale House, Arncliffe
Callow Hall, Ashbourne
Little Barwick House, Barwick
Lindeth Fell, Bowness-on-Windermere
Frogg Manor, Broxton
Aynsome Manor, Cartmel
Uplands, Cartmel
Castleman, Chettle
Tor Cottage, Chillaton
Ashwick House, Dulverton
Bel Alp House, Haytor
At the Sign of the Angel, Lacock
Langar Hall, Langar
Bindon Country House, Langford Budville
Lewtrenchard Manor, Lewdown
Lea Hill, Membury
Beetle and Wedge, Moulsford-on-Thames
Ees Wyke, Near Sawrey
Stone House, Rushlake Green
Innsacre Farmhouse, Shipton Gorge
Plumber Manor, Sturminster Newton
Priory, Wareham
Gilpin Lodge, Windermere

Scotland
Monachyle Mhor, Balquhidder
Dunain Park, Inverness

Wales
Ynyshir Hall, Eglwysfach
Tyddyn Llan, Llandrillo
Portmeirion, Portmeirion
Maes-y-Neuadd, Talsarnau

Ireland
Temple Country House, Ballymote
Cromleach Lodge, Castlebaldwin
Hilton Park, Clones
Assolas, Kanturk
Currarevagh House, Oughterard
Coopershill, Riverstown
Ballymaloe House, Shanagarry

HOTELS WITH RURAL CHARM
Simple style

England
Frog Street Farm, Beercrocombe
Blackmore Farm, Cannington
Nobody Inn, Doddiscombsleigh
Bolebroke Mill, Hartfield
Hill Top Farmhouse, Haworth
Oak Tree Farm, Hopwas
Mizzards Farm, Rogate
Innsacre Farmhouse, Shipton Gorge
Howtown, Ullswater

Scotland
Sheiling, Ullapool

Ireland
Kylenoe, Ballinderry

HOTELS BY THE SEA
Luxury

England
Burgh Island, Bigbury-on-Sea
St Martin's on the Isle, St Martin's
Island, Tresco

HOTELS BY THE SEA
Medium price or simple

England
Henley, Bigbury-on-Sea
Treglos, Constantine Bay
Crantock Bay, Crantock
Tregildry, Gillan
Port Gaverne, Port Isaac
Garrack, St Ives
Talland Bay, Talland-by-Looe
Trebrea Lodge, Tintagel
Nare, Veryan

Scotland
Balcary Bay, Auchencairn

Wales
Porth Tocyn, Abersoch
Druidstone, Broadhaven

Channel Islands
White House, Herm

Ireland
Zetland House, Cashel Bay
Rosturk Woods, Mulranny

WALKING AND MOUNTAIN HOTELS

England
Seatoller, Borrowdale
Mill, Mungrisdale
Hazel Bank, Rosthwaite
Wasdale Head, Wasdale Head

Scotland
Summer Isles, Achiltibuie

Wales
Pen-y-Gwryd, Nantgwynant

HOTELS WITH GOOD SPA OR LEISURE FACILITIES

England
Hartwell House, Aylesbury
Bath Priory, Bath
Budock Vean, Budock Vean
Highbullen, Chittlehamholt
Wallett's Court, Dover
Penmere Manor, Falmouth
Moonfleet Manor, Fleet
One Aldwych, London
Chewton Glen, New Milton
Garrack, St Ives
Vineyard, Stockcross
Cliveden, Taplow
Bishopstrow House, Warminster
Holbeck Ghyll, Windermere
Middlethorpe Hall, York

Scotland
Kinloch House, Blairgowrie
Isle of Eriska, Eriska

Wales
Bodysgallen Hall, Llandudno

Ireland
Dunraven Arms, Adare
Sheen Falls Lodge, Kenmare
Temple House, Moate
Rathmullan House, Rathmullan
Mount Juliet, Thomastown

HOTELS WITH FISHING

England
Callow Hall, Ashbourne
Holne Chase, Ashburton
Highbullen, Chittlehamholt
Combe House, Gittisham
Arundell Arms, Lifton
Prince Hall, Two Bridges

Scotland
Kinnaird, Dunkeld
Forss House, Forss
Taychreggan, Kilchrenan
Sheiling, Ullapool

Wales
Tyddyn Llan, Llandrillo
Lake, Llangammarch Wells
Llangoed Hall, Llyswen

Ireland
Caragh Lodge, Caragh Lake
Enniscoe House, Crossmolina
Sheen Falls Lodge, Kenmare
Delphi Lodge, Leenane
Newport House, Newport
Currarevagh House, Oughterard

HOTELS FOR GOLFERS

England

Budock Vean, Budock Vean
Highbullen, Chittlehamholt
Lea Hill, Membury
Chewton Glen, New Milton
New Hall, Sutton Coldfield

Scotland

Greywalls, Gullane

Wales

Lake, Llangammarch Wells

Channel Islands

Atlantic, St Brelade

Ireland

Beaufort House, Beaufort
Hilton Park, Clones
Enniscoe House, Crossmolina
Currarevagh House, Oughterard
Mount Juliet, Thomastown

HOTELS WITH TENNIS (T) AND/OR SWIMMING (S)

England

Regent, Ambleside (S)
Eagle House, Bathford (T)
Lodge, Bathford (S)
Burgh Island, Bigbury-on-Sea (T,S)
Mallory Court, Bishop's Tachbrook (T,S)
Blakeney, Blakeney (S)
Lindeth Fell, Bowness-on-Windermere (T)
Woolley Grange, Bradford-on-Avon (T,S)
Frogg Manor, Broxton (T)
Budock Vean, Budock Vean (T,S)
Ravenwood Hall, Bury St Edmunds (T,S)
Brockencote Hall, Chaddesley Corbett (T)
Gidleigh Park, Chagford (T)
Tor Cottage, Chillaton (S)
Highbullen, Chittlehamholt (T,S)
Treglos, Constantine Bay (S)
Corse Lawn House, Corse Lawn (T,S)
Cloth Hall Oast Cranbrook (S)
Delbury Hall, Diddlebury (T)
Summer Lodge, Evershot (T,S)
Evesham, Evesham (S)
Moonfleet Manor, Fleet (T,S)
Fowey Hall, Fowey (S)
Manoir aux Quat'Saisons, Great Milton (T)
Congham Hall, Grimston (T,S)
Hambleton Hall, Hambleton (T,S)
Mill at Harvington, Harvington (T,S)
Hassop Hall, Hassop (T)
Homewood Park, Hinton Charterhouse (T,S)
Combe House, Holford (T,S)
Oak Tree Farm, Hopwas (S)
Hunstrete, Hunstrete (S)
Bindon Country House, Langford Budville (T,S)
Mizzards Farm, Rogate (S)
Boscundle Manor, St Austell (S)
Nanscawen House, St Blazey (S)
Ennys, St Hilary (T,S)
St Martin's on the Isle, St Martin's (S)
Star Castle, St Mary's (S)
Priory Bay, Seaview (T,S)
Charlton House, Shepton Mallet (T)
Soar Mill Cove, Soar Mill Cove (T)
Gabriel Court, Stoke Gabriel (T,S)
Plumber Manor, Sturminster Newton (T)
New Hall, Sutton Coldfield (T)
Hermitage, Swinburne (T)
Talland Bay, Talland-by-Looe (S)
Calcot Manor, Tetbury (T,S)
Island, Tresco (T,S)
Nare, Veryan (T,S)
Watersmeet, Woolacombe (T,S)
Mount Royale, York (S)

Scotland
Old Mansion House, Auchterhouse (T,S)
Todhall House, Dairsie (S)
Mackeanston House, Doune (T)
Kinnaird, Dunkeld (T)
Isle of Eriska, Eriska (T)
Inverlochy Castle, Fort William (T)
Greywalls, Gullane (T)
Dunain Park, Inverness (S)
Ardanaiseig, Kilchrenan (T)
Skirling House, Skirling (T)
Baile-na-Cille, Timsgarry (T)

Wales
Porth Tocyn, Abersoch (T,S)
Penpont, Brecon (T)
Bodysgallen Hall, Llandudno (S,T)
Lake, Llangammarch Wells (T)
Llangoed Hall, Llyswen (T)
Portmeirion, Portmeirion (T,S)
Conrah Country House, Rhydgaled (S)

Channel Islands
White House, Herm (T,S)
Atlantic, St Brelade (T,S)
Longueville Manor, St Saviour (T,S)

Ireland
Dunraven Arms, Adare (S)
Caragh Lodge, Caragh Lake (T)
Zetland House, Cashel Bay (T)
Rock Glen, Clifden (T)
Beech Hill House, Derry (T)
Castle Leslie, Glaslough (T)
Glin Castle, Glin (T)
Marlfield House, Gorey (T)
Assolas Country House, Kanturk (T)
Park Kenmare, Kenmare (T)
Sheen Falls Lodge, Kenmare (T)
Glenview House, Midleton (T)
Rosturk Woods, Mulranny
Rathmullan House, Rathmullan
Tinakilly House, Rathnew (T)
Coopershill, Riverstown (T)
Ballymaloe House, Shanagarry (T,S)
Mount Juliet, Thomastown (T)

HOTELS WITH FRIENDLY INFORMALITY (Run like a private house)

England
Frog Street Farm, Beercrocombe
Chilvester Hill House, Calne
Coach House at Crookham, Crookham
Nonsuch House, Dartmouth
Delbury Hall, Diddlebury
Old Rectory, Hopesay
Grey Cottage, Leonard Stanley
Hazelwood House, Loddiswell
Stone House, Rushlake Green
Strattons, Swaffham

Scotland
Todhall House, Dairsie
Apple Lodge, Lochranza
Viewfield House, Portree
Skirling House, Skirling
Talisker House, Talisker

Wales
Old Rectory, Bettws Gwerfyl Goch
Tŷ Isaf, Llanfachreth
Old Rectory, Llansanffraid Glan Conwy

Ireland
Kylenoe, Ballinderry
Temple House, Ballymote
Hilton Park, Clones
Castle Leslie, Glaslough
Cullintra House, Inistioge
Delphi Lodge, Leenane
Roundwood House, Mountrath
Coopershill, Riverstown

HOTELS THAT WELCOME CHILDREN

England
Rothay Manor, Ambleside
Cavendish, Baslow
Harington's, Bath
Royal Crescent, Bath
Eagle House, Bathford

Blakeney, Blakeney
Woolley Grange, Bradford-on-Avon
Old Rectory, Campsea Ashe
Gidleigh Park, Chagford
Corse Lawn, Corse Lawn
Evesham, Evesham
Moonfleet Manor, Fleet
Fowey Hall, Fowey
Manoir aux Quat'Saisons, Great Milton
Hambleton Hall, Hambleton
Holdsworth House, Halifax
Homewood Park, Hinton Charterhouse
Bindon Country House, Langford Budville
Great House, Lavenham
42 The Calls, Leeds
Arundell Arms, Lifton
Holdfast Cottage, Little Malvern
Hazelwood House, Loddiswell
Basil Street, London
Connaught, London
22 Jermyn Street, London
Meudon, Mawnan Smith
Beetle and Wedge, Moulsford-on-Thames
Mill, Mungrisdale
Bank House, Oakamoor
Pen-y-Dyffryn, Rhydycroesau
St Enodoc, Rock
Seaview, Seaview
Charlton House, Shepton Mallett
Soar Mill Cove, Soar Mill Cove
Cliveden, Taplow
Calcot Manor, Tetbury
Island, Tresco
Nare, Veryan
Watersmeet, Woolacombe

Scotland

Old Mansion House, Auchterhouse
Darroch Learg, Ballater
Kirkton House, Cardross
Enmore, Dunoon
Forss House, Forss
Inverlochy Castle, Fort William
Duisdale, Isle Ornsay
Tigh an Eilean, Shieldaig
Old Pines, Spean Bridge
Baile-na-Cille, Timsgarry

Wales

Porth Tocyn, Abersoch
Garthmyl Hall, Garthmyl
Cawdor Arms, Llandeilo
St Tudno, Llandudno
Egerton Grey, Porthkerry

Channel Islands

St Brelade's Bay, St Brelade

Ireland

Hilton Park, Clones
Sheen Falls Lodge, Kenmare
Roundwood House, Mountrath
Coopershill, Riverstown
Ballymaloe House, Shanagarry
Inch House, Thurles

HOTELS THAT WELCOME DOGS

England

Holne Chase, Ashburton
Lodge, Bathford
Bibury Court, Bibury
Halmpstone Manor, Bishop's Tawton
Blakeney, Blakeney
Bracken House, Bratton Fleming
Ravenwood Hall, Bury St Edmunds
Coach House at Crookham, Crookham
Ashelford, East Down
Glewstone Court, Glewstone
Holdsworth House, Halifax
Northleigh House, Hatton
Heddon's Gate, Heddon's Mouth
22 Jermyn Street, London
Cottage in the Wood, Malvern Wells
Morston Hall, Morston
Mill, Mungrisdale
Hall, Newton-le-Willows
Beechwood, North Walsham
Port Gaverne, Port Isaac
Arkleside, Reeth

Pen-y-Dyffryn, Rhydycroesau
Boar's Head, Ripley
Innsacre, Shipton Gorge
Swan, Southwold
Strattons, Swaffham
Cliveden, Taplow
Prince Hall, Two Bridges
Inn at Whitewell, Whitewell

Scotland
Auchendean Lodge, Dulnain Bridge
Enmore, Dunoon
Ednam House, Kelso
Beechwood House, Moffat
Maridon House, Oban
Tigh an Eilean, Shieldaig
Creagan House, Strathyre
Baile-na-Cille, Timsgarry

Wales
Bear, Crickhowell
Cawdor Arms, Llandeilo
Lake, Llangammarch Wells

HOTELS FOR GOURMETS

England
Fischer's Baslow Hall, Baslow
Lettonie, Bath
Mallory Court, Bishop's Tachbrook
Waterside Inn, Bray
Gidleigh Park, Chagford
Gravetye Manor, East Grinstead
Michael's Nook, Grasmere
White Moss House, Grasmere
Manoir aux Quat'Saisons, Great Milton
Hambleton Hall, Hambleton
Northcote Manor, Langho
Capital, London
Mr Underhill's, Ludlow
Morston Hall, Morston
Beetle and Wedge, Moulsford-on-Thames
Chewton Glen, New Milton
Seafood Restaurant, Padstow
Yorke Arms, Ramsgill-in-Nidderdale
Sandgate, Sandgate
Charlton House, Shepton Mallet
McCoy's, Staddlebridge
Plumber Manor, Sturminster Newton
Castle, Taunton
Howard's House, Teffont Evias
Sharrow Bay, Ullswater
Old Beams, Waterhouses
White House, Williton
Winteringham Fields, Winteringham

Scotland
Summer Isles, Achiltibuie
Three Chimneys, Colbost
Inverlochy Castle, Fort William
Cross, Kingussie
Airds, Port Appin
Altnaharrie, Ullapool

Wales
Old Rectory, Llansanffraid Glan Conwy
Carlton House, Llanwrtyd Wells
Plas Bodegroes, Pwllheli

Channel Islands
Longueville Manor, St Saviour

Ireland
Marlfield House, Gorey
Park, Kenmare
Sheen Falls Lodge, Kenmare
Rathmullan House, Rathmullan
Ballymaloe House, Shanagarry

HOTELS WITH FACILITIES FOR ♿

England
Rothay Manor, Ambleside
Hartwell House, Aylesbury
Mallory Court, Bishop's Tachbrook
Leathes Head, Borrowdale
Millstream, Bosham
Lindeth Fell, Bowness-on-Windermere
Bracken House, Bratton Fleming
Blackmore Farm, Cannington
Brockencote Hall, Chaddesley Corbett
Coach House at Crookham, Crookham

Evesham Hotel, Evesham
Holdsworth House, Halifax
Northcote Manor, Langho
42 The Calls, Leeds
Malmaison, Leeds
Cadogan, London
One Aldwych, London
Meudon, Mawnan Smith
Malmaison, Newcastle upon Tyne
Beeches, Norwich
Burgoyne, Reeth
Garrack, St Ives
Greenway, Shurdington
Stonor Arms, Stonor
New Hall, Sutton Coldfield
Leeming House, Watermillock
Grange, York

Scotland
Kirkton House, Cardross
Forss House, Forss
Malmaison, Glasgow
Dunain Park, Inverness
Old Pines, Spean Bridge

Wales
Milebrook House, Knighton

Ireland
McCausland, Belfast
Seaview House, Ballylickey
Hibernian, Dublin
Sheen Falls Lodge, Kenmare
Glenview House, Midleton
The Narrows, Portaferry
Rathmullan House, Rathmullan
Churchtown House, Rosslare

Hotels with facilities for weddings

A civil wedding licence is necessary for hotels in England and Wales. In Scotland and Ireland it is not necessary. Please see the end of Facilities for hotels where you can get married.

Hotels that offer a Christmas package

So many hotels now offer a Christmas package that we no longer have the space to list them here. When a hotel tells us that it offers a package, we give that information under Terms.

How we choose our hotels

We are often asked how we select our entries. A fair question, since the hotels included in the *Guide* cater for a wide range of ages, incomes, tastes and prejudices. Moreover, they have been nominated by a miscellaneous collection of individuals of varying tastes. Though we have records going back over 25 years, we do not know the quality of judgment of everyone who writes to us. How then can there be any coherent standard behind our choices?

There is no single standard. Our own tastes are eclectic, and the only thing which all these hotels have in common is that the editors would be happy to stay in them. Nevertheless, the process of selection is not arbitrary. Among the factors which assist us are the following:

• The consensus of recent reports on a hotel that already has an entry in the *Guide*, and the tone of the nominating letter in the case of a candidate for first-time selection. If someone whose judgment we know and trust tells us of an exciting find or that a particular hotel does not deserve its entry, he or she obviously carries more weight than a nominator or complainant out of the blue.
• The hotel's brochure. Its pitch will usually reveal the kind of custom it is hoping to attract, and its photographs or drawings, while no doubt always aiming to beguile, may tell us instantly that this one is not for us.
• Menus. Very instructive in subtle as well as in obvious ways.
• Hoteliers' responses to our questionnaire. We invite them to expand on their answers by telling us what sort of custom they hope to attract. Not all take the trouble to do so; those who do are very helpful.
• Whether and how a hotel features in other guides.
• Inspections. In cases of doubt (due to unconvincing or ambivalent reports or lack of feedback), we carry out an anonymous inspection. We have a limited inspection budget, but a number of long-time readers have generously volunteered to do unreimbursed inspections for us.

No hotel is considered unless the nominator or inspector has spent a night in one of its rooms and had the opportunity to assess the sorts of thing that a tour with a clipboard will not reveal: noisy plumbing; thin walls; whether breakfast is as good as dinner; how effective the bedside lighting is; how comfortable the beds are; intangibles of atmosphere.

Of course, such a system is open to error, but the fact that we get far more endorsements than blackballs encourages us to think that we are on the right lines. No guide can afford to inspect hotels with the frequency needed to guarantee total reliability. But we are convinced that the way we operate, by reader recommendation backed up by independent inspection, is not only the most honest, but also the most reliable, method of selecting exceptional hotels.

One of the occupational hazards of our trade is the collusive or inspired report. A common practice is for hotels to give departing guests a report form and invite them to send us an 'unsolicited' recommendation. Sometimes we receive a rash of fulsome reports on a particular establishment, all from people who have never written to us before. Some hotels photocopy our report forms, and, having prevailed on their guests to fill them in, post them to us in a batch. One hotel designed a special postcard for the purpose. Over the years, we have developed a sophisticated nose for this sort of try-on. So we would advise any hotel tempted to try it, not to waste their time or ours.

Hotels are dropped from the *Guide* when it is clear from our reports that there has been a fall in standards or – a tricky question this – when we feel that they are no longer offering value for money. We also omit a hotel after a change of ownership or management, if we do not have enough evidence that the new regime is maintaining previous standards. And hotels are dropped – sometimes unfairly – when we have had inadequate feedback. We are used to getting a spate of letters asking: Why on earth have you left out —?' If the case is well made, we reinstate the place in the next edition.

As we have said repeatedly over the years, we beg all those who find the *Guide* useful to make a habit of sending us reports after staying in a *Guide* hotel. We rely on the generosity and judgment of all our readers. So please do send us a few lines by post, fax or email, telling us about your likes and dislikes or even just saying we have got the place right (or wrong). Letters are the lifeblood of this guide. Who knows, you could even win one of the 24 bottles of champagne given annually to the writers of the best reports.

How to read the entries

Length Entries vary greatly. A long one does not necessarily imply an especially good hotel, nor a short one a marginal case. Sometimes it takes many words to convey a place's special flavour, and sometimes we quote an amusing report at length. City hotels usually get less space than country ones, because the surroundings matter less in a town, and because when a hotel is in a relatively remote area, we like to comment on the location.

Names At the end of each entry we give the names or initials of people who have nominated that hotel or endorsed its entry in an earlier edition of the *Guide*. We don't give the names of inspectors, of correspondents who wish to be anonymous, or of those who have written adverse reports, though these are just as important as the enthusiastic ones.

Maps and index Each entry is listed under the name of the town or village. If you remember a hotel's name but not its location, please consult the alphabetical list of hotels at the end of the book.

Facilities The factual material varies in length. Some hotels have many facilities, others few. Most hotel bedrooms nowadays have telephone, TV and an *en suite* bathroom; many have tea-making facilities. If any of these is vital to you, please discuss it with the hotel at the time of booking. A 'double room' may be double- or twin-bedded; you should mention which you prefer. If you have strong pro- or anti-duvet feelings, this should be discussed. We try to provide accurate information about opening times, but hotels, particularly small ones, sometimes close on the spur of the moment. And they don't always give us reliable information about which credit cards they take. Please check with the hotel if this is vital to you.

Italic entries These describe hotels which are worth considering but which we feel, for various reasons – inadequate information, lack of feedback, ambivalent reports – do not at present deserve a full entry.

Shortlist This is intended to plug gaps in the maps, particularly in large cities where we have few, or insufficient, entries. *We must emphasise that they do not necessarily meet our normal criteria.* We are grateful for comments on these hotels, and nominations for new hotels.

Traveller's tales These tales of disaster are for the amusement of our readers, and none relate to hotels currently in the *Guide*. They have *no connection* with the entry immediately above.

Symbols We do not provide a lot of information in hieroglyphic form. Days and months are abbreviated; 'B&B' means bed and breakfast, 'D,B&B' means dinner, bed and breakfast, and 'alc' is *à la carte.* A 'set meal' can be no-choice or *table d'hôte*. The 'full alc' price is the hotel's estimate per person for a three-course meal with a reasonably priced half bottle of wine, service and taxes; 'alc' indicates the price excluding wine. We say: 'Unsuitable for disabled', when a hotel tells us that, and we list under 'Special Hotels' places which claim to have full facilities for the disabled. But it is *vital* that you check details with the hotel. We have a 'New' label for hotels making their debut in the *Guide* or being readmitted after an absence, and a 'Budget' label for hotels which offer dinner, bed and breakfast at around £50 per person, or B&B for about £30 and dinner for about £20.

Vouchers These enable readers to obtain a discount at many *Guide* hotels. On the tear-out card in the centre of the book, you will find six vouchers which may be used at any hotel with ***V*** at the end of its entry. A voucher entitles you to a discount of 25 per cent of the normal price for bed and breakfast (or the price of a room if the hotel charges for breakfast separately). You can't use it if you are already on a bargain break or special deal, and you will be expected to pay the full price for all other services. The discount will apply whether you use the voucher for one night or for a longer visit, and it is for one room. You must produce two vouchers if you are booking two rooms. The vouchers remain valid till the publication of the 2003 edition in September 2002. *IMPORTANT: You MUST request a voucher booking at the time of reservation, and participating hotels may refuse a voucher reservation or accept the voucher for one night only if they expect to be fully booked at the normal room price at that time.*

Tariffs These can be complicated. Some hotels have a standard rate for all rooms, regardless of season and length of stay, but many operate a complex system depending on season, length of stay, what sort of facilities are offered, and whether the room is in single or double occupancy. And most British hotels offer a variety of breaks. When figures are given without mention of a single or a double room they indicate the range of tariffs per person; otherwise we give a room rate. The lowest price is what you pay for the simplest rooms, sharing a double, or out of season, or both; highest rates are for the 'best' rooms, and for high season if the hotel has one. Meal prices are per person. But inevitably, the tariffs quoted are not totally reliable. We ask hotels, when they complete our questionnaire in the spring of one year, to make an informed guess at their tariffs for the following year – not easy. Many hotels prefer to quote their current rates. Please *don't* rely on the figures printed. You should *always* check at the time of booking and not blame the hotel or the *Guide* if prices differ from those printed.

How to contact us:
By mail: From anywhere in the UK write to Freepost PAM 2931, London W11 4BR (no stamp is needed)
From outside the UK: Good Hotel Guide, 50 Addison Avenue, London W11 4QP, England
By telephone or fax: 020-7602 4182
By email: Goodhotel@aol.com

Special offers If you wish to spend two days or more at a hotel, it is worth asking about special offers. These can be amazing value, and may apply throughout the year. Many city hotels cater for business visitors during the week and offer much reduced weekend rates.

Location We try to give accurate information especially with out-of-the-way places. Please say if you find the directions inadequate.

As usual, we ask readers to tell us of any errors of omission or commission. The entries are written in good faith, but inevitably, after we have gone to press, some hotels close or change hands. We are hugely grateful to the readers who take the trouble to write to us, enabling the *Guide* to meet the needs of travellers as well as it can.

A partisan view of rival guides and hotel groups

This guide, unlike many of its competitors, takes no advertising, no hospitality and no payment of any kind. It pays the cost of all its inspections, always an anonymous overnight stay. Only by operating in this way can we preserve our reputation for independent judgment, built up over a quarter of a century.

In many bookshops and hotel bedrooms you will find lavishly illustrated publications masquerading as independent guides. Only when you read the small print do you find an acknowledgement that hotels pay 'a contribution' or 'a registration fee' to be included. The glossy Johansens guides, for example, charge hotels up to £2,500 for an entry. Not surprisingly, you will find not a word of criticism in these guides. He who pays the piper calls the tune and more often than not writes the words. The 'paid-for' guides are, in fact, little more than advertising sheets, but it is dismaying that few ordinary buyers, and even some specialist travel book shops, know the difference between a genuinely independent guide and one that is not.

We prize our own independence and that of the hotels we report on. Almost all the establishments in the *Guide* are independently owned and run. There are exceptions: some large hotels, and some in cities, are in the hands of managers. Some others, eg, the *César*-winning *Hotel Barcelona*, Exeter, belong to a small group.

Our experience is that chain hotels do not often provide the personal style that our readers seek, so they rarely qualify for these pages. But we do include three: *New Hall* (Thistle), Sutton Coldfield; *Shelley's* (Grace Hotels), Lewes; and *Leeming House* (Heritage Hotels), Watermillock.

Many *Guide* hotels belong to a consortium for marketing purposes. The most famous, and by far the most expensive, is Relais & Châteaux, French-owned but worldwide. It includes grand castles, lush country houses and gourmet restaurants, all privately owned. But so strong is the Relais brand image that they are sometimes mistaken for a chain. Some travellers in search of luxury use the Relais booklet extensively or exclusively. Others steer clear, not caring for the swank – and sometimes the snootiness – which they detect in these posh places. The Relais contingent in the UK are in general impressive, and more dependable in our view than their associates across the Channel and in the United States. But it is said that fewer British hotels are now joining, due to the high cost and the fact that it is regarded as something of an old boys' network, out of tune with the more flexible approach to food, children and dress codes of the younger hoteliers. Because the style is so distinctive, we always mention a hotel's membership in its *Guide* entry. We also mention hotels' membership of Pride of Britain, a small, upmarket, British consortium.

The worldwide Best Western group is an association of about 400 independent hotels, less homogeneous than that of the groups mentioned above. A few of its members are included in the *Guide*. The self-explanatory Relais du Silence, long established on the Continent, has some members in the UK, of which we include a few.

Many *Guide* readers choose to stay in guest houses and B&Bs operated in private homes, because they are more personal and, on the whole, much cheaper than hotels. They vary in sophistication. Some function alone, others belong to a group: a leading one is Wolsey Lodges, a non-profit-making consortium named after Henry VIII's cardinal who toured the country expecting to be entertained in style. Its members are defined as 'an Englishman's home where you are welcome to stay as a guest for a night or more'. It has more than 200 members in the UK, and a few on the Continent. They cater for travellers who enjoy socialising with their hosts and eating in dinner-party style with fellow guests. There are some splendid examples of the species in these pages. The Hidden Ireland association, which operates on the same principles, provides some of our most popular Irish entries.

The AA guide recommends hotels which pay a fee to be inspected. But, confusingly, it also includes paid advertisements from some of them. Its standards are not those prized in these pages: we once saw a TV programme in which an AA inspector berated a hotelier for not having 'captive coat hangers'. These are an abomination as far as many *Guide* readers are concerned: 'Do they think we are thieves?' one inspector wrote.

As usual, if a hotel or a restaurant-with-rooms has a *Michelin* star, or a *Bib Gourmand* (for a good meal at a moderate price), we mention this in the text. When we list an inn that also has an entry in our sibling publication, the *Good Pub Guide*, we mention that fact.

London

Hazlitt's, London

The disconcerting thing about hotels in London is how many belong to large groups. These are often faceless and anonymous (you might be in any city in the world); managers are frequently moved around, creating little sense of continuity, and ownership is subject to change. The 22 hotels featured in this chapter, we believe, combine character with consistent standards. Some are traditional but there are also several quirkier establishments offering something a little different from the norm. Our *César* goes to a charming B&B hotel, hidden away in the heart of Soho, whose youthful staff are informal but helpful. Prices in London can be alarming, and among the selection in our Shortlist at the back of the book are a few cheaper alternatives.

LONDON **Map 2:D4**

Basil Street Hotel
8 Basil Street
London SW3 1AH

Tel 020-7581 3311
Fax 020-7581 3693
Email info@thebasil.com
Website www.thebasil.com

'A delight,' say visitors this year, praising the 'undoubted quality of the management and staff' of this old-established hotel in Knightsbridge – the manager, Charles Lagares, and the head chef, Julio Fernandez, are both new this year. 'You can sit in the bar or lounges and pretend to be an old buffer. The dining room is candlelit, and cooking is classic English. Privacy is maintained. The atmosphere militates against the use of mobile phones. All very un-London, and none the worse for that.' Other comments: 'Cosy, ideally situated, good value.' 'The rooms are real, not a designer's concept of a hotel room. There are always familiar faces among the staff.' The public rooms have antiques, oriental rugs, mirrors and paintings. Traditional meals, served by formally dressed waiters, and accompanied at night by a pianist, include duck terrine with Cumberland sauce and Melba toast; grilled Dover sole; roast rack of lamb; desserts on a trolley. House wines are reasonably priced. Female guests have their own domain, the Parrot Club. At breakfast, you are waited on, and nothing is packaged. The bedrooms (not lavishly endowed with extras) vary greatly (some singles are very small), but many rooms are smoke-free, and refurbishment is ongoing. Some spacious doubles have antiques and a large bathroom; some baths are large, too. There are some two-bedroomed family suites (children are welcomed). Some rooms get noise from traffic, a nearby fire station or neighbouring bedrooms, but those overlooking a courtyard are quiet; many are double-glazed, and earplugs can be provided. (*Jonathan and Michelle Ray, MD*)

Open All year.
Rooms 5 family, 45 double, 30 single.
Facilities Lift. Lounge bar, ladies' club, dining room (pianist at night); function facilities. Only public areas accessible to ♿.
Location Central, near Knightsbridge. 2 parking spaces (book in advance); public car park nearby. (Underground: Knightsbridge)
Restrictions No smoking in 40 bedrooms. Dogs by arrangement; not in public rooms.
Credit cards Amex, MasterCard, Visa.
Terms (*Excluding VAT on accommodation*) Room: single from £141, double from £209, family from £286. Breakfast £10–£14.50. Set lunch £19, dinner £25; full alc £35. Extra bed for child: £20. Concessions to regular visitors; long-stay rates; special rates Aug, winter, bank holidays, Christmas, Easter, New Year.

The Cadogan
75 Sloane Street
London SW1X 9SG

Tel 020-7235 7141
Fax 020-7245 0994
Email info@cadogan.com
Website www.cadogan.com

Discretion is the order of the day at this Victorian building near Sloane Square. It could as easily be an embassy or a private club; a polite notice in the lobby requests that mobile phones be switched off, and the hotel's literature proclaims its historic association with Oscar Wilde and Lillie Langtry, without explaining the cause of either's notoriety in Victorian London. Langtry entertained the Prince of Wales in rooms that are now incorporated within the hotel; Wilde was arrested in room 118 in 1895, on a charge of homosexuality. The atmosphere is formal but friendly; it is a hideaway on the doorstep of some excellent shopping, equidistant from Peter Jones, Harvey Nichols and the Conran shop. The hotel is one of a small group of distinguished buildings owned by Historic House Hotels Ltd (see also *Hartwell House*, Aylesbury; *Middlethorpe Hall*, York; *Bodysgallen Hall*, Llandudno, Wales). It is luxurious in a traditional way, with panelled public rooms, Arts and Crafts wallpaper, antiques, lots of sofas and armchairs. Most bedrooms are air-conditioned; they have fine cotton sheets, floral fabrics, fresh flowers. Guests tell of being 'well looked after by the friendly staff'. The lounge is a popular place for tea. The Edwardian-style restaurant is run by Graham Thompson, who says he enjoys cooking offal but caters for conservative tastes with dishes like sauté of wild mushrooms with fried quail's eggs; fillet of brill with mustard lentils and crispy potatoes; apple tart with vanilla ice cream. Guests have access to the large gardens in Cadogan Place opposite, which many rooms overlook. A new manager, Milton Hussey, was due to arrive in summer 2001, so we'd like more reports, please.

Open All year. Restaurant closed Sat midday.
Rooms 4 suites, 54 double, 7 single. 1 adapted for ♿. All air-conditioned.
Facilities Lift, ramps. Drawing room, bar, restaurant; function facilities. No background music. Access to gardens opposite: tennis. Civil wedding licence.
Location Central (rear rooms quietest). Meter parking; NCP car park opposite. (Underground: Sloane Sq, Knightsbridge)
Restrictions No smoking in 16 bedrooms. Dogs by arrangement.
Credit cards Amex, MasterCard, Visa.
Terms (*Excluding VAT on accommodation*) Room: single/double £190, suite £270–£350. Breakfast: continental £12, English £16.50. Set lunch £18.90, dinner £27; full alc £49. Child in parents' room: under 5, free. Weekend rates. Theatre, Christmas packages.

The Capital
22 Basil Street
London SW3 1AT

Tel 020-7589 5171
Fax 020-7225 0011
Email reservations@capitalhotel.co.uk
Website www.capitalhotel.co.uk

This 'grand hotel in miniature', where 'a liveried footman greets guests, and an open fire burns in the front hall', stands in a busy little street near Harrods. The owner, David Levin, has presided for over 30 years; son Joseph is now managing director of the family company (it includes also two restaurants, and simpler *L'Hotel* (*qv*), almost next door). A main draw for many visitors to *The Capital* is its restaurant, awarded its second *Michelin* star this year for the classic French cooking of Eric Chavot. At dinner there is a five-course set meal at £60, or an *à la carte* menu with seven choices for each course: starters at £18 (eg, warm smoked haddock with aioli potatoes and deep-fried quail eggs), main courses at £22 (eg, roasted saddle of rabbit and sweet onion pastilla); desserts at £9 (eg, caramel and coffee melting pot with crunchy puffed wheat). The simpler lunch is thought good value (£26.50). Meals are served amid a Nina Campbell decor of chandeliers, mirrors, frosted-glass window panes, honey-coloured walls and tapestry chairs. There is a pale-panelled bar for drinks and after-dinner coffee. The bedrooms (many have recently been redecorated) are lavish, with heavy fabrics, original oil paintings, flowers, double glazing, a marble bathroom and 24-hour room service. The manager is Olivia Hetherington. More reports, please.

Open All year.
Rooms 8 suites, 28 double, 12 single.
Facilities Lift. Lounge, bar, restaurant; 2 private dining rooms, business facilities. No background music. Unsuitable for ♿.
Location Central (rooms double-glazed; rear ones quietest). Garage for 12 cars (£25 per night). (Underground: Knightsbridge)
Restriction Dogs at management's discretion; not in public rooms.
Credit cards All major cards accepted.
Terms [2001] (*Excluding VAT on accommodation, 'discretionary' 12½% service charge on meals*) Room: single £180–£196.23, double £190–£287.88, suite £440.62. Breakfast £12.50–£16.50. Set lunch £26.50, dinner £60; full alc £67. Weekend rates. Christmas package.

The Connaught
Carlos Place
London W1Y 6AL

Tel 020-7499 7070
Fax 020-7495 3262
Email info@the-connaught.co.uk
Website www.savoy-group.co.uk

Duncan Palmer, only the sixth general manager in the 104-year history of this red brick Victorian hotel (it is now owned by the Savoy Group), is presiding over a multi-million-pound makeover. In keeping with its 'discreet and attentive' style, regular visitors have been consulted by the designer, Nina Campbell, on the redecoration, and the style remains traditional, though the dress code has been relaxed. 'Jeans and plimsolls' are now allowed in the reception area, but men must wear jacket and tie in the restaurant at lunch, and after 6 pm in the public rooms. The drawing room is now a bar (wood-panelled, with butterscotch paint, antique wall lights), where lunches and afternoon teas are served. A light supper is available in the smaller lounge, dramatically redecorated in red. The bedrooms and suites, off a five-storey wood-panelled staircase under a cupola, remain traditional, with large damask armchairs, flower-patterned curtains, big antique mirrors, crisp sheets on a huge bed, a marble bathroom with a large bath and big cakes of soap. The affluent clientele includes foreign royalty, famous actors, international businessmen, drawn by the old-fashioned style and 'lack of snootiness – all the staff are friendly'. Children are welcomed. Michel Bourdin is to retire after presiding for 26 years over the *Michelin*-starred kitchen. His deputy, Jerome Ponchelle, who also has a classic French background, steps up in January 2002. Change is likely to be gradual in both the mahogany-panelled restaurant, grandly elegant (arched windows, a huge crystal chandelier), and the more intimate, green-walled Grill Room. Tail-coated waiters provide entertainment, as they wheel trolleys, carve meat, heat sauces over flames. From the huge breakfast menu you can order kedgeree, grilled chicken, and much more. A fitness studio in the attic is new, and guests may use the swimming pools of the sister hotels, *The Berkeley* and *The Savoy*. No grounds, but Mount Street Gardens, shaded by plane trees, are round the corner, and Hyde Park is near. Some traffic noise, but it dies down at night, and rooms are air-conditioned. One of the *Guide*'s original seven hotels. More reports, please.

Open All year.
Rooms 22 suites, 47 double, 23 single. All air-conditioned.
Facilities Lift. 2 lounges, bar, Grill Room, restaurant; private dining room, function/meeting rooms; fitness studio. Free use of health facilities at *The Berkeley*, *The Savoy*, *Claridge's*. No background music.
Location Central. NCP parking nearby. (Underground: Bond St, Green Pk)
Restriction No dogs.
Credit cards All major cards accepted.
Terms (*Excluding VAT on accommodation, 15% service charge on breakfast*) Room: single £280–£345, double £390–£425, suite £695–£1,670. Breakfast £16.50–£22.50. Set lunch £22.50–£33.50, dinner £58; full alc from £60. Luxury breaks. Christmas package.

Dukes Hotel NEW
St James's Place
London SW1A 1NY

Tel 020-7491 4840
Fax 020-7493 1264
Email enquiries@dukeshotel.com
Website www.dukeshotel.com

'An excellent hotel, calm, quiet, exclusive. Attentive service, not too frosty, but somehow rather special. Bedrooms quiet, though some a bit small. Public rooms quiet too. Breakfast first rate. An oasis in St James's.' 'The hidden-away lounge, with a small Zen-like garden, was a delight.' An old-established hotel, managed by Andrew Phillips, which stands behind a small courtyard in a side street, convenient for shops, palaces, parks, art galleries and theatres. The owner, David Naylor-Leyland, owns two other smart *Guide* hotels, *The Franklin*, and *Egerton House*. *Dukes* has a loyal American clientele. The bar is famous for its martinis. Staff includes butlers and valets. There is a health club with steam room, cardio-vascular exercise equipment, beauty treatments, etc. The bedrooms are traditional in decor, but with voicemail, two-line telephone, etc, for the business traveller. All suites have a south-facing drawing room; the penthouse suite has wide views to Buckingham Palace and the Houses of Parliament. Room-service meals are served from 7 am to 11 pm. We'd like reports on the restaurant, please. The chef, Steve Robinson, serves modern British dishes, eg, sea bass with a lime and ginger salt crust, egg noodles and red pepper; honey-roasted peppered duck with sarladaise potatoes and pak choi. Desserts include pear brûlée with pear sorbet; cherry and almond flan. (*Susan Hill, Robert Sandham*)

Open All year.
Rooms 7 suites, 55 double, 27 single. Air-conditioning.
Facilities Lift. Drawing room, bar, dining room, breakfast/private dining room; health club. No background music. Unsuitable for ♿. Civil wedding licence.

Location Central, in St James's. (Underground: Green Pk)
Restrictions No smoking in some bedrooms. No dogs.
Credit cards All major cards accepted.
Terms (*Excluding VAT*) Room: single from £195, double from £225, suite from £425. Breakfast from £11. Full alc £37. ***V***

Durrants
George Street
London W1H 5BJ

Tel 020-7935 8131
Fax 020-7487 3510
Email enquiries@durrantshotel.co.uk
Website www.durrantshotel.co.uk

One of London's oldest privately owned hotels, opened in 1790, and run by the Miller family since 1921. It is one of the select set that has featured in all 25 editions of the *Guide*. The Georgian facade unites the original four terraced houses: the legacy is 'a fascinating rabbit warren' of public rooms and bedrooms. Small panelled lounges with leather settees and chairs lead off a quaint, rambling corridor. Original paintings, prints and engravings of London hang above antique furniture. 'The polish on the brass is a wonder to behold, and there is not a finger mark on the sparkling glass panels in the doors,' says one visitor. Another thinks it 'remarkably well-staffed, reminiscent of another era'. The bedrooms are well maintained, but they vary greatly – some are small: the largest, at the front, get some traffic noise. At the back, 'you would not think you were in central London'. An American guest was pleased to find 'an efficient shower, for once'. Twenty rooms were refurbished this year, as well as the Spy Room where breakfast is served. A new head chef, Pascal Vallée, serves traditional English–French cuisine in the panelled restaurant. The short daily set menu might include cream of watercress soup with lemon and parsley croutons; steak-and-kidney pie; roast supreme of salmon. The long *carte* offers more ambitious dishes, eg, fillet of beef, cèpe and goat's cheese polenta with caramelised shallots; also grills. The barman is 'very helpful, providing sandwiches after theatre or for a late lunch'. Breakfast has 'decent marmalade and excellent smoked haddock'. Women travelling alone are welcomed, and so are children (high chairs, cots, babysitters, early suppers are available). *Durrants* has a 'wonderfully convenient location' behind Oxford Street. The Wallace Collection is opposite; the Wigmore Hall is close by. The family also own the *Red Lion,* Henley-on-Thames (*qv*). (*SH, and others*)

Open All year. Restaurant closed for dinner 25 Dec.
Rooms 4 family, 68 double, 16 single. 33 air-conditioned. 7 on ground floor.
Facilities 2 lifts. Lounges, bar, breakfast room, restaurant; function rooms. No background music.
Location Central (rear rooms quietest). Public car park 5 mins' walk. (Underground: Bond St, Baker St)
Restrictions No smoking in breakfast room. Guide dogs only.
Credit cards Amex, MasterCard, Visa.
Terms (*Excluding 12½% 'optional' service charge*) Room: single from £92.50, double from £145, suite from £285. Breakfast: continental £10.50, English £15.50. Set lunch/dinner £22; full alc £45.

Egerton House
17–19 Egerton Terrace
London SW3 2BX

Tel 020-7589 2412
Fax 020-7584 6540
Email bookings@egertonhousehotel.co.uk
Website www.egertonhousehotel.co.uk

A tall Victorian town house overlooking two tree-lined squares, in a quiet setting but close to Knightsbridge. It is owned by David Naylor-Leyland (see also *The Franklin* and *Dukes*). Its fans write warmly of the helpful staff and attractive decor: 'The chintzy style may seem dated compared with the new boutique hotels, but that makes it refreshingly different. Fabrics are of superior quality, antique furniture is real not repro, marble bathrooms are impressive.' Power showers, a two-line telephone with voicemail, and a modem link are among the modern attributes. The bedrooms vary in size; Room 25, which looks out to the mews behind Brompton Road, is small, with a tiny bathroom. An 'excellent breakfast' (fresh orange juice, good coffee, a variety of bread and rolls) is taken in the bedrooms, or in a pretty basement room. Afternoon tea is served in the drawing room, with its marble fireplace, stuccoed walls, oil paintings; there is a rather pricey' honesty bar. The room-service menu ranges from toasted sandwiches to a mixed grill. A newspaper is included in the rates (regular visitors' preferences are recorded on a database). A new manager, Christine Pimentel, arrived in spring 2001, so we'd like more reports, please.

Open All year.
Rooms 21 double, 8 single. All air-conditioned.
Facilities Lift. Drawing room, honesty bar, breakfast room; private dining room. No background music. 24-hour room service. Unsuitable for ♿.
Location Central. Valet parking. (Underground: Knightsbridge, South Kensington)
Restriction No dogs.
Credit cards All major cards accepted.
Terms [2001] (*Excluding VAT*) Room: single £115–£160, double £145–£250. Breakfast £10– £16. Full alc (room service) £30. Easter, Christmas, summer holiday rates.

The Franklin NEW
20 Egerton Gardens
London SW3 2DB

Tel 020-7584 5533
Fax 020-7584 5449
Email bookings@franklinhotel.co.uk
Website www.franklinhotel.co.uk

A large red brick building facing a leafy private garden where guests may sit on a bench and read, and which some bedrooms overlook through large bay windows. It is now a town house hotel, owned by David Naylor-Leyland (see also *Egerton House* and *Dukes*). The decor is in the style of a luxurious private house: antiques, oil paintings, ornaments, heavy curtains, open fires. But power showers are there, too, as well as business facilities (fax, etc) to keep the working traveller happy, and a computer room gives free Internet access. *The Franklin* has many devotees. 'We love it,' say one American couple who regularly stay for three weeks. 'The staff are so helpful; minor things go wrong, but they are so promptly and charmingly sorted out that we have become very fond of *The Franklin*.' Tea and snacks can be served in the drawing room, and there is an extensive room-service menu. The Knightsbridge shops are a short walk away.

Open All year.
Rooms 15 suites, 23 double, 9 single. Air-conditioning.
Facilities Lifts. Morning room, drawing room, bar, breakfast/function room; computer room. 2½-acre garden. Unsuitable for ♿.
Location Central. (Underground: South Kensington, Knightsbridge)
Restrictions No smoking: breakfast room, some bedrooms. No dogs.
Credit cards All major cards accepted.
Terms Room: single £140–£160, double £185–£210, suite £215–£325. Breakfast: continental £10, English £16. Full alc £30.

The Goring
Beeston Place
Grosvenor Gardens
London SW1W 0JW

Tel 020-7396 9000
Fax 020-7834 4393
Email reception@goringhotel.co.uk
Website www.goringhotel.co.uk

César award in 1994

'Let's hear it for *The Goring*,' says a visitor this year who 'liked it a lot'. 'Everything seemed smooth, and they were extremely friendly.' George Goring is the third generation of his family to run the hotel built by his grandfather in 1910 close to Buckingham Palace. The style is traditional, even sedate, but the welcome is much commented on. 'I was astonished, upon entering, at the immediate and detailed attention to one's presence,' writes another visitor. Mr Goring believes that one of the many advantages of private ownership is the ability to retain long-serving staff: the doorman has been here for 33 years; the general manager, William Cowpe, for 30; others, including a porter and chambermaid, for more than 20. Each bedroom is individually designed, with mouldings, striped wallpaper, writing desk and easy chairs, and a bathroom in marble and wood. Many look over a private garden (not for guests' use); some have a balcony, where breakfast can be served on fine days. One visitor thought his room was excellent but 'to find a large stuffed sheep at the foot of the bed is a bit of a shock' – a reference to the replicas which migrate between public rooms and bedrooms and add a welcome touch of eccentricity to a formal establishment. Mr Goring is often seen supervising in the restaurant, which provides 'a very cosseting experience', the food 'not too old-fashioned, not too trendy'. A long menu features a mixture of traditional and modern, eg, lobster bisque, or salad of crab with a grapefruit jelly; grilled Dover sole, or smoked haddock and leek tart. The wine list is 'extensive and fairly priced'. Bar lunches are served, and tea may be taken in the lounge. A Pride of Britain member. (*Michael and Anne Forrest, Brian Pullee, CR*)

Open All year.
Rooms 7 suites, 47 double, 20 single. All air-conditioned.
Facilities Lift, ramps. Lounge, bar, terrace, restaurant (pianist in evening); function facilities. Free use of nearby health club. Civil wedding licence.
Location Central, near Buckingham Palace (front rooms double-glazed). Garage, mews parking. (Underground: Victoria)
Restriction No dogs.
Credit cards All major cards accepted.

Terms Room: single £199–£218, double £240–£264, suite £323–£411. Breakfast: continental £12.50, English £16.50. Bar meals. Set lunch £29, dinner £38. Christmas, Easter, weekend breaks.

Halkin Hotel
5 Halkin Street
London SW1X 7DJ

Tel 020-7333 1000
Fax 020-7333 1100
Email res@halkin.co.uk
Website www.halkin.co.uk

Behind a sober Georgian-style facade, the decor of this small hotel in a residential street in Belgravia is the last word in postmodern Italian designer chic. Many weekday guests are here on business: a Reuters area supplies up-to-date financial news. The hotel is much admired for its 'understated style', and 'extremely nice young staff'. Dressed by Armani, they are 'warm and friendly, without a hint of attitude'. The stylish designer rooms, on five storeys, are reached along curved black-walled corridors; they have a sitting area, fax, video, two telephone lines, email, voicemail, 24-hour room service. Each floor is themed to a natural element: water, air, fire, earth and sky. 'Our quiet room at the back was big and well appointed; its bathroom had a separate shower,' say visitors this year. Another reporter liked the 'glorious toiletries'. Major changes have taken place: the restaurant, refurbished and enlarged, was due to reopen in July 2001. The *Michelin*-starred chef Stefano Cavallini has left: his replacement is Australian David Thompson, who specialises in Thai cuisine, and was working on his menu as the *Guide* went to press. His reputation at his *Darley Street* restaurant in Sydney is based on dishes like chu-chu (red curry) of scallops and deep-fried smoked trout on a bed of betel leaves. Light meals are served in the bar, the lobby (where a harpist plays at night) and the bedrooms. The Singaporean owner, Christina Ong, also owns the 155-bedroom *Metropolitan* in Park Lane, with a similarly minimalist decor and a staff dressed by Donna Karan.

Open All year.
Rooms 19 suites, 22 double.
Facilities Lift. Lobby, bar, restaurant; private dining/meeting room; gym.
Location Central (double glazing). Public car park 60 yds. (Underground: Hyde Park Corner)
Restriction No dogs.
Credit cards All major cards accepted.
Terms [2001] Room: single/double £285, suite £425–£625. Child in parents' room: under 12, free. Breakfast £16–£19. Set lunch £30, dinner £50–£60. Weekend rates.

Hazlitt's
6 Frith Street
London W1D 3JA

Tel 020-7434 1771
Fax 020-7439 1524
Email reservations@hazlitts.co.uk
Website www.hazlittshotel.com

César award: London hotel of the year

Much restoration, notably of the original Georgian panelling, has recently taken place at this quirky little B&B hotel without diminishing its charms. No lift (it is a conversion of three 18th-century listed

Soho houses), but it is otherwise up to date, 'and equipped with all the necessary modern communications and life support systems', including air-conditioning, and triple-glazed windows on the busy street side. Named for the essayist, who died here in 1830, it is popular with people in film, fashion, music and publishing. The bedrooms are named after famous residents and visitors to the house; most are light, with a high ceiling, though some look on to a dark inner courtyard. Mary Barker (named for the poet who lived in No. 5) was 'dark but charming' with a bigger, lighter bathroom/dressing room. All have prints and plants, an 18th- or 19th-century bed (many are four-poster or half-tester), and good linen. Some bathrooms have a claw-footed freestanding bath. An 'excellent' breakfast, continental with fresh-baked rolls and pastries or 'Reveille' (with yogurt, honey and muesli), is brought to the bedroom, room-service snacks (baguettes with exotic stuffings, pasta, blinis, etc) are available, and *Hazlitt's* has a residential liquor licence. The young, informal staff are 'extremely helpful', and the receptionist was particularly praised this year. Dogs are allowed in bedrooms and public rooms. Within easy walking distance are theatres, museums and countless restaurants. *The Gore*, in South Kensington, and *The Rookery*, in Clerkenwell (see Shortlist for both), are also owned by the *Hazlitt's* proprietor, Peter McKay.

Open All year, except Christmas.
Rooms 1 suite, 19 double, 3 single. 3 on ground floor.
Facilities Sitting room. No background music. Unsuitable for ♿.
Location Central (rear rooms quietest). NCP nearby. (Underground: Tottenham Court Rd, Leicester Sq)
Credit cards All major cards accepted.
Terms [2001] (*Excluding VAT*) Room: single £155, double £195, suite £300. Breakfast £8.95. Weekend rates.

L'Hotel
28 Basil Street
London SW3 1AS

Tel 020-7589 6286
Fax 020-7823 7826
Email reservations@lhotel.co.uk
Website www.lhotel.co.uk

'Very cosy, ideally situated; good value.' This upmarket B&B, owned by David Levin of *The Capital* (*qv*), next door but one, was liked again this year for its 'no-frills atmosphere, and very helpful reception'. It is relatively inexpensive for this part of London, and it aims for 'an ambience of quietness and discretion', without a large staff and lots of facilities. The manager is Nathalie Jarnot. Reception at night is shared with *The Capital*; there is no residents' lounge. The bedrooms have a French country-style decor: pale colours, patterned wallpaper, pine furniture, wooden shutters, good fabrics, but some guests have found the lighting dim. Each room has a kettle, crockery and a fridge; best ones have a gas fire. A continental or English breakfast is served between 7.30 and 10.30 am in the basement wine bar, the *Metro*, run by the sister hotel's *Michelin*-two-starred chef, Eric Chavot. It is open to the public for bistro-style meals (soups, salads, omelettes), and has a jazzy modern decor: granite, chrome and leather (service was again thought to be slow this year). Wines of quality are sold by the glass. Afternoon teas are served between 3.30 and 5.30 pm. Rooms above the *Metro* can be noisy; the ones at the top are probably the most peaceful. (*Wendy and Dr Michael Dods*)

Open All year. *Metro* closed Sun, bank holidays, except for residents' breakfast.
Rooms 1 suite, 11 double. 1 on ground floor.
Facilities Lift. Reception, wine bar (pop/classical background music at meals).
Location From underground Knightsbridge, Harrods' exit, turn left into Hans Cresc, then 1st left. Rear rooms quietest. NCP opposite.
Restriction No dogs.
Credit cards All major cards accepted.
Terms [2001] (*Excluding VAT*) B&B: double £155, suite £175. English breakfast £7.50. Full alc £25. Child in parents' room: £15–£20.

Knightsbridge Green Hotel
159 Knightsbridge
London SW1X 7PD

Tel 020-7584 6274
Fax 020-7225 1635
Email theKGHotel@aol.com
Website www.theKGHotel.co.uk

The narrow entrance off Knightsbridge has been given a feeling of light and space, as a lounge has been added in what had been an adjacent travel agency. There is a very private feel to this small hotel, close to Hyde Park, that has been owned by the Marler family for over 30 years. 'As always, the courteous staff were helpful in all ways. The friendliness is appreciated after a long journey,' reports a visitor from the Channel Islands. 'The no-smoking policy is a plus.' An American regular regards this as a 'home from home in London'. The spacious double rooms are good value so close to Harrods and Harvey Nichols. The best accommodation is in large suites 'somewhat plainly furnished, but well provisioned', with a double bedroom, a sitting room and a large tiled bathroom. The quietest rooms, at the back, overlook a courtyard, but all are double-glazed. The air-conditioning was 'a great relief' during a heatwave. The manager, Paul Fizia, writes that towels have been replaced after a comment in the *Guide* last year, and all pillows and blankets are new. An 'excellent and fresh' breakfast is delivered to the room: 'express' at 7 am, with croissants, and continental or cooked from 7.30 am on weekdays, between 8 and 10 on Sunday. The Club Room on the first floor provides free tea and coffee during the day. Reception is staffed from 7.30 am to 10.30 pm, and porters are on duty between 7 am and 8 pm. The Marler family also own the *St Enodoc Hotel (qv)* at Rock, Cornwall. (*Dr Mary Tilden-Smith, MG*)

Open All year.
Rooms 12 suites, 9 double, 7 single. All air-conditioned.
Facilities Lift. Reception (background radio), lounge, Club Room (complimentary refreshments 9 am–8 pm). Access to nearby health club. Unsuitable for ♿.
Location Central (rooms double-glazed; quietest ones at rear). NCP car park nearby. (Underground: Knightsbridge)
Restrictions No smoking. No dogs.
Credit cards All major cards accepted.
Terms Room: single £110, double £145, suite £170. Breakfast: express £3.50, continental £7, English £10.50. *V*

Langorf Hotel
20 Frognal
Hampstead
London NW3 6AG

Tel 020-7794 4483
Fax 020-7435 9055
Email langorf@aol.com
Website www.langorfhotel.com

'A charming Edwardian hotel that delivers style and hospitality that other more expensive London establishments should envy,' writes a visitor who has adopted this 'oasis of hospitality' as his London base. Caroline Haynes – 'energetic, personable and caring' – is the manager. The *Langorf* consists of three red brick houses close to Finchley Road underground station – four stops on the Jubilee Line to Oxford Circus. Though 'not at all smart', it has good-sized, pleasantly decorated bedrooms, some suitable for a family. The rooms at the back are quietest; some bathrooms are small. Plenty of choice at the buffet breakfast, served in a room overlooking the sloping rear garden ('a bit unkempt,' says a report this year). There is a licensed bar and a 24-hour room-service snack menu. *Casa Giovanni*, a nearby Italian restaurant, is recommended. Street parking only, said to be expensive. The Freud museum is close by, Hampstead village is five minutes' walk. (*John R Hester*)

Open All year.
Rooms 31 double. 2 on ground floor. Also 5 self-catering apartments.
Facilities Lift. Lounge, bar, breakfast room (classical background music). Walled garden. Unsuitable for ♿.
Location Between Finchley Rd and Fitzjohn's Ave. Street parking. (Underground: Finchley Rd)
Restrictions No smoking in breakfast room. No dogs.
Credit cards All major cards accepted.
Terms B&B: single £82, double £98–£130. Child in parents' room: under 8, 50% reduction. Winter rates. Christmas package.

The Leonard
15 Seymour Street
London W1H 7JW

Tel 020-7935 2010
Fax 020-7935 6700
Email the.leonard@dial.pipex.com
Website www.theleonard.com

The atmosphere is 'unquestionably hospitable' in this tucked-away gem' close to Marble Arch. Four Grade II listed 18th-century town houses have been sensitively converted, by the Iranian owners, into a smart hotel where antiques, fine fabrics, paintings, plants and flowers combine with the latest technology: video, hi-fi and (in the suites) a dedicated line for fax or modem. The manager, Angela Stoppani, and her staff are 'keen to assist at all times'. Accommodation is mostly in suites; some are large, with a kitchenette. Rooms at the front can be noisy. The high-quality bedlinen and power showers are appreciated. The café/bar, with sofas and dining tables, serves breakfast, and drinks and light Mediterranean-style meals all day. But one visitor complained: 'The menu never changes.' And 'the lobby could be made more inviting'. There is a small exercise room. Guests may do their laundry in the utility room. Ten rooms are being added in a new fifth floor.

Open All year.
Rooms 20 suites, 11 double. Some on ground floor. 10 more planned for Oct 2001.

Facilities Lift. Lobby, café/bar (open 7 am–11 pm; varied background music at night); 24-hour room service; function facilities; exercise room. Access to garden square with tennis.
Location Central, near Marble Arch (rooms double-glazed). NCP car park 2 mins' walk. (Underground: Marble Arch)
Restrictions No smoking in 4 bedrooms. No dogs.
Credit cards All major cards accepted.
Terms Room: single £235, double £258, suite (1–2 bedrooms) £329–£705. Breakfast: continental £13.50, English £18. Full alc £35. Weekend, Christmas rates.

Miller's
111a Westbourne Grove
London W2 4UW

Tel 020-7243 1024
Fax 020-7243 1064
Email enquiries@millers.uk.com
Website www.millers.uk.com

Antiques are the overriding theme as you would expect for a hotel owned by Martin Miller, author of the antiques guide that bears his name. You enter by a maroon door beside a launderette. A staircase hung with shabby rugs brings you to 'a dimmed sanctuary, a complete contrast to the busy world outside' (it is near Notting Hill Gate). The large drawing room, recently redecorated, is filled with old furniture, ornaments, busts, bric-a-brac, paintings. It has a huge oak fireplace; candles often burn at night, supplementing the light from French brass chandeliers. A staircase, with maroon walls densely hung with pictures and prints 'quaintly modern or antiquated risqué', leads to the bedrooms. Each is named after an English poet. They are theatrically furnished, with heavy brocades and velvets and a lavish bed, but also equipped with voicemail, and a TV with video. Dust cannot be kept at bay in such a decor, and housekeeping may not be perfect, but the atmosphere is hospitable and informal. Guests are given a key, and told to help themselves to drinks from an honesty bar. Breakfast, served round one large table, is largely self-service: you toast your own bagel, help yourself to fruit and yogurt, make your own tea. One warning: if you give your credit card number to guarantee a booking, £200 will be blocked on your account a week before your arrival. Mr Miller, who often visits, also owns *Chilston Park*, at Lenham, Kent, also antique-filled and eccentric, with staff in period dress. Carl Vockins is the new manager. More reports, please.

Open All year.
Rooms 1 suite, 4 double.
Facilities 2 lounges, drawing/breakfast room (classical background music all day). Unsuitable for ♿.
Location Above *Rodizio Rico* restaurant (entrance in Hereford Road). (Underground: Notting Hill Gate, Bayswater, Queensway)
Restrictions No smoking in some bedrooms. No dogs.
Credit cards All major cards accepted.
Terms (*Excluding VAT*) B&B: single £126–£144, double £140–£160. Corporate rates on application. Lounge may be hired for functions. ***V***

For details of the Voucher scheme see page xxx.

Number Sixteen
16 Sumner Place
London SW7 3EG

Tel 020-7589 5232
Fax 020-7584 8615
Email reservations@numbersixteenhotel.co.uk
Website www.numbersixteenhotel.co.uk

A town house hotel, comprising four adjacent Victorian buildings, in a residential street near South Kensington underground station. It was taken over in June 2000 by Kit and Tim Kemp, who own a small group of luxury hotels in London, including *The Pelham* close by; they have installed Justin Pinchbeck as manager. 'It is still a good choice,' say visitors this year. But another couple felt that the earlier spirit was now missing – 'no fresh flowers, in the past they were spectacular' – and that redecoration was needed. The location 'is great, with a neighbourhood feel', access to good transport round London and direct underground trains to Heathrow airport. A major asset is the pretty garden, with flowers, a fountain, tables and chairs, which the quietest rooms overlook; breakfast, tea and drinks are served here in fine weather. The bedrooms 'vary in size and desirability'; some bathrooms may be small. There is a lounge (yellow, chintzy, cheerful), a library (cranberry red with shelves to browse through and an honesty bar). Children are welcomed (babysitters can be arranged). Restaurants of all sorts are close by – *Hilaire* is warmly recommended. Prices are no longer quoted inclusive of VAT. More reports, please.

Open All year.
Rooms 5 suites, 23 double, 9 single. 4 on ground floor.
Facilities Lift. Drawing room, library with honesty bar (classical background music), conservatory. Small garden. Unsuitable for ♿.
Location Central (quietest rooms overlook garden). Pay parking 5 mins' walk. (Underground: South Kensington)
Credit cards Amex, MasterCard, Visa.
Terms (*Excluding VAT*) B&B: single £100–£120, double £120–£170, suite £160–£220. Christmas, Easter, summer packages.

One Aldwych
1 Aldwych
London WC2B 4RH

Tel 020-7300 1000
Fax 020-7300 1001
Email sales@onealdwych.co.uk
Website www.onealdwych.com

'Expensive but worth it.' The staff in this chic hotel, in a prime position opposite Waterloo Bridge, are as young and smart as many of the clientele. The building – once a newspaper office, later a bank – has been stylishly converted, with cutting edge technology and modern decor. Two restaurants to see and be seen in: *Axis*, found 'superb' this year, serving a modern European menu, in a spacious room on the lower ground floor, and *Indigo*, lighter, more informal, on a balcony overlooking the lobby. Here, the chef will prepare special dishes for children (the hotel welcomes them, particularly at the weekend). The huge lobby has a giant statue of an oarsman in his boat, 'trendy, if tortured, flower arrangements', and a bar that serves 'inventive cocktails'. Bedrooms are equipped with modem plugs, fax lines, mobile phones, etc; fibre-optic lights allow discreet reading in bed; fresh flowers and fruit are replenished daily. Some rooms are small. There is a gym, and an 18-metre lap swimming pool with underwater music; personal trainers are available, and two suites have their own private gym. Private travellers, as well as those on business, have almost all enjoyed the 'understated style'. 'The staff were genuinely friendly.' 'Excellent soundproofing. Great choice at breakfast' (continental, healthy or English). The 'high-energy' *Cinnamon Bar*, opening on to Aldwych, serves pastries, sandwiches, fruit juices. Many theatres, and the Royal Opera House, are within an easy walk. (*NM Mackintosh, Robert Sandham*)

Open All year.
Rooms 12 suites, 93 double. 6 adapted for ♿. All air-conditioned.
Facilities Lifts. Lobby, 2 bars, coffee bar, 2 restaurants (background jazz in *Axis*), private dining rooms; function facilities; newsagent, florist. Health club: indoor swimming pool, sauna, gym. Civil wedding licence.
Location Central, where Aldwych meets the Strand (rooms triple-glazed). Valet parking. (Underground: Charing Cross, Waterloo)
Restrictions No smoking in some bedrooms. Guide dogs only.
Credit cards All major cards accepted.
Terms [2001] (*Excluding VAT*) Room: double £270–£355, suite £445–£1,140. Breakfast £12.50–£17.50. Set lunch/dinner (2 to 3 courses): *Axis* £20.75–£24.75; full alc: *Axis* £35–£40, *Indigo* £30. Reductions for children under 16. Weekend breaks.

Pembridge Court
34 Pembridge Gardens
London W2 4DX

Tel 020-7229 9977
Fax 020-7727 4982
Email reservations@pemct.co.uk
Website www.pemct.co.uk

Spencer and Churchill, two ginger cats with prima donna tendencies, welcome guests to Derek and Karen Mapp's unpretentious but 'eminently well-run' 19th-century town house. The Portobello Road market is close by. The long-serving manager, Valerie Gilliat, oversees a 'friendly and considerate' staff. The bedrooms, decorated in 'mock-Victorian style', vary greatly in size: some are very small, and two singles lack air-conditioning. One visitor found the decor 'tired', but most rooms have been thought 'pleasant to live in, well soundproofed, with lights just about adequate for reading'. There is a 'cheerful, light lounge'. The basement restaurant, *Caps* (decorated with cricketing memorabilia), serves light meals to residents and their guests. The help with bags is appreciated; also the 'swift and efficient' service, and the 'excellent bacon' and lack of background music at breakfast. Restaurants of all kinds are nearby; there is good transport to the West End and the City. Visitors are offered discounted rates at the Mapps' other hotel *Cross House*, Padstow, Cornwall. More reports, please.

Open All year.
Rooms 17 double, 3 single. Some on ground floor. 18 air-conditioned.
Facilities Lounge, bar/restaurant (taped background music evenings). Unsuitable for ♿.
Location Side street off Notting Hill Gate. (Underground: Notting Hill Gate)
Restriction No dogs in public rooms, or unattended in bedrooms.
Credit cards All major cards accepted.
Terms [2001] B&B: single £125–£165, double £160–£195. Family rates on application. Reductions 24 Dec–1 Jan. ***V*** (1 night only)

The Portobello
22 Stanley Gardens
London W11 2NG

Tel 020-7727 2777
Fax 020-7792 9641
Email info@portobello-hotel.co.uk
Website www.portobello-hotel.co.uk

Supermodels, film stars and rock musicians frequent Tim Herring's bohemian hotel created from two six-floor Victorian terrace houses on a residential street in Notting Hill. They are drawn by a quirky decor (gilt mirrors, military pictures, marble fireplaces, potted palms, Edwardiana, cane and wicker furniture, etc) and some exotic bedrooms, which are often redesigned. 'The laid-back style that I love is almost unchanged, and the themed bedrooms really are special; you should discuss them carefully when booking,' says a returning visitor. 'The Moroccan room is very special' adds a report this year. The Round Room, with its round bed, was created for Alice Cooper; he kept his boa constrictor in its large freestanding Edwardian bathing machine. Room 22, facing the garden at the rear (no access for regulars), is 'so quiet, an amusing bathroom, a quaint mix of furnishings'. Scary and Sporty Spice were the first to experience the two Japanese water garden basement suites, each with an oversized bath. Breakfast disappointed one reporter: 'Fresh orange juice, but inferior toast, and packet butter and jams.' Porterage and room service operate only between 8 am and 4 pm, but reception is open day and night, as is the restaurant/bar, supervised by the co-owner and manager/chef Johnny Ekperigin. Parking is awkward. Tim Herring also owns *Julie's Restaurant*, and *Julie's Bar*, enjoyed for their 'slightly decadent' '60s feel, in nearby Clarendon Cross (known for its arty little shops). Portobello Road, with its famous Saturday market, is close by. (*IE, NM Macintosh, SB*)

Open 2 Jan–24 Dec.
Rooms 9 suites, 11 double, 4 single. Some on ground floor.
Facilities Lift. Lounge/bar, restaurant (open 24 hours to residents); background music. Access to health club nearby. Unsuitable for ♿.
Location Central. Meter parking. (Underground: Notting Hill Gate)
Credit cards Amex, MasterCard, Visa.
Terms B&B: single £140, double £150, suite £350. Full alc £15–£20.

A number of organisations in London offer B&B in private homes. They include:
At Home in London, 70 Black Lion Lane, London W6 9BE. *Tel* 020-8748 1943, *fax* 020-8748 2701, *email* info@athomeinlondon.co.uk, *website* athomeinlondon.co.uk. B&B in over 70 private homes in central and west London, priced according to location. All close to public transport. B&B (2 nights min.): single £29–£65, double £52–£90.
Uptown Reservations, 41 Paradise Walk, London SW3 4Jl. *Tel* 020-7351 3445, *fax* 020-7351 9383, *email* enquiries@uptownres.co.uk, *website* www.uptownres.co.uk. Upmarket accommodation in private homes in central London. B&B: single £65, double £85. Family rooms, studios, 1-bedroom apartments also available.

Tophams Belgravia
28 Ebury Street
London SW1W 0LU

Tel 020-7730 8147
Fax 020-7823 5966
Email tophams_belgravia@compuserve.com
Website www.tophams.co.uk

A popular choice, offering central accommodation at a reasonable price, *Tophams* 'is a very pleasant place. But, like most things, it is not perfect.' Two otherwise satisfied guests had to wait for breakfast in a room that 'couldn't hold everybody at busy times'; a third, who arrived with two other couples, found Rooms 1, 2 and 3, described to her as 'garden rooms', 'airless and claustrophobic' – one of the couples was moved to Room 36 at the front which was refurbished and 'very acceptable'. Most of the rooms in this family-owned hotel have been upgraded, but it still has a 'delightfully old-fashioned' atmosphere, says one of its most loyal fans. 'The friendly staff have been there for ages and by now know us,' says another regular. Marianne Topham, of the third generation, runs it with her husband Nicholas Kingsford. Their aim is to evoke 'the charm of an English country house', despite the busy central London location. Mirrors, pictures and pieces of china adorn the small public rooms; there are floral sofas and armchairs in the lounge. The bedrooms are mostly small, but 'tastefully done'; some have a 'new, beautifully appointed' bathroom. Four singles lack facilities *en suite*, but bathrobes are provided for the trip down the corridor. The basement brasserie (open to the public) has a short menu, including, eg, fried halloumi with roasted vegetables and lavosh bread; fillet of beef with bordelaise sauce; baked apple and toffee pie. The position of rooms varies widely, from those at the rear or in the mews (quiet) to those at the front, overlooking the street (noisy). (*Ran Ogston, WS, DB*)

Open All year, except Christmas, New Year.
Rooms 1 suite, 31 double, 8 single (4 not *en suite*). Some on ground floor.
Facilities Ramp, lift. Sitting room, bar, brasserie; light background music, private dining/function room.
Location Central (front rooms double-glazed). Limited private parking (£20 per day). (Underground: Victoria)
Restrictions No smoking in some bedrooms. Guide dogs only.
Credit cards All major cards accepted.
Terms B&B: single £90–£115, double £100–£170, family (for 4) £260. Full alc £24.

---

22 Jermyn Street
22 Jermyn Street
London SW1Y 6HL

Tel 020-7734 2353
Fax 020-7734 0750
Email office@22jermyn.com
Website www.22jermyn.com

César award in 1996

Unusually for London, here is an upmarket establishment that encourages children to stay. Pets are welcome, too, at Henry Togna's small hotel in a prime position in St James's. The secret, apart from Mr Togna's family-friendly attitude, is that 13 of the 18 rooms are suites and can be converted to two bedrooms. 'Thank goodness for sofa beds,' says Mr Togna. 'On one night we had 56 bodies, from ancient to just born, in our 18-bedroom hotel.' Visitors continue to appreciate the service. 'Having walked Jermyn Street all my life, what a treat it was to find this jewel,' writes an American. 'Henry Togna and his staff are excellent and no small item goes unnoticed.' The ultimate in hi-tech – fax/modem lines, Internet MasterCard, a CD-ROM library, private voicemail and an individual email address for every guest – 'is combined with personal care. Business visitors appreciate 'the sheer practicality' of the services provided. The in-house newsletter makes theatre, exhibition and restaurant recommendations. Mr Togna is a fitness fanatic: his guests may use the sporting facilities at a nearby club, borrow a mountain bike, or go jogging with him in St James's Park. His art-historian niece, Louise Hayward, conducts tours of art galleries. The decor is an appealing blend of contemporary furniture and fabrics with antiques. No public rooms, but light room-service meals (salads, pasta, fish-cakes, sandwiches) can be served. West End theatres, shops and eating places of all kinds are nearby. (*AMK, KG, and others*)

Open All year.
Rooms 13 suites, 5 double. All air-conditioned. 24-hour room service.
Facilities Lift. Reception (classical background music); small conference facilities. Access to nearby health club (swimming pool, gym, squash courts).
Location Central. Valet parking (expensive). (Underground: Piccadilly Circus)
Restriction No smoking in reception and corridors.
Credit cards All major cards accepted.
Terms [2001] (*Excluding VAT*) Room: £210, suite £295–£335. Extra bed £50. Child in parents' room: under 7, free. Breakfast £11.55. Room-service full alc £30–£45.

See also SHORTLIST

****

Traveller's tale Hotel in Scotland. The person dealing with reception appeared to be drunk (we could smell it). She was incapable of taking in my letter of confirmation, and twittered about asking 'what I wanted'. A second employee appeared, a young waitress, quite arrogant, who barely offered an apology. This reception, combined with an earlier mistake over my booking, seemed to indicate that office arrangements were somewhat wanting.

****

Traveller's tale Hotel in Ireland. Our bedroom was not vacuum-cleaned in four days. It was full of flies when we arrived and, though we asked them to spray the room while we were out the next day, there were even more flies when we returned. On Saturday evening, the bathwater was tepid (due no doubt to a party of 26 walkers all taking a bath at the same time). The staff – willing, cheerful and hardworking – had clearly received no training.

****

England

Painswick Hotel, Painswick

This year's list of *César* winners again illustrates the enormous variety of hotels that we feature in the English section. We are encouraged by how many traditional hotels and inns have sought to keep up with the times, developing lighter, modern menus and upgrading rooms and facilities. We include some grand country houses but also many more informal places where the owners have a strong presence and offer much of the atmosphere of a private home. Our selection reflects the spread of the modern designer chains – where the rooms are striking and contemporary and the restaurants are lively – though individual hotels are only listed when the reports from readers and inspectors match up to our standards. Another development over our 25-year history is the popularity of restaurants-with-rooms: we have some outstanding examples across the country, though sometimes we warn that the quality of the food is inevitably rather better than that of the rooms. We continue to feature some simple but very popular B&Bs and unsophisticated guest houses. This year we have made a special effort to find more 'proper hotels' but we acknowledge that some readers continue to prefer the personal touch to be found, along with good value, in the smaller places.

ABBOTSBURY Dorset — Map 1:D6

Abbey House BUDGET
Church Street
Abbotsbury DT3 4JJ

Tel 01305-871330
Fax 01305-871088
Email info@theabbeyhouse.co.uk
Website www.theabbeyhouse.co.uk

'A magical setting – beautiful and quiet, with wonderful views. Breakfast outside on a late May morning was memorable.' More praise this year for Jonathan and Maureen Cooke's small guest house, 'a place of enchantment'. 'The long, low building is set in a large and lovely garden. The views towards the huge golden-stoned tithe barn, abbey ruins, roofs liberally sprinkled with white doves, are stupendous,' reported our inspector. The core of this 'modest and unspoilt place' was once an infirmary serving the nearby Benedictine abbey; extensions were added during the 17th and 18th centuries. Inside are old flagstoned floors, wide panelled doors, authentic windows. Bedrooms, three of which have been redecorated, vary in size and style. 'Ours was spacious, looking over the lovely view; it had chintzy armchairs, lacy cloths on round tables, Impressionist-style paintings.' Another visitor had a 'very romantic' attic room, with its bathroom across a hall. The 'charming owners' are 'obviously happy in what they are doing'. Breakfast is 'a feast', with everything from home-made muesli to smoked haddock. Light lunches and cream teas are served on the lawn in fine weather. Concerts are sometimes held in the garden. Evening meals are available only for house parties, but the village has several pubs, including *The Ilchester Arms* (a long-standing main entry in the *Good Pub Guide*). Abbotsbury is known for its sub-tropical gardens and its ancient swannery (established by the monks over 600 years ago). The panoramic expanses of Chesil Bank are 15 minutes' walk away, and the monument to Admiral Hardy – Nelson's flag captain at the battle of Trafalgar – is worth viewing. (*Nigel M Mackintosh, and others*)

Open All year. Restaurant open for lunch Apr–Oct; closed at night, except for house parties.
Rooms 1 family suite, 4 double. No telephone.
Facilities Lounge, breakfast room, tea room. No background music. 1½-acre grounds: stage for plays/classical concerts. Sea 15 mins' walk. Unsuitable for ♿.
Location Abbotsbury is on B3157 halfway between Weymouth and Bridport. Turn left at sign to Swannery; after 100 yds left through abbey arch; *Abbey House* on right. Train: Dorchester/Weymouth; then taxi.
Restrictions No smoking. No dogs.
Credit cards None accepted.
Terms B&B: double £60–£65, suite £65–£70. Set lunch £10. Child in parents' room: under 13, 50% of adult rate. Christmas package. House parties catered for. 1-night bookings sometimes refused high season.

If you find details of a hotel's location inadequate, please tell us.

ALFRISTON East Sussex *See SHORTLIST* Map 2:E4

ALSTON Cumbria Map 4:B3

Lovelady Shield
Nenthead Road
nr Alston CA9 3LF

Tel 01434-381203
Fax 01434-381515
Email enquiries@lovelady.co.uk
Website www.lovelady.co.uk

'A lovely place,' say *Guide* correspondents after their eighth annual visit to this handsome white 19th-century house. It stands among trees in a remote position in the High Pennines near Alston, England's highest market town; the river Nent borders its grounds. 'The situation is superb, the surrounding countryside is stunning, the welcome was first class,' others wrote. The 'unfussy service' and 'family atmosphere' are liked, and the owners, Peter and Marie Haynes, are 'truly hospitable'. But there were some caveats too: some bedrooms (several are small) may be in need of new beds and redecoration, and one couple was surprised to be charged for bottled water from the hotel's own spring. The chef (for the past ten years), Barrie Garton, serves 'classical English dishes, with a Continental influence', eg, scrambled eggs with woodland mushrooms; roasted organic suckling pig with sage, honey and almonds; poached pear in elderflower syrup, stuffed with soft caramel. Portions are generous, with good ingredients. Vegetarians are catered for, with advance notice. At breakfast there is freshly squeezed orange juice, and cooked dishes such as kedgeree (ordered in advance) and Cumberland sausages. 'The dawn chorus was unforgettable.' A good base for exploring Hadrian's Wall and the Borders. (*Dr and Mrs James Stewart, JT, and others*)

Open All year.
Rooms 11 double, 1 single.
Facilities 2 lounges, bar, restaurant. No background music. 3-acre grounds: river, fishing, croquet. Golf, riding nearby. Unsuitable for ♿. Civil wedding licence.
Location 2½ miles E of Alston. Take A689 to Nenthead. Hotel 2 miles on left, at junction with B6294.
Restrictions Smoking banned in restaurant, 1 lounge, 'actively discouraged' in bedrooms. No dogs in public rooms.
Credit cards Amex, MasterCard, Visa.
Terms B&B from £70; D,B&B from £90. Set lunch £19.50, dinner £33. Child in parents' room: under 2, free; 2–16, £20. 3-night breaks. Christmas package. *V*

AMBERLEY West Sussex Map 2:E3

Amberley Castle
Amberley
nr Arundel BN18 9ND

Tel 01798-831992
Fax 01798-831998
Email info@amberleycastle.co.uk
Website www.amberleycastle.co.uk

The portcullis comes down at midnight at Joy and Martin Cummings's Norman castle. As it is surrounded by a 60-foot wall and a dry moat, admission can be difficult after this, but the suites in the stone-built *Bishopric* in the moat have their own entrance. Other luxurious bedrooms are distributed between a manor house and the castle, which stands on a bend of the river Arun, and has views over the South Downs from its battlements. The decor is 'splendidly OTT', with heavy drapes, much panelling. Many bedrooms have a four-poster; some have a gas log fire; some have a spa bath. The public rooms have antique furniture and suits of armour, and one visitor commented on 'the owners' propensity to decorate every room possible with cuddly toys'. The restaurant is formal (men must wear a jacket and tie in the evening), and ambitious. The new chef, James Peyton, promoted from *sous-chef*, maintains an 'eclectic English' style, eg, quenelle of smoked haddock and scallop tartare; South Down rabbit with grain mustard creamed potatoes; honey-glazed breast of duck with sour cherry chutney. White peacocks stalk the lovely gardens where two lakes are home to black swans and ducks. There is a pond with Koi carp; also two goats, three alpacas and two miniature Shetland ponies in a paddock. A colony of jackdaws has nested in the castle for ten centuries. Family pets include two Pyrenean mountain dogs, a Persian chinchilla and Sam and Buca, the parrots. Guests can arrive by helicopter. Nearby are water meadows full of flora and fauna, and the South Downs Way (good walking); also Arundel Castle, Petworth, Parham and Goodwood houses, and the Sussex coast. Pride of Britain member. More reports, please.

Open All year.
Rooms 6 suites, 13 double. 5 in *Bishopric*.
Facilities Hall, 2 lounges, library, 2 restaurants; function facilities. No background music. 12-acre grounds: gardens, tennis, putting, croquet, dry moat, ponds, wildlife. Beach 10 miles. Unsuitable for ♿. Civil wedding licence.
Location SW of village 4 miles N of Arundel. Train to Amberley.
Restrictions No smoking: restaurant, bedrooms. No children under 12. No dogs.
Credit cards All major cards accepted.
Terms [2001] Room: double £145–£300, suite £275–£325. Breakfast £10–£16.50. Set lunch £15, dinner £38–£45; full alc £55. Min. 2-night booking weekends. Castle breaks. Christmas, New Year packages.

AMBLESIDE Cumbria — Map 4: inset C2

Kent House NEW/BUDGET
Lake Road
Ambleside LA22 0AD

Tel 015394-33279
Fax 015394-31667
Email mail@kent-house.com
Website www.kent-house.com

Richard and Margaret Lee are 'perfect hosts', says one regular visitor to this Lakeland guest house in an elevated position in a one-way street in the centre of town. Other correspondents call it 'small, but not claustrophobically cosy' and write of reasonable prices and an evening meal, cooked by Mr Lee, that is 'delicious, and good value'. The bedrooms are 'decorated with flair', and equipped with useful extras (eg, shoe-cleaning kit) and 'paperback books that you would be happy to read'. The Lees promise freshly baked bread most mornings, to accompany the hearty breakfast, and the set dinner (at 6.30 for 7 pm) might consist of broccoli and Stilton quiche; pan-fried duckling breast with a thyme and honey sauce; strawberries with shortbread pastry, fromage frais and raspberry coulis. White plastic tables and chairs stand under parasols on a flowery small terrace above the road; here summer drinks or tea (with home-made cakes) are served. (*Miss DM Cairns, Willa Speiser, Caroline Capewwell*)

Open All year.
Rooms 6 double.
Facilities Lounge, dining room. No background music. Small terrace garden. Lake Windermere 15 mins' walk. Unsuitable for ♿.
Location Central. 300 yds from post office; in one-way system. Train: Windermere (5 miles); then taxi/bus.
Restrictions No smoking. No dogs in public rooms.
Credit cards MasterCard, Visa.
Terms B&B £24–£35; D,B&B £40.50–£54.50. Set dinner £20. Christmas package. Advance 1-night bookings for Sat sometimes refused. *V*

Regent Hotel
Waterhead Bay
Ambleside LA22 0ES

Tel 015394-32254
Fax 015394-31474
Email lit@regentlakes.co.uk
Website www.regentlakes.co.uk

A traditional hotel, which the Hewitt family has owned for many years. So faithful is its clientele that it runs a 'Regulars Club', offering reduced rates. It stands opposite the slipway at Waterhead Bay on Lake Windermere. In summer, hanging flower baskets adorn the front. 'It is very welcoming, with good food and service,' writes its most devoted fan in 2001. 'Redecoration of the public areas has resulted in a more contemporary style without loss of comfort.' She recommends the 'classic' bedrooms – 'clean, comfortable and bright, with a king-size bed, and a small but adequate bathroom'. Another visitor was less happy with Room 5 ('admittedly the last available'), complaining of worn decor and the smell of cigarette smoke. In the 'pleasant split-level restaurant', the five-course dinner has ample choice, and portions are generous. 'We have never had a meal we didn't like: starters of fish pie; smoked venison salad; grilled prawns; main courses of good fish, beef, lamb, steak, accompanied by appetising combinations of sauces and vegetables. Desserts are lip-smackingly delicious (there is always a hot one). The wine list gives good variety and is reasonably priced.' Service is by 'well-trained Australian and New Zealand staff'. But several visitors thought breakfast less good: 'packets of jam and butter, and inferior juices' but 'a good choice of fruits and cereals'. 'An excellent location for walking; good value for money.' The lake is visible from a top room with a balcony; spacious suites, also with a balcony, overlook the flowery courtyard. The newest rooms are in a building in the garden. Some rooms overlook the road (busy by day, but quiet at night). There is good accommodation for families. The swimming pool has closed; guests are now given free membership of a local leisure club. (*Shirley Tennent, and others*)

Open All year, except Christmas.
Rooms 3 suites, 24 double, 3 single. 10 in courtyard, 5 in garden. 7 on ground floor.
Facilities Ramp. Lounge, sun lounge, bar, restaurant (pianist twice weekly). Courtyard, ½-acre garden. Access to local leisure centre. Near Lake Windermere: sailing, waterskiing, fishing.
Location S of centre on A591 Kendal–Keswick, at Waterhead Bay. Garden-facing rooms quietest. Train: Windermere (5 miles); taxi/bus.
Restrictions No smoking: restaurant, some bedrooms, 1 lounge. No dogs in public rooms.
Credit cards MasterCard, Visa.
Terms B&B £39–£64.50; D,B&B £60–£82. Set lunch £15, dinner £27.50. Child in parents' room: under 12, B&B £12.50. Lakeland breaks. 1-night bookings sometimes refused Sat. *V*

Rothay Manor
Rothay Bridge
Ambleside LA22 0EH

Tel 015394-33605
Fax 015394-33607
Email hotel@rothaymanor.co.uk
Website www.rothaymanor.co.uk

César award in 1992

'As good as the *Guide*'s description, and better than we expected. In short, admirable.' 'An all-time favourite.' Praise has come consistently for many years for this listed Lakeland Regency house, once the home of a prosperous Liverpool merchant. It is one of just seven hotels that have been recommended in every edition of the *Guide* – its *César* was for 'maintaining traditional hotel virtues'. 'Efficient and well kept but also relaxed. Not pretentious. Ambleside can be crowded and noisy, with too many cars; *Rothay Manor* is far enough away from the centre to escape this.' Many original architectural features have been retained, notably the first-floor veranda with cast iron railings that overlooks the immaculate gardens. Inside are smart lounges and 'an atmosphere of calm', despite the one-way traffic system nearby. Bedroom windows are double-glazed, and the quietest rooms are on the garden side. Most are spacious, with a country house decor, fruit and bottled water. The lounges have open fires, deep carpets and 'squashy chairs'. The hotel is run by brothers Nigel and Stephen Nixon with their wives. Colette Nixon and Jane Binns run the restaurant, which has had a *Good Food Guide* entry for many years, thanks to the quality of its traditional cooking: 'The best scallops ever, fish (char) from Lake Windermere.' There is a separate vegetarian menu. A wine is recommended to accompany each dish. Few half bottles 'but they let me have a full bottle and charged only for what I drank'. Dinner is by candlelight, on polished wooden tables with heavy glass and tableware. A traditional Sunday lunch is served; on weekdays there is a light lunch menu or soup and sandwiches. Afternoon teas are lavish and 'good value'. 'The best hotel breakfast I have known: freshly squeezed orange juice, eggs perfectly cooked, excellent toast, excellent butter and marmalade.' Special meals are provided for hildren, as are cots, high chairs and baby-listening. (*William Rodgers, SP, and others*)

Open 8 Feb–3 Jan.
Rooms 3 suites (in annexe, 20 yds), 13 double, 2 single. 2 suitable for ♿.
Facilities Ramp. 2 lounges, 2 dining rooms; meeting/conference facilities. No background music. 1-acre garden: croquet. Free use of local leisure centre. Lake Windermere: sailing, waterskiing, fishing.
Location On A593 to Coniston, ¼ mile SW of Ambleside. Train: Windermere (5 miles); then taxi/bus.
Restrictions No smoking: restaurant, 1 lounge. No small children in restaurant at night. No dogs.
Credit cards All major cards accepted.
Terms [2001] B&B: single £65–£76, double £110–£137, suite £150–£172; D,B&B: single £80–£104, double £140–£192, suite £180–£227. Set lunch £14–£18, dinner £25–£32. Winter rates, special interest breaks (painting, music, etc). Christmas package. 1-night bookings refused Sat.

Rowanfield
Kirkstone Road
Ambleside LA22 9ET

Tel 015394-33686
Fax 015394-31569
Email email@rowanfield.com
Website www.rowanfield.com

Philip and Jane Butcher are the 'very friendly' owners of this small, white-walled guest house in a late Regency farmhouse. The setting is 'gorgeous', above Lake Windermere, on the road to Kirkstone Pass; it has panoramic views from 'the hundreds' to 'Coniston Old Man' and beyond. It is decorated in cheerful period style. The lounge has a wood-burning stove, books, maps and games. The bedrooms have bright colours and patterned wallpaper; some have a sitting area, and the family room has a patio balcony; there are low-beamed or sloping ceilings in some; all have TV. The dining room has the original flagstone floor, a grandfather clock, an old pine dresser. An 'excellent dinner' at 7, cooked by the host, is sometimes available; when it is not, the Butchers can suggest local restaurants. Guests make their choice, by 5 pm, of dishes like creamed parsnip soup; pan-fried mullet with Moroccan spices; hot lemon sponge pudding in a lemon syrup, served with cream. Unlicensed: bring your own wine. At breakfast, there is freshly squeezed orange juice, home-made muesli and bread, American-style pancakes and a Cumberland spread. Stagshaw Gardens (National Trust) are nearby; also Dove Cottage and Rydal Mount. More reports, please.

Open End Mar–end Nov, Christmas, New Year. Dinner not always available.
Rooms 8 double. No telephone.
Facilities 2 lounges, dining room (classical background music at dinner); drying room. ½-acre garden. Lake Windermere 1½ miles. Unsuitable for ♿.
Location NE of Ambleside. Turn off A591 towards Kirkstone almost opposite *Bridge House*; *Rowanfield* ½ mile on right. Train: Windermere; taxi.
Restrictions No smoking. No children under 8. No dogs.
Credit cards MasterCard, Visa.
Terms B&B: single £55–£67, double £65–£100; D,B&B: single £69–£91, double £115–£148. Set dinner £24. Christmas package. 1-night bookings occasionally refused.

AMPLEFORTH North Yorkshire — Map 4:D4

Shallowdale House
West End, Ampleforth
nr York, YO62 4DY

Tel 01439-788325
Fax 01439-788885
Email stay@shallowdalehouse.demon.co.uk
Website www.shallowdalehouse.demon.co.uk

'Utterly wonderful', this small guest house stands in a 'quite glorious position' on a sheltered south-facing slope of the Hambleton hills. 'It has been exquisitely decorated, in a very personal style,' says a regular visitor this year, and the charming hosts, Phillip Gill and Anton van der Horst, 'treat their guests as friends'. Every room of the house, built above green lawns in 1962, has spectacular views of the surrounding unspoilt countryside. The three bedrooms are 'attractive and spacious'; 'each is equally delightful'. The owners serve dinner, by arrangement, preparing 'domestic-eclectic' food 'of very high quality', using local seasonal ingredients, eg, roulade of peppers and aubergines; slow-roasted cushion of Moors lamb; iced Armagnac parfait. There is a modest wine list. Dinner is served at 7.30 pm by candlelight, at separate tables; coffee is taken by a log fire in a lounge with antique furniture and floral fabrics. Breakfast 'is excellent', with home-made bread, cakes and biscuits. Ampleforth, in the North York Moors National Park, is famous for its Benedictine priory and public school. A good base for visiting Castle Howard, Newby Hall, the ruins of Byland, Rievaulx and Fountains abbeys, etc. Lawrence Sterne was curate in the delightful village of Coxwold, six miles away, where he wrote part of *Tristram Shandy*. (*Andrew Warren, Philip Spertus, and others*)

Open All year, except Christmas, New Year. Occasional closures in winter.
Rooms 3 double. No telephone.
Facilities Drawing room, sitting room, dining room. No background music. 2½-acre grounds. Unsuitable for ♿.
Location 20 miles N of York. At W end of Ampleforth, on turning to Hambleton. Bus from York.
Restrictions No smoking. No children under 12. No dogs.
Credit cards MasterCard, Visa.
Terms B&B: single £32.50–£55, double £65–£80; D,B&B: single £55–£77.50, double £110–£125. Set dinner £22.50. Reductions for 3 or more nights. 1-night bookings refused bank holiday weekends.

APPLETHWAITE Cumbria — Map 4: inset C2

Underscar Manor
Applethwaite
nr Keswick CA12 4PH

Tel 017687-75000
Fax 017687-74904

'If there's an afterlife, it will look something like *Underscar* on a spring evening,' says an admirer of this Italianate Victorian house, which 'has bags of charm'. The setting 'is breathtaking', in large wooded grounds (where red squirrels and kites can be seen) in the Lake District National Park. From the grounds and many rooms there are 'stunning views' across Derwentwater to the mountains beyond.The food is thought 'excellent' too (the owners, Pauline and Derek Harrison, also own *Moss Nook*, a well-known Manchester restaurant). With Gordon Evans, they 'run a slick professional operation, to which they give an air of lovable eccentricity'. Teddy bears are everywhere – one is seated at the disklavier grand piano in the hall, which sometimes tinkles away during dinner. 'Crystal chandeliers and frilly cushions add to the charm' (some find it OTT). The best bedrooms overlook the view, as does the ornate conservatory dining room, where smart dress is expected at dinner. Elaborate modern dishes are served by the chef, Robert Thornton (Mrs Harrison's brother), eg, fish pie gateau with king prawns, spinach and parsley sauce; medallions of venison with a chartreuse of vegetables and foie gras, wild mushrooms, caramelised apple, polenta pancake and Calvados sauce. For dessert you could choose the 'selection of small sweet tastings' – seven little puddings on a plate. The wine list is 'impressive, but lacks a selection of wines by the glass'. Breakfast is 'excellent, with fresh orange juice and hot dishes cooked to order'. There are 25 timeshare apartments in a building adjacent to the hotel, and a spa with an indoor swimming pool, health and beauty facilities, and a bistro. (*VH*)

Open All year, except 3 days after New Year.
Rooms 11 double.
Facilities Hall (pianist occasionally in evening), 2 lounges, restaurant; spa (indoor swimming pool, bistro, etc). 40-acre grounds: gardens, woodland, stream; Derwentwater, fishing, water sports 1½ miles; golf nearby. Unsuitable for ♿.
Location Off A66, 1½ miles N of Keswick. Train: Penrith; taxi.
Restrictions No smoking in restaurant. No children under 12. No dogs.
Credit cards Amex, MasterCard, Visa.
Terms D,B&B double £180–£250. Set lunch £25, dinner £30; full alc £50. Special breaks by arrangement. Christmas package. 1-night bookings refused Sat, public holidays.

ARNCLIFFE North Yorkshire — Map 4:D3

Amerdale House
Arncliffe, Littondale
Skipton BD23 5QE

Tel 01756-770250
Fax 01756-770266
Website www.amerdalehouse.co.uk

César award in 1995

'A delightful place to stay, in wonderful countryside.' 'Nigel and Paula Crapper are a unique team, and make their guests very welcome.' 'Their staff are attentive and kindly.' 'My ideal hotel. It's so peaceful. Comfortable in any weather. Very good value for money.' Many tributes came again this year to this Victorian manor house in one of the quietest backwaters of the Yorkshire Dales. The Crappers have presided for 15 years. The place is 'by no means luxurious', and the comfortable bedrooms vary in size; some are small; three are on the second floor (no lift); most look down Littondale. 'The ambience is relaxing; reception rooms are well proportioned and maintained, each with an open fire and plenty to read.' 'The highlight is Nigel's cooking; presentation is superb, service is discreet. One night the menu included warm herbed chicken salad; seafood casserole; sea bass with delicate and unusual vegetables; chocolate tart.' The ingredients for the four-course dinner are sourced locally whenever possible; there are always three choices of starter and two of main course. Vegetarians should make their needs known in advance. Wine prices range from £9.50 to £79 a bottle; there are good selections from France and the New World. Breakfast, 'a leisurely affair', includes black pudding and Cumberland sausage, also freshly squeezed orange juice and decent toast. 'Nigel's scrambled eggs are the best ever, and he makes his own delicious marmalade.' All around is excellent walking and birdwatching – the Crappers provide local maps, guide books, picnic lunches, a boot box in the porch, help with drying clothes. Fountains Abbey, Harewood House and Skipton Castle are nearby; a spectacular 14-mile drive will take you to the start of the Settle–Carlisle Railway. (*JP Marland, Jennifer Davis, Trevor Lockwood, Stephen Potts*)

Open Mid-Mar–mid-Nov. Restaurant closed midday.
Rooms 11 double. 1 in converted stables.
Facilities Lounge, library, bar, restaurant. No background music. 2½-acre grounds. Unsuitable for ♿.
Location 17 miles NW of Skipton. Fork left off B6160 to Arncliffe. Local bus.
Restrictions No smoking in restaurant. No dogs.
Credit cards MasterCard, Visa.
Terms [2001] D,B&B £70.50–£74.50. Single supplement £10. Set dinner £30. Special breaks: 4 nights for price of 3. 1-night bookings refused some weekends.

ASHBOURNE Derbyshire — Map 3:B6

Callow Hall
Mappleton
Ashbourne DE6 2AA

Tel 01335-300900
Fax 01335-300512
Email reservations@callowhall.co.uk
Website www.callowhall.co.uk

'The owners are pleasant; staff are attentive. There is always someone around to help, but you don't feel constantly observed. The atmosphere is agreeably informal, but everything is under control. Expensive, but excellent value.' A report this year on this 'handsome building, with an air of 19th-century solid comfort'. It is 'beautifully sited', in large grounds at the southern edge of the Peak District National Park, above the valley of the river Dove and its tributary, the Bentley brook (with fishing rights for trout and grayling). Other visitors called it 'an oasis of peace, away from the nearby tourist bustle'. The 'unpretentious owners' are David, Dorothy and Anthony Spencer. Mrs Spencer is usually at reception; father and son are the chefs. They do not offer flunkey-type service – you may have to carry your cases; bedrooms are not serviced at night. The interior is 'pleasingly simple': with rugs on polished floors, stags' heads, bowls of flowers and pot-pourri, 'it has the atmosphere of a well-used family home'. Some of the old furniture is heavily carved. The bedrooms, up a wooden staircase, are named after members of the family. 'They are of two categories: the smaller ones are well decorated and cosy; the larger ones, worth the extra money, have lots of space to relax in.' Home-made biscuits, fruit and mineral water, are replenished daily. 'Excellent dinners' are served in a large room with views: 'Interesting main courses, like venison en croûte; imaginative fish courses, eg, battered cod with tomato coulis; delicious desserts, such as tarte Tatin.' Bread is home-baked, sausages and salmon home-smoked. 'First-class breakfasts' have freshly squeezed orange juice, leaf tea, 'perfect poached eggs'. Children are welcomed. Functions are sometimes held. The grounds 'are being restored to their Victorian glory'. Holly, 'an affectionate yet restrained' Labrador, will accompany visitors on walks. Nearby sights: Chatsworth, Kedleston, Hardwick Hall, Haddon Hall, Calke Abbey, Alton Towers. (*Stephen Potts*)

Open All year, except 25/26 Dec.
Rooms 1 suite, 15 double. 1, on ground floor, equipped for ♿.
Facilities Lounge, bar, restaurant; function/conference facilities. No background music. 42-acre grounds: garden, woodland, farm, stables; river, fishing (tuition available).
Location ½ mile from Ashbourne: A515 to Buxton; sharp left at top of 1st hill by *Bowling Green* pub, 1st right to Mappleton; cross bridge; drive on right. Train: Derby; taxi.
Restrictions No smoking in restaurant, some bedrooms. No dogs in public rooms.
Credit cards All major cards accepted.
Terms [2001] B&B: single £85–£110, double £130–£165, suite £190. Set Sun lunch £20.50, dinner £38; full alc £39.50. Weekend, midweek breaks. *V*

ASHBURTON Devon — Map 1:D4

Holne Chase
Ashburton
nr Newton Abbot TQ13 7NS

Tel 01364-631471
Fax 01364-631453
Email info@holne-chase.co.uk
Website www.holne-chase.co.uk

César award in 1999

'Highly recommended for people with dogs, looking to be wined and dined and walk among some of Dartmoor's most beautiful landscapes.' A visitor this year sums up the attractions of this quirky former hunting lodge on a large estate in the Dartmoor National Park. Guests are likely to be met by Batty the basset hound and Sebastian Hughes, who owns and runs the hotel with his wife, Philippa. He will probably pick up your bags and escort you, talking non-stop, to your room. This is a batty sort of place. The hound has her own website, www.batty-basset.co.uk, and 'a slightly mad pony roams around, and likes to join you for tea on the terrace'. Some find the bluff approach unsympathetic, but fans think *Holne Chase* 'excellent in every way'. 'They drove us to the top of a hill for a good walk down, and even offered to lend us a car.' Dog-owners are accommodated in the stables (these rooms have a sitting room, but walls may be thin). Front bedrooms in the main house look across the wooded valley to distant hills. Some rooms are quite small, with a small bathroom. The river Dart (with fishing rights) runs through the grounds; there is a pond with ducks and geese, and acres of woodland with wild flowers, animals and birds. The food has been thought 'a bit pretentious' in the past. As we went to press, we learned that the style of cooking was being changed to 'something more appropriate for a country hotel'. There will be a smaller selection, of daily-changing dishes, eg, cuts of meat off the bone. Wines are 'good, if expensive'. Several visitors this year wrote of slow breakfast service. The Hugheses own three other *Guide* hotels: *Duke's*, Bath, *The Little Admiral*, Dartmouth, *St Olaves*, Exeter. (*Mark Foster, DJO and HP Owen, Jonathan Mirsky, BJ Hanbury, and others*)

Open All year.
Rooms 8 suites, 9 double. 6 in stables 200 yds. 1 on ground floor.
Facilities Ramp. Lounge, bar, restaurant; private dining/meeting room. No background music. 70-acre grounds in 300-acre estate: river Dart (fly-fishing), croquet, putting.
Location From N and E: M5 to Exeter, A38 to 2nd Ashburton turn-off; pass Pear Tree garage on left; after 2 miles cross Holne bridge; hotel ¼ mile on right. From Plymouth: leave A38 at 1st Ashburton turn-off. Train: Newton Abbot; taxi.
Restrictions No smoking in restaurant. No children under 12 at dinner. No dogs in public rooms.
Credit cards Diners, MasterCard, Visa.
Terms B&B: single £95, double £130–£150, suite £170. Set lunch £20, dinner £34.50. Special breaks. Christmas, New Year, painting, etc. 1-night bookings refused weekends. ***V***

ASHFORD Kent *See SHORTLIST* — Map 2:D5

ASHWATER Devon — Map 1:C3

Blagdon Manor
Ashwater EX21 5DF

Tel 01409-211224
Fax 01409-211634
Email stay@blagdon.com
Website www.blagdon.com

'A sociable place', Tim and Gill Casey's Grade II listed 17th-century manor house stands in large grounds, deep in the countryside on the Devon/Cornwall border. They run it in house-party style. Guests dine together round a large rosewood table at 8 pm, and the hostess's 'delicious home cooking' is admired. No choice until dessert, on a three-course menu, eg, toasted goat's cheese with a chicory and orange salad; cod on lemon mash, with roasted peppers; mixed berries poached in spiced red wine, or home-made sorbet. Chintzy fabrics and fresh flowers complement the old building's oak beams and slate flagstones. There is a 'gorgeous library', a snooker table in the bar, and a large log fire in the drawing room in winter. 'It is *so quiet,*' said a fan. 'No sound of traffic, only birds and cows. Lovely grounds.' A child-free zone: no one under 16 is admitted. You can see Dartmoor in one direction, in the other the Cornish coast, ten miles away. Local attractions include Rosemoor and other gardens, and many National Trust properties. More reports, please.

Open All year, except Christmas.
Rooms 7 double.
Facilities Lounge, library, games room, bar/snooker room, dining room; 2 meeting rooms. No background music. 8-acre grounds: gardens, golf practice,

croquet, helipad. Shooting, riding, fishing nearby. Unsuitable for ♿.
Location 6 miles NE of Launceston. A388 towards Holworthy. Past Chapman's Well and 1st sign to Ashwater. Right at 2nd sign; 1st right (signposted Blagdon/Viza). House on right.
Restrictions Smoking in library and bar only. No children under 16. Dogs by arrangement, not in public rooms.
Credit cards Amex, MasterCard, Visa.
Terms B&B: single £60–£70, double £95–£110. Set dinner £21.

AYLESBURY Buckinghamshire — Map 2:C3

Hartwell House
Oxford Road
nr Aylesbury HP17 8NL

Tel 01296-747444
Fax 01296-747450
Email info@hartwell-house.com
Website www.hartwell-house.com

A rich history attaches to this magnificent, honey-coloured, Grade I listed mansion, part Jacobean, part Georgian, with a grand interior. King Louis XVIII of France held court in exile here in the early 19th century. As a hotel (Relais & Châteaux), it is much visited by the rich and famous (eg, Bill Clinton, the Emperor of Japan), and often used for corporate events. It was restored to its former glory by Historic House Hotels (see also *Middlethorpe Hall*, York, *The Cadogan*, London, *Bodysgallen Hall*, Llandudno). It stands in a huge park with a chapel, a trout lake, statuary, a ha-ha. 'The combination of an architecturally distinguished building and a fine setting must make this one of the most attractive hotels in the UK,' one fan wrote. Guests enter through an 18th-century baroque great hall, to find a Jacobean central staircase, fine paintings and plasterwork, chandeliers, a maze of corridors. The huge best bedrooms have large windows, panelling and tapestries. The King's Room has a double aspect, yellow curtains and four-poster bed. *Hartwell Court*, a converted stable block, houses some newer rooms (some are duplexes), also a spa with a swimming pool, a small gym, and a buttery for light lunches. The atmosphere is formal – men must wear jacket and tie in the restaurant at night – but the courteous manager, Jonathan Thompson, and his 'uniformly pleasant' staff are regularly praised. The chef, Daniel Richardson, describes his style as 'British, simple, not messed about with' – main courses include grilled salmon with hollandaise sauce; rump of lamb with a kidney and rosemary risotto; grilled steak with béarnaise sauce. *Hartwell House*'s summer breaks include free entry into local stately homes (Waddesden Manor, Blenheim Palace, etc). (*TH, and others*)

Open All year.
Rooms 13 suites, 32 double, 1 single. Some in stable block. Some on ground floor.
Facilities Lift, ramp. 4 drawing rooms, bar, 3 dining rooms; conference facilities; spa: swimming pool, whirlpool, sauna, beauty salon, bar/buttery. No background music. Pianist in vestibule, Fri/Sat evening. 94-acre grounds: tennis, croquet, lake (fishing), woodlands.
Location 2 miles S of Aylesbury on A418 towards Oxford; hotel on right. Train: Aylesbury; taxi.
Restrictions No smoking: dining rooms, morning room, some bedrooms. No children under 8. No dogs in public rooms or main house bedrooms.

Credit cards MasterCard, Visa.
Terms [2001] Room: single £140–£145, double £225–£235, suite £325–£335. Breakfast £12.50–£16.90. D,B&B £160–£225 per person. Set lunch £22–£29, dinner £46. Special breaks: winter, spring, summer, spa. Christmas, New Year house parties. *V* (Sun–Thurs)

BAMPTON Devon — Map 1:C5

Bark House
Oakfordbridge
Nr Bampton EX16 9HZ

Tel 01398-351236
Website www.barkhouse.co.uk

Owner/chef Alastair Kameen runs this old Exe valley stone house, once used to store bark chippings for a tannery, as a reasonably priced small hotel. The atmosphere is 'inviting', says a visitor this year. 'Service is at all times courteous.' 'Their wish to meet our needs was utmost,' says another enthusiastic report. 'Our large and comfortable bedroom overlooked a main road, but it was silent at night.' The food is much admired. 'A dinner party-style menu was cooked superbly, and served in the intimate dining room. The ingredients were natural, fresh and of the highest quality.' The cooking, which 'has a light touch' is 'inventive but not flashy' – a melon and muscatel soup was refreshing and tasty'. A choice of two main courses is generally offered (perhaps halibut with a dill and vermouth cream sauce, or casserole of chicken with wine, spices, prunes and apricots). Breakfast, 'equally good and substantial', has home-baked bread and porridge made from home-milled oats. Morning tea can be brought to the room or DIY; 'children of considerate parents' are welcomed. Guests can take tea and drinks in the pretty terraced garden. *Bark House* does its best to welcome guests with a mobility problem, but due to its age, it has no facilities for wheelchairs. Good walking nearby, and the north and south Devon Coastal Paths are about 40 minutes away by car. (*TW Groves, Ruth Fasht*)

Open 'Most of the year' but generally closed Mon, Tues in summer.
Rooms 5 double. Also one 2-bedroomed self-catering cottage.
Facilities Lounge, dining room (light classical background music at night). 1¼-acre garden. Unsuitable for ♿.
Location Hamlet 3 miles W of Bampton. On A396, 9 miles N of Tiverton. Train: Tiverton Parkway.
Restrictions No smoking: restaurant, bedrooms. No dogs in public rooms.
Credit cards None accepted.
Terms [2001] B&B £39.50–£51.75; D,B&B (min. 2 nights) £65.75–£73. Set dinner £25. Christmas, New Year packages. 1-night bookings occasionally refused.

BARNARD CASTLE Co. Durham — Map 4:C3

Homelands BUDGET
85 Galgate
Barnard Castle DL12 8ES

Tel 01833-638757
Email homelands@barnard-castle.fsnet.co.uk

'The epitome of an excellent guest house.' Mrs Irene Williamson runs a friendly and flexible place. Saturday visitors, who arrived to find that the restaurant was fully booked, appreciated her 'kindly gesture' of serving a Sunday evening meal (when the restaurant is normally closed) on their return eight days later. 'She told us we were to be accommodated in the garage; this turned out to be a meticulous conversion at the bottom of the charming garden, blissfully quiet.' This 'marvellous place' makes a good base for visiting this market town on the river Tees (it takes its name from the ruins of a 12th-century castle, built for Barnard Balliol, a cohort of William the Conqueror). Charles Dickens is one of many famous visitors to be commemorated with a blue plaque, and the famous Bowes Museum is housed in a French Renaissance-style mansion on the town's outskirts. *Homelands*'s restaurant, open to the public and attracting diners from nearby hotels, looks over the garden. The cooking, on a short, weekly-changing menu, is admired: 'Leek and cheese tartlet with wonderfully light pastry; succulent pork fillet; tender, rare beef.' Mr Williamson 'knows about wine and serves it properly'; several good choices are available by the glass. The house is filled with antiques ('there to be used, not just looked at') and pictures. Front bedrooms overlook a road that is busy by day but quiet at night. All rooms have double glazing, a colour-coordinated decor, TV, thoughtful extras. Some are 'compact' with a small shower room. 'Close to perfection in the small town hotel bracket,' was an inspector's verdict. 'Exceptional quality at a budget price.' Very popular. Book well ahead. (*GH Pells, and others*)

Open All year, except Christmas, New Year. Restaurant closed midday, Sun night.
Rooms 3 double (1 in garden), 2 single.
Facilities Lounge, restaurant (light classical background music at night). Small garden. Unsuitable for ♿.
Location Central (rooms double-glazed). Bus-stop opposite.
Restrictions No smoking: restaurant, bedrooms. No children under 6. No dogs.
Credit cards None accepted.
Terms B&B: single £22–£30, double £43–£50. Set dinner £16.50.

BARNSTAPLE Devon — Map 1:B4

Lynwood House
Bishop's Tawton Road
Barnstaple EX32 9EF

Tel 01271-343695
Fax 01271-379340
Email info@lynwoodhouse.co.uk
Website www.lynwoodhouse.co.uk

'Two springer spaniels provide a homely touch' to a restaurant-with-rooms which was once a Victorian gentleman's residence, on the edge of the market town. This is the Roberts family home: John is in charge of the front-of-house; his wife, Ruth, and son, Matthew, are the chefs. The building, fronted by gravel parking, is not particularly attractive but it is 'warm, and personally run', with an 'unpretentious, lived-in feel', and the owners (for 34 years) are 'extremely professional hoteliers'. The bedrooms are well equipped, with a cafetière, fresh milk, biscuits, fruit, etc, and 'the showers really are high powered'. The restaurant, redecorated this year, is popular with locals. It specialises in fish dishes, eg, 'chunky fish soup' (thought 'delicious'); seafood pot; smoked haddock pancake. Breakfast, in a small, pleasant upstairs room, includes freshly squeezed orange juice; 'really good' scrambled eggs with smoked salmon; home-made marmalade. Light lunches are served in the bar. Beaches, the RHS Rosemore garden, and the Royal North Devon Golf Club (the oldest in England) are nearby. More reports, please.

Open All year; restaurant closed Sun to non-residents.
Rooms 5 double.
Facilities Lounge, bar, breakfast room, restaurant (light classical music). Beaches, golf nearby. Unsuitable for ♿.
Location ½ mile SE of centre. Car park. Regular buses, courtesy car, from station.
Restrictions No smoking: restaurant, 2 bedrooms. Dogs by arrangement.
Credit cards Amex, MasterCard, Visa.
Terms B&B: single £47.50, double £67.50. Full alc £30–£35. 2-day break: D,B&B double £220. ***V***

BARWICK Somerset — Map 1:C6

Little Barwick House
Barwick, nr Yeovil
BA22 9TD

Tel 01935-423902
Fax 01935-420908
Email reservations@barwick7.fsnet.co.uk
Website www.littlebarwickhouse.co.uk

César award: Restaurant-with-rooms of the year

'A real find.' 'A delightful place. Oh, so smart, but not "cutting edge".' 'The food is superb, with no hint of flashiness. Very good value.' 'We like everything about it.' 'They call it a restaurant-with-rooms, which correctly plays up the restaurant, but unnecessarily plays down the hotel. The staff are pleasant and non-stuffy.' 'A peaceful stay. The garden is beautifully kept and restful.' Just some of the praise which has come this year for this 'charming Georgian house' in a 'lovely quiet location' in an interesting village near Yeovil. Tim and Emma Ford have been here only two years, and the bedroom refurbishment is nearly complete (bathrooms have a power shower). They 'make a perfect couple'; 'she is a charming young hostess'. They met while working at *Sharrow Bay*, Ullswater, and later worked at *Summer Lodge*, Evershot (*qqv*). Using 'excellent raw materials' on menus with plenty of choice, Tim Ford cooks dishes like ravioli of langoustine with crayfish sauce; roasted sea bass with baby fennel and girolles; apricot délice with white peach sorbet. 'On the comprehensive wine list, most bottles are under the £20 mark.' The dining room has bare floorboards, a large mirror, white cloths on tables. The lounge is 'bright and comfortable'; there is a 'cosy bar'. Breakfast includes generous glassfuls of fresh orange juice and 'wonderful scrambled eggs'; 'not a portion-pack of cereal in sight'. A room at the top may be small. Winter breaks are good value. Barwick is noted chiefly for the 18th-century follies – pillars, towers and arches – on the edge of its park. There are plenty of houses and gardens to visit nearby; the Dorset coast is 30 minutes' drive away. (*Bryan and Mary Blaxall, Heather Sharland, Revd Andrew Kleissner, Col AJW and Mrs HM Harvey, Prof. Robin Winter, PNM Jebb, and many others*)

Open All year, except 2 weeks Jan. Only for lunch on 25 Dec. Restaurant closed to non-residents Sun evening/Mon.
Rooms 6 double.

Facilities Lounge, bar/snug, restaurant, conservatory. No background music. 3½-acre garden: terrace, croquet. Only public rooms accessible for ♿.
Location Left off A37 Yeovil–Dorchester at 1st roundabout. Hotel ¼ mile on left. Train: Yeovil, 2 miles.
Restrictions No smoking: restaurant, bedrooms. No dogs in public rooms.
Credit cards Amex, MasterCard, Visa.
Terms B&B £46.50–£65; D,B&B £66.50–£73.50. Set lunch £14.95, dinner £28.95. Reductions for 2 nights or more. *V*

BASLOW Derbyshire — Map 3:A6

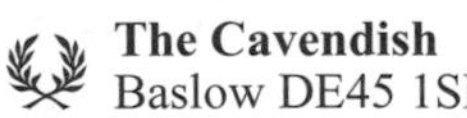

The Cavendish
Baslow DE45 1SP

Tel 01246-582311
Fax 01246-582312
Email info@cavendish-hotel.net
Website www.cavendish-hotel.net

César award: Traditional hotel of the year

'One of our favourite hotels,' writes a devotee in 2001. She loves the combination of 'delightful service, informality, efficiency and location'. Twenty-five years old this year, and run since the beginning by the 'ever-charming' lease-holder, Eric Marsh, *The Cavendish* stands on the northern edge of the Duke and Duchess of Devonshire's Chatsworth estate in the Peak District National Park. A busy road passes in front, but the bedrooms overlook Chatsworth Park, with its ancient trees, river and garden; guests can reach it by walking through a field. 'The staff must be among the nicest in the country. They all get on with whatever needs doing. If the porter isn't around, a waiter will rush over to help with cases. Reception is charming. We like the flexible pricing structure.' Major changes have taken place on the gastronomic front. *Sous-chef* Chris Allison has been promoted to head chef; the main restaurant, renamed *The Gallery*, has been given a simpler decor and a more modern style of cooking. 'Colours are vibrant; it is light and spacious; nothing impedes the bucolic views of the gardens and park. We ate excellent asparagus soup; potted salmon loaf with roquette salad, artistic and tasty; robust braised lamb shank; delicious carpaccio of beef.' *The Garden Room,* 'even more casual than before', has a new, lighter menu. The lounges, furnished with antiques, have lavish flower arrangements, and log fires in winter. Mr Marsh's collection of paintings, 'ranging from Victorian fine art to 20th-century graffiti', hangs throughout; 300 are in *The Gallery*. A bronze figure on the lawn commemorates the millennium. The older bedrooms are in a former inn; others are in the Mitford wing, named after the duchess's famous family. Some have 'a generous sitting area', though bathrooms may be 'a bit old-fashioned', and lighting 'romantic, but dim'. One pleasure is 'to sit at your dressing table and see Chatsworth Park reflected in the mirror'. Breakfast, served all morning, has 'really good home-made marmalade', Buck's Fizz, fresh orange juice, a wide variety of cooked dishes. Eric Marsh owns *The George* (*qv*) in nearby Hathersage. (*Padi Howard, and others*)

Open All year.
Rooms 1 suite (usually let by the month), 23 double.
Facilities Lounge/bar, 2 restaurants (varied background music); private dining

room, conference room. 1-acre grounds: putting. River, fishing nearby. Unsuitable for ♿.
Location On A619 in Chatsworth grounds. M1 exit 29. Train: Chesterfield; taxi.
Restrictions No smoking: restaurants, some bedrooms. No dogs.
Credit cards All major cards accepted.
Terms Room: single £95–£115, double £125–£145, suite £195; D,B&B: £110–£166 per person. Breakfast £12.55. Alc from £22.45. Winter bonus weekends: stay 2 nights, Sun is free. Romantic breaks. Christmas package. 1-night bookings sometimes refused in summer.

Fischer's Baslow Hall *Tel* 01246-583259
Calver Road *Fax* 01246-583818
Baslow DE45 1RR

César award in 1998

'Always a pleasure. Service is unfailingly attentive and pleasant. The owners are true professionals,' writes a regular visitor this year. 'An impeccable welcome; superlative food,' says another guest at Max and Susan Fischer's Edwardian stone manor house. It stands up a winding chestnut tree-lined drive on the edge of the Chatsworth estate. There have been major changes: a new building, *The Garden House*, provides five new bedrooms; there is a new reception in the main house, and a more formal residents' lounge. In the original building, antiques and country pine furniture are set off by bold colours, good fabrics, fresh flowers and bowls of pot-pourri. Some bedrooms are very small, others 'spacious and light' – 'our bathroom had a huge Victorian bath, with a soup plate-sized shower head'. The new rooms, in contrast, have a computer modem point. Residents wishing to dine must reserve a table; they can choose between the *Michelin*-starred restaurant (where men are expected to wear a jacket and tie) and the bistro, *Café-Max* (*Michelin Bib Gourmand*), in the two front rooms. 'Fresher than fresh ingredients' are used 'with herbs that enhance the flavour of the ingredients'. Modern European specialities include rabbit terrine wrapped in Parma ham; pig's trotter stuffed with chicken and morel mushrooms. The fresh fruit Pavlova 'is exquisite'. Even the brasserie dishes are 'quite elaborate, with rich sauces'. There is an extensive and fairly priced wine list. 'Impeccable breakfasts' have freshly squeezed orange juice, fresh fruit, home-baked bread and croissants. 'The gardens are a joy; the Japanese-style sunken garden has matured interestingly.' A good base for walking and climbing. Local stately homes include Chatsworth, Hardwick and Kedleston halls. (*Francine and Ian Walsh, and others*)

Open All year, except 25/26 Dec. Restaurant closed Sun evening; café closed Sat evening/Sun.
Rooms 1 suite, 10 double. 5 in *Garden House*.
Facilities Lounge, bar, breakfast room, restaurant, café; function facilities. No background music. 5-acre grounds. Unsuitable for ♿. Civil wedding licence.
Location A623 Baslow–Stockport. Last entrance on right within village boundary. Train: Chesterfield, 12 miles; taxi.
Restrictions No smoking: restaurant, bedrooms. No children under 12 in restaurant after 7 pm. No dogs.
Credit cards All major cards accepted.

Terms B&B: single £100, double £150. English breakfast £8.50. Set lunch (2 to 3 courses) £20–£24, dinner £48. Winter 2-night packages. Weekend breaks. 1-night bookings sometimes refused.

BASSENTHWAITE LAKE Cumbria — Map 4: inset C2

The Pheasant
Bassenthwaite Lake
nr Cockermouth
CA13 9YE

Tel 017687-76234
Fax 017687-76002
Email pheasant@easynet.co.uk
Website www.the-pheasant.co.uk

'A most pleasant experience,' says a regular *Guide* correspondent of her visit to this 400-year-old inn. Set back from the lake among trees, in the unspoilt northern part of the Lake District, it aims to care for guests 'in a traditional manner at reasonable prices'. Other visitors liked the 'combination of atmosphere and comfort'. The manager, Matthew Wylie, and his staff are 'very helpful'. 'We could not fault our newly refurbished room. The next day's weather forecast was delivered to us each evening. We greatly enjoyed the food – traditional, with a bit of *nouvelle*.' In the beamed dining room, chef Malcolm Ennis offers, eg, pheasant, chicken liver and brandy pâté; fillet of cod on smoked salmon cream sauce; hazelnut and chocolate roulade with raspberry and kirsch coulis. But one resident would have liked the possibility of choosing a one-course meal without having to pay the price of a three-course one. The little bars, 'pleasantly old-fashioned and pubby', serve good lunches (soups, potted shrimps, venison sausage, etc). The lounges have rugs on parquet floors; antiques, log fires. The renovation of the remaining bedrooms should be complete by early 2002. Good walking in all directions. (*Elizabeth Sandham,* Good Pub Guide)

Open All year, except Christmas Day.
Rooms 2 suites, 12 double, 3 single. 1 on ground floor. 2 in garden lodge. TV on request.
Facilities 3 lounges, bar, dining room. No background music. 20-acre grounds. Lake 200 yds, fishing.
Location 6 miles E of Cockermouth. ¼ mile off A66 to Keswick. Train: Penrith, 30 miles.
Restrictions No smoking: dining room, 1 lounge. No children under 8. Dogs in lodge only.
Credit cards MasterCard, Visa
Terms B&B £53–£80; D,B&B (min. 2 nights) £71–£98. Set lunch £15.75, dinner £21.95; full alc £35. 15% discount on 3-night stays, July, Aug. 1-night bookings refused weekends. ***V***

****

Traveller's tale Hotel in Somerset. The atmosphere of this place depends on the character of the host. He is jolly, but he is often abroad, working as an engineer. In his absence the atmosphere is funereal.

****

BATH Somerset **Map 2:D1**

Apsley House
141 Newbridge Hill
Bath BA1 3PT

Tel 01225-336966
Fax 01225-425462
Email info@apsley-house.co.uk
Website www.apsley-house.co.uk

'Definitely charming; all the staff were very pleasant,' says a visitor this year to this upmarket B&B where David and Annie Lanz aim to create the atmosphere of a private home. It was built as a country house for the Duke of Wellington, a mile from the centre. The setting is now urban, but inside the house retains its period feel, and is furnished with antiques and original oil paintings appropriate to its date. Breakfast, served at separate tables in a tall-windowed room that overlooks the small garden, 'is good, with wonderfully cheerful service'. It includes smoked salmon, strawberries and melon in season, large pots of preserves; vegetarians are catered for. There is a smart drawing room, and a bar. Some bedrooms are large and 'pretty, without being too chintzy'; one has an immense bathroom, a fireplace, and French windows opening on to the garden, where tables and chairs stand on the lawn. But one small attic room was thought 'overpriced' this year. No evening meals, but Bath has a huge variety of eating places. (*Suzy Bridges, and others*)

Open All year, except Christmas.
Rooms 9 double.
Facilities Lounge, bar, breakfast room: background radio/CDs all day. ½-acre garden. Unsuitable for ♿.
Location 1 mile W of centre. A4 (Upper Bristol Rd, Newbridge Rd); left into Apsley Rd. Car park. Bus/taxi from centre.
Restrictions No smoking: breakfast room, lounge, some bedrooms. No children under 5. No dogs.
Credit cards All major cards accepted.
Terms [2001] B&B: single £60–£75, double £75–£130, family £95–£130. 2-night breaks; off-season breaks. 1-night bookings sometimes refused.

The Bath Priory
Weston Road
Bath BA1 2XT

Tel 01225-331922
Fax 01225-448276
Email bathprioryhotel@compuserve.com
Website www.thebathpriory.co.uk

'A magnificent city hotel, once an ancient priory, that has been extended several times, creating an architectural jigsaw puzzle given harmony by a splendid garden, part formal, part country herbaceous.' This Grade II listed Georgian Gothic-style building stands in large grounds on the edge of the city. The centre can be reached by a short bus ride or a walk through Victoria Park. Owned by Andrew Brownsword (owner also of Bath Rugby Club), and managed by Tim Pettifer, it is liked for the 'cosy opulence' of the public rooms, with their large oil paintings (many are portraits), antiques, chandeliers, flower arrangements and log fires. For many guests, the highlight is the 'wonderful food', served in the Gothic Room (with antiques and fine paintings though one reader thought it gloomy), in a garden room or an orangery. The chef, Robert Clayton, well deserves his *Michelin* star, says a visitor this year for his 'modern and unfussy yet strikingly presented' food. The hotel's vegetable, herb and fruit garden supplies the kitchens, and Mr Clayton's philosophy is: 'When properly prepared, the simplest of foods can have the most exquisite taste.' The three-course menu changes daily, and might include ravioli of poached lobster bound with a scallop mousse; roast best end of organic lamb with Jerusalem artichokes; warm chocolate fondant with a malted milk ice cream. The wine list is wide ranging. The bedrooms vary in size (one couple reported an overheated one over the boiler room); the 'superior' ones are 'seriously comfortable and very pretty'. 'One of the best we've had in Britain,' one guest wrote. Rooms that overlook the gardens are peaceful; others can get traffic noise. There is an open-air swimming pool, and a spa with an indoor pool (in the style of a Roman bath) and a gym. (*Adrian Turner, BW*)

Open All year.
Rooms 3 suites, 24 double, 1 single. Some on ground floor.
Facilities 2 lounges, restaurant; conference facilities. No background music. Spa: indoor swimming pool, gym, sauna, etc. 4-acre grounds: swimming pool, croquet.
Location 1 mile W of centre, off A4 to Bristol. From E take London Rd to The Paragon; right into Lansdown Rd, 3rd left into Julian Rd; continue along Crescent La, Weston Rd (park on left, golf course on right). Hotel 300 yds on left, after mini-roundabout at junction with Park La.
Restrictions No smoking: restaurant, some bedrooms. Guide dogs only.
Credit cards All major cards accepted.
Terms [2001] B&B: single £145, double £230–£290, suite £320; D,B&B: single £170, double £285–£345, suite £375. Set lunch £27.50, dinner £45; full alc from £37.50. Weekend breaks. Christmas package.

Duke's NEW
Great Pulteney Street
Bath BA2 4DN

Tel 01225-463512 and 787960
Fax 01225-483733
Email info@dukesbath.co.uk
Website www.dukesbath.co.uk

A small Palladian-style hotel: every bedroom has an aristocratic name: Wellington, Grafton, Marlborough, etc. It was recently taken over by Philippa and Sebastian Hughes of *Holne Chase*, Ashburton (*qv*). They have extensively refurbished, and Martin Blunos is supervising the restaurant, *Fitzroy's*, giving it a less formal style than his other Bath restaurant, *Lettonie* (*qv*). The manager is Niall Edmondson. 'The situation is excellent, on one of the city's most elegant streets, away from the bustle but close to the Pulteney Bridge,' says an inspection report in 2001 which is positive, but with some caveats. 'A very nice hotel, both smart and comfortable, decorated with period furniture, prints and portraits. The staff are very friendly, and service was helpful, though it was not altogether clear who was in charge, and there were some glitches. Our attic room had lovely views over hills, and a masculine decor, brown, with botanical prints, leather chairs, nautical-style chests. The small bathroom had fluffy towels.' Other bedrooms, and the suites, are larger. 'The small dining room in the basement is rather dark, done in a colonial style, with decorative elephant screens to give privacy. Dinner was not cheap, and we did not think it special: borscht, and crispy duck with roasted red pepper salad were both a little bland; salmon with creamed leeks was nice but not outstanding. But chocolate fondant with rosemary-infused ice cream was good, and breakfast was excellent: good croissants, delicious scrambled eggs. A few teething problems, and the hotel is not yet quite at ease with itself, but we would stay here again.' Dog-owners can exercise their pets in Henrietta Park, opposite. More reports, please.

Open All year.
Rooms 5 suites, 17 double, 1 single. Some on ground floor, 1 adapted for ♿.
Facilities Lounge, bar, restaurant. No background music. Courtyard, garden.
Location 5 mins' walk from centre. Parking permits available (£5 a night).
Restrictions No smoking in restaurant. No dogs in public rooms.
Credit cards Diners, MasterCard, Visa.
Terms B&B: single £145, double £185, suite £225. Set lunch £20, dinner £30; full alc £37.

Haringtonʼs Hotel
8–10 Queen Street
Bath BA1 1HE

Tel 01225-461728
Fax 01225-444804
Email post@haringtonshotel.co.uk
Website www.haringtonshotel.co.uk

'A matchless small hotel, seriously addictive,' is the verdict of one regular visitor to this unassuming place. It consists of a group of 18th-century houses on a cobbled street in the middle of town and is liked for its 'agreeably informal style', and the warmth of the owner/managers, Susan and Desmond Pow, 'who have a knack for making guests feel at home'. Their staff 'are unfailingly attentive and friendly'. The bedrooms have pastel colours and cable TV, and are 'surprisingly quiet, considering the hotel's position in the centre of Bath'. Some are up a steep spiral staircase (no lift; this is a listed building). Breakfast 'is served with a smile'; 'very good coffee' is on tap all day. The pleasant little café', open to the public, serves reasonably priced light meals – pasta, curries, salads, etc, until 8 pm and drinks until midnight. Many other eating places are nearby. Parking is awkward: after unloading on the pavement outside, you must drive to the long-term car park, five minutes' walk away. All the city's main attractions – the Roman Baths, the Abbey, the Assembly Rooms and the Theatre Royal – are close by. (*Ann Evans*)

Open All year, except Christmas.
Rooms 12 double, 1 single.
Facilities Café/bar (mixed background music all day). Tiny courtyard. Unsuitable for ♿.
Location Central, near Queen Sq. From George St, turn into Milsom St. Right after *Jolly's* into Quiet St; 1st left into Queen St. Long-term car park in Charlotte St, 200 metres (£5 for 24 hours).
Restrictions Smoking in bar only. No dogs.
Credit cards All major cards accepted.
Terms B&B: single £65–£88, double £88–£118. Full alc £20. 1-night bookings sometimes refused Sat.

Give the *Guide* positive support. Don't leave feedback to others.

Haydon House
9 Bloomfield Park
Bath BA2 2BY

Tel 01225-444919
Fax 01225-427351
Email stay@haydonhouse.co.uk
Website www.haydonhouse.co.uk

Built of traditional Bath stone, and run by its 'warm and helpful' owners, Gordon and Magdalene Ashman-Marr, this B&B is a semi-detached Edwardian house in a quiet residential area above the city. With free street parking on the doorstep, a dovecote in front, and a colourful rear garden (with statues), it is a useful base for visiting the city. The centre is an easy walk down to the centre, a steepish walk back (or you can take a bus). 'Big bow windows face the street; an indoor fountain gurgles,' say inspectors. 'Our large, high-ceilinged bedroom had all the necessary accessories (trouser press, sherry, tea tray, shortbread, etc). Its decor was pink and blue, the bed was very comfortable, the bathroom was luxurious. Pigeons nesting under the window cooed from the early hours, and the bathroom pipes clunked from about the same time.' The lounge is crammed with family photos, china ornaments, plants and dried flowers. The host, 'eccentricity personified', keeps up a flow of conversation while serving the communal breakfast. 'No skimping' – a huge choice includes pancakes with maple syrup, whisky or rum porridge, scrambled eggs with smoked salmon, eggs Benedict, home-made mango-and-orange marmalade, all served with good china, silver and crystal. Vegetarian and vegan options can be arranged, and a continental breakfast can be taken in the bedroom. The large top room, with a sitting area, is suitable for a family. But Room 4 is said to be very small, with a tiny shower room. Help is offered with theatre and dinner reservations. The golden retrievers, Cloud and Cobweb, 'are an integral part of our organisation', say the Ashman-Marrs.

Open All year.
Rooms 5 double.
Facilities Sitting room, study (soft classical background music), breakfast room, terrace. ½-acre garden. Sports/leisure centre nearby. 'Not really suitable for ♿, but they are welcome by prior arrangement.'
Location From centre take A367 (to Exeter) *c.* ½ mile up Wells Rd. Right into shopping area (*Bear* pub on right). At end of short dual carriageway fork right into Bloomfield Rd; Bloomfield Pk 2nd right. Street parking. Bus 14 from centre.
Restrictions No smoking. Children by arrangement. No dogs.
Credit cards Amex, MasterCard, Visa.
Terms B&B: single £50–£70, double £70–£103, family £90–£135. 3 nights for price of 2 (except Fri/Sat, bank holidays) Nov–Mar. 1-night bookings occasionally refused weekends. ***V***

Lettonie
35 Kelston Road
Bath BA1 3QH

Tel 01225-446676
Fax 01225-447541
Email sian@lettonie.co.uk
Website www.lettonie.co.uk

Neither chef/*patron* Martin Blunos nor his wife, Siân (front-of-house), was in attendance at their *Michelin* two-star restaurant-with-rooms when our inspector called this year, but service and food were 'of the highest quality'. The honey-coloured Georgian gentleman's residence is on a hill two miles out of Bath. The public rooms and bedrooms have glorious views over the green Kelston valley. 'We were warmly greeted by Andrew, in charge that day, who took our bags. He later served us pre-dinner drinks in the bar (with lots of leather sofas, traditional furnishings). The friendly young Scottish *sommelier* offered a choice of six wines by the glass. A New Zealand Sauvignon Blanc was crisp and fruity.' The restaurant is formed from two formal Georgian rooms in a mirror image of each other: traditional table settings, discreet lighting, soft modern jazz. 'Service, by a young French waitress, was attentive, friendly, never obtrusive.' The three-course set menu (£47.50) comes with entertaining embellishments, eg, a tea cup of tangy broccoli soup as an *amuse-gueule*. 'Mr Blunos cooks with wit, imagination, and references to his Latvian roots. Delicious borscht terrine, a variation of a traditional soup, was served with shredded beef and onion pirags (Latvian dough balls). Crab ravioli was lightly dressed with a cognac cream sauce. The main course of lamb cutlets and individual shepherd's pie (with a crisp pastry base and a creamy potato topping) was spot-on: inventive, but not over-elaborate. The pre-dessert "egg soldier" was another joke – a brown eggshell, filled with vanilla cream and topped with mango mousse. This light touch continued with desserts like blood orange terrine; warm apple and vanilla savarin.' The rear bedrooms are large and light. Our inspector's cheaper room at the front was cramped, with dim lighting and a tiny bathroom. 'But the comfortable bed had crisp cotton sheets, there was a silver bowl of fruit, bottles of Madeira and mineral water, and traffic noise was baffled by a high wall. Continental breakfast is served in the room. The waitress staggered in with tray loaded with good coffee, fresh orange juice, a bowl of yogurt, a pot of honey, pastries, croissants, home-made strawberry preserve. There was nowhere to put it, but we cleared a side table, and picnicked on the bed. When we checked out, we were given a packet of warm pirags. *Lettonie* may be expensive, but it is a great treat.'

Open All year, except 2 weeks over Christmas, 2 weeks Aug, Sun, Mon.
Rooms 4 double (for restaurant guests).
Facilities Reception, bar, restaurant, private dining room; background music. 1-acre garden.
Location 2 miles NW of Bath on A431 to Kelston, Bristol.
Restrictions No smoking: restaurant, bedrooms. No dogs.
Credit cards All major cards accepted.
Terms B&B double £95–£150. Set lunch £25, dinner £47.50. ***V***

The Queensberry
Russel Street
Bath BA1 2QF

Tel 01225-447928
Fax 01225-446065
Email enquiries@bathqueensberry.com
Website www.bathqueensberry.com

César award in 2000

'We really enjoyed our stay.' 'Everything very spruce; most pleasant staff.' Stephen and Penny Ross's upmarket small hotel, composed of adjoining town houses (designed by John Wood for the Marquis of

Queensberry in 1772) is in a residential street near the Assembly Rooms. One younger couple found the service 'genuinely warm without being obsequious (we arc under 30, and occasionally get treated as undesirables in upmarket hotels)'. Flower baskets hang in front in summer. 18th-century stucco ceilings, cornices and panelling set off a contemporary decor and modern watercolours. The drawing room is 'particularly pretty in rust and yellow' (teas are served here). Some bedrooms, and the small bar, open on to courtyard gardens at the rear. The stairways are elegant with a dark blue carpet and cream paintwork. On the first floor, bedrooms are large ('ours was tasteful and uncluttered, decorated in primrose and dark blue'; 'our bathroom was the size of a bedroom in our London flat'). Higher up, rooms are smaller and cheaper. Light meals and a continental breakfast can be brought to the bedrooms. A cooked breakfast is served in the 'light and cheerful' basement *Olive Tree* restaurant (with pink walls, and rugs on a tiled floor). 'We loved it. Lunch was good and the ambience delightful.' At night, candles burn, and modern British/Mediterranean dishes, eg, terrine of rabbit saddle; roasted belly of organic pork with green pea purée; gratin of blood oranges and blueberries, are accompanied by 'reasonably priced' wines. 'Super food in quiet and luxurious surroundings.' Jason Horn has been promoted to head chef. Parking is difficult, but careful instructions are given. (*Nicholas Kind, Brian and Eve Webb, James L Clarke, and others*)

Open All year, except 4 days over Christmas. Restaurant closed midday bank holiday Mon.
Rooms 29 double. Some on ground floor.
Facilities Lift. Drawing room, bar, restaurant (background jazz at lunch and dinner); meeting room. 4 courtyard gardens.
Location 100 yds from Assembly Rooms. Take Bennett St left off Lansdown Rd, then 1st right. Street parking.
Restrictions No smoking in restaurant. Guide dogs only.
Credit cards MasterCard, Visa.
Terms [2001] B&B: single £90–£120, double £115–£210. English breakfast £9.50. Set lunch £13.50–£15.50, dinner £24; full alc £45. Winter breaks. 1-night bookings refused weekends.

Royal Crescent Hotel
16 Royal Crescent
Bath BA1 2LS

Tel 01225-823333
Fax 01225-339401
Email reservations@royalcrescent.co.uk
Website www.royalcrescent.co.uk

'For views, setting and friendly service, this is one of the best,' is one comment on this 'landmark hotel' owned by Cliveden Ltd (see also Taplow). Composed of two adjoining Georgian houses and the Palladian villas in the peaceful gardens behind, it stands in all its Georgian splendour in the middle of John Wood's glorious crescent, looking down across the city. No hotel sign; guests are greeted by 'impeccably mannered doormen in tails' and valet parking. Chandeliers, antiques, fine paintings and lavish flower arrangements fill the grand public rooms. The suites are grand, too, and lavishly equipped, and most doubles are large, with a 'tastefully restrained' decor, TV concealed in a cabinet, drinks in decanters, 'a pleasing variety of toiletries' in the bathroom. Only one restaurant now: *Pimpernel's*, with hand-printed wallpaper depicting garden follies, in the dower house. Here, chef Steven Blake serves contemporary English dishes 'with a flavour of the East', eg, spare rib terrine with Thai green rice; halibut with fine noodles, coconut and coriander nage. Vegetarians have their own menu. One visitor this year wrote of 'extremely small portions – but the puddings were elegantly presented'. There is a plunge pool in the garden, a Bath House for soothing Japanese-style treatments, a 17-piece gym (new this year), a launch for cruising on the Kennet and Avon Canal, a hot-air balloon for aerial sightseeing. Children are welcomed (babysitting can be arranged), and so are dogs. Not cheap, with lots of extras on the bill. Weddings and all manner of other functions are catered for. A new manager, Kevin Poulter, arrived this year, so we'd like more reports, please.

Open All year.
Rooms 16 suites, 29 double. In 5 buildings. Some on ground floor.
Facilities Lift, ramps. Hall/bar, drawing room, library, restaurant (occasional background music); function facilities. 1-acre garden: Bath House, gym, open-air plunge pool. River launch, hot-air balloon trips, theatre tickets arranged. Civil wedding licence.
Location ½ mile from centre. From Circus, exit to Brock St; hotel at centre of crescent (no hotel sign; entrance to left of magnolia). Valet parking.
Restrictions No smoking: restaurant, 9 bedrooms.
Credit cards All major cards accepted.
Terms [2001] Room: double £220, suite £420–£800. Breakfast £17.50. Set lunch £18–£25; full alc £60. 2-night rates. Christmas, New Year packages. 1-night bookings sometimes refused weekends.

Sydney Gardens Hotel NEW
Sydney Road
Bath BA2 6NT

Tel 01225-464818 and 445362
Fax 01225-484347
Email book@sydneygardens.co.uk
Website www.sydneygardens.co.uk

'The location is perfect. It is beautifully and comfortably furnished. The service is friendly.' An inspection report in 2001 'unreservedly recommends' Geraldine and Peter Beaven's small B&B in their listed Italianate Victorian house (they have been here five years). 'Our double room, attractive in yellow and green, was quiet, looking over the garden, but some rooms get noise from a railway line. The public areas are lovely too: unusual pieces of furniture and antique objects, eg, an old-fashioned cash register, Art Deco lamps, indicate a collector's eye. There is a wide iron staircase, a delightful lounge. Plants are everywhere. The impression is of space and light. In the breakfast room, most attractive, with expensive drapes on windows, mirrors, a beautiful fireplace, there was a central table with a large selection of cereals, fruit, good jam and honey in pots. The cooked breakfast was superb. The owners' charming daughter waited on us.' Sydney Gardens are accessible through a gate off the small, neat grounds, and the city centre is a short walk away.

Open All year, except Christmas.
Rooms 6 double.

Facilities Lounge, breakfast room. Small garden. Access to adjacent park with tennis, canal walks. Unsuitable for ♿.
Location From A4, left on to A36 to Exeter/Wells. Cross Avon. 4th right, pass Holburne Museum on left. Turn left. House 200 yds up slope, on left. From S, A36 takes you past the door. Parking.
Restrictions No smoking. No children under 4. Dogs by arrangement.
Credit cards Amex, MasterCard, Visa.
Terms [2001] B&B: single £55–£75, double £69–£80.

Tasburgh House NEW
Warminster Road
Bath BA2 6SH

Tel 01225-425096
Fax 01225-463842
Email hotel@bathtasburgh.co.uk
Website www.bathtasburgh.co.uk

'Comfortable, unintimidating, with fantastic views', this small hotel is on the edge of the city, in large grounds that slope down to the Kennet and Avon Canal. Here, guests can walk or jog along a towpath, or enjoy a 'gourmet picnic', provided by the owners, Susan and David Keeling – they live downstairs with a dog and a parrot. They recently lavishly redecorated the Victorian red brick building, which they bought in a run-down condition. 'A friendly welcome from Mr Keeling; Mrs Keeling is very good-looking and smiling,' said our inspectors. 'Our bedroom was quiet, with a swagged and draped decor, repro furniture (rather a lot of it for a not very big space), a four-poster with miles of blue and green material, mirrors, oil paintings, a teddy bear dressed to reflect the room's name, Tennyson. The bathroom was lighter, and cheery; it had a window looking down the hill. At night, the lights of the city twinkled in the distance. A comfortable Z-bed, with dark blue bedding, was provided for our young son (he thought the room "very grand").' Pre-dinner drinks are served in a drawing room where guests may play a baby grand piano or browse through newspapers. The apricot-walled dining room has 'colossal curtains', a marble fireplace and potted plants. The Keelings' daughter, Antonia, is chef, cooking, eg, chargrilled tiger prawns with a chilli sauce; seared salmon fillet with an olive crust and smashed basil; towering ice-cream sundae with fudge sauce. 'The food was very good, but portions were enormous, particularly for a child. At breakfast, served by waitresses wearing white gloves, we had boiled eggs (just right) and toast (hot).' Meals are served on a terrace in fine weather. From the bus-stop outside the house, it is a five-minute journey to the centre; or you can walk along the canal. 'We specialise in small groups,' write the Keelings, who are 'happy to help with sightseeing'.

Open All year. Lunch not served.
Rooms 11 double, 1 single. 2 on ground floor.
Facilities Drawing room, dining room, conservatory/terrace; classical background music all day; 7-acre grounds: canal walks, private mooring, pontoon. Unsuitable for ♿.
Location On A36 to Warminster, ½ mile E of Bath.
Restrictions No smoking. No dogs.
Credit cards All major cards accepted.
Terms [2001] B&B: single £52, double £55–£98; D,B&B: single £75.50, double £102–£145. Set dinner £23.50–£25. Discount on 2 or more nights midweek. Christmas package. 1-night bookings refused weekends.

BATHFORD Somerset — Map 2:D1

Eagle House BUDGET
Church Street
Bathford BA1 7RS

Tel 01225-859946
Fax 01225-859430
Email jonap@eagleho.demon.co.uk
Website www.eaglehouse.co.uk

'The welcome and the house were warm on a particularly cold weekend. The views across the valley to the outskirts of Bath were splendid, the breakfast was plentiful and good, and the owners could hardly have been more helpful.' An enthusiastic endorsement this year for John and Rosamund Napier's informal B&B in a quiet street in a conservation village three miles east of Bath (a frequent bus service runs between the two). The listed Georgian building, by John Wood the Elder, is grand; the Napiers are not. The decor is informal rather than *soigné*: 'Old furniture (good, but not too smart) and family possessions are scattered everywhere.' The Napiers welcome families and dogs. High chairs, baby-listening and children's suppers are available; the large, wildish garden has a tree house, a sandpit, a Tarzan swing and a grass tennis court. The two-bedroomed cottage, with its own walled garden and kitchen, is particularly good for a family. In the main house, each room is named after a tree: Pear is large, 'pretty and sprigged', with pine furniture, a garden view and a pristine bathroom. A curving staircase leads up from the hall. The handsome drawing room has a fine marble fireplace and moulded ceiling. If guests bring their own drinks, they can take them by the log fire – the Napiers will supply ice. Breakfast, served until 10 am on weekdays, 10.30 on Sunday, is plentiful. In winter, guests with a bird's name for a surname, eg, gosling, sparrow, wren, get a discount (size of discount relative to size of bird). (*Dr F Peter Woodford, and others*)

Open 4 Jan–20 Dec.
Rooms 1 suite, 6 double, 1 single. 2 in cottage with sitting room, kitchen, walled garden.
Facilities Drawing room, breakfast room. No background music. 2½-acre garden: tennis, croquet, sandpit, tree house, swings. Golf, hot-air ballooning, riding, boating, etc, nearby. Unsuitable for ♿.
Location Up Bathford Hill past *Crown* pub. 1st right (Church St), house is 200 yds on right behind high stone wall and wrought iron gates (conservation area; no sign permitted). Do not go to Eagle Lodge. Ample parking. 4 buses an hour from Bath.
Restrictions No smoking: breakfast room, bedrooms. Dogs not allowed in public rooms if other guests object.
Credit cards MasterCard, Visa.
Terms [2001] B&B: single £38–£54, double £52–£82, suite £76–£98. Cooked breakfast £3.40. Child in parents' room free. Winter breaks 1 Nov–Easter. 1-night bookings sometimes refused. *V*

Lodge Hotel
Bathford Hill
Bathford, Bath BA1 7SL

Tel 01225-858467
Fax 01225-858172
Email lodgethe@aol.com
Website www.lodgehotelbath.co.uk

Keith and Mary Johnson's B&B, a listed Georgian house, is on Bathford's steep hill (with some traffic by day, but quiet at night). It stands in a large landscaped garden (with a swimming pool), and it makes a 'restful base' from which to tour Bath and the West Country. Mrs Johnson is 'genuinely welcoming' and visitors enjoy the 'family atmosphere' with dogs and cats (visitors' dogs are welcome in the bedrooms but not the public rooms). Tea is served free of charge to arriving guests. Breakfast includes a buffet with exotic fruits, cereals, yogurt, 'and a huge and varied cooked plateful'. Some rooms have been redecorated, but one visitor this year wrote of one that was in need of a facelift. A double bed may turn out to be two twins latched together, but guests like the complimentary sherry. 'The most important "extra" is the care and concern given by Mary,' says one visitor. I can't praise her enough for this home-from-home approach.' The Johnsons own a narrowboat on the Kennet and Avon Canal, which guests may hire by the day. They specialise in house parties, and are knowledgeable about local attractions, eating places, etc. (*MB, and others*)

Open All year.
Rooms 1 suite, 5 double. 1 on ground floor.
Facilities Lounge, breakfast room. No background music. 3-acre garden: swimming pool (heated May–Oct). River, canal ¼ mile: fishing, boating; golf nearby.
Location M4 exit 18; A46 towards Bath to roundabout at end of dual carriageway; under railway bridge; 1st left, then straight up hill; house on right, 100 yds after *Crown* inn. Ample secure parking. Train: Bath; bus/taxi, or they will meet.
Restrictions No smoking in breakfast room. No dogs in public rooms.
Credit cards MasterCard, Visa.
Terms B&B: single £55–£65, double £65–£120, suite £120. Child in parents' room: under 5, free. 10% reduction for 3 nights. 1-night bookings sometimes refused Sat. *V*

BEAMINSTER Dorset — Map 1:C6

The Bridge House
Prout Bridge
Beaminster DT8 3AY

Tel 01308-862200
Fax 01308-863700
Email enquiries@bridge-house.co.uk
Website www.bridge-house.co.uk

Peter Pinkster runs a small hotel in a former priest's house, parts of which date back to the 13th century – thick walls, mullioned windows, old beams and inglenook fireplaces have survived. It has been praised by visitors for the friendly welcome, and the restaurant has a busy local trade. One visitor this year reported a problem with reception, though her stay 'was pleasant', and the rooms were 'attractive and well-appointed'. The bedrooms are spread throughout the main house, converted stables and a new wing; those by the road get some traffic noise; rear ones are quiet. 'Views vary: lovely garden on one side, light industry on the other.' Linda Paget uses home-grown herbs for her English/international menu, served in the panelled dining room, eg, king prawns wrapped in smoked bacon; duck confit with parsnip purée and a honey and ginger sauce; treacle tart. There is a vegetarian menu and a good choice of reasonably priced wines. Light lunches are served in a conservatory (where the green plastic chairs have now been replaced by wooden ones) or in the walled garden in summer; tea is taken by a fire on winter afternoons. A good breakfast includes freshly squeezed orange juice. Beaminster, pronounced Bemminster, is a pretty, if busy, town in the middle of Hardy country. Parnham House, now the John Makepeace Furniture Workshops, is three-quarters of a mile to the south; many stately homes and gardens are within easy reach; and the coast is six miles away. More reports, please.

Open All year, except New Year.
Rooms 13 double, 1 single. 5 in coach house. 4 on ground floor.
Facilities Sitting room, bar, sunroom, restaurant; patio. No background music. ½-acre walled garden.
Location 2 mins' walk from centre (2 front rooms double-glazed). Private car park. Train: Crewkerne, 8 miles; taxi.
Restrictions No smoking: restaurant, bedrooms. No dogs in public rooms, unattended in bedrooms.
Credit cards All major cards accepted.
Terms B&B: single £50–£91, double £98–£128; D,B&B (min. 2 days): single £78–£113, double £146–£176. Set lunch £10.25–£14.25, dinner £25.50–£28.50. Winter breaks. Christmas package. 1-night bookings sometimes refused. *V*

BEAULIEU Hampshire — Map 2:E2

Master Builder's House
Buckler's Hard
Beaulieu SO42 7XB

Tel 01590-616253
Fax 01590-616297
Email res@themasterbuilders.co.uk
Website www.themasterbuilders.co.uk

'Superb position, very comfortable, competent staff.' In charming New Forest setting, in time-warp village on the Beaulieu river: old hotel (Best Western), recently refurbished by owners of The George, *Yarmouth* (qv). *25 bedrooms: 'gorgeous' ones in main building; small, less attractive ones in wing. Lounge, bar; pleasant patio with views of water; sloping 1-acre garden; boat available for charter; conference facilities. Good French cooking by Denis Rhoden in attractive* Riverview Restaurant *and brasserie. No background music. Civil wedding licence. 'Could be super, but management uncoordinated,' says visitor this year, 'and menu hardly changed during a week's visit.' Unsuitable for ♿. Amex, MasterCard, Visa accepted. No dogs in restaurants. B&B: single £115, double £155, suite £205; D,B&B (min. 2 nights) £90–£120 per person. Set lunch from £13.95, dinner £29.50; full alc from £36.25 [2001]. More reports, please.*

BEERCROCOMBE Somerset — Map 1:C5

Frog Street Farm BUDGET
Beercrocombe, Taunton TA3 6AF

Tel/Fax 01823-480430

César award in 1988

The deep rural Somerset setting, and the exuberant charm of the hostess, combine to make this small guest house an enduring favourite with *Guide* readers. Henry and Veronica Cole's listed 15th-century farmhouse, very personally run, never accommodates more than six guests at one time. It is on a working farm, with fields and woods on one side, orchards on the other. Recent accolades: 'Here small is truly beautiful.' 'A welcoming, comfortable home. Guests leave as friends.' Most peaceful.' 'There can't be many places of this quality where two people can stay and be fed for less than £100 a day.' Dinner, by arrangement, at 7 pm, is generally served at separate tables, but guests may eat together if they prefer. Mrs Cole's country cooking is much admired: 'succulent fillet steak and mouth-watering lemon meringue pie'; 'excellent wild salmon'. No licence; bring your own wine. Breakfast includes 'perfectly cooked bacon and eggs'. There is a large lounge, with beams and a wood stove. Henry Cole is a racehorse trainer and the horses in the fields around are 'worth studying, even if you are not a betting type'. Plenty of National Trust properties in the area: Barrington Court, Montacute, Brampton D'Evercy and Tintinhull; the busy market town of Ilminster is nearby; the north and south coasts are about 21 miles away. More reports, please.

Open Apr–Oct.
Rooms 1 suite, 2 double. No telephone/TV.
Facilities 2 lounges, dining room. No background music. 130-acre working farm: garden, trout stream. Unsuitable for ♿.
Location 7 miles SE of Taunton. M5 exit 25. Take A358 past the *Blackbrook Tavern* to Ilminster. In Hatch Beauchamp, at *Hatch Inn*, take Station Rd, *not* Beercrocombe. Keep left about 1 mile. Farm on left, signposted down No Through Road.
Restrictions No smoking. Children by arrangement; not under 11. No dogs.
Credit cards None accepted.
Terms B&B: single £30–£35, double £54–£60. Set dinner £18. Weekly rates. 1-night bookings sometimes refused weekends.

BIBURY Gloucestershire — Map 3:E6

Bibury Court
Bibury
nr Cirencester GL7 5NT

Tel 01285-740337
Fax 01285-740660
Email info@biburycourt.co.uk
Website www.biburycourt.co.uk

On the edge of this lovely village, in romantic grounds, stands this graceful Tudor manor house, much extended in the 17th century. It is run by its owners, Andrew and Anne Johnston and Jane Collier, on country house lines. With the 'very efficient' general manager, Simon Gould, 'who bears more than a passing resemblance to Groucho Marx', and a long-serving staff, they aim 'to provide good food and wine in informal and comfortable surroundings'. Many bedrooms have a four-poster bed. Some other beds may be 'a bit narrow', and lighting can be dim, but bathrooms are well equipped; hot water is plentiful, and one bath 'is big enough to swim in'. The panelled lounge has a flagstone floor, large chairs and sofas, and an open fire. The restaurant is quite small, but there is a conservatory for summer dining. The gardens stretch down to the river Coln (with trout fishing). Tom Bridgeman, the chef, serves elaborate dishes, eg, asparagus spears layered in Parmesan wafers with herb hollandaise sauce; roast lamb with an apricot and garlic farce; blueberry and almond tart with clotted cream. Light lunches and afternoon teas are served. Breakfast is continental, full English, vegetarian or Jacobean (with cold meats and pickled walnut chutney). This is a locally popular venue; functions are often held, and outside lunchers and diners are catered for. Charles Dickens is said to have based events in *Bleak House* on long-running legal disputes over the ownership of *Bibury Court*. William Morris's house at Kelmscott is nearby. More reports, please.

Open All year.
Rooms 1 suite, 17 double. 1 on ground floor.
Facilities Lounge, bar, restaurant, conservatory, TV/snooker room. No background music. 7-acre grounds: 'secret garden', orchard; on river Coln, fishing.
Location Village centre, behind church.
Restriction No smoking: restaurant, conservatory. No dogs in restaurant.
Credit cards All major cards accepted.
Terms [2001] B&B £57.50–£100; D,B&B (min. 2 nights) £82.50–£120. English breakfast £5.95–£7.25. Light lunches. Set dinner £29.50. Christmas package. 1-night bookings refused Sat.

BIGBURY-ON-SEA Devon — Map 1:D4

Burgh Island Hotel
Burgh Island
Bigbury-on-Sea TQ7 4BG

Tel 01548-810514
Fax 01548-810243
Email reception@burghisland.com
Website www.burghisland.com

César award in 1993

'A fantasy world of the 1920s', this large, white Art Deco building stands on a private island in Bigbury Bay. At high tide it is 'romantically cut off', and guests are carried across on a sea tractor; at low tide they cross a causeway on foot or in the hotel's Land Rover. In its heyday, the hotel was visited by Edward, Prince of Wales, with Mrs Simpson, and by Agatha Christie. It has been lovingly restored by Tony and Beatrice Porter: furniture and fittings are in period style, down to the last milk jug. It is all 'fabulous' and great fun; 'you are pampered from the moment you arrive'. Accommodation is in suites with one or two bedrooms; most have a balcony and a sea view. There is also a two-roomed cottage on the beach. 1920s cocktails are served in the peacock-domed palm court. Tea is taken in a glassed-in sun lounge, and dinner is served in a 1920s ballroom – in deference to its splendour, guests are asked to dress formally. On Saturday they dance the Charleston, accompanied by a local band called Pennies from Devon. The new chef, Chris Egelnick, serves English dishes with a Mediterranean slant, eg, ceviche of mackerel with tapenade; poached salmon with asparagus; panna cotta with plums braised in port. There is a natural swimming pool in the rocks below the hotel, and a private beach with water sports. (*SJ, LW*)

Open All year, except Jan, and Sun–Thurs in Feb.
Rooms 15 suites. Also 2-bedroomed house on beach.
Facilities Lift. Sun lounge, palm court/cocktail bar, restaurant, ballroom; 1930s original recordings played; live music/dinner-dance Sat. On 26-acre private

island: natural sea swimming pool; beach, water sports; tennis; 14th-century inn; helipad; access to private club (with heated swimming pool) on mainland beach. Unsuitable for ♿. Civil wedding licence.
Location Leave A38 at Modbury exit. Hotel arranges transfer. Lockup garage on mainland.
Restrictions No smoking at breakfast. No children under 7 at dinner. No dogs.
Credit cards All major cards accepted.
Terms D,B&B £124–£150. Set lunch £22, dinner £38–£45. Christmas package.

The Henley *Tel/Fax* 01548-810240
Folly Hill
Bigbury-on-Sea TQ7 4AR

'A peaceful, relaxed little hideaway.' 'The people are so charming.' There is high praise this year for Martin Scarterfield's small hotel, which is 'unpretentious, but sets high standards'. This Edwardian holiday cottage has been completely renovated, and is 'spick and span', with a conservatory dining room that has 'the most wonderful sea views'. The interior is attractive, with dark red walls and old furniture, well polished, in the hall; a pleasant small sitting room with games, books and magazines; Lloyd Loom chairs. Binoculars are provided. Set in a small terraced garden above the Avon estuary, *The Henley* looks across to Burgh Island and beyond. A private path ('only suitable for mountain goats,' says an older guest) leads down the cliff to a sandy beach. The bedrooms are small 'but with everything one needs', and 'even our side room had lovely views'. The front-of-house welcome comes from Petra from Hanover, 'slim and elegant', with 'irresistible charm and efficiency'; 'two friendly dogs add to the atmosphere'. Guests are invited to come to the drawing room at 7 pm so that the dishes from the small menu can be individually cooked for 7.30. 'The food was very good, especially the soups.' The fish is fresh, and the vegetables 'retain such wonderful flavour'. Parsnip and cranberry soup might be followed by cod with king prawns and garlic butter sauce; coffee pecan sponge pudding. 'The wine list is modest but well chosen.' 'An excellent breakfast, too, with local bacon and good coffee.' There is limited family accommodation. Dogs are welcomed. 'Outstanding value for money.' (*Brian and Eve Webb, Heather Sharland, CR*)

Open Feb–Dec.
Rooms 6 double.
Facilities 2 lounges, bar, veranda dining room; jazz/classical background music at night; garden; steps to beach. Golf, sailing, fishing, coastal path nearby. Unsuitable for ♿.
Location 5 miles S of Modbury. Through Bigbury; past golf course. Hotel on left as road slopes down to sea.
Restrictions No smoking. No dogs in public rooms.
Credit cards Amex, MasterCard, Visa.
Terms [2001] B&B: single £43–£50, double £76–£80. D,B&B: single £59–£65, double £100–£110. Set dinner £20. Off-season reductions.

Report forms (Freepost in UK) are at the end of the *Guide*.

BIGGIN-BY-HARTINGTON Derbyshire — Map 3:B6

Biggin Hall BUDGET
Biggin-by-Hartington
Buxton SK17 0DH

Tel 01298-84451
Fax 01298-84681
Email bigginhall@compuserve.com
Website www.bigginhall.co.uk

James Moffett, a 'courteous owner', runs an unpretentious small hotel in his 'sympathetically converted' 17th-century stone house (with narrow mullioned windows), peacefully set in the Peak District National Park. Its chief glory is the position: you can walk straight out on to the Tissington Trail and over fields to the dales. 'The value is outstanding,' says a visitor this year. Most bedrooms are spacious, with old beams and chintz, TV, a telephone with a modem socket, a well-appointed bathroom. Some accommodation is in buildings in the grounds. All rooms have a small fridge. Two small singles share a bathroom. Dinner, served in 'a friendly, if brisk, manner', is at 7 pm, in a room with a picture window. Mark Wilton's cooking is 'simple but tasty', and the atmosphere is congenial. 'Talk takes place between guests, and there is a good view across the fields, if you get the right table.' Two choices (one vegetarian) of main course, perhaps poached fillet of salmon, or sweet and sour vegetables with herbed couscous. Desserts include crêpes Suzette; queen of puddings; there is a good cheeseboard. Wines are well priced. The continental breakfast includes cereals, dried fruits, home-made croissants; guests not on a special break pay £4.50 for a large cooked plateful. Cream teas are available. The winter break includes mulled wine at night, porridge for breakfast, and a picnic lunch. Groups of doctors are often entertained. Even in Mr Moffett's absence, 'his staff, particularly the young chef, were more than up to the job'. Convenient for visiting Ashbourne, Buxton and Bakewell; Chatsworth and Haddon Hall, and Alton Towers (16 miles away). (*Robert Hill, Trevor Lockwood*)

Open All year.
Rooms 17 double, 2 single. 10 (4 on ground floor) in annexes.
Facilities Sitting room, library, dining room; meeting room. No background music. 7-acre grounds: croquet. River Dove 1½ miles. Not really suitable for ♿.
Location ½ mile W of A515. 8 miles N of Ashbourne. 8 buses daily.
Restrictions No smoking: dining room, library, some bedrooms. No children under 12. No dogs in main house.
Credit cards Amex, MasterCard, Visa
Terms B&B: single £50–£70, double £54–£130; D,B&B £39–£85 per person. English breakfast £4.50. Set dinner £15.50. Winter breaks. Christmas package. 1-night bookings sometimes refused. *V*

BIRMINGHAM West Midlands — Map 2:B2

Hotel du Vin & Bistro NEW
25 Church Street
Birmingham B3 2NR

Tel 0121-236 0559
Fax 0121-236 0889
Email info@birmingham.hotelduvin.com
Website www.hotelduvin.com

The fourth in the Hotel du Vin group, opened April 2001, is an artful conversion of the former Birmingham and West Midlands Eye Hospital, an ornate red brick Victorian building just off St Philip's Cathedral Square. It has a grand entrance with giant pillars offset by *trompe l'oeuil* stonework and a ceiling fresco. Our inspector thought it lived up to the group's aim of providing a stylish but unpretentious atmosphere: 'The young, well-trained staff clearly enjoy their work. We were greeted by a young porter in a black Armani suit, who dealt with our pre-booked valet parking. The equally friendly receptionist chatted as she showed us to our room.' The bedrooms, named after wine producers, and spread over five floors, vary in size but all have a large bath (some freestanding), power shower, bathrobes, fluffy towels. 'Ours, Rosemount, on the first floor, overlooked the central courtyard, so was very quiet. It was long, with the bathroom down several steps, and rather dark, not helped by the modern colour scheme (beige, mauve and dark green), though there were good spotlights. The enormous bed had crisp Egyptian cotton sheets, wonderful pillows, a light duvet. There was a CD-player, kettle, cafetière, teapot, a range of coffees and teas.' An attractive Bubbly Bar, with plump sofas, has a choice of 50 champagnes; there is also a basement bar, with leather sofas. The bistro, with wooden floors and tables, serves modern British dishes with a Mediterranean slant. 'A warm baguette on a wooden tray was brought before we ordered. Seared scallops with ginger and rocket were excellent, so were our main courses: tender pink rump of lamb on a potato rösti; salt beef on a bed of Puy lentils. Service was friendly and well paced. The *sommelier* did not seem too disappointed when we ordered the house red, a soft French Syrah well priced at £12.95, rather than explore his extensive list. Both bar and bistro were blissfully free of background music. Breakfast was a feast: big jugs of fresh fruit juices, cereals, fruit salad, yogurt, even date and banana cake, excellent coffee and tea, a fry-up cooked to order, and a basket of crisp granary toast, croissants and pastries.' Within walking distance are shops, art galleries, museums and theatres.

Open All year.
Rooms 11 suites, 55 double. 5 suitable for ♿.
Facilities Lift. Bistro, 2 bars; spa; courtyard. No background music.
Location Central, near St Philip's Cathedral (quietest rooms overlook courtyard). Valet parking (£10 a night).
Restriction Guide dogs only.
Credit cards All major cards accepted.
Terms Room: single/double £110, suite £175. Breakfast £8.50– £11.50. Full alc £35. Christmas package.

See also SHORTLIST

BISHOP'S TACHBROOK Warwickshire — Map 3:D6

Mallory Court
Harbury Lane
Bishop's Tachbrook
nr Leamington Spa CV33 9QB

Tel 01926-330214
Fax 01926-451714
Email reception@mallory.co.uk
Website www.mallory.co.uk

'A relaxing break in a beautiful hotel, where care is taken with the overall picture, and the detail is impressive.' 'We love it – an inspiration and a delight.' Praise again this year for Jeremy Mort and Allan Holland's Lutyens-style mansion (Relais & Châteaux), where 'cares of the day slip away and one cannot help but relax and luxuriate'. The large terrace is ideal for taking lunch or tea under sunshades; it overlooks an ornamental water garden. 'The combination of the grounds and the surrounding countryside falling away on two sides is perfection.' There is an outdoor swimming pool, a tennis court, a croquet lawn. Allan Holland has handed over charge of the kitchen to Steven Love, an ex-Roux scholar with an impressive pedigree. He serves a modern British/French menu in the oak-panelled dining room, eg, seared scallops wrapped in pancetta with an artichoke broth; canon of lamb with confit tomato and crispy sweetbreads; and 'perfect desserts' like caramelised apple mousse with an apple and lemon sorbet. But one writer would have appreciated a wider selection of wines. 'Refurbishment has given the public rooms a lighter, brighter look.' The bedrooms are immaculate; the older ones are lavishly decorated. Eastcote 'is lovely, with a double aspect and impressive plumbing; instant hot water every time'. 'The new suites are slightly simpler in style, with beautiful fabrics and textures.' Many beds 'are Olympic'. The smallest rooms face the car park; upgrades are common at quiet times. Breakfast is good with 'the best-ever kippers'. Light lunches and lavish afternoon teas are served; room service operates from 7 am to 11.30 pm. Birmingham, Warwick and Stratford-upon-Avon are nearby. Local attractions include Charlecote Park, Packwood House, Snowshill Manor; the Cotswolds are within 40 minutes' drive. (*John and Kate Gibbon, Pat and Jeremy Temple, FW*)

Open All year.
Rooms 8 suites, 10 double. 1 with access for ♿.
Facilities Ramps. 2 lounges (automatic piano plays some evenings), conservatory, restaurant, private dining room; conference centre. 10-acre grounds: unheated swimming pool, tennis, squash, croquet. Civil wedding licence.
Location 2 miles S of Leamington Spa. M40 exit 13 (from S), 14 (from N). Hotel off B4087 to Harbury. Train: Leamington Spa; then taxi.
Restrictions No smoking in restaurant. No children under 9, except babies with own cot. No dogs.
Credit cards All major cards accepted.
Terms [2001] B&B: single £175–£250, double £185–£320. English breakfast £10. Bar lunches. Set lunch £27, dinner £38.50; full alc £60. Child in parents' room: free. 2/3-day winter breaks. Christmas package.

BISHOP'S TAWTON Devon — Map 1:C4

Halmpstone Manor
Bishop's Tawton
nr Barnstaple EX32 0EA

Tel 01271-830321
Fax 01271-830826
Email charles@halmpstonemanor.co.uk
Website www.halmpstonemanor.co.uk

There is a restful atmosphere in the family home of Charles and Jane Stanbury on a working farm in the rolling hills of north Devon. But regulars also like the professional management, though it is run more like a private home than a hotel. 'No false intimacy; we were called "Sir" and "Madam" throughout our visit, which we like,' one visitor wrote. Help with luggage, and complimentary tea with cake in the lovely sitting room, with its squashy sofas, antiques, family photos and log fire, are also appreciated. 'Fresh flowers everywhere. A lovely dining room panelled and candlelit, only five tables, elegantly set with old-fashioned chunky cutlery, crisp table napkins.' Mrs Stanbury's four-course dinners are admired too: they might feature fresh crab and cucumber salad; saddle of roe deer with a cream sauce – along with 'delectable home-grown vegetables'. Breakfast includes fresh orange juice and home-made preserves. Most bedrooms are spacious, with a traditional decor, and they are supplied with sherry, biscuits and other extras; two have a four-poster. From a patio there are views of the moors. Plenty to visit nearby, including Lydford Gorge, Lynton and Lynmouth, Rosemoor and Marwood gardens – you need a car. More reports, please.

Open All year, except Christmas, New Year, Feb. Lunch by arrangement.
Rooms 5 double.
Facilities Lounge, bar, dining room. No background music. ½-acre garden. Unsuitable for ♿.
Location 4 miles SE of Barnstaple. A39 to Bideford for 300 yds. A377 to Exeter/Crediton. Through Bishop's Tawton; opposite petrol station turn left on to minor road; follow signs for 2 miles. Train: Barnstaple; taxi.
Restrictions No smoking: dining room, some bedrooms. No children under 12.
Credit cards All major cards accepted.
Terms B&B: single £70, double £100–£140. D,B&B: single £95, double £150–£190. Set lunch/dinner £25 (£30 to non-residents).

BLACKBURN Lancashire *See SHORTLIST* Map 4:D3

BLACKPOOL Lancashire Map 4:D2

Raffles NEW/BUDGET *Tel* 01253-294713
73/75 Hornby Road *Fax* 01253-294240
Blackpool FY1 4QJ

'Excellent establishment', 'a real bargain', flower-fronted, bay-windowed, in road of many hotels near centre. 'Amazingly cheery, helpful hosts', Graham Poole and Ian Balmforth (he is chef). Huge breakfast, 5-course evening meal (from 5 pm) by arrangement (£10); 'easy listening' background music in public rooms. Lounge, bar. Parking. No smoking: dining room, some bedrooms. Amex, MasterCard, Visa accepted. 17 rooms. B&B £21–£28.

See also SHORTLIST

> We quote either prices per room, or else the range of prices per person – the lowest is likely to be for one person sharing a double room out of season, the highest for a single room in the high season.

BLAKENEY Norfolk Map 2:A5

The Blakeney Hotel
Blakeney
nr Holt NR25 7NE

Tel 01263-740797
Fax 01263-740795
Email reception@blakeney-hotel.co.uk
Website www.blakeney-hotel.co.uk

'The setting is wonderful. It is efficient and smart. Rooms are scrupulously clean.' And families with young children have all they need, from high chairs and baby-sitting to early evening meals, at this long-established hotel on the quayside of the East Anglian yachting and holiday town. Off-season, it is popular with older visitors: 'We (in our mid-50s) always feel that we lower the average age of the clientele by ten years,' says one regular. The indoor swimming pool, and the 'lovely walks' along the estuary, particularly at low tide, are great attractions. Two lounges – one upstairs – have fine views over the estuary towards Blakeney Point. The decor, particularly of the bedrooms and bathrooms, may seem 'a bit dated' to some, but many rooms have a sea view; those in the modern annexe have the use of a patio overlooking the garden. Staff 'are cheerful' (many have been here for years), but sightings of owner or management are still said to be rare. And one visitor thought the pool area 'needed attention' and would have liked more pictures on the walls. The food is traditional; it has been thought variable this year. 'First dinner disappointing; thereafter it got better and better.' 'Very good fish, delicious potatoes, but some dishes bland.' Light lunches are served on weekdays; on Sunday a choice of roasts forms the centrepiece of the menu. The local smoked kipper is recommended at breakfast. Good birdwatching at the National Trust's Blakeney Point nature reserve; boat trips to see the seals can be arranged. Blickling Hall, Holkham Hall, and the North Norfolk steam railway at Sheringham are nearby. (*Richard Purish, Graham Snowdon, Alan Green; also Mr and Mrs Michael Richards, and others*)

Open All year.
Rooms 51 double, 8 single. 10 in annexe across drive. Some on ground floor.
Facilities Lift, ramps. Lounge, sun lounge, bar, restaurant; function facilities; indoor swimming pool, spa bath, sauna, mini gym; games room. No background music. ¼-acre garden: table tennis, swings. Sailing, fishing, water sports, golf, tennis nearby.
Location On quay. Off A149 coast road, 8 miles W of Sheringham. Train: Sheringham; taxi.
Restrictions No smoking: restaurant, sun lounge. Only guide dogs in public rooms.
Credit cards All major cards accepted.
Terms [2001] B&B £58–£100; D,B&B (min. 2 nights) £67–£116. Light lunches Mon–Sat. Set Sun lunch £13, dinner £20; full alc £30. 2- to 7-day breaks. Senior citizen breaks. Christmas, New Year packages. 1-night bookings usually refused Fri/Sat.

Hotels are dropped if we lack positive feedback. If you can endorse an entry, please do so.

BLOCKLEY Gloucestershire — Map 3:D6

The Old Bakery — *Tel/Fax* 01386-700408
High Street, Blockley
nr Moreton-in-Marsh GL56 9EU

'Linda Helme is a perfectionist, and nowhere is this more evident than in her cooking,' says a visitor to this small guest house. 'Beautifully converted' from a row of four cottages built around 1800, it is modelled on a French restaurant-with-rooms by the 'hands-on' hostess (she earlier worked in publishing). The 'great atmosphere' is praised; so are the 'immaculate bedrooms' ('a nice touch was the small thermos of fresh milk'), and the house is furnished with antiques, 'interesting pictures, lots of books and comfortable chairs'. In the handsome dining room, which looks through French windows on to the immaculate small garden, 'fine food is attractively presented in well-judged quantities'. Ms Helme recently visited Australia and New Zealand, and the result is a Pacific Rim influence in her dishes, eg, lamb cutlets on spicy sweet potatoes with a chilli and mint salsa; grilled pineapple with mango and ginger sorbet. 'Her great strength is in her meat cookery,' says a report this year. Some 'exciting New World wines' have been added to the cellar (the mark-up is low). Dinner is a set four-course menu based, when possible, on local and organic ingredients. 'Delicious breakfasts' have freshly squeezed orange, and 'scrambled eggs to die for'. A cottage across a lane is let for self-catering (its residents can dine at *The Old Bakery*). Blockley, said to be one of the most unspoiled villages in the Cotswolds, is well placed for excursions: Stratford-upon-Avon is 14 miles away, Cheltenham 15, Oxford 35. Hidcote, Sudeley Castle and many other attractions are nearby. (*PE Carter, Sara Price, CN and DY*)

Open Feb–Nov. Closed 2 weeks in June. Dining room closed to non-residents.
Rooms 1 suite, 2 double. No telephone. Self-catering cottage across lane.
Facilities Sitting room, study/bar, dining room. No background music. Garden: courtyard, patio. Unsuitable for ♿.
Location Corner of High Street and School Lane. Towards Broadway, turn right off A44 at Bourton-on-the-Hill. Follow signs to Blockley village centre. Parking.
Restrictions No smoking. No children under 12. No dogs.
Credit cards Amex, MasterCard, Visa (all with 2% surcharge).
Terms [2001] D,B&B £60–£100. 1-night bookings occasionally refused weekends.

BORROWDALE Cumbria — Map 4: inset C2

The Leathes Head BUDGET — *Tel* 017687-77247
Borrowdale — *Fax* 017687-77363
Keswick CA12 5UY
Email enq@leatheshead.co.uk
Website www.leatheshead.co.uk

'A wonderful experience. Our dietary requirements were met superbly, and the owners were helpful in advising us about walks, and the whereabouts of red squirrels and their behaviour.' Continuing praise this year for Roy and Janice Smith's gabled Lakeland stone Edwardian house in a 'great location', high up in wooded grounds outside Borrowdale. Set well back from the road to Keswick, it has extensive views of the spectacular surrounding countryside. Popular with serious walkers and climbers, the house is furnished in keeping with its age, and original features – stained glass, old fireplaces and plasterwork – have been retained. Tea and drinks are served in a sunroom, furnished with wicker armchairs, that overlooks the garden. Books, local guidebooks and games are scattered around. Smoking is 'strictly limited' to the lounge and bar. The chef, David Jackson, changes his menus daily. They might include seared tuna; fillet of lemon sole rolled with seafood mousseline; sticky date pudding. 'Vegetarians should be pleased with dishes such as baked capsicum stuffed with vegetable and tomato ragout, or Chinese vegetable hotpot.' Guests have access, for a small fee, to a nearby leisure club. Children are welcomed: there are family rooms, and high tea for the very young (but no baby-listening service). The owners write: 'Roy will help with mountain bike repairs (he previously ran a mountain bike business); Janice, a qualified physiotherapist, will sooth aching muscles and joints.' (*FG Millen, and others*)

Open Feb–Nov, Christmas, New Year.
Rooms 11 double. 2 on ground floor, 1 with facilities for ♿.
Facilities Ramp. Lounge, bar, restaurant, sunroom; light classical background music at night. 3-acre grounds: sun terrace, children's play area, woodland. Bicycle/boat hire; lake, water sports nearby. Temporary membership of local leisure club.
Location 3½ miles S of Keswick on B5289. Train: Penrith; then bus.
Restrictions Smoking in lounge and bar only. No children under 7. No dogs.
Credit cards MasterCard, Visa.
Terms D,B&B £49.50–£69.50. Set dinner £19.50. Spring, summer, autumn breaks. Christmas, New Year packages. 1-night bookings sometimes refused. *V* (half board only)

Seatoller House BUDGET
Borrowdale
Keswick CA12 5XN

Tel 017687-77218
Fax 017687-77189
Email seatollerhouse@btconnect.com
Website www.seatollerhouse.co.uk

With 'marvellous walks from the door', this popular guest house has a beautiful setting at the head of the Borrowdale valley. Much loved by hikers and climbers for its 'homely atmosphere', the 350-year-old house, set in a 'nice garden', is owned by Lake Hunts Ltd. It has been run for the last two years by manager/chefs Jay and Morven Anson. They provide high standards in a 'quiet and happy environment'. 'A warm welcome, attention to detail, very good cooking.' Meals are served at two long oak tables. Dinner, announced by a gong, is at 7 pm. No choice on the menu (though special diets can be catered for). Roasted tomato and aubergine soup; beef and Jennings ale casserole; sticky toffee bread and butter pudding are typical fare. There is a short, well-chosen wine list; coffee comes with fudge or truffles. Breakfast, at 8.30, is hearty. The bedrooms are simple, but all have facilities *en suite*. Three were redecorated this year. (*JW, and others*)

Open Mar–Dec. Dining room closed midday and Tues.
Rooms 9 double. 2 on ground floor. 1 in garden annexe. No telephone/TV.
Facilities Lounge, library, tea room, dining room, drying room. No background music. 2-acre grounds: pond. Unsuitable for ♿.
Location 8 miles S of Keswick on B5289. Train: Penrith; regular buses.
Restrictions No smoking: dining room, some bedrooms. No dogs in public rooms.
Credit cards MasterCard, Visa.
Terms B&B (not Sat) £28.50–£30.50; D,B&B £39.50–£41.50. Set dinner £11. Packed lunches available. Weekly rates.

BOSHAM West Sussex — Map 2:E3

The Millstream
Bosham Lane
Bosham, nr Chichester PO18 8HL

Tel 01243-573234
Fax 01243-573459
Email info@millstream-hotel.co.uk.
Website www.millstream-hotel.co.uk.

'Very friendly and well run.' 'Good but not snooty.' This hotel, managed for many years by Antony Wallace, consists of a small manor house linked to an 18th-century malt house cottage, in tranquil grounds by a stream with ducks. 'We were part of a largish bridge group and were very well looked after, which isn't always the case. Best of all, my reading glasses were posted back to me within 24 hours, without a phone call prompt.' The decor is pretty, with pale colours, antique and period furniture, potted plants and unexceptional pictures. 'The comfortable bedrooms show great attention to detail.' Two suites, recently renovated, are in a thatched waterside cottage in the corner of the garden. The chef, Bev Boakes, who has presided for over a quarter of a century, serves a 'delicious' fixed-price English and French menu with plenty of choice. Starters might include duck galantine filled with apricots and pistachio nuts, or a salad of hot chorizo sausage and mozzarella cheese; the main course could be pan-seared breast of duck, or roast fore-rib of beef carved from the trolley. A vegetarian menu is also available. The 'outstanding restaurant manager' has been here for many years. Only caveat: 'Lounge accommodation could be improved with more comfortable chairs.' Bosham, pronounced Bozzum, is full of history: its church was visited by King Harold before he set off to visit Duke William of Normandy in 1064 (this is depicted in the Bayeux Tapestry), and the incident of King Canute and the tide is said to have occurred here. Goodwood, Petworth and Arundel Castle are not far. Hotel guests visiting the Chichester theatre can order a late supper. (*Juliet Sebag-Montefiore, Mr and Mrs WH Baily*)

Open All year.
Rooms 3 suites (2 in garden cottage), 27 double, 5 single. 7 on ground floor, 1 equipped for ♿.
Facilities Lounge (pianist Fri, Sat evenings), bar, restaurant; classical background music 10.30 am to 10.30 pm in public rooms; conference room. 1-acre garden, stream. Civil wedding licence.
Location In village 3½ miles W of Chichester. Follow signs to hotel. Car park. Station/bus-stop in village.
Restrictions No smoking: restaurant, most bedrooms. No dogs in public rooms.

Credit cards All major cards accepted.
Terms B&B: single £75–£80, double £120–£125, suite £160–£170; D,B&B (min. 2 nights) £60–£103 per person. Set lunch £16, dinner £23.50. Midweek rates. Bridge, Christmas, New Year packages. 1-night bookings refused Sat.

BOURNEMOUTH Dorset *See SHORTLIST* **Map 2:E2**

BOWNESS-ON-WINDERMERE Cumbria **Map 4: inset C2**

Fayrer Garden House
Lyth Valley Road
Bowness-on-Windermere
LA23 3JP

Tel 015394-88195
Fax 015394-45986
Email lakescene@fayrergarden.com
Website www.fayrergarden.com

Beautiful, large gardens, good food and friendly staff draw devotees back year after year to Iain and Jackie Garside's Victorian house, half a mile above Lake Windermere. The best bedrooms have a distant lake view; some are large, and many have a spa bath; some also have a four-poster. Ground-floor rooms have a French window opening on to a terrace. The decor is traditional, with patterned carpets, lots of pink. The restaurant is popular with non-residents, and was busy even on a Sunday evening when our inspector called. Edward Wilkinson's modern British cooking is enjoyed: main courses include roast local beef; marinated escalopes of turkey; smoked haddock baked in lemon and herbs. The moderately priced wine list has a choice of six house wines, and plenty of half bottles. 'The cheerful staff made the place; they were laid-back, but in a pleasant way.' Breakfast is a buffet with packaged orange juice, fresh fruit salad, prunes and apricot compote. Bowness is a busy tourist centre on Lake Windermere – many lake boats set out from here, and the roads can become congested in season. More reports, please.

Open All year, except 6–18 Jan.
Rooms 4 suites, 12 double, 2 single. 5 on ground floor. 1 suitable for ♿.
Facilities Lounges, lounge bar, restaurant; piano/assorted background music at night. 5-acre grounds. Lake ½ mile: fishing, boating, etc; free use of local leisure centre; golf nearby. Civil wedding licence.
Location 1 mile S of Bowness on A5074.
Restrictions No smoking: restaurant, lounge, some bedrooms. No children under 5 in restaurant at night.
Credit cards Amex, MasterCard, Visa.
Terms B&B £40–£90; D,B&B £55–£105. Set lunch £14.95, dinner £29.95. Christmas package. 1-night bookings sometimes refused weekends.

Lindeth Fell
Lyth Valley Road
Bowness-on-Windermere LA23 3JP

Tel 015394-43286
Fax 015394-47455
Email kennedy@lindethfell.co.uk
Website www.lindethfell.co.uk

Pat (Air Commodore) and Diana Kennedy's early 19th-century house, set at the end of a tree-lined drive well above the bustle of Windermere, offers good value – 'no nasty surprises when you settle the bill'. 'You feel like a guest in someone's house,' says one regular. The gardens, with their small lake and banks of rhododendrons, are especially good in spring and early summer, when they are open to the public (other fine gardens, including the Lakeland Horticultural Society's own, are nearby). Many outdoor activities may be enjoyed in the large grounds (see below). On warm days, tea and drinks are served on a terrace. The house itself is spacious, with 'good places for sitting around in'. The lounges have family photographs, bric-a-brac, watercolours, books and magazines, a log fire. One has a fine plaster ceiling and large windows looking over the treetops towards distant Windermere. Steven Marsden serves five-course dinners in a dining room with lake views: chargrilled black pudding on basil mashed potato; mildly spiced monkfish with curried prawns and mango salsa; lemon posset and shortbread fingers, all feature on his extensive menus. There is always a vegetarian main course. Bedrooms vary in size and are priced accordingly. The best ones have a lake view; top ones are quite small, with a sloping ceiling. 'The considerate hosts are ever-available; the staff make the guest feel truly cared for.' The English Tourism Council gave the hotel a Gold Award for quality in 2000. More reports, please.

Open All year.
Rooms 12 double, 2 single. 1, on ground floor, suitable for ♿.
Facilities Ramp. Hall, 2 lounges, dispense bar, 3 dining rooms. No background music. 7-acre grounds: gardens, tennis, croquet, putting, bowls, tarn. Lake Windermere 1 mile: free fishing; golf nearby.
Location 1 mile S of Bowness on A5074. Train/bus to Windermere.
Restrictions No smoking: dining rooms, 1 lounge. No children under 7 in dining rooms at night. No dogs in house.
Credit cards MasterCard, Visa.
Terms [2001] B&B: single £40–£66, double £80–£130; D,B&B: single £50–£72.50, double £100–£178. Light lunch/picnic. Set lunch £13.50, dinner £23. Off-season rates. Christmas package. 1-night bookings sometimes refused weekends. *V*

BRADFORD West Yorkshire *See SHORTLIST* **Map 4:D3**

BRADFORD-ON-AVON Wiltshire **Map 2:D1**

Woolley Grange
Woolley Green
Bradford-on-Avon BA15 1TX

Tel 01225-864705
Fax 01225-864059
Email info@woolleygrange.com
Website www.woolleygrange.com

This was the first of Nigel Chapman's Luxury Family Hotels group, which aims to offer a child-friendly environment combined with civilised comforts for adults (see also *Moonfleet Manor,* Fleet, and *Fowey Hall,* Fowey). Louise Collier is the manager. The Jacobean manor house stands in large grounds on the edge of a lovely Wiltshire town; bedrooms have been fitted into the old structure. Some are spacious, others small but 'cleverly designed'; some have a gas log fire; some can be arranged to form an inter-connecting suite. Parents pay by the room, squeezing in as many children as they can tolerate. From 10 am to 6 pm a nanny runs a playroom for small children, where their meals are served; babysitting is available in the evening. A huge Victorian hen-house has games for older children, and there are plenty of attractions outdoors (see below). Informal antiques and amusing primitive paintings adorn the public areas. In the panelled hall there are newspapers, magazines, comics for children. When small children are settled in bed, parents sit down to a candlelit dinner with dishes like pan-fried calf's liver with white bean, basil and chorizo cassoulet, garlic fritters; rump of veal, oxtail dumpling with cèpe, shallot and port sauce; chocolate and raspberry tart with white chocolate sauce. The kitchen is supplied by an organic garden. Light meals are served in the conservatory. The attractive building and 'happy atmosphere' have long been admired, but staying here is not cheap, and reports are again mixed this year: 'The rooms are lovely,' says one visitor, but another complained of a 'threadbare carpet, and large gaps between the window and frame'. The food is said to vary from very good to poor'. Breakfast can be 'chaotic with long waits'. 'The whole set-up is willing but amateur,' is one view. More reports, please.

Open All year.
Rooms 3 suites, 19 double, 1 single. 9 in courtyard. 1 on ground floor.
Facilities Ramp. 3 lounges, restaurant, conservatory; children's nursery, games rooms. No background music. 14-acre grounds: swimming pool, tennis, badminton, croquet, children's play area. Cycling, riding, golf, fishing, hot-air ballooning nearby.
Location 1 mile NE of Bradford-on-Avon on B3105. Train: Bath/Bradford-on-Avon/Chippenham.
Restriction No smoking: restaurant, some bedrooms.
Credit cards All major cards accepted.
Terms [2001] B&B: single £90, double £105–£190, suite from £180. Light meals available. Set lunch £15.50–£20, dinner £34.50; full alc £40. Children free in parents' room. Christmas, New Year, winter, 7-night packages. 1-night bookings refused weekends.

BRAMPTON Cumbria — Map 4:B3

Farlam Hall
Brampton CA8 2NG

Tel 016977-46234
Fax 016977-46683
Email farlamhall@dial.pipex.com
Website www.farlamhall.co.uk

César award in 2001

'A special place. The impression is strong of having been invited to stay in a private home, an impression in no way diminished by having to part with a cheque when saying goodbye.' More praise for this 'excellent hotel' (Relais & Châteaux), run by two families, the Quinions and Stevensons. Set in a landscaped Victorian garden with tall trees, a stream and a pond with a fountain, it is approached up a sweeping drive past an ornamental lake. 'We arrive with a sense of relief, knowing that good food and a warm welcome await, from whichever member of the family is on duty. The elder Quinions are in a class of their own when it comes to courtesy,' says a returning visitor. The 'pampering atmosphere' and 'lack of pretension' are admired. The public rooms are ornately Victorian, with dark wallpaper, heavy furniture, trimmings and ornaments. The 'very comfortable bedrooms', decorated with a mixture of stripes and floral designs, are priced according to size (best ones have a whirlpool bath). All have high-quality linen, good lighting, fresh fruit, books and magazines. Those on the road hear traffic, but windows are double-glazed; in other rooms you might hear 'the soothing sounds of the countryside through an open window'. Drinks are served in the lounge (no bar). Dinner, cooked by Barry Quinion, who learnt his trade in Switzerland and at the *Waterside Inn,* Bray (*qv*), is 'classic country house, a friendly though formal affair' (male guests are asked to wear a tie; waitresses are in long dresses). Typical dishes include terrine of pheasant and pistachio; tenderloin of pork with plum bavarois. Wines by the glass are reasonably priced, and 'the evening can end with a warming Armagnac by the fire'. Brampton has an old church, mostly 13th-century, and an ancient border fortress, Naworth Castle. A good base for walking, birdwatching, riding, garden-visiting, etc, and for sightseeing: Hadrian's Wall and associated archaeological digs are within easy reach. (*PJH Govier, Margaret Watson, and others*)

Open All year, except 25–30 Dec. Restaurant closed midday (light lunch for residents by arrangement).
Rooms 12 double. 1 in stables. 2 on ground floor.
Facilities Ramps. 2 lounges, restaurant. No background music. 12-acre grounds. Golf, riding, birdwatching nearby. Unsuitable for ♿.
Location On A689, 2½ miles SE of Brampton (*not* in Farlam village). Some rooms double-glazed. Train: Carlisle; taxi.
Restrictions 'We ask guests not to smoke in restaurant and bedrooms.' No children under 5.
Credit cards MasterCard, Visa.
Terms [2001] D,B&B £120–£140. Light/packed lunches by arrangement. Set dinner £32.50. Special breaks. *V*

BRATTON FLEMING Devon — Map 1:B4

Bracken House BUDGET
Bratton Fleming
nr Barnstaple EX31 4TG

Tel 01598-710320
Fax 01598-710115
Email holidays@brackenhousehotel.com
Website www.brackenhousehotel.com

Woodland and paddocks surround this Victorian rectory, a small lake in the grounds is inhabited by mallards, and the hens on the lawn provide fresh eggs. The owners of this little guest house, Prue and Lawrie Scott, are wildlife enthusiasts, who enjoy sharing this interest with their visitors. They look after injured owls, and Lawrie Scott often gives a talk about owls. The decor is in keeping, with owl ornaments and plenty of taxidermy. Readers appreciate the informal ambience, the 'genuinely warm welcome', with free tea and cakes, and the 'glorious setting' in rolling country high on the western edge of Exmoor, with views to the distant Taw estuary and Hartland Point. The library is well supplied with local information, and there is a small bar in the drawing room. Smoking is now banned throughout. Six of the eight bedrooms, which vary greatly in size, have a new waxed pine decor ('the melamine has disappeared,' say the Scotts); bathrooms have a power shower. After a substantial English breakfast (fresh orange juice, all manner of cooked dishes), guests make their choice from the dinner menu (always with a vegetarian course). The Aga-cooked meal, served between 7 and 7.30 pm, might include beetroot consommé; casserole of beef in red wine; then comes a choice of at least three desserts, including a hot pudding. Dogs are welcomed. Sunday-to-Sunday bookings are preferred. Fine beaches, the Rosemoor and Marwood Hill gardens, and two National Trust properties, Arlington Court and Knightshayes Court, are nearby. More reports, please.

Open Apr–Oct. Dining room closed midday.
Rooms 8 double. 2 on ground floor; 1 suitable for ♿. No telephone. 1 self-catering cottage.
Facilities Ramps. Drawing room/bar, library, dining room; light classical background music early evening. 8½-acre grounds. Riding, boating nearby.
Location Edge of village 7 miles NE of Barnstaple. Bus from Barnstaple.
Restrictions No smoking. No children under 12.
Credit cards MasterCard, Visa.
Terms B&B £32–£45; D,B&B £50–£63. 1-night bookings sometimes refused.

BRAY Berkshire — Map 2:D3

The Waterside Inn
Ferry Road
Bray SL6 2AT

Tel 01628-620691
Fax 01628-784710
Email reservations@waterside-inn.co.uk
Website www.waterside-inn.co.uk

In an idyllic waterside setting, where well-fed ducks and swans paddle in the Thames, this is one of only two British *Michelin* three-starred restaurants. Michel Roux and his son, Alain, with chef Mark Dodson, preside over a 'truly exceptional establishment' (Relais & Châteaux). The cooking has been called 'unashamedly grand'. 'It should be visited by every food lover at least once,' one correspondent wrote (but you need to be well heeled). Others wrote of 'sauces rich but sublime in their intensity, cheeses outstanding in their range, presentation and quality', and a wine list that was 'impressive and not intolerably priced'. But eyebrows have been raised at the practice of giving only the host a menu with prices. At dinner, you could opt for the five-course *menu exceptionnel* at £74 (excluding an 'optional' service charge) or go *à la carte*. Sample dishes: terrine of foie gras with poached figs; lobster medallions with a white port and ginger sauce; dôme au deux chocolats et ses framboises (or you could choose a selection of six desserts). 'Smart casual' clothing is expected. The 'friendly welcome from the carefully trained, young French staff' is praised. Drinks are served in a summer house by the water, or on an electric launch. The suite, La Rivière, and the two best bedrooms, La Terrasse and La Tamise, overlook the river (the latter two share a terrace). Le Nid Jaune, 'small but pleasant', has a warm decor of orange and honey, a wrought iron four-poster bed and a shower room.

Breakfast, served in the bedroom, 'is just right after the indulgence of the night before: a large wooden tray with orange juice, yogurt, coffee or tea, croissants, jam, petits pains au chocolat, all excellent'. Some reporters find the whole experience 'very '70s', and corporate visitors sometimes adversely affect the atmosphere of the restaurant. Windsor Castle is five miles away; Heathrow airport is a 20-minute drive. (*PH, and others*)

Open All year, except 26 Dec–31 Jan. Closed bank holidays, Mon, and Tues except Tues night 1 Jun–31 Aug.
Rooms 1 suite (in cottage, 30 yds), 8 double.
Facilities Restaurant; private dining room; launch for drinks/coffee. No background music. Unsuitable for ♿. Civil wedding licence.
Location On Thames, just SE of Maidenhead. M4 exit 8/9 towards Maidenhead Central. 2nd roundabout turn towards Windsor/Bray. Left after ½ mile on to B3028. In Bray 2nd right into Ferry Rd; hotel on left. Train: Maidenhead; then taxi.
Restrictions No children under 12. No dogs.
Credit cards All major cards accepted.
Terms (*Excluding 'optional' 12½% service charge*) B&B: single/double from £160, suite £290. Set 3-course lunch: Wed–Sat £33.50, Sun £49.50; *menu exceptionnel* (lunch/dinner) £74; alc £100.

BRIGHTON East Sussex — Map 2:E4

The Dove Waldorf NEW/BUDGET
18 Regency Square
Brighton BN1 2FG

Tel 01273-779222
Fax 01273-746912
Email dovehotel@dovehotel.free-online.co.uk
Website www.brighton.co.uk/accommodation

In a 'once elegant square, still mostly handsome despite the plethora of lookalike B&Bs on all sides', this terraced, bay-windowed house is described by its owner, for the past two years, Christina Waldorf, as 'a modest family hotel'. Like her predecessor, under whom it had a *Guide* entry for many years, she is Polish – 'very friendly, very efficient,' says an inspector in 2001. 'Our room, the best, had a huge bow-fronted window and a balcony looking over the square. The decor was nothing special, and it lacked frills, but the bathroom was large, adequately lit and the water was hot. Breakfast, in an attractive basement room, included yogurt with nuts and honey, decent coffee and toast, and all options of the full English variety. We thought it good value. The car park underneath the square will be a bonus to many.' The bedrooms are priced according to size and position; those at the back are smaller.

Open All year.
Rooms 8 double, 1 single.
Facilities Breakfast room (classical background music). Unsuitable for ♿.
Location Central, in square opposite West Pavilion. NCP car park under square.
Restrictions No smoking. No dogs.
Credit cards Amex, MasterCard, Visa.
Terms B&B: single £32–£39, double £50–£95. 1-night bookings refused Sat in season.

We need detailed fresh reports to keep our entries up to date.

Topps
17 Regency Square
Brighton BN1 2FG

Tel 01273-729334
Fax 01273-203679
Email toppshotel@aol.com

In quiet square near sea and conference centre: Regency building, carefully restored: 'a decent B&B'. New owner this year, Audrey Heard, with Wolfgang Schrimpf as manager. 15 bedrooms, most with gas coal fire, 3 no-smoking, 2 with balcony, some on ground floor. Lift, lounge. 'Lots of attention to detail; friendly owners. Nice and quiet.' Guide dogs only. NCP car park close by. All major credit cards accepted. B&B: single £49–£69, double from £84.

See also SHORTLIST

BRISTOL — Map 1:B6

Hotel du Vin & Bistro
The Sugar House
Narrow Lewins Mead
Bristol BS1 2NU

Tel 0117-925 5577
Fax 0117-925 1199
Email info@bristol.hotelduvin.com
Website www.hotelduvin.com

An imaginative conversion of three derelict buildings, one a sugar warehouse, as the third *Hotel du Vin & Bistro*. A glassed canopy entrance opens to a reception desk beside a 100-foot chimney; there are generous public areas and a sweeping steel and oak staircase. Modern sculptures and paintings 'enhance the sense of style'. This is a city-centre hotel – it faces 'a depressing 1960s shopping centre with raised walkways and concrete office blocks' – which necessarily means noise. Front rooms overlook a busy road. One visitor had a broken night's sleep thanks to 'car alarms, even a fight outside the hotel' but our inspector found that thick curtains and double glazing dampened the sound as the street fell quiet in the night. The rooms are minimalist – colours are cream, slate and chocolate – with low beds on a wide wooden frame, and white Egyptian cotton sheets. They vary in size; some are on two levels. One reporter thought the front-of-house staff 'efficient but rather impersonal', but the mainly French restaurant staff 'very friendly'. The bistro is central to the experience, tables generally packed, even on Sunday night, and the food is highly regarded. A pigeon main course was 'magnificent', served rare and tender with creamed cabbage and truffle mash, and bream with cucumber, aubergine and ravioli was 'outstanding'. The wine list is serious, with some expensive choices, but a round and fruity Chilean Cabernet Sauvignon was 'good value'. Breakfast 'was all it should be' with a good red fruit salad on the buffet table, organic yogurt and a comprehensive basket of *Viennoiseries*. (*John and Margaret Speake, Sally Bailey, Moray Nairn, and others*)

Open All year.
Rooms 10 suites, 30 double.
Facilities Lift. Lounge, library, billiard room, bar, bistro. No background music.
Location City centre (front rooms get traffic noise). From motorways and A4,

follow signs to centre. Pass House of Fraser department store on left. After *c.* 400 yds hotel is visible on opposite side of carriageway. Follow road to traffic lights (keep in right-hand lane). Right at war memorial (doubling back). Hotel on small side road after 200 yds. Parking.
Restriction No dogs.
Credit cards All major cards accepted.
Terms Room: single/double £109–£130, suite £160–£225. Breakfast: continental £8.50, English £11.50. Full alc £35–£40.

See also SHORTLIST

BROCKENHURST Hampshire — Map 2:E2

Whitley Ridge Hotel NEW
Beaulieu Road
Brockenhurst SO42 7QL

Tel 01590-622354
Fax 01590-622856
Email whitleyridge@brockenhurst.co.uk
Website www.whitleyridge.co.uk

In 5-acre grounds on B3055, 4 miles S of Lyndhurst, in the New Forest, close to river Lymington: Rennie and Susan Law's Georgian former royal hunting lodge, wisteria-clad. 2 lounges in country house style, bar 'with atmosphere of gentlemen's club'; good views. 14 bedrooms (1 on ground floor), well furnished, spotless, with modern bathroom (some get noise from trains). Good English/French cooking (and vegetarians catered for) in bay-windowed dining room (background CDs at night). Friendly owners, but reception thought 'frosty' this year. Mature grounds: tennis. Unsuitable for ♿. Closed New Year. No smoking: restaurant, lounges. No dogs in public rooms. All major credit cards accepted. B&B £51–£70; D,B&B £66–£86. Set lunch £14.50, dinner £25.50 [2001]. More reports, please. *V* *(midweek Nov–Mar)*

BROXTED Essex *See SHORTLIST* — Map 2:C4

BROXTON Cheshire — Map 3:A5

Frogg Manor
Nantwich Road
Broxton, Chester CH3 9JH

Tel 01829-782629
Fax 01829-782459

César award in 1997

The owner John Sykes describes himself as 'only mildly eccentric' and visitors who find him 'flamboyant and delightful' are impressed with his 'very high standards of service' and 'real individual style'. 'A unique blend of home comforts, friendly atmosphere and culinary delights,' writes one. Mr Sykes is manager, chef and self-styled 'chief frog', dedicated to 1930s/1940s music (of which there is an 'inexhaustible collection') and to frogs – several hundred (ceramic, straw, brass, etc) are scattered around the house. The bedrooms are plush and themed: a lavishly canopied four-poster is the centrepiece of the

Wellington suite, and the Churchill suite has an 'amazing bathroom' (dramatic in black and white). All rooms are stocked with shoe-cleaning kit, toothbrushes, dressing-gowns, tea, coffee, biscuits and hangover cures. Cotton sheets are standard; Irish linen ones are supplied on request. Public rooms are 'sumptuously comfortable, and elegantly decorated' (strong colours, antiques, lavish flower arrangements). 'The cooking is excellent' as is the wine list. The menus offer a wide range of dishes, eg, Serbian pepper (baked with mozzarella cheese); Auntie Mary's Sunday afternoon melon and prawns; breast of duck served in Singapore, Normandie or Newmarket style; fillet of beef Bombay. It includes vegan as well as vegetarian dishes. Dinner is announced by a bugle call and served between 7 and 10 pm; you should make clear at what time you want to eat. A light supper can be arranged for latecomers. Breakfast *à la carte* (remember to order toast) is served round the clock from Monday to Saturday, and between 9 and 10.30 am on Sunday. The garden is romantically floodlit at night, and it has views across Cheshire to the Welsh mountains. (*Stewart Griffin, NDVR, BT*)

Open All year.
Rooms 1 suite, 5 double.
Facilities Lounge, bar lounge, restaurant (1930s/40s background music); private dining room; conference facilities. 10-acre grounds: tennis. Unsuitable for ♿. Civil wedding licence.
Location 12 miles SE of Chester. From A41, take A534 to Nantwich. Hotel on right.
Restriction No smoking in restaurant. Dogs in 1 bedroom only; not in public rooms.
Credit cards All major cards accepted.
Terms [2001] Room: single £50–£100, double £70–£150. Alc breakfast *c.* £10. Set lunch £19.80, dinner £35. Discounts for more than 1 night (except Christmas, New Year). *V*

BUDOCK VEAN Cornwall — Map 1:E2

Budock Vean Hotel
Budock Vean, nr Mawnan Smith
Falmouth TR11 5LG

Tel 01326-252100
Fax 01326-250892
Email relax@budockvean.co.uk
Website www.budockvean.co.uk

'A pet Labrador amongst hotels; reliable, friendly, soothing, certain to provide a warm welcome,' says a regular visitor. 'Very well run, like a Swiss mountain hotel,' add inspectors. Other reports speak of the 'caring, long-serving staff' at this traditional resort hotel. You approach past a nine-hole golf course; brightly coloured flowers stand in neat beds. A walk down the hill past a lovely water garden leads to the estuary. The hotel's owners, the Barlow family, also own *Treglos*, Constantine Bay (*qv*). Martin and Amanda Barlow are the resident directors ('much in smiling evidence'). Bedrooms (with flowery fabrics and patterned carpet) lead off corridors enlivened by a collection of prints. 'They are comfortable, well equipped, efficiently serviced during dinner.' Not everyone likes the 'draconian' enforcement of the dress code – men must wear a jacket and tie at dinner. 'The food is very good in a traditional way; fish is a strong point; good roast beef; a decent vegetarian dish every night', elaborate puddings follow, and a 'scrumptious cheeseboard'. Lots of good wines at around £14 a bottle. Breakfast has 'an adequate buffet, freshly cooked eggs, bacon, etc, good toast'. *Budock Vean* does not promote itself as a hotel for young children (no playground or playroom), but families are welcomed, 'provided the peace of fellow guests is respected', and they must follow rules about children's use of the swimming pool and restaurant. Three famous gardens: Trebah, with a lovely beach, Glendurgan and Carwinion, are nearby. (*Mary Woods, Nancy Drucker; also Mrs C Cootes, and others*)

Open All year, except Jan.
Rooms 1 suite, 50 double, 7 single.
Facilities Lift. 3 lounges, 2 bars, restaurant (pianist at night), snooker room. 65-acre grounds: country club: bar, restaurant, health spa, 9-hole golf course, covered swimming pool, tennis, croquet, archery, river frontage, water sports, etc. Unsuitable for ♿. Civil wedding licence.
Location 6 miles S of Falmouth. A39 to Hillhead roundabout; right to Mawnan Smith. Follow brown signs to Trebah Garden; hotel ½ mile on.
Restrictions No smoking in dining room. No children under 7 in bar or main restaurant after 7 pm. No dogs in public rooms.
Credit cards MasterCard, Diners (*2% surcharge*), Visa.
Terms [2001] B&B: single £42–£89, double £84–£178; suite £169–£243; D,B&B from £52 per person. Bar lunches. Set lunch £14.50, dinner £26.50. Special breaks: golf, Valentine, etc. Christmas, Easter tariffs. *V* (on half-board stay)

BURFORD Oxfordshire — Map 2:C2

The Lamb
Sheep Street
Burford OX18 4LR

Tel 01993-823155
Fax 01993-822228

'Traditionally charming from the outside, unusually relaxed and efficient within.' 'It is beautifully run, very "hands-on" but inconspicuously so. Everything you could wish for in a small country hotel and then some.' Resounding praise this year for Richard and Caroline de Wolf's 'lovely old inn', full of 15th-century character, with mullioned windows, polished oak floors, flagstones, chintzes, oriental rugs, antiques, polished brass and an open fire in its main lounge. 'It might seem twee at first, but *The Lamb* is actually very jolly and comfy,' writes one enthusiastic visitor. The picture-postcard village makes 'a marvellous base for exploring the Cotswolds'. 'An old-fashioned but busy dining room, with sweet waitresses in frilly aprons, and very courteous but unobtrusive management.' Pascal Clavaud's cooking is 'rich but good with a wide range of modern British dishes' – 'good value too'. The menu might include roast scallops on spiced couscous with curry oil and crispy green onions; grilled sole with anchovies, lime butter and timbale of wild rice; sticky toffee pudding with butterscotch sauce. 'Service was excellent, and the food well cooked and presented. A most reasonably priced wine list.' A small paved courtyard behind the inn leads to a walled garden, where neat lawns are surrounded by flowering shrubs and small trees. The public bar ('great atmosphere') serves good snacks on weekdays and a formal Sunday lunch. One big bedroom (The Barn) 'has a beautiful old wooden bed, sloping ceilings, beams, and a bathroom with a good lazy bath'. Some rooms are up narrow steps. (*Hannah MacDonald, John Marland; also* Good Pub Guide)

Open All year, except 25/26 Dec.
Rooms 15 double.
Facilities 3 lounges, bar, restaurant. No background music. Courtyard; ½-acre garden. River fishing ½ mile. Unsuitable for ♿.
Location 500 yds from centre. Parking. Bus from Oxford. Nearest station 8 miles.
Restrictions No smoking in restaurant. No dogs in restaurant.
Credit cards MasterCard, Visa.
Terms [2001] B&B: single £70–£85, double £105–£125; D,B&B: single £85–£100, double £145–£155. Set lunch (Sun) £22, dinner £28. Various breaks. 1-night bookings sometimes refused weekends.

BURNHAM MARKET Norfolk — Map 2:A5

The Hoste Arms
The Green
Burnham Market PE31 8HD

Tel 01328-738777
Fax 01328-730103
Email thehostearms@compuserve.com
Website www.hostearms.co.uk

The North Norfolk coast has developed a reputation as Chelsea-on-sea as the London wealthy set has forced property prices ever higher. This 300-year-old inn stands on the green of a lovely village with a plethora of upmarket shops. Lord Nelson used to collect his dispatches here, and it has served as court assizes, auction house and brothel. Now, it is the chosen watering hole for the Range Rover set. Paul Whittome is a 'not uneccentric' host who warns in his brochure: 'Please speak up. I am very deaf and this is sometimes mistaken for rudeness.' He and his wife, Jeanne, run a lively establishment, with upmarket bedrooms, a large shell collection, and a small art gallery. 'Not the place for a quiet weekend' – it is 'busy, even at breakfast'. The bar 'is also the village pub'; residents have a conservatory lounge. In the restaurant (with wooden floors and panels, tables close together) guests are fed in relays. The Australian chef, Andrew McPherson, serves brasserie-style dishes, eg, collops of monkfish with aromatic rice and a ginger sauce; spicy Szechwan chicken with egg noodles; steak and chips. 'The menu is ambitious, and generally successful, but the keen, very young staff need more supervision,' one couple wrote. But another report tells of a disappointing meal. The bedrooms vary: one couple had a 'lovely, large' one overlooking the green, but its bedside lighting was much too dim'. Rooms in an extension look through French windows on to the garden, where

there are 'chairs for summer drinkers, and children running around'. The annexe (formerly the town's station), a short walk away, has 'small but adequate' bedrooms; a car will take its residents to the inn for meals. (*R and L Cooper,* Good Pub Guide, *and others*)

Open All year. Restaurant closed midday 1 Jan.
Rooms 10 suites, 13 double, 5 single. 6 in annexe. Some on ground floor.
Facilities Conservatory lounge, 4 dining rooms; conference facilities. No background music. ¼-acre garden: summer restaurant. Sea, bird sanctuaries, golf nearby. Unsuitable for ♿.
Location Central. Large car park. Train: Norwich/Kings Lynn; taxi.
Restrictions No smoking in 3 dining rooms. 'Not suitable for noisy or badly behaved children, but charming ones are warmly welcomed.'
Credit cards MasterCard, Visa.
Terms B&B £45–£102; D,B&B (min. 2 nights) £93–£150. Bar meals. Full alc £30. Child under 15 in parents' room: £15. Christmas package. 1-night bookings refused Saturday.

BURPHAM West Sussex — Map 2:E3

The Burpham — *Tel* 01903-882160
Burpham, nr Arundel BN18 9RJ — *Fax* 01903-884627

A visitor arriving on a wet Saturday night with floods alarmingly close to the road was cheered 'by an excellent welcome – the staff were friendly and somewhat proud to be running the hotel without the benefit of the owners' presence (annual vacation)'. This is a good sign, for those who meet George and Marianne Walker find him 'great fun' and her 'charming'. Their small country hotel, in what was an 18th-century shooting lodge of the Dukes of Norfolk, stands 'at the end of the longest cul-de-sac in Sussex, which ensures peace and quiet'. 'The house is comfortable, warm, well aired, and stocked with flowers, even in February.' The bedrooms, with lots of velour, are well equipped, though lighting may be dim, and some bathrooms may be small. The stairs are steep. 'Tasty nibbles' are served in the bar before dinner. The English/French/Swiss food (influenced by the Swiss origins of Mrs Walker) is considered 'quite wonderful'; 'outstandingly good'. 'Luscious fresh scallops in a delicious sauce' are singled out for praise. The only disappointed diner (over-cooked duck in Mrs Walker's absence) did enjoy the scallops and thought breakfast 'superb'. A conservatory has views across the croquet lawn and the South Downs, and allows guests to breakfast and dine in a 'blaze of sunshine'. The bar area can get crowded. Burpham (pronounced Ber′-fum) has a Norman church and a cricket pitch on which WG Grace once played; Arundel Castle and Peter Scott's Wildfowl Trust are close by; Chichester and Goodwood are within easy reach. Good walking all around. (*Julia Fiehn, Barry Rogers, and others*)

Open All year, except 25 Dec, last week Jan, 1st week Feb. Restaurant closed midday, Sun and Mon evening.
Rooms 9 double (1 on ground floor), 1 single.
Facilities Hall, lounge, bar, restaurant, conservatory; light classical background music at night; small conference room. ½-acre garden: croquet. Coast 6 miles: sand/shingle beaches, safe bathing. Unsuitable for ♿.
Location NE of Arundel. Left off A27 Arundel–Worthing towards

Warningcamp/Burpham just after railway bridge. Hotel on right after 2½ miles (look for sign on A27).
Restrictions No smoking: restaurant, some bedrooms. No children under 12. No dogs.
Credit cards Amex, MasterCard, Visa.
Terms [2001] B&B £42.50–£55; D,B&B £67.50–£80. Set dinner (2–3 courses) £21–£25. Special breaks; Stress Remedy breaks. *V*

BURRINGTON Devon — Map 1:C4

Northcote Manor
Burrington, nr South Molton
EX37 9LZ

Tel 01769-560501
Fax 01769-560770
Email rest@northcotemanor.co.uk
Website www.northcotemanor.co.uk

Up meandering drive through 20-acre wooded grounds with apple orchard: serene wisteria-clad 18th-century manor house overlooking sweeping lawns. Pride of Britain member, recently refurbished by owner, David Boddy: elegant decor with country house feel. Managed by Karen Dawson; her husband, Chris, formerly of Ynyshir Hall, *Eglwysfach, Wales (*qv*), is chef. Lounge, lounge/bar (light classical music sometimes). Modern cooking and personal attention in restaurant with large medieval-style murals, wine list specialising in New Zealand vintages. Civil wedding licence. 18-hole golf course adjacent; fishing in river Taw. Unsuitable for ♿. No smoking: restaurant, lounge, some bedrooms. No children under 12. No dogs in public rooms. All major credit cards accepted. 11 bedrooms. B&B from £82.50. Set lunch £25, dinner £35.* *V*

BURY ST EDMUNDS Suffolk — Map 2:B5

The Angel NEW
Angel Hill
Bury St Edmunds IP33 1LT

Tel 01284-714000
Fax 01284-714001
Email sales@theangel.co.uk
Website www.theangel.co.uk

Much has changed at this creeper-clad inn on the town's central square since Charles Dickens stayed here while writing *The Pickwick Papers*, 'but at heart it is still a historic town-centre coaching inn', writes the director, Robert Gough. For the past two years he has overseen the refurbishment and expansion of the old building, which stands opposite the ruined abbey (the town is named for King Edmund the Martyr, who was murdered by Danes in the 9th century). Twenty-three air-conditioned bedrooms have been added in a former ballroom. 'They are quiet, comfortable, and well designed; our very large bathroom had the biggest bath we have ever come across,' writes a regular correspondent this year, restoring *The Angel* to the *Guide*. 'The hotel is comfortable, well furnished. The new decor in the main restaurant is attractive, if startling, with dark blue walls. Service is deft; and the whole air is that of trying to please the guest. All the staff are charming.' The chef, Simon Barker, has come from the Gough family's other hotel, *The Marlborough*, Ipswich (*qv*). 'His cooking is very good: seared scallops in filo pastry were out of this world; duck breast was pink and tender. The red house wine was very good. Breakfasts were excellent, though preserves are in small pots.' There is a less formal restaurant in the 12th-century undercroft. Tea, coffee and drinks are served in the large lounge. Bedroom decor ranges from traditional (some four-posters) to contemporary. Jazz evenings are held. (*Moira Jarrett*)

Open All year.
Rooms 2 suites, 55 double, 4 single. Some on ground floor, with access for ♿.
Facilities Lounge, bar (background jazz all day), restaurant, brasserie; function facilities. Civil wedding licence.
Location Central. Follow signs for tourist information centre. Parking.
Restriction No smoking in main restaurant.
Credit cards All major cards accepted.
Terms B&B: single £82, double £114–£144, suite £180; D,B&B: single £100, double £140–£160, suite £240. Set lunch £16, dinner £25; full alc £45. Winter packages. Sunday-night rates. Christmas package. *V*

Ounce House
Northgate Street
Bury St Edmunds IP33 1HP

Tel 01284-761779
Fax 01284-768315
Email pott@globalnet.co.uk
Website www.ouncehouse.co.uk

Good fabrics, antiques, pictures and prints, and inviting colour schemes abound in Simon and Jenny Pott's civilised B&B in a Victorian merchant's house. Many of the public areas were redecorated this year. Guests have the use of a bay-windowed drawing room with a large fireplace, and a library with TV, an upright piano and an honesty bar. There is a useful parking area in front of the house, which is on a busy road; the quietest of the three bedrooms overlooks the walled garden. Breakfasts are 'perfectly cooked and presented'. Dinner can be served if numbers are sufficient. It is taken communally, and traditional: four courses, eg, English onion soup with goat's cheese croutons; Aldeburgh fish pie with prawn sauce; chocolate marquis; cheese. The 'warm and helpful' Mrs Pott is an excellent source of information on local history. The town has many handsome buildings, including the Theatre Royal, the second oldest working theatre in the country. Ickworth House (National Trust) is nearby. More reports, please.

Open All year.
Rooms 3 double.
Facilities Drawing room, snug, bar/library, dining room. No background music. ½-acre walled garden. Unsuitable for ♿.
Location Central (rear room quietest). Leave A14 (formerly A45) at 2nd Bury exit. Left at 1st roundabout into Northgate St; house at top of hill. Private parking. Collection arranged from station.
Restrictions Smoking in bar/library only, 'provided guests light a candle'. No dogs.
Credit cards All major cards accepted.
Terms [2001] B&B: single £60–£70, double £85–£95. Set dinner (by arrangement, for 4 or more) £24–£26. Weekend rates; reductions for 3 or more nights.

All our inspections are carried out anonymously.

Ravenwood Hall
Rougham, nr Bury St Edmunds
IP30 9JA

Tel 01359-270345
Fax 01359-270788
Email enquiries@ravenwoodhall.co.uk
Website www.ravenwoodhall.co.uk

'A very happy place. The staff are most friendly. Our small son loved the informality.' 'Wholeheartedly recommended: comfortable, quiet bedrooms; a wonderful non-stuffy atmosphere.' 'Stuart Turner, the general manager, did his utmost to ensure that everyone had an excellent stay.' There is much praise this year for Craig Jarvis's unpretentious hotel in a large park just outside Bury St Edmunds. The building dates back to Tudor times; 16th-century wall paintings, ornately carved oak woodwork, and inglenook fireplaces testify to its age. A 'country air' is added by cricketing gear, tennis rackets and a mixed collection of pictures and prints. Bearded goats, horses and ponies graze in a paddock, and the large gardens have an open-air swimming pool, tennis courts and a croquet lawn. The best bedrooms are in the main house. 'Antique and period furniture successfully blend with modern luxuries (thick towels and good bubble bath).' Dean's Room, suitable for a small family, is 'decked out in simple good taste'. St Edmunds, with its canopied bed, 'would be charming for a romantic night away'. Rooms in converted stables are smaller, cheaper and less attractive, but handy for wheelchair users and dog-owners; some have a glass door leading on to the garden. In the heavily beamed, pink-walled dining room (once the Great Hall), the cooking of the new chef, David White, is 'classic English, with a modern twist', eg, home-smoked duck sausage on a spicy plum sauce, or Mediterranean fish soup with rouille croutons; supreme of turbot on white crab and lemongrass risotto, or braised shank of lamb with confit of root vegetables. 'Not too *nouvelle*, but inventive.' 'Very good vegetarian main courses.' Portions are a bit large for some. A blackboard menu of simpler, 'also very good', dishes is served in the bar, and cream teas are available. At breakfast, the menu ranges from porridge to bacon *froize* (a kind of pancake). Weddings and functions are held in a pavilion. Mr Jarvis also owns the *Black Lion*, Long Melford (*qv*). (*Felicity Chadwick-Histed, JR Williams, Julie and Mark Thomas, IJ*)

Open All year.
Rooms 14 double. 7 in mews. Some on ground floor.
Facilities Ramps. Lounge, bar, restaurant; function suite; classical background music in public areas all day. 7-acre grounds: swimming pool, tennis, croquet. Golf nearby; hunting, shooting available. Civil wedding licence.
Location Off A14, 3 miles SE of Bury St Edmunds. Bus to Rougham.
Restrictions No smoking: restaurant, bedrooms. No dogs in public rooms.
Credit cards All major cards accepted.
Terms B&B: single £71–£84, double £93–£103. Bar meals. Set lunch (Sun)/dinner £21.50; full alc £45. Christmas package.

> Hotels often book you into their most expensive rooms or suites unless you specify otherwise. Even if all room prices are the same, hotels may give you a less good room in the hope of selling their better rooms to late customers. It always pays to discuss accommodation in detail when making a reservation, and to ask for a free upgrade on arrival if the hotel isn't full.

BYLAND ABBEY North Yorkshire — Map 4:D4

The Abbey Inn NEW
Byland Abbey
nr Coxwold YO61 4BD

Tel 01347-868204
Fax 01347-868678
Email jane@nordli.freeserve.co.uk
Website www.bylandabbeyinn.com

An appealing new venture in a hamlet in the North York Moors National Park. This creeper-covered old inn (built in the 16th century by the Benedictine brothers of nearby Ampleforth) stands opposite Byland's ruined Cistercian abbey. Its owners (since 1997), Jane and Martin Nordli, have now added three luxurious bedrooms. 'The Abbots Retreat, with a four-poster bed and sitting area, was one of the nicest rooms we have ever stayed in,' says one enthusiastic report. 'Fabulous attention to detail: wine, chocolates, flowers, this week's *Hello*; scrummy bath products in a black and white bathroom to die for. The views of the floodlit abbey are the icing on the cake.' The Priors Lynn has a half-tester bed; The Monks Rest has a brass one. 'A very friendly host and hostess; scrumptious food' (eg, broccoli and hazelnut mousse with Parma ham; fillet of venison on a celeriac purée with a black cherry sauce; caramelised oranges with cream). A series of eating areas has big fireplaces, carved oak seats, polished wooden tables. Breakfast, ordered the evening before, is brought to the bedroom. Functions can be held in a marquee in the garden. Not suitable for the infirm: the old building has steep steps. The delightful village of Coxwold is nearby. (*Mrs CA Pattoll, Sue Stuart; also Catherine Hayden,* Good Pub Guide*, and others*)

Open All year. Restaurant closed Sun night, Mon midday.
Rooms 1 suite, 2 double.
Facilities Bar, restaurant; background jazz/classical music; library/function room. Large patio: facilities for marquee; large garden. Unsuitable for ♿.
Location 2 miles W of Ampleforth. From A19 York–Thirsk, right at sign to Coxwold; in village, turn left at sign to Byland Abbey. Parking.
Restrictions No smoking in 2 dining rooms. No dogs.
Credit cards MasterCard, Visa.
Terms B&B: single £40–£70, double £70–£100, suite £110. Full alc £25. *V*

CALNE Wiltshire — Map 2:D2

Chilvester Hill House
Calne SN11 0LP

Tel 01249-813981 and 815785
Fax 01249-814217
Email gill.dilley@talk21.com
Website www.chilvesterhillhouse.co.uk

Cesar award in 1992

A long-time *Guide* favourite – 'the private house of a professional family,' say its owners, Gill and John Dilley. It is a Wolsey Lodge member in a Victorian house built for the land agent of Lord Lansdowne, the owner of nearby Bowood estate. The Dilleys, loved for their 'charm and slight eccentricity', sometimes breed beef cattle, which graze in the fields around the large garden. Indoors are antiques, and mementos of many years in the Middle East. No brochure – prospective visitors are sent a chatty letter discussing facilities and food preferences. The set dinner (eg, smoked trout fillets with horseradish cream; grilled chicken breast with wine and mushroom sauce; orange- and cardamom-flavoured rhubarb fool) is served round one large table. Couples may be separated to encourage conversation; the Dilleys often join their guests for pre-dinner drinks, or afterwards for coffee. No obligation to eat in; help is given with reservations at local eating places. 'The rooms cannot be faulted,' writes a devotee (they are equipped with a hot drinks tray, biscuits, etc), 'and as in a visit to a country house, beds are turned down during dinner.' *En suite* bathrooms have a hand-held shower only, but a large shower room is available (bathrobes are provided). The breakfast, once awarded 11 out of 10 by Derek Cooper, 'is "what you like when you like it"; most guests settle for something between 8 and 9 am'. On offer are fresh grapefruit, cereals, locally produced bacon, kippers, kidneys, tomatoes, mushrooms, eggs any way, plus home-made jams and preserves. Dr Dilley has encyclopaedic local knowledge: sights include the Neolithic stone circle at Avebury, the National Trust village of Lacock, the Slimbridge Wildfowl Trust. (*Chris Kay*)

Open All year, except possibly 1 week autumn and/or spring.
Rooms 3 double. No telephone.
Facilities Drawing room, sitting room with TV, dining room. No background music. 2½-acre grounds (also 5 acres used for cattle). Golf, riding locally. Unsuitable for ♿.
Location From Calne, A4 towards Chippenham. Right after ½ mile to Bremhill; drive immediately on right (gateposts with stone lions).
Restrictions No smoking in dining room. Generally no children under 12, except babes in arms. No dogs in house.
Credit cards All major cards accepted.
Terms B&B: single £45–£55, double £75–£85. Packed/snack lunches. Set dinner *c.* £20–£25. 10% discount for B&B if 1 week or more.

CAMBRIDGE Cambridgeshire *See SHORTLIST* Map 2:B4

CAMPSEA ASHE Suffolk Map 2:C6

The Old Rectory *Tel/Fax* 01728-746524
Campsea Ashe
nr Woodbridge IP13 0QL

César award in 1992

Owner/chef Stewart Bassett, with long-time manager, Tina Moorford, runs his creeper-covered Georgian house informally as a restaurant-with-rooms and a Wolsey Lodge. 'Homely and unpretentious', it stands in a large garden with statuary, by the church in a village not far from Aldeburgh. 'Warm hospitality, excellent cooking. Thoroughly deserves its place in the *Guide*,' said a recent report. Visitors value its relaxed atmosphere', 'old-world comfort' and eccentric charm, and above all the reasonably priced food and 'amazing wine list'. Dinner (24 hours' notice is required) is served by candlelight at 7.30: in winter it is in the old-style dining rooms, in summer in a conservatory.

Guests sit at well-spaced bare wooden tables on big rattan chairs. The three-course, no-choice menu might include pan-fried halibut on a bed of spinach with butter sauce, or braised spiced lamb with roasted almonds. Breakfast includes an extensive buffet. In the large drawing room, high ceilings and grand antiques are set off by rich terracotta walls, and there is an honesty bar. Bedrooms range from a large four-poster room overlooking the churchyard to a small double above the garden; the one above the kitchen can be noisy. Budget B&B accommodation is offered in a cottage in the village, good for a family. Children are welcomed, though there are no special facilities for them. 'Well-behaved dogs' are accepted, but not in the dining room. Guests should not arrive between 2 and 4 pm. House parties, weddings and conferences are catered for. Plant propagation courses for gardeners are held. The RSPB reserve at Minsmere is nearby. (*KL, JW*)

Open All year, except Christmas, 3 weeks Feb/Mar. Restaurant closed midday, Sun evening; bedrooms sometimes closed Sun.
Rooms 6 double, 1 single. 1 in garden. No telephone/TV (payphone in hall).
Facilities Drawing room with TV, honesty bar, restaurant; function facilities. No background music. 4½-acre garden: croquet. Riding, golf nearby; sea at Aldeburgh, 10 mins' drive. Unsuitable for ♿.
Location By church in village 1½ miles E of A12 on B1078. Train: Wickham Market, via Ipswich.
Restrictions No smoking. No dogs in public rooms.
Credit cards All major cards accepted.
Terms [2001] B&B: single £45, double £65–£75. Set dinner (24 hours' notice required) £19. Child in parents' room: under 3, free; 3–10, B&B £10. Plant propagation courses. 1-night bookings refused Sat if dinner not taken.

CANNINGTON Somerset — Map 1:B5

Blackmore Farm BUDGET
Blackmore Lane
Cannington
nr Bridgwater TA5 2NE

Tel 01278-653442
Fax 01278-653427
Email dyerfarm@aol.com
Website www.dyerfarm.co.uk

'Everything was quite splendid,' wrote returning visitors to this 'truly wonderful' pink-washed medieval manor house. Ann and Ian Dyer offer traditional farmhouse B&B in their family home, Grade I listed, with a lovely little chapel attached. They are generous hosts: 'Tea and delicious home-made sponge cake are served free to arriving guests. There were endless goodies (fruit, biscuits, chocolates) in our large bedroom. We stayed with our young grandchild for a total cost of £50.' The old house, on a quiet lane on a large working farm not far from the M5, retains many original features: heavy latched doors, stone archways, mullioned windows, a spiral stone staircase, garderobes and oak beams; old pewter pots, hay forks and nasty looking man-traps' are scattered about. 'You feel you have stepped back into the past.' The four bedrooms are simply furnished 'in quiet good taste'; they look over fields or the farmyard. The West Room has Gothic arches and an oak four-poster bed. The Gallery has oak panelling and beams, and a sitting room down a flight of steps. The Solar has three single beds and a shower. A room in a converted barn is adapted for disabled visitors. At breakfast, in the Great Hall, guests eat together at a long refectory table by a massive sandstone fireplace. 'It was very good, with fruit, yogurt, scrambled egg with smoked haddock, and a vegetarian option.' 'A good pub for dinner is five minutes' walk away', and there are plenty of restaurants nearby. You can watch the cows being milked from a gallery, play croquet in the garden, and visit a cottage nearby where Coleridge once lived. A good base for exploring the Quantocks, the west Somerset coast and Exmoor. (*Ray and Angela Evans*)

Open All year.
Rooms 1 suite, 3 double. 1, on ground floor, adapted for ♿. No telephone.
Facilities Lounge/TV room, breakfast room. No background music. 1½-acre garden in 750-acre farm: croquet, children's play area. Coarse fishing, riding, golf, cycling nearby.
Location From Bridgwater: A39 to Minehead; after 3 miles left at Tincknells into Blackmore La. Farm ¾ mile on left, after *Maltshovel* pub. Train: Bridgwater, 4 miles; irregular bus service.
Restrictions No smoking. No dogs.
Credit cards MasterCard, Visa.
Terms B&B: single £30–£40, double £45–£55, suite £55–£60.

CANTERBURY Kent — Map 2:D5

The Canterbury Hotel
71 New Dover Road
Canterbury CT1 3DZ

Tel 01227-450551
Fax 01227-780145
Email canterbury.hotel@btinternet.com

Canterbury Cathedral is a ten-minute walk away and the 'garden of England' lies just beyond, but this Victorian red brick house on the busy Dover road is French in style. The manager, M. Boizot, and his young staff are French, as is the restaurant *La Bonne Cuisine*, which is hung with Renoir prints. The decor is attractive (blue and yellow predominate). The bedrooms are on three floors – some are spacious – and have bright colours and a small but gleaming bathroom; 'boiling hot water, even at midnight'. There is a new French chef this year, M. Supparo, who presents a traditional menu, eg, foie gras de canard; noisettes d'agneau en croûte; lasagne de lotte; poire au vin rouge. Breakfast, however, is a very English affair. Drinks and bar snacks are served in the lounge or on a patio. The busy road and constant background music are among the drawbacks, but the hotel has much to recommend it, not least its car park and useful location. More reports, please.

Open All year.
Rooms 20 double, 3 single.
Facilities Lift. Lounge, bar, restaurant; background 'relax music' all day; small conference facilities. Small garden. Unsuitable for ♿.
Location On A2, ½ mile S of centre. Car park. Train to Canterbury East.
Restrictions No smoking in reception. No children under 6 in restaurant at night. No dogs in public rooms.
Credit cards All major cards accepted.
Terms B&B: single £55–£80, double £75–£105. Set dinner £16.50–£21.50. 2-night breaks. Christmas package.

See also SHORTLIST

CARLISLE Cumbria **Map 4:B2**

Avondale BUDGET
3 St Aidan's Road
Carlisle CA1 1LT

Tel/Fax 01228-523012
Email beeanbee@hotmail.com
Website www.beeanbee.co.uk

'Wonderful in every way,' says a visitor who has regularly visited Michael and Angela Hayes's civilised small guest house over many years. 'They could not be more hospitable.' 'It is one of the most comfortable guest houses I have used,' says another reporter, who spends much time on the road. The large Edwardian house retains many original features – fireplaces, stained glass, elaborate ceilings, door handles, etc – and has a 'very pretty' decor to match. It is on a quiet road in a residential area, not far from the centre. All three bedrooms have TV; the largest room, overlooking the garden, has a bathroom *en suite*; the other two have access to one bathroom. The 'delicious breakfasts' include 'expertly cooked fresh eggs'. A simple evening meal is available by arrangement. It is 'traditional, wholesome and uncomplicated', say the owners, eg, carrot and coriander soup; goulash with new potatoes; fresh fruit salad. Portions are generous. Unlicensed; bring your own wine. No brochure, but the owners send a detailed description, and they now have a website. 'We tend to take older children whose parents are happy for them to sleep in a separate room,' say the Hayeses. (*Gay Firth, ME*)

Open All year, except Christmas.
Rooms 3 double, 1 with bathroom *en suite*, 2 with access to 1 bathroom. No telephone.
Facilities Sitting room, dining room. No background music. Small front and rear gardens. Unsuitable for ♿.
Location From M6 exit 43 enter Carlisle. Turn right just past church on right after 4th traffic lights. Parking. Train/bus stations nearby.
Restrictions No smoking. No dogs.
Credit cards None accepted.
Terms (*Not VAT-rated*) B&B £20–£40. Evening meal £9. Child accommodated free in parents' room.

Number Thirty One
31 Howard Place
Carlisle CA1 1HR

Tel/Fax 01228-597080
Email bestpep@aol.com
Website www.number31.freeservers.com

More than 20 years of experience at the top end of the hotel and restaurant business has been brought by Philip and Judith Parker to the different demands of running a small guest house. They renovated a Victorian terraced house on a tree-lined street in the town centre, and have created a 'relaxed environment' that is 'something special' according to *Guide* readers. Their lounge is crammed with knick-knacks and souvenirs of travel; there is a small patio garden. Only three bedrooms: the Blue Room, at the rear, is the largest; the Green Room has an oriental-style decor; from the Yellow Room in front, the owners claim, you can see the Pennines on a fine day. Breakfast specialities include home-made muesli; kedgeree with saffron rice. A three-course, no-choice evening meal is served by arrangement, at separate tables, and the food is thought 'well presented, and good value'. Philip Parker says he cooks' in the Floyd manner, with glass in hand (normally nothing stronger than sparkling water)'. Virtually everything is home made; ingredients are bought each day. 'We avoid produce with additives; trout and salmon are smoked on the premises when I catch them; breakfast sausages are made to a Cumbrian recipe.' Each dish is described at length on the unusual menu: main courses include spiced lamb fillets on sweet potato mash; pan-fried tournedos of beef on a nest of polenta. The Parkers regularly transport their guests to and from the railway station; they have a stock of books on tape for the blind. (*P and HR, JMW*)

Open 1 Mar–1 Nov.
Rooms 3 double. No telephone.
Facilities Lounge, dining room/library (dinner background music chosen by guests). Small patio. Unsuitable for ♿.
Location From M6 exit 43 take Warwick Rd towards Carlisle. Howard Pl is 1st right after 5th traffic lights. Free parking with permit. Parkers will meet train/bus (10 mins' walk).
Restrictions No smoking. No children under 16. No dogs.
Credit cards Amex, MasterCard, Visa.
Terms [2001] B&B: single £55, double £75–£90. Set dinner £25.

See also SHORTLIST

CARTMEL Cumbria — Map 4: inset C2

Aynsome Manor
Cartmel
nr Grange-over-Sands
LA11 6HH

Tel 015395-36653
Fax 015395-36016
Email info@aynsomemanorhotel.co.uk
Website www.aynsomemanorhotel.co.uk

César award in 1998

'We loved it,' says one of many enthusiastic reports this year on this traditional hotel run by two generations of the Varley family: Chris and his wife, Andrea, with his parents, Tony and Margaret. Other praise: 'They have got it just right.' 'Welcoming and unstuffy, with excellent service; outstandingly good food.' 'When we saw the prices we wondered, "What's the catch?" – there wasn't one.' The 16th-century house is in a picturesque village on the edge of the Lake District, 'an area of little traffic and considerable interest'. A great attribute is 'the perfect silence of the surrounding countryside, particularly at night'. The decor is cheerful – patterned carpets and period furniture in the two spacious lounges (one has a fine old marble fireplace). The bedrooms vary in size; some are suitable for a family; a top-floor one is heavily beamed with sloping ceilings and not much view; two are in a cottage with a sitting room, across the cobbled courtyard. In the oak-panelled restaurant, with its large bay windows, moulded plaster ceiling and oil paintings, dinner (at 7 pm) is quite formal: jacket and tie are expected of male diners. The English country house cooking of Nicholas Stopford might include crab and prawn fish-cakes on cucumber linguine; salmon, lemon sole and monkfish on chive mash; calorific pies and gateau desserts on a trolley. On Sunday there is a traditional lunch, and a supper with soup and a cold buffet. 'Excellent cooked breakfasts with superior coffee.' Some visitors would have liked a no-smoking lounge, but the lack of muzak is appreciated. Cartmel's ruined 12th-century priory is close by. Local attractions include Holker Hall, Levens Hall and Sizergh Castle. (*Dr G and Mrs C McDade, CC Schofield, JM Hope, PE Carter; also GL Featherstone*)

Open 1 Feb–2 Jan. Lunch served Sun only.
Rooms 12 double. 2 in cottage (with private lounge) across courtyard.
Facilities 2 lounges, cocktail bar, dining room. No background music. ¼-acre garden. Lake Windermere 4 miles: water sports. Golf nearby. Unsuitable for ♿.
Location 12 miles from M6 exit 36. Leave A590 at Cartmel sign. Hotel on right, ½ mile before village. Train: Grange-over-Sands, 3 miles; taxi.
Restrictions Smoking banned in restaurant, discouraged in bedrooms. No children under 5 at dinner. No dogs in public rooms, unattended in bedrooms.
Credit cards Amex, MasterCard, Visa.
Terms D,B&B: single £60–£72, double £99–£124. Set Sun lunch £14, dinner £18.50. Child in parents' room: under 5, £6; 5–12, £25 (half board). Weekend, midweek, Christmas breaks; bonus breaks for returning guests. 1-night bookings occasionally refused. *V*

Uplands
Haggs Lane, Cartmel
nr Grange-over-Sands LA11 6HD

Tel 015395-36248
Fax 015395-36848
Email uplands@kencomp.net
Website www.uplands.uk.com

The food is the highlight of the stay at this 'peaceful place', a restaurant-with-rooms on a hillside with views across a patchwork of fields to Morecambe Bay. The pebble-dashed house, decorated in contemporary style, is approached through a tiny courtyard, Italianate in feel, with plants in pots and tubs, small statues, clematis over an archway. The resident marmalade cats, Basil and Teddy, have been joined by Mabel, 'a sweet-tempered Jack Russell who is more than happy to take guests for walks', and 'well-behaved dogs' are welcome visitors here, say the hosts, Tom and Di Peter. Deer, squirrels, pheasants and badgers are sometimes seen in the grounds. Mr Peter's modern cooking, in country style, is 'sometimes ambitious, mostly superb; pricey but good value'. The second course is a tureen of soup (it might be roasted red pepper and tomato, or broccoli and Stilton) brought to each table with a warm home-baked wholemeal loaf. Main courses, accompanied by five vegetables, might be baked fillet of sea bass with chive and lemon sauce, or roast saddle of hare with a rich Madeira sauce. 'Standards are high,' say regular visitors, and the 'good-humoured service' is praised. At breakfast, a toaster is placed on each table. The bedrooms are on the small side, but pretty; three have a small shower room, the others a bathroom; two enjoy the view. A hilly golf course with lovely views is adjacent. Cartmel village, with its 12th-century priory and racecourse, is a mile away. Grange-over-Sands, the Victorian resort on Morecambe Bay, is two miles. Local stately homes: Holker Hall, with an award-winning garden; Levens Hall ('magnificent topiary').

Open Mar–Dec (except some days in July). Restaurant open for lunch Thurs–Sun, for dinner daily, except Mon.
Rooms 5 double.
Facilities Lounge, restaurant. No background music. 2-acre grounds. Golf nearby; Lake Windermere 6 miles. Unsuitable for ♿.
Location In Cartmel, opposite *Pig & Whistle*, take road to Grange-over-Sands for 1 mile; hotel on left. Parking. Train: Grange-over-Sands; taxi.
Restrictions No smoking: restaurant, 2 bedrooms. No children under 8. No dogs in public rooms.
Credit cards Amex, MasterCard, Visa.
Terms D,B&B £66–£89. Set lunch £16, dinner £29.50. Reductions (£10–£20) for 2 nights or more Nov–Apr. Christmas package. 1-night bookings occasionally refused Sat. *V*

CASTLE CARY Somerset — Map 2:D1

Bond's NEW

Ansford Hill
Castle Cary BA7 7JL

Tel/Fax 01963-350464
Email bonds-bistro@faxvia.net

'We found it so good. Excellent value; wonderful, interesting food. A very pleasant bedroom (No. 7); a well-lit bathroom – important if you like reading in the bath.' Yvonne Bond is chef and her husband, Kevin, is front-of-house, in their bistro-with-rooms, a listed, creeper-covered, Georgian coaching inn, in an agreeable mid-Somerset town (its name refers to its Norman castle, now in ruins, and its river, the Cary). An inspector, restoring it to the *Guide*, reports: 'The dining room is smart, with plants, interesting objects (eg, antique cheese dishes), square and round tables, a fireplace, posters and old prints. The attractive bar has an open fire and some tiny tables. No residents' lounge. Our compact bedroom had an old-fashioned decor (1980s textiles, striped wallpaper with a frieze at the top). Water pressure was weak, and towels were on the small side, but the bath was deep and wide. The buffet breakfast was remarkable, with huge choice: fruit compote, yogurt, cereals in urns, smoked salmon, ham, quiche Lorraine and much more. Exceptional home-made bread at both breakfast and dinner. The welcome was pleasant. Mr Bond, with a faint "ex-forces" aura, is a courteous host, on excellent terms with his local customers. Service at dinner was by nice young girls. Mussels were plump and perfectly cooked; rack of lamb was tender and pink; we finished with rhubarb and frangipane tart with flavourful raspberry sorbet.' Cheese is a special feature. The short wine list includes 'some excellent bottles at moderate prices'. Mr Bond 'will gladly show you his immaculate classic cars and charming garden'. Some traffic noise in front rooms, but the house is set back from the road. (*Mrs FE Dryden, and others*)

Open All year, except Christmas, New Year.
Rooms 7 double.

Facilities Lounge/bar, bistro; background modern piano music at night. ¼-acre garden. Unsuitable for ♿.
Location 1 mile N of Castle Cary, on A371, 300 yds from station. Large car park.
Restrictions No smoking in bistro. No children under 8, except babies. No dogs.
Credit cards MasterCard, Visa.
Terms [2001] B&B: single £58, double £69.50. Light lunch £6; full alc dinner £25. *V*

CHADDESLEY CORBETT Worcestershire — Map 3:C5

Brockencote Hall
Chaddesley Corbett
nr Kidderminster DY10 4PY

Tel 01562-777876
Fax 01562-777872
Email info@brockencotehall.com
Website www.brockencotehall.com

A late Victorian mansion in a peaceful English setting has been transformed over 15 years into a country house hotel with a distinct Gallic flavour, by its owners, Alison and Joseph Petitjean. The landscaped grounds (with a half-timbered Tudor dovecote and ornamental lake) were part of an estate that dates back to the 17th century. A modern French menu is served by the 'impeccably polite', mainly French staff ('a level of conversational French is an advantage,' says one reporter, tongue in cheek). The chef, Jérôme Barbancon, formerly worked at the *Michelin*-starred *Charlton House*, Shepton Mallet (*qv*). His dishes include squab pigeon and foie gras; loin of venison with braised chicory; bitter chocolate moelleux with pistachio ice cream. Coffee and petits fours are included in the price. House wines are reasonably priced. 'Only disadvantage: the menu does not change, and it lacks plain food.' The spacious public rooms are formal, with honey-coloured panelling, open fires, potted plants. The large bedrooms, 'perfect for a woman on her own', have fresh flowers, fruit, sherry, up-to-date magazines and an impressive bathroom – some have a spa bath. One visitor thought breakfast 'extremely good', but 'not for those in a hurry'. Weekend breaks include reflexology treatment. Chaddesley Corbett village has a harmonious blend of 16th- to 19th-century houses; its old church is part Norman. Nearby is Harvington Hall, a moated 16th-century manor house. A good base for visiting Warwick Castle, Cadbury World and West Midlands Safari Park. (*Sue Davies, Becky Goldsmith, John J Jenkins, and others*)

Open All year.
Rooms 17 double. Some on ground floor; 1 adapted for ♿.
Facilities Lift, ramp. Hall, 3 lounges, conservatory, restaurant; function facilities. No background music. 70-acre grounds: gardens, lake, croquet, tennis. Golf nearby.
Location On A448 Kidderminster–Bromsgrove. M42 exit 1 (southbound only); M5 exit 4. Train: Kidderminster; taxi.
Restrictions No smoking in restaurant. Guide dogs only.
Credit cards All major cards accepted.
Terms [2001] B&B: single £110–£130, double £135–£170; D,B&B: single £137.50–£157.50, double £190–£225. Set lunch (2–3 courses) £12–£15, dinner £27.50; full alc £50. Child in parents' room: under 12, free. Short breaks; aromatherapy, shooting, golfing breaks. Christmas package. *V*

CHAGFORD Devon — Map 1:C4

Gidleigh Park

Chagford TQ13 8HH
Tel 01647-432367
Fax 01647-432574
Email gidleighpark@gidleigh.co.uk
Website www.gidleigh.com

César award in 1984 and 1989

Michael Caines's two-star *Michelin* cooking may attract those in the know to deepest Devon, but the food is complemented by the hands-on approach to hotel-keeping of *Gidleigh*'s owners, Paul and Kay Henderson. This combination of a Devonian cooking modern French dishes and an American couple creating a classic British country house hotel (Relais & Châteaux) may seem unlikely, but it continues to be admired for its unashamed luxury. 'The long-term staff are charming, always there if needed, but they don't hover,' writes one regular, who always departs 'wondering how soon we can fund another visit'. Even a visitor who found the cooking 'old-fashioned and ludicrously fussy' was lavish in his praise. 'Our room, No. 2, was magnificent, with a broad bay window overlooking the gardens. The bed was large and comfy; sheets and blankets were of the highest quality. There was a large dressing area, an excellent marble bathroom.' The bedrooms are priced by size and view; some are small; courtyard-facing ones are cheapest. In the lounges are wood fires, rich fabrics, antiques and water-colours of Dartmoor. Wellington boots and fishing rods in the hall, ticking clocks and purring Siamese cats add a homely touch. Michael Caines's dishes 'show great confidence, culinary talent and balance, with no coarseness or forcing of flavour', writes a reporter who can be an acerbic judge of restaurant standards. 'We enjoyed Jerusalem artichoke and truffle soup, full of flavour and with the texture of velvet; pan-fried red mullet with olives, tomato, and fennel cream sauce, a marriage made in heaven.' Save room for such puddings as millefeuille of crême brûlée. The 'Falstaffian wine list' is wide ranging, and fairly priced, with a 'superb' choice of wines by the glass, and many half bottles. Light lunches are available. The house, built in 1928 in mock-Tudor style, is rather severe, but the gardens, with the river Teign running through, croquet lawns and a lime walk, are 'absolutely stunning'. 'This is when *Gidleigh*'s magic works its spell.' (*PH, AT, and others*)

Open All year.
Rooms 2 suites, 12 double. Also 3-room cottage, 350 yds.
Facilities Hall, lounge, bar, 2 dining rooms. No background music. 45-acre grounds: gardens, croquet, tennis, bowls, putting, walks. Fishing, riding nearby. Unsuitable for ♿.
Location Approach from Chagford, *not* Gidleigh. From main square, facing Webbers with Lloyds Bank on right, turn right into Mill St. After 150 yds fork right; downhill to Factory Crossroad; straight across into Holy St; follow lane 1½ miles to end. Train: Exeter, 20 miles; then taxi.
Restrictions No smoking in restaurant. No children under 7 in restaurant. No dogs in public rooms.
Credit cards MasterCard, Visa.
Terms D,B&B: single £275–£440, double £400–£500, suite £430–£500. Set dinner £70. Winter discounts. Walking holidays, wine weekends, hunting, shooting and fishing organised. 1-night bookings sometimes refused.

CHELTENHAM Gloucestershire — Map 3:D5

Hotel Kandinsky NEW
Bayshill Road, Montpellier
Cheltenham GL50 3AS

Tel 01242-527788
Fax 01242-226412
Email info@hotelkandinsky.com
Website www.hotelkandinsky.com

Having wooed affluent parents with their successful Luxury Family Hotels format (see *Woolley Grange*, Bradford-on-Avon, etc), Nigel Chapman and Nicholas Dickinson are now courting the MINT ('middle income, no tie') market with Alias Hotels. This was the first, opened in 2000, in a stately white Regency building on a tree-lined street in the Montpellier area of Cheltenham. The manager is Lorraine Jarvie. Inspectors in 2001 found much to praise: 'The decor is an eclectic mix of old and new, spotlights and chandeliers, chrome and timber, Art Deco and antique, potted plants, interesting mirrors, wood or tile floors, Kandinsky prints. All is done with panache. Our bedroom was large and airy, with huge, long windows, plain, natural linen fabrics, a natural hessian carpet, a comfortable queen-size bed with Italian wall-fixed modern lights, ideal for reading. A large wardrobe housed the TV, CD-player, video, etc. The spotless bathroom was large, with black and white tiles. The bar, open all day, serves sandwiches out of normal restaurant hours. The *Café Paradiso*, a long, light room, has unusual, very comfortable Spanish chairs, polished wood tables close together, old wooden high stools, and a wood-fired pizza oven. We ate very good antipasti, a vast pizza, nicely grilled salmon, excellent bread. The *U-bahn* nightclub in the basement, very dark, has retro-style chairs and tables, a small dance floor and a bar. But you are not aware of noise from it elsewhere in the building. Service by the young staff was generally good; it lacked polish in some quarters, but they made up for this in willingness and pleasantness; front-of-house was slightly disorganised. The value for money is excellent.' Some bedrooms and bathrooms at the top are small. The second hotel in the group, *The Barcelona*, Exeter, also makes its *Guide* debut this year.

Open All year.
Rooms 2 suites, 38 double, 8 single.
Facilities Lift. Lounge, bar, restaurant, nightclub; ethnic background music in public areas all day. Garden.
Location ¼ mile from centre. Parking.
Restrictions No smoking: restaurant, some bedrooms. No dogs.
Credit cards All major cards accepted.
Terms [2001] Room: single £60–£70, double £65–£85, suite £110–£150. Breakfast £7.95–£10.95. Full alc £35. Weekend D,B&B rates.

Hotel on the Park
Evesham Road
Cheltenham GL52 2AH

Tel 01242-518898
Fax 01242-511526
Email stay@hotelonthepark.co.uk
Website www.hotelonthepark.co.uk

Darryl Gregory's Regency town house 'is gorgeous, with fine antiques', one visitor wrote. It looks to Pittville Park across a busy tree-lined road (rear bedrooms are quietest). The decor (swagged and tasselled curtains, mirrors and ticking clocks in the public rooms) is in keeping with the age of the house. Large bedrooms and bathrooms, as stylish as the rest, are reached up a curving staircase. But despite the formality of the surroundings, we regularly get reports of the kindness to children: 'When my 12-year-old daughter was hungry, the receptionist got the *sous-chef* to make her a tempting bacon butty; and they sent back a soft toy we had left behind.' The French windows of the drawing room and library look over the trim rear garden ('we liked the lop-eared rabbit'). But another visitor, while praising hotel, bedroom and reception, was critical of the breakfast, and thought the dinner 'pretentious'. The restaurant, run as a concession by Simon Hulstone, serves contemporary British dishes on a short weekly-changing menu (called 'Concept of the Kitchen'), eg, smoked haddock with curried potato terrine; loin of salmon, crayfish and spring onion risotto with tomato beurre blanc; coconut beignets with exotic fruit salsa. There is also an *à la carte* menu. Mr Gregory keeps a boat on the river Severn, six miles away. (*KG, Gwen Griffiths, and others*)

Open All year.
Rooms 2 suites, 10 double.
Facilities Drawing room/bar, library, restaurant (background jazz/classical music). Small garden. Unsuitable for ♿.
Location 5 mins' walk from centre. On A435 towards Evesham (front rooms double-glazed). Car park. Cheltenham station, 2 miles; then taxi.
Restrictions Smoking banned in restaurant, library, discouraged in bedrooms. No children under 8. Small dogs only, by arrangement; not in public rooms.
Credit cards All major cards accepted.
Terms [2001] Room: single £79.50, double £99.50, suite £129.50–£159.50; D,B&B double £155–£215. Breakfast £6.25–£8.25. Set lunch £15.95, dinner £21.50; full alc £36. Child in parents' room: £15. 2-day breaks.

The Wyastone
Parabola Road
Cheltenham GL50 3BG

Tel 01242-245549
Fax 01242-522659
Email reservations@wyastonehotel.co.uk
Website www.visitcheltenham.gov.uk

The welcome is warm at this small hotel in a quiet tree-lined avenue, five minutes' walk from the centre of Cheltenham. 'Friendly reception, a comfortable room, a bathroom with a window, a first-class position,' says an endorsement this year. The owners, Mr and Mrs Howard, run the hotel 'like a private house'. 'Dinner was freshly cooked and efficiently served.' Mr Howard's simple menu has starters like prawn cocktail or chicken liver pâté; main courses include grilled salmon or sirloin steak; for dessert you could choose hot chocolate pudding or 'A slice of Kiss of the Blarney'. If you prefer to dine out, the Howards will help with reservations. There is a pink-walled lounge, and in summer you can have a drink by the pond (with a fountain and Koi carp) in the secluded patio garden. (*Mr G Smith, RV*)

Open All year, except 24 Dec–2 Jan. Dining room closed midday.
Rooms 2 family, 7 double, 6 single.
Facilities Lounge, bar/TV room, dining room (light background music at mealtimes). Patio garden. Unsuitable for ♿.

Location Central. Parking. Cheltenham station; then taxi.
Restrictions No smoking: dining room, bedrooms. No dogs.
Credit cards Diners, MasterCard, Visa.
Terms [2001] B&B: single £55, double £78, family £95. Snacks available. Full alc dinner £19.50.

See also SHURDINGTON and SHORTLIST

CHESTER Cheshire — Map 3:A4

The Chester Grosvenor NEW
Eastgate
Chester CH1 1LT

Tel 01244-324024
Fax 01244-313246
Email chesgrov@chestergrosvenor.co.uk
Website www.chestergrosvenor.co.uk

A large, luxurious hotel, gabled and half-timbered, in the historic centre of the city, near the walls and many shops. Owned by the Duke of Westminster's Grosvenor Estates, it is managed by Jonathan Slater. It is 'highly commended' this year: 'The welcome was warm; service was outstanding. When I ordered a gin and tonic on arrival, it was brought to the bedroom seconds after we reached it, even before our luggage – a clear sense of priority! Our large bedroom and bathroom were spotless. The room-service supper was outstanding; the weekend rate was good value. We felt like guests, not customers.' There are two restaurants (in both you need to reserve a table). The Parisian-style *La Brasserie* produces salads, sandwiches, grills and a children's menu; in the *Michelin*-starred *Arkle* (named for the famous racehorse owned by Anne, Duchess of Westminster), chef Simon Radley serves, eg, foie gras in three styles; braised ox cheek; apple charlotte. The lounge, decorated in shades of gold, has antiques and oil paintings. Coffee, light lunches, teas and drinks are served in the library. High chairs and cots are supplied for children. Residents may use a country club (with indoor and outdoor swimming pools, gym and sauna) on the outskirts of the city. (*Christopher Smith*)

Open All year. *Arkle* restaurant closed 25–31 Dec; 1–22 Jan.
Rooms 11 suites, 85 double.
Facilities Lift, ramps. Drawing room, library, 2 bars, brasserie (jazz Sat night/Sun), restaurant (background piano/CDs); function facilities; leisure suite: gym, sauna, solarium; beauty salon. Access to local country club.
Location City centre, by Eastgate Clock. NCP car park adjacent.
Restrictions No smoking: *Arkle* restaurant, some bedrooms. Guide dogs only.
Credit cards All major cards accepted.
Terms [2001] Room: single £158.62–£182.12, double £229.13–£276.12, suite £411.25–£528.75. Breakfast £14.50. Set lunch £30, dinner £45; full alc £56. Weekend rates. Christmas package.

See also SHORTLIST

> The 'New' label is used both for debutantes and for hotels which have been readmitted to the *Guide* this year.

CHETTLE Dorset — Map 2:E1

Castleman
Chettle
nr Blandford Forum DT11 8DB

Tel 01258-830096
Fax 01258-830051
Email chettle@globalnet.co.uk
Website www.castlemanhotel.co.uk

'A lovely, characterful place. A haven of peace and quiet.' 'A genuine curiosity. The atmosphere is resolutely individual, shaped by the family and its locality. Very country-folk oriented.' 'Exceptional value.' This restaurant-with-rooms is the dower house of a Queen Anne manor house ('an outstanding specimen of English Baroque', according to Pevsner) that is open to the public in summer. Chettle, in a designated area of outstanding natural beauty on the edge of Cranborne Chase, is one of the few remaining feudal villages in England. It has been owned by the Bourke family for over 150 years. Edward Bourke and Barbara Garnsworthy run the *Castleman* in unfussy style. She is chef; her brother, Brendan, is the manager. 'We have never tried to be a "country house hotel", with manicured gardens, full room service, etc,' they say. 'We aim to offer good food, wine and accommodation at sensible prices.' The house, 'comfortable in all ways', has been carefully converted while preserving period features – a porticoed doorway, galleried hall, carved staircase, plasterwork ceilings, a Jacobean fireplace; there are some interesting 17th-century paintings. Bedrooms are 'plain but not sparse'; service is 'attentive without pomp'. The 'excellent, relatively simple' food is admired, eg, venison, bacon and pigeon terrine; pork fillet with Dijon mustard, cider and cream; toffee and banana sponge with butterscotch sauce. Vegetarians are well catered for. No breakfast menu; orange juice is freshly squeezed, and you can have more or less whatever you want ('very good scrambled eggs'). Good walks from the door; Salisbury, and many historic houses, including Wilton, Kingston Lacy, Stourhead and Longleat, are within easy reach; plenty of sporting activities available (see below). (*NM Mackintosh, Felicity Chadwick-Histed*)

Open Mar–Jan. Closed Christmas.
Rooms 8 double.
Facilities 2 drawing rooms, bar, restaurant. No background music. 2-acre grounds: stables for visiting horses/dogs. Golf, riding, fishing, shooting, cycling nearby. Only restaurant suitable for ♿.
Location Village 1 mile off A354 Salisbury–Blandford; hotel signposted. Train: Salisbury; taxi.
Restrictions No smoking: restaurant, 1 drawing room. No dogs.
Credit cards MasterCard, Visa.
Terms B&B: single £45, double £65–£75. Set Sun lunch £15; full alc £25. Discount for 3 or more nights.

CHICHESTER West Sussex *See SHORTLIST* — Map 2:E3

If the *Guide* is unavailable, or poorly displayed, in your local bookshop, please complain to the manager and/or let us know.

CHILLATON Devon — Map 1:D3

Tor Cottage
Chillaton, nr Lifton
PL16 0JE

Tel 01822-860248
Fax 01822-860126
Email info@torcottage.co.uk
Website www.torcottage.co.uk

Maureen Rowlatt ('a strong, warm person') welcomes guests to her upmarket B&B in a secluded Devon valley with a trug filled with fresh fruit, a bottle of Cava, and luxury chocolates. She promises badgers, buzzards and butterflies as well as deer and pheasants, and wild flowers in spring and summer. Filled with antiques, good fabrics, fresh flowers, ornaments and family photographs, the house is in large wooded grounds with a stream, Shetland ponies and wildlife. Bridleways lead from the grounds to Dartmoor and the Tamar valley. There is a swimming pool in the garden, available all day to visitors (after 11.30 am they might find themselves sharing it with Mrs Rowlatt or some of her friends). The suite is upstairs in the cottage; other bedrooms are in the garden; one is decorated in Art Deco style; it has a 'beautiful black and white bathroom' and a private conservatory. All have a log fire, CD-player, a fridge and a private terrace; two have a king-size bed. 'Everything is done in exquisite taste,' said inspectors. Breakfast is served in a 'delightful conservatory'. It has good kedgeree, 'super scrambled eggs with smoked salmon' and can be served also in the bedroom; in summer it can be taken alfresco on a new terrace. Vegetarians are catered for. Very popular with the garden-loving Japanese (one of whom wrote: 'It is like we visit to aunt's house'). Dinner is not served, except by arrangement for group bookings, but reservations can be made in nearby restaurants – *Neil's*, in Tavistock, is recommended.

Open All year, except 2 weeks over Christmas.
Rooms 1 suite (in main building), 3 double (in garden). No telephone.
Facilities 2 sitting rooms, conservatory, breakfast room (background music according to guests' taste). 18-acre grounds: 2-acre garden, swimming pool (generally open May–Sept), stream, bridleway, walks. River, fishing ½ mile; boating, canoeing 6 miles. Unsuitable for ♿.
Location ½ mile S of Chillaton. At village square, with pub and shop on left, drive 300 metres up hill towards Tavistock. Take drive on right, marked 'Bridlepath. No Public Vehicular Access'. Cottage gate at end of unmade road.
Restrictions No smoking. No children under 16. Guide dogs only.
Credit cards MasterCard, Visa.
Terms [2001] (Min. 2 nights) B&B double/suite £115. Winter breaks: 3 nights for the price of 2.

****

Traveller's tale Hotel in Surrey. At this hotel, they are suffering from Staff Loneliness Syndrome. This unfortunate affliction is easily spotted: members of staff gather for a nice little chat at a time when they should be working. No amount of waving, or attempts at eye-contact, can interrupt this ritual until the participants decide they are ready to break off their discussions and focus on the customer.

****

CHIPPING CAMPDEN Gloucestershire — Map 3:D6

Seymour House NEW

High Street
Chipping Campden GL55 6AH

Tel 01386-840429
Fax 01386-840369
Email enquiry@seymourhousehotel.com
Website www.seymourhousehotel.com

Recommended 'for a comfortable, reasonably priced weekend', this old stone house stands 'at the quiet end of the ancient High Street', says its nominator. 'It has a calm feel, with attentive but unobtrusive service; the staff had time for a friendly word. Fresh milk was brought in a small vacuum jug each evening for early morning tea.' *Seymour House* has facilities for weddings and conferences, and a special relationship with the Royal Shakespeare Company at nearby Stratford-upon-Avon – ticket and meal reservations can be made for residents. There is a spacious lounge; casual meals are served in the bar or on the lawn. In the restaurant, guests dine under an ancient vine, and the manager/chef, Felice Tocchini, presides over a pasta club, with monthly pasta-making demonstrations. His menus are cosmopolitan: Cornish rack of lamb on beetroot fritters, supreme of chicken with spiced couscous, and grilled red snapper were all enjoyed this year ('our only problem was deciding what to order'). The bedrooms (some are beamed) have period furnishings, flowery fabrics, wall-to-wall carpets; suites have a four-poster. (*Susan Hill, Stuart G Pratt*)

Open All year.
Rooms 4 suites, 11 double. 4 in cottage. 2 on ground floor.
Facilities Lounge, bar, restaurant; 'easy-listening' background music; conference room. ½-acre garden. Unsuitable for ♿. Civil wedding licence.
Location Central. Car park approached via Back Ends (lane parallel to High St).
Restrictions No smoking in restaurant. No dogs.
Credit cards Amex, MasterCard, Visa.
Terms B&B: single £72.50, double £95–£120, suite £150–£190. Set 2-course lunch £9.75; full alc £26. Christmas package. *V*

CHITTLEHAMHOLT Devon — Map 1:C4

Highbullen Hotel

Chittlehamholt
Umberleigh EX37 9HD

Tel 01769-540561
Fax 01769-540492
Email info@highbullen.co.uk
Website www.highbullen.co.uk

César award in 1991

'The atmosphere is of being welcomed into a home. The situation is outstanding.' Hugh and Pam Neil's Victorian Gothic mansion, high above the Mole and Taw valleys, with views towards Exmoor and Dartmoor, has many fans. They are attracted by the sporting amenities – fishing, tennis, swimming (though the indoor pool is very small), and the 18-hole golf course, free to residents, that surrounds the buildings. 'The friendly atmosphere rubs off on the guests, the bar becomes a lively centre of conversation in which the proprietors join each evening,' says one devotee, though some visitors find that it can be packed with golfing groups and feel that more care should be given to the tennis courts. But golf widows are comfortable in the warm public rooms', and regular visitors appreciate the no-frills style and the excellent value for money'. Most accommodation is in houses and cottages in the grounds. These rooms are simple, and sound insulation can be poor. The best bedrooms are in the main house; many have a good view, but some bathrooms may be 'a bit dated'. In the large restaurant, the Neils's daughter, Colette Potter, serves traditional English dishes on a daily-changing menu: eg, chargrilled smoked salmon; pork chop with ginger and orange sauce; sticky toffee pudding. The wine list is a fascinating document.' Breakfast, mainly self-service, has a large buffet; cooked dishes cost extra. Rosemoor Garden, Dartington Hall, and Arlington Court, Killerton House and Knightshayes (all National Trust) are within half an hour's drive. Colette Potter also owns *Stumbles*, a restaurant with ten bedrooms in South Molton, nearby. (*RA Joseph, and others*)

Open All year.
Rooms 38 double, 2 single. 25 in cottages/converted farm buildings. Some on ground floor.
Facilities Lounge, library; bar, billiard room, restaurant; no background music; indoor swimming pool, steam room, sunbed, exercise room, table-tennis, squash. 100-acre grounds: woodland, garden, croquet, putting, 2 swimming pools, 18-hole golf course, indoor tennis (golf/tennis tuition), 10 miles river fishing (ghillie available). Unsuitable for ♿.
Location M5 exit 27. A361 to South Molton. B3226 for 5 miles, up hill to Chittlehamholt; through village, ½ mile to hotel. Train: Tiverton Parkway, then taxi; Exeter St David's to connect with North Devon branch line to King's Nympton – hotel will meet.
Restrictions No smoking in restaurant. No children under 8. No dogs.
Credit cards MasterCard, Visa.
Terms D,B&B £75–£95. Cooked breakfast £5. Set lunch £15, dinner £27.50. Midweek reductions. Off-season breaks.

CLANFIELD Oxfordshire — Map 3:E6

The Plough at Clanfield NEW
Bourton Road
Clanfield OX18 2RB

Tel 01367-810222
Fax 01367-810596
Email ploughatclanfield@hotmail.com

'Attractive old listed manor house, in pleasant surroundings', recently extended by 'very nice' owners, John and Rosemary Hodges (she is chef). In village 15 miles SW of Oxford, between Witney and Faringdon, at junction of A4095 and B4020. Cottagey decor, good repro furniture. Pretty Shires Restaurant, *low-ceilinged and candlelit, serves English cooking. Open 7 Jan–24 Dec; restaurant closed Mon midday. 12 bedrooms (1 on ground floor); lounge/bar, restaurant; classical background music all day. 1½-acre garden. No smoking: restaurant, bedrooms. No children under 12. No dogs in bedrooms. All major credit cards accepted. B&B: single £82.25, double £95–£110, suite £125; D,B&B: single £105.75, double £160–£175, suite £190. Set lunch £19, dinner £32.50. More reports, please.*

COLCHESTER Essex *See SHORTLIST* Map 2:C5

COLN ST-ALDWYNS Gloucestershire Map 3:E6

The New Inn At Coln
Coln St-Aldwyns
nr Cirencester GL7 5AN

Tel 01285-750651
Fax 01285-750657
Email stay@new-inn.co.uk
Website www.new-inn.co.uk

'It is unusual to find such a civilised inn,' says the *Good Pub Guide*. Travellers have been welcomed at this creeper-clad building in a pretty Cotswold village since Elizabethan times. Brian and Sandra-Anne Evans now preside with a young staff. The front door opens into the cosy bar, 'where staff and regulars alike survey and/or salute in equal measure'. The new chef, Alastair Ward, cooks in eclectic modern style, and we'd be grateful for reports on his work. You must book for the split-level restaurant, which has open fires, low beams and oriental rugs. Here you might order boudin of chicken with spinach and apple sauce; panache of seafood and shellfish; baked brill with sweet chilli lime butter sauce; individual lemon tarts. You can ask for main courses to be plainly cooked. The 'first-class, well-priced' wine list, and the wide range of ales and malt whiskies earn regular plaudits. Vegetarian dishes, as well as such traditional fare as fish and chips and pork and leek sausages, are served in the long bar with its inglenook fireplace. There is a small residents' lounge and a terraced garden. The bedrooms in the main house are small; one, by the bar, is noisy. Larger, quieter and more modern rooms are in a converted dovecote. The riverside walk to Bibury is recommended. Well placed for visiting Westonbirt, Bath, and William Morris's house at Kelmscott.

Open All year.
Rooms 13 double, 1 single. 6 in dovecote. 1 on ground floor.
Facilities Lounge, bar, breakfast room, restaurant; conference/function facilities; terrace. No background music. River 100 yds; golf nearby.
Location In village 8 miles E of Cirencester, between Bibury and Fairford.
Restrictions No smoking in restaurant. No children under 10 in restaurant or accommodation. Dogs in dovecote rooms and bar only.
Credit cards Amex, MasterCard, Visa.
Terms B&B: single £72, double £99–£125; D,B&B £71.50–£98.50 per person. Bar meals. Set lunch £18.50–£22.50, dinner £23.50–£27.50. Midweek breaks. Christmas package. 1-night bookings refused Sat.

COLWALL Worcestershire Map 3:D5

Brook House BUDGET
Walwyn Road
Colwall, nr Malvern WR13 6QX

Tel/Fax 01684-540604

Maggie Powell's 'superior B&B', in 17th-century Grade II listed house, gabled, half-timbered, recently refurbished. In 2½-acre grounds (highly rated by Royal Horticultural Society), with mini-*

arboretum, stream, lovely landscaped gardens, wide views of Malvern hills. 'The delightful hostess cannot do enough for you,' said nominator. 3 bedrooms (Lemon, Pink and Green), with en suite *bathroom, TV. Good breakfast (English or continental). Morning room with TV available to guests. No background music. Colwall station ½ mile. Closed Christmas, New Year. Unsuitable for ♿. No smoking. No dogs. Credit cards not accepted. B&B £29.50–£39.50. More reports, please.*

CONSTANTINE BAY Cornwall **Map 1:D2**

Treglos Hotel
Constantine Bay
Padstow PL28 8JH

Tel 01841-520727
Fax 01841-521163
Email enquiries@treglos-hotel.co.uk
Website www.treglos-hotel.co.uk

César award in 1994

'There is an excellent "let's go back" feel about it. Many of the staff feel like old friends. Wally Vellacott, front-of-house and restaurant manager, has been there over 25 years.' Owned by the Barlow family for 36 years, and run by Jim and Rose Barlow, this traditional hotel continues to receive warm praise. Smaller and less smart than the family's other hotel, at Budock Vean (*qv*), it provides 'old-fashioned comfort (log fires, early morning tea brought to the room)', and welcomes all generations, offering school holiday packages, and bridge holidays in low season. The garden has secluded corners for sitting, a play area for children, and a small indoor swimming pool. The position is 'superb', overlooking Constantine Bay and Trevose Head. A wide sandy beach, popular with surfers, is ten minutes' walk away, and there is easy access to the coastal footpath. As at the sister hotel, men must wear a jacket and tie in public areas after 7 pm. Dinners include lots of fresh fish, meat dishes like roast lamb on an apple and pear compote; braised venison in a poivrade sauce with juniper-scented plums; and some rich desserts. Breakfast has a buffet with 'excellent choice', and the freshly cooked local bacon, haddock and kippers are warmly commended. So is the afternoon tea, served on a west-facing terrace. The decor – brick fireplaces, log fires, chintzy furniture, patterned carpets – is conventional, but it is renewed each year. Bedrooms have light colour schemes and built-in white furniture. The single rooms are small, but a 'lovely double, with large balcony' was enjoyed – 'the views alone make the visit worthwhile'. Eight golf courses are within a 40-minute drive (one is two minutes away). (*Ian Dewey, and others*)

Open 14 Mar–mid-Nov.
Rooms 4 suites, 34 double, 6 single. Some on ground floor. 4 self-catering flats, 1 bungalow, in grounds.
Facilities Lift, ramps. 2 lounges, bridge room, TV room, restaurant; children's den, snooker room; indoor swimming pool, whirlpool. No background music. 2-acre grounds: croquet, badminton, children's play area, boathouse with table-tennis, etc. Sandy beach, golf, tennis, riding, water sports nearby.
Location 3 miles W of Padstow. Avoid Bodmin, Wadebridge. From crossroads at St Merryn take B3276. Turn right by Constantine Bay stores: hotel 50 yds on right. Train: Bodmin; then bus/taxi.

Restrictions No smoking: dining room, 1 lounge. No children under 7 in dining room after 7 pm. No dogs in public rooms.
Credit cards MasterCard, Visa.
Terms [2001] D,B&B £63–£85. Bar lunches. Child in parents' room during school holidays, half-term: £17–£27.50. Weekly rates. Weekend, midweek breaks. Bridge, golf packages. *V* (not bank holidays or weekends)

COOKHAM DEAN Berkshire — Map 2:D3

The Inn on the Green NEW
The Old Cricket Common
Cookham Dean SL6 9NZ

Tel 01628-482638
Fax 01628-487474
Email reception@theinnonthegreen.com
Website www.theinnonthegreen.com

On green of tiny village just W of Stanley Spencer's Thames-side home town, Cookham (3 miles N of Maidenhead): old inn, recently renovated as restaurant-with-rooms. 'Reasonable, if rich' Anglo-French modern cooking by Derek Moran in attractive beamed dining room; friendly service by young French waiters; 'well cared-for wines'. Courtyard meal service in summer. But inspectors found reception cool and bedroom 'lacking a personal touch', despite ancient beams, beautiful bed, good lighting. Breakfast mixed, but 'perfect smoked haddock with poached egg'. Frequent weddings, receptions, functions held. 10 bedrooms (with Sky TV, modem points). Lounge bar, public bar, courtyard; large car park. Closed early Jan. No background music. Amex, MasterCard, Visa accepted. B&B: single £85–£95, double £120–£150. Set 3-course lunch/dinner £20; full alc £40.

CORFE CASTLE Dorset — Map 2:E1

Mortons House NEW
45 East Street
Corfe Castle BH20 5EE

Tel 01929-480988
Fax 01929-480820
Email stay@mortonshouse.co.uk
Website www. mortonshouse.co.uk

In an attractive old village dominated by the ruins of a Norman castle, this Elizabethan manor house stands in a walled garden. The original stone fireplace is still in place in the entrance hall; the oak-panelled drawing room has wooden friezes carved by Indonesian sailors. Inspectors this year were impressed by the 'happy atmosphere' created by the 'new and enthusiastic' owners, Andy Hageman and Edwin Clayton (they took over in October 2000). 'A very well-run hotel. Extremely friendly reception; useful local advice. Spacious public rooms; decor pleasant and understated (no swords or ploughshares), blazing log fire, good prints, many with a historical theme. A quiet, well-planned bedroom with chintz fabrics, white cotton sheets, no fussy ornaments to be pushed aside.' They were not too keen on the breakfast ('carton orange juice, metal teapots, tasteless scrambled eggs, but well-made brown toast'), but were impressed by the work of the chef, Dan Giles, at dinner: 'A sensibly limited set-price menu: celeriac soup, just right; huge tender steak, perfectly under-cooked, with lovely creamy spinach; cappuccino brûlé that caused great delight; lovely cheesecake. Service was quiet, attentive and cheerful; just the right pauses between courses.' Chairs and tables stand in a paved courtyard. Lots to do in this pretty part of the country; the beautiful Purbeck coast is a few miles' walk away (good birdwatching); an old steam railway is close by; stately homes include Parnham and Athelhampton.

Open All year.
Rooms 2 suites, 15 double, some with spa bath. Planning sought for ♿ suite.
Facilities 2 lounges, bar, 2 dining rooms (soft background music if requested); conference/function facilities. 1-acre garden. Beaches 4 and 5 miles.
Location In village on A351 Wareham–Swanage. Car park. Train: Wareham; taxi/bus.
Restrictions: No smoking: restaurant, bar, bedrooms. No dogs.
Credit cards All major cards accepted.
Terms B&B: double £84–£130, suite £150–£170; D,B&B: double £94–£182, suite £202–£222. Set lunch £12.50–£16, dinner £26; full alc £30–£35. 1-night bookings sometimes refused. Winter and summer breaks; Christmas package.

CORNHILL-ON-TWEED Northumberland — Map 4:A3

See SHORTLIST

CORSE LAWN Gloucestershire — Map 3:D5

Corse Lawn House
Corse Lawn GL19 4LZ

Tel 01452-780771
Fax 01452-780840
Email hotel@corselawnhouse.u-net.com
Website www.corselawnhousehotel.co.uk

'The manager, Giles Hine, has two young children, hence the calm and welcoming approach to us and our toddler,' writes a visitor this year. 'The bistro was opened for us each evening at 6 pm. Food was of good quality all round.' Giles's parents, Denis and Baba Hine, of the brandy family, have owned this Queen Anne Grade II listed building, set back from the green of a village near Tewkesbury, for almost a quarter of a century. The ornamental pond in front, now inhabited by assorted wildfowl, began life as a coach wash into which a stagecoach with four horses could be driven and turned around. Though much extended, the place maintains a country house air. It is generally admired for its 'relaxed style', though one reporter found some of the staff 'very cold', and the decor may be 'a bit dated'. The bedrooms, named for a brandy or a local village, are mostly large, with a king-size bed, good storage, home-made biscuits, real tea and coffee, an 'excellent bathroom'. Mrs Hine and Andrew Poole run the kitchen, which serves both the formal restaurant and the brightly upholstered bistro. The cooking is 'traditional mid-Channel', eg, salmon and smoked haddock fish-cake; roast lamb provençale. A vegetarian menu is available. Bread is home-baked. The wine list has 'some first-class choices at a reasonable cost'. The bistro has a good range of light meals, which are also available from room service. 'A superb breakfast', served until 10 in the restaurant, 11 in the bedroom, includes fresh orange juice, mango with lime, home-made yogurt, eggs and bacon, and kippers ('but not in the bedroom'). Cots, high chairs and baby-listening are provided for small children. In the grounds are a tennis court, a 'lovely' covered swimming pool, croquet, horses in a paddock, and the family's two dogs. Local attractions: Tewkesbury Abbey, the Westonbirt Arboretum, the Wildfowl Trust and Wetlands Centre at Slimbridge. (*Felicity Chadwick-Histed, and others*)

Open All year, except Christmas.
Rooms 2 suites, 16 double, 1 single. 5 on ground floor.
Facilities 2 lounges, bar, bistro, restaurant; 2 private dining rooms. No background music. 12-acre grounds: croquet, tennis, badminton, covered swimming pool. Golf, fishing, riding nearby. Civil wedding licence.
Location 5 miles SW of Tewkesbury on B4211.
Restrictions No smoking in restaurants. No children under 6 in restaurant at night. No dogs in restaurants.
Credit cards All major cards accepted.
Terms B&B: single £80, double £125, suite £160; D,B&B: single £95, double £165, suite £200. Set lunch £16.50–£18.50, dinner £27.50; full alc £35.50. 2-day breaks. *V*

COVENTRY West Midlands *See SHORTLIST* — Map 2:B2

CRACKINGTON HAVEN Cornwall — Map 1:C3

Manor Farm BUDGET

Tel 01840-230304
Crackington Haven EX23 0JW

'The ambience is first class, and nothing is too much trouble; standards are still of the highest order,' reports a second-time visitor to this Domesday-old stone manor house in a small village on the rocky north Cornish coast. It is run in house-party style by Paul and Muriel Knight who 'are most welcoming hosts'. The 'splendid house', surrounded by farmland, is 'wonderfully quiet at night'. Visitors admired its 'elegant atmosphere' (mullioned windows, old beams, log fires and antique furniture). 'The decor is delightful; the gardens are immaculate.' Guests tend to 'change' or 'dress' for dinner. Drinks are at 6.30; the 'delicious and attractively presented' dinner is at 7, served at one large table, using porcelain, silver, good glass. No choice; a four-course menu might offer chicken pâté with a touch of ginger; lamb ragout with garlic bread topping; bread-and-butter pudding with clotted cream; cheese and biscuits. Wines are 'well priced'. Coffee and chocolates follow in the lounge. A farmhouse breakfast is served at 8.30 am. The sea is a mile away, and the South West Coastal Path runs nearby, in a designated area of outstanding natural beauty. (*John and June Astle-Fletcher, JA*)

Open All year, except Christmas and New Year. Dinner not served in Aug.
Rooms 3 double. No telephone/TV.
Facilities Lounge, TV room, music room, bar, dining room. No background music. 2-acre garden in 25-acre farmland. Sea 1 mile. Unsuitable for ♿.
Location From Wainhouse Corner on A39 follow signs to Crackington Haven. At beach turn inland, ignoring Highcliff Rd; after 1 mile left into Church Park Rd, then 1st right.
Restrictions No smoking. No children. No dogs.

Credit cards None accepted.
Terms B&B £30–£45; D,B&B £48–£63. Set dinner £18. 1-night bookings refused bank holidays.

CRANBROOK Kent — Map 2:E4

Cloth Hall Oast

Cranbrook TN17 3NR — *Tel/Fax* 01580-712220

Mrs Katherine Morgan, who ran the picturesque, part-Tudor Old Cloth Hall, *SE of Cranbrook, for 18 years, has moved, with her antiques, family portraits, travel souvenirs, four-poster bed, etc, into newly converted adjoining barn/oast house/stables. 5-acre garden: heated swimming pool. Closed Christmas, New Year. Unsuitable for ♿. Children by arrangement. No dogs. Credit cards not accepted. 3 bedrooms (no telephone; no smoking). B&B only: double room £85. Visitors to the previous set-up admired the 'warm welcome; splendid country breakfasts; tranquil setting'. We'd like reports, please.*

Kennel Holt

Goudhurst Road
Cranbrook TN17 2PT

Tel 01580-712032
Fax 01580-715495
Email hotel@kennelholt.demon.co.uk
Website www.kennelholt.co.uk

'Strongly recommended,' says a visitor in 2001 to this 'small, friendly' house, part Tudor, part Edwardian, which stands in an 'idyllic' garden, with a pond, topiaried yew hedges, and a croquet lawn, in the Weald of Kent. The owners, Neil and Sally Chalmers, write: 'No large conference suites, no health and fitness centre; we want you to feel at home' – though small 'upmarket' conferences and functions are catered for. The bedrooms have antiques, exposed timbers and mullioned windows; two have a four-poster. Guests have the use of a beamed lounge, and an oak-panelled library with an honesty bar, Edwardian books, and a large collection of vinyl discs and CDs. Neil Chalmers cooks 'modern dishes with a strong French/Italian influence', eg, spaghettini with piquant sauce and seared seafood; roasted herb-crusted lamb loin with a spicy bean and vegetable stew. There are some well-priced wines. 'Excellent, romantic, unusual', 'very nice owners', 'a wonderfully quiet setting', are recent comments, but one business visitor this year, not wanting to take the full set menu, found the service 'inflexible'. Twenty-eight houses and 37 gardens open to the public, notably Sissinghurst, are within easy reach. The Channel Tunnel is a 40-minute drive away. (*Richard Creed*)

Open All year, except 1 week Jan. Restaurant closed Mon.
Rooms 8 double, 2 single. 1, with separate entrance, on ground floor.
Facilities Hall, sitting room, library; occasional varied background music; restaurant; private dining/meeting room. 5½-acre grounds. Golf, fishing nearby. Unsuitable for ♿.
Location 1 mile NE of Cranbrook, off A262. Train: Staplehurst, 4 miles.
Restrictions No smoking in restaurant. No children under 7, except babies; no children under 10 at dinner. No dogs.
Credit cards MasterCard, Visa.

Terms (*Excluding 10% 'optional' service charge added to meal bills*) B&B: single £90, double £150–£195. Set dinner £27.50–£32.50. 3-night breaks in low season. 1-night bookings refused weekends May–Sept.

CRANTOCK Cornwall — Map 1:D2

Crantock Bay Hotel NEW/BUDGET
West Pentire, Crantock
nr Newquay TR8 5SE

Tel 01637-830229
Fax 01637-831111
Email stay@crantockbayhotel.co.uk
Website www.crantockbayhotel.co.uk

'A well-run hotel with long-serving staff, long-standing owners' – it celebrated its half-century in 2001. The setting is 'unrivalled', on the West Pentire headland (National Trust), facing the Atlantic and a huge sandy beach. Sheltered coves, surf, rock pools and caves make it good for a family holiday, and there is walking from the door – the South West Coast Path runs through the garden. The owners of this unpretentious place, David and Brenda Eyles, have a loyal clientele; children are welcomed, and so are dogs, though not in the public rooms. The hotel was dropped from last year's *Guide* after some critical reports, notably of the cooking, but supporters have rallied to the defence. 'The food has markedly improved,' says one report. 'It is perfectly acceptable, sometimes excellent, with a good-value wine list,' says another (a sample menu includes smoked chicken mousse with an apricot sultana salad; grilled whiting with sweet chilli sauce; profiteroles with butterscotch sauce). A guest on a three-generation holiday wrote of the 'charming proprietors, hard-working, amiable staff, and excellent facilities – washing and ironing, paperback books, toys, a fridge on each landing'. Bedrooms are comfortable, with adequate facilities, although some can feel 'a bit cramped'. Second-floor rooms are recommended for best coastal views – 'if you don't mind the stairs'. Lunch is a self-service buffet; freshly baked scones and home-made biscuits are served with afternoon tea. Mr Eyles ('a tall, military figure') impresses guests with his encyclopaedic local knowledge – he likes to do the round of breakfast tables, discussing the day's plans. A large extension houses a warm swimming pool, toddlers' pool, sauna and exercise room. Entertainments (slide shows, dances, etc) are organised in season, and special breaks of all kinds are offered. Crantock, a mile away, is a pretty old village with an ancient church and thatched cottages. Six golf courses, the Eden Project and the Lost Gardens of Heligan are nearby. (*Richard Creed, S Gillian Comins, Bryan and Mary Blaxall*)

Open 1 Apr–31 Oct, winter weekends, New Year.
Rooms 24 double, 9 single. 1 suitable for ♿.
Facilities 2 lounges, bar, bar lounge, restaurant (quiet classical background music sometimes); games room, indoor swimming pool, exercise room; dances, competitions, children's parties in season. 4½-acre grounds: tennis, croquet, children's play area, putting, donkeys. Sea, sandy beach, safe bathing 200 yds. Riding, golf nearby.
Location 5 miles SW of Newquay, 1 mile beyond Crantock: do not turn right into village centre; keep on West Pentire road for 1 mile. Train: Truro; hotel will meet.
Restrictions No smoking: restaurant, 1 lounge. No dogs in public rooms.

Credit cards All major cards accepted.
Terms D,B&B £43–£73. Lunch from £5; set dinner £19.50. Discounts for returning visitors. Child in parents' room: under 2, free. Winter weekends, spring garden breaks. *V*

CRICKET MALHERBIE Somerset — Map 1:C6

The Old Rectory NEW
Cricket Malherbie, nr Ilminster
TA19 0PW
Tel 01460-54364
Fax 01460-57374
Email theoldrectory@malherbie.freeserve.co.uk
Website www.malherbie.freeserve.co.uk

A Grade II listed 16th-century thatched house with many original features, in a conservation hamlet surrounded by farmland, on the edge of an area of outstanding natural beauty. The owners, Michael and Patricia Fry-Foley, are 'an erudite couple', says an inspector (they formerly worked at the Royal Opera House, Covent Garden). 'She cooks like a dream; he, full of charm, gets the balance between pleasant chat and intrusive mateyness spot on.' The Fry-Foleys belong to the campaign for real food. 'Ninety per cent of produce is local, much of it organic,' they write. Dinner, by arrangement, is at 8, communally served round a large, polished table, from a no-choice menu. 'The food was imaginative, tempting to look at, perfectly seasoned: choux pastry case with mushroom and ham; local pheasant, mange tout with pine nuts and pak choi; pear tart with chocolate sauce; cheese with grapes. Lovely glass and china. Breakfast had plenty of choice (smoked salmon, designer sausages, etc), home-made jams and marmalade, no nasty plastic packages. The sitting room is heavily beamed, cosy, with slightly jarring modern lamps and paintings, lots of informative books. No background music – hooray! We loved our bedroom: huge bed, William Morris curtains, soothing shades of green and biscuit, Chinese silk pictures, pretty (but inadequate) bedside lights, efficient bathroom; total quiet apart from birdsong. For a comfortable stay in peaceful surroundings, this would be hard to beat. We were sorry to leave.' Stately homes (Montacute, Tintinthull, etc) are close by; the south Dorset coast is within a half-hour drive.

Open All year, except Christmas. Dining room closed midday.
Rooms 5 double. No telephone.
Facilities Sitting room, dining room. No background music. 1¼-acre garden. Unsuitable for ♿.
Location 2 miles S of Ilminster, 10 miles SE of Taunton. From A303 junction, A358 S towards Chard. After Donyatt, left towards Ilminster, right to Cricket Malherbie. House on left. Train: Crewkerne; taxi.
Restrictions No smoking. No children under 16. Guide dogs only.
Credit cards MasterCard, Visa.
Terms B&B: single £48, double £75–£85. Set dinner £19.50. *V*

CROOKHAM Northumberland — Map 4:A3

The Coach House at Crookham BUDGET
Crookham
Cornhill-on-Tweed
TD12 4TD

Tel 01890-820293
Fax 01890-820284
Email thecoachhouse@englandmail.com
Website www.coachhousecrookham.com

César award in 1997

Lynne Anderson, a 'hostess with the mostest', runs her guest house in personal style. It has excellent facilities for the disabled – everywhere is accessible to wheelchairs. And children are welcomed. 'We don't pretend to offer hotel-type service or atmosphere,' says Ms Anderson. 'We aim to cater for guests as if for visiting friends.' The cluster of old farm buildings, built around a courtyard, is set back from a road not far from the site of Flodden Field. The decor may be nothing special, but there is no doubting the kindness of the owner and her staff, and their generous style: tea and home-made cakes are produced free of charge on guests' arrival, dogs are looked after if their owners wish to spend a day in Edinburgh, an hour's drive away. Plenty of praise came this year: 'Extremely comfortable.' 'A relaxed atmosphere, due in large part to the personality of the hostess.' 'Our room was spacious and well kitted out.' Others are 'small but adequate'. All are 'plainly but pleasantly furnished'; they have white cotton bed linen, fresh flowers and a large bathroom; most have a fridge; there are adjoining rooms, good for a family. A 'lovely terrace' looks over a field and damson trees. Good pictures hang in the public rooms. Tea and drinks are taken in the former coach house, with a beamed ceiling and huge arched windows. Dinner, at 7.30, is 'sound home cooking', served at antique tables in a former smithy with large fireplaces. 'Particularly good starters, [eg, avocado soup with coriander, chilli and crème fraîche] and puddings.' No regular choice of main course (it might be roast pork or quail), but individual needs are catered for. Soups, ice creams, etc, are home-made; eggs are free-range; meat is locally reared. Generous breakfasts include kedgeree, devilled kidneys. The Pennine Way passes close by. 'Cragside house and gardens, near Rothbury, are worth a visit, and the ramparts of Berwick-on-Tweed are good for a walk.' (*John Crisp, GH Pells, Susan Aglionby, Janet Austin*)

Open Easter–end Oct.
Rooms 7 double, 2 single. Some adapted for ♿.
Facilities Lounge with honesty bar, library, 2 dining rooms; terrace. No background music. 3-acre grounds. Golf, fishing, riding, gliding, birdwatching nearby.
Location On A697, 3½ miles N of Milfield. Bus from Berwick-on-Tweed.
Restrictions No smoking: dining rooms, lounge. No dogs in public rooms, unattended in bedrooms.
Credit cards MasterCard, Visa (*4% surcharge*).
Terms B&B £25–£39; D,B&B £42.50–£56.50. Set dinner £17.50.

Don't keep your favourite hotel to yourself. The *Guide* supports; it doesn't spoil.

CUCKFIELD West Sussex — Map 2:E4

Ockenden Manor
Ockenden Lane
Cuckfield
nr Haywards Heath RH17 5LD

Tel 01444-416111
Fax 01444-415549
Email ockenden@hshotels.co.uk
Website www.hshotels.co.uk

Conveniently near Gatwick airport (13 miles), this Pride of Britain member is owned by Sandy and Anne Goodman (see also *The Spread Eagle*, Midhurst). Tucked into a quiet corner of the bustling main street of this pretty village, the 16th-century house, part stone, part half-timbered, stands in mature gardens with views over the downs. The long-serving, 'charming manager', Kerry Turner, is regularly praised. 'His staff make every effort to be obliging,' says a visitor this year, who thought her visit 'good value'. Others wrote: 'The comfort of our room was matched by the brilliantly clean and well-appointed bathroom. The grounds, though well maintained, had a natural appearance. We were treated as guests rather than customers.' The public rooms are luxurious: much panelling; antiques, flowers and an open fire in the drawing room; an inglenook fireplace in the bar; heraldic stained glass and an embossed ceiling in the dining room, which is candlelit at night. There has been another change of chef: Steve Crane, formerly at *The Spread Eagle,* serves 'modern French' dishes, eg, Jerusalem artichoke soup with wild mushroom ravioli; cod fillet with cheese and mustard sauce; tulip of fresh fruits with vanilla ice cream. There is a vegetarian menu, a 'tasting menu', and an 'excellent wine list'. 'Very good breakfasts.' Some bedrooms (some have long, low beams) are in the old house; larger, less characterful ones are in a later wing. Some rooms may need refurbishing, but one suite had a facelift this year. A good base for visiting Brighton and Glyndebourne. Many famous houses and gardens (eg, Nymans and Leonardslee) are nearby, so is Mannings Heath golf club, and the Bluebell steam railway runs from Sheffield Park, 18 miles away. (*Romney Bathurst, and others*)

Open All year.
Rooms 3 suites, 18 double, 1 single.
Facilities Bar, lounge, restaurant; function facilities. No background music. 9-acre grounds: croquet. Golf nearby. Unsuitable for ♿. Civil wedding licence.
Location In village 2 miles W of Haywards Heath. B2115 from A23. Drive into village; hotel at end of Ockenden La. Train: Haywards Heath; taxi/bus.
Restrictions No smoking in restaurant. No dogs.
Credit cards All major cards accepted.
Terms B&B: single £99, double £132–£200, suite £240–£270. Set lunch £18.50; full alc £39–£50. 2-day breaks all year. Christmas, New Year packages. 1-night bookings sometimes refused Sat. *V*

CULLOMPTON Devon — Map 1:C5

Upton House BUDGET
Cullompton EX15 1RA

Tel/Fax 01884-33097

The 'friendly owner', Fay Down, has lovingly restored this 'beautiful old house' in a quiet country setting in the Culm valley. She runs it as an upmarket B&B – 'a wonderful place to stay,' say visitors. 'The lounge and dining room are of the quality of a smart hotel.' The 17th-century building has old beams, an inglenook fireplace and antique furniture. 'The family's rooms are on the other side of the hall so there is privacy for the guests. Our bedroom and bathroom was large and well-appointed.' Breakfast is served round one large table in a panelled room where an inscription by an 18th-century workman can be read. Plenty of eating places are within a radius of two miles – the *Merry Homes* restaurant is recommended. Mrs Down's husband, Chris, formerly an amateur jockey, and their son, Richard, breed racehorses on the 180-acre organic farm (lots of wildlife) that surrounds the house. The Exmoor National Park is close. (*J and AH*)

Open All year, except Christmas, New Year.
Rooms 3 double. No telephone.
Facilities Lounges, conservatory, breakfast room. No background music. Large garden. On 180-acre farm: 2 coarse fishing lakes, stabling. Walking, riding, golf nearby. Unsuitable for ♿.
Location SE of Tiverton. From M5, exit 28, go towards Cullompton. Left to Broadclyst; follow main street through town. Take left turn, Meadow Lane, signposted Sports Centre. Next T-Junction turn right, cross motorway bridge. Next left, signposted Plymtree. *Upton* is up next lane on left.
Restrictions No smoking. No children under 12. No dogs.
Credit cards None accepted.
Terms [2001] B&B £20–£27.

DARLINGTON Co. Durham ***See SHORTLIST*** **Map 4:C4**

DARTMOUTH Devon **Map 1:D4**

The Little Admiral
27/29 Victoria Road
Dartmouth TQ6 9RT

Tel 01803-832572
Fax 01803-835815
Email info@little-admiral.co.uk
Website www.little-admiral.co.uk

In small side street back from waterfront, near covered market: old hotel restored by Sebastian and Philippa Hughes of Holne Chase, *Ashburton (*qv*). Attractive lounge with fireplace; bar/brasserie, serving 'traditional food with French influence' (eg, fish-cakes with new potatoes; steak with Stilton cream sauce). No background music. 10 small but pretty bedrooms on 1st and 2nd floors (no lift), all with bath or shower ('big, fluffy bath sheets'). Limited parking (reserve in advance). No smoking: brasserie, bedrooms. Diners, MasterCard, Visa accepted. B&B: single £55–£60, double £60–£120. Full alc £22. New manager, Russel Brown, and chef, Guy Balligeant, this year. More reports, please.* *V*

Italicised entries are for hotels on which we need more feedback – either because we are short of detailed or recent reports, or because we have had ambivalent or critical comments.

Nonsuch House
Church Hill, Kingswear
Dartmouth TQ6 0BZ

Tel 01803-752829
Fax 01803-752357
Email enquiries@nonsuch-house.co.uk
Website www.nonsuch-house.co.uk

César award in 2000

'Excellent in every way. The setting is superb,' said visitors last year to this small, upmarket guest house run by Kit Noble with his parents, Geoffrey and Patricia. Reporters this year agree: 'The hospitality is warm. The owners are discreet and extremely pleasant. The colourful decor is very appealing: canary yellow walls, royal blue plain carpets, interesting ornaments and lovely books enliven what could have been a staid building. We lay on the balcony in the sun, befriended by the three house dogs and Michael, the cat.' Other praise: 'Visitors are made to feel part of the family.' 'Great value.' 'High standards.' *Nonsuch House* comprises two Edwardian villas on a hillside reached by car or by a ferry from Dartmouth. Every room overlooks the view across the river to the harbour with fields beyond, and also out to sea. The Nobles promise 'no piped music, no artificial flowers, no UHT milk cartons'. An evening meal – 'simple, nicely presented, and ample' – is available. A fish main course might be preceded by chicken liver parfait or watercress soup, and followed by chocolate mousse with fresh fruit. No liquor licence – bring your own wine. In summer, meals are served in a 'lovely conservatory', with balconies looking over the garden and the view. In the bedrooms 'everything is of quality – nice old furniture; good lights, fresh flowers, home-made biscuits'. Breakfast has 'excellent coffee and proper bread', fresh orange juice, home-made muesli. If you wish to dine out, there are many eating places in Dartmouth, including the famous *Carved Angel*, and the *Little Admiral* (see previous entry). The booking procedure is liked: 'No deposit required; a hand-written letter of confirmation. No reception desk, just an airy hallway and the friendliest of welcomes.' (*Eve and Brian Webb*)

Open All year, except 1st 2 weeks Jan. No dinners served in Nov.
Rooms 3 double. No telephone.
Facilities Lounge, dining room, conservatory. No background music. ¼-acre garden: patio. Rock beach 200 yds; sailing nearby. Unsuitable for ♿.
Location 2 miles before Brixham, on A3022, take A379 Dartmouth/Kingswear. After mini-roundabout, fork left to A3205 downhill. Through woods, left up Higher Contour Rd, down Ridley Hill to *Nonsuch* at hairpin bend ('look for the first available parking place'). Ferry to Dartmouth (5 mins' walk).
Restrictions No smoking: dining room, bedrooms. No children under 7. No dogs.
Credit cards MasterCard, Visa.
Terms B&B: single £52.50–£60, double £65–£80. Set dinner £21. 3-day off-season rates. Christmas, New Year, Easter breaks. 1-night bookings refused summer weekends. *V*

In your own interest, always check the tariffs with a hotel when booking.

DEDHAM Essex — Map 2:C5

Dedham Hall & Fountain Restaurant
Brook Street, Dedham
nr Colchester CO7 6AD
Tel 01206-323027
Fax 01206-323293
Email sarton@dedhamhall.demon.co.uk

'Beautifully situated' in Constable country (Flatford Mill is two miles away), this unusual establishment is a combined guest house, restaurant and art school. The owners, Wendy and Jim Sarton, are 'very professional', said an inspector who admired the 'excellent food and pleasantly relaxed atmosphere – everything is on a generous scale'. A small 15th-century house, a larger 18th-century one, and a barn (where painting courses are held) stand in 'idyllic gardens' with chickens, white geese in a large pond, daffodils on lawns in spring, and a view of Dedham's church tower. The artists are accommodated in the former stables and piggeries. 'Lovely paintings hang in the book-filled lounge where we were given tea in pretty cups with wonderful gooey chocolate cake.' The guests' bedrooms (no keys are given) are dotted around. 'Ours, large, old-fashioned, slightly shabby, had William Morris wallpaper, books, a large bathroom, a power shower.' Some rooms are approached through the kitchen, where 'a bank of Agas emits delicious smells'. The 'large, elegant' restaurant (with pale pink tablecloths on well-spaced tables, candles and flowers) is locally popular; you should reserve your table when booking accommodation. The cooking is 'very good, not exotic', eg, starters like avocado salad with Stilton and pine nuts, or grilled sardines with mustard mayonnaise; main courses like breaded pork fillet with fresh tomato sauce, or spinach and cream cheese pancakes. Home-baked bread 'comes with lashings of butter'. Wines are 'good and moderately priced'. Breakfast (in a room also used by the students) has 'toast out of this world', bowls of sliced fresh fruit, 'wonderful bacon'. Paintings by Sir Alfred Munnings may be seen in his home, Castle House, nearby. Plenty of local interest: Ickworth, Kentwell and Melford halls; Beth Chatto's garden, Colchester (eight miles away). More reports, please.

Open All year, except Christmas, New Year, 2 weeks Jan.
Rooms 5 double, 1 single. Also 10 in annexe for painting holidays. No telephone. Some ground-floor rooms.
Facilities 2 lounges, 2 bars, dining room, restaurant; studio. Classical background music sometimes. 6-acre grounds: pond, fields.
Location 1 min's walk from centre; end of High St, on left. Train: Manningtree (can be met).
Restrictions No smoking: restaurant, some bedrooms. No dogs.
Credit cards MasterCard, Visa.
Terms B&B: single £45, double £75; D,B&B: single £65, double £115. Set dinner £23.

Maison Talbooth
Stratford Road, Dedham
nr Colchester CO7 6HN
Tel 01206-322367
Fax 01206-322752
Email mtreception@talbooth.co.uk
Website www.talbooth.com

The Milsom family offer country house accommodation in this pink-washed Victorian mansion (Pride of Britain) to run alongside their nearby riverside restaurant, *Le Talbooth*. Breakfast is served on giant trays in the bedrooms, and snacks and drinks are generally available during the day, served in a large drawing room with a gas fire, squashy chairs and settees. But the separation can lead to a 'lack of a social atmosphere', one visitor thought. The gastronomic action takes place at *Le Talbooth*, a half-timbered former weaver's cottage by a bridge over the river Stour. It is a ten-minute walk away on a narrow country road: a courtesy car takes guests there or to the Milsoms' other restaurant, *The Pier at Harwich* (*qv*). Daniel Clark, the restaurant's head chef since 1999, prepares dishes like terrine of corn-fed chicken and veal sweetbread; breast of Norfolk duck; banana bread-and-butter pudding. 'We know that guests, on some occasions, prefer simpler dishes such as smoked salmon or a plain grilled steak. These are always available,' writes the managing director, Paul Milsom. A Sunday barbecue on a wet July evening, 'very organised', had 'excellent salads'. *Maison Talbooth* is a peaceful place. Its bedrooms are named for poets. The most lavish is Shakespeare, with a terrace leading into the garden (mainly lawn, with loungers). Milton looks over the vale. Tennyson, Brooke and Kipling are smaller and cheaper. All have a sitting area, lavish fabrics and wallpaper, mineral water and reading matter. One visitor this year commented on a 'bath like a swimming pool – and the others I glanced at were even bigger, round and enormous'. The family recently bought back the *Dedham Vale Hotel*, and reopened it in April 2001 as *Milsoms*, a 15-room hotel with a bar/bistro, thought 'excellent' this year. (*M and SA*)

Open All year. Restaurant closed Sun evening Oct–May.
Rooms 1 suite, 9 double. 5 on ground floor.
Facilities Drawing room, function facilities. No background music. 3-acre grounds: croquet. Restaurant, bar, garden on banks of Stour, 10 mins' walk (courtesy car provided). Civil wedding licence.
Location 6 miles NE of Colchester, just E of A12-exit Stratford St Mary. Train: Colchester; taxi.
Restrictions Smoking discouraged in restaurant during mealtimes. No dogs.
Credit cards All major cards accepted.
Terms (*Excluding 10% service charge on meals*) B&B: double £155–£190, suite £170–£210. Cooked breakfast £7.50. Set lunch £21, dinner £27; full alc £45. 2-night breaks. Christmas package. 1-night bookings refused Sat.

DENT Cumbria — Map 4:C3

Stone Close BUDGET — *Tel* 015396-25231
Main Street
Dent — *Email* accommodation@stoneclose.co.uk
nr Sedbergh LA10 5QL — *Website* www.stoneclose.co.uk

Dent is a picturesque old village, with narrow cobbled streets lined by old stone houses with small windows and window boxes, in the Yorkshire Dales National Park. Here, two whitewashed houses have been turned into this tea shop and 'delightful B&B' (also an information point). Flagstone floors, exposed beams, cast iron ranges, pine furniture, and 'charming owners', Kay and Peter Rushton, combine to create an 'exceptional atmosphere', says a devoted regular. 'People must realise that this is not a hotel (it is something nicer).' It offers 'amazing value'. The 'delicious home baking' is renowned. Teas and meals (home-made soups, salads, baked potatoes, etc, on blackboard menus) are served all day until early evening. A 'first-rate' three-course evening meal, accompanied by a small selection of wines, is available for residents by arrangement, eg, chicken and broccoli crumble, or lamb with garlic and mint; treacle tart, or elderflower and raspberry cheesecake. Of the four simple, pretty bedrooms, one has facilities *en suite*; the others have a washbasin and access to a bathroom ('you can see down the lovely Dee valley while showering'). Residents have their own lounge, with comfy sofas. Breakfast is a well-presented wholefood affair with a vegetarian option. The independent Dent Brewery, close by, produces 'excellent beer' for the local pubs. More reports, please.

Open Feb–Dec. Tea shop closed midweek Nov–early Dec, Jan–mid-Mar.
Rooms 3 double, 1 single. 1 with bathroom. No telephone (payphone available).
Facilities Residents' lounge, tea room/restaurant (classical background music all day). River, fishing 300 yds. Unsuitable for ♿.
Location Centre of village 4 miles SE of Sedbergh. Car park adjacent. Train: Dent, Oxenholme; the Rushtons can arrange cheap fares.
Restrictions No smoking. No dogs in public rooms.
Credit cards MasterCard, Visa.
Terms [2001] B&B £19.50– £25.75. Full alc supper £17. 1 night free in a stay of 5 or more. 1-night bookings sometimes refused.

DIDDLEBURY Shropshire — Map 3:C4

Delbury Hall
Diddlebury
Craven Arms SY7 9DH

Tel 01584-841267
Fax 01584-841441
Email wrigley@delbury.com
Website www.delbury.com

'We were made very welcome. The atmosphere was relaxed, the owners were friendly but not imposing. The house, grounds and setting presented a nostalgic reminder of life "above stairs".' 'Good food; charming hosts.' Two enthusiastic reports came this year on this Georgian red brick house in a hamlet near Ludlow. The owners, Lucinda and Patrick Wrigley, write: 'This is a family home, with children, pets and household activities.' They do not offer hotel-type facilities, and they treat their visitors like personal, rather than paying, guests. The house stands by a small lake with ornamental ducks, in a large estate amid lovely countryside. It has flowery gardens, a tennis court, a trout fishery with two stocked ponds, and a small farm and vegetable garden. The interior is impressive: fine plasterwork, family portraits and an open-string oak staircase leading to a spectacular gallery, but the atmosphere is informal. In house-party style, guests help themselves to drinks in the large sitting room – 'no spirit measures!' Dinner is communal, served by candlelight. Patrick Wrigley's cooking is thought 'excellent, expertly prepared with fresh ingredients'. No choice, but he likes to discuss the menu in advance. Regular dishes include home-smoked salmon or duck; rack of lamb with rosemary gravy and onion and mint purée; oranges in caramel. The wine list is 'first-class and well priced'. Breakfasts are 'exemplary'. The bedrooms are large, with antique furniture. Because the Wrigleys did not wish to damage their graceful proportions, only the four-poster room has facilities *en suite*; each of the others has a private bathroom. Close by are Offa's Dyke, Much Wenlock, Wenlock Edge and Stokesay Castle. (*Michael Olney, Sir John Johnson*)

Open All year, except Christmas. Lunch not served.
Rooms 4 double. 1 *en suite*, 3 with private bathroom.
Facilities Drawing room, sitting room, dining room; children's playroom. No background music. 12-acre grounds in 80-acre parkland: tennis, lake, trout fishery, dovecote. Unsuitable for ♿. Civil wedding licence.
Location In village NE of Craven Arms. Follow signs to trout fishery, then *Delbury Hall*. Train: Ludlow, 8 miles, Craven Arms, 5 miles.
Restrictions No smoking: dining room, bedrooms. No dogs in house (kennels available).
Credit cards MasterCard, Visa.
Terms [2001] B&B £50–£60. Set dinner £32. 1-night bookings sometimes refused bank holidays.

DODDISCOMBSLEIGH Devon — Map 1:C4

The Nobody Inn BUDGET
Doddiscombsleigh
nr Exeter EX6 7PS

Tel 01647-252394
Fax 01647-252978
Email inn.nobody@virgin.net
Website www.thenobodyinn.com

César award in 2001

There are no half-measures from the bearded landlord Nick Borst-Smith, also a wine merchant. He keeps 700 wines (20 available by the glass at any time); also 240 whiskies, real ale, farm cider, and more than 50 Devon cheeses. This 'lovely old inn' got its name after an earlier, unfriendly landlord locked the door against weary travellers on this twisting Devon lane, so they would assume that nobody was in. It is a 'marvellously unchanging' place, say its fans, welcoming locals and overnight visitors, and offering 'good value'. The lounge bar has inglenook fireplaces, low beams, Windsor chairs, carriage lanterns, hunting prints, and a 'civilised atmosphere, enhanced by the friendly enthusiasm of the service and the lack of piped music and fruit machines'. It serves interesting dishes, eg, Blue Vinny cheese soup; pork stuffed with ostrich pâté. The restaurant, with its red carpet and red-fringed lamps, features spicy Nobody Soup; rainbow trout with almonds; lamb's liver sautéed with thyme, onion and garlic. Only seven bedrooms: some simply furnished ones are above the pub. Their lighting may be a bit dim, and towels rather small, but extras include a drinks tray with whisky, sherry and gin, and a hot-water bottle – 'but don't expect to get to sleep before closing time'. The better, larger rooms are in *Town Barton*, a Georgian manor house 150 yards away. They have a fridge containing the ingredients for a continental breakfast. But if you opt for this you miss a 'splendid affair', served in the bar, with freshly squeezed orange juice, hot toast made to order, and 'the best ever fry-up'. Cannonteign Falls, Castle Drogo and the Teign Valley golf course are nearby. (*KM,* Good Pub Guide*, and others*)

Open All year, except 24–26 Dec. Restaurant closed midday, Sun evening/Mon night.
Rooms 7 double. 3 (1 on ground floor) in *Town Barton* 150 yds.
Facilities Bar, restaurant. No background music. 3-acre grounds; patio.
Location 6 miles SW of Exeter, off A38 at Haldon Hill. Local buses (sometimes) from Exeter.
Restrictions No smoking in restaurant. No children under 14. No dogs.
Credit cards Amex, MasterCard, Visa.
Terms [2001] B&B: single £22–£38, double £70. Full alc £22.

DORCHESTER Dorset — Map 1:C6

Casterbridge Hotel
49 High East Street
Dorchester DT1 1HU

Tel 01305-264043
Fax 01305-260884
Email reception@casterbridgehotel.co.uk
Website www.casterbridgehotel.co.uk

Rita and Stuart Turner are the 'hospitable proprietors' of this unassuming B&B hotel which has been in the Turner family (who also own *The Priory*, Wareham, *qv*) for more than 80 years. It is on Dorchester's busy high street, which the smart little lounge overlooks, but the four front bedrooms are double-glazed, and the building rambles backwards to a quiet courtyard with a fountain. Regulars agree that the hotel is 'very good value for money'. The attractive larger bedrooms have a big bed, and there is good family accommodation. Some singles are tiny, with a low doorway. The 'very English' breakfast, with cereals, muffins, fresh fruit, and a good choice of cooked dishes, including kedgeree, is 'good and generous'. No restaurant, but tea and coffee are available all day, guests may picnic in the conservatory, and there are plenty of eating places nearby. The *Mock Turtle*, up the hill, is warmly recommended. Loading and unloading a car can be tricky but the hotel offers help and advice. Outings, guided walks and chauffeur-driven tours of local sights are arranged for guests who arrive by train. The historic county town of Dorset (the model for Thomas Hardy's Casterbridge) has many 17th- and 18th-century houses and some Roman remains. (*JB*)

Open All year, except 25/26 Dec.
Rooms 10 double, 4 single. 5 in annexe across courtyard; 2 on ground floor, with access for ♿ (but no other facilities).
Facilities Ramps. Lounge, bar/library, breakfast room, conservatory. No background music. Small courtyard. Sandy beach, bathing 8 miles.
Location Main street, 100 yds below town clock (front rooms double-glazed). 2 garages; free parking 7 pm–8 am and Sun in public car park in adjacent street. Station 1 mile.
Restrictions No smoking: breakfast room, 11 bedrooms. No dogs.
Credit cards All major cards accepted.
Terms B&B: single £40–£55, double £58–£90. Discounts for extended stays. Winter weekend breaks. ***V***

> Deadlines: nominations for the 2003 edition of this volume should reach us not later than 25 May 2002. Latest date for comments on existing entries: 1 June 2002.

Yalbury Cottage NEW
Lower Bockhampton
nr Dorchester DT2 8PZ

Tel 01305-262382
Fax 01305-266412
Email yalbury.cottage@virgin.net
Website www.smoothhound.co.uk/hotels/yalbury

Heather and Derek Furminger's 'small, select hotel', a conversion of two old cottages, 'is the place for peace and serious cosseting', writes a fan, bringing it back to the *Guide*. 'Long, low, thatched and pretty', it stands in a flower-filled garden near Dorchester, in a tiny village with 20 or so houses and a pretty bridge over the river Frome; no pub, no church, no shop. 'While not luxurious, it provides good accommodation for those not wedded to muzak and king-size beds.' Inside are inglenook fireplaces and low, beamed ceilings. Spacious bedrooms, 'almost Shaker in feel', with pretty bedclothes and pine furniture, are in a discreet modern wing. 'The attentiveness and helpfulness of the owners and their staff is noteworthy.' The cooking of Russell Brown 'is of good dinner-party type, delicious, well balanced, with fresh vegetables' (modern English dishes, eg, brill with olive oil-crushed potatoes, roast cherry tomatoes, herb butter sauce; loin of lamb with bubble and squeak cake and red wine jus). 'Dinner is at a pre-arranged time – no hardship as the lounge is so comfortable.' 'Breakfast includes fresh orange juice, proper toast, proper kippers.' Cream teas are served, in the garden in fine weather. Lovely walks through Hardy country (the village is 'Mellstock' in *Under the Greenwood Tree*, and his birthplace is nearby). (*Pauline Simonis, Philip and Gill Kogan, Col. and Mrs AJ Harvey, Bryan and Mary Blaxall*)

Open 1 Feb–28 Dec. Restaurant closed for lunch.
Rooms 8 double.
Facilities Lounge, restaurant. ½-acre garden. No background music. Only restaurant suitable for ♿.
Location In hamlet 2 miles E of Dorchester, 1 mile S of Hardy's cottage. Turn S off A35 Bournemouth–Dorchester. Train: Dorchester; then taxi.
Restrictions No smoking: restaurant, bedrooms. No dogs in public rooms.
Credit cards MasterCard, Visa.
Terms B&B £43–£55; D,B&B (min. 2 nights) £70–£82. Set dinner £27. Christmas package. 1-night bookings refused Sat May–Oct. *V* (Nov–Apr)

DOVER Kent — Map 2:D5

Wallett's Court
West Cliffe
St Margaret's-at-Cliffe
Dover CT15 6EW

Tel 01304-852424
Fax 01304-853430
Email wc@wallettscourt.com
Website www.wallettscourt.com

High above the sea, in a designated area of outstanding natural beauty, stands this Grade II* listed mainly Jacobean manor house. The owners for many years, Chris and Lea Oakley, have handed over management to their son, Gavin, and Colin Kirkwood. The Domesday-old building has an ancient staircase, a carved wood porch, a 17th-century wall painting, a priest hole in the roof, exposed brickwork, moulded plaster fireplaces. There are black wood-burning stoves, antiques and leather sofas in the large lounge. *Wallett's Court* has many fans, often one-nighters travelling to or from the Continent. 'It is always wonderful,' they write. 'All the staff are friendly.' 'Even in summer candles were lit in the bar, creating a delightful atmosphere.' 'The restaurant is lovely' – it is popular with well-heeled local diners. Chris Oakley is now 'semi-retired' from the kitchens; Stephen Harvey's cooking is thought 'outstanding', 'well presented'. The long *prix-fixe* menu includes dishes like scallops on a butternut squash mousse; local sole with a basil olive crust on peperonata and tomato sauce; hot gingerbread soufflé with marmalade ice cream. Or you could try the five-course no-choice gourmet menu at £40, the vegetarian menu or the short bar/room-service menu. Breakfast, in a conservatory, includes eggs from the family's farm nearby, toasted granary bread, home-made preserves. Early departers can be served from 7 am. The bedrooms vary greatly (several were renovated this year). Those in the main house have the most character: Eleanor of Castile, large, with an oak-panelled four-poster bed, is named for one former visitor. Most rooms are in converted barns; some are small, with a tiny shower, and floorboards may be creaky. Four rooms above the leisure centre in a converted barn are well kitted out, but some might get noise from the spa. The small swimming pool has a swim-trainer jet: 'you can swim on the spot, fighting the current'. A 'pleasant and pastoral' walk leads to St Margaret's-at-Cliffe; go a short way further for views over the chalk cliffs and across the Channel. Canterbury is 15 miles away. (*LB, and others*)

Open All year.
Rooms 2 suites, 15 double. 13 in converted barns, stables, cottages.
Facilities Lounge, bar, restaurant (classical background music on quiet evenings), conservatory. 7-acre grounds: spa (swimming pool, sauna, steam room), tennis, croquet, jogging trail, tree house. Sea 1 mile (by footpath). Golf nearby. Unsuitable for ♿.
Location 3 miles N of Dover. From A2 take A258 to Deal. 1st right to West Cliffe; hotel ½ mile on right, opposite church. Train: Dover Priory; then bus 90.
Restrictions No smoking: restaurant, 8 bedrooms. No children under 8 in restaurant after 8 pm. No dogs.
Credit cards All major cards accepted.
Terms B&B: single £75–£110, double £90–£130, suite £130–£150. Set lunch £17.50, dinner £35–£40.Christmas packages. *V*

See also SHORTLIST

DULVERTON Somerset **Map 1:B5**

Ashwick House
Dulverton TA22 9QD

Tel/Fax 01398-323868
Email ashwickhouse@talk21.com
Website www.ashwickhouse.co.uk

César award in 1994

'Excellent. We went with high expectations and were not disappointed.' 'The success is due to the outstanding dedication of the proprietor.' 'Tremendous value for money.' Warm endorsements this year for this quirky Edwardian house, high above the Barle valley. The owner/manager/chef, Richard Sherwood, runs it 'more like a private house than a hotel'. Visitors find the situation 'delightful' – 'we had a marvellous three-hour walk from the door' – and the house 'beautifully furnished and maintained'. 'Our room was one of the most comfortable we have come across. Tremendous attention to detail.' The galleried hall has the original William Morris wallpaper and huge stained-glass windows. In the lounge, a fire crackles, a grandfather clock ticks, and there are 'inviting sofas'. Informative handwritten notes can be found everywhere. In the spacious bedrooms, 'everything has been thought of' – fresh fruit, mineral water, Scrabble, binoculars, a CD-player and speak-your-weight scales. At night, a cartoon-character hot-water bottle warms your bed. At dinner, each table gets a personalised menu, presented as a scroll, and the cooking has been called 'uniformly excellent'. No choice of main course: after 'the chef's little spinach and pecan nut filled crêpe', it might include spring lamb with a port wine sauce; strawberry Bavarian cream dessert with Cointreau. Wines are fairly priced. Breakfast has freshly pressed apple juice, free-range eggs and brown toast, and the menu carries the day's weather forecast. On fine days, guests eat outdoors on the south-facing terrace. The dramatic landscape of Exmoor is all around, and nearby places to visit include Dunster Castle, Knightshayes, and Selworthy thatched village. (*DG Stevens, AHE, JD*)

Open All year.
Rooms 6 double.
Facilities 2 lounges, library, dining room; terrace. No background music. 6-acre grounds: water garden, croquet, woodland. Unsuitable for ♿.
Location 2½ miles NW of Dulverton. Take B3223 towards Lynton; up steep hill, over 2 cattle grids; signpost on left. Train: Tiverton Parkway; then bus.
Restrictions No smoking: dining room, library, 2 bedrooms. No children under 8. No dogs in house.
Credit cards None accepted.
Terms B&B £48–£64; D,B&B £60–£84. Set lunch £14.95, dinner £21.75. 2- to 5-day breaks. Christmas, New Year house parties. *V*

DUNWICH Suffolk — Map 2:B6

The Ship Inn BUDGET
St James Street
Dunwich, nr Saxmundham IP17 3DT
Tel 01728-648219
Fax 01728-648675

Everyone is made welcome at this 'delightful old brick pub, with a good bustling atmosphere' in a 'charming old village' (once a thriving medieval port). It is run by Stephen John and Ann Marshlain, with a friendly staff. The 'cosy main bar' is furnished with benches, pews, captain's chairs and wooden tables on its tiled floor, a wood-burning stove and nautical memorabilia. There is a conservatory, a sunny rear terrace and a large garden. Meals are very simple (eg, fish pie crumble; steak and chips; lasagne, followed by 'scrumptious home-made puddings'). The bedrooms, upstairs, are pretty (patchwork quilts and flowery fabrics; best ones have views of sea and marsh. 'Plenty of books and board games.' Breakfasts 'are wonderful, including squeeze-your-own orange juice'. The RSPB bird sanctuary at Minsmere is nearby. (Good Pub Guide)

Open All year, except Christmas after midday.
Rooms 3 double. No telephone.
Facilities Conservatory, bar, breakfast room, restaurant. No background music. Large garden, patio. Beach 2 mins' walk. Unsuitable for ♿.
Location Centre of village, 4 miles SW of Southwold.
Restrictions No smoking in restaurant. No children under 14 in bar. No dogs in restaurant.
Credit cards MasterCard, Visa.
Terms [2001] B&B: single £45–£50, double £60. Set lunch £15, dinner £20. 2-day breaks in winter (except school holidays).

DURHAM Co. Durham *See SHORTLIST* Map 4:B4

EAST DOWN Devon Map 1:B4

Ashelford

East Down, nr Barnstaple
EX31 4LU

Tel 01271-850469
Fax 01271-850862
Email accommodation@ashelford.co.uk
Website www.ashelford.co.uk

'Someone wishing to "escape from it all" could stay here and walk for miles without ever leaving the estate,' said a visitor to Tom and Erica McClenaghan's upmarket guest house. It stands amid pasture and woodland, and has wide views across the National Trust's Arlington Court, two miles away, to Exmoor. 'The peace and quiet is amazing, with Exmoor ponies in a paddock, lovely walks.' Three bedrooms are in the 17th-century farmhouse, and a converted barn makes a 'superb suite', with a sitting room upstairs, a six-foot antique bed, views of a lily pond and stream – 'so romantic'. One bathroom has an extra-long antique bath. All rooms are provided with a fridge, spare toothbrushes, hangover powders, etc; wellies and walking sticks can be borrowed. Tea on arrival comes with home-made cake. There are log fires and TV in the guests' sitting rooms, and a reasonably priced bar. The stars can be viewed through an eight-inch telescope. A home-cooked evening meal can be arranged – 'portion control is unknown here'. Local produce is cooked in 'old-fashioned style', say the McClenaghans. No children, but dogs are welcome – there is an outside bath for them, and kennels are available. The north Devon coast is ten minutes' drive away. More reports, please.

Open All year. Lunch not served.
Rooms 1 suite, 4 double. 2 in barn. No telephone.
Facilities 2 lounges, snug, 2 dining rooms; occasional background music 'to suit guests'. 70-acre grounds: garden, water garden, pasture, woodlands. Horse riding nearby. Unsuitable for ♿.
Location 6 miles NE of Barnstaple. Turn off A39 just N of Shirwell, signed Upcott, Churchill; follow next sign to Churchill; *Ashelford* on right.
Restrictions No smoking in dining room before 10 pm, or in bedrooms. No children under 18.
Credit cards MasterCard, Visa.
Terms B&B double £94–£141. Set dinner (by arrangement) £30.

EAST GRINSTEAD West Sussex **Map 2:D4**

Gravetye Manor
Vowels Lane
East Grinstead RH19 4LJ

Tel 01342-810567
Fax 01342-810080
Email info@gravetyemanor.co.uk
Website www.gravetyemanor.co.uk

César award in 1991

The carefully restored grounds (open only to the hotel's visitors) are magnificent – they were designed by William Robinson, pioneer of the English natural garden. And the creeper-covered Elizabethan manor, run for four decades by Peter Herbert and his wife Sue, wins regular plaudits. 'It never disappoints; "cosseting" just begins to describe the service,' one visitor wrote. Another guest described the dining room as 'one of the best I have visited'. There are 'lots of nice country house touches' in this Relais & Châteaux member: home-made biscuits at tea, served by an open fire in the Tudor drawing room with its carved wooden ceiling; fruit, books and magazines in the 'soothing bedrooms'. Most rooms are large, but a single above the kitchen is said to get cooking smells and some noise. Mark Raffan serves traditional English and classical French dishes in the *Michelin*-starred restaurant, offering two *table d'hôte* menus, one longer and more expensive than the other (coffee and petits fours are £4 extra). The cheaper menu might include warm camembert and tomato tart, or langoustine tortellini; pan-fried sea bass with herb-crushed potatoes and baby fennel, or roast squab pigeon with truffled potatoes; orange mousse with lemongrass jelly and citrus ginger salad, or cheese. The much-admired wine list is huge, with some 'eyebrow-raising prices'. Light lunches, with limited choice, are available. 'Lovely berries with natural yogurt' are available for breakfast. Not cheap, 'but for a special occasion, it is hard to beat'. Gatwick is 20 minutes' drive away. Local attractions include the gardens of Wakehurst Place, Leonardslee and Sheffield Park. (*Michael Kavanagh, and others*)

Open All year. Restaurant closed to non-residents Christmas night.
Rooms 17 double, 1 single.
Facilities 3 sitting rooms, bar, restaurant; private dining room. No background music. 30-acre grounds: gardens, croquet, 3-acre trout lake (fishing). Unsuitable for ♿.
Location 5 miles SW of East Grinstead, off B2110 to West Hoathly. Train: East Grinstead, 5 miles, Gatwick Airport, 12 miles; taxi.
Restrictions No smoking in restaurant. No children under 7, except babies. No dogs in house (kennels in grounds).
Credit cards MasterCard, Visa.
Terms [2001] Room: single £95–£150, double £160–£300. Breakfast £14–£16. Set lunch £27, dinner £37 or £52. Off-season rates. 1-night bookings refused Sat.

British hotels nowadays have private facilities in most bedrooms. And many have TV, baby-listening and tea-making facilities. To save space we do not list all of these; if any is particularly important to you, please discuss with the hotel.

EAST STOKE Dorset — Map 2:E1

Kemps
East Stoke
nr Wareham BH20 6AL

Tel 01929-462563
Fax 01929-405287
Email kemps.hotel@lineone.net
Website www.smoothound.co.uk/hotels/kemps

'Paul and Gillian Warren are welcoming hosts,' say visitors to the small hotel/restaurant they run in an extended Victorian rectory overlooking the Frome valley and Purbeck Hills. Some redecoration has taken place this year. 'Our bedroom was large and comfortable, with a pleasant view of the garden.' The rooms in the main house are 'traditionally comfortable'. Some rooms are in a purpose-built annexe; some of these have a spa bath, and one has a four-poster bed. There are also rooms in a coach house set well back from the nearby road and railway, but these are the least popular; some bathrooms are tiny, and sound insulation can be poor. The restaurant, with its west-facing conservatory overlooking the garden and 'well-trained staff', is popular with locals, particularly for Sunday lunch, and *Kemps* specialises in weddings and parties. The menu, which changes daily, offers modern dishes, eg, spiced lamb koftas with lemon, chilli, rosemary and garlic on a tomato sauce; beef and kidney in a Stilton puff pastry basket. A vegetarian option is available. Breakfast includes a buffet with fresh fruit, toast made from home-made bread, unpackaged jams, marmalades and butter. The National Trust coastline is nearby; so is entertainment for all tastes: Monkey World, a tank museum, Corfe Castle. (*Betty and Harry Alton, DG*)

Open All year. Restaurant closed Sat midday.
Rooms 15 double. 4 in coach house, 6 in annexe. 2 adapted for ♿.
Facilities Lounge, study, bar, restaurant (light classical background music); function/conference facilities. 1½-acre garden: pond. Sea, safe bathing 10 mins' drive.
Location On A352, 5 miles W of Wareham.
Restrictions Smoking banned in dining room, discouraged in bedrooms. Dogs by arrangement.
Credit cards MasterCard, Visa.
Terms [2001] B&B £42–£77. Set lunch £10.95, dinner £21.95; full alc £28. Child in parents' room: under 7, free; 7–12, £5; 13 and over, £15. 2-night breaks. Christmas package. 1-night bookings sometimes refused. *V*

ERPINGHAM Norfolk — Map 2:A5

The Ark
The Street
Erpingham NR11 7QB

Tel 01263-761535

Sheila and Michael Kidd run a restaurant-with-rooms that has a 'home-spun air', in their brick and flint house on a small country road. Mrs Kidd is an 'imaginative and enthusiastic' chef while her husband runs the front-of-house and is *sommelier* and waiter. 'The dinner was superb – we had six courses between us, all excellent,' reports a visitor this year. The Elizabeth David-influenced country cooking includes, eg, mackerel marinated in sweet soy on grilled aubergine and sesame purée; partridge stuffed with mushrooms with a cep and red wine sauce; glazed apple and japonica pancake with vanilla ice. Vegetarians are well catered for. Everything, from bread to chocolates, is home-made, and the large garden supplies many of the organic ingredients. The wine list ranges from reasonably priced house wines up to the £80 mark. The small dining room has 'a homely atmosphere: attractively laid tables, an open fire, a lovely Edwardian inlaid cabinet'. 'Only 36 covers, ensuring a personal touch,' write the Kidds. The lounge is warmed by a wood-burning stove. Both have been redecorated this year; so have all three bedrooms. These are 'eccentrically planned and somewhat lacking in privacy: one opens off the lounge, the other off the tiny hall'; one has a private garden. The Attic Room, suitable for a family, and reached up a narrow, twisting staircase, is 'arranged as a pleasant sitting room-cum-bedroom', and has a bathroom under the eaves. Breakfast, served round one large table, is at flexible times. No menu, but it includes freshly squeezed orange juice, fresh croissants, home-baked bread, home-made marmalade, local bloaters and kippers. 'Recommended for gourmets, but not perhaps for honeymooners. Very good value.' The grounds of Wolterton Park, close by, and Mannington Hall, two miles to the north-west, merit a visit. Blickling and Felbrigg halls (both National Trust) and some wonderful beaches are nearby. Also worth visiting: the tiny church at Ingworth, with its thatched roof and original box pews. (*David Lodge, MJ*)

Open All year, except part of Oct, Christmas, part of Jan.
Rooms 3 double. 2 with *en suite* facilities; 1 with adjacent bathroom. 1 on ground floor. No telephone.
Facilities Lounge, bar, restaurant, breakfast/private dining room. No background music. 1-acre garden: croquet. Sea 7 miles.
Location 4 miles N of Aylsham. Left off A140, just before Alby Centre. Parking.
Restrictions No smoking: restaurant, bedrooms. Dogs in garden bedroom only, not in public rooms.
Credit cards None accepted.
Terms D,B&B: single £70–£80, double £125–£145. Set lunch £16, dinner (2 to 4 courses) £22–£28. Off-season breaks.

The Saracen's Head BUDGET *Tel* 01263-768909
Wolterton, nr Erpingham *Fax* 01263-768993
Aylsham NR11 7LX *Website* www.broadland.com/guest/aylsham/saracen

Norfolk-born and bred, Robert Dawson-Smith is a landlord with character. He 'welcomes all comers with warmth', and promises: 'No piped music or fruit machines, no chips, peas or scampi, just fresh and delicious fare.' One visitor writes: 'Not a place for those who want to be fussed over; the approach is casual and friendly.' Built as a coaching inn for the Walpole family in 1806, it has a 'comfortably bold' decor: candles, log fires, plants, 'all kinds of interesting artefacts'. The 'charmingly old-fashioned patio' has 'the feel of a Tuscan farmhouse'. This is a popular local eating place, with a menu that changes at every meal; booking is advised. Morston mussels are a speciality –

sometimes served with cider and cream. Other dishes suggest the flavour of the fare offered: real rare ruddy ribs of roast beef; fried Gunton venison with red fruit. Herbs and tomatoes are liberally used. 'Heavenly puddings', eg, nutty banana and Marsala crumble; old-fashioned treacle tart. The two-course weekday lunch is 'amazing value' at £5.50. In summer, meals are served alfresco. Three of the bedrooms, reached up steep steps, are in the roof; they have rounded dormer windows, sloping ceilings, simple pine furniture. Breakfast includes freshly squeezed orange juice, fresh fruit, fresh bread, good kippers. Wine tastings, and shows of work by local artists are held. The Blickling estate is close by (Mr Dawson-Smith also manages its pub, the *Buckinghamshire Arms*). Other local attractions: the gardens of Wolterton Park and Mannington Hall, the north Norfolk coast, Holkham Hall and Norwich. This is a rich area for windmill and railway enthusiasts. (Good Pub Guide*; also CS Jones*)

Open All year, except 25 Dec.
Rooms 4 double. No telephone.
Facilities Parlour, 2 bars; function room. No background music. 1-acre grounds: courtyard. Unsuitable for ♿.
Location Turn W off A140 to Erpingham. Do not bear right towards Aldborough; go straight on, passing church on left and following signs to Itteringham. Pub ½ mile on right, in field.
Restrictions Smoking discouraged in eating areas, banned in bedrooms. Dogs by arrangement, not in public rooms.
Credit cards All major cards accepted.
Terms B&B: single £35–£40, double £40–£60. Set lunch from £5.50; full alc £25. Winter breaks. 1-night bookings sometimes refused weekends.

EVERSHOT Dorset — Map 1:C6

Summer Lodge
Evershot DT2 0JR

Tel 01935-83424
Fax 01935-83005
Email reservations@summerlodgehotel.com
Website www.summerlodgehotel.com

César award in 1985

Nigel and Margaret Corbett have been 21 years at this long-time *Guide* favourite (Relais & Châteaux), in the former dower house of the Earls of Ilchester. It is commended again this year for 'continuing high standards', but there are changes in senior management. Thierry Lepinoy ('very charming') has joined as manager from *Chewton Glen* (*qv*); David Richards took over as head chef in April 2001. 'The welcome and personal attention is very gratifying,' says one visitor. 'Still a delight, very comfortable,' says another. The ambience and decor are 'friendly, cosy rather than grand'; the house is 'beautifully furnished, very warm'. Mrs Corbett's flower arrangements are much admired. Several 'annoyances' were reported this year including problems with hot water. 'A small effort would turn a very good hotel experience into an almost perfect one,' is one view. Bedrooms are well appointed, if sometimes 'a bit cluttered'. Most are large, but No. 5 is small. Lighting may be too soft for some, but the 'incredibly thick towels' are appreciated. We'd like reports on the 'modern English' cooking, served on a daily *table d'hôte* menu and a *carte,* eg, seared oak-smoked salmon on a salad of white crab and pineapple; roast chump of lamb on spring onion mash with Madeira jus; glazed strawberries in champagne sabayon with red fruit sorbet. Many of the staff are 'French, young and well trained'. Breakfast is 'outstanding' with 'the finest raspberry jam in the world'. Children are welcomed. Not cheap, but the half-board prices include early morning tea, a newspaper, a lavish cream tea. Shooting parties are sometimes accommodated. There is good walking in a large deer park nearby. Local attractions include Parnham House, Stourhead, Hardy's cottage, Cerne Abbas, Montacute House and Kingston Lacy. Ten golf courses are within 25 miles. (*Edwin Prince, Heather Sharland, Michael and Anne Forrest, Brian and Lesley Knox, Brian and Eve Webb, and others*)

Open All year.
Rooms 1 junior suite, 13 double, 3 single. 6 in coach house 20 yds (3 on ground floor, 2 with private terrace). Also 2-bedroomed cottage.
Facilities Ramps. 2 lounges, bar, restaurant. No background music. 4-acre grounds: garden, swimming pool, croquet, tennis. Golf, fishing, hunting nearby; sea, shingle beach 12 miles. Civil wedding licence.
Location 10 miles NW of Dorchester. Entering village turn left into Summer Lane; drive on right. Train: Yeovil/Dorchester; taxi.
Restrictions No smoking in restaurant. No dogs in public rooms. No children under 8 in restaurant at night.
Credit cards All major cards accepted.
Terms B&B: single £95–£135, double £135–£295; D,B&B (min. 2 nights): single £125–£165; double £195–£395. Set lunch £12.50–£19.75, dinner £42.50; full alc £50. Off-season breaks. Christmas, New Year packages. 1-night bookings occasionally refused Sat. *V*

EVESHAM Worcestershire — Map 3:D6

The Evesham Hotel — *Tel* 01386-765566
Cooper's Lane, off Waterside — *Fax* 01386-765443
Evesham WR11 6DA — *Freephone* 0800-716969 (reservations only)
Email reception@eveshamhotel.com
Website www.eveshamhotel.com

César award in 1990

'A delightful three-generation weekend, the most enjoyable family get-together we have ever had. The hotel brought out the best in all of us; on Sunday the children, aged between seven and 20 months, had to be dragged away.' 'The hospitality is as good as ever.' Yet more praise for a popular hotel, where 'humour is evident throughout'. John and Sue Jenkinson (who celebrate a quarter-century here this year) say they offer 'a light-hearted approach to comfort (comfort always comes first)'. She is responsible for the design of some remarkable themed rooms. Alice in Wonderland has toadstool tables, a tiny front door set low in a wall, gnomes sitting on beams, a mad hatter's tea party. A 'fabulous' Tropical Island room has a fish tank under the basin; the Egyptian Room has mummies (including a teddy) and hieroglyphs; Mulberry Cottage is spacious, with facilities for the disabled. Children under 12 are charged according to age and amount of food eaten. The eccentric approach shows 'intelligence, and warmth to all comers'. The Jenkinsons, supported by a long-serving staff, 'try to establish a balance by not having too many children at the same time'. The popular restaurant offers exotic fare from around the world (jokingly explained on the menu), eg, Maltese quail; pork Sanchez. Plainer fare is also served, and there are always seven vegetarian main courses. 'Food was excellent, though we included one veggie, one on a gluten-free diet, another avoiding all fat.' But one diner thought the restaurant lighting could have been 'more subtle'. Lunch includes a 50-dish buffet. The huge wine list avoids, on principle, French and German vintages. 'Breakfast is freshly cooked, none of that congealed buffet.' (*Joan and David Bates, Sandie Llewelyn-Jones, Deborah Boyle, FG Millen*)

Open All year, except 25/26 Dec.
Rooms 3 suites (1 suitable for ♿), 32 double, 5 single. 10 on ground floor. Cottage 30 yards.
Facilities Lounges, bar, restaurant; function facilities; small indoor swimming pool. No background music. 2½-acre grounds: croquet, putting, swings, trampoline.
Location Off Riverside Rd. 5 mins' walk from town centre, across river. Parking. Station 1 mile.
Restrictions No smoking: restaurant, 1 lounge, 25% of bedrooms, pool area. No dogs in public rooms.
Credit cards All major cards accepted.
Terms B&B: single £65–£79, double £103–£108, suite £152–£164; D,B&B (min. 2 nights) £58–£74 per person. Full alc £28. Child in parents' room: under 12, £2 or £3 for each year of life, depending on season (eg, £12 for a 6-year-old in winter). 1-night bookings sometimes refused weekends.

EXETER Devon — Map 1:C5

Hotel Barcelona NEW
Magdalen Street
Exeter EX2 4HY

Tel 01392-281000
Fax 01392-281001
Email info@hotelbarcelona-uk.com
Website www.hotelbarcelona-uk.com

César award: Designer hotel of the year

'Gloriously stylish; a great asset for Exeter.' An inspector's enthusiastic verdict on this 'design-led' hotel, the newest of Nigel Chapman and Nicholas Dickinson's Alias Hotels group (see also the *Kandinsky*, Cheltenham, and the child-friendly group of *Woolley Grange*, Bradford-on-Avon, etc). Mr Chapman writes: 'Converting a Victorian eye hospital has been interesting; the late 19th-century passion for light and space helped.' His collection of '60s psychedelic posters fills the building, and his '50s *films noirs* can be watched in the nightclub, *Kino*. 'No beauty outside (municipal brickwork, grey-painted woodwork), the building has been transformed into a dazzling modern hotel with a definite touch of the Gaudís: bright paintings and posters, a superb bar (once the waiting room) with yellow and red '50s sofas and chairs, lots of chrome, fab cocktails, great-value "foodles" (eg, garlic king prawns, smoked fish platter). The sunny *Café Paradiso* restaurant overlooks an acre of walled garden. It is fantastic: a chef rolls dough and cooks pizzas in a wood-burning pizza oven imported from Naples. Fish and meat are charred on a wood-burning grill, and the antipasti are a gourmet feast. The building smells of wood smoke and fresh carpet, and the young staff are eager and very helpful.' Every room has a CD-player and video. 'My small single was beautifully furnished (gorgeous bedcover and rug, very Spanish). The bathroom was fabulous: fluffy towels, gleaming fittings. Traffic noise from the main road woke me early, but double glazing is to be installed. Some odd gurgles in the water pipes remind you of the hotel's origins.' Meals are served on the large terrace in fine weather. The managers are Nikki and Jon Broom. As with the other hotels in the group, any number of children stay free in their parents' bedroom. A sister hotel in Manchester, the *dAdA*, is planned for early 2002.

Open All year.
Rooms 39 double, 7 single. Some on ground floor.
Facilities Ramp. Lift. 2 lounges, restaurant; background jazz; private dining room; nightclub; meeting facilities; large terrace. 1-acre garden.
Location (They will send map.) 5 mins' walk from centre (front rooms get traffic noise), near Cathedral Green. Parking.
Restrictions No smoking in restaurant. No dogs unattended in bedrooms.
Credit cards All major cards accepted.
Terms Room: single £70, double £80–£90. Breakfast £3.50–£10.50. Full alc £30. Weekend rates. Child in parents' room: free.

St Olaves NEW
Mary Arches Street
Exeter EX4 3AZ

Tel 01392-217736
Fax 01392-413054
Email info@olaves.co.uk
Website www.olaves.co.uk

'Superb. Lovely rooms, lovely decor. Wonderful food. Beautiful dining room, snug bar and sitting room. Staff are charming.' 'Good value for a city hotel. Good situation.' Praise by two seasoned travellers for this 'haven of tranquillity' in the centre of the bustling city. Once a Georgian merchant's house, and Grade I listed, it stands in a walled garden with a fountain and mulberry tree. It was taken over a year ago, and extensively renovated, by Sebastian and Philippa Hughes, the owners of *Holne Chase*, Ashburton (*qv*). A lovely spiral staircase rises towards a glass dome; original features – fireplaces, cornices, ceiling roses – have been carefully restored, and the decor is in keeping, with flowery fabrics and antiques, but also power showers. Anthony Ware is the manager; Graham Beal is the chef, producing dishes such as seafood and saffron risotto; calf's liver with bubble and squeak; sticky toffee pudding. Close to shops, and the cathedral is five minutes' walk away. Some bedrooms are 'very small'. (*Val Hennessy, Sue Davies*)

Open All year.
Rooms 2 suites, 12 double, 1 single. Some on ground floor.

Facilities Lounge, bar, restaurant. No background music. 1-acre garden. Civil wedding licence.
Location Central. Parking.
Restrictions No smoking in restaurant. No dogs in public rooms.
Credit cards Amex, MasterCard, Visa.
Terms B&B: single/double £95–£115, suite £125–£145; D,B&B: single from £96, double from £142, suite from £182. English breakfast £8. Set lunch (2 courses) £14.50, dinner (2–3 courses) £14.50–£17.50; full alc £34. Christmas package. *V*

FALMOUTH Cornwall — Map 1:E2

Greenbank Hotel NEW
Harbourside
Falmouth TR11 2SR

Tel 01326-312440
Fax 01326-211362
Email sales@greenbank-hotel.com
Website www.greenbank-hotel.com

Traditional hotel, 400 yds from centre: old white building above the sea (wide views across harbour to the Roseland peninsula). Recently extensively refurbished by new owners (a small leisure company); managed by William Pound. 'Very welcoming, up-to-date in comfort and facilities; helpful young staff.' Flagstoned foyer, curving staircase, lounge, bar, restaurant; background CDs; framed Wind in the Willow *prints, letters from Napoleonic era, Florence Nightingale's entry in hotel's register. Small waterfront garden. 54 bedrooms: many are spacious, with modern bathroom; some face quiet road. Good food: much local fish; 'exciting desserts'. Civil wedding licence. No smoking: restaurant, 20 bedrooms. No dogs in public rooms. All major credit cards accepted. B&B: single £57–£72, double £90–£145, suite £125–£175; D,B&B £60–£102.50 per person. Set lunch £12.50; full alc £27.50 [2001].* *V* (*Oct–Apr*)

Penmere Manor
Mongleath Road
Falmouth TR11 4PN

Tel 01326-211411
Fax 01326-317588
Email reservations@penmere.co.uk
Website www.penmere.co.uk

Andrew Pope and Elizabeth Rose's Georgian country house, now a traditional hotel (Best Western), stands amid subtropical gardens and woodland near the south Cornwall coast, about a mile from the town centre. Sandy beaches are a mile away. The decor may be 'somewhat anodyne', but it is a 'dependable place, with a happy atmosphere', says one report. Another visitor writes of 'great friendliness, a truly beautiful room, *and* our child was positively enjoyed'. The food is 'unpretentious, varied and good, served with enthusiasm', and eating arrangements are flexible. Chef James Spargo has rejoined after five years away. *Bolitho's Restaurant* has a long four-course menu that changes daily: many seafood starters, a sorbet to follow, and a wide choice of main courses (several with a supplementary charge); you pay according to number of courses taken. There is also a menu devoted to local lobster (ranging from plain grilled to 'Auld Reekie'). You can lunch or dine more informally in the bar in the leisure club, which also has a gym, a large indoor swimming pool, solarium, beauty treatments, etc. The walled garden shelters a heated outdoor pool. The best bedrooms, in the garden wing, are spacious, with a sitting area and king- or queen-size bed. There are conference and business facilities. Falmouth golf club is nearby (booking necessary), as are Land's End, Pendennis and St Mawes castles; vouchers are available for free entry to Trebah Gardens at Mawnan Smith. (*HJMT, Kathy Burges*)

Open All year, except 24–27 Dec.
Rooms 26 double, 11 single.
Facilities 2 lounges (guitar player or pianist Apr–Oct), bar, restaurant; conference/function facilities; leisure club: gym, solarium, beauty room; indoor and outdoor swimming pools. 5-acre grounds: children's play area. Beach, sailing, windsurfing, golf nearby. Unsuitable for ♿. Civil wedding licence.
Location 1 mile SW of Falmouth. From Truro: A39 towards Falmouth, right at Hillhead roundabout. After 1 mile, left into Mongleath Road. Train: Penmere, 1 mile; local buses.
Restrictions No smoking: restaurant, bedrooms. No dogs in public rooms.
Credit cards All major cards accepted.
Terms [2001] B&B £56–£73; D,B&B £78–£95. Full alc £31. Off-season breaks. *V*

FERRENSBY North Yorkshire — Map 4:D4

The General Tarleton
Harrogate Road
Ferrensby
nr Knaresborough HG5 0PZ

Tel 01423-340284
Fax 01423-340288
Email gti@generaltarleton.co.uk
Website www.generaltarleton.co.uk

'The food is quite exceptional,' says an endorsement this year for this 18th-century inn in a village with a duck pond, and red brick cottages standing in flowery gardens. Named for Sir Banastre Tarleton, barrister, soldier (said to be the only successful British general in the American War of Independence) and MP, it has been transformed by Denis and Juliet Watkins and John Topham (he is the chef with Jason Moore) into a 'thoroughly modern' operation. The versatility is admired: 'It is a genuine local, serving locals. If you want, you can join them, or eat the superior food served in the bar' (this occupies the original pub, with its alcoves, oak beams, and big old fireplace). The *Dining Room* serves a similar menu (eg, ham hock and foie gras terrine; chargrilled venison with parsnip and potato mash; chocolate and orange torte). It has exposed stone walls; upholstered high-backed chairs, smartly set tables, and a wide-ranging wine list. A fixed-price 'early bird menu' is served between 6 and 7.30 pm. Service is by 'friendly young staff'. The bedrooms, in a new extension, 'are superior chain-like in design', but they have attractive fabrics, cheerful prints, good lighting, and a functional bathroom. The 'very good breakfast', taken in a glass-roofed courtyard, includes freshly squeezed juices, toasted walnut bread and unsalted butter (but one visitor disliked the accompanying music). No residents' lounge. The owners' other old inn, the *Angel* at Hetton, near Skipton, is run on similar lines, but it has no bedrooms. Harrogate and York, the Yorkshire dales and moors are nearby. (*Mr and Mrs RT Johnson, Ran Ogston*)

Open All year, except 25 Dec.
Rooms 14 double. Some on ground floor.
Facilities Reception lounge, bar/brasserie, restaurant, covered courtyard (classical background music); small conference facilities.
Location 2 miles NE of Knaresborough. From A1, take A6055 to Knaresborough. The inn is 4 mins' drive, on right.
Restrictions No smoking: restaurant, courtyard, bedrooms. No dogs in public rooms.
Credit cards Amex, MasterCard, Visa.
Terms [2001] Room: single/double £65. Breakfast £9.95. Bar meals. Set Sun lunch £17.50, dinner £25; full alc £35. Champagne, golfing, gourmet, sport, shopping breaks.

FLEET Dorset — Map 1:D6

Moonfleet Manor
Fleet Road, Fleet
nr Weymouth DT3 4ED

Tel 01305-786948
Fax 01305-774395
Email info@moonfleetmanor.com
Website www.moonfleetmanor.com

'A welcoming balance of luxury and informality, to suit all the family. Superb food, friendly staff; first-class childcare arrangements. The Christmas package was outstanding.' So say parents of four small sons (earlier they had enjoyed a 'wonderful' fortnight's summer holiday here). 'I have never seen my well-travelled grandchildren happier than they are here,' writes another visitor this year to this Georgian manor house. The location 'is great', overlooking Chesil Beach and Lyme Bay, though the grounds may 'need attention'. Neil Carter manages it for the Luxury Family Hotels group (see also *Woolley Grange,* Bradford-on-Avon, *Fowey Hall,* Fowey). Any number of children can stay free in their parents' room. 'Flexibility is the key. Children can eat in the restaurants (before 7.30) or lie on the floor in the TV room, burger in one hand, Nintendo keypad in the other.' The chef, Tony Smith, serves 'Anglo-French modern' dishes in the formal dining room and the *Verandah* café, eg, breast of duck on garlic-crushed potatoes; panache of seafood on stir-fried basmati rice with a saffron cream sauce. Wines are almost exclusively from the New World. Service can be 'disorganised' at times. Facilities include a 'Den' with full-time nannies, an indoor swimming pool, aromatherapy treatments, a new indoor play area with table tennis, soft tennis and snooker, and a huge sandpit. Large, comfortable public rooms have a colonial feel – one reporter described the decor as 'Gothic-seaside Raj', and the lounge as 'shabby exotic'. Bedrooms vary in size; some may seem 'a little cramped', but all have now been refurbished. Strong currents rule out sea bathing, but there are good walks in either direction along the Coast Path; Weymouth beach, 'Punch and Judy and all, is great', and the views at night 'are wonderful'. (*Claire and Andrew Bowles, KH, and others*)

Open All year.
Rooms 9 suites, 28 double, 1 single. 6 in 2 annexes. 3 on ground floor.
Facilities Lift. 2 lounges, 2 restaurants; meeting room; games room/nursery; disco; indoor swimming pool, sauna, solarium, sunbed, aromatherapy,

snooker. No background music. 5-acre grounds: children's play areas, tennis, bowls, squash, badminton. Riding stables, golf, sailing nearby.
Location 5 miles W of Weymouth. A354 from Dorchester. Right at Manor roundabout to Weymouth centre; right at Chafey's roundabout to Chickerell/Bridport; through golf course to Wessex roundabout, left to Chickerell, right at junction; 1.7 miles to Moonfleet mini-roundabout; turn left; 2 miles on towards sea. Train: Weymouth; taxi.
Restrictions No smoking in restaurant. No dogs in public rooms.
Credit cards All major cards accepted.
Terms [2001] B&B: single £75, double £95–£200, suite £200–£280; D,B&B: single £80–£90, double £105–£235, suite £200–£315. Child in parents' room: charged for meals only. Bar meals. Set Sun lunch £15, dinner £28. Spring, autumn breaks. Christmas package. 1-night bookings refused weekends.

FLETCHING East Sussex — Map 2:E4

The Griffin Inn NEW
Fletching, nr Uckfield
TN22 3SS

Tel 01825-722890
Fax 01825-722810
Website www.thegriffininn.co.uk

Nigel and Bridget Pullan's 400-year-old inn stands on the main street of the pleasant old Sussex village where Simon de Montfort is said to have camped on the eve of the Battle of Lewes in 1264. It is probably not the place for a long stay (there's no lounge), but the *Good Pub Guide* likes the 'good, bustling atmosphere' of the 'beamed and quaintly panelled bar rooms', though it adds that there can be long waits for meals at busy times. Much local organic produce appears on the menus in the bar and the more expensive restaurant, where our inspectors, on a busy Saturday night, enjoyed the 'modern eclectic' cooking. 'Fennel, celeriac and coconut soup, and timbale of crab both excellent, followed by sea bass with tagliatelle. The recommended Mercurey was drinkable. We thought they should have made one of the dining rooms smoke-free. Our bedroom in the stable block was tiny, dominated by a five-foot four-poster; the door to the well-designed shower would not shut, but someone had taken the trouble to paint a jolly mural; there were attractive curtains, very good bedlinen. At breakfast, coffee was poor, but home-made croissants and marmalade were splendid. Service was by consistently friendly staff.' Children are welcomed: 'We have a large garden, trees to climb, banks to roll down, and a children's menu,' says the brochure. The Prince of Wales recently stopped for a quick drink at the *Griffin*, a visit commemorated by a large photograph. A good base for visiting Glyndebourne, Bateman's, Bodiam Castle, etc.

Open All year, except Christmas Day. Restaurant closed Sun night.
Rooms 8 double. 4 in coach house. 2 on ground floor. No telephone.
Facilities Bar (live duo Fri night, Sun lunch), restaurant. 1½-acre garden.
Location Centre of village 3 miles NW of Uckfield. Train: Haywards Heath, 8 miles; taxi.
Restrictions No smoking in bedrooms. No dogs: bedrooms, restaurant.
Credit cards All major cards accepted.
Terms [2001] B&B double £85–£120. Set Sun lunch £19.50; full alc £28–£32. Midweek package: 3 nights for the price of 2. *V*

FLITWICK Bedfordshire ***See SHORTLIST*** **Map 2:C3**

FOWEY Cornwall **Map 1:D3**

Fowey Hall
Hanson Drive
Fowey PL23 1ET

Tel 01726-833866
Fax 01726-834100
Email info@foweyhall.com
Website www.foweyhall.com

'Must be the best all-round hotel we have visited. How they manage to combine true luxury with the demands of young children is beyond us. Not cheap, but the value is undeniable. It rained throughout our visit, but *Fowey Hall* is prepared for every eventuality. The staff endured our four-year-old son's attempts at piano playing with fortitude and charm.' A rave report this year on Nigel Chapman and Nicholas Dickinson's hotel, with directors Tim and Hazel Brocklebank, in an Italianate Victorian mansion which may have been the model for Toad Hall – some bedrooms are named after characters in *The Wind in the Willows*. A member of the Luxury Family Hotels group, it specialises in welcoming families, and you can cram as many children as you like into your room for no charge. The building is 'appealing, with a big pillared portico, huge terrace with a wonderful view over rooftops to the estuary'. Public rooms have baroque plasterwork, panelling, marble fireplaces, oriental rugs, potted plants, 'a hotchpotch of furniture, much of it repro Jacobean'. There are two 'cosy lounges' and a child-free 'quiet room'. The Four Bears Club has trained nannies who will take children off their parents' hands for several hours during the day. In the large grounds there is a courtyard with tractors, bicycles, sandpits, slides; a shallow swimming pool is in a conservatory. 'Our bedroom was eclectically furnished, and splendidly comfortable. Room service was exemplary.' Some rooms in the attics (no lift) have a steeply sloping ceiling and no view. 'Every meal was meticulously prepared, with the accent very much on fish.' The chef, Tony Duce, presides over two restaurants: the 'lovely and light' *Palm Court* (home-made soups, salads, seafood) and the 'more staid' dining room. Its daily changing set menu might include pressed duck with date chutney; grilled mullet on couscous with shellfish sauce; set custard with soft berries. The young staff are 'uniformly pleasant', and the aromatherapist, Tina, is strongly recommended. Early morning tea and a newspaper are included in the price. The Eden Project is ten minutes' drive away. (*Michael Kavanagh*)

Open All year.
Rooms 11 suites, 13 double. 8, some on ground floor, in coach house.
Facilities Drawing room, library, billiard/meeting room. 2 restaurants (background music); nursery (supervised 10 am–6 pm), games room. 5-acre grounds: garden: covered heated swimming pool (with ramp), croquet, badminton. Sea 10 mins' walk. Civil wedding licence.
Location Top of town: arriving in Fowey, at mini-roundabout, go straight ahead towards centre, down ravine. Right into Hanson Dr; hotel on right. Parking. Train: Par; bus.
Restrictions No smoking in restaurants. No dogs in public rooms.
Credit cards Amex, MasterCard, Visa.

Terms [2001] B&B: double from £155, suite £205–£270; D,B&B: double £145–£195, suite £175–£310. Set dinner £29.50. Children free in parents' room. Christmas package. 1-night bookings sometimes refused.

FRANT Kent **Map 2:D4**

The Old Parsonage
Church Lane, Frant
nr Tunbridge Wells TN3 9DX

Tel/Fax 01892-750773
Email oldparson@aol.com
Website www.theoldparsonagehotel.co.uk

A 'grand Georgian rectory': it was built for the third son of the local peer, Lord Abergavenny, in the 18th century, and it remained in clerical hands until 1989 when Mary and Tony Dakin took over. They run an 'excellent-value establishment', say *Guide* readers. 'Tony Dakin's outstanding black-and-white photographic portraits line the staircase. Elsewhere are sepia photos of the old village of Frant – a lot of it still mercifully unchanged.' Two sets of oak double doors lead into a grand hall; the spacious bedrooms are up an equally grand staircase. 'Our room, nicely furnished, had views over the Kent Weald. The shower room *en suite* was small (but we had been told of this in advance).' There are antiques throughout the house, a large lounge, and a Victorian conservatory, where tea and drinks are served. Only caveat: 'Heating a little on the sparse side for early October.' A balustraded terrace leads to the walled garden. Breakfast, served at a refectory table in a high-ceilinged room, is continental (ham, cheese and croissants), or English (eggs, bacon, etc, or kedgeree). No evening meal, but two pubs are on the doorstep. Or you could try the *Hotel du Vin & Bistro* at Tunbridge Wells (*qv*), two miles away. Frant is a conservation village on a ridge with extensive views. Its green, surrounded by superb timber-framed and Georgian houses, 'makes a perfect setting for cricket'. Sightseeing within a 15-mile radius includes Hever, Bodiam and Leeds castles, Penshurst Place, Ightham Mote, Bateman's, Chartwell, Sissinghurst. (*Mrs BR Emberson, TG*)

Open All year, except Christmas.
Rooms 4 double. No telephone.
Facilities Drawing room, conservatory; classical background music morning/evening; breakfast room. 2-acre grounds: terrace, lawns, croquet. Lake, trout-fishing 3 miles; reservoir, leisure facilities 5 miles. Unsuitable for ♿.
Location By church in village 300 yds off A267, 2½ miles S of Tunbridge Wells. Train: Tunbridge Wells; bus/taxi.
Restrictions Smoking in conservatory only. No children under 7. Dogs allowed in bedrooms if owners bring a blanket; only guide dogs allowed in public rooms.
Credit cards MasterCard, Visa.
Terms B&B: single £49–£59, double £69–£79. 1-night bookings refused weekends in season.

****

Traveller's tale Hotel in Manchester. Our bedroom was very nice, and we settled down to a pre-dinner nap. A chambermaid came to ask if we wanted our beds turned down. I had to tell her we were already in the beds.

****

GATESHEAD Tyne and Wear — Map 4:B4

Eslington Villa NEW/BUDGET
8 Station Road, Low Fell
Gateshead NE9 6DR

Tel 0191-4876017
Fax 0191-4200667
Email admin@eslingtonvilla.fsnet.co.uk

Nick and Melanie Tulip have for many years run this 19th-century villa as a hotel and restaurant – 'heritage with attitude', they call it. It has been on the *Guide*'s shortlist for some years, but recently a major refurbishment took place, and two enthusiastic reports came: 'It was comfortable, with an appropriate decor. The staff were friendly. The restaurant was excellent. At £60, half board was good value. A pleasant, large, leafy garden.' 'Ask for a room in the new extension. The food has returned to its former high standards with a new head chef (Barry Foster). Starters such as Caesar salad and gravad lax particularly good. Service excellent, even when the restaurant is full with large parties.' Main courses on the *table d'hôte* menu might include salmon with fresh asparagus, chargrilled steak with French fries. Bedroom decor ranges from traditional to contemporary. Background jazz in public rooms at all times. (*Michael Wace, Dr Norman Waterman*)

Open All year. Closed bank holidays.
Rooms 17 double. 3 in annexe.
Facilities Lounge, conservatory, restaurant; background jazz; conference/function facilities. 2-acre garden. Unsuitable for ♿.
Location 2 miles from centre. From A1 to Newcastle, at roundabout between North and South Kingsway take Eastern Ave past Team Valley Trading Est, to Station Rd. Car park.
Restrictions No smoking in some bedrooms. No dogs.
Credit cards All major cards accepted.
Terms [2001] B&B: single £54.50–£65, double £59.50–£75. Set lunch £13, dinner £18.50, alc £35.

GATWICK West Sussex *See SHORTLIST* — Map 2:D4

GILLAN Cornwall — Map 1:E2

Tregildry
Gillan, Manaccan
nr Helston TR12 6HG

Tel 01326-231378
Fax 01326-231561
Email trgildry@globalnet.co.uk
Website www.tregildryhotel.co.uk

César award in 1998

'Its underlying strength is the quality of service.' 'Huw and Lynne Phillips obviously enjoy looking after their guests.' 'They have the knack of making everyone feel special.' 'Their staff back them up superbly.' 'The welcome and the feeling of being well looked after remains in the mind long after the holiday is over.' 'All the words of praise seem to have been used up in previous editions of the *Guide*, but are all well deserved.' Another large batch of plaudits this year for this civilised small hotel. Set above Gillan Creek, it has panoramic views of the Helford river, Falmouth Bay and beyond. A private path leads down to a small stony cove; the coastal path is nearby. Sandy beaches, eg, the National Trust's Poldhu, are reached via winding Cornish lanes. The decor creates a warm Mediterranean ambience: apricot walls, white paintwork; wicker/rattan furniture. Large lounges, divided into separate areas, have sofas, fresh flowers, panoramic views in all directions, glossy magazines, books about local flowers, birds, etc. The bedrooms are bright, well lit; even the small ones have 'wonderful views'. The ground-floor room, entered via the restaurant, is the least liked ('not very private'). Huw Phillips provides 'modern British cooking with French influences' on 'well-balanced menus', eg, filo basket of garlicky mushrooms; grilled trout on hazelnut butter; always a vegetarian dish. The restaurant has well-spaced tables and wide archways, and comments on the food range from 'imaginative' to 'superb'. The short wine list has 'something for everyone'. But one visitor found the piped music 'intrusive'. Breakfast includes freshly squeezed orange juice, 'whisky porridge of just the right consistency, creamy scrambled eggs'; also 'low fat' alternatives. A small selection of sandwiches is available during the day. The hotel, approached along narrow lanes, is ten miles off the main road. 'This lack of instant access contributes to the much-loved tranquillity.' (*Andrew Wiltshire, RW Harvey, Susan Roffe, Shirley Tennent, Michele Brown, Andrew Long; also MJ Dodd, Vincent and Heather Finnamore*)

Open Mar–Oct.
Rooms 9 double, 1 single.
Facilities 2 lounges, bar, restaurant (light classical background music during dinner). 4-acre grounds. Private path to coastal path and cove: bathing, sailing, fishing, windsurfing. Golf nearby. Unsuitable for ♿.
Location 12 miles SE of Helston. Take A3083 towards the Lizard. 1st left for St Keverne; follow signs for Manaccan/Gillan.
Restrictions No smoking: restaurant, 1 lounge, bedrooms. No children under 8. No dogs in public rooms.
Credit cards MasterCard, Visa.
Terms D,B&B £65–£85. Set dinner £24. 3- to 7-night breaks. 1-night bookings sometimes refused.

GITTISHAM Devon — Map 1:C5

Combe House
Gittisham
nr Honiton EX14 3AD

Tel 01404-540400
Fax 01404-46004
Email stay@thishotel.com
Website www.thishotel.com

A Grade I listed Elizabethan manor house (with 19th-century additions), 'set comfortably' in its own parkland. 'It is delightful, with a real country feeling,' says a visitor this year. The 'charming owners', Ruth and Ken Hunt, have been restoring it from a neglected condition. Backed by venerable trees, it stands on a hill at the end of a mile-long drive bordered with camellias and rhododendrons, in a vast Devon estate of woodland, meadows, pastures with Arabian horses. The panelled public rooms, 'large and comfortable', 'not intimidatingly grand', have huge fireplaces with Grinling Gibbons-style carvings, coats of arms, plastered ceilings, ancestral portraits. 'The antique furniture looks meant to be used rather than admired; arrangements of garden flowers are prolific.' There is praise this year (with some caveats – cool bedrooms, slow service at breakfast). The rooms vary (some may still need 'a spruce-up'). A dog-owner enjoyed a rear suite with direct access to the garden: 'It had a nice lived-in feel, a king-size bed, a *chaise longue*, a homely lounge, also with a bed.' Another room was 'a warm haven – sprigged fabric on walls, paint in two shades of yellow, tall shuttered windows'. But another guest complained of a small room overlooking the kitchen and boiler room (her charge was waived). Chef Philip Leach wins praise for his 'marvellous food'. 'My pigeon breast salad and grilled brill were attractively presented and perfectly cooked; my wife's fish starter and roast partridge were just as satisfactory. Service was confident and friendly.' But one visitor would have liked more changes on the menu. Breakfast, served until 10 am, has good thick toast, 'perfectly poached egg with smoked haddock'. There are toys, games and an early supper for children (the Hunts have a boy and a girl). Gittisham is a picture-book village, with thatched cottages with cream and green walls and a Saxon church. Nine golf courses are within easy reach, and the hotel has one and a half miles of fishing on the river Otter. (*Val Hennessy, JW, Andrew Wiltshire, and others*)

Open All year.
Rooms 3 suites, 12 double.
Facilities Great Hall, sitting room, bar (background music on request), restaurant, private dining room. 10-acre garden in 3,500-acre estate. Fishing on river Otter; coast 9 miles. Only restaurant suitable for ♿. Civil wedding licence.
Location 2 miles SW of Honiton. Train: Honiton from London (Waterloo).
Restrictions No smoking: restaurant, 4 bedrooms. 'Well-behaved' dogs in 2 bedrooms, not in restaurant.
Credit cards All major cards accepted.
Terms [2001] B&B £65–£123. Set lunch £12–£16, dinner £29.50. Child in parents' room: under 12, £15. Midweek, seasonal breaks. Christmas, New Year packages. 1-night bookings refused Fri, Sat.

GLEWSTONE Herefordshire — Map 3:D4

Glewstone Court
Glewstone
nr Ross-on-Wye HR9 6AW

Tel 01989-770367
Fax 01989-770282
Email glewstone@aol.com
Website www.smoothhound.co.uk

'Delightfully informal, yet comfortable and efficient,' says a visitor this year to Bill and Christine Reeve-Tucker's hotel/restaurant. It stands in wooded grounds with mature fruit orchards, and a Cedar of Lebanon reputed to be the oldest in the West of England. The owners welcome families with children and dogs – they have dogs and cats of their own. The house is listed (Georgian in origin, with Regency wings), but its decor is homely (log fires, photos, old pictures and an abundance of family clutter). CDs of '20s, '30s and '40s music are often played in the public rooms, but they will be turned off on request. The bedrooms, named after the owners' daughters and nieces (Victoria, Lucy, Clementine, Poppy, etc), are mostly spacious, if sometimes a bit 'frayed around the edges'. They have stencilled walls, floral drapes and a big bed. 'Our room was large and comfortable, with good views and excellent cupboard space, but its bathroom was cramped,' is one comment. The large drawing room/bar has French windows opening on to the garden; informal lunches and dinners are served here, from an extensive menu. The Georgian restaurant (Mrs Reeve-Tucker is chef) serves 'modern English/classic French' meals with lots of choice, eg, spinach and crab roulade with rocket and cress salad; breast of duck stuffed with wild mushrooms, with a Madeira jus; chocolate marquise with strawberries. Sunday lunch is a family occasion (reduced rates for children under ten; no charge for occupants of high chairs). Breakfast, served until 10 am, includes thick granary toast and scrambled eggs with smoked salmon. Conferences and functions are held. The setting is secluded, but the A40 is less than half a mile away. The river Wye (with canoeing and fishing) is near, and there is good walking. Well placed for touring the Brecon Beacons, Hay-on-Wye, the Cotswolds. More reports, please.

Open All year, except 25–27 Dec.
Rooms 7 double, 1 single.
Facilities Hall, drawing room/bar, restaurant; private dining room; conference/function facilities. Background jazz/swing in public rooms. 3-acre grounds: croquet. Only restaurant suitable for ♿.
Location 3 miles SW of Ross-on-Wye. Turn right off A40 Ross–Monmouth (dual carriageway), signposted Glewstone. Hotel ½ mile on left.
Credit cards Amex, MasterCard, Visa.
Terms [2001] B&B: single £45–£75, double £90–£105. Set Sun lunch £14, dinner £26. Child in parents' room: in cot, free, otherwise B&B £15. 2-day breaks, except bank holidays. 1-night bookings sometimes refused. *V* (not Fri, Sat, bank holidays, Cheltenham races)

GLOSSOP Derbyshire — Map 3:A6

The Wind in the Willows
Derbyshire Level
off Sheffield Road
Glossop SK13 7PT

Tel 01457-868001
Fax 01457-853354
Email info@windinthewillows.co.uk
Website www.windinthewillows.co.uk

'Elegant and friendly. We had a peaceful weekend,' wrote a visitor to Ian and Alison Wilkinson's Victorian house. With a willow tree in its garden and bedrooms called after Kenneth Grahame characters, it stands by a nine-hole golf course at the foot of Snake Pass, on the edge of the Peak District National Park. Inspectors liked the 'atmosphere of a smart family home'. There are 'delightful antiques' everywhere; multi-patterned carpets and curtains in the lounge, also flowers, books, glossy magazines, a huge oak dresser stocked with drinks, an open fire. 'Lots of dark wood and excellent lighting in our beautifully furnished bedroom, Toad Hall, and a copy of Thomas Crapper's *Flushed with Pride* in the bathroom.' Another couple found this room airless in summer, and thought the place 'lacked ambience', but 'dinner was beautifully cooked, and portions just right'. The menu, served in a blue and beige dining room, might include red pepper soup; honey-roast duck breast with a port and redcurrant sauce; chocolate and orange cake with chocolate sauce and whipped cream. 'Cooked breakfast exceptionally good, and top marks for freshly squeezed orange juice, but the continental version was sparse.' The bedrooms vary in size; Mr Mole, at the top, is 'cosy'. Old Glossop is mainly 17th-century, with narrow streets and pretty houses; the town centre, and the cotton mills which brought prosperity, were built in the early 19th century. Chatsworth and Haddon Hall are 40 minutes' drive away. More reports, please.

Open All year. Restaurant closed for lunch.
Rooms 12 double.
Facilities Drawing room with dispense bar, study, dining room; conference room. No background music. 1-acre garden, 4 acres fields; fishing lodge. Golf course adjacent; pot-holing, riding, gliding, boating nearby. Unsuitable for ♿.
Location 1 mile E of Glossop. Turn off A57 opposite *Royal Oak* pub. Hotel 400 yds on right. Train: Glossop; then taxi.
Restrictions No smoking: restaurant, study. No children under 10. No dogs.
Credit cards All major cards accepted.
Terms B&B: single £74–£94, double £99–£121. Set dinner £25. *V*

GOLCAR West Yorkshire — Map 4:E3

The Weavers Shed

Knowl Road, Golcar
nr Huddersfield HD7 4AN

Tel 01484-654284
Fax 01484-650980
Email info@weavers-shed.demon.co.uk

'High-quality bedroom and excellent food.' 'One of our favourites. Dinner was terrific. Nice owners and staff.' Two fresh endorsements came this year for this restaurant-with-rooms in a stone-built village south of Huddersfield. The accent is on the modern cooking of chef/*patron* Stephen Jackson and his co-chefs, Ian McGunnigle, Robert Jones and Cath Sill; each is responsible for one course. The garden supplies much of the fruit, herbs and vegetables used in the kitchen. A pamphlet in the bedrooms lists the local suppliers of meat, fish and game. 'Despite the high aspirations, there is a homely Yorkshire feel,' says one visitor. The restaurant, in a former cloth-finishing mill, has a flagstone floor, old beams, and framed menus from famous restaurants on the walls. The cooking, on a 'sensibly short' *carte*, is modern, with first courses like caramelised tomato tart; tortellini of chicken and morel mushrooms, and main dishes such as braised belly of old-breed pork; chargrilled saddle of Worsbrough red deer. To end, you might choose warm Eccles cake, banana tarte Tatin, or cheese. The bedrooms, each named after a local textile mill, are in a substantial house next door. Original features – old fireplaces, moulded ceilings, etc, have been retained. 'Not luxuriously furnished but comfortable, spacious, tasteful, with neutral fabrics, good lighting, lots of storage, big bathroom with quality goodies and bathrobes. Excellent cooked breakfast prepared by a real chef. Amazing value.' Golcar is not particularly attractive, but there is much to see nearby. (*David and Kate Wooff, Michael Williamson, and others*)

Open All year, except 25/26 and 31 Dec. Restaurant closed Sun, Mon.
Rooms 5 double. In adjacent house. 2 on ground floor.

Facilities Lounge/bar, restaurant; jazz/light classical background music; function/conference room. Garden.
Location 3 miles W of Huddersfield. Turn on to B6111 off A62 towards Oldham. They will send detailed directions. Parking.
Restriction No dogs.
Credit cards MasterCard, Visa.
Terms B&B: single £40–£50, double £55–£65. Set lunch £12.95; full alc £29. 2-day breaks.

GRANGE-IN-BORROWDALE Cumbria — Map 4: inset C2

The Borrowdale Gates
Grange-in-Borrowdale
Keswick CA12 5UQ

Tel 017687-77204
Fax 017687-77254
Email hotel@borrowdale-gates.com
Website www.borrowdale-gates.com

'Good food, without being ripped off' and 'unbeatable views of the lake' continue to draw praise for Terry and Christine Parkinson's extended Victorian house. 'It never fails to live up to expectations,' say its most devoted fans. Visitors enjoy the 'warm welcome' (though one or two reported that they had not met the owners) and the 'wonderful setting', in wooded grounds on the edge of a hamlet in the Borrowdale valley, at the head of Derwent Water. With craggy peaks close by, this is a good base for walking and climbing. The public areas have been extensively redecorated, and the result is 'very comfortable, if not very individual', reports a guest, who loved the almost 180-degree view from picture windows in the open-plan restaurant, lounges and bar. There are antiques, books and magazines, plants and flowers; log fires in winter. Michael Heathcote's long menu includes starters like Cumbrian goat's cheese tartlet, or tian of avocado and Icelandic prawns; main courses might be délice of turbot, or chargrilled beef on a potato galette with wilted spinach; then come elaborate puddings. There is a 'splendid selection of home-made breads, and cheeses, local and French'. The most characterful bedrooms are in the main building; others are in a 1970s extension. Many rooms have good views, but one overlooks the car park. A word of advice: 'At busy periods, fix your dinner time when making your reservation.' (*Ran Ogston, John and Margaret Myring, Claire Lavery*)

Open 1 Feb–2 Jan.
Rooms 26 double, 3 single. 10 on ground floor.
Facilities Ramp. 4 lounges, bar, restaurant. No background music. 2-acre grounds. Derwent Water 10 mins' walk: boating, fishing, windsurfing, etc.
Location SW of Keswick. Take B5289; after 4 miles turn right over double hump-back bridge at Grange. Hotel ¼ mile on right. Bus or taxi from Keswick.
Restrictions No smoking in restaurant. No children under 7 in restaurant at night. No dogs.
Credit cards Amex, MasterCard, Visa.
Terms B&B £42.50–£75; D,B&B £50–£95. Set Sun lunch £15.50, dinner £33; full alc £47.80. Child in parents' room: under 3, free; 4–8, £17.50; 9–12, £22.50. Off-season breaks. Christmas, New Year packages. 1-night bookings sometimes refused.

GRASMERE Cumbria — Map 4: inset C2

Michael's Nook
Grasmere LA22 9RP

Tel 015394-35496
Fax 015394-35645
Email m-nook@wordsworth-grasmere.co.uk
Website www.grasmere-hotels.co.uk

'Upon a forest side at Grasmere Vale/there dwelt a shepherd, Michael was his name.' Wordsworth is the inspiration for the name of this hotel 'of character', a substantial Lakeland stone house on the steep slopes of Greenbank Fell. It stands in large, landscaped grounds. The owner, Reg Gifford, a former antiques dealer, has furnished the mahogany-panelled public areas with his collection of furniture, oriental rugs, prints and porcelain (he also keeps Crufts-winning Great Danes). There is a grand piano in the lounge, a spinet in the hall; also splendid flower displays, potted plants 'and the occasional glimpse of an exotic cat'. 'Everything was perfect,' says a visitor in 2001. The *Michelin*-starred dining room has white cornices, deep red walls, a collection of antique tables, and a log fire. Chef Michael Wignall serves modern French-influenced dishes, eg, assiette of foie gras and duckling; turbot with poached morels and asparagus; chocolate and orange fondant. There is a menu of British cheeses. Vegetarians are catered for, given notice. The wide-ranging wine list includes many half bottles. The cooking is 'superb, modish, technically impressive and attractively presented'; 'portions just right'. Breakfast is 'just as good' (freshly squeezed juices, leaf tea, impeccably cooked dishes; also cold meats, cheeses, etc), and the staff 'go out of their way to comply with guests' requirements'. A mahogany staircase leads up to bedrooms of varying sizes, furnished in elegant country house style, and with a modern bathroom. Some have a balcony; one suite has a private patio. Good walks start from the door; guests may use the health facilities and swimming pool at the sister hotel, the *Wordsworth*, down the hill; and there is free golf at a local championship course. Wordsworth's house, Dove Cottage, and Beatrix Potter's home at Near Sawrey are close by. (*DW, PMR d'Adhémar de Labaume, and others*)

Open All year.
Rooms 2 suites, 12 double.
Facilities Hall, drawing room, bar, 2 dining rooms; conference room. No background music. 3-acre garden adjoining 10-acre woodland: croquet. Access to leisure facilities at the *Wordsworth* nearby. Free river/lake fishing nearby. Unsuitable for ♿. Civil wedding licence.
Location Turn up between *Swan* hotel and its car park on A591 just N of village. Hotel 400 yds on right. Train/bus: Windermere; bus/taxi.
Restrictions No smoking in restaurant. Children by arrangement. No dogs.
Credit cards All major cards accepted.
Terms D,B&B £90–£205. Set lunch £37.50, dinner £48. Midweek, weekend breaks off-season. Christmas, New Year house parties. 1-night bookings refused Sat, bank holidays. *V*

Most hotels have reduced rates out of season and offer 'mini-break' rates throughout the year. It is always worth asking about special terms.

White Moss House *Tel* 015394-35295
Rydal Water, Grasmere LA22 9SE *Fax* 015394-35516
Email sue@whitemoss.com
Website www.whitemoss.com

Peter and Sue Dixon run this grey-stoned creeper-covered house (once bought by William Wordsworth for his son, Willie) as a restaurant-with-rooms. It is set in classic Wordsworth country, with excellent walking all around; the poet's two homes, Dove Cottage and Rydal Mount, are within a mile. Mr Dixon and co-chef Robert Simpson serve a fixed-price, five-course dinner at 7.30 for 8 pm (except Sundays) with no choice until dessert. They are admired for their 'unshowy interpretation of English country house cooking', eg, baby fennel, apple and almond soup; bombe of brill with a centre of British brie wrapped with smoked salmon, chervil sauce; fillet of Angus beef marinated with real ale; cabinet pudding with fluffy lemon sauce, or chocolate hazelnut cream slice. British cheeses with home-baked oat biscuits round off the meal. The wine cellar has a choice of over 300 bins, and plenty of wines are available by the glass. After dinner, guests take coffee in a small lounge. The house looks to Rydal Water across the A591, but windows are double-glazed, and there is little traffic at night. The most peaceful bedrooms are in the cottage up the hill, which is let as a unit. In the main house, bedrooms are small, with a tiny bathroom; they are packed with extras, including herbal bath-salts, fresh flowers, books, magazines, a sewing kit, trouser press, etc. Breakfast continues the English theme, with kippers, Cumberland sausage, etc. A popular venue for private house parties, birthdays, reunions and other celebrations. More reports, please.

Open Feb–end Nov. Closed Christmas, New Year. Restaurant closed midday, Sun night.
Rooms 7 double, 2-room cottage on hillside (10 mins' drive or footpath).
Facilities 2 lounges, restaurant; terrace. 1-acre garden. Near Rydal Water, river Rothay: swimming, fishing, boating. Free use of nearby leisure club. Unsuitable for ♿.
Location 1 mile S of Grasmere on A591 (heavy lorries banned; double glazing; cottage rooms quietest). Train: Windermere, 8 miles; bus to door.
Restrictions No smoking in restaurant. No small children in restaurant. Dogs in cottage only.
Credit cards MasterCard, Visa.
Terms [2001] D,B&B £50–£92. Set dinner £30. Off-season breaks. 1-night bookings occasionally refused.

GRASSINGTON North Yorkshire Map 4:D3

Ashfield House BUDGET *Tel/Fax* 01756-752584
Summers Fold *Email* info@ashfieldhouse.co.uk
Grassington *Website* www.ashfieldhouse.co.uk
nr Skipton BD23 5AE

When I arrived on a wet Yorkshire afternoon, it was a real delight to walk into the warm sitting room with a good fire,' says a visitor this year to Linda and Keith Harrison's 17th-century guest house. It stands up a little cobbled drive a few yards from Grassington's main square.

'The owners' gentle, unassuming and friendly stamp is everywhere.' 'They put the comfort of their guests first.' Colourful flower baskets hang around the front door in summer. The decor is simple: bare stone walls, beams, old oak and pine furniture, log fires, modern fabrics. The bedrooms are small ('but the excellent housekeeping more than compensates'); most have an efficient (if small) shower room *en suite;* one has a private bathroom adjacent. The home-cooked dinner (no choice of main course) is served punctually at 7 pm at separate tables. 'Meals are straightforward; the food is fresh, and beautifully cooked'. eg, roast onion salad with shavings of Parmesan; seafood bake with puff pastry topping; orange and cardamom jelly, or cheese. Some ingredients are home-produced. The wines 'are brilliant value'. The walled garden is a peaceful refuge when the village is crowded with day-trippers. Rupert, the resident cat, presides. 'Good for walkers, drivers, cyclists and lovers of Yorkshire comfort.' (*HJM Tucker, John and Margaret Myring, and others*)

Open New Year, end Jan–end Nov. Restaurant closed midday. Sat, also Wed in season.
Rooms 7 double. No telephone (pay-phone available).
Facilities 2 lounges (1 with honesty bar), dining room; drying room. No background music. ¼-acre garden. River, fishing ¼ mile. Unsuitable for ♿.
Location 50 yds off village square: turn left into Summers Fold when coming *up* main street. Parking. Train/bus: Skipton, via Leeds; bus.
Restrictions No smoking. No children under 5. Guide dogs only.
Credit cards MasterCard, Visa.
Terms B&B £32–£55. Set dinner £17. Child in parents' room: 50% of adult rate. Seasonal breaks. Dickensian festivities in Dec. 1-night bookings sometimes refused.

GREAT DUNMOW Essex — Map 2:C4

The Starr
Market Place
Great Dunmow CM6 1AX

Tel 01371-874321
Fax 01371-876337
Email starrrestaurant@btinternet.com
Website www.zynet.co.uk/menu/starr

A handsome old building, green-walled, with black-framed windows, facing the marketplace of an Essex village. It has been run for years as a restaurant-with-rooms by Brian and Vanessa Jones. Mark Fisher serves a 'modern menu with a French accent' – it changes daily – in the beamed dining room, which has uneven floors, small windows and a bright conservatory extension. Seafood is a speciality, eg, sautée of fresh scallops and king prawns; poached fillet of brill in red wine with roast shallots. But there are more robust choices, too, such as lamb's sweetbread fritters on red onion marmalade; pink duck breast on rosemary jus with leek mousse. The bedrooms, in a courtyard stable block, are well supplied with local information, books, magazines, mineral water, etc. Some have antique or period furniture and a bed with a brass or wooden board; the Oak Room has a four-poster with a free-standing Victorian bath at its foot, as well as a separate shower room. One visitor found the Blue Room 'very small' and over-priced. But another praised 'the outstanding service and attention to detail'. There is some noise from passing traffic. Breakfast is good. Easton Lodge, with beautiful gardens, is close by. Stansted airport is 15 minutes' drive away. More reports, please.

Open All year, except 1st week Jan.
Rooms 8 double, all in rear courtyard.
Facilities Reception/bar, restaurant, conservatory; function/conference facilities. No background music. Unsuitable for ♿.
Location Central (some traffic noise). Courtyard parking. Train: Bishop's Stortford, 8 miles, Stansted airport, 15 miles; then taxi.
Restrictions No smoking: restaurant, bedrooms. No dogs in public rooms.
Credit cards All major cards accepted.
Terms B&B: single £65, double £105. Set lunch £16.50–£25, dinner £24–£35. Weekend rate for diners. *V*

GREAT MILTON Oxfordshire — Map 2:C3

Le Manoir aux Quat'Saisons
Church Road
Great Milton OX44 7PD

Tel 01844-278881
Fax 01844-278847
Email lemanoir@blanc.co.uk
Website www.manoir.co.uk

César award in 1985

'The attention to detail is relentless, the food remarkable, but the staff's ability to get the atmosphere exactly right is the most impressive feature here.' 'Wonderful. Service of the highest level. Breakfast was fabulous.' Some of this year's comments on Raymond Blanc's famous *domaine* (Relais & Châteaux) in a village near Oxford (the manager is Philip Newman-Hall). 'It takes a Frenchman to bring out the best in an English country house hotel,' said another experienced traveller. 'Visitors are welcomed in the car park, by a porter who phones reception. There you are greeted by name, and shown around by an enthusiastic receptionist.' 'The gardens have matured beautifully, with sleeping ducks by the pond and a fabulous kitchen garden'. This provides fresh produce for M. Blanc's *Michelin* two-star conservatory-style restaurant, renowned for such sophisticated dishes as watercress salad with pan-fried duck foie gras; roast wild partridge with black pudding; Calvados soufflé baked in an apple. There is a seasonally changing *à la carte* menu, a four-course lunchtime *menu du jour*, and a seven-course *menu gourmand* ('the dishes are balanced but the cumulative effect can be rich') at night. Vegetarians are catered for, and the young have their own appetising menu: 'We don't just tolerate children, we welcome them,' is the *Manoir*'s philosophy. Toys and garden games are provided. Emily Todhunter has decorated the bedrooms in 'cutting-edge modern' style. Opium, with saffron and red silk and warm lighting, looks over a Zen garden. Mermaid Rose has a 'very romantic' bathroom, reached by spiral stairs, with side-by-side bathtubs. Other rooms are more traditional. Prices – and expectations – are high, and some visitors had minor reservations (some feel the amount of outside business leads to an 'impersonal feel'), but most wrote of 'the highest quality'. (*David Wooff, Sarah Randolph, and others*)

Open All year.
Rooms 13 suites, 19 double. 23 in garden buildings. Some on ground floor.

Facilities 2 lounges, champagne bar (background music), restaurant; function room; cookery school. 27-acre grounds: gardens, croquet, tennis, lake, fishing. Civil wedding licence.
Location 8 miles SE of Oxford. From London: M40 exit 7, from Birmingham exit 8a; left on to A329 towards Wallingford; 2nd right to Great Milton. From Oxford: A40 exit for Thame; right on to A329 towards Wallingford, 2nd right. Train: Oxford; taxi; limousine service from London, Gatwick, Heathrow.
Restrictions No smoking in restaurant; no dogs in house (free kennels).
Credit cards All major cards accepted.
Terms B&B: single/double £245–£395, suite £395–£750. Cooked breakfast £6 supplement. Set lunch £45, dinner £89; full alc £100. Midweek breaks, residential cookery courses. Christmas package. 1-night bookings refused Sat May–Aug.

GREAT SNORING Norfolk — Map 2:A5

The Manor House
Barsham Road
Great Snoring
Fakenham NR21 0HP

Tel 01328-820597
Fax 01328-820048
Email gtsnoringmanorho@cs.com
Website www.norfolkcountryhouse.co.uk

The name has changed (it was formerly *The Old Rectory*), and Rosamund and William Scoles are now in sole charge of this fascinating old building where they offer 'country house accommodation'. It stands in a large walled garden with old trees (a large beech is floodlit at night). Tudor in origin, with Victorian additions, it has two hexagonal towers and a terracotta frieze with alternating male and female carved heads, possible portraits of the Shelton family who built it. Inside are polished floor tiles, lots of dark wooden furniture, and flowers, and oriental carpets and rich red flowered wallpaper in the large lounge. The bedrooms vary in size: some are quite small; others are spacious. They are comfortable rather than luxurious, but all have bath, telephone and TV; early morning tea is brought to the room. Guests now have the use of a 'butler's pantry' for tea-making, and a shower room has been made on the first floor. Dinner is served in a room with mullioned windows, heavy beams, and oak tables set with good silver, plate and glass. No written menu and no choice of main course – cooking is traditional English (eg, smoked goose breast, or baked banana with Stilton fondue; salmi of pheasant; dark chocolate and cherry pudding, or hot lemon pudding). The house is often used for group bookings. A good base for visiting the Heritage Coast, Sandringham and Holkham Hall. More reports, please.

Open All year, except 24–27 Dec. Dining room closed midday.
Rooms 6 double.
Facilities Drawing room, dining room. No background music. 1½-acre walled garden. Golf nearby. Unsuitable for ♿.
Location Behind church on road to Barsham, in village off A148, 3 miles NE of Fakenham. Train: King's Lynn, 23 miles.
Restrictions No smoking in dining room. Children by arrangement. No dogs.
Credit cards Amex, MasterCard, Visa.
Terms B&B: single £78–£85, double £97–£105. Set dinner from £25.

GRIMSTHORPE Lincolnshire — Map 2:A3

Black Horse Inn NEW
Grimsthorpe, nr Bourne
PE10 0LY

Tel 01778-591247
Fax 01778-591373
Email dine@blackhorseinn.co.uk

An old coaching inn, built in 1717: the owner/chef Brian Rey, and his wife, Elaine, have recently redecorated the eating areas. 'The bedrooms need a facelift, which no doubt they will get in due course,' says an inspection report. 'But much thoughtfulness has gone into them. Our room was cluttered, and everything seemed to be decorated with roses, but the fridge contained fresh milk, cheese, water. Corridors are narrow, with patterned carpeting and dark paint: small windows, mirrors, and wall lights permanently on keep them from being gloomy. The bar is light and attractive. Of the two dining rooms, one is charmingly furnished in yellow and blue; the other has original stone walls, beams, open fireplaces. They have wooden tables and chairs, parquet floors, tapestries on metal curtain poles, sumptuous drapes over the windows (advertising fabrics from a local warehouse). Our meal was thoroughly enjoyable: the restaurant menu was ambitious, the bar menu only slightly less so; the cooking was competent. We had foie gras and chicken liver parfait with red onion jam, and risotto of shellfish and cockles; timbale of honey-glazed duck breast, and sea bream with sautéed scallops. The duck was pink, the bream moist and delicious. Every dish was beautifully presented; portions were generous. The wine list was thoughtfully designed, showing wines first by the glass, then by type. Breakfast, equally good, was again served by the hostess. Generous portions, including two eggs each, good sausages, proper toast, butter and marmalade.' A *Good Pub Guide* Lincolnshire dining pub of the year in 2000.

Open All year. Restaurant closed Sun night/Mon (bar meals available).
Rooms 1 suite, 5 double.
Facilities Lounge, bar, 2 dining rooms. 1-acre garden. Unsuitable for ♿.
Location NW of Peterborough; 4 miles NW of Bourne.
Restrictions No smoking in restaurant. No dogs.
Credit cards All major cards accepted.
Terms B&B: single £50, double £69, suite £95. Full alc: bar £20, restaurant £28. Christmas package.

GRIMSTON Norfolk — Map 2:A5

Congham Hall
Lynn Road
Grimston, King's Lynn PE32 1AH

Tel 01485-600250
Fax 01485-601191
Email reception@conghamhallhotel.com
Website www.conghamhallhotel.co.uk

'Wonderful in every way. Manager Andrew Chantrell and the staff are especially friendly. They treat you as one of the family, asking how you slept, if you had a good day. They meet you with an umbrella if it is raining.' Praise again this year from most visitors to this handsome Georgian house (Pride of Britain), on an unspoilt estate near King's Lynn. It stands in manicured grounds, with a flower-filled front garden, a large herb garden, and a cricket pitch. The hotel is flourishing under the ownership of Von Essen Hotels (see also *Ston Easton Park*, Ston Easton, and *The Mount Somerset*, Lower Henlade). 'The garden suite could not be bettered as regards space, decor, and attention to detail,' says another report. 'From the conservatory restaurant, we watched wildlife – barn owls, pheasants, squirrels, rabbits – and a sinking sun.' 'The food is excellent, and if you stay several days, they ask if they can provide anything special.' The chef, James Parkinson, who has worked with Gordon Ramsay, serves modern dishes, eg, boudin of pheasant with a leek risotto; medallions of monkfish wrapped in Parma ham with coriander noodles and a velouté of ginger; pineapple tarte Tatin with coconut ice cream and a passion fruit coulis. 'Breakfast was excellent, too: delicious fruit compote, granary bread, home-made marmalade.' The spacious public rooms have flowers, herb baskets, modern nude bronzes. A white-painted 'serpent' staircase leads to chintzy bedrooms, stocked with flowers, potpourri, books, etc. 'Our spacious, comfortable room was prettily decorated, and had a lovely view of a field where horses grazed' (but some rooms are small). Conferences and weddings are catered for. Nearby attractions: Sandringham, Houghton Hall, the RSPB reserve at Titchwell. (*Sally Burt*, *AB*)

Open All year.
Rooms 2 suites (1 on ground floor), 11 double, 1 single.
Facilities Lounge, bar, restaurant; conference room. No background music. 30-acre grounds: herb garden, unheated swimming pool, orchards, stables, cricket pitch. Coast 12 miles. Unsuitable for ♿. Civil wedding licence.
Location 6 miles NE of King's Lynn. Right towards Grimston off A148; hotel 2½ miles on left. Do *not* go to Congham. Train: King's Lynn; taxi.
Restrictions No smoking: restaurant, bedrooms. No children under 7 at dinner. No dogs in house (kennels available).
Credit cards All major cards accepted.
Terms B&B: single £85, double £130–£175, suite £205–£230; D,B&B £95–£145 per person. Set lunch £15.50, dinner £34. Special breaks. Christmas package. 1-night bookings occasionally refused Sat. *V*

GUILDFORD Surrey *See SHORTLIST* **Map 2:D3**

GULWORTHY Devon **Map 1:D3**

The Horn of Plenty *Tel/Fax* 01822-832528
Gulworthy *Email* enquiries@thehornofplenty.co.uk
nr Tavistock PL19 8JD *Website* www.thehornofplenty.co.uk

Michelin-*starred restaurant-with-rooms 3 miles W of Tavistock. In wisteria-covered stone Georgian house, up long drive through 4½-acre grounds with garden, orchards, stunning views of Tamar valley. Chef Peter Gorton is co-owner with Paul and Andie Roston (they also own the* Carved Angel *restaurant, Dartmouth). 'Some of the best cooking in the West Country' (eg, grilled sea bass with asparagus, tomato confit and prawn sauce; fillet of beef topped with a roasted garlic and parsley soufflé); 'exceptionally helpful' staff. Drawing room, lounge, library; light background music throughout. Civil wedding licence.*

10 bedrooms; 6 spacious ones, with balcony, small bathroom, are in stable block; 4 are on ground floor. Closed Christmas; restaurant closed Mon midday. Smoking in drawing room only. No children under 10 at dinner. No dogs in public rooms. Amex, MasterCard, Visa accepted. B&B: single £95–£190, double £120–£200. Set lunch £18.50, dinner £40; full alc £55. More reports, please.

HALIFAX West Yorkshire **Map 4:D3**

Holdsworth House
Holdsworth
Halifax HX2 9TG

Tel 01422-240024
Fax 01422-245174
Email info@holdsworthhouse.co.uk
Website www.holdsworthhouse.co.uk

The Pearson family have owned this 17th-century manor house for over 30 years. Sisters Kim Pearson and Gail Moss are now in charge, with manager Peter Phillips. A trusted *Guide* correspondent found lots to admire: 'A truly magnificent house. Public rooms and bedrooms full of character and arranged with exquisite taste. The atmosphere is unique. The decor cannot be faulted, and maintenance is good. A delicious meal.' The outlook from the sides and back is uninspiring, however, due to the location north of the city centre. Old buildings frame an attractive courtyard. Inside, panelling, mullioned windows, oil paintings, log fires and oak furniture 'make you feel that you have stepped into a Dutch painting'. The lounge/bar, in a converted stable, is 'light, smart, immensely pleasant to sit in'. The restaurant is formal with candlelight, fresh flowers, sparkling glass and silverware, impeccable napery. Chef Neal Birtwell serves a mixture of modern and traditional dishes, eg, wild mushroom risotto; fried calf's liver with garlic-crushed potato, and he will produce a simple grill on request. Desserts include orange and Grand Marnier soufflé; cappuccino brûlé. One visitor, while admiring the food and the friendliness, found meal service a bit disjointed: 'Because of a big function in another room, staff kept disappearing.' The bedrooms, in a well-crafted modern wing, vary greatly in size (some may be a bit small). Superior rooms have a brass or a four-poster bed. Good modern bathrooms. Children are welcomed. The gardens have been landscaped to a 17th-century design; a Grade II listed Jacobean gazebo can be hired for small functions. During the week, the clientele is mainly business-oriented, but weekend breaks are good value. Nearby attractions: the Eureka Children's Museum, Halifax, the Brontë parsonage, Haworth, the David Hockney art gallery, Saltaire. (*FW, MW*)

Open All year, except Christmas. Restaurant closed Sat and Sun midday.
Rooms 5 suites, 23 double, 12 single. 2 adapted for ♿.
Facilities Lounge/bar, restaurant (jazz/classical background music); 4 private dining rooms, function room. 4-acre garden: gazebo. Golf nearby. Civil wedding licence.
Location 2½ miles N of centre. Take A629 Keighley road. Right after 1½ miles on to Shay La. Hotel 1 mile on right. Train: Halifax, 5 miles, Leeds, 13 miles; taxi.
Restrictions No smoking: restaurant, some bedrooms. No dogs in public rooms.

Credit cards All major cards accepted.
Terms B&B: single £87, double £107, suite £138; D,B&B: single £92.50, double £125, suite £152. English breakfast £8.25. Set lunch £10; full alc £32.75.

HALNAKER West Sussex — Map 2:E3

The Old Store BUDGET
Stane Street, Halnaker
nr Chichester PO18 0QL

Tel/Fax 01243-531977
Email alandavis@theoldstore.fsnet.co.uk

'Perfect for exploring this area of the South Downs; I have been in hotels costing three or four times as much that were not as good,' says a visitor this year to Alan and Iris Davis's modest and welcoming B&B. The red brick 18th-century Grade II listed house was once the village store and bakery of the adjacent Goodwood estate. One bedroom is suitable for a family. All rooms have a lavatory and shower *en suite* ('the wooden loo seat rather than the usual plastic' was much appreciated by one guest). One couple enjoyed the view from their room across fields to Chichester cathedral. Another visitor had the single, 'very clean and in good order; it was on the road, but windows were double-glazed'. The 'excellent breakfast' includes free-range eggs cooked in many ways, locally made sausages, home-made marmalade, but one visitor complained of a lack of wholemeal toast. Plenty of interesting sightseeing: Arundel, Petworth, Fishbourne Roman palace, etc. (*Simon Small, and others*)

Open All year, except possibly during holiday Jan–mid-Feb.
Rooms 6 double, 1 single. 1 on ground floor. No telephone.
Facilities Lounge, breakfast room. ¼-acre garden. Unsuitable for ♿.
Location 4 miles NE of Chichester, on A285 to Petworth. Bus from Chichester.
Restrictions No smoking. No dogs.
Credit cards MasterCard, Visa.
Terms [2001] B&B: single £25–£28, double £50–£55. Child in parents' room: under 5, free; 5–12, 50% of adult rate. 1-night bookings sometimes refused.

HAMBLETON Rutland — Map 2:B3

Hambleton Hall
Hambleton
Oakham LE15 8TH

Tel 01572-756991
Fax 01572-724721
Email hotel@hambletonhall.com
Website www.hambletonhall.com

César award in 1985

Tim and Stefa Hart have presided over their immaculately presented Victorian pile since 1979, and their 'benign and alert' stewardship has earned a reference in the *Guide* ever since. Perhaps this is because of an attitude to staff and guests expressed in their literature: 'We have no intention of being taken in by all the kind words that have been written about us; we know that every day is a new day, in which we have to recreate the magic.' Visitors praise the 'impeccable service', and the 'glorious setting' on a peninsula in Rutland Water, the largest man-made lake in northern Europe, with fishing, sailing and water sports. The swimming pool and terrace, where breakfast or drinks may be taken in fine weather, 'are perfectly placed from which to enjoy the views'. The decor is sophisticated: fine fabrics, good antiques and paintings, flowers everywhere. The *Michelin*-starred cooking of Aaron Patterson is appreciated too ('fish is a particularly strong suit'). Dinner was the best ever. Poached tails of langoustines with chilled essence of tomato made a perfect start – each flavour separate, intense, perfectly balanced. Then, roasted fillet of sea bass with basil-flavoured pasta and a fennel and vanilla sauce – heaven! Caramelised lemon tart with compote of blackberries gave a wonderfully fresh finish. The wine waiter recommended a different glass of wine with each course – an excellent idea. The set lunch was equally impressive and tremendous value.' 'Every possible luxury' is supplied in the bedrooms. The best ones overlook Rutland Water ('even the loo has a view'); some, particularly one called Chota (Urdu for 'small'), are not large. The Croquet Pavilion suite guarantees extra seclusion, and would be good for a family – children are welcomed. Some famous stately homes – Burghley, Belton, Boughton and Belvoir – are nearby; so is the superb garden of the late Geoff Hamilton at Barnsdale. Tim Hart also owns a restaurant, *Hart's*, in Nottingham. (*SD, AB, and others*)

Open All year.
Rooms 1 2-bedroomed suite, with kitchenette, in pavilion (40 metres), 15 double.
Facilities Lift, ramp. Hall, drawing room, bar, restaurant; small conference facilities, 2 private dining rooms. No background music. 17-acre grounds: swimming pool, tennis, cycling; helipad; lake: trout fishing, windsurfing, sailing. Riding, shooting by arrangement. Civil wedding licence.
Location 3 miles E of Oakham. Follow Hambleton sign off A606 to Stamford. Train: Peterborough/Kettering/Oakham (branch line); taxi.
Restrictions No smoking: restaurant, 1 bedroom. 'Children in the restaurant must be old enough to sit on a proper chair and stay there.' No dogs in public rooms, or unattended in bedrooms.
Credit cards MasterCard, Visa.
Terms B&B: single £150–£175, double £200–£335, suite £450–£600. English breakfast £12. Set lunch £16.50, dinner £35; full alc £55. Winter rates. Christmas package. 1-night bookings sometimes refused Sat.

HAMSTERLEY FOREST Co. Durham — Map 4:C3

Grove House BUDGET
Hamsterley Forest
nr Bishop Auckland DL13 3NL

Tel 01388-488203
Fax 01388-488174
Email xov47@dial.pipex.com
Website www.come.to/grovehouse

Surrounded by beautifully kept gardens, Helene Close's unusual guest house stands in a valley with two small rivers on either side; beyond are 5,000 acres of mixed woodland and moorland. The house is full of treasures: the remarkable backplate of the dining room fire, brought from France by the original owners, was once in a royal palace of the Valois; much of the furniture, including Art Deco chairs, 1920s lamp fittings, etc, was brought from Germany by Mrs Close's grandfather, escaping in 1939. 'A place of unusual delights,' said a visitor who enjoyed its 'away-from-it-allness', deep in a green forest. The accommodation is in one wing of a grandiose shooting lodge, built about 1820 by a member of the Surtees family. The bedrooms are 'large, stylish, comfortable and home-like, with such generous touches as lotions and potions in big bottles in the bathroom, rather than teeny packages'. The lounge is 'very comfy', with an open fire, TV, stereo, family mementos. Dinner is served at flexible times in a 'splendidly eccentric' room hung with portraits. 'The five-course evening meal (no choice) was delicious: mushrooms picked that morning in the forest, and sautéed; duck with a blackcurrant coulis; a delectable sweet of baked bananas with a caramel sauce, lemon ice and pancake; a selection of local cheeses (£2.50 extra). Not hotel food at all, but sympathetic home-entertaining cooking.' No licence; bring your own wine. At breakfast 'the sideboard is weighed down with fruit, cereals, etc, and there is a wide range of cooked dishes to follow'. Good walking; mountain bikes can be borrowed. The former gardener's cottage is let on a self-catering basis. Barnard Castle is 20 minutes' drive away; Durham is half an hour. (*HR, Dr AB, and others*)

Open All year. Dining room closed for lunch (packed lunch available).
Rooms 3 double. No telephone/TV. 1 self-catering cottage.
Facilities 2 lounges, dining room. No background music. 1½-acre grounds. Unsuitable for ♿.
Location From A68 turn W to Hamsterley village (ignore signs for Hamsterley Forest). Through village, continue for 2 miles to sign for 'The Grove'; follow road to right, then left; after ½ mile, turn right at *Grove House* sign. Continue *c.* 2½ miles. House is across old stone bridge.
Restrictions No smoking. No children under 8. No dogs. No drinks licence.
Credit cards None accepted.
Terms B&B £26.50–£36.50. Set dinner £22.50. Child in parents' room: B&B £18. Weekly rates.

HARROGATE North Yorkshire — Map 4:D4

Ascot House
53 Kings Road
Harrogate HG1 5HJ

Tel 01423-531005
Fax 01423-503523
Email admin@ascothouse.com
Website www.ascothouse.com

'Modest and friendly comfort' is offered in owner/manager Stephen Johnson's small hotel in a Victorian house. It is in a street of small hotels, a short walk away from the spa town's conference and exhibition centre. The decor is traditional; there is an open fire in the formal little sitting room; the restaurant has chandeliers and a moulded ceiling. The bar is getting a new carpet, possibly because the existing red floral one offended a visiting writer. The bedrooms are small but 'properly thought out', with a good bathroom. 'In the distinctly elegant dining room we had good, genuine food, including an excellent breakfast, with helpful service. Highly recommended,' says a visitor. The set-price menus, with choice, are traditional too, eg, peppered smoked mackerel; fried sirloin steak with a shallot and bacon cream sauce. The *carte* is more adventurous (dishes like deep-fried baby camembert with a red onion marmalade; salmon with a pesto crust with provençale roasted vegetables). Cots, high chairs and toys are provided for young children. Small conferences are held, 'but they are not obtrusive'. *Fawlty Towers* nights are held, with professional actors playing the leading roles: 'Normally, nothing lands on the floor, unless Manuel tries helping to clear away,' writes Mr Johnson. (*RO, and others*)

Open All year, except New Year, 27 Jan–10 Feb. Lunch not served.
Rooms 15 double, 4 single.
Facilities Lounge, bar lounge (soft taped music), restaurant; banqueting room. Small garden. Unsuitable for ♿. Civil wedding licence.
Location Central (side and back rooms quietest). Follow signs for centre/conference centre. In Kings Rd, pass exhibition centre; *Ascot House* on left, immediately after open park area up hill. Car park.
Restriction No dogs in public rooms.
Credit cards All major cards accepted.
Terms B&B: single £52–£63, double £78–£98; D,B&B (min. 2 nights): single £65–£78, double £102–£128. Set dinner £15.95; full alc £23. Child in parents' room: under 14, B&B £5. Stay 6 nights, get B&B free on the 7th. Christmas package. 1-night bookings occasionally refused.

Cutlers on the Stray NEW/BUDGET
19 West Park
Harrogate HG1 1BL
Tel 01423-524471
Fax 01423-506728
Website www.cutlers-brasserie.com

An old coaching inn which looks across a road to Harrogate's famous green-belt Stray. It has been converted by the director/chef Rick Hodgson to a brasserie with bedrooms. Guests sit on white chairs at wood-topped tables to consume dishes like smoked duck and orange salad; grilled scallops with hollandaise sauce; dark chocolate tart with white chocolate sauce. Many items can be ordered in 'starter' or 'main' portions; children have their own menu. In the bar, residents and locals can drink wine, beer or tea. The bedrooms (six of them look over the Stray) have been refurbished and supplied with fancy toiletries, a CD-player and a laptop link. 'Their decor contrasts dramatically with the exterior,' says a report this year. 'Our room was very Mediterranean, in bright yellows and oranges, with a pristine black-and-white tiled bathroom. The breakfast was superb, with everything from fresh pastries to eggs Benedict.' Other visitors liked the 'informal, yet stylish atmosphere', the good food and the 'unfailingly helpful' staff. (*Martin Hodgson, Paul and Gillian Stephens, David Rolfe; also Jennie Austen*)

Open All year.
Rooms 1 suite, 18 double. 1 designed for ♿.
Facilities Reception lounge, bar, brasserie; background music all day.
Location Across road from the Stray, 5 mins' walk from centre. Limited parking.
Restriction No smoking in some bedrooms. Guide dogs only.
Credit cards Amex, MasterCard, Visa.
Terms B&B: double £60–£95, suite £95–£125. Full alc £22. Christmas package. *V*

See also SHORTLIST

HARTEST Suffolk **Map 2:C5**

The Hatch BUDGET *Tel/Fax* 01284-830226
Pilgrims Lane, Cross Green
Hartest IP29 4ED

'A very pretty B&B in a peaceful rural location.' Enthusiasm from Belgian visitors this year for this 15th-century timber-framed and thatched cottage on what was once the Pilgrims' Way to Bury St Edmunds – it is now a dead-end lane. It stands in a 'lovely garden', filled with old English roses, by a large paddock populated by 'splendid grazing horses'. 'Most of all we enjoyed the warm hospitality. We relaxed (with nice tea and cake) in a charming sitting room and slept in a lovely bedroom. The house is tastefully furnished with antiques.' The owners, Bridget and Robin Oaten, run it with 'care and attention to detail'. Both the dining room and drawing room have an inglenook fireplace, and views of 'idyllic Suffolk countryside'. The bedrooms have goose-down duvets, linen sheets, fresh flowers, a decanter of sherry, fruit, sweets, quality toiletries. 'Old beams add to the ambience; tall people should mind their head.' The suite has its own entrance off the drive. Breakfast includes home-baked scones, chocolate muffins, and a daily-changing selection of fresh fruit and compotes. In winter, Bridget Oaten occasionally prepares an evening meal by arrangement, particularly for regular clients and *Guide* readers. She describes her cooking as 'English with French and North American influences'. There is a good pub, *The Crown*, on the village green, and plenty of restaurants are within 15 minutes' drive. Bury St Edmunds is seven miles away; Ickworth (National Trust) and Melford Hall, a turreted Tudor mansion, are also within striking distance. (*Sandra and Evert Beyers, JDC*)

Open All year, except Christmas, occasional closures; dinner sometimes served Oct–Mar.
Rooms 1 suite (on ground floor), 1 double, 1 single. Telephone in suite.
Facilities Drawing room, dining room. No background music. 1-acre garden and meadows. Unsuitable for ♿.
Location From Bury St Edmunds: A143 S towards Haverhill; left on B1066; left after 6 miles, after Hartest sign, at cluster of cottages on corner; house is 1st down lane, on right.
Restrictions No smoking. No children under 9, except babies. Dogs in suite only; not in public rooms.
Credit cards None accepted.
Terms (*Not VAT-rated*) B&B: single £35–£45, double/suite £60–£70. Set dinner £12.50–£25. Weekly rates. 1-night bookings occasionally refused.

The 'Budget' label by a hotel's name indicates an establishment where dinner, bed and breakfast cost around £50 per person, or B&B about £30 and an evening meal about £20. These are only a rough guide, and do not always apply to single accommodation, nor do they necessarily apply in high season.

HARTFIELD East Sussex — Map 2:E4

Bolebroke Mill *Tel/Fax* 01892-770425
Perry Hill, Edenbridge Road *Email* bolebrokemill@btinternet.com
Hartfield TN7 4JP *Website* www.bolebrokemillhotel.co.uk

'Very quaint,' says a visitor this year to David Cooper's B&B, a skilfully converted Domesday-old watermill, with an Elizabethan barn and mill house. It was used as a location for the 1995 film *Carrington* (starring Emma Thompson and Jonathan Pryce). It is 'an idyllic spot', set well back from a busy road up a winding track. A tree-lined stream, with ducks and geese, flows under the mill towards the Ashdown Forest; its 'new' building (17th-century) continued to grind corn until 1948. Each of the five bedrooms is different, 'furnished with cottagey charm, with dried flower arrangements and rustic beams'. They all have facilities *en suite,* TV, a coolbox with fresh milk for early morning tea. Three rooms, including the Honeymooners' Hayloft with its four-poster bed, are in a barn. Two are up 'seriously steep' loft ladders in the white weather-boarded mill. Both buildings have a spacious sitting room, comfortable sofas and bookshelves, and a 'startling array of agricultural implements, hunting trophies, African carvings and weaponry, suggesting a former overseas life'. Breakfast, served at two large tables in the tile-hung brick Mill House, includes 'adventurous' dishes like huge stuffed mushrooms or fruit pancakes, as alternatives to a traditional fry-up; jams are home-made. Its steep stairs and changes of level make *Bolebroke* 'suitable only for the nimbler sort of guest', but those who are sufficiently spry agree: 'Very quiet at night.' 'Very romantic, if a bit faded.' Pooh Bridge at AA Milne's former home down the road is much visited, leading to defoliation of the nearby trees; you should bring your own twigs if you wish to play Pooh Sticks. Chartwell, Sissinghurst, Glyndebourne, Hever Castle, and countless other attractions are nearby. (*SGP*)

Open 10 Feb–22 Dec.
Rooms 5 double. 2 in mill, 3 in barn. No telephone.
Facilities 2 lounges, breakfast room. No background music. 6½-acre grounds: garden, millpond, rowing, woodland walks. Unsuitable for ♿.
Location A264 East Grinstead–Tunbridge Wells for 6 miles. Right at crossroads on to B2026 towards Hartfield. After 1 mile, just past garden centre, left into unmade lane. Follow signs.
Restrictions No smoking. No children under 7. No dogs.
Credit cards All major cards accepted.
Terms B&B: single £60–£73, double £66–£79. 10% reduction for 3 or more days. 1-night bookings refused Sat.

HARVINGTON Worcestershire — Map 3:D6

The Mill at Harvington *Tel/Fax* 01386-870688
Anchor Lane, Harvington *Email* millatharvington@aol.com
nr Evesham WR11 5NR

'Wonderful. No praise too high for the welcome, food and service.' 'We think it excellent.' More plaudits this year for the 'helpful' owners, Simon and Jane Greenhalgh and Richard and Susan Yeomans, who provide an atmosphere of 'quiet elegance' in their hotel converted from a Georgian house and red brick mill. All the bedrooms overlook the wooded garden and river, where guests may fish for chub, roach, dace and barbel, watch such wildlife as herons, hare, pheasants and minks, or simply enjoy the recently extended grounds. The fixed-price menu has a wide choice, with dishes like wild mushroom tartlet; terrine of game birds; ragout of seafood; braised local pheasant. The wine list is 'extensive, with a modest mark-up'. Light lunches and dinners (eg, baked egg with mushrooms; sausages and mash) are available in the informal *Chestnut Tree* conservatory café. Breakfasts, which include freshly squeezed orange juice, are enjoyed. A nine-hole, par three golf course opened on the doorstep in spring 2001. Local attractions include Stratford-upon-Avon, only ten miles away, the medieval castles of Warwick, Kenilworth and Sudeley, and the Cotswolds. (*Dr Norman Waterman, Mrs P Ormsby*)

Open 3 Jan–24 Dec.
Rooms 21 double. 6 in garden annexe. Some on ground floor.
Facilities Lounge, conservatory/café (background recorded piano), restaurant; private dining room, function facilities. 8-acre grounds: heated swimming pool, tennis, 200 yds river frontage, fishing. Golf adjacent.
Location On river Avon. Turn SE off Norton–Bidford Rd, opposite Harvington village. Down Anchor Lane; hotel 3rd left. Train: Evesham; taxi.
Restrictions No smoking in restaurant. No children under 10. No dogs.
Credit cards All major cards accepted.
Terms [2001] B&B: single £63–£75, double £84–£125. Set lunch £14.45, dinner £25; full alc £21. 2-night breaks. 1-night bookings sometimes refused. ***V***

HARWICH Essex — Map 2:C5

The Pier at Harwich
The Quay
Harwich CO12 3HH

Tel 01255-241212
Fax 01255-551922
Email info@pieratharwich.co.uk
Website www.pieratharwich.com

The Milsom family of *Maison Talbooth*, Dedham (*qv*), own this handsome Victorian building overlooking the confluence of the Stour and the Orwell on Harwich's waterfront. It was built in the style of a Venetian palazzo to accommodate passengers on the packet boat to Holland. In summer, tables and chairs stand on the pavement in front. The views are dramatic, particularly at night, when Felixstowe, opposite, lights up. The manager/chef, Chris Oakley, runs it as two restaurants-with-rooms with a 'cheerful and informal' staff. 'Food, service and accommodation are all excellent.' Others wrote of 'first-rate meals, with wines to match, at not outrageous prices'. The *Harbourside* restaurant on the first floor, with a decor both 'nautical and tasteful', serves oysters, lobster from its own tanks, and fish cooked in a variety of ways. Many dishes can be ordered in a large or a smaller portion, priced accordingly. A pianist sometimes plays. On the ground floor, the *Ha'penny Bistro* provides fish and chips, baked haddock, chargrilled steak and so on (its muzak was thought 'irritating' this year). The bar is smart, with smoked glass, granite bar tops and a copper ceiling. Breakfasts have good cooked dishes, 'but the continental version is less satisfying (no fruit or yogurt)', says an inspector. The bedrooms, on the top floor, have a pastel decor, and are 'well furnished, large and smart'. Front ones have 'an exciting view of the estuary and its shipping'. Seven 'brilliant' new rooms (including a suite with a bow window and a telescope) and an attractive large lounge (with beams, squashy sofas, newspapers, and a fireplace) are in the adjacent building, formerly the *Angel* pub. (*Sandra M Ford*)

Open All year.
Rooms 4 suites, 10 double. 7 in adjacent building.
Facilities Lounge, restaurant (varied piped music during week; pianist weekends), bistro. Unsuitable for ♿. Civil wedding licence.
Location On quay. Parking. Train: Harwich Town, 5 mins' walk.
Restrictions No smoking in restaurant. Guide dogs only.
Credit cards All major cards accepted.
Terms [2001] (*Excluding 10% service charge on meals*) B&B: single £68–£105.50, double £91–£111, suite £161; D,B&B: single £90–£127.50, double £136–£156, suite £205. English breakfast £5.50. Set lunch £18, dinner £20.50; full alc £38. Christmas package.

HASSOP Derbyshire — Map 3:A6

Hassop Hall
Hassop
nr Bakewell DE45 1NS

Tel 01629-640488
Fax 01629-640577
Email hassophallhotel@btinternet.com

The owner, Thomas Chapman, has presided since 1975, with his sons and daughter, over this grey, bow-windowed building. It is a stately pile, full of history, but our inspector found a 'real family atmosphere'. She liked the 'absence of the trappings of self-conscious luxury', and the unpretentious style. Built of local stone, it has 'a beautiful setting' in the Peak District National Park. The public rooms have carved plaster ceilings, stone fireplaces, good views, open fires and family photos; there is a panelled bar. The service is friendly: 'Our cases were carried; Mr Chapman came to chat, without being intrusive; the waitress was charming.' In the long, attractive dining room, the extensive menu is traditional, eg, curried prawns, or potted shrimps; Dover sole, or roast duckling. Desserts come on a trolley. Breakfast (continental or English) is served in bedrooms (they have a traditional chintzy decor; the best ones look over fields). Functions are held (a ballroom adjacent to the house is under renovation). Guests have access to a 60-acre arboretum. Local stately homes include Haddon Hall, Chatsworth, Eyam Hall. Sheffield is 17 miles away. More reports, please.

Open All year, except Christmas/New Year; restaurant closed Sun night/midday Mon.
Rooms 1 suite, 13 double.
Facilities Lift, ramp. Hall (pianist Fri, Sat evening), lounge, bar, 3 dining rooms; conference/function facilities. 5½-acre grounds: tennis; helipad; access to arboretum, golf nearby. Civil wedding licence.
Location 2½ miles N of Bakewell. From M1 exit 29: Chesterfield town

centre; A619 to Baslow, A623 to Calver. Left at traffic lights on to B6001. Hassop 1 mile.
Restrictions Smoking discouraged in restaurant, banned in lounge. Dogs at management's discretion; not in public rooms.
Credit cards All major cards accepted.
Terms [2001] B&B: single £86.95–£158.95, double £94.90–£168.90; D,B&B: single £114.70–£193.20, double £150.40–£237.40. Child in parents' room: £10. Set lunch £15.90–£21.75, dinner £27.75–£34.25. £5 reduction per person for 2-night stays 1 Nov–31 Mar.

HASTINGS East Sussex *See SHORTLIST* Map 2:E4

HATCH BEAUCHAMP Somerset Map 1:C5

Farthings NEW
Hatch Beauchamp
Nr Taunton TA3 6SG

Tel 01823-480664
Fax 01823-481118
Email farthing1@aol.com
Website www.farthingshotel.com

A restaurant-with-rooms in a pretty white-painted Georgian house, in a historic little Somerset village. It stands near a road in a large, well-tended garden, opposite the cricket ground. A wrought iron balcony runs along the front, colourful in summer with plants in pots and hanging baskets. 'It is welcoming, not smart,' says an inspector in 2001, returning it to the *Guide*. 'Guests are looked after in a family way. Food is outstanding (not "fashionable"), at moderate prices.' The owners, Stephen and Hilary Murphy, who took over in February 2000, are redecorating ('they have a taste for artificial flowers'). Most bedrooms are large: Bay 'is beautiful', with a bathroom up a spiral staircase. 'Our room, overlooking the garden, had a Victorian feel, a well-appointed bathroom.' A fridge on the landing contains fresh milk, fruit juices, etc. All the public rooms have a log fire in cold weather. The lounge, not large, is bright, with big sofas; newspapers and magazines lie around. 'The attractive dining room has pale green-and-cream striped walls, green tablecloths overlaid with cream; good cutlery and glasses. Mr Murphy really can cook. The food was impeccably sourced; duck was a revelation, all meat and crisp skin, served with a plum and orange sauce; steak was thick and pink with a good mushroom sauce; vegetables were fresh and well cooked. Ice cream was home-made. Breakfast, nicely laid out, had fresh orange juice (seconds offered), wonderful scrambled eggs, excellent sausages. The owners are delightful.' They write: 'We attract guests of the 40-plus age group; usually on a three- or four-night break.' Close by is Hatch Court, a Palladian mansion set in award-winning gardens in a large deer park; also several golf courses, and many National Trust properties. A good stop-over on the way to the West Country (the M5 is three miles away). (*Jean Bligh, Michael and Maureen Heath, and others*)

Open All year.
Rooms 1 suite (in cottage), 9 double.
Facilities Lounge, bar, 2 dining rooms, private dining room; 'easy listening'

background music. 3-acre grounds. Children's playground across road; golf, fishing, riding nearby. Unsuitable for ♿. Civil wedding licence.
Location Centre of village 5 miles SE of Taunton, signposted from A358 to Ilminster. Train: Taunton; taxi.
Restrictions No smoking. No small children at dinner. Dogs by arrangement; not in public rooms.
Credit cards Amex, MasterCard, Visa.
Terms [2001] B&B: single £64, double £94, suite £120. Set Sun lunch £14.99, dinner £23.50. Christmas, New Year packages. *V*

HATHERLEIGH Devon — Map 1:C1

Pressland Country House NEW/BUDGET
Hatherleigh, nr Okehampton
EX20 3LW

Tel 01837-810871
Fax 01837-810303
Email accom@presslandhouse.co.uk
Website www.presslandhouse.co.uk

Owned by Gill and Graham Giles, who formerly ran a catering business in Berkshire: large Victorian house amid fields, off A386, 2 miles S of Hatherleigh (old Devon market town), 5 miles N of Okehampton. Traditional decor. Lounge, bar, dining room; background jazz/classical music. 1½-acre garden, with wide views of Dartmoor. 'A first-class experience. Good value. Exceptional dinners, outstanding breakfasts,' says nominator. Open 25 Mar–22 Dec; restaurant closed to non-residents Mon, Thurs, Sun. No smoking. No children under 12. No dogs. MasterCard, Visa accepted. 5 double bedrooms. B&B £22–£36; D,B&B (min. 2 nights) £34–£55. Set dinner £18 [2001].

HATHERSAGE Derbyshire — Map 3:A6

The George
Hathersage S32 1BB

Tel 01433-650436
Fax 01433-650099
Email info@george-hotel.net
Website www.george-hotel.net

The young manager, Gerald Chislett, runs a tight ship, and standards are high at this 500-year-old inn, now owned by Eric Marsh of *The Cavendish*, Baslow (*qv*). 'The decor is sympathetic with the age of the building, preserving original stone walls, oak beams, open fires, and there are many good antiques,' our inspectors reported. 'Our bedroom was large and light, with a pristine decor, pleasant pictures, lovely fabrics, a functional bathroom. The restaurant is stunningly decorated, in dark blue and terracotta.' Aiming for the feel of an upmarket brasserie, it is open much of the day, serving breakfast until noon, coffee, snacks, lunches and suppers until 10 pm. Chef Ben Handley's menus include 'Best of British meat', eg, aromatic belly of pork with watercress salad; terrine of pressed ham and poached chicken with pear and lemon chutney; also 'From the Deep Blue' (fish dishes) and 'From the Plantation' (vegetarian). 'Sinful but worth it' desserts include citrus tart with caramel sauce and berry sauce; lemon brûlé with blueberry ice cream. Breakfast has 'very good pastries', but some of the hot dishes may be 'a bit hit and miss'. All bedrooms have a sitting area and a desk. The village has connections with Charlotte Brontë, who often visited – she called it Morton in *Jane Eyre* (the hotel was owned by one James Eyre in her day). More reports, please.

Open All year.
Rooms 15 double, 4 single.
Facilities Lounge, restaurant (background contemporary CDs); 2 function rooms. Courtyard. Only restaurant accessible for ♿. Civil wedding licence.
Location 8 miles N of Bakewell, in village centre (rear rooms quietest). Parking.
Restrictions No smoking in restaurant. Dogs at management's discretion, in 2 bedrooms only.
Credit cards All major cards accepted.
Terms [2001] B&B: single £59.50–£69.50, double £89.50–£119.50; D,B&B £69.75–£89.50 per person. Full alc £30–£35. Midweek reductions. Off-season break: stay 2 nights, get the 3rd free. Christmas package. 1-night bookings occasionally refused. *V*

HATTON Warwickshire — Map 3:C6

Northleigh House BUDGET
Five Ways Road
Hatton, Warwick CV35 7HZ

Tel 01926-484203
Fax 01926-484006
Website www.northleigh.co.uk

'Accommodation is comfortable, thoughtful and spacious. The owner is generous, with a pleasing manner.' There is a 'warm welcome' from Sylvia Fenwick at her unpretentious B&B on a small road in countryside just north of Warwick. A note in the brochure reads: 'If you should need anything, a larger table perhaps, a hot-water bottle or laundry service, just ask.' Ms Fenwick is a keen decorator, and each of the bedrooms has a different colour theme. 'The ground-floor Italian Room (light blues and browns) was comfortable and homely, with a smart, well-equipped bathroom.' The Blue Room (the priciest) has a king-size bed in a blue-curtained alcove, blue sofas, pine furniture, a huge bathroom and a kitchenette. Each room has a fridge, TV and a fan heater. The panelled lounge has a wood-burning stove, books and original paintings. The 'delicious breakfast', with a toaster on each table, is served in a spacious room overlooking the garden (there is also a fenced paddock, 'nice for dogs'). A local map, and information about local pubs and restaurants, are provided. 'Excellent value for money.' Warwick Castle is five miles away; Stratford-upon-Avon is 12; Birmingham is a 30-minute drive. (*SD, Jonathan and Deborah Oxley*)

Open Feb–mid-Dec.
Rooms 6 double, 1 single. 1 with kitchenette. 2 on ground floor. No telephone (payphone available).
Facilities Sitting room, breakfast room. No background music. 1½-acre grounds: garden, paddock. Unsuitable for ♿.
Location 5 miles NW of Warwick off A4177. At Five Ways roundabout take Shrewley road for ½ mile.
Restrictions No smoking. Dogs by arrangement, not in public rooms.
Credit cards MasterCard, Visa.
Terms [2001] B&B: single £36–£43, double £52–£62.

HAWES North Yorkshire — Map 4:C3

Simonstone Hall NEW
Simonstone, nr Hawes
DL8 3LY

Tel 01969-667255
Fax 01969-667741
Email hotel@simonstonehall.demon.co.uk
Website simonstonehall.com

Imposing grey stone former hunting lodge, gabled and tall-chimneyed, splendidly located in North Wensleydale, 1 mile N of small market town. Gothic staircase, original fireplaces, ancestral portraits, genuine antiques, cheese-dish collection, white-panelled dining room; background CDs. 4-acre grounds (croquet). 'Lots of character, charming reception, cheerful bar staff, pleasant waitresses, agreeable lounge', but inspectors this year reported a poor breakfast and had reservations about dinner, recommending instead meals in the 'atmospheric bar'. Pets accepted. No smoking: restaurant, bedrooms. Amex, MasterCard, Visa accepted. 20 rooms (2 on ground floor). B&B: single £50–£60, double £120–£170; D,B&B: single £75–£85, double £170–£220. Full alc £35. Extension to be completed by summer 2001, so we'd like more reports, please.

HAWKSHEAD Cumbria — Map 4: inset C2

Rough Close BUDGET
Hawkshead LA22 0QF

Tel 015394-36370
Fax 015394-36002

'Tony and Marilyn Gibson always amaze us with their happiness and warmth, delightful menus, lovely garden and quiet comfort.' Very relaxing. Totally spoiling. We will go back for years to come.' Warm endorsements this year for the Gibsons' unpretentious guest house which stands above Esthwaite Water; from its garden there are views of fells and woodland. It has many regular visitors, drawn by the beautiful setting, the unpretentious comfort, the friendliness of the owners, and the 'excellent value for money'. The five-course dinner at 7 pm is English 'with some European influence', eg, tomato and orange soup; chicken thighs with apricots in a green peppercorn sauce; Eve's pudding with cream. The Gibsons share the cooking, and Mr Gibson serves at table and acts as wine waiter (each menu suggests a wine, priced at about £12.50, to match the food). Substantial breakfasts are served between 8.45 and 9.15 am. All the bedrooms have private facilities, but one (large and warm) bathroom is across the landing. A minor road is nearby, but noise is not usually a problem. There is good walking from the grounds, and excellent birdwatching, and the Gibsons can advise about local attractions – they include Beatrix Potter's home, Hill Top; Hawkshead Grammar School (attended by William Wordsworth, now a museum); the restored steam yacht, *Gondola*, which operates on Coniston Water. (*Margaret and David Nicholls, Mrs S Burns*)

Open Mar–Nov. Lunch not served.
Rooms 5 double. No telephone.
Facilities Lounge, bar, dining room. No background music. 1-acre garden: *boules*. Lake, boating, fishing nearby. Unsuitable for ♿.

Location 1¼ miles S of Hawkshead on Newby Bridge road. Infrequent bus service.
Restrictions No smoking: dining room, bedrooms. No children under 12. No dogs.
Credit cards MasterCard, Visa.
Terms B&B £28.50–£32; D,B&B £41.50–£45. Single rate by negotiation. Set dinner £14. Reductions for long stays. 1-night bookings sometimes refused.

HAWORTH West Yorkshire — Map 4:D3

Hill Top Farmhouse BUDGET — *Tel* 01535-643524
Haworth Moor, Haworth BD22 0EL

'We reached this isolated farmhouse on the moor above Haworth just as a blizzard hit; the Foxes awaited us with the door wide open.' Our inspector this year adds to the acclaim for Brenda Fox's 17th-century farmhouse with wide views over farms, villages and the Lower Laithe Reservoir to the distant hills. These are the moors where the Brontë sisters walked, and there is a timeless quality (except for the electricity) to the 'relaxed and homely' atmosphere of this informal guest house. 'The large lounge/dining room is striking, furnished with 18th-century carved furniture, and a collection of antique crockery and ornaments.' There is also a 'smaller, cosier' sitting room. This is very much the home of Mrs Fox and her husband Alan: 'You are treated as friends. Mr Fox sits with you by the fire, a cheerful bustle emanates from the kitchen with Radio 4 on around the clock, and Mrs Fox emerges now and again to give her views on the latest news.' Packed lunches are available by arrangement, and so is an evening meal: 'Straightforward home cooking: pea and ham soup; roast chicken and potatoes, with mushroom gravy and a separate dish of broccoli and two kinds of green beans; bilberry pie and cream; coffee came with white chocolate mints.' Vegetarians are catered for. No licence; bring your own wine. 'Our classic country bedroom had oldish furniture, antique bric-a-brac, TV, lovely fresh flowers and a minute shower room.' Breakfast has a limited choice of cooked dishes. Haworth parsonage is 15 minutes' walk away; the Keighley and Worth Valley Railway (of *Railway Children* fame) is nearby.

Open All year.
Rooms 3 double, all with shower. No telephone.
Facilities Lounge, lounge/dining room (soft background music). Large grounds. Unsuitable for ♿.
Location From Haworth take minor road to Colne; 1st turning left (signed Peniston Hill Country Park). *Hill Top* is 1st building on right.
Restrictions No smoking. No dogs in house.
Credit cards None accepted.
Terms [2001] B&B £23; D,B&B £35.50.

> The second volume of the *Guide*, containing nearly 1,000 Continental hotels, will be published early in 2002. Deadline for reports on Continental hotels: 30 September 2001; for new nominations: 14 September 2001.

Weaver's
15 West Lane
Haworth BD22 8DU

Tel 01535-643822
Fax 01535-644832
Email colinjane@aol.com
Website www.weaversmallhotel.co.uk

'Nothing changes except regular variations on the menu. Still my favourite place,' writes a returning visitor to this restaurant-with-rooms on a cobbled street behind the Brontë Parsonage Museum. The owner/chefs, Colin and Jane Rushworth, may have lost their *Michelin Bib Gourmand* this year, but readers still enthuse about their traditional and modern British regional cooking. Regulars appreciate the re-working of the menu: 'A few old favourites are kept, and new dishes are introduced – a sign that someone really enjoys cooking.' 'The food was excellent, particularly the smoked haddock soup. It was followed by the best lamb we have had for a long time. The vegetables were very good. Excellent sweets followed.' Using fresh, and mostly local, ingredients, the Rushworths serve such dishes as marinated salmon with potato salad; fisherman's pie; green leaf, bean and egg fritter. Home-made puddings include sticky toffee pudding; nanny's meringue. The wine list is wide-ranging, with a good selection of half bottles, and a low mark-up. 'Our stay was most enjoyable because all the elements were there to make it so – 'hospitality, high standards, a friendly and efficient atmosphere.' Old photographs, modern paintings, antiques, bric-a-brac, and mementos of the spinners' craft fill the house, once a barn and a row of weavers' cottages. The bar and lounge 'can be crowded in a friendly sort of way'. The 'stylish and idiosyncratic' bedrooms, up a narrow staircase, have lace-trimmed pillowcases, fresh milk, a cafetière with ground coffee, TV. They 'are maintained to a high standard'. (*Chris Kay, Derek Wheal, and others*)

Open All year, Tues–Sat from 6.30 pm, except 22 Dec–8 Jan. Lunches for groups by arrangement.
Rooms 2 double, 1 single.
Facilities Bar/lounge, restaurant. Mixed '50s/'60s background music at night. Unsuitable for ♿.
Location By Brontë Parsonage Museum: use its pay-and-display car park. Ignore sign for Brontë village/Tourist Information. Train: Keighley; then bus/taxi.
Restrictions No smoking in restaurant, bedrooms. No dogs.
Credit cards All major cards accepted.
Terms B&B: single £55, double £80. Set menu (except Sat) £14.50; full alc £28. *V*

HAYTOR Devon — Map 1:D4

Bel Alp House
Haytor
nr Newton Abbot TQ13 9XX

Tel 01364-661217
Fax 01364-661292

'Really charming, with beautiful new bathroom, excellent home cooking, amazing views.' 'Excellent in every way'. Fresh praise this year for this Edwardian country house, high on a hill on the south-east edge of Dartmoor. Our inspectors, too, were charmed by the 'really warm welcome, fresh, simple food and cosy atmosphere'. One of its chief glories is the panoramic view across fields, a church, faraway towns to the distant sea – it is worth paying extra for one of the large front bedrooms. The house was much altered in the 1920s by its then owner, the tobacco millionairess Dame Violet Wills, and the interior is light and spacious, with arches, bay windows, stained glass and a homely decor. It is run in a generous spirit by its owners, Mary and Jack Twist. She is the cook, he the solicitous front-of-house. 'The level of personal attention is high, but they are never intrusive.' Dinner is served on a glassed-in balcony – 'as we ate, we watched the sunset and the twinkling lights of far-away houses – magical'. The hand-written, two-choices-per-course menu might include lentil soup, or fillet of trout; steak medallions with mushroom and wine gravy, or cod with a tomato pesto herb crust; masses of vegetables. Mealtimes are flexible – 'they urged us to lie in on Sunday, if we wished'. Breakfast has toast made from home-made bread, 'excellent cafetière coffee', good cooked dishes. There is direct access to the moor from the grounds. Charlie, the golden retriever, will take guests for walks. Many local attractions: houses, gardens, the Lydford Gorge, etc. (*Freddie Stockdale, Margaret Snow, EW Gibbons*)

Open All year.
Rooms 1 suite, 7 double. 1 on ground floor.
Facilities Lounge, sitting room, bar, restaurant; background music if requested; snooker table in basement; patio. 8-acre grounds. Riding, golf nearby.
Location From A38: A382 to Bovey Tracey, B3387 to Haytor/Widecombe. After 1½ miles, cross cattle grid on to moor; fork left after 500 yds into hotel drive, crossing 2nd cattle grid. Train: Newton Abbot; taxi.
Restrictions No smoking: restaurant, bedrooms, lounge. No dogs unattended in bedrooms, or in dining room.
Credit cards All major cards accepted.
Terms B&B: single £60–£75, double £120, suite £150. Packed lunch available. Set dinner £25. 10% discount for 3 or more nights. 1-night bookings refused bank holiday weekends.

HEDDON'S MOUTH Devon — Map 1:B4

Heddon's Gate Hotel
Heddon's Mouth, Parracombe
Barnstaple EX31 4PZ

Tel 01598-763313
Fax 01598-763363
Email info@hgate.co.uk
Website www.hgate.co.uk

César award in 1990

'Definitely a gem. Beautiful setting, friendly staff. Every other guest seemed to have been there many times before.' A tribute this year to Robert and Heather Deville's Swiss/Victorian lodge which has a remote setting, in large grounds with steeply terraced gardens, on the edge of Exmoor. Regulars love the old-fashioned decor: 'The bar with its stags' antlers and black leather furniture; the lounge walls hung with tapestries, the '20s shop mannequin, dressed as a waitress, standing by a case of china dogs. But there is nothing dingy or dusty about the period atmosphere.' The personal service (beds turned down at night, etc) is appreciated too, and the 'friendly atmosphere: like-minded people to chat with, and plenty of laughter in the bar'. The price includes afternoon tea with home-made cakes, and after-dinner coffee with 'luscious hand-made chocolates'. Guests are expected to take dinner. With limited choice, it is served promptly at 8 pm. Mr Deville's daily-changing menu is traditional 'and excellent' (main courses like beef braised in red wine with sautéed mushrooms; sea bass with saffron sauce). Breakfast, brought to the table rather than self-service, 'deserves special mention, with excellent choice from figs to boiled eggs with "soldiers"' (also freshly squeezed orange juice, local bacon and kippers). Packed lunches are available. The bedrooms, named for their original use – Grandmama's, Nursemaid's, etc – vary greatly and are priced accordingly. Some are large, with a spacious bathroom. The cottages in the garden are convenient for dog-owners. There is good walking in the 'superb coastal countryside'. The Watersmeet estate and Arlington Court (both National Trust) are near. (*John and Margaret Speake, JP Berryman, and others*)

Open Easter–early Nov. Dining room closed for lunch.
Rooms 4 suites (3 in cottages, on ground floor), 9 double, 1 single.
Facilities Lounge, bar lounge, library, piano/card room, dining room; table-tennis room. No background music. 20-acre grounds. River, fishing, riding, pony-trekking nearby. Sea ¾ mile. Not really suitable for ♿.
Location 6 miles W of Lynton. From A39, after 3 miles, take road to Woody Bay/Martinhoe; follow signs for *Hunter's Inn*; hotel drive on right. Train/coach: Barnstaple, 16 miles; taxi.
Restrictions No smoking in dining room. Children 'must be old enough to dine with parents at 8 pm'. Dogs by arrangement, not in dining room, or unattended in bedrooms.
Credit cards MasterCard, Visa.
Terms [2001] D,B&B £68–£84. Set dinner £26. Child in parents' room: 50% of adult rate. Weekly rates. 3-day breaks. 1-night bookings occasionally refused.

HENLEY-ON-THAMES Oxfordshire — Map 2:D3

The Red Lion
Hart Street
Henley-on-Thames RG9 2AR

Tel 01491-572161
Fax 01491-410039
Email reservations@redlionhenley.co.uk
Website www.redlionhenley.co.uk

The Miller family of *Durrants*, London (*qv*), own this creeper-clad 16th-century red brick inn, looking over the Royal Regatta course on the river Thames. 'Any hotel which can remain cheerful and efficient during its busiest period is surely worth its entry,' one visitor wrote. Under the new manager, Richard Vowell, it continues to be admired: 'The guest comes first,' is one comment. The public rooms have antique panelling and furniture; there are flagstones, an open fire and rowing memorabilia in the bar. The riverside restaurant serves a mix of modern and traditional dishes: carpaccio of lamb and monkfish roasted in pancetta appear on the *table d'hôte* menu; pea and ham soup, and roast beef and Yorkshire pudding at Sunday lunch. Dishes are 'well presented, and unpretentious, with good service'. But one visitor thought the cooked breakfast 'not up to the standard of the main meals – best stick to the continental'. The traditional bedrooms, 'full of creature comforts', have flowery fabrics, prints on walls, rugs on wooden floors, a marble-tiled bathroom, and there are some impressive antique beds. Some rooms get noise from the busy bridge, close by, but double glazing helps to keep out the sound of traffic. (*Peter Jowitt, BS*)

Open All year.
Rooms 23 double, 3 single.
Facilities Lounge, bar, restaurant (classical background music); conference/function facilities. On river: boat hire, picnics arranged. Unsuitable for ♿.
Location By Henley bridge (rooms double-glazed). Trains to Henley from London, Reading. Large car park.
Restriction No dogs.
Credit cards Amex, MasterCard, Visa.
Terms [2001] (*Excluding 'optional' 10% service charge on meals*) Room: single £99–£105, double £145–£150. Breakfast £8.50–£12.50. Set lunch/dinner (2 to 3 courses) £12.50–£16; full alc £35. *V*

See also SHORTLIST

HEREFORD Herefordshire — Map 3:D4

Castle House NEW
Castle Street
Hereford HR1 2NW

Tel 01432-356321
Fax 01432-365909
Email info@castlehse.co.uk
Website www.castlehse.co.uk

The Left Bank Village, the brainchild of a 'very charming' Dutch business man, Dr Albert Heijn, on the banks of the river Wye, is an ambitious project to regenerate a neglected area of this ancient city. It comprises a restaurant, brasserie, shops, and this small, luxurious hotel in two sensitively restored Grade II listed town houses. With an exterior of pale cream stone, dark green wrought iron balconies, and a portico, it stands close to the cathedral (home of the Mappa Mundi and the Chained Library). 'A winner on all counts,' one couple wrote. Sadly, the much-admired manager, Ben Jager, died in March 2001, shortly before our inspectors visited, but they found it 'very pleasant, with very polite staff' and an attractive decor: polished wood floors, bright rugs, lavish fabrics, massive flower arrangements, elegant, wide staircase. The bedrooms (many are suites) aim to illustrate the joint history of Great Britain and the Netherlands (names like Cavalier, Orange). 'Charles II was a blend of technology, imagination and contemporary design: a supremely comfortable bed, a tapestry with rather violent hunting scenes; a fridge, a music system.' The menus (described as 'Anglo-French with a hint of fusion') offer some complicated dishes like cappuccino of white beans and truffle, tortellini of foie gras; pork and pancetta tournedos, goat's cheese mash, sun-blushed tomato beignet. 'Go for the simpler main courses,' is our inspectors' suggestion. 'Puddings were all exquisite.' Privacy is guaranteed in the secluded gardens that overlook an ancient moat. (*Selwyn and Rebecca Goldsmith, and others*)

Open All year.
Rooms 10 suites, 1 double, 4 single. 1 suitable for ♿.
Facilities Lounge, bar, restaurant; classical background music. Garden.
Location ½ mile from centre. Follow signs for city centre east; *Castle House*. Parking.
Restrictions No smoking in restaurant. No dogs in restaurant.
Credit cards Amex, MasterCard, Visa.
Terms [2001] B&B: single £90, double £155, suite £165–£210. English breakfast £8.50. Set lunch £18.95, dinner £29.95. Christmas package. *V*

HINTON CHARTERHOUSE Somerset — Map 2:D1

Homewood Park
Hinton Charterhouse
Bath BA2 7TB

Tel 01225-723731
Fax 01225-723820
Email res.@homewoodpark.com
Website www.homewoodpark.com

Long-term manager Frank Gueuning and his 'charming staff' please visitors with their 'seamless service' in a classic country house hotel a few miles from Bath. The ivy-clad, grey stone, mainly 18th-century building is in a village on the edge of the Limpley Stoke valley, a designated area of outstanding natural beauty. It has fine fabrics, antiques, oriental rugs, and works by local artists. Log fires burn in the lounge and bar in cold weather. The restaurant will be on its toes this year having lost its *Michelin* star. Chef Nigel Godwin serves elaborate modern English fare, eg, roasted Cornish sea scallops with soused cucumber tagliatelle, pancetta wafers and a Bloody Mary sorbet; Trelough duck with sarladaise potatoes and candied apples with boudin made from its gizzards, truffled chicory and a calvados jus; apple parfait and baby toffee apples. The menus change with the season, and Mr Godwin makes his own marmalade. Breakfast includes freshly squeezed juices, delicious croissants and brioches, and 'beautifully presented' yogurt with fresh fruit. Most bedrooms are spacious, and overlook the immaculate garden. There is a secluded swimming pool, 'long enough to swim in'. Children are welcomed. Some traffic noise from the busy road nearby. More reports, please.

Open All year.
Rooms 2 suites, 3 junior suites, 14 double. 1 on ground floor.
Facilities Drawing room, bar, restaurant. No background music. 10-acre grounds: swimming pool, tennis, croquet. Civil wedding licence.
Location 6 miles SE of Bath, opposite Hinton Priory. A46 from M4; A36 to Warminster; left at 2nd turning to Freshford. Some traffic noise (rooms double-glazed). Train: Bath; then taxi.
Restrictions No smoking in restaurant. Guide dogs only.
Credit cards All major cards accepted.
Terms [2001] B&B: single £75–£109, double £99–£180, suite £115–£250; D,B&B: single £112–£146, double £173–£213, suite £189–£324. Set lunch £19.50, dinner (2–3 courses) £36–£47; full alc £55. 2-day breaks. Christmas package. 1-night bookings sometimes refused weekends.

HOCKLEY HEATH Warwickshire Map 3:C6

Nuthurst Grange
Nuthurst Grange Lane
Hockley Heath B94 5NL

Tel 01564-783972
Fax 01564-783919
Email info@nuthurst-grange.co.uk
Website www.nuthurst-grange.com

David Randolph and Karen Seymour run this red brick Edwardian house in a large village on the Stratford-upon-Avon Canal as a hotel/restaurant. 'Extremely comfortable, with good food, efficient reception, excellent service,' wrote experienced travellers. With a terrace, creeper-clad walls, bay windows with leaded panes, dormer windows in the roof, it stands amid landscaped gardens, fountains, ponds and a herb garden; you approach by a mile-long tree-lined drive. The front looks across the M40, half a mile away (some traffic noise, but handy for Birmingham), to open country. The public rooms have lavish fabrics, stylish flower arrangements, lots of pink. Two light sitting rooms overlook the garden. The spacious bedrooms are traditional, with flowery fabrics, period furniture, fruit, 'useful extras', and a bathroom with an air spa bath. Mr Randolph has recruited Ben Davies to run the kitchen; his modern British dishes are served at well-spaced tables on a three-course menu with three choices for each course: eg, salad of spiced guineafowl and pancetta with grain mustard; fillet of red mullet on a bed of braised lentils, leeks and asparagus; lemon bavarois with poached red fruits. Or you can eat off a four-course menu and pay according to the number of courses taken. 'Breakfast is good and efficiently served. They prefer you to take it in the bedroom, but will serve it in the dining room if asked.' 'Suitable for children who are well behaved,' says the brochure. A popular venue for weddings, small meetings, and functions. Three impressive castles, Warwick, Broughton and Berkeley, are nearby. (*J and TH, SD*)

Open All year, except 24–26 Dec.
Rooms 1 suite, 14 double. Some on ground floor.
Facilities Ramps. 2 lounges, restaurant; function/private dining rooms. No background music. 7½-acre grounds: herb garden, croquet, ponds, woodland; helipad. Riding, tennis, golf, clay-pigeon shooting, canal boating nearby. Civil wedding licence.
Location 10 miles NW of Warwick. Off A3400 ½ mile S of Hockley Heath. Turn right at hotel sign.
Restrictions No smoking: restaurant, 1 lounge. Dogs by arrangement, not in public rooms.
Credit cards All major cards accepted.
Terms B&B: single £135, double from £155, suite £185. Set lunch £25.50, dinner £36.50; full alc lunch £45. Weekend breaks: D,B&B £79.50 per person. ***V***

HOLFORD Somerset Map 1:B5

Combe House BUDGET
Holford
nr Bridgwater TA5 1RZ

Tel 01278-741382
Fax 01278-741322
Email enquiries@combehouse.co.uk

'The hotel and surrounding scenery are picturesque and peaceful. The food is good, the staff are friendly.' A report this year on Denice and

John Page's converted 17th-century tannery. Long, low and still with its waterwheel, it is at the end of a narrow lane in a combe that leads up to the Quantock hills. This is a hotel for walkers and lovers of the countryside rather than those seeking luxury. Another visitor liked its 'air of having grown rather than been designed, and ambience of a homely country house' but thought the decor in the public rooms – log fires, beams, creaking stairs and floors, patterned carpets, and 'a variety of furniture apparently bought at long-ago auctions' – 'rather tired'. The long-serving chef, Lynn Gardner, serves 'impressive' traditional English dinners, eg, home-made soup; Victorian chicken pie with green peppers, mushrooms and cream; hazelnut meringue. The wine list is 'extensive with a good price range'. Room 5, the largest, has good wardrobe space and decent reading lights, but 'the bath-water was rather tepid'. Some rooms are small. Breakfasts are 'very good and very large, all the usual staples; we particularly enjoyed the sausages'. Packed lunches and cream teas ('lashings of cream and jam') are available. No nightlife, 'just the ripple of the stream through the gardens, the sound of wind in the trees, the song of birds'. A rock beach is nearby; Cleeve Abbey and Dunster Castle are within 20 minutes' drive. (*Paul and Samantha Evans, Richard Green, and others*)

Open Mid-Feb–end Dec; Closed Mon–Thurs Nov, Dec, Feb.
Rooms 1 suite, 11 double, 4 single. 1 on ground floor.
Facilities 2 lounges, bar, restaurant. No background music. 3-acre grounds: tennis, covered swimming pool, stream. Golf, riding, walking, rock beach nearby. Unsuitable for ♿.
Location A39 Bridgwater–Minehead. Turn between *Plough Inn* and Holford garage. Left at T-junction, left at fork; hotel on right. Train: Bridgwater, Taunton; local bus.
Restrictions No smoking: dining room, 1 lounge, bedrooms. No dogs in public rooms.
Credit cards Amex, MasterCard, Visa.
Terms B&B: single £33–£41, double £66–£106, suite £77–£106; D,B&B £53–£73 per person. Bar lunches from £2.50. Set dinner £20. 2- to 5-night breaks. Christmas, New Year packages. 1-night bookings refused bank holidays. *V*

HOLNE Devon — Map 1:D4

Church House Inn NEW/BUDGET
Holne TQ13 7SJ

Tel 01364-631208
Fax 01364-631525
Website www.churchhouse-holne.co.uk

14th-century white-walled inn, in 'great setting' in Dartmoor National Park. New, 'very hospitable' owners, Jan and Tony Skerritt and Jane and Paul Silk (who also run the village shop), have redecorated public areas. Sitting room with books, 2 bars. Restaurant (no-smoking) serves 'traditional adventurous' cooking à la carte*; 'very good breakfast'; bar lunches. No background music. No garden. Dogs welcomed (no charge). Unsuitable for ♿. MasterCard, Visa accepted. 6 bedrooms, 4 with facilities* en suite*. B&B £27–£30. Full alc £25.*

HOPE Derbyshire — Map 3:A6

Underleigh House BUDGET
off Edale Road
Hope S33 6RF

Tel 01433-621372
Fax 01433-621324
Email underleigh.house@btinternet.com
Website www.underleighhouse.co.uk

Philip and Vivienne Taylor and their 'delightful Border terrier, Tess', are 'really welcoming hosts', say visitors this year. They offer B&B in this conversion of a 19th-century barn and cottages near a Domesday-old village in the Hope valley. The award-winning breakfast, served around a large oak table in a beamed, flagstoned room, 'is lovely', with plenty of choice, including home-made fruit conserve, muesli and preserves. The Aga-cooked porridge is warmly recommended. The bedrooms were refurbished when the Taylors took over last year; they have plenty of toiletries, and views over the lovely surrounding countryside or the garden; most beds are king-size. Drinks are served in a large lounge with a log fire, or on a terrace surrounded by flowers. Plenty of hostelries are close at hand for supper. Maps and packed lunches are provided (you can walk in the Peak District National Park from the door), and there is good birdwatching nearby. (*Madeline and Richard Green, Don Parker*)

Open All year, except Christmas, New Year.
Rooms 1 suite, 5 double. 2 on ground floor.
Facilities Lounge, breakfast room. No background music. ¾-acre garden. Not really suitable for ♿.
Location 1 mile from Hope: from A6187, opposite church (with *Old Hall* pub on corner), take road to Edale for *c.* ⅔ mile. After *Cheshire Cheese* pub and bridge, beyond S-bend sign, take lane on left. Keep right; house is 1st on right.
Restrictions No smoking. No children under 12. Guide dogs only.
Credit cards MasterCard, Visa (*5% surcharge*).
Terms [2001] B&B: single £33–£46, double £60–£66, suite £70–£80. 3-night rates. 1-night bookings refused Sat in season.

HOPESAY Shropshire — Map 3:C4

The Old Rectory
Hopesay, Craven Arms SY7 8HD

Tel 01588-660245
Fax 01588-660502
Email villar.oldrectory@virgin.net

César award in 2001

Roma and Michael Villar's 17th-century grey stone rectory, wisteria-draped, stands in landscaped gardens by a 12th-century church in a hamlet above the Clun valley. It is much admired as 'a lovely retreat' and for 'high standards which never slip'. 'From the first greeting we felt like welcome guests. The owners could not have been more kind,' one couple wrote. The house has been 'beautifully restored, with a perfect balance between formality and informality'. An Aga-cooked evening meal is served at 8 pm at a polished oak refectory table. The cooking is 'quite sophisticated, using the freshest products'. Tomato and feta cheese salad, and seared sea bass with orange and vermouth sauce might be followed by 'chocolate roulade to die for'. 'We regularly order good wine – here it is not a rip-off.' The silhouette of the hill seen from the dining room as the sun sets 'is the final touch to make dinner a rare treat'. The drawing room has an Adam fireplace, Georgian sash windows opening on to a terrace, antique and period furniture, and a self-service drinks trolley. The spacious bedrooms have TV, up-to-date magazines, armchairs; two have an emperor-size bed. 'Perfectly timed and cooked' breakfasts include home-made preserves, fruit compote, home-baked bread, traditional cooked items. Afternoon tea, with home-made biscuits and cakes, is included in the rates. Hotel facilities should not be expected (guests wanting to arrive before 4 pm need to make prior arrangements). There is much to enjoy in this lovely part of west Shropshire, including birdwatching from local RSPB hides and in the rectory garden; Powis and Stokesay castles, Offa's Dyke and Long Mynd are near. Also recommended: the 'wheely wonderful cycling' offered by Patchfield Farm, Elton: 'Excellent bikes, and miles of virtually flat cycling through quiet lanes and voluptuous countryside.' (*P and EH, and many others*)

Open All year, except Christmas/New Year.
Rooms 1 suite, 2 double. No telephone.
Facilities Drawing room, dining room. Terrace. No background music. 2-acre garden. Unsuitable for ♿.
Location 4 miles W of Craven Arms. B4368 to Clun; at Aston-on-Clun turn right over humpback bridge to Hopesay. Hotel 1½ miles, by church.
Restrictions No smoking. No children under 16. No dogs.
Credit cards None accepted.
Terms B&B £40. Set dinner £22.

HOPWAS Staffordshire — Map 3:C6

Oak Tree Farm — *Tel/Fax* 01827-56807
Hints Road
Hopwas, nr Tamworth B78 3AA

'A wonderful place to stay': this B&B is a 'little rural oasis', say *Guide* readers. 'The welcome from the hostess, Sue Purkis, is warm and homely'; 'she has a genius for hospitality, and provides a tranquil environment'; 'her staff are excellent.' The renovated farmhouse, in a pretty village, stands in grounds between the river Tame (coarse fishing) and a canal (good walks). 'A cornucopia of a hanging basket sways in the breeze; swallows swoop; a cat blinks on the lawn.' There is a swimming pool in a conservatory, and a lounge with a wood-burning stove. Spotless bedrooms, 'tastefully decorated' and good sized, have a sofa, armchairs, TV, a desk, books, magazines and much else. The 'splendid breakfast', which includes freshly baked bread and newspapers, is served from 7 am until 10. The village has two good pubs (one is open all day). The market town of Tamworth, across the river, has an old castle, a Norman church and a snow dome for indoor skiing. Lichfield, the cathedral city and birthplace of Samuel Johnson, is five miles away; Drayton Manor pleasure park is nearby; Birmingham is 13 miles. (*Tim, Kimberly and Anastasia Andreadis, Sarah Plevin, Mr and Mrs A Mathews; also Mrs M MacGregor*)

Open All year, except Christmas, New Year.
Rooms 6 double, 1 single. 5 in barn. No telephone (payphone available).
Facilities Drawing room, breakfast room; conservatory with swimming pool; small conference facilities. No background music. 4-acre grounds on river, fishing. Golf nearby. Unsuitable for ♿.
Location From A51, turn into Hints Rd at *Tame Otter* pub. Last house on left at fork in road. Train: Tamworth; taxi.
Restrictions No smoking. No children. No dogs in public rooms.
Credit cards Amex, MasterCard, Visa.
Terms B&B: single £57, double £75.

HORLEY Surrey **Map 2:D4**

Langshott Manor
Langshott
Horley RH6 9LN

Tel 01293-786680
Fax 01293-783905
Email admin@langshottmanor.com
Website www.langshottmanor.com

'A wonderfully romantic place to stay before a Gatwick flight. Very attentive staff and fine facilities.' This Grade II listed timber-framed Elizabethan manor house stands in a traditional English garden with roses, herbaceous borders and a lake – but not on the Gatwick flight path. Owned by Peter and Deborah Hinchcliffe and managed by Kenneth Sharp, it is an airport hotel with a difference, a world apart from the chain hotels nearby. It has sturdy chimneys, leaded windows, beamed ceilings, wooden staircases and fresh flowers. 'The building is charming and the gardens are a marvel,' says one report. 'The lounges are warm and inviting.' The poshest bedrooms are in the main house. Those in the converted mews may have less character, but they are comfortable, and have views over gardens or fields and treetops. Some bathrooms have a four-poster bath. Chef Stephen Toward serves 'modern European' menus in the hotel's *Mulberry Restaurant*. Dishes include tomato and red pepper bisque; poached Cornish turbot with a champagne, parsley and mustard cream sauce; apricot tarte Tatin. 'Excellent breakfast.' The rates include a week's free parking at a nearby airport car park. Many packages are offered, including visits to famous gardens and houses (Wisley, Wakehurst Place, Bateman's, etc); learning to fly, using a flight simulator; trips to horse races. (*MD, Robert Sandham, RN*)

Open All year.
Rooms 1 suite, 14 double. 8 in mews 50 yds. Some on ground floor.
Facilities Ramps. 3 lounges (piano/CDs, evenings), restaurant; conference/private dining room. 3-acre garden: croquet. Courtesy car to Gatwick Airport (2½ miles). Unsuitable for ♿. Civil wedding licence.
Location From A23 in Horley: Ladbroke Rd (3rd exit off large roundabout by *Chequers* hotel) to Langshott. Hotel ½ mile on right. Train: Gatwick; taxi.
Restrictions No smoking: restaurant, 1 lounge, bedrooms. No dogs in house (kennels available).
Credit cards All major cards accepted.
Terms B&B: single £145–£245, double £165–£275, suite £245–£275. Set lunch £25, dinner £37.50; full alc £55. Special breaks. Christmas package. *V*

HUDDERSFIELD West Yorkshire *See SHORTLIST* Map 4:E3

HULL East Yorkshire *See SHORTLIST* Map 4:D5

HUNSTRETE Somerset Map 2:D1

Hunstrete House
Hunstrete, Chelwood
nr Bath BS39 4NS

Tel 01761-490490
Fax 01761-490732
Email user@hunstretehouse.co.uk
Website www.hunstretehouse.co.uk

Many changes have taken place at this country house hotel owned by North American Country Inns and managed by David Hennigan. Some of the public rooms have been redecorated, and most of the bedrooms have been given a make-over, with improved lighting and a 'more guest-friendly' layout. There is a new chef, Philip Hobson, formerly *sous-chef* at *The Bath Priory* (*qv*). His first task, with his 'modern British, European-influenced' cooking is to regain a lost *Michelin* star. His dinner menu might include millefeuille of gratinated monkfish; roast loin of venison with Savoy cabbage and speck; blackcurrant crème brûlée with liquorice ice cream. The 18th-century grey stone building, 'small for a country house', stands on the edge of the Mendip hills, in huge grounds with woodland, a deer park, a heated swimming pool, magnificent gardens – 'some of the most interesting we know' – with a flourishing *potager*. The public rooms have chandeliers, antiques, mirrors, portraits, open fires. Bedrooms are luxurious too, and 24-hour room service is available. A day at Bath racecourse can be arranged, with two horse-racing correspondents. 'Expensive, but very good value,' was a verdict last year. We'd like more reports, please.

Open All year.
Rooms 2 suites, 20 double. 11 in courtyard. Some on ground floor.
Facilities Drawing room, library, bar, restaurant (classical background music). 92-acre grounds: gardens, swimming pool, tennis, woodland, deer park, pond, fishing. Civil wedding licence.
Location 7 miles SW of Bath, 10 miles SE of Bristol. From Bath: A4 towards Bristol; A39 through Marksbury; A368 towards Weston-super-Mare. Turn off at Historic House signpost.
Restrictions No smoking: restaurant, some bedrooms. No dogs.
Credit cards All major cards accepted.
Terms B&B: single £80–£115, double £125–£230, suite £240–£265. Set lunch £19.95; full alc £55. Christmas package. 1-night bookings sometimes refused.

HUNTINGDON Cambridgeshire Map 2:B4

The Old Bridge
1 High Street
Huntingdon PE29 3TQ

Tel 01480-424300
Fax 01480-411017
Email oldbridge@huntsbridge.co.uk

'Stylish and civilised', this handsome, creeper-covered 18th-century building belongs to a small group of Fenland inns described as 'a partnership of chefs'. The owner, John Hoskins, a Master of Wine, writes: 'We try to offer individuality and some luxury in every room.' Formerly a bank, *The Old Bridge* stands by the river Ouse, hedged in by a busy traffic system, but the bedrooms have triple glazing and air-conditioning, and the riverside garden provides a relatively peaceful retreat. The 'combination of informality and efficiency' is admired; manager/chef Martin Lee and his wife, Jayne, lead an international staff. The decor is traditional: fine fabrics, good prints, period furniture. The bar lounge is popular for its real ales. Meals are served in the panelled dining room or the less formal terrace room with murals. The cooking is 'excellent, imaginative', but unpretentious, based on local ingredients: starters like quail eggs and Parma ham with spring onion salad, or crab boudin with Swiss chard and tarragon; main courses could be pot-roast chicken with morel mushrooms, sweet potato and leeks, or braised shoulder of lamb with rosemary, tomato, roasted root vegetables and mashed potato. The 'outstanding wine list' includes some good-quality wines by the glass. Morning coffee and afternoon tea are served, with appetising cakes and cookies. 'Our bedroom was very comfortable,' says a visitor this year. 'Morning tea, delivered to the room, came with delicious, really fresh orange juice, and thin shortcake biscuits.' Breakfast 'is good too, with plenty of choice and good service'. Croissants, muffins, bread and black pudding are home-made every day. On weekdays, conferences are catered for. A good base for visiting Ely, the Fens and the bird reserves of the Ouse Washes. (Good Pub Guide, *Pamela Haley*)

Open All year.
Rooms 18 double, 6 single. 2 on ground floor.
Facilities Lounge, bar, 2 restaurants; conference facilities. No background music. Terrace, 1-acre garden; on river bank: fishing, mooring. Civil wedding licence.
Location 500 yds from centre. From Cambridge/Godmanchester cross bridge to inner ring road, turn left; hotel on left. Car park. Station 10 mins' walk.
Restrictions No smoking: restaurant, bedrooms. No dogs in public rooms.
Credit cards All major cards accepted.
Terms B&B: single £80–£95, double £100–£160; D,B&B £70–£120 per person. Full alc £28. Christmas package.

ILFRACOMBE Devon — Map 1:B4

Strathmore Hotel NEW/BUDGET
57 St Brannock's Road
Ilfracombe EX34 8EQ

Tel 01271-862248
Fax 01271-862243
Email strathmore@ukhotels.com
Website www.strathmoreukhotels.com

'We speak French, Italian, Greek and Arabic,' writes the polyglot resident owner, Stella Metaxas, of this friendly little hotel. It stands near the centre of an unspoiled Victorian resort on the north Devon coast. The nominator adds: 'They could not be more caring. My evening meal was superb; the main course of baked salmon had the most delicious potatoes ever. When I mentioned how much I had liked the honey at breakfast, they gave me a pot of it to take home.' Other traditional dishes include avocado and prawns in Marie Rose sauce; roast pork; meringues with strawberries and cream. Children and pets are welcomed. The bedrooms have pastel colours and flowered fabrics. The dining room is strikingly done in shades of red. Green iron tables and chairs, and parasols stand on a flowery patio. Boats to Lundy Island set out from the town harbour. (*Murray Elkington*)

Open All year.
Rooms 1 family, 5 double, 1 single.
Facilities Lounge, TV room, bar, restaurant; varied background music. Patio; outdoor barbecue. Unsuitable for ♿. Sea 10 mins' walk.
Location 8 mins' walk from centre; near Bigglescombe Park. Car park.
Restriction Smoking in bar and lounge only.
Credit cards MasterCard, Visa.
Terms [2001] B&B: single £25–£33, double £40–£56, suite £56–£60; D,B&B £34.95–£47.95. Set dinner £14.95. Special breaks Oct–Mar. Christmas package.

ILMINGTON Warwickshire — Map 3:D6

The Howard Arms NEW
Lower Green, Ilmington
nr Stratford-upon-Avon CV36 4LT

Tel/Fax 01608-682226
Email howardarms@virgin.net
Website www.howardarms.com

Well known to readers of earlier editions of the *Guide* who visited them at *Cotswold House*, Chipping Campden, Robert and Gill Greenstock, with manager Martin Devereux, are now running a much simpler operation on the green of this quiet village just south of Stratford-upon-Avon. In their 400-year-old stone-built inn, they aim 'to provide food of excellent quality at inexpensive prices, in informal surroundings', and in 2001 the *Good Pub Guide* chose it as Warwickshire Dining Pub of the Year. Our correspondents enjoyed the 'innovative modern cooking', served in the heavy-beamed dining room – 'no frills, just good food, ordered at the bar from a blackboard menu', and the 'buzzing atmosphere and sophistication'. Main dishes might be grilled plaice with grain mustard and tarragon butter, or calf's liver with onions, bacon and balsamic dressing; home-made desserts follow, eg, 'Mrs G's toffee meringue'; pear and apple crumble with custard. Only three bedrooms, decorated in 'antique country style'. 'They are delightful, with every attention to detail, but uncluttered and simple; very superior for posh pub accommodation.' A traditional cooked breakfast is included in the rates. Service can be 'a bit strained' at busy times. The garden 'is lovely in summer, with fruit trees sheltering the lawn and a colourful herbaceous border', and there is good walking in the nearby hills. (*Emma Merriam*)

Open All year, except 25 Dec.
Rooms 3 double. No telephone.
Facilities Snug, bar, dining bar. ½-acre garden. Unsuitable for ♿.
Location Green of village 4 miles NW of Shipston on Stour. Parking.

Restrictions No smoking: dining room, snug, bedrooms. No children under 10 overnight. No dogs.
Credit cards MasterCard, Visa.
Terms [2001] B&B: single from £45, double £84; D,B&B double £118. Full alc £25–£28. 2-day breaks. 1-night bookings refused weekends.

IPSWICH Suffolk — Map 2:C5

The Marlborough
Henley Road
Ipswich IP1 3SP

Tel 01473-257677
Fax 01473-226927
Email reception@themarlborough.co.uk
Website www.themarlborough.co.uk

Owned by Mrs Mary Gough (see also *The Angel*, Bury St Edmunds), this Victorian town house is in a residential area of Ipswich, across a busy road from Christchurch Park. 'It is one of our favourite hotels,' wrote a returning visitor. 'The staff, headed by Nancy Innes, the charming manager, as usual bent over backwards to be helpful.' Simone, at reception, wins special mention – 'she doubles as waitress, barman, early morning coffee server and so on.' Shaun Thurlow has been promoted to head chef, replacing Simon Barker, who has transferred to *The Angel*. He maintains 'the usual high standard'. 'We had really fresh sea bass, tender pink duck breast, excellent chicken. Desserts are consistently good, including toffee and banana crème brûlée. An innovation is a selection of freshly baked bread instead of rolls.' Guests are charged according to number of courses taken. Coffee comes with 'delicious home-made fudge'. The restaurant has well-spaced tables, good napery; it gives access to the pretty garden where alfresco meals are served in summer. The bedrooms have period furniture, good reading lights and television sets with a low maximum volume guaranteeing the neighbouring rooms peace. Business visitors are catered for during the week; there are good weekend reductions. Musical evenings are held in summer. Ipswich, the birthplace of Cardinal Wolsey, and the possible home of Chaucer, is a busy inland port and agricultural centre on the river Orwell. Despite modernisation, it retains some fine old buildings. (*Moira Jarrett*)

Open All year.
Rooms 1 suite, 17 double, 4 single. Some on ground floor.
Facilities Ramps. Lounge, bar, restaurant; 'easy-listening' background music all day; private dining room, small conference room. ½-acre garden. Civil wedding licence.
Location 1 mile SW of centre, off A1214 (rear rooms quietest). Parking.
Restrictions No smoking in restaurant. No dogs in public rooms.
Credit cards All major cards accepted.
Terms [2001] B&B: single £29.50–£80.15, double £59–£113.30, suite £80–£135. D,B&B £54.45–£105.10 per person. Set lunch £17.95, dinner £25.95; full alc £40. Child in parents' room: under 12, free. Christmas, New Year, Easter packages. *V*

> If you think we have over-praised a hotel or done it an injustice, please let us know.

KIMBOLTON Herefordshire **Map 3:C4**

Lower Bache House BUDGET *Tel* 01568-750304
Kimbolton *Email* leslie.wiles@care4free.net
nr Leominster HR6 0ER

The setting is 'ravishingly beautiful': this 17th-century half-timbered farmhouse and granary 'sits invitingly' in its little Herefordshire valley, surrounded by fields and woodland. It has been sympathetically restored by Rose and Leslie Wiles who run it as a friendly country guest house. 'A good place in which to be involuntarily marooned,' writes a visitor this year. 'The lovely old building offered a cool escape from the hot afternoon sun. In the mornings, fresh air, and the sounds of birds filled the bedroom.' Family dogs and cats roam around. 'My bedroom had a sitting area with squashy sofa, writing desk, TV, kettle, etc, and a modern shower room. Over 40 prints hung on the walls, and the bookshelves were laden with interesting things to read.' The sitting/dining room, with a vaulted ceiling, a flagstone floor, and 'exciting features', notably the old cider mill wheel, has been furnished with antiques. Organic ingredients are used in imaginative cooking, eg, grilled tiger prawns with a garam masala and turmeric mayonnaise; guineafowl roasted with garlic, sage and rosemary. Vegetarians are catered for. Dinner must be ordered by midday; preferences are discussed in advance. Much of the produce is home-grown. 'Breakfast is an organic experience of home-made items of every kind, all delicious.' The check-out time of 10 am is a bit early for some. Much interesting sightseeing nearby: castles, gardens, Hereford cathedral with the Mappa Mundi, etc. (*Trevor Lockwood*)

Open All year.
Rooms 4 double. 1, on ground floor, across courtyard. No telephone.
Facilities Lounge/dining room. No background music. 14-acre grounds: meadows, wildlife. Walking, cycling, riding, golf, horse racing, fishing nearby.
Location 4 miles NE of Leominster. From A4112 between Kimbolton and Leysters, follow signs to Lower Bache.
Restrictions No smoking. No children under 8. No dogs.
Credit cards None accepted.
Terms B&B: single £39.50, double £59. Set dinner £15.50–£21.50. Bargain breaks. Christmas package.

KINGSBRIDGE Devon **Map 1:D4**

Buckland-Tout-Saints NEW *Tel* 01548-853055
Goveton, nr Kingsbridge *Fax* 01548-856261
TQ7 2DS *Email* buckland@tout-saints.co.uk
Website www.tout-saints.co.uk

A serene Queen Anne manor house near Kingsbridge, in a 'gorgeous out-of-the-way setting' reached by winding Devon roads. 'It well deserves an entry in the *Guide*,' says an inspector, 'though my "superior" single bedroom was distinctly less posh than the ones shown in the brochure, and the background music played all evening and at breakfast was very irritating. The public rooms were lovely (all wood panelling), the staff were charming, and my dog was made very welcome.' But she thought the food on the long menu 'over-priced – goat's cheese starter very small; baked brill was dry, with a stingy serving of vegetables'. The grounds, though not large, 'are lovely', but 'the helipad is very near the house'. Captain Mark Trumble and his wife, Julia, the owners since 1999, have restored old plasterwork and Adam doors; the panelling in the bar was created from pews from the Carfax church, Oxford. Open fires, a chessboard laid out ready for play, and a 'teddy Tout-Saints' in every bedroom add to the feel 'that you are in a gracious home, not a hotel'.

Open 5 Feb–8 Jan.
Rooms 2 suites, 8 double.
Facilities Lounge (live jazz monthly), bar, 2 dining rooms (background music); function suite. 4½-acre grounds: croquet, *pétanque*, putting. Golf, sailing, fishing, beaches nearby. Civil wedding licence. Unsuitable for ♿.
Location 2 miles NE of Kingsbridge, signposted. Left off A381 from Totnes. Train: Totnes; taxi.
Restriction No smoking: restaurant, bedrooms.
Credit cards MasterCard, Visa.
Terms B&B £55–£120; D,B&B £95–£130. Set lunch £18, dinner £25; full alc £25. Christmas package. ***V***

KINGTON Herefordshire — Map 3:C4

Penrhos Court
Kington HR5 3LH

Tel 01544-230720
Fax 01544-230754
Email martin@penrhos.co.uk
Website www.penrhos.co.uk

Martin Griffiths and Daphne Lambert have lovingly restored a tranquil collection of ancient buildings to create a smoke-free eco-friendly hotel. Ms Lambert, the chef, runs the first organic restaurant in Britain to gain the Soil Association's symbol, and while her cooking might be 'too healthy' for some, she won praise this year from a committed carnivore. 'All the vegetarian members of our party thought the food was fine. Over four evenings we had lentil soup, Jerusalem artichoke soup, tofu, polenta, mushrooms, salads, chicken for those of us who need meat. The organic wine was enjoyed.' There are choices at dinner, served under subdued lighting at rustic wooden tables: sweet potato soup, or tomato, olive and feta salad might be followed by mackerel with apples, cider and cream, supreme of chicken with ratatouille, or marinated tofu with red rice pilaff. 'The puddings were outstanding – we tried them all; the chestnut, raisin and brandy ice cream was the best ever.' The flagstone-floored Cruck Hall (not too easy to heat in winter) dates from the time of Edward I; there is an Elizabethan wing, and a large modern one, 'beautifully integrated with the rest'. They are set around a pond (home to moorhens, coots and mallards) off a road in the hilly Welsh borders. Bedrooms, named after local birds, are large; some are huge, with lovely views. 'Old-fashioned comfort and creaky wooden floors combine with modern conveniences such as TV, and a shower that would measure up to the most exacting standards.'

Breakfast has freshly squeezed fruit and vegetable juices; a loaf of wholemeal bread at each table, organic honey and preserves. No fry-up, but Welsh rarebit or tofu sausages. Daphne Lambert runs a school of food and health; gardening weekends are held with the organic gardener, Bob Flowerdew. The 'helpful host' will recommend good walks and pubs for lunch. Close by are the Hergest Croft Gardens; also castles, stately homes, and Offa's Dyke. (*Anthony Stern, and others*)

Open All year. Lunch not served.
Rooms 15 double. Some on ground floor.
Facilities Ramps. Cruck Hall, Elizabethan room, snug, restaurant; function facilities. No background music. Garden. Civil wedding licence.
Location W of Leominster. ½ mile E of Kington, on A44.
Restrictions No smoking. No dogs.
Credit cards Amex, MasterCard, Visa.
Terms B&B: double £90, suite £100; D,B&B double £152–£163. Set dinner £31.50; full alc £38.50. 2-night breaks. Christmas package.

KNUTSFORD Cheshire — Map 4:E3

Belle Epoque BUDGET
60 King Street
Knutsford WA16 6DT
Tel 01565-633060 and 632661
Fax 01565-634150
Email info@thebelleepoque.com

'Superb food in an eccentric and exotically decorated dining room with stupendous tall flower arrangements on every table; helpful staff.' Run by Nerys Mooney with her sons, David (the chef) and Matthew, this brasserie-with-rooms was once a coffee house. The building (with a quirky tower) is considered to be the crowning achievement of Richard Harding Watt, a well-travelled Manchester glove merchant/architect, active locally at the turn of the 19th century. It has a dramatic Art Nouveau decor: deep green and purple walls, mirrored alcoves, a Venetian glass floor. Fabrics are lavish; tables have heavy cloths, good cutlery and glassware, wicker chairs. David Mooney (who has worked with Raymond Blanc and Marco Pierre White) serves menus that embrace all influences', eg, rillettes of rabbit; goat's cheese with spring onion pancakes; venison and peach pie; Cheshire cheese sausage; fish and chips. There is a terrace for alfresco meals. 'Our room, up about three narrow, difficult (with heavy bags) staircases, was cramped, with a poor bathroom. Despite the discomfort, the extreme idiosyncrasy and high culinary standards made the stay memorable.' One bedroom has French doors leading on to the roof terrace – 'here, we breakfasted in privacy on two sunny mornings'. There could be aircraft noise from Manchester airport. With cobbled alleys, courtyards, and narrow streets rich in antique shops, pubs and interior designers, Knutsford is a small commuter town, 18 miles from Manchester. Mrs Gaskell, who grew up here, used it as the model for *Cranford*. It has two Palladian mansions (both National Trust): Tatton Park, in large grounds with gardens by Humphry Repton and a working farm, and Tabley House. (*James L Clarke, GE*)

Open All year, Mon–Fri only, except Christmas, New Year. Brasserie closed Sat lunch, bank holidays, possibly all day Sun.
Rooms 6 double.
Facilities Restaurant (background music); function rooms; terrace, roof garden. Unsuitable for ♿.
Location Town centre. Street parking. Regular trains from Manchester.
Restrictions No smoking in 1 dining room. No children under 12. No dogs.
Credit cards All major cards accepted.
Terms [2001] B&B: single £50, double £60. Full alc £25.

Longview
51 and 55 Manchester Road
Knutsford WA16 0LX

Tel 01565-632119
Fax 01565-652402
Email enquiries@longviewhotel.com
Website www.longviewhotel.com

'The owners and staff are charming,' says a visitor this year to Pauline and Stephen West's small hotel, endorsing earlier praise: 'welcoming atmosphere'; 'good value'. Composed of two Victorian houses separated by a private home, and decorated in Victorian style (Staffordshire china, flowery curtains, patterned wallpapers), it looks across a busy commuter road to a wide common. Quietest bedrooms are at the rear (front windows are double-glazed). The double rooms vary from 'cosy' to 'premium'; most have mahogany Victorian-style furniture, and they have been thoughtfully equipped (with nail brush, pincushion, 'full-bodied towels', a clothes brush, etc). But some walls are thin, and steps to the rooms are steep. The two new suites look over a private garden; one has its own terrace. There is a small cellar bar. The restaurant is frequented by locals, and serves careful, reasonably priced, traditional cooking, eg, king prawns in garlic butter; game casserole; chocolate terrine; also good vegetarian dishes. Light meals can be taken in the bar or the bedrooms. 'Substantial breakfast.' Visit the local stately home, Tatton Park. (*GL Ellis, MM Reeves; also John Gibbon*)

Open Jan–Dec. Restaurant closed midday; also Sun, bank holidays.
Rooms 2 suites, 18 double, 6 single. 13 in annexe (2 doors away).
Facilities Bar (light background music), restaurant. Small grounds. Unsuitable for ♿.
Location On road to Manchester (front rooms double-glazed). 10 mins' walk from station (regular commuter trains).
Restrictions No smoking in restaurant. No dogs in public rooms.
Credit cards All major cards accepted
Terms B&B: single £50–£69.50, double £69.50–£99, suite £125–£135. Full alc £23.50.

> Readers with mobility problems might like to know of the *Smooth Ride Guides,* which publish information about many hotels with facilities for the disabled. *Tel* 01279-777966, *fax* 01279-777995, *email* july.ramsey@virgin.net, *website* www.easyspace.com/banner.

LACOCK Wiltshire Map 2:D1

At the Sign of the Angel
6 Church Street
Lacock, Chippenham SN15 2LB

Tel 01249-730230
Fax 01249-730527
Email angel@lacock.co.uk
Website www.lacock.co.uk

César award in 1989

Quintessentially English, this 15th-century half-timbered inn has been run by the Levis family for almost 50 years. It stands in the middle of a lovely wool village, now preserved in its entirety by the National Trust. With low doorways and beams, oak panelling, antique furniture, open fires, and squeaky floorboards, it is not for those seeking luxury. It is liked for its 'no-frills style and intimacy', 'friendly but not gushing' service, and peaceful garden. But one guest thought that help with luggage should have been offered. 'Eccentric, with old uneven floors; no keys to the bedroom though they can be locked from the inside,' writes one reader this year. Others enjoy the very good service, very good food, great wine list' and 'great atmosphere' but again there is a grumble about the lack of a smoking ban, particularly in the restaurant. Bedrooms may be small, but they are full of character. Inevitably, the sound insulation between some rooms is imperfect, and some rooms get noise from the kitchens below. The quietest ones are probably those in the garden cottage across a stream. Chef/*patronne* Lorna Levis and co-owner/*sous-chef* George Hardy preside over a restaurant that is often busy with visitors enjoying the 'robustly satisfying English cooking, using excellent local produce'. But one diner, who sent her beef back because it was rare, thought the chefs 'dictatorial'. Home-made soups; ham hock with honey mustard sauce; meringues with clotted cream and strawberries are typical of the traditional menu. There is always a roast of the day, and a vegetarian option. 'Breakfasts are wonderful.' One recommendation/caution: 'It is important to like cats: two black and white ones spend most of their time in the lounge upstairs, while Henry, who is ginger, will sit on your lap at breakfast.' (*LW, and others*)

Open 1 Jan–23 Dec.
Rooms 10 double. 4 in garden annexe. 4 on ground floor. 1 suitable for ♿.
Facilities Lounge, 3 dining rooms. No background music. Civil wedding licence. Garden: stream.
Location 7 miles S of M4 exit 17; E of A350 Chippenham–Melksham. Garages, off-street parking. Train: Chippenham, 3 miles.
Restrictions No smoking in bedrooms. No dogs in public rooms.
Credit cards All major cards accepted.
Terms B&B: single £68–£85, double £99–£137.50. Full alc £30.

****

Traveller's tale Hotel in Lincolnshire. The bedroom was fine, if cramped, but there was no hot water – indeed, there was little water at all. When we came down to breakfast, we commented on this. The owner had the audacity to say: 'You should have said you wanted the hot water on.' Could it not have been anticipated that we would wish to shower before breakfast?

****

LANGAR Nottinghamshire — Map 2:A3

Langar Hall
Langar NG13 9HG

Tel 01949-860559
Fax 01949-861045
Email langarhall-hotel@ndirect.co.uk
Website www.langarhall.com

César award in 2000

Imogen Skirving has called in the decorators at her ever-popular hotel. She promises that the 'faded gentility', even scruffiness, will bc vanquished. The small bar has been extended, the study refurbished, and a new bedroom ('not too pink') is dedicated to the memory of a regular guest, Barbara Cartland. It looks over the adjacent churchyard. Richard Firmstone, who previously looked after marriages and receptions, has been promoted to general manager. But the mild eccentricity that secured our *César* can be expected to continue as Ms Skirving keeps her finger on the pulse. The old brick house, 'quaint, wood panelled and almost wallpapered with pictures and cartoons', stands by the ancient church of a village in the Vale of Belvoir (pronounced Beaver). Housekeeping may not always be immaculate, but *Langar Hall* is loved for its personal style, and is favoured by lawyers and Test Match Special commentators as a retreat from nearby Nottingham. The large, most expensive rooms are in the main house. Barristers resembles an old-fashioned solicitor's office. Bohemia, dedicated to the Arabian Knights, and with love poetry inscribed on its bathroom, is recommended for the romantic. One six-foot-tall guest found the bed in Lilac a bit short. In the busy restaurant, the chefs, Toby Garratt and Chris Ansell, serve simply cooked dishes using organic ingredients and light sauces, eg, wood pigeon and mushroom tart; roast turbot, roast duck, or saddle of venison; passion fruit tart or iced coffee soufflé; the cheeseboard features Colston Bassett, the Stilton cheese made a mile away. 'Service at dinner was prompt and friendly, but at breakfast it was very slow. We were puzzled by the 5% "optional" service charge, but we paid up.' Other reporters thought breakfast 'excellent'. The occasional opera performances after dinner have been dropped, but not the annual open-air Shakespeare production. New trees have been planted in the large grounds in which are gardens, canals, medieval fishponds, a croquet lawn and an adventure play area for children. (*Anthony Stern, and others*)

Open All year.
Rooms 1 family, 9 double, 1 single. 1 on ground floor.
Facilities Ramp. Drawing room, library, bar, dining room, private dining room; small conference facilities. No background music. 30-acre grounds: gardens, children's play area, croquet, ponds. Civil wedding licence.
Location 12 miles SE of Nottingham (hotel will send directions). Train: Grantham or Nottingham; link to Bingham, 3 miles.
Restriction No smoking: restaurant, bedrooms.
Credit cards All major cards accepted.
Terms (*Excluding 5% discretionary service charge*) B&B: single £70–£97.50, double £140–£185, family £210–£320. Cooked breakfast £7.50. Set lunch £10, dinner £20; full alc £35. 2-night weekend breaks: 25% reduction. *V*

LANGFORD BUDVILLE Somerset — Map 1:C5

Bindon Country House
Langford Budville
nr Wellington TA21 0RU

Tel 01823-400070
Fax 01823-400071
Email stay@bindon.com
Website www.bindonhouse.com

'It has a happy atmosphere. Reception is always warm, the owners and their staff are most courteous, and the food is excellent.' A report this year on this 'splendidly bizarre' house (Pride of Britain). It dates back to the 17th century, but in Victorian days it was given the appearance of a baroque Bavarian hunting lodge. It stands in large grounds with formal gardens, woodland, a small swimming pool, a hot tub, a croquet lawn and a chapel. Though only ten minutes from the M5, it is deep in Somerset countryside, next to the 180-acre Langford Heath nature reserve. Wellington, the town from which the Iron Duke took his title, is nearby, and the hotel's 'personable young owners', Lynn and Mark Jaffa, have turned it into something of a shrine to him: pictures of the battles that he fought, and memorabilia of his life, adorn the public rooms. The oak-panelled bar and the 'intimate restaurant' are called Wellington and Wellesley, respectively – the 'rather staid' drawing room (with heavy drapes and dark furnishings) is Bonaparte. The bedrooms are named for famous Wellingtonian victories: Waterloo, Talavera, Douro, etc. They vary in size, but all are well equipped and 'most comfortable'. 'Delicious canapés' come with pre-dinner drinks. The chef, Patrick Roberts, from Brittany, serves modern dishes on a short *carte* and a set menu with plenty of choice, eg, seared scallops on broccoli purée, onion Tatin and rabbit consommé; grilled sea bass with roast vegetables, tagliatelle and cappuccino of peas; chocolate soufflé with orange sorbet. 'And if one wants something else, it is provided at no extra charge.' A child-friendly place – the Jaffas are parents themselves (there are high teas for the young). Dunster Castle, Barrington Court and Hestercombe house and gardens are within driving distance. (*CHN Mackey*)

Open All year.
Rooms 2 junior suites, 10 double. Some on ground floor.
Facilities Hall (pianist on Sat), lounge, TV room, bar, restaurant, 2 conference rooms. No background music. 7-acre grounds: kitchen garden, swimming pool, croquet, chapel, woodland. Nature reserve adjacent. Civil wedding licence.
Location 4 miles NW of Wellington. B3187 towards Langford Budville. After 4 miles, follow sharp left-hand bend into village. Through village; right towards Wiveliscombe; right at next junction. After 1 mile, pass Bindon Farm; hotel 450 yds further (next right). Train: Tiverton, 7 miles, or Taunton.
Restrictions No smoking: restaurant, lounge. No dogs in public rooms.
Credit cards All major cards accepted.
Terms [2001] B&B double £95–£155; D,B&B £60–£105 per person. Set lunch £12.95, dinner £29.95; full alc £45. Child sharing with parents charged for meals only. Midweek break. Christmas package. *V*

For details of the Voucher scheme see page xxx.

LANGHO Lancashire Map 4:D3

Northcote Manor
Northcote Road, Langho
Blackburn BB6 8BE

Tel 01254-240555
Fax 01254-246568
Email admin@northcotemanor.com
Website www.northcotemanor.com

Luscious pictures of food adorn the glossy brochure for Nigel Haworth and Craig Bancroft's informally run red brick Victorian house. They proclaim the priorities at this *Michelin*-starred restaurant-with-rooms: the focus is on the food; service can be 'haphazard' at times. One couple was 'favourably impressed despite a poor welcome'. One guest was surprised to be shown to Room 10, with a poor outlook and faulty lights, when the place was not full. Other bedrooms are said to have 'ravishing views', and most are spacious, with good fabrics, old furniture, ornaments and games. Some are up a handsome wooden staircase; some are down 'a maze of corridors'. The dining room has yellow walls, and crockery specially designed by Wedgwood; daytime views over a Japanese-style flowerbed 'add another dimension'. Nigel Haworth, who describes his cooking as 'modern British with rustic undertones', has researched old regional recipes, eg, black pudding and buttered pink trout with mustard and watercress sauce; beef with marrowbone, tarragon jus and honey-roast potatoes; apple crumble soufflé. Many vegetables and herbs are grown organically in the garden. The wide-ranging wine list has a 'fine selection of half bottles'. The house, set in wooded grounds, looks across to Pendle Hill, above the county town of Clitheroe. The busy A59 is close by (windows are double-glazed). Breakfast includes freshly squeezed orange juice, 'artistically arranged' fresh fruit, black and white puddings, and 'delicious wholemeal bread'. Good walking nearby in the Ribble valley and the Forest of Bowland; also ruined abbeys, interesting museums, and historic villages – many associated with witches. (*Peter and Audrey Hutchinson, WKW, FW*)

Open All year, except 25 Dec, 1 Jan, some bank holiday Mondays.
Rooms 1 suite, 13 double. 4 on ground floor.
Facilities Ramp. Lounge, drawing room, bar, restaurant (background jazz); private dining/meeting room. 2-acre garden. Civil wedding licence.
Location From M6 exit 31, follow signs to Skipton, Clitheroe. At 1st set of traffic lights, turn left on to A59. Straight ahead at roundabout at Mellor. After 8 miles turn left, immediately before large roundabout at Langho. Train: Preston, 14 miles; bus/taxi.
Restrictions No smoking: restaurant, some bedrooms. No dogs.
Credit cards Amex, MasterCard, Visa.
Terms (*Excluding 'optional' 10% service charge*) B&B: single £80–£110, double £100–£130, suite £130–£150. Set lunch £16, dinner £25–£40; full alc £54. Gourmet breaks.

There are many expensive hotels in the *Guide*. We are keen to increase our coverage at the other end of the scale. If you know of a simple place giving simple satisfaction, do please write and tell us about it.

LANGLEY MARSH Somerset Map 1:B5

Langley House
Langley Marsh
Wiveliscombe
nr Taunton TA4 2UF

Tel 01984-623318
Fax 01984-624573
Email user@langley.in2home.co.uk

Peter (the chef) and Anne Wilson, a 'nicely tactful' couple, have presided for over 15 years at their restaurant-with-rooms – a gold grasshopper sign marks the entrance. Their Grade II listed Georgian house stands in large grounds, with mature gardens, a pond and a tiny stream, on the edge of the Exmoor National Park. Some might find the style old-fashioned, but the flexible way children are handled was admired this year, and the decor 'emphasises comfort as well as elegance', using vibrant colours, notably in the pink-walled drawing room. Antique furniture, heavy fabrics, and fresh and dried flowers abound. The medium-sized bedrooms, up a curved staircase, have a floral decor, patterned wallpaper, good lighting. After drinks in the lounge, dinner is from 8 on weekdays, at 8.30 on Saturday, in the small, beamed pink and green dining room. Three courses on weekdays, four (including cheese) at the weekend. Fresh local ingredients are cooked with herbs and vegetables from the walled garden. The style is Modern British, eg, sea bass with a herb crust on leeks with beurre blanc; lamb with onion and cassis purée. No choice on the menu until dessert, perhaps chocolate parfait or elderflower and elderberry syllabub. Morning tea is brought to the bedroom. Hot toast comes with cooked dishes at breakfast. Extra charges, for after-dinner coffee and chocolates, newspapers, etc, can bump up the bill. The Brendon hills are nearby; so are some famous gardens: Knightshayes, Stourhead, Montacute, etc. More reports, please.

Open All year.
Rooms 1 family, 6 double, 1 single.
Facilities 2 lounges, restaurant, conservatory, private dining room. 4-acre garden: croquet. Unsuitable for ♿.
Location B3227 to Wiveliscombe; right at town centre, signposted Langley Marsh; house ½ mile to N, on right. Train: Taunton; bus to Langley Cross.
Restrictions No smoking: restaurant, 2 bedrooms. No dogs in public rooms.
Credit cards Amex, MasterCard, Visa.
Terms [2001] B&B: single £77.50–£87.50, double £93–£127.50, family £142.50–£155; D,B&B £74–£105 per person. Set dinner (3–4 courses) £27.50–£32.50. Discount for 2 nights or more. 1-night bookings sometimes refused weekends, bank holidays. *V*

LASTINGHAM North Yorkshire Map 4:C4

Lastingham Grange
Lastingham YO62 6TH

Tel 01751-417345 and 417402
Fax 01751-417358
Email reservations@lastinghamgrange.com
Website www.lastinghamgrange.com

César award in 1991

'It was six years since our last visit; we found it as good as ever.' A tribute this year from regular *Guide* readers to a hotel that has been a regular in the *Guide* since the first issue. The owners, Dennis and Jane Wood, attract many loyal visitors who love its 'homely atmosphere', and find it 'wonderfully quiet'. The outstanding dedication' of Mr Wood is praised, and the 'conscious effort to treat every guest as an individual – from the outset one is addressed by name'. 'The Woods are most informative about the area.' A major attraction is the 'marvellous position' in the North York Moors National Park; you can step straight out on to the moor. The 17th-century stone-walled farmhouse, built round a courtyard, is surrounded by gardens, mature trees and fields. The well-maintained decor is thoroughly traditional (patterned carpets everywhere; flowery fabrics and wallpaper in the 'spotless bedrooms'). The food is traditional though 'not fuddy-duddy', 'good, if not gourmet', with dishes like avocado vinaigrette, or curried egg and apple; 'excellent baked skate wings', or grilled fillet steak béarnaise. There is always a vegetarian main course. Mr Wood is 'very attentive in the dining room, without being intrusive'. Not cheap, but newspapers, morning coffee, afternoon tea and shoe-cleaning are included. Children are welcomed – they have their own adventure playground. The village, where St Cedd built an abbey in the 7th century, makes an excellent base for walking. Nearby attractions include Castle Howard, and Rievaulx and Fountains abbeys. (*Anne and Denis Tate*, *Ann H Edwards, HRL*)

Open Beginning Mar–end Nov.
Rooms 10 double, 2 single.
Facilities Hall, lounge, dining room; laundry facilities. No background music. 10-acre grounds: garden, adventure playground. In National Park, near moors and dales; riding, golf, swimming nearby. Unsuitable for ♿.
Location 5 miles NE of Kirkbymoorside. 2 miles E of Kirkbymoorside, turn N off A170 towards Appleton-le-Moors.
Restrictions No smoking in dining room. No dogs in public rooms.
Credit cards All major cards accepted.
Terms [2001] B&B: single £85–£89, double £160–£168; D,B&B: single £102–£115, double £190–£210. Light/picnic lunches available. Set lunch £17.75, dinner £32.75. Child in parents' room: under 12, free. Reductions for long stays. Winter breaks.

LAVENHAM Suffolk — Map 2:C5

The Great House
Market Place
Lavenham CO10 9QZ

Tel 01787-247431
Fax 01787-248007
Email info@greathouse.co.uk
Website www.greathouse.co.uk

Owner/chef Régis Crépy and his wife, Martine, run a Gallic restaurant-with-rooms in this 16th-century house with a Georgian facade, where the poet Stephen Spender once lived. It overlooks Lavenham's medieval marketplace. 'The food is excellent,' reports a visitor who also enjoyed the croissants and pain au chocolat at breakfast. 'Wonderful; charming though not luxurious,' says another. Accommodation is mainly in suites; the best ones have antiques, old beams and a smart new bathroom; homelier ones are on the top floor. 'We liked the thoughtful details, eg, halogen lights in the four-poster, enabling us to read in bed. Wonderful to have a separate sitting room.' 'Room 2 was pleasant, but noisy on a Saturday night.' The 'consistently courteous service' by the French staff is praised. 'They genuinely like and welcome children, and treat them as mini-adults.' Traditional French dishes are served in the oak-beamed, candlelit dining room, with its bare floorboards and original inglenook fireplace. Parmesan risotto with cèpes, parsley and garlic; veal with wild mushrooms, poached quail's eggs and a Madeira sauce, might feature on the *carte*; the *prix-fixe* menu offers plenty of choice and good value. Light lunches are served from Tuesday to Saturday; Sunday lunch is a set three-course affair. The mainly French wine list has some reasonably priced bottles. There is a small sitting room/bar, a patio, where alfresco meals are served, and a walled garden. The restaurant is popular – book a table when reserving your room. The Crépys also own another restaurant at Bury St Edmunds, *Maison Bleue at Mortimers*. (*IB, Felicity Chadwick-Histed*)

Open Feb–Dec. Restaurant closed Sun night/Mon.
Rooms 4 suites, 1 double.
Facilities Lounge/bar, restaurant (French background music). ½-acre garden: patio, swings. Unsuitable for ♿.
Location By Market Cross, near Guildhall. Public car park. Bus 753, Colchester–Bury.
Restrictions No smoking: restaurant, bedrooms. No dogs in public rooms.
Credit cards Amex, MasterCard, Visa.
Terms [2001] B&B: single £55–£130, double £70–£140. Set lunch £9.95–£15.95, dinner £19.95; full alc: lunch £18, dinner £38. Midweek breaks. Child in parents' room: under 2, free; 3–12, £15. 1-night bookings refused Fri/Sat.

Lavenham Priory
Water Street
Lavenham CO10 9RW

Tel 01787-247404
Fax 01787-248472
Email mail@lavenhampriory.co.uk
Website www.lavenhampriory.co.uk

Tim and Gilli Pitt ('very nice, chatty and helpful') have lavishly restored a medieval priory – 'the title was first held by Benedictine monks in the 13th century – 'to recreate its appearance as an Elizabethan merchant's home. 'It has ended up a dream,' said our inspector. You enter through a 'wonderful garden', with herbs and old roses, to the timber-framed house. The Great Hall has a Tudor inglenook fireplace, antique furniture, and an oak Jacobean staircase, and plenty of comfortable sofas and chairs, 'not over the top, just comfortable'. The five 'bedchambers' have unusual beds – four-poster, *lit bateau* or polonaise. 'Everything is done with taste. Our bedroom was huge, romantic, with a soaring ceiling. The bathroom, oh so pretty, had a large slipper bath, and there was a separate shower room with a

power shower.' Breakfast is served round a large table in another antique-filled room. 'You squeeze your own orange juice, and make your own toast from good bread; there is a buffet with fresh fruit, compotes, etc; and well-cooked egg dishes, etc.' In summer, breakfast and drinks (the Pitts have a licence to sell alcohol) are served in the herb garden. No dinners, but there are good restaurants very near, eg, *The Great House* (see above). Guests can sit in the Great Hall or a lounge (with TV, videos and books); both have an inglenook fireplace.

Open All year, except Christmas, New Year.
Rooms 5 double. No telephone.
Facilities Great Hall, reading room, breakfast room. No background music. 3-acre garden: courtyard, herb garden. Unsuitable for ♿.
Location Central. From A1141 to Lavenham turn by *Swan* on to Water St; right after 50 yds into private drive. Parking.
Restrictions No smoking. No children under 10. No dogs.
Credit cards MasterCard, Visa.
Terms [2001] B&B: single £59–£69, double £78–£108. Sat supplement: £10. 1-night bookings refused Sat.

LEAMINGTON SPA Warwickshire *See SHORTLIST* Map 2:B2

LEDBURY Herefordshire *See SHORTLIST* Map 3:D5

LEEDS West Yorkshire Map 4:D4

---

42 The Calls

42 The Calls
Leeds LS2 7EW

Tel 0113-244 0099
Fax 0113-234 4100
Email hotel@42thecalls.co.uk
Website www.42thecalls.co.uk

César award in 1995

'It still beats most luxury hotels by reason of the comprehensive (and very personal) information pack, the reliable services and, above all, the efficient and very friendly staff.' Praise from a returning visitor for this unusual hotel in a former warehouse in the waterfront area of central Leeds. Another wrote of 'the nice touches in the bedrooms: best pillows and sheets, proper shower, CD-player, good soundproofing, etc' that 'make the place'. The founder, Jonathan Wix, this year opened a 68-bedroom hotel in the former *Scotsman* building in Edinburgh, and one visitor wondered whether 'attention to detail was slipping' in his absence – 'a bottle of lukewarm champagne had been left in our bedroom' – but concluded: 'Though less "cutting edge" than it once was, it remains a very pleasant place.' The decor is modern, with original paintings everywhere, and smart, air-conditioned public rooms. Bedrooms vary from 'study' to 'Director's' (these 'are exceptional'). All have satellite TV, three telephones, a lavish bathroom. Many overlook the river Aire (with fishing rights – you might find a rod by the window). 'Breakfast, in a beautiful riverside room, offers freshly squeezed orange juice, fruit compotes, cereals, lovely fresh bread, good coffee', also juicy kippers, nine types of exotic sausage (eg, wild boar and black sheep). *Brasserie 44,* which serves 'excellent, straightforward', Mediterranean-style food, was awarded a *Michelin Bib Gourmand* this year. The restaurant, *Pool Court at 42* (*Michelin* star), serves Jeff Baker's 'classically inspired modern cooking' (eg, creamed eggs with shaved truffle; sautéed calf's liver with polenta and pancetta; organic lemon sponge with mandarin sorbet) in black and white surroundings. It has a waterfront balcony for summer meals. The hotel is business-orientated during the week; at weekends it offers generous reductions. Difficult to find by car, but they will send a map. Nearby are Victorian arcades and shops, including the northern branch of Harvey Nichols. (*Kate and David Wooff, Anne-Marie Sutcliffe, IGC Farman, and others*)

Open All year, except New Year, possibly Christmas. *Pool Court* closed Sat and Sun midday, bank holidays.
Rooms 3 suites, 36 double, 2 single. 1 suitable for ♿.
Facilities Lift. Lounge, 2 bars, breakfast room, restaurant, brasserie; background music; conference facilities.
Location Central, near Corn Exchange (rooms double/triple-glazed; quietest ones overlook river). Valet parking (£4.95 a day weekends, £8.95 weekdays).
Restriction No dogs in public rooms.
Credit cards All major cards accepted.
Terms (*Excluding 10% service charge on meals*) Room: single £105, double £138, suite £195. Breakfast £8.95–£12.50. Set meals (restaurant) £29.50–£37.50; full alc: brasserie £28, restaurant £32. Child in parents' room: £5. 1-night bookings refused bank holidays, some weekends. *V*

Haley's
Shire Oak Road
Headingley, Leeds LS6 2DE

Tel 0113-278 4446
Fax 0113-275 3342
Email info@haleys.co.uk
Website www.haleys.co.uk

Regional Loo of the Year for 10 years running is one of the awards that John Appleyard's popular hotel in Headingley has claimed. This turreted Victorian House wins regular acclaim, too, from visitors who like 'the quiet surroundings, well-trained young staff', the efficient manager, Tim Howard, the 'lack of sycophancy' and the free parking. It is popular with business visitors, so offers good weekend rates. The house, named for a local stonemason prominent at the turn of the 19th century, has been carefully restored to its original splendour. There are open fires, period furniture, lavish drapes in the public rooms; pictures everywhere, many with a cricketing theme in honour of the famous cricket ground nearby. 'A delightful atmosphere, very comfortable bedrooms.' The rooms in the turrets are large, with a bay window. The one in the garden has 'well-designed period touches', a tiny lobby/lounge and a decent-sized bathroom. Extras include a trouser press, two phones in every room, an ironing board, Harrogate toffee and a cuddly toy dog. Chef Jon Vennell changes his menu monthly in the restaurant (open to the public), which has a striking brown-and-cream decor. His modern cooking might include chicken and thyme sausage; grilled John Dory; always a vegetarian option; duo of raspberry and mango parfait. Breakfast is Yorkshire or continental. (*AB*)

Open All year, except 26–30 Dec. Restaurant closed midday Mon–Sat, to non-residents Sun evening.
Rooms Two 2-roomed suites, 18 double, 9 single. 7 in *Bedford House*, next door.
Facilities Ramp. Lounge/bar, library, restaurant; function/meeting room. Jazz/classical background music 6 pm–11.30 pm. Small front and back lawns. Unsuitable for ♿. Civil wedding licence.
Location 2 miles N of centre. Turn off A660 Leeds–Otley between Yorkshire and HSBC banks in Headingley. Parking.
Restrictions No smoking: restaurant, library, some bedrooms. Guide dogs only.
Credit cards All major cards accepted.
Terms [2001] B&B: single £60–£110, double £75–£140, suite £185–£230. D,B&B: £64–£141.50 per person. Set Sun lunch £14.50, dinner £26.50; full alc £38. Weekend breaks. *V*

Malmaison
Sovereign Quay
Leeds LS1 1DQ

Tel 0113-398 1000
Fax 0113-398 1002
Email leeds@malmaison.com
Website www.malmaison.com

Contemporary chic holds sway in this 'trendy part of the city' within walking distance of the shops, including Harvey Nichols, the Yorkshire Playhouse and the heritage trail along the river Aire. The *Malmaison* formula of cutting-edge style – taupe and grey are the predominant colours in the public areas and the bedrooms – is supported by 'informal but very good service' in the French-style brasserie. This is hailed as the brightest star in a small chain: 'An excellent all-rounder,' one visitor wrote. Our inspector praised the 'high-quality finish in the bedrooms', the 'superb firm beds' and 'the best background lighting I have ever found in a hotel'. The 'striking gas-effect fire' in the restaurant is 'very cosy on a cold evening'. 'Good robust comfort food, accompanied by modern jazz' is served in 'a meeting point for both fun and business'. One visitor thought the vegetarian choices were limited: only one vegetarian main course (roasted artichoke and black-eye bean soup) in a selection of 11 dishes like roast lamb niçoise with tapenade jus; citrus chicken with bang bang sauce. The room-service breakfast, 'served sushi-style in a black tray', may be 'a bit trendy' for some (pastries rather than toast and marmalade) but a cooked breakfast is served in the brasserie. Also liked: the 'cool' CD player in the rooms (discs can be borrowed from reception for a refundable deposit) and the availability of Sky MovieMax – 'a definite plus for parents with teenagers'. (*Mr and Mrs Nigel Primrose, Sarah de Lisle, and others*)

Open All year.
Rooms 1 suite, 97 double, 2 single. 5 suitable for ♿.
Facilities Lift. Lounge, bar, brasserie; background jazz/blues; gym.
Location Central. Some rooms might get noise from bars opposite.
Restrictions No smoking in some bedrooms. No dogs.
Credit cards All major cards accepted.
Terms [2001] Room: single £89, double £115–£120, suite £150. Breakfast £8.75–£10.75. Set lunch £9.95; dinner (2 courses) £10.95; full alc £30.

LEONARD STANLEY Gloucestershire — Map 3:E5

The Grey Cottage BUDGET — *Tel/Fax* 01453-822515
Bath Road, Leonard Stanley
Stonehouse GL10 3LU

César award in 1999

Regular visitors have been saddened by the death of Andrew Reeves ('such a gentleman') last year. His widow, Rosemary, continues to offer the hospitality that secured our *César* award. 'She is doing a magnificent job; her warm personality and joy at greeting us made us feel so welcome,' reports one couple. 'Tea and cake awaited us in the sitting room, warmed by a log fire.' The small, simple stone guest house, 170 years old, was once the meeting place for the local Methodist movement. Its colourful flower garden, enclosed by a nine-foot yew hedge, is dominated by a 100-foot sequoia, planted in 1865. The spacious bedrooms are 'warm, airy, spotlessly clean and so comfortable'. 'Everything we needed: tea/coffee tray with biscuits, TV, wireless, books, tourist leaflets, maps and guide books.' One room has its bathroom down a short hall. Dinner, by arrangement, is served at a polished table in front of a log fire, or in a conservatory. No choice; preferences are discussed in advance, and local produce, organic when possible, is used. 'It was yummy,' say visitors who enjoyed lettuce and ginger soup; Wiener schnitzel with chive mash, parsnip purée and baked squash mornay; raspberry Bavarian cream with brown sugar meringue. Breakfast offers freshly squeezed orange juice, kedgeree, smoked salmon with scrambled eggs, home-made jams. A Norman church is all that remains of the medieval priory that once stood in the village. Local attractions include the Wildfowl and Wetlands Trust at Slimbridge, Berkeley Castle, the Westonbirt Arboretum. (*Sue and Colin Raymond, and others*)

Open All year, except occasional holidays. Advance booking essential.
Rooms 2 double, 1 single. No telephone.
Facilities Sitting room with TV, conservatory, dining room. No background music. ¼-acre garden. Unsuitable for ♿.
Location 3 miles from M5 exit 13. 3 miles SW of Stroud. 1 mile S of A419, between King's Stanley and Leonard Stanley. Train: Stonehouse, 1½ miles; then local bus. Parking.
Restrictions No smoking: dining room, bedrooms. No dogs.
Credit cards None accepted.
Terms B&B: single £38–£40, double £52–£60. Set dinner £20. Reductions for 3 nights or more.

LEWDOWN Devon — Map 1:C3

Lewtrenchard Manor — *Tel* 01566-783256
Lewdown — *Fax* 01566-783332
nr Okehampton EX20 4PN
Email stays@lewtrenchard.co.uk
Website lewtrenchard.co.uk

A romantic stone house (Pride of Britain) in a 'superbly tranquil' setting – large grounds with an avenue of beech trees, a lake with swans, a dovecote, a sunken garden. It is the 'Victorian–Elizabethan fantasy' (with ornate plaster ceilings, oak panelling, stained glass, huge fireplaces, portraits, antiques, brass door handles) of the Revd Sabine Baring-Gould, author of the hymn 'Onward, Christian Soldiers' (he is buried in the little church at the end of the drive). The South African owners, James and Sue Murray ('they have trenchant views on certain subjects'), run it in house-party style. Many plaudits came this year: 'Comforting and welcoming, with considerate hosts, much in evidence.' 'We loved the smell of beeswax and wood smoke. The lounge was all that a lounge should be.' 'A memorable visit; a lovely room overlooking the garden.' The bedrooms are off a long music gallery, reached by a fine wooden staircase. Best ones overlook the garden. Some are quite small, and one bathroom may need a facelift. No keys on doors, but you can bolt yourself in. Jason Hornbuckle has returned to the kitchens. 'Dinner at £32 was reasonable value, given the level of competence and the additional bits and pieces. The style is elaborate, but the effect is balanced' (eg, pigeon breast with stuffed baby cabbage and foie gras; sea bream with squid risotto and pesto; apple tarte Tatin with crème caramel and caramel sauce. 'During our four-day stay, we were consulted about preferences, and given main courses that did not appear on the menu.' 'Breakfast made the long journey worthwhile: fresh orange juice in crystal glasses; ambrosial porridge with Devon cream.' Ben, the black Labrador, and Meggie, the Jack Russell, are in attendance. Nearby are Cothele House, Buckland Abbey, the Lydford Gorge, good fishing. (*Andrew Wardrop, Pauline Simonis, Zara Elliott; also NR Ham*)

Open All year.
Rooms 1 suite, 8 double.
Facilities Stair lift. Lounge, bar, restaurant (classical background music), breakfast room; ballroom. 31-acre grounds: croquet, lake (fishing from boat). Clay-pigeon shooting, river fishing nearby. Civil wedding licence.
Location S of A30 Okehampton–Launceston. Take slip road for A386 Tavistock–Plymouth. Right at T-junction, immediately left on to old A30, signposted Bridestowe/Lewdown. Left, after 6 miles, at sign to Lewtrenchard.
Restrictions No smoking in restaurant. Children under 8 by arrangement. No dogs in public rooms.
Credit cards All major cards accepted.
Terms [2001] B&B: single £90–£110, double £120–£165, suite £175. Set lunch/dinner £32. 2-day off-season rates. Christmas house party. 1-night bookings refused bank holidays.

LEWES East Sussex — Map 2:E4

Berkeley House BUDGET
2 Albion Street
Lewes BN7 2ND

Tel 01273-476057
Fax 01273-479575
Email rp.berkeleyhse@lineone.net
Website www.berkeleyhousehotel.co.uk

Owners Roy Patten and Stephen Johnson share the passion for opera that attracts guests looking for budget accommodation with character close to Glyndebourne. 'They are delightful and considerate hosts – 'they lent my father a pair of cufflinks to replace those forgotten,' said one guest. The cream Grade II listed house is part of a Georgian terrace in a small side street. Its admirers enjoy its offbeat style and good value. Some bedrooms are small 'but perfectly adequate for one night; very clean with a good little loo and shower room'. The one at the top 'is not for the arthritic or overly tall'. Room 4 (the suite), however, is 'spacious, with a comfortable double bed and plenty of the important things such as mineral water, kettle, hot chocolate, hairdryer and wardrobe hanging space, but without the unimportant ones like trouser presses and minibars'. Another visitor hailed 'the thoughtfulness of such extras as an electric fan, bottled water, an alarm clock'. An 'excellent' cooked breakfast, served on Jeff Banks crockery in a bijou room overlooking the micro-garden, 'is a pleasant morning-after experience'. Drinks, tea and coffee are available 'at all reasonable times'. The county town of East Sussex has lots of antique shops. Splendid walking on the South Downs Way is a mile away; Brighton and Charleston Farmhouse are 20 minutes' drive. (*Simon Willbourn, HJM Tucker, Jean Deinhardt, and others*)

Open All year, except Christmas and New Year.
Rooms 1 suite, 4 double. All with shower. No telephone.
Facilities Lounge, breakfast room. No background music. Roof terrace. Leisure centre, outdoor swimming pool nearby. Unsuitable for ♿.
Location Central. Limited private parking opposite (advance booking advised); public car park nearby.
Restrictions No smoking: breakfast room, 1 bedroom. No children under 8. No dogs.
Credit cards All major cards accepted.
Terms B&B: single £40–£50, double £50–£60, suite £75. 1-night bookings sometimes refused Sat May–Sept. *V*

Shelleys
High Street
Lewes BN7 1XS

Tel 01273-472361
Fax 01273-483152
Email info@shelleys-hotel-lewes.com
Website www.shelleys-hotel-lewes.co.uk

An attractive Georgian building with an elegant interior. It stands on Lewes High Street and is 'very much part of the town's life'. The 'grand and spacious' house was once the home of the poet's aunts; it now belongs to a small group, Grace Hotels. It is liked for its 'good ambience' and good food (main courses such as steamed canon of lamb, or chargrilled swordfish, are served by the chef, Robert Pierce). The nominator found it 'delightfully stylish'; also welcoming. 'Breakfast, excellent in all respects, had fresh ingredients and a good, but not fussy, choice,' said another visitor. 'The manager, Graeme Coles, gives personal, yet discreet, attention to guests. Prices are steep, but it was a faultless stay.' The restaurant, overlooking the garden, 'is smart, with white linen tablecloths, good cutlery and glasses'. Bar lunches, morning coffee, afternoon teas and room-service meals are available, and there are benches and tables in the quiet rear garden. Chintzy fabrics and pastel colours in the bedrooms; some have a four-poster; some look over the high street, but all windows are double-glazed. (*RP*)

Open All year.
Rooms 1 suite, 17 double, 1 single.

Facilities Lounge, bar, restaurant (light background music at lunch and dinner); 2 function rooms. 1-acre garden. Only public areas accessible to ♿. Civil wedding licence.
Location Central (rooms double-glazed). Car park. Train/bus stations nearby.
Restrictions No smoking: restaurant, some bedrooms. No dogs in public rooms.
Credit cards All major cards accepted.
Terms Room: single £135, double £180, suite £250. Breakfast £10.50–£13.50. Set lunch £18, dinner £30; full alc £45. Short breaks. Christmas package. 1-night bookings occasionally refused. *V*

LIFTON Devon — Map 1:C3

The Arundell Arms

Lifton PL16 0AA

Tel 01566-784666
Fax 01566-784494
Email reservations@arundellarms.com
Website www.arundellarms.com

'We always welcome a chance to stay here. From a catering point of view, in bar and restaurant, it is in a class of its own.' So says a returning visitor to this creeper-covered coaching inn, in a small Devon town just off the A30. The owner (for 41 years), Anne Voss-Bark, is much in evidence, with all the elegance you might expect of a former actress – 'she is charming, thoroughly professional'. Her husband, the former political broadcaster, Conrad Voss-Bark, died this year aged 87, but she is supported by the manager (for 23 years), Sally Hill, and a long-serving staff. Mrs Voss-Bark, an expert fly-fisher, has 20 miles of fishing on the Tamar and four of its tributaries, and a three-acre stocked lake. Fishing courses of all kinds are offered (you need to book early). The ghillies are 'knowledgeable and entertaining'; picnic hampers are provided. Families and non-sporting guests are also welcomed; off-season packages of all kinds are offered, and functions and conferences are catered for. Much refurbishment of the public areas has taken place; the restaurant's light, contemporary look enhances high ceilings and large windows. The much-admired chef (for 21 years), Philip Burgess (assisted by Nick Shopland), serves main courses like roast beef fillet with rosemary crust; casserole of monkfish, sea bass, brill and lobster with asparagus, leeks and parsley. The bedrooms vary greatly (some, on the road, are plain). A suite is new (and popular) this year. The terraced rear garden (with one of the few remaining cockpits in England) has new flowerbeds, and seating for alfresco meals. Local sightseeing: Castle Drogo, Cothele, Lanhydrock, the Eden Project. (*Leonard Leech*)

Open All year, except 3 nights over Christmas.
Rooms 1 suite, 19 double, 7 single. 5 in annexe opposite. 4 on ground floor.
Facilities Ramp. Lounge, cocktail bar, public bar, 2 dining rooms (taped background music); conference/meeting rooms; games room, skittle alley. ½-acre garden. 20 miles fishing rights on river Tamar and tributaries, 3-acre stocked lake, fishing school.
Location Half mile off A30, 3 miles E of Launceston (road-facing rooms double-glazed). Train: Exeter, 40 miles; taxi.
Restrictions No smoking in restaurant. No dogs in restaurant.
Credit cards All major cards accepted.

Terms [2001] B&B £46.50–£76.50; D,B&B (min. 2 nights) £73–£93. Bar meals from £3.50. Set lunch £18–£22.50, dinner £30–£37.50. Child in parents' room: under 16, free. 2–6-night breaks all year. Off-season breaks: sporting, gourmet, etc. *V*

LINCOLN Lincolnshire — Map 4:E5

D'Isney Place Hotel
Eastgate
Lincoln LN2 4AA

Tel 01522-538881
Fax 01522-511321
Email info@disneyplacehotel.co.uk
Website www.disneyplacehotel.co.uk

No connection with a Hollywood mouse: this red brick Georgian town house is named for the local worthy, John D'Isney, who built it in 1735. It was later given a Victorian extension, and David and Judy Payne now run it as a B&B. The medieval wall of the cathedral close forms the southern boundary of the garden. The style is intimate: no public rooms; breakfast is served in the bedrooms. 'Our room was spacious, with a view over the garden to the cathedral, a well-equipped bathroom, and a large table where we sat to enjoy the excellent bacon and eggs,' says a visitor this year. Fresh orange juice and fruit come also, on trays with fresh flowers and bone china. 'The most luxurious B&B we know, refreshingly consistent over many years,' say regular visitors. The bedrooms vary greatly in size and style: some have a view across the town to country. One has a four-poster bed, two have a spa bath; some are suitable for a family; the simplest ones have a shower. Some rooms get traffic noise (but they have double glazing), others are 'remarkably quiet'. Service is 'unobtrusive but solicitous'. The weekend breaks are good value. For meals, the *Wig and Mitre*, a pub/café/restaurant ('very good, busy and cheerful'), and *Seely's* ('a bit quieter') were enjoyed this year. Or you could try *The Jew's House* (one of the oldest inhabited buildings in Britain). The castle and the Usher Gallery are close by. (*HJM Tucker, J and JW, JC*)

Open All year.
Rooms 1 suite, 15 double, 1 single. 2 in cottage annexe with sitting room, kitchen, dining room. Some on ground floor.
Facilities Ramps. No background music. 1-acre garden.
Location By cathedral. Front rooms double-glazed; back ones quietest. Small car park; street parking after 6 pm. Bus, taxi from station.
Restriction No smoking in 15 bedrooms.
Credit cards All major cards accepted.
Terms [2001] B&B: single £55–£75, double £87–£107, suite £107. Weekend breaks. *V*

LISKEARD Cornwall — Map 1:D3

Pencubitt House BUDGET
Lamellion
Liskeard PL14 4EB

Tel/Fax 01579-342694
Email claire@penc.co.uk
Website www.penc.co.uk

'A quiet hotel, very relaxing. My favourite in the south-west. There is always a warm welcome. The food is exceptional, beautifully presented.'

A regular visitor's praise for this Victorian wool merchant's house. It stands in mature gardens in elevated position, with lovely views of East Looe valley, on the edge of the old market town. Michael Kent (the chef) and wife Claire (front-of-house) have completely refurbished the house since they bought it in a run-down state, five years ago. Plenty of sitting areas: two spacious sitting rooms (one with an open fire), and a veranda. The decor is traditional: patterned carpets on staircases; oriental rugs in the lounges. This year, Michael Kent has won a West Country award for his modern British cooking, served by candlelight (eg, warm goat's cheese with roast red peppers; braised shoulder of lamb with rosemary sauce; caramelised rice pudding, Armagnac prunes and raisins). Diners not wishing to make decisions can opt for the six-course Surprise Menu. Half a dozen National Trust properties are within a half-hour drive; the Eden Project is 20 minutes away. (*Peter Sawyer*)

Open All year, except Christmas, New Year.
Rooms 4 double, 1 single.
Facilities 2 lounges, bar, restaurant (classical background music). 3-acre garden. Unsuitable for ♿.
Location At Liskeard, follow 'Park and Ride for Looe' signs. Hotel a short way past railway station, off B3254. Parking.
Restrictions No smoking: restaurant, bedrooms. No children under 12. No dogs in public rooms.
Credit cards MasterCard, Visa.
Terms B&B £30–£40; D,B&B £52–£62. Set lunch/dinner £20; full alc £30. 2/4-day breaks. *V*

LITTLE MALVERN Worcestershire — Map 3:D5

Holdfast Cottage
Marlbank Road
Little Malvern WR13 6NA

Tel 01684-310288
Fax 01684-311117
Email holdcothot@aol.com
Website www.holdfast-cottage.co.uk

'We appreciated the service and the attention we received,' writes a visitor this year to Stephen and Jane Knowles's 17th-century cream-and-brown guest house with Victorian extensions. Others wrote: 'How very good it is.' 'We liked the cottage style, complete with low beams of the "duck or grouse" variety, and the homely feel.' 'The proprietors were extremely helpful, preparing late night feasts and ordering taxis.' There is a 'great view' of the Malvern hills from the wisteria-covered terrace – the cottage is set back from the road between Little Malvern and Pershore. You enter through a plant-filled conservatory into a small hall with low black beams and the original cast iron range. The diminutive Victorian-style bar and the candlelit dining room, now redecorated in soft green, overlook the garden. The bedrooms, reached up little staircases, are small too. Many have been redecorated this year with less chintz – 'more calm and welcoming,' say the owners. The rooms with the most character are in the older part of the house. Mrs Knowles provides 'very good and well-presented' dinners. Five choices for each course, eg, mushrooms baked with cream; roast duck breast with morello cherry and red wine sauce. Rolls are home-baked, ice creams home-made, herbs home-grown.

Breakfast 'is beautifully served, in a serene yet efficient atmosphere'. Children are welcomed. Sir Edward Elgar is buried in the Roman Catholic cemetery in the village. Gloucester, Worcester, Hereford and Tewkesbury, Eastnor Castle and Little Malvern Court are all within easy reach. (*Dennis A Dyer, Elizabeth Wallace-Dunlop, P Inman and R Fisher; also Dr Norman Waterman, and others*)

Open All year, except Christmas, 1st 2 weeks Jan.
Rooms 7 double, 1 single.
Facilities Hall, lounge, conservatory, bar, restaurant. No background music. 2-acre grounds: croquet, Wendy house, small wood. Unsuitable for ♿.
Location On A4104 halfway between Welland and Little Malvern. Train: Great Malvern; taxi.
Restrictions No smoking: restaurant, bedrooms. No dogs in public rooms.
Credit cards MasterCard, Visa.
Terms [2001] B&B £41–£50; D,B&B £66–£68. Set dinner £25. Short breaks all year. 1-night bookings refused Sat in season. *V*

LITTLE PETHERICK Cornwall — Map 1:D2

Molesworth Manor BUDGET — *Tel* 01841-540292
Little Petherick — *Website* www.molesworthmanor.co.uk
nr Padstow PL27 7QT

Handsome Grade II listed 17th-century stone rectory, 2 miles SE of Padstow. Converted into manor house in 19th century, now an informal B&B. Peter Pearce and Heather Clarke have handed over to their daughter, Jessica Clarke, and her partner, Geoff French. 11 bedrooms, varying in grandness; most are spacious, some have antiques. Ground-floor lounges for reading, TV and music. Afternoon tea on terrace; breakfast in conservatory (lavish cold buffet). No dinners, but table laid for guests who bring own food. Plenty of pubs, bistros and restaurants nearby, including the* Seafood Restaurant *(*qv*), Padstow. Open Feb–Oct; Nov–Jan by arrangement. Unsuitable for ♿. No smoking. No dogs. No background music. Credit cards not accepted. B&B £25.50–£34.50; £5 supplement for single night [2001]. More reports, please.*

LITTLE SHELFORD Cambridgeshire — Map 2:C4

Purlins NEW/BUDGET — *Tel/Fax* 01223-842643
12 High Street — *Email* dgallh@ndirect.co.uk
Little Shelford CB2 5ES

A B&B in a delightful village near Cambridge. The owners, David Hindley and his Irish wife, Olga, run it by themselves. He is a musician who does research on birdsong; she was a music librarian. 'This is our home. We are a very small affair, and cannot offer many luxuries or a full range of amenities,' they write. Guests are expected to be out of the house between 10.30 am and 5 pm, and they should not check in before 5 without prior notice. Inspectors had an 'immaculate bedroom, not large', overlooking the garden (with large visiting pheasants). 'The freshly cooked breakfast was better than that offered in many posh hotels (good thick brown toast; excellent scrambled eggs).' Served between 7.30 and 9 am, it can be vegetarian, traditional or continental. A good restaurant, *Sycamore House*, is close by (you need to book well in advance), and the helpful Hindleys will advise on other local eating places. Printed notes: 'Please turn off the lights', etc, greet visitors when they return from dinner. Slight noise sometimes, from the M11, nearby, but windows are double-glazed. The house was designed by Mr Hindley in 1978 and is based on a medieval manor house, with some bedrooms leading off a gallery. Guests may sit in a conservatory overlooking the wooded grounds.

Open 1 Feb–16 Dec. Sometimes closed for owners' breaks.
Rooms 3 double, 1 single (for occasional use). 2 on ground floor.
Facilities Conservatory lounge, breakfast room. No background music. 2-acre garden.
Location 5 miles S of Cambridge, in village off M11 (exits 10, 11). Hourly bus to Cambridge by door; station ½-hour's walk. Parking.
Restrictions No smoking. No children under 8. No dogs.
Credit cards None accepted.
Terms [2001] B&B: single £44–£48, double £50–£58. 1-night bookings occasionally refused.

LIVERPOOL Merseyside *See SHORTLIST* — Map 4:E2

LIVERSEDGE West Yorkshire — Map 4:D3

Healds Hall Hotel NEW

Leeds Road
Liversedge WF15 6JA

Tel 01924-409112
Fax 01924-401895
Email healdshall@ndirect.co.uk

Half a mile from old industrial town in Spen valley, on A62, SW of Leeds: Tom and Nora Harrington's 'cheerful, hard-working' hotel, with 'enjoyable staff'. 24 bedrooms (some on ground floor), 'comfortable, sensibly equipped'. Good food, straightforward wine list (and continuous background music) in restaurant (no-smoking) and bistro. Lounge, 2 bars, conference/banqueting suite (wedding receptions, discos held); garden. Only guide dogs in public rooms. All major credit cards accepted. B&B: single £45–£59, double £65–£75. Full alc £26–£30 [2001]. *V*

LODDISWELL Devon — Map 1:D4

Hazelwood House BUDGET

Loddiswell
nr Kingsbridge TQ7 4EB

Tel 01548-821232
Fax 01548-821318
Website www.seekers.org

'We had a great time in a distinctive setting. Five open fires, personal attention which was not intrusive, excellent cooking, and guests who, in the relaxed atmosphere, enjoyed each other's company.' Returning visitors enjoyed seeing in the New Year at this Victorian house informally run by Jane Bowman, Gillean Kean and Anabel Farnell-Watson. They are involved in the Dandelion Trust (see also *Woodwick*

House, Evie, Scotland), which organises conservation and cultural projects in the UK, and 'Through Heart to Peace' projects in Ethiopia and central Europe. They run a busy programme of courses (eg, bereavement; corn circles) and concerts (the Medici String Quartet often appears). There are also weekends with entertainments (jazz, painting, story-telling, philosophy, etc). The house stands in a beautiful Devon valley, amid meadows and woods that slope down to the river Avon. It is not at all smart. It does not offer hotel facilities; some bedrooms are small, only two have facilities *en suite*, and heating is by electric fires (no central heating). But the 'genuinely warm hospitality', 'non-commercial atmosphere', and 'feeling of peace and friendliness' are loved by its devotees, and children are welcomed. The decor is a 'delightful mix' of simple furniture, antiques and paintings. The short menu is based on organic ingredients. Vegetarians are well catered for. There is a small selection of wines (some are organic). Water comes from the house's own spring. 'Two or three cats roam around, and the small terrier loves having her tummy tickled.' (*Ken and Liz Bartlett, CR*)

Open All year.
Rooms 1 suite, 10 double, 5 single. 2 with facilities *en suite*. 1 on ground floor. No telephone/TV. 6 self-catering cottages.
Facilities Hall, telephone room, drawing room, library/TV room, dining room; chapel; function/conference facilities. 67-acre grounds, river, boathouse.
Location 1 mile N of Loddiswell. From California Cross on B3207 Dartmouth–Modbury take road to Kingsbridge/Loddiswell. Left after *c.* ¾ mile to Hazelwood. Down lane; entrance gate with stone pillars on right. Train: Totnes, 14 miles; taxi.
Restrictions No smoking: dining room, bedrooms. Dogs by arrangement.
Credit cards Amex, MasterCard, Visa.
Terms (*Excluding VAT*) B&B £25–£50. Set lunch from £10, dinner from £15; full alc from £25. Child in parents' room: under 4, free; 4–12, 50% of adult rate. Negotiable rates for parties, groups, etc. Christmas, New Year packages.

LONG MELFORD Suffolk — Map 2:C5

Black Lion NEW
Church Walk, The Green
Long Melford CO10 9DN

Tel 01787 312356
Fax 01787 374557
Email blacklionhotel@ravenwoodhall.co.uk
Website www.ravenwoodhall.co.uk

'A pleasantly situated former inn'; it overlooks the large green of this Suffolk village. It was recently taken over by Craig Jarvis, the owner of *Ravenwood Hall*, Bury St Edmunds (*qv*); bedroom renovation is in progress. Inspectors in 2001 were critical of the reception ('no help with luggage, and they tried to give us one of the least good rooms'), but thereafter they found much to enjoy: 'The decor is attractive: walls dark red or peach; white paint, Hogarth prints. Our bedroom had a country feel, sloping ceiling, pale blue walls, pine furniture.' Two dining rooms: one informal, with wooden chairs and tables; the other formal: good wooden furniture, portraits, red curtains ('but they were drawn on a summer's evening which made a gloomy effect'). 'The menu is a bit pretentious, but the food was well cooked: we enjoyed scallops with salad, and duck liver parfait; liver and bacon, and sirloin steak. Breakfast a bit mixed, but the smoked haddock was good. We did not see anyone in a position of authority, but we had a pleasant stay.' Light bar meals are available; cream teas are served in the walled garden. Good family accommodation; children's menus, toys, etc.

Open All year.
Rooms 1 family, 9 double.
Facilities Lounge, bar; classical background music all day; restaurant. Walled garden. Unsuitable for ♿.
Location 3 miles SW of Lavenham. On green, by church. Car park.
Restrictions No smoking: restaurant, bedrooms. No dogs in restaurant.
Credit cards Amex, MasterCard, Visa.
Terms B&B: single £90, double £115. Bar meals. Full alc £35. 2-night breaks. Christmas package.

LORTON Cumbria — Map 4: inset C2

New House Farm
Lorton
Cockermouth CA13 9UU

Tel/Fax 01900-85404
Email hazel@newhouse-farm.co.uk
Website www.newhouse-farm.co.uk

Hazel Thompson 'is an enthusiastic hostess who runs a very well-organised small country guest house', says a traveller this year. 'No TV. Bliss! We can't praise Hazel highly enough,' others wrote. She has furnished her 17th-century Grade II listed whitewashed farmhouse with style. Antiques, silver and bright colours in the small lounges complement original oak beams and rafters, flagstone floors and open stone fireplaces. All is spotless; service is 'very professional'. 'Not a hotel. You are definitely in someone's house.' Lorton Vale, in the north-west corner of the Lake District National Park, is a majestic setting – 'there are three lakes within three miles. There is traffic on a country road in front of the house, 'but the two main bedrooms at the rear are perfectly quiet'. The home-cooked dinner (no choice) might consist of local Solway shrimps; cream of tomato soup; pheasant cooked in cider; rhubarb crumble with cream. There is a short wine list. 'Excellent breakfasts' include fresh grapefruit pieces, juicy prunes, eggs and bacon, home-made marmalade. Lunches and teas are served in the café, in a converted barn. Bedrooms, of varying sizes, are 'cosy', with 'marvellous views'. 'Ideal for dog-owners' (their pets are allowed the run of the grounds but not the public rooms). There is easy access to Loweswater, Crummock Water, Buttermere and the fells, and good birdwatching. (*Robert Ager, and others*)

Open All year.
Rooms 5 double. 1 in stable, 3 yds. Telephone available. No TV.
Facilities 3 lounges, dining room. No background music. 14-acre grounds: garden, streams, woods, field. 3 lakes within 3 miles. Unsuitable for ♿.
Location On B5289, 2 miles S of Lorton.
Restrictions No smoking. No children under 6. No dogs in public rooms.
Credit cards MasterCard, Visa.
Terms B&B £40–£52; D,B&B £58–£74. Packed lunch £6.50. Set dinner £22.

Reduced rates for 3 nights or more. Christmas package. 1-night bookings sometimes refused.

Winder Hall BUDGET
Low Lorton
Cockermouth CA13 9UP

Tel/Fax 01900-85107
Email stay@winderhall.co.uk
Website www.winderhall.co.uk

With only six bedrooms, Mary and Derek Denman's upmarket country guest house, in a village in the quiet Lorton vale, is 'a restful place', said the nominator. The Grade II listed building, named for the family who built it, is 14th-century in origin with later additions. Thick Tudor walls, Victorian mullioned windows, and a huge fireplace with a priest-hole give it plenty of character. The bedrooms, all different, 'are beautiful'. Two have a king-size four-poster; all have flowers and chocolates. The grounds run down to a stretch of the river Cocker crossed by an old bridge. The rates include afternoon tea and an evening drink, served in the large drawing room. Dinner, ordered after breakfast, is at 7.30 pm in the oak-panelled dining room. Two choices of starter and main course, eg, cheese and broccoli soup, or melon with Cumbrian mature royal ham; seared salmon with new potatoes, or aubergine cannelloni. Desserts might be sticky toffee pudding, or mango and lime cream meringue. The short wine list has some reasonably priced house wines. Breakfast has a cold buffet, smoked fish, egg dishes, home-made preserves. Maps and advice about local walks are provided. More reports, please.

Open All year, except Christmas, and some days in Jan.
Rooms 6 double. Some on ground floor. No telephone.
Facilities Lounge with honesty bar, dining room (baroque background music mealtimes). ½-acre grounds on river Cocker. Unsuitable for ♿.
Location From Keswick: A66 west, then B5292 Whinlatter Pass. At T-junction with B5289 left to Low Lorton. House on right, past *Wheatsheaf Inn.*
Restrictions No smoking. No children under 8. No dogs.
Credit cards MasterCard, Visa.
Terms D,B&B £43–£56. B&B available at quiet times. Child in parents' room: 8–10, £8; 11–15, £12. 1-night bookings sometimes refused.

LOUGHBOROUGH Leicestershire — Map 2:A3

Old Manor NEW
11 Sparrow Hill
Loughborough LE11 1BT

Tel 01509-211228
Fax 01509-211128
Email bookings@oldmanor.com
Website www.oldmanor.com

In this industrial and university town, Roger Burdell has run a restaurant for over 15 years, well known for his modern Mediterranean cuisine. The old house looks over an ancient churchyard in the old town. Four years ago, some upstairs rooms were converted into bedrooms and a bridal suite. 'Mr Burdell, who seems to run the operation almost single-handed, was a friendly, calm and helpful host,' says an inspection report on this characterful place. 'Our bedroom was good-sized, if not smart, and it could have done with double glazing, as it was on a one-way traffic system. But the beds were comfortable, and there was plenty of hot water in the tiny, if functional shower [earlier problems with water have been sorted out]. The public rooms are more attractive, decorated in Mediterranean style: rugs on wooden floors; shuttered windows, large mirrors creating a spacious feel; fresh flowers and plants everywhere. Our excellent dinner (there had been no pressure on us to dine in) included baked mushrooms with polenta, pancetta and pecorino cheese; lamb with garlic, rosemary, anchovy and wild mushroom gravy. Imaginative and delicious puddings, eg, brandy snap basket with peach, lemon and ricotta ice cream and peach sauce. Breakfast is light, continental or full, with a good selection of cereals, proper toast, butter and preserves in small dishes. A haven for anyone needing to visit Loughborough, and a good base for exploring Nottinghamshire and Leicestershire.' Strictly no-smoking. Some bedrooms are small; one has a floral-draped half-tester bed. Some of the furniture is antique; some has been made by the multi-talented owner, who describes the decor as 'rich and earthy'.

Open All year. Restaurant closed midday. Sun dinner for residents only, by arrangement.
Rooms 8 double. 2 across courtyard.
Facilities Lounge, dining room/bar; background music in public areas at breakfast and dinner. Small courtyard. Unsuitable for ♿.
Location Central: Loughborough is 10 miles N of Leicester. Enter from A6 south. At traffic lights past Jarvis hotel (*King's Head*), right on to Baxter Gate. At traffic lights by Bar 32, left on to Sparrow hill. Hotel is 1st main building on right. Car park.
Restrictions No smoking. No dogs.
Credit cards Amex, MasterCard, Visa.
Terms [2001] Room: single £75–£88, double £95–£105, suite £105–£150. Breakfast £6–£10.50. Set dinner £27.50–£32.50.

LOWER BEEDING West Sussex — Map 2:E4

South Lodge NEW
Brighton Road
Lower Beeding
nr Horsham RH13 6PS

Tel 01403-891711
Fax 01403-891766
Email enquiries@southlodgehotel.co.uk
Website www.exclusivehotels.co.uk

Wisteria-clad Victorian mansion on 93-acre estate (with 2 lakes, tennis, croquet) on A281. 6 miles S of Horsham. 'Glorious views' but slight traffic noise. 'Staff extremely friendly, lovely bedroom, excellent cooking' (English with Mediterranean influences by Lewis Hamblet), but 'expensive wines'. Splendid public rooms (wooden floors, moulded ceilings, old-fashioned furniture, chandeliers). Lounge (pianist some evenings), library bar, snooker room, oak-panelled dining room (no smoking). 41 luxurious bedrooms (1 suitable for ♿), all large, bar one called Ronnie Corbett. Good breakfast buffet. Small conferences and weddings held. Golf at Mannings Heath, close by. No children in restaurant at night. No dogs. All major credit cards accepted. B&B: single £174, double £199–£374. Set lunch £24–£26, dinner £37.50; full alc £70. New manager, Mr Kirby, arrived in spring 2001, so we'd like more reports, please. *V*

LOWER HENLADE Somerset — Map 1:C5

The Mount Somerset
Lower Henlade
Taunton TA3 5NB

Tel 01823-442500
Fax 01823-442900
Email info@mountsomerset.co.uk
Website www.mountsomersethotel.com

Original features carefully preserved in Tudor house made over by 19th-century Italian architect, now owned by Countess von Essen (see also Congham Hall, *Grimston,* Ston Easton Park, *Ston Easton). High up in Blackdown Hills ('memorable views'), 3 miles E of Taunton. Friendly young managers, Scott and Tracy Leeming; 'soothing atmosphere'. Lounge, large bar; classical background music. 6 suites, 5 double rooms, lavishly decorated, even OTT. Chef Ritchie Herkes serves modern dishes. Reasonably priced wines. Good breakfast buffet. Conservatory, 2-acre grounds. Conference/function facilities. No smoking: restaurant, 2 bedrooms. Unsuitable for ♿. No dogs. All major credit cards accepted. B&B: single £95, double £155, suite £175. Set lunch £20, dinner £30; full alc £40. No recent reports, we'd like some please.*

LUDLOW Shropshire — Map 3:C4

Dinham Hall
by the castle
Ludlow SY8 1EJ

Tel 01584-876464
Fax 01584-876019
Email info@dinhamhall.co.uk
Website www.dinhamhall.co.uk

Beautifully proportioned Georgian house in 'tranquil spot', in 1-acre walled garden (with parking), near castle: views of Teme valley, and 'some of Ludlow's loveliest houses and gardens'. Owned by the Mifsuds of The Lake, *Llangammarch Wells, Wales (*qv*); managed by Alexander Grainger. 15 bedrooms, 1 on ground floor – best ones have elaborate drapes, four-poster, etc, but may need updating; 2 are in cottage. 2 lounges, elegant restaurant (no smoking), with French chef, Olivier Bossut. His cooking has been called 'exciting and diverse'. Hearty breakfasts. Helpful staff. No background music. Civil wedding licence. Unsuitable for ♿. No dogs in public rooms. All major credit cards accepted. B&B £60–£85; D,B&B £75–£115. Set lunch £15, dinner £2; full alc £35.* ***V***

Mr Underhill's
Dinham Weir
Ludlow SY8 1EH

Tel 01584-874431
Website www.mr-underhills.co.uk

César award in 2000

Ludlow has three *Michelin*-starred restaurants, but only this one offers accommodation – the owner/chef Christopher Bradley, and his wife, Judy, run it with a small staff, and 'without the trappings associated with many smart country house hotels'. They put no pressure on residents to dine in every night, and will help with meal reservations elsewhere. 'The place is charming,' say its most devoted fans. 'Bedrooms (the soundproofing has been improved) are simple, and there are only two small sitting areas, but standards are high. Judy Bradley is a natural hostess.' Others wrote: 'Food excellent, wines excellent, breakfast excellent; all very reasonably priced.' The setting 'is delightful', below the ramparts of Ludlow Castle, beside the river Teme, though this brought two bouts of flooding, necessitating much redecoration, in 2000. Herons, otters, kingfishers, and wild salmon have all been spotted from the dining room, where 'modern, intensely flavourful' cooking is served amid a decor of yellow walls, rusty red carpet, sumptuous drapes depicting fruit and flowers. No choice on the menu until dessert (you should discuss preferences in advance). Dishes enjoyed this year: asparagus on broad bean risotto with champagne; wild venison with sauce poivrade; 'stunning desserts', eg, rice pudding ice cream with rhubarb lemon tart; all followed by an 'excellent cheeseboard', 'delicious petits fours and good coffee'. In fine weather, meals are served in the courtyard. The bedrooms have good pine furniture, natural fabrics, a large bed, crisp linen, a small but 'well-arranged' bathroom, and a view across the river to Whitcliffe Common. Breakfast includes fresh orange juice, home-made muesli, organic bacon, sausage and eggs. Frodo, alias Mr Underhill, the British Blue cat who gave his name to the restaurant, is no more, but two descendants are to take his place. (*Padi and John Howard, Anne and Denis Tate*)

Open All year. Restaurant generally closed Tues.
Rooms 6 double.
Facilities 2 small lounge areas, restaurant; function facilities. No background music. ¼-acre courtyard garden on river: fishing, swimming. Unsuitable for ♿.
Location Below castle on bank of river Teme. Station ½ mile. Parking for residents.
Restrictions No smoking: restaurant, bedrooms. No dogs.
Credit cards MasterCard, Visa.
Terms B&B: single £60–£90, double £75–£120. Set lunch/dinner £27.50. 1-night bookings refused some Sats. *V* (not weekends)

Number Twenty Eight
28 Lower Broad Street
Ludlow SY8 1PQ

Tel 01584-876996
Reservations 0800 0815000
Fax 01584-876860
Email ross@no28.co.uk
Website www.no28.co.uk

'Our fourth visit. There can be no more hospitable hosts. The management is faultless,' says a report in 2001 on Patricia and Philip Ross's unusual B&B. Other visitors wrote: 'It is beautiful and original; we left restored and happy.' It consists of a number of small houses in a quiet street close to the river Teme. The breakfast room and two bedrooms are in *Number Twenty Eight*, early Georgian with 13th-century origins; other rooms, and three new suites, are in Tudor cottages and a small Victorian terrace. Each house has a garden, and a sitting room with an open fire, family photographs, books, maps, etc. Bathrooms have been added with respect for the houses' origins; all are well provided with toiletries and useful items like plasters and razors. The rooms are 'charming, spotless and well organised', though some are quite small, and one bathroom 'might be uncomfortable for a large person'. The owners' 'kindness and genuine concern for guests' comfort' is praised. 'Daisy, the resident Labrador, regarded us with benign affection.' A continental breakfast is available in the bedrooms, which are equipped with a fridge and a toaster; a cooked breakfast is 'competently served by Mr Ross'; the marmalade 'is made by a leading light of the Women's Institute'. Parking can be awkward. No shortage of eating places: Ludlow has three *Michelin*-starred restaurants. It is also well endowed with historic buildings (its entire centre is Grade II listed). A good base for touring Shropshire and the Welsh Marches. (*Ann Evans, RW, and others*)

Open All year.
Rooms 3 suites, 6 double, in 6 separate houses.
Facilities 3 sitting rooms, breakfast room (classical background music sometimes). 4 gardens. Unsuitable for ♿.
Location 200 yds from centre; near Ludford Bridge. They will meet train.
Restrictions No smoking. No dogs in main house.
Credit cards MasterCard, Visa.
Terms B&B: single £70–£90, double £75–£90, suite £75–£100. 1-night bookings refused weekends.

LYME REGIS Dorset *See SHORTLIST* — Map 1:C6

LYMINGTON Hampshire — Map 2:E2

Stanwell House
14 High Street
Lymington SO41 9AA

Tel 01590-677123
Fax 01590-677756
Email sales@stanwellhousehotel.co.uk
Website www.stanwellhousehotel.co.uk

'A very good atmosphere throughout. Excellent, professional service. Highly recommended.' 'Very helpful receptionist.' Fresh praise this year for Jane McIntyre's Georgian coaching inn. Flag flying, it stands on the main street of this port and yachting station at the mouth of the river Lymington where it reaches the Solent. This visitor arrived during the extensive redecoration carried out in early 2001: 'The reception area was transformed into a flagstone-floored hall with a wonderful lilac sofa.' Bright colours – fuchsia, amethyst, burgundy – are everywhere, and lavish use of silk and velvet. The bedrooms in the main building are often of a strange shape and size. 'Our suite, overlooking the courtyard, was perfect, with a large balcony – a lovely sunny spot in summer.' But one visitor thought that his room in an extension did not live up to the style of the rest: 'its cheap fittings made it overpriced.' Another guest had a room that was 'tiny and boxlike'. In the bar/bistro spread over three rooms, the food was found 'excellent and reasonably priced', 'as good as the wine'. Chef Ian McLelland's menus might include Solent brown crab with shellfish jelly and cucumber salad; wild sea bass with oyster velouté; caramelised breast of duck with macadamia nuts and couscous. The conservatory lounge, with flagstones, plants, antiques and bric-a-brac, buzzes with locals taking morning coffee or afternoon tea. A clothing store sells goods by Mulberry, Burberry and others. Two bedrooms are in a cottage, a few minutes' walk from the quay. A 50-foot yacht, *Alpha of Devonport*, is available for charter. Parking can be awkward. A good base for visiting the New Forest, and touring Dorset. Winchester and Salisbury are not far. 'Small, well-behaved' dogs are allowed. (*Sue Davies, and others*)

Open All year.
Rooms 5 suites, 22 double, 1 single. Some on ground floor. 2-bedroomed cottage nearby.
Facilities Conservatory lounge, bar, bistro, restaurant; background music. Conference facilities. Walled garden; patio. Private yacht. Unsuitable for ♿. Civil wedding licence.
Location High street (rear rooms quietest). Train: Brockenhurst (main line), 6 miles; Lymington 200 metres. Public car park opposite.
Restrictions No smoking: restaurant, some bedrooms. No dogs in restaurant.
Credit cards All major cards accepted.
Terms [2001] B&B: single £60, double £110, suite £150; D,B&B: single £85, double £160, suite £200. Set dinner £25. Child in parents' room: from £15.

LYNDHURST Hampshire — Map 2:E2

Le Poussin at Parkhill NEW
Beaulieu Road
Lyndhurst SO43 7FZ

Tel 02380-282944
Fax 02380-283268
Email sales@lepoussinatparkhill.co.uk
Website www.lepoussin.co.uk

The *Michelin*-starred chef Alex Aitken and his wife, Caroline, have moved their renowned restaurant, *Le Poussin*, from Brockenhurst (their son, Justin, is managing the original, now called *Simply Poussin*). Here, in a Georgian former hunting lodge, they are running a restaurant-with-rooms which bowled over the nominator. 'The emphasis is on food, but it is a lovely hotel, beautifully situated, well appointed, with very helpful staff, memorable meals – at a price! The entrance is welcoming, luxurious, but in a homely way (flowers, pots of orchids, magazines). Our room, No. 1, the largest, had a huge French sleigh bed, good antique-style furniture, large TV. In the big lounge, with plenty of armchairs for sinking into, and French windows leading on to a lawn, we took tea in front of a fire. In the very pretty restaurant, we dined on velouté soup with truffle; tomato Tatin with brill; breast of poussin with foie gras and prunes, all delicious, and not too heavy. A young couple brought their beautifully behaved baby to dinner; the head waiter could not do enough for them. Breakfast was let down by commercial orange juice, but had wonderful coffee and croissants, fresh fruit salad, platters of cheeses, meat, etc. Service was French, charming, highly professional.' No set menus: the half-board rate includes two courses from the *carte*. Some bedrooms have a sitting area; cheaper ones are smaller, and 'cottagey'. (*Heather Sharland*)

Open All year, except 2–15 Jan.
Rooms 4 suites, 9 double, 1 single. 5 in coach house.

Facilities Lounge, library, 2 bars, restaurant. No background music. 13-acre grounds: swimming pool, fishing lake. Unsuitable for ♿. Civil wedding licence.
Location 1¼ miles SE of Lyndhurst on B3056.
Restrictions No smoking: restaurant, lounge, 5 bedrooms. No dogs in public rooms.
Credit cards Amex, MasterCard, Visa.
Terms [2001] (*Excluding 10% service charge on meals*) B&B £45–£75; D,B&B £70–£100. English breakfast from £7.50. 2-course meal: lunch £15, dinner £29.50. Midweek breaks. Christmas package.

MALVERN WELLS Worcestershire — Map 3:D5

The Cottage in the Wood
Holywell Road
Malvern Wells WR14 4LG

Tel 01684-575859
Fax 01684-560662
Email proprietor@cottageinthewood.co.uk
Website www.cottageinthewood.co.uk

Glorious views over the Severn valley can be enjoyed at this Georgian dower house. It stands amid shrubbery and woods, high on the slopes of the Malvern Hills. From the grounds you can walk straight out to a nine-mile range of the hills, and more than 100 miles of tracks. 'Excellent, with friendly staff in a lovely setting,' writes one visitor this year. 'Fine foods, good wine selection and a well-planned, if small room.' The owners, John and Sue Pattin, and their family run the hotel 'with effective, natural team work', says another guest, who thought the breakfast 'excellent in every respect'. The public rooms have antiques, and picture windows overlooking the view. The restaurant, run by Dominic Pattin, has Indian paintings, well-spaced tables, and a 'correct atmosphere'. One reporter found the cooking 'too ambitious and complex', and meat portions too large, with too few vegetables, but the kitchen will cook dishes plainly if asked, and others enjoyed their meal, especially the fish and the 'discreetly original' meat dishes. Half-board rates include three courses from the long, monthly-changing *à la carte* menu (eg, sausage of wild mushrooms on wilted spinach; saddle of venison on sautéed leeks; prune and Armagnac tart). The wine list includes many half bottles, and three pages of English wines – a refund is promised if you try one and don't like it. The bedrooms vary greatly; the best ones, in the main house, have a traditional decor, home-made shortbread, Malvern water; most have binoculars. There are plans for replacing the annexe, which has less appealing accommodation, with a 16-room building. Guests have access to the local golf and squash clubs. (*BA Howard, and others*)

Open All year.
Rooms 20 double. 4 in Beech Cottage 70 yds, 8 in Coach House 100 yds.
Facilities Lounge, bar, restaurant; function facilities. No background music.

7-acre grounds. Golf, squash nearby. Unsuitable for ♿.
Location Off A449 to Ledbury, 3 miles S of Malvern; turning is 500 yards N of B4209 junction, on opposite side of road. Do not approach from S end of Holywell Rd. Train: Great Malvern.
Restrictions No smoking in restaurant. No dogs in main house.
Credit cards Amex, MasterCard, Visa.
Terms B&B: single £77–£87, double £97–£155; D,B&B (min. 2 nights) £63–£99 per person. Set lunch £11.95–£16.95; full alc £39.50. Bargain breaks. Christmas, New Year packages. 1-night bookings sometimes refused Fri/Sat. *V*

MANCHESTER — Map 4:E3

Eleven Didsbury Park — *Tel* 0161-448 7711
11 Didsbury Park — *Fax* 0161-448 8282
Didsbury Village — *Email* enquiries@elevendidsburypark.com
Manchester M20 5LH — *Website* www.elevendidsburypark.com

Owner Eamonn O'Loughlin 'is much in evidence' at his designer hotel, a member of the Planet consortium. 'His delightful Irish manner contributes much to the informal atmosphere,' says our inspector. His wife, Sally, 'equally charming', is responsible for the 'fairly minimal' modern style: public rooms have white walls, large steel-framed mirrors, a huge stone fireplace topped by three large stones, coffee tables made of old trunks, goldfish in a tall bowl, fresh flowers. 'We loved the bedroom decor, especially the bathroom, which was up four steps,' says a visitor this year. 'Everyone was eager to be helpful.' The Victorian town house is in a conservation area, an easy walk to Didsbury green, and a 20-minute bus ride to the city centre. 'Our bedroom had white walls, a beige carpet, dark polished furniture, an extra-large bed, a small wardrobe, a CD-player.' Breakfast is in a 'pleasant, airy' room with framed montages of cutlery. One guest, who dislikes paying extra, thought it 'disappointing', but others liked the 'interesting selection of cooked dishes' (eg, a full Irish breakfast of black pudding, white pudding and potato cake; eggs Benedict). Individual pots of preserves have replaced the packaged variety complained about last year, and the bedrooms now have a minibar. There is a new manager, Michelle Holbrook. No restaurant, but you can order dishes from a 'Deli Menu' (salads, soups, pasta, etc), the hotel's car will ferry guests to local restaurants, and the owners sometimes hold a barbecue in the garden. (*Suzy Bridges, and others*)

Open All year.
Rooms 1 junior suite, 13 double.
Facilities Lounge, veranda, breakfast room; background radio/CDs all day. Large walled garden: croquet, putting; rooftop terrace. Unsuitable for ♿.
Location 3 miles from centre (regular buses). From A34 take A5145 (Wilmslow Rd); right up Didsbury Pk. Parking.
Restrictions No smoking: breakfast room, 11 bedrooms. No dogs in public rooms.
Credit cards All major cards accepted.
Terms Room: single £99.50–£115.50, double £105.50–£125.50, suite £135–£155.50. Breakfast £8.50–£10.50.

See also SHORTLIST

MARKINGTON North Yorkshire — Map 4:D4

Hob Green
Markington
nr Harrogate HG3 3PJ

Tel 01423-770031
Fax 01423-771589
Email info@hobgreen.com
Website www.hobgreen.com

Reached up a tree-lined drive, this large white 18th-century house near Ripon 'is no great beauty', but it is enhanced by its setting in a huge estate, with extensive floral and vegetable gardens (it has won a 'Yorkshire and Humberside in Bloom' prize). It was turned into a hotel in 1982 by the long-time owners, the Hutchinson family, who write: 'Guests here are guests, not numbers on a booking chart.' They have a new manager this year, Christopher Ashby. 'Well-appointed' and traditional (Best Western), *Hob Green* is liked for its 'good value, excellent service, and high standard of cooking'. The public rooms have an old-fashioned style: original panelling and moulding, antiques, fresh flowers, open fires; also views across the valley. No bar: drinks are served in the hall or the lounge. 'You should not make too great an inroad into the crudités, given the size of the main courses at dinner.' These are 'traditional English/French classical', with a wide choice, eg, seared calf's liver with a red onion butter sauce; rack of lamb with redcurrant and rosemary sauce; puddings might be plum and brandy fool with shortbread hearts; pecan pie with maple syrup. There is a 'decent selection of reasonably priced wines'. The bedroom decor varies from traditional (draped curtains, period furniture, some four-posters) to modern. 'Room 1 was large and attractive, with a good view, a minibar containing fresh milk, lots of bathroom goodies.' Plenty of choice for breakfast. Conferences and functions are catered for. Within 20 minutes' drive are Fountains Abbey, Ripley Castle, the cathedral city of Ripon, and many other attractions. More reports, please.

Open All year.
Rooms 1 suite, 7 double, 4 single.
Facilities 3 lounges, restaurant; function facilities. No background music. 800-acre grounds: garden, croquet, farm, woodlands. Unsuitable for ♿. Civil wedding licence.
Location SW of village which is 9 miles N of Harrogate. From Harrogate: A61 to Ripon; B6165 to Pateley Bridge. After 1 mile turn right at sign to Fountains Abbey. After 2 miles, right at *Drovers' Inn*; hotel 1 mile further. Look for brown signs.
Restrictions No smoking: restaurant, bedrooms. No dogs in public rooms.
Credit cards All major cards accepted.
Terms [2001] B&B: single £85–£90, double £95–£110, suite £120. Set lunch £7.50–£13.95, dinner £24.50; full alc £37.50. Christmas package.

> Please make a habit of sending a report if you stay at a *Guide* hotel, even if it's only to endorse the existing entry.

MAWNAN SMITH Cornwall Map 1:E2

Meudon
Mawnan Smith
nr Falmouth TR11 5HT

Tel 01326-250541
Fax 01326-250543
Email wecare@meudon.co.uk
Website www.meudon.co.uk

'A good family hotel, very comfortable.' 'Well-trained and managed staff in all departments.' 'Good food.' Comments this year on this thoroughly traditional hotel, run by its owners, father and son Harry and Mark Pilgrim, with Shaun Davie. It consists of a mellow stone mansion connected by a glassed-in 'bridge' (which doubles as a sun lounge) to a utilitarian modern bedroom wing. Its chief glories are its subtropical garden, which was laid out in the 18th century by Capability Brown, and its location in 200 acres of protected Cornish coastline between the Fal and Helford rivers, at the head of a valley leading down to a private beach. The decor is conventional (patterned carpets and wallpaper in the public rooms), and the old-fashioned style is appreciated: cases carried, beds turned down at night, shoes cleaned, early morning tea brought to the room (tea-making facilities are also available). The bedrooms are spacious and well equipped, but not luxurious; the suites are 'particularly good'. All the beds are twins, and the Pilgrims do not charge a single-occupation supplement. Breakfast is of a 'calorific nature', including black pudding with a huge mixed grill; lashings of toast and coffee. Afternoon tea is taken outdoors, or by a log fire in the lounge. The restaurant is supervised by head waiter David Pitcher, 'kind, friendly, very professional', 'with eyes everywhere'. Alan Webb, the long-serving chef, offers a traditional five-course dinner, with lots of choice: sorbet in the middle, fish, steaks, etc, to follow (lobster and crab can be specially ordered – you pay extra); 'particularly good vegetables'; a trolley of old-fashioned desserts; an excellent cheeseboard, and a decent range of reasonably priced wines. Another lovely garden, Trebah, and the Eden Project are close by. (*Anne and Denis Tate, Mr K Newton, Ken and Mildred Edwards; also Roger Hughes*)

Open 1 Feb–3 Jan.
Rooms 3 suites, 26 double. 16 on ground floor (some suitable for ♿). Self-catering cottage.
Facilities Lift, ramps. 3 lounges, bar, restaurant. No background music. 10-acre grounds: gardens, private beach. Golf, riding, windsurfing nearby.
Location 4 miles S of Falmouth. From Truro: A39 towards Falmouth for about 9 miles. Turn off at Hillhead roundabout, following signs for Meanporth (*not* Mawnan Smith). Follow narrow, winding road (marked 'Unsuitable for long vehicles'). Hotel on left ½ mile after Meanporth beach, 1 mile before Mawnan Smith. Car park. Train: Truro; taxi/hire car.
Restriction No dogs in public rooms.
Credit cards All major cards accepted.
Terms [2001] D,B&B (min. 2 nights): single £49.50–£95, double £99–£190. Suite £60 supplement. B&B only (not in low season): £10 deducted per person. Set lunch from £12.50, dinner from £25.50; full alc from £40. Reductions for children in adjoining rooms July/Aug. 3-day breaks. Christmas package. *V*

MELBOURN Cambridgeshire Map 3:C4

Sheene Mill Hotel & Brasserie NEW
Station Road
Melbourn SG8 6DX

Tel 01763-261393
Fax 01763-261376
Email steven@stevensaunders.co.uk
Website www.stevensaunders.co.uk

The celebrity chef Steven Saunders and his wife Sally ('both young and keen, with youthful tastes') have given a major facelift to this pretty black-and-white timbered building which bestrides the river Mel in a quiet village near Cambridge. Each of the bedrooms (all have a river view) has been done by a different designer: the suite is by David Emmanuel; the Water Room (Tracy Wilson) has portholes, a waterbed, and a blue-and-orange decor. 'The Garden Room (Anna French) has a fabulous view of the idyllic garden (with pond, ducks, huge old trees),' writes our inspector. 'Its colour scheme of cream, lime green and orange created a fresh feeling. The fabrics were of high quality, but the furniture had a bit of a DIY feel (badly fitting wardrobe doors and drawers), and the bathroom was very small, and awkwardly planned. In the restaurant, where "smart casual clothing" is expected of diners, the atmosphere was lively, tables a bit close, service attentive but not intrusive. You eat *à la carte*: one starter was over-flavoured, but rump of veal with pesto juices was one of the best pieces of meat I have had in a long time, and roasted cod with crispy onions and pea broth was excellent. We slept well; creaks from the old building were minimal; ducks made the loudest noise. Breakfast was not up to the standard of dinner. Reception was correct if not overly warm; we did not see the owners or meet the manager.' Light lunches and coffee are served in a conservatory; in cold weather the adjacent bar areas are warmed by log fires.

Open All year, except 25/26 Dec. Restaurant closed 1 Jan.
Rooms 1 suite, 7 double, 1 single.
Facilities Lounge, bar, conservatory, restaurant; light jazz/piano at night. 3-acre garden: terrace, river. Unsuitable for ♿. Civil wedding licence.
Location 2 miles NE of Royston; 10 miles SW of Cambridge. King's Cross–Cambridge train stops at Melbourn station (10 mins' walk).
Restrictions No smoking: restaurant, some bedrooms. Guide dogs only.
Credit cards Amex, MasterCard, Visa.
Terms B&B: single £75, double £80–£95, suite £110. Set lunch £11.50; full alc £30. Painting, cookery courses.

MEMBURY Devon Map 1:C5

Lea Hill Hotel
Membury, nr Axminster
EX13 7AQ

Tel 01404-881881
Fax 01404-881890
Email reception@leahillhotel.co.uk
Website www.leahillhotel.co.uk

'A delightfully tranquil setting away from main thoroughfares; we were made to feel very welcome by the genial hosts.' Visitors love the peaceful location of Sue and Chris Hubbard's 14th-century thatched longhouse, reached by narrow rural roads. It has a beautiful position on a Devon hilltop in a designated area of outstanding natural beauty. From the large grounds there are wide views of woodland and meadows. Inside the handsome building are ancient beams, flagstone floors and inglenook fireplaces. The 'first-class cooking' of the Hubbards' son, James, is also admired. The 'delightful wood-beamed dining room', on two levels, is open to the public. It has wooden tables and chairs, fat candles, fresh flowers. The four-course dinner is 'imaginative, well prepared and presented'. A sample menu includes local goat's cheese with fried wontons and white truffles; quail with pear fondant and celeriac crisps; home-made marmalade ice cream. On Sunday evening, when the restaurant is closed, a 'Lea Hill Platter' is served in the bar. 'Breakfasts as good as I've had anywhere,' was another compliment. The buffet has freshly squeezed orange juice, and cooked dishes include local bacon, sausages and black pudding, Manx kippers, poached smoked Finnan haddock. Most bedrooms are in 'tastefully converted' barns; many have a private garden or patio. 'Ours was furnished in pleasing floral design'; they are well equipped and have 'excellent lighting'. Membury, a pretty village on the borders of Devon, Somerset and Dorset, was a Quaker centre in the 17th and 18th centuries; it has a Quaker burial ground and meeting house. The coast and an abundance of National Trust properties are close by. (*Grahame Hattam*, *JL, BB*)

Open Mid-Mar–Dec. Restaurant closed midday, Sun.
Rooms 2 suites, 9 double. 9 in 2 barns. Most with private patio or garden.
Facilities 2 small lounges, bar, restaurant; light classical background music; meeting room; terrace. 8-acre grounds: garden, 9-hole par 3 golf course. Riding, fishing nearby; sea, safe beaches 10 miles. Unsuitable for ♿.
Location 2½ miles NW of Axminster. From *George Hotel* take road to Membury. Through village, past trout farm. House on right after ½ mile. Train: Axminster; hotel will meet.
Restrictions Smoking in bar only. No children. Dogs by arrangement; not in public rooms except bar.
Credit cards Amex, MasterCard, Visa.
Terms [2001] B&B £54–£68; D,B&B £76–£89. Set dinner £27. 3 nights for the price of 2 sometimes. Christmas package. 1-night bookings refused bank holidays. *V*

MIDHURST West Sussex **Map 2:E3**

The Spread Eagle NEW
South Street
Midhurst GU29 9NH

Tel 01730-816911
Fax 01730-815668
Email spreadeagle@hshotels.co.uk
Website www.hshotels.co.uk

Once a 15th-century coaching inn in this old market town, the Spread Eagle now belongs to Anne and Sandy Goodman's select Historic Sussex Hotels group (see also *Ockenden Manor*, Cuckfield). They have added a health centre in a modern extension – it draws both residents and locals (you need to book the special treatments in advance). 'Very relaxing; a lovingly cared for old building, informally run, but five-star treatment; delightful bedroom with eccentric plumbing. Breakfast the only letdown,' says a visitor this year. Others, travelling with a one-year-old son, wrote: 'We got everything we wanted – comfort, simple luxury, a spacious, attractive room – without breaking the bank. Service was fast, friendly, efficient. The female deputy manager was outstanding.' An inspector adds: 'The lounge, pleasantly shabby, has faded leather armchairs, open fire, no sign of a decorator's hand. Walls are uneven plaster, white or terracotta; floors are dark oak. There are stairs up, stairs down, winding corridors, suits of armour, and a large conservatory, warm enough to sit in on a winter's day.' Most bedrooms are on the small side. Some are old, 'with sloping floorboards, four-poster, creaky cupboards'; others, 'not luxurious, but warm', are in a new wing; some get traffic noise. 'Room 3 adjoins the Jacobean hall, popular for weddings – best check the situation if you want a quiet time.' 'Very good' modern cooking by Lee Williams, eg, sea bass with ginger nage; roast lamb with ratatouille. 'We thought the *table d'hôte* pricey, but as part of the half-board package it was good value.' The Goodmans' other Midhurst hotel, *The Angel*, currently being refurbished, has an informal brasserie. (*Mrs J Murray, Kate Price, and others*)

Open All year.
Rooms 1 suite, 38 double. 4 in Market House.
Facilities Lounge, lounge bar, conservatory, restaurant; 3 private dining rooms. No background music. 1-acre garden. Unsuitable for ♿. Civil wedding licence.
Location Central (some rooms get traffic noise). Car park. Train: Haslemere; bus.
Restrictions No smoking: restaurant, some bedrooms. No dogs in public rooms.
Credit cards All major cards accepted.
Terms B&B double £110–£210; D,B&B £49–£115 per person. Set lunch £18.50, dinner £35; full alc £55. Midweek, weekend breaks. Christmas package. 1-night bookings refused weekends. *V*

MILBORNE PORT Dorset — Map 2:E1

The Old Vicarage BUDGET
Sherborne Road
Milborne Port DT9 5AT
Tel 01963-251117
Fax 01963-251515
Email theoldvicarage@milborneport.freeserve.co.uk
Website www.milborneport.freeserve.co.uk

A 'good-looking' neo-Tudor Victorian house in a village near Sherborne. It stands in large grounds, with a round pond, and views of an 11th-century stone church, gentle hills, horses and Friesian cattle in a field. 'The A30 runs through the interesting ancient village, but a faint hum of traffic can be heard in the house only when the windows are open,' say inspectors in 2001. 'A wide, handsomely carved and carpeted staircase leads up to three bedrooms (the others, smaller and cheaper, are in a coach house). Ours was green, peach and yellow, with a canopied bed; the bathroom was vividly decorated in jade and yellow; some slightly erotic Indian batik pictures hung on the walls. In the spacious lounge, the quantity of furniture, curtains, pictures, antiques, oriental pots, easy chairs, books, games and ornaments, plus a piano, gave the right feel of clutter for a Victorian house.' In the conservatory restaurant, where dinner is served only at weekends, the owner/chefs, Anthony Ma and Jörgen Kunath, serve dishes from around the world on an eclectic menu. 'The cooking was pleasurable and good value, with no pretension to *haute cuisine*: flavoursome baked mushroom with a nutty cheese top; venison with a brandy and peppercorn sauce; marinated lamb with mint and white wine sauce; delicious apricot and apple crumble. Bread was varied and excellent at dinner and breakfast.' The wine list is 'interesting and well priced'. Only caveat: 'We disliked the UHT milk in the bedroom, and the wrapped butter pats at breakfast.' 'Jörgen is a mine of information about local sights' (they include Montacute, Parnham and Stourhead). 'Chinese, German, French and Spanish are all spoken here,' say the polyglot owners.

Open Feb–Dec. Restaurant closed Sun–Thurs.
Rooms 6 double, 1 single. 4 (some on ground floor) in coach house (20 yds).
Facilities Lounge with drinks trolley (classical background music at night), dining room. 3½-acre grounds. Unsuitable for ♿.
Location 3 miles NE of Sherborne, on A30 at W end of village. Train: Sherborne; taxi.
Restrictions No smoking: dining room, bedrooms. No children under 5. Dogs in coach house only, not in public rooms.
Credit cards Amex, MasterCard, Visa.
Terms [2001] B&B £27–£48; D,B&B £43–£68. Set dinner £21.90. Weekend breaks. 1-night bookings sometimes refused weekends.

MILTON KEYNES Buckinghamshire *See SHORTLIST* Map 2:C3

MORSTON Norfolk Map 2:A5

Morston Hall
Morston, nr Blakeney
NR25 7AA

Tel 01263-741041
Fax 01263-740419
Email reception@morstonhall.com
Website www.morstonhall.com

Galton and Tracy Blackiston are 'involved at all stages' in the running of their restaurant-with-rooms in a flint-stoned Jacobean house on the North Norfolk coast. He runs the *Michelin*-starred kitchen which, for many, is the main reason for a visit. Using local produce, the cooking is a combination of modern British and classical French, eg, seared calf's liver on sautéed artichokes with rich beef jus and Alsace bacon; fillet of cod with herb crust; roast rack of milk-fed lamb on braised cabbage; orange tart with blood orange sorbet. Dinner, a four-course no-choice menu, is 'at 7.30 for 8'. Portions are 'not over large, so you can enjoy the meal without feeling bloated'. Breakfast includes home-made bread, fresh orange juice, 'excellent' local smoked haddock and kippers. Cream teas are served. There are mixed reports about the bed-rooms this year. Most are spacious and well furnished, with a CD-player, a video, and a large bathroom; those in the attic have a sloping ceiling. Some rooms may be 'curiously laid out' and one is said to be 'very small'. Lighting may be rather dim, and one visitor complained of noise from the laundry. A peaceful garden has a lily pond and fountain, roses and a croquet lawn. Children are welcomed (toys, high chairs, cots are provided). Dogs are welcomed too: a small charge is made for those accommodated in the house, but kennels are free. Morston is in a designated area of outstanding natural beauty – the estuary is two minutes' walk away; local attractions include the Blakeney Point seal sanctuary, Sandringham, Felbrigg and Blickling halls, Sheringham Park and 'some wonderful churches'. (*Anne and Denis Tate, G and AS, and others*)

Open Feb–1 Jan. Restaurant closed for lunch, except Sun.
Rooms 1 suite, 5 double.
Facilities 2 lounges, conservatory, restaurant. No background music. 3½-acre garden: pond, croquet. Sea, beaches, sailing, birdwatching nearby. Only restaurant suitable for ♿.
Location On A149 coast road, 2 miles W of Blakeney. Private parking. Train: Sheringham, via Norwich; then taxi.
Restrictions No smoking in restaurant. No dogs in public rooms.
Credit cards All major cards accepted.
Terms D,B&B £100–£140. Set Sun lunch £22, dinner £36. Child in parents' room: under 3, free, over 3: B&B £20. 3-night off-season breaks. Cookery courses. 1-night bookings sometimes refused Sat.

MOULSFORD-ON-THAMES Oxfordshire — Map 2:D3

The Beetle and Wedge — *Tel* 01491-651381
Ferry Lane — *Fax* 01491-651376
Moulsford-on-Thames OX10 9JF

César award in 1993

'What a great place.' 'The best fresh-from-the-cook food I have enjoyed for some time.' The setting of Richard and Kay Smith's old inn is 'magical', in manicured lawns on the stretch of the river immortalised by Kenneth Grahame in *The Wind in the Willows.* Jerome K Jerome lived here while he wrote *Three Men in a Boat*. There is a distinct Frenchness of style, in the welcome to children, the emphasis on food, and the style of the cooking (Mr Smith's co-chef is Olivier Bouet). The mainly French young staff are 'enthusiastic and courteous'. Other comments: 'Outstanding. Lovely grounds.' 'Expert service and management.' The restaurants use locally grown produce, organic where possible, and menus vary according to supplies. The conservatory-style *Dining Room*, overlooking the river, serves sophisticated main courses and luscious desserts, eg, game consommé with pheasant dumplings and morels; sea bass with spinach and béarnaise sauce; warm gooey chocolate pudding with almond milk ice cream. The wine list, strong on Italian and French vintages, has no half bottles, but a 'dipstick' policy applies: order a whole bottle and pay for what is consumed plus £1.25. The informal *Boathouse* restaurant, which has a different chef and kitchen, serves charcoal grills, salads, casseroles and traditional puddings, in large portions. It has a terrace for summer meals, and is often crowded at the weekend. 'Our guests thrive on a relaxed style of eating,' write the Smiths. 'Meal reservations are advisable.' Most bedrooms have river views; some are large. Mrs Smith often redecorates. The style is a mixture of old and modern – a huge bed, a sofa, heavy curtains, a 'glorious, old-fashioned bath' and 'delicious home-made biscuits, replenished during the evening turn-down service'. Breakfast, served from 7.30 until 11, includes freshly squeezed orange juice, porridge, 'well-timed' smoked haddock and 'perfectly poached' eggs; also kidneys and black pudding, 'excellent coffee', and 'the chunkiest marmalade I have ever encountered'. 'Our children loved feeding the ducks and swans.' A good base for visiting Henley, Oxford and the Cotswolds. Heathrow airport is 50 minutes' drive away. (*KG, David Taylor, D Barnett, and others*)

Open All year.
Rooms 10 double. 4 in cottage. 2 on ground floor.
Facilities Lounge, 2 restaurants; private dining/function room. No background music. ½-acre grounds on river; terrace, jetty.
Location From M4 junction 12 take A4 S; at 2nd roundabout take A340 Pangbourne/Streatley/Moulsford. In village turn to river on Ferry La. Parking. Train: Reading/Goring; then taxi.
Restrictions No smoking: *Dining Room*, bedrooms. Dogs by arrangement.
Credit cards All major cards accepted.
Terms [2001] B&B: single £97.50–£127.50, double £165–£185. Bar meals. Set Sun lunch £40; full alc £35–£45. Champagne weekends; cooking tutorials; Christmas, New Year breaks. *V*

MUNGRISDALE Cumbria — Map 4: inset C2

The Mill Hotel
Mungrisdale
Penrith CA11 0XR

Tel 017687-79659
Fax 017687-79155
Email quinlan.themill@bushinternet.com
Website www.themillhotel.com

César award in 1993

Richard Quinlan extends 'a personal welcome from the initial phone call' to this converted 17th-century former mill cottage, still with its millrace, waterfall and trout stream. A popular, family-friendly hotel, it stands in a peaceful hamlet at the foot of the Skiddaw range of mountains. There is walking through 'delightful woodland' from the door. The public rooms are small, and they can be crowded at times. The sitting room has an open fire; there is a sunroom, and a small reading room with 'a catholic selection of reading matter'. Some bedrooms are small, too, with a small bed. Tables in the dining room are close together, encouraging conviviality. Dinner is served at 7 pm by Mr Quinlan; his wife, Eleanor, is the chef. The five-course dinner, with choice, might include smoked trout, spinach and salmon terrine; butternut squash and apple soup; fillet of sea bass with salsa verde, or Jamaican black-eye bean hotpot; puddings such as steamed treacle pudding, or Eve's pudding with peaches and vanilla. Bread is home-baked every day. The 'sheer professionalism of the Quinlans' is regularly admired. 'It is matched by their concern that guests really enjoy their stay.' Breakfasts are 'first class'. Dogs are welcomed by arrangement. The Penrith exit of the M6 is only 12 miles away. A good base for climbing, birdwatching, hang-gliding, etc. (*AF*)

Note: Not to be mistaken for the *Mill Inn*, with which it confusingly shares an entrance.

Open 1 Mar–1 Nov. Dining room closed for lunch.
Rooms 9 double, 6 with facilities *en suite*. 2 on ground floor. No telephone.
Facilities Lounge, reading room, sunroom, dining room (classical background music during dinner); drying room. 2-acre grounds: millrace, waterfall, trout stream. Golf 3 miles; Ullswater, fishing, sailing 5 miles.
Location Small village 2 miles N of A66 Penrith–Keswick. M6 exit 40.
Restrictions No smoking in dining room. No dogs in public rooms.
Credit cards None accepted.
Terms B&B £29–£39; D,B&B £59–£69. Set dinner £28.50. Reductions for 5 or more nights. *V*

NANTWICH Cheshire *See SHORTLIST* Map 3:B5

NAYLAND Suffolk Map 2:C5

The White Hart

11 High Street
Nayland CO6 4JF

Tel 01206-263382
Fax 01206-263638
Email nayhart@aol.com
Website www.whitehart-nayland.co.uk

Owned by Michel Roux (see *The Waterside Inn*, Bray), this old inn 'teaches the English how to run a hotel and restaurant', according to an enthusiastic visitor this year. 'The staff are marvellous, always pleased to help, obviously well trained.' The setting could not be more English, in the high street of a small Suffolk town (with colour-washed houses and a milestone obelisk) 15 minutes' drive from Colchester and Sudbury. Standing in a garden on the river Stour, *The White Hart* dates back to the 15th century; in 1789 its frontage was changed to make a tunnel entrance through which carriages could pass. It is run in personal style by the French manager, Franck Deletang, and his wife. They have a young child, and guests' children are welcome here: 'We took our one-year-old daughter and they made every effort to ensure that she enjoyed her stay.' The bedrooms are decorated in contemporary style, with bright checked fabrics and a king-size bed. 'It is all very French,' said our inspector. 'Our room, not large, was smart in blue and yellow.' *Michelin* awards a *Bib Gourmand* for the classical cooking of Neil Bishop. He provides informal lunches (eg, soups; moules marinière; confit of rabbit legs), and sophisticated dinners (dishes like twice-cooked goat's cheese soufflé; grilled wood pigeon with wild mushrooms and juniper sauce; chocolate crème brûlée. Breakfast 'is flexible in respect of timing and content, reflecting the "can do, will do" approach of the staff'. 'It was delicious, with fresh orange juice, large French-style coffee cups, perfectly cooked eggs.' 'Great value; at no point did we feel we were being ripped off.' Functions are held (a marquee is sometimes erected on the terrace). Beautiful Suffolk countryside is all around. (*James Colegrave; also Sara Price*)

Open 4 Jan–26 Dec. Restaurant closed Mon, except bank holidays.
Rooms 5 double, 1 single.
Facilities Lounge, bar, restaurant; background jazz; private dining/function rooms, terrace. Garden on river. Unsuitable for ♿. Civil wedding licence.
Location 6 miles N of Colchester, in village on A134. Car park. Buses from Sudbury, Ipswich, Colchester.

Restrictions No smoking in bedrooms. No dogs.
Credit cards All major cards accepted.
Terms B&B: single £66, double £71.50; D,B&B (midweek) £47.50–£57.50 per person. Set lunch £11.50–£13.50, dinner £16.50–£20.50; full alc £29.50. *V*

NEAR SAWREY Cumbria — Map 4: inset C2

Ees Wyke

Near Sawrey
nr Ambleside LA22 0JZ

Tel/Fax 015394-36393
Email eeswyke@aol.com
Website www.smoothhound.uk/hotels/eeswyke

Hard-working owners Margaret and John Williams run their late Regency mansion (much altered in the 20th century) in the vale of Esthwaite as a guest house. It was once the holiday home of Beatrix Potter, who loved it so much she moved to the village; her farmhouse, Hill Top, managed by the National Trust, is nearby. *Ees Wyke* looks across fields towards Esthwaite Water and distant hills. A gentle Border collie, Ruff, is in attendance. 'Excellent value for money, in an idyllic spot,' says a regular visitor. The consistent standards are admired as well as the 'good-humoured atmosphere'. Others wrote of the 'fresh and homely' decor (with tasseled lampshades and fringes, open fires, a medley of furniture in the bedrooms); 'everywhere is immaculate'. Each room is named for its colour scheme, and all but one have a lake view. They are good-sized and well decorated, with a 'compact but charming bathroom'. In the two pleasantly furnished sitting rooms, guests assemble for drinks at 7 pm, and socialise after a leisurely dinner. The cooking was found 'well above average, with good raw materials, impressive timing'. 'Modern dishes, skilfully prepared' might include cream of tomato, pear and tarragon soup; paupiette of turkey filled with orange and apricot; 'guests talk freely between the well-spaced tables'. Breakfast is 'startlingly copious'; 'the fried eggs are a picture'; 'Mrs Williams circulates with a groaning platter of mushrooms, black pudding, kidneys, fried bread, three kinds of sausage; guests choose what they fancy'. (*Don Parker, DW, and others*)

Open Mar–Dec.
Rooms 8 double. 1 on ground floor. No telephone.
Facilities 2 lounges, restaurant. No background music. 2-acre garden. Access to lake: fishing, boating. Unsuitable for ♿.
Location On edge of village 1½ miles SE of Hawkshead, on road to Windermere ferry. Local bus from Windermere.
Restrictions No smoking in restaurant. No children under 8 at dinner. No dogs in public rooms.
Credit cards None accepted.
Terms B&B £50. Set dinner £15 (£25 to non-residents). Weekly rates. Christmas, New Year house parties.

By sending us reports you automatically qualify for the Report of the Year competition. Each of 12 winners is awarded a bottle of champagne and a free copy of the *Guide*.

Sawrey House
Near Sawrey
nr Ambleside LA22 0LF

Tel 015394-36387
Fax 015394-36010
Email enquiries@sawrey-house.com
Website www.sawrey-house.com

In peaceful setting in 3-acre gardens next to Beatrix Potter's home, Hill Top: Colin and Shirley Whiteside's Victorian country house (original features, eg, stained glass retained). Period furniture, log fires, views of lake, forest and mountains. 'Warm, but unobtrusive' welcome. Ambitious cooking; extensive, reasonably priced wine list in restaurant (with pianist or CDs). 11 well-equipped bedrooms, some on ground floor. Smoking in bar only. No children under 8. No dogs in public rooms. Open mid-Feb–mid-Nov, Christmas, New Year. MasterCard, Visa accepted. B&B £45–£48; D,B&B £60–£68. Set dinner £30. More reports, please.

NEW MILTON Hampshire — Map 2:E2

Chewton Glen
Christchurch Road
New Milton BH25 6QS

Tel 01425-275341
Fax 01425-272310
Email reservations@chewtonglen.com
Website www.chewtonglen.com

'Fantastic.' 'Expensive, but value for money.' Martin and Brigitte Skan's luxurious 'hotel, health and country club' on the edge of the New Forest has had a *Guide* entry ever since our first edition. The Skans have stayed at the forefront of British hotel-keeping by combining innovation with traditional values. They were ahead of the pack with health and sporting facilities, and they cater for an international moneyed clientele. The restaurant has a *Michelin* star, and managing director Peter Crome and his large team are 'unfailingly helpful and charming'. 'Wonderful, with lovely staff, very good food,' one visitor wrote. Another found the golf course 'immaculate, and pleasantly under-used'. The restaurant, named for Captain Marryat (he wrote *The Children of the New Forest* here), has a 'warm, intimate feeling'. Pierre Chevillard's 'cooking with a light touch' is 'refreshingly modern, but with no hint of unnecessary trendiness', eg, timbale of crab and avocado; pork cheeks and lobster; baked monkfish on rosemary-flavoured polenta. The menu also includes vegetarian and 'wellness' choices. Breakfast can be healthy (skimmed milk, wholemeal toast, decaffeinated coffee), traditional English (with New Forest sausages), or luxurious (champagne, scrambled eggs and smoked salmon). Large lounges have antiques and fine fabrics. Suites and bedrooms, some vast, are equally lavish, and stocked with fruit (constantly replenished), sherry, biscuits, toiletries, huge towels, bathrobes. Some have a balcony or terrace; the two-storey suites in the coach house have a private garden. The sea is a short walk away, along a footpath. (*Paul Hingston, John Gibbon, and others*)

Open All year.
Rooms 19 suites, 43 double. Some on ground floor.
Facilities Ramps. 3 lounges (pianist in one, Fri/Sat evening), bar, restaurant; function rooms; snooker room; health club: indoor tennis, swimming pool,

gymnasium, beauty salon. 180-acre grounds: swimming pool, tennis, croquet, 9-hole golf course, lake, jogging course, helipad; bicycle hire. Beach, fishing, sailing, shooting, riding nearby. Chauffeur service. Civil wedding licence.
Location M27 to A31. Turn left towards Emery Down, right on to A35 (*don't* follow New Milton signs); after 11 miles, turn off to Walkford/Highcliffe. As you leave Walkford, road dips; turn into Chewton Farm road (immediately before roundabout sign). Entrance on right. Bus service nearby. Station 5 mins' drive.
Restrictions No smoking: restaurant, 1 lounge. No children under 6. No dogs (kennels nearby).
Credit cards All major cards accepted.
Terms B&B: single £250–£275, double £250–£405, suite £480–£720; D,B&B: single £345–£365, double £395–£420, suite £630–£870. Set lunch £35, dinner £55. 5-night breaks. Healthy breaks. Christmas, Easter, golfing packages. Min. 2-night bookings at weekends.

NEW ROMNEY Kent — Map 2: E5

Romney Bay House NEW
Coast Road, Littlestone
New Romney TN28 8QY
Tel 01797-364747
Fax 01797-367156

César award in 1997

'Superb, friendly, with very good service.' 'Excellent, wonderfully quiet. The hosts, their staff, their dog and two cats were all welcoming. My bedroom was lovely.' These compliments came this year for Jennifer and Helmut Gorlich. They put their hotel on the market a year ago, but it has not sold, and fans say that it is as good as ever (but you should check the position if you want to book). Built by Sir Clough Williams-Ellis for the American actress and Hollywood gossip columnist Hedda Hopper, the white-walled, red-roofed house looks out over a mile of sand and pebble beaches. Behind, a golf course stretches into the distance. 'The isolated spot with its vast skyscapes and seascapes make one feel miles from the hurly-burly of everyday life,' visitors wrote. 'No shelter from wind nor shade from sun.' The no-choice dinners cooked by Jennifer Gorlich are thought 'delicious and generous' (portions are too large for some). 'Wonderful fresh fish, light seasonal puddings.' The 'lively host' acts as wine waiter and takes a genuine interest in his guests. Antiques, pictures, and an 'astonishing number of knick-knacks' fill the house. At night, white candles burn in the public rooms, and a log fire crackles in the lounge. One bedroom in the new extension has almost floor-length windows, with views of the sea; another room has a 'corner-ways-on bath of an old style – a deliberate oddity'. Breakfast is served until late. The continental version includes cold meats, cheese, fruits, croissants and 'excellent marmalade'; full English is available too. Cream teas are served, on the terrace in fine weather. From the 'lookout', a first-floor lounge at the front of the hotel, there are wide views along the coast, and an old telescope for viewing. The Channel Tunnel is 20 minutes' drive away. (*BA Orman, Miss J Northcote, E and P Thompson, Marion and Glyn Harper*)

Open All year, except Christmas. Restaurant closed 2 weeks mid-June, occasional evenings.

Rooms 10 double. No telephone.
Facilities 2 sitting rooms (radio sometimes played), bar, dining room, dining conservatory; small function facilities. 2-acre garden: tennis, croquet, *boules*. Opposite sea (safe bathing), fishing, golf course. Unsuitable for ♿.
Location From New Romney follow signs to Littlestone; at sea, turn left. Continue as far as possible. Hotel alone, opposite sea, on left. Train: Ashford; then taxi.
Restrictions No smoking: restaurant, 1 sitting room, bedrooms. No children under 14. No dogs.
Credit cards Diners, MasterCard, Visa.
Terms B&B: single £60–£95, double £80–£149. Light lunches. Set dinner £29.50. Midweek breaks Nov–Mar. 1-night bookings generally refused weekends.

NEWBURY Berkshire *See SHORTLIST* — Map 2:D2

NEWCASTLE UPON TYNE Tyne and Wear — Map 4:B4

Malmaison

The Quayside
Newcastle upon Tyne NE1 3DX

Tel 0191-2455000
Fax 0191-2454545
Email newcastle@malmaison.com
Website www.malmaison.com

One seasoned traveller, who has stayed at all five *Malmaison* hotels in Britain (see also Glasgow, Leeds and Shortlist), rates the Newcastle one as the best. Others write: 'This is *the* place to stay in the city centre, ultra-modern, ultra-stylish.' The 'enthusiastic young staff' are praised, so is the 'value for money, particularly at the weekend'. But one correspondent wrote of a reservation not honoured. The former Co-operative Society warehouse is in the newly developed Quayside area. Tall and square, it has an Art Deco-style metal canopy over the entrance. It is run with a light touch; eg, instead of a 'Do not disturb' sign you get one saying 'Leave me alone'; a lift with recorded announcements in French takes you up to the bedrooms. The ground-floor lobby is smart in beige and cream, with mirrors, wall-to-wall carpeting, bold contemporary furniture, taped jazz. The long reception desk has 'cheerful and unpretentious' staff. The bedrooms, all different, have a plain decor: striped fabrics, striped wallpaper, well-designed contemporary wooden furniture, a CD-player, interesting artwork, decent wines in the minibar, a well-planned bathroom with a deep bath and a power shower. Some rooms are quite small; suites on the seventh floor have wide views. The dimly lit bar has wooden Venetian blinds, tables with blue lamps. The brasserie, overlooking the river, serves uncomplicated French dishes on a frequently changing menu, eg, eggs Benedict; salmon fish-cake; seared loin of tuna. Breakfast 'is lovely' – it includes freshly squeezed orange juice, fruit, cheese. A high-tech gym and a spa are in the basement. (*DB, HW, and others*)

Open All year.
Rooms 18 suites, 98 double. 6 adapted for ♿.
Facilities Lifts. 2 lounges, café/bar, brasserie; modern jazz 24 hrs; gym, spa; function facilities.

Location ½ mile from centre; on quayside, by law courts. Under Tyne bridge; head E for 200 yds. Parking (£2 for 24 hours).
Restrictions No smoking in some bedrooms. Guide dogs only.
Credit cards All major cards accepted.
Terms [2001] Room: single/double £115, suite £125. Breakfast £8.50–£10.75. Set lunch £10–£15, dinner £15–£20. Full alc £25–£30.

NEWLYN Cornwall — Map1:E1

Higher Faugan NEW

Chywoone Hill
Newlyn TR18 5NS

Tel 01736-362076
Fax 01736-351648
Email reception@higherfaugan-hotel.co.uk
Website www.higherfaugan-hotel.co.uk

New owners, Andrew and Cyndi Bell, took over this hotel in July 2000. The house, which looks towards Mount's Bay and St Michael's Mount, was built in 1904 for the artist Stanhope Forbes, founder of the Newlyn School of Art, and his wife, Elizabeth. Its gardens, with a dell and an Italian sunken garden, appear in many of their paintings. Now, they contain also a swimming pool and an 18-hole putting green. 'Our stay was perfection,' say the nominators, 'more like staying in a gentleman's home than a hotel.' Art books, games and bowls of sweets lie around in the public rooms, where the feel is 'more 1950s than 2000s'. Bedrooms 'are spotless'; they look over the gardens; some see the sea beyond. In the dining room, 'tables are immaculately laid, but lighting is a bit dim'; a conservatory extension leads on to the grounds. The 'jolly young chef', Amy Brown, serves English cooking: local fish, simply grilled, is a speciality; also local wild boar steak; 'superb crab ramekins'. Special diets are sympathetically catered for. Artistic groups sometimes take the place over. (*Barry and Ina Lambe*)

Open All year.
Rooms 10 double, 1 single.
Facilities Lounge, snug, bar, games room, studio, dining room. 10-acre grounds: croquet, tennis, putting, swimming pool. Beach 1½ miles.
Location ¾ mile SW of Penzance. Entrance on right on Chywoone Hill (B3315). Bus-stop 250 yds.
Restrictions No smoking in restaurant. No dogs in public rooms.
Credit cards All major cards accepted.
Terms B&B: single £55–£65, double £80–£115; D,B&B: single £65–£75, double £100–£130. Set lunch £5.50, dinner £17.95; full alc £22.50. Christmas package.

NEWTON-LE-WILLOWS North Yorkshire — Map 4:C3

The Hall

Newton-le-Willows
nr Bedale DL8 1SW

Tel 01677-450210
Fax 01677-450014

A handsome Georgian house on the edge of a tiny Bedale village. Its 'very friendly' owner, Oriella Featherstone, runs it in house-party style, providing 'peace, quality, attention to detail', and 'delicious dinner party-style cooking'. 'It is a real joy to stay here,' said our inspector (her only criticism was 'dim bedside lighting'). The decor is theatrical ('a bit OTT' for some tastes): continental antiques and *objets d'art*, tapestries, oriental rugs, heavy curtains fill the rooms. Rose-patterned fabrics and floral prints in the spacious bedrooms (Apollo, Aphrodite, etc) echo the roses in the secluded garden (with ancient copper beeches, ponds and streams, it is set amid fields good for dog-walking). The suite has a seven-foot bed. Guests help themselves from an honesty bar; tea, coffee and home-made fruitcake are always available in the kitchen. An evening meal, by arrangement, is served round one large table; guests are consulted about their needs in advance (vegetarians are catered for). No choice of main course (it might be smoked fish in a creamy sauce; game casserole; chicken with mushrooms in a white wine sauce). There is a choice of puddings, eg, chocolate pot, or sherry trifle, and of cheeses. Coffee and mints are taken by a fire in the 'snug'. Breakfast, served at flexible times, includes local bacon and sausages, thick brown toast, sometimes goose eggs. Mulligan, a Fell terrier, will accompany visitors on a walk. The owner's car is sometimes available to collect guests from Teesside airport or Darlington station. A good base for visiting the Dales, castles, ruined abbeys, gardens, and local racecourses. The A1 and the Middleham moors are ten minutes' drive away.

Note: This village is not to be confused with the Merseyside town of same name.

Open All year.
Rooms 1 suite, 2 double. No telephone.
Facilities Drawing room, TV room/snug, breakfast room, dining room. Classical/modern background music morning/evening. 12-acre grounds: 2-acre gardens, stables and fields for visiting horses. Golf, fishing, riding, cinema and Georgian theatre nearby. Unsuitable for ♿.
Location In village 3 miles W of Bedale. From A1 go W on A684, through Bedale; pass golf course on left, sports centre on right; take 1st left towards Newton-le-Willows; turn right at T-junction. After 500 yds, in front of *Wheatsheaf Inn*, turn left; house on right. Train: Darlington; taxi (or they will meet).
Restrictions No smoking: breakfast room, bedrooms. No children under 13 except by prior arrangement. No dogs in public rooms.
Credit cards None accepted.
Terms B&B £40–£50. Set dinner £25. Christmas house party can be booked.

NORTH BOVEY Devon — Map 1:D4

Blackaller Hotel
North Bovey
nr Moretonhampstead TQ13 8QY

Tel 01647-440322
Fax 01647-441131
Email peter@blackaller.fsbusiness.com
Website www.blackaller.co.uk

'A perfect antidote to a hectic lifestyle. Peaceful, relaxing, away from it all.' Another resounding endorsement for this converted woollen mill on the edge of a delightful village (with granite and thatch houses and a large green with oak trees) at the end of a long lane half a mile from Dartmoor National Park. The 'charming, unassuming host', Peter Hunt, 'is an ideal front-of-house'. He 'is a very special person who makes the hotel what it is – it echoes his character'. In his spare time he keeps bees, spins wool from his own Jacob sheep, and plays the sitar. The four-course dinners, by arrangement, are cooked by Hazel Phillips, the 'jolly hostess', and accompanied by reasonably priced New World wines. They are 'well balanced, with plenty of fresh vegetables and colour', eg, warm smoked haddock and prawn flan; Devon lamb rack with couscous and red pepper chutney; strawberry semifreddo with a raspberry coulis. A vegetarian meal can be ordered. Breakfast has home-produced yogurt, muesli and honey, toast made from 'chunky brown bread'. Antiques, china, flowers and family photos give a homely air to the public rooms. Only three bedrooms are available now (some are up a steep staircase). They have a simple decor: oak beams, pine furniture, quality fabrics, and a bright bathroom. Cream teas are served, alfresco in fine weather. Garden chairs and tables are dotted about on the smooth lawn; it leads down to the river Bovey, where you might see a kingfisher flash by. Castle Drogo (National Trust) is close by; good walking all around. (*Alan and Pippa Daniels*)

Open Mar–Dec; closed New Year. Dinner by arrangement.
Rooms 3 double. No telephone/TV.
Facilities Lounge, bar (classical background music at night), restaurant. 3-acre garden on river: limited trout fishing. Golf nearby. Unsuitable for ♿.
Location From Moretonhampstead follow sign to North Bovey. Sign on wall at edge of village. Train: Exeter, 14 miles; hosts will meet.
Restrictions No smoking. No children under 13. No dogs in public rooms.
Credit cards None accepted.
Terms B&B £31–£40. Set dinner £23. Special breaks: autumn, spring, Christmas, walking, bird photography. *V*

NORTH MOLTON Devon — Map 1:B4

Heasley House BUDGET

Heasley Mill
North Molton EX36 3LE

Tel 01598-740213
Fax 01598-740677
Email info@heasley-house.co.uk

'A gem of a small country guest house. The warmth of John and Jane Ayres's greeting complements the homely atmosphere. They combine friendliness with total professionalism.' 'Everything was excellent. Our American friends wondered how they do it at these prices. Our student son and his girlfriend arrived in an elderly truck with a large dog, and were made most welcome.' This Grade II listed Georgian dower house, once the residence of local copper mine captains, has had many enthusiastic reports this year. It stands in a small garden in a hamlet on the southern edge of Exmoor National Park. Visitors like the 'well-appointed bedrooms containing all the little extras that make one feel at home'. Pre-dinner drinks are served in the drawing room, and a four-course set menu featuring traditional English country cooking is served in a room hung with horse brasses and old hunting prints. 'Starters ranged from delicious smoked mackerel pâté to warming leek and potato soup; desserts included mouth-watering Pavlova; peaches soaked in brandy.' The main course is served by agreement; alternatives, including vegetarian dishes, are available. The wine list is 'excellent'. Breakfast is 'superb English', 'carefully prepared to order'. The area 'is a naturalist's paradise' with Exmoor ponies, red deer and badgers. (*Tom Hulton, A Bruce; also HW Langley*)

Open 1 Apr–1 Feb. Lunch not served.
Rooms 1 suite, 7 double. 1 on ground floor.
Facilities 2 sitting rooms, dining room. No background music. ¾-acre garden. Fishing, shooting, riding nearby. Unsuitable for ♿.
Restrictions Smoking in TV room only. No children under 12.
Location In hamlet just N of North Molton, 11 miles E of Barnstaple.
Credit cards MasterCard, Visa.
Terms [*To 1 Apr 2002*] B&B £29–£53. Set dinner £19.50. *V*

NORTH WALSHAM Norfolk — Map 2:A6

Beechwood BUDGET
Cromer Road
North Walsham NR28 0HD

Tel 01692-403231
Fax 01692-407284
Email beechwood-hotel.co.uk
Website www.beechwood-hotel.co.uk

'The staff are exceptionally pleasant,' says an endorsement this year for Don Birch and Lindsay Spalding's red brick, ivy-clad 200-year-old house. Once a doctor's residence, it is now a small hotel, which has been completely redecorated by the 'charming owners'. They say they guarantee peace by taking no large groups, wedding parties or conferences. The 'friendly ethos' and 'willing service' are admired; so are the two 'adorable Airedale dogs', Clem and Emily. Chef Steven Norgate cooks a long menu in 'New World' style, eg, duck rillettes on a bed of pickled cucumber and onion; breast of chicken with tiger prawns and a bacon and tarragon cream sauce; always an interesting vegetarian main course. Dishes may be cooked more simply on request. 'Delicious and varied.' 'One dinner was excellent; the next good,' guests have written. 'Breakfast was enjoyable.' Spacious bedrooms have big sash windows, antique or period furniture. One has a four-poster, another a freestanding slipper bath. 'The small garden, with shrubs, a long lawn and a sunken area, is beautiful.' In winter, visitors on a two-day weekend break can stay on Sunday night as well with no charge for B&B, provided that they dine in. Lord Nelson was educated in this market town (its church is the second largest in Norfolk). A good base for exploring the Norfolk broads. Sandy beaches are nearby, also Blickling, Holkham and Felbrigg halls (National Trust) and Sandringham. 'The knowledgeable owners will advise about outings.' (*John Hillas, VF*)

Open 7 Jan–23 Dec. Restaurant closed Sat midday.
Rooms 10 double. Some on ground floor.
Facilities Lounge, bar, restaurant; light classical background music at mealtimes. 1-acre garden. Sea 5 miles. Golf, sailing, tennis, riding nearby. Unsuitable for ♿.
Location Approaching North Walsham on B1150 from Norwich, turn left at first set of traffic lights, right at the next set; *Beechwood* is on left.
Restrictions Smoking in bar only. No children under 10.
Credit cards MasterCard, Visa.
Terms B&B £35–£70; D,B&B £42–£85. Set lunch £12.50, dinner £26. Short breaks. 1-night bookings sometimes refused weekends. *V*

NORTON Shropshire — Map 3:C5

Hundred House
Bridgnorth Road
Norton TF11 9EE

Tel 01952-730353
Fax 01952-730355
Email hphundredhouse@compuserve.com
Website www.hundredhouse.co.uk

César award: Utterly enjoyable mild eccentricity

Offering 'consistently good food and service', this red brick old inn stands by the village bowling green. Its quirky style, combined with 'professional management and good humour', is much enjoyed. It is family-run, by Henry Phillips (who says he likes to brew beer and make damson gin), with his wife, Sylvia, and their sons, David and Stuart. Dried flowers and herbs hang from beams in the panelled public rooms. Cast iron pots hang in open fireplaces. Upstairs is a riot of colour: stairs carpeted with bright patchwork, and with equally bright walls, lead to the bedrooms, most of which have a swing made of iron, with a crushed velvet seat, suspended from a wooden beam. Inspectors liked their room: 'It had an ornate glass chandelier, gold-painted ceiling paper, walls that were mauve with a pattern of stencilled gold hearts and cupids. The colourful carpet had a small, busy pattern, and the bed had a patchwork quilt that matched the curtains. The bathroom was functional.' The 'modern European' cooking has earned an entry in the *Good Food Guide 2001* (main courses like cassoulet of wild boar with venison sausage and a tomato and white wine sauce; lobster with basil and brandy bisque sauce; desserts include apricot and almond pie; pear and mascarpone trifle (or you could choose 'the ultimate dessert', comprising all eight puddings on the menu). Brasserie-style meals are served in the bar and at wooden tables in series of tile-floored small rooms. 'You can order as much or as little as you like', and there are vegetarian dishes and a children's menu. Wines are reasonably priced, with a good selection served by the glass. Breakfast may be less satisfying than dinner. The house stands in an old-fashioned garden with roses, shrubs, a 'teddy bear's picnic', a large herb garden with a memorial corner. A busy road passes by, 'but double glazing muffled the sound and there was not much traffic at night'. (Good Pub Guide*, and others*)

Open All year.
Rooms 9 double, 1 single.
Facilities Reception lounge, bar, restaurant. No background music. 1-acre grounds. Unsuitable for ♿.
Location 6 miles S of Telford on A442. Train: Telford; bus/taxi.
Restriction Dogs by arrangement, not in public rooms.
Credit cards MasterCard, Visa.
Terms B&B: single £75, double £99–£125; D,B&B: single £85, double £120. Full alc £27. Child in parents' room: B&B free. 10% reduction for more than 5 nights. Christmas package. 1-night bookings sometimes refused. *V*

If you have had recent experience of a good hotel, B&B or inn that ought to be in the *Guide*, please write to us as soon as you can. Report forms are to be found at the back of the book.

NORWICH Norfolk — Map 2:B5

The Beeches
2–6 Earlham Road
Norwich NR2 3DB

Tel 01603-621167
Fax 01603-620151
Email reception@beeches.co.uk
Website www.beeches.co.uk

An unpretentious hotel, owned by Keith and Lis Hill and their daughter Kate, and run with an 'unfailingly courteous' staff. Two of its three old buildings front on to a busy road (rooms are double-glazed); the third stands on the edge of the romantic Grade II listed Plantation Garden, designed in the 19th century by William Trevor, in a wooded hollow. It has terraces, balustrades, a huge Gothic fountain in a pond with ducks and frogs, mock ruins and a massive rockery. The best bedrooms are quiet, with a lofty ceiling. 'My room was smallish, immaculate, with a tiny shower room, nylon cover on duvet, excellent lighting,' writes an inspector. 'It was approached up a staircase with a bright red patterned carpet. All the staff were friendly. I had an excellent fixed-price dinner (watercress and walnut salad; trio of fish in a creamy sauce; poached pear), very reasonably priced at £15. But the 'easy listening" background music was inappropriate for such good cooking. And breakfast, which was adequate and well served, was accompanied by Radio 2. Walking in the garden at dusk and in the early morning was magical.' Snacks can be served in the bar or bedroom. The cathedral is a 20-minute walk away.

Open All year, except Christmas. Restaurant closed midday.
Rooms 28 double, 8 single. In 3 buildings. 10 on ground floor. 1 designed for ♿.
Facilities Lounge, bar, restaurant; 'light' background music; meeting room. Access to 3-acre Plantation Garden.
Location On B1108 (rooms double-glazed), 10 mins' walk W of centre. Parking.
Restrictions No smoking: restaurant, bedrooms. No children. No dogs.
Credit cards All major cards accepted.
Terms [2001] B&B: single £54–£59, double £70–£88. Set dinner £15; full alc £28. 1-night bookings occasionally refused Sat.

By Appointment
25–29 St George's Street
Norwich NR3 1AB

Tel 01603-630730

César award in 1999

'We have stayed at Tim Brown and Robert Culyer's restaurant-with-rooms twice. We were struck both times by their effusive yet totally genuine welcome and their willingness to do more than we would have asked to make our stay as comfortable as possible.' This 'enjoyably eccentric' place wins yet more praise this year. 'For us, there is nowhere else to stay in Norwich,' wrote another visitor. The 15th-century merchant's house in the historic city centre has a labyrinthine layout. You enter under an arch at the back of the street, through a tiny courtyard with a Della Robbia relief on the wall, and straight into the kitchen. The decor has been described as 'Merchant Ivory, emphasised by trunks and panama hats'. The restaurant is in four rooms, dotted around the house. The menus, displayed on gilt-framed blackboards, and read out by Mr Culyer 'with the aplomb of a circus ringmaster' before each meal, include, eg, sautéed Cajun spiced prawns with crème fraîche; fillet of beef wrapped in bacon and topped with Dijon mustard and brown sugar; steamed lemon and honey sponge pudding. There is a separate vegetarian menu. The bedrooms are 'a riot of Victoriana'. 'Ours was cram packed with minutiae of bygone eras and starched nightwear of yesteryear.' Bathrooms are 'exotic but efficient' (one is a floor below its bedroom, adjacent to the loo used by diners in the restaurant). 'Tim and Robert left loving goodnight notes with chocolates.' They hope to add three new bedrooms this year, subject to planning permission. At breakfast there is a choice of smoked salmon with scrambled eggs, fillet steak, fried eggs, mushrooms, sausages, bacon. (*Oliver and Kate Longstaff, RH, and others*)

Open All year. Restaurant closed lunchtime, Sun and Mon evenings.
Rooms 3 double, 1 single. 3 more planned.
Facilities 2 lounges, restaurant (jazz/classical background music at night). Tiny courtyard. Unsuitable for ♿.
Location Central; corner of St George's St and Colegate (windows double-glazed).
Restrictions No smoking: restaurant, bedrooms. No children under 12. No dogs.
Credit cards MasterCard, Visa.
Terms [2001] B&B: single £70, double £95. Full alc £31.95.

See also SHORTLIST

NOTTINGHAM Nottinghamshire — Map 2:A3

The Lace Market Hotel
29–31 High Pavement
Nottingham NG1 1HE

Tel 0115-8523232
Fax 0115-8523223
Email reservations@lacemarkethotel.co.uk
Website www.lacemarkethotel.co.uk

The hilltop Lace Market area of the city has cobbled streets and tall town houses. Here, two Georgian red brick buildings (once a probation office and a lace factory) have been turned into this designer hotel. Managed by Mark Cox, it has an 'easy-going atmosphere', a 'pleasant young staff'. The modern decor uses brown, yellow and olive green, and 'the odd bit of feng shui, including vases of goldfish'. 'The location is great,' said our inspectors – it is next to St Mary's, 'a gem of a church', and opposite the lovely 18th-century Galleries of Justice (the basement entrance has the inscription 'County Gaol' in stone). 'Our bedroom had high ceilings, four tall sash windows, good views, a spacious bathroom, CD-player, tape deck, voicemail, a desk.' The hotel's fashionable restaurant, *Merchant's,* serves Sunday brunch all day, and on weekdays a brasserie menu, eg, saffron tagliatelle with seared scallops; sea bass stuffed with Thai vegetables; sweetbreads and poached chicken wrapped in pastry with lobster and tarragon sauce; 'an impressive selection of cheeses with very good bread'. At breakfast there is a good buffet, with fresh orange juice, 'delicious treacly compotes, but poor bread'; the salmon fish-cakes are recommended, but some find the accompanying jazz irritating. In this lively area, 'the intermittent yodelling of revellers' on a Saturday night might disrupt sleep. 'The weekend rates are excellent value.' (*Jonathan and Michelle Ray, and others*)

Open All year, except Christmas.
Rooms 3 suites, 23 double, 3 single. 24-hour room service.
Facilities Lift. Bar/café, restaurant; 'easy listening' background music all day; private dining room, boardroom. Unsuitable for ♿.
Location City centre (rooms double-glazed). Follow signs for Galleries of Justice; hotel is opposite. No private parking.
Restrictions No smoking in reception. No dogs in public rooms, except bar.
Credit cards All major cards accepted.
Terms Room: single £69–£89, double £89–£115, suite £145–£169. Breakfast £2.95–£10.95. Set lunch £7.50–£9.90; full alc £30. Off-season and weekend rates. 1-night bookings sometimes refused.

See also SHORTLIST

OAKAMOOR Staffordshire — Map 3:B6

Bank House BUDGET

Farley Lane
Oakamoor
nr Stoke-on-Trent ST10 3BD

Tel/Fax 01538-702810
Email john.orme@dial.pipex.com
Website www.smoothhound.co.uk/hotels/bank

John and Muriel Egerton-Orme run a guest house 'with a house-party ambience' on the outskirts of a village below a steep hill on the edge of the Peak District National Park. 'They are thoughtful owners, food is excellent, bedrooms are splendid,' said one report. Mrs Egerton-Orme won an AA award for the best landlady in the UK in 1996. The house was constructed by its owners in the style of a Derbyshire manor house, using bricks and stone quoins from a much older building on the site. There are pastoral views from the lovely grounds (with a formal garden, a bog garden and ponds), but Alton Towers is only a mile away. No brochure – a personal letter is sent to each prospective guest, explaining the accommodation in detail. Only three bedrooms: two can accommodate a family of four (one has a four-poster bed, another a spa bath). There is a hall with a grand piano, a drawing room and a library; also a large, friendly dog and some cats (if you are averse to pets you should advise the hosts when booking). In fine weather, meals can be served on a terrace. Breakfast, 'where you like it, when you want it', includes home-made breads, pastries and preserves; also porridge, fruit, all manner of cooked dishes. A simple four-course evening meal is available by arrangement (eg, eggs mimosa, or cream of nettle soup; pheasant casserole, or beef Wellington). The hosts often eat with their guests, or join them for a drink. There are also eating places of all sorts nearby, and good walking from the door. The Staffordshire Way is close by; also many stately homes – Chatsworth, Haddon and Kedleston halls, etc. More reports, please.

Open All year, except Christmas week. Lunch not served.
Rooms 3: 1 can accommodate 3; 2 can accommodate 4. Telephone on request.
Facilities Hall, drawing room, library (both with TV), dining room. No background music. 1-acre grounds: garden, water garden, bog garden, woodland. Walking, golf, riding, cycling, etc, nearby. Unsuitable for ♿.
Location From A50: B5030 at Uttoxeter. Follow signs to Alton Towers via Alton village. Pass theme park main entrance on right. After 400 yds turn left signed Farley (narrow lane). After ¾ mile, 2nd house on left (name on gate piers).
Restrictions No smoking. Dogs by arrangement.
Credit cards Diners, MasterCard, Visa.
Terms [2001] B&B: single £45–£54, double £60–£78. Set dinner (by arrangement) £22. Reductions for longer stays. Child in parents' room: under 5, £10; 5–12, £14; over 12, £16. 1-night bookings occasionally refused. *V* (midweek only)

ORFORD Suffolk — Map 2:C6

Crown and Castle NEW

Orford, nr Woodbridge
IP12 2LJ

Tel 01394-450205
Fax 01394-450176
Email crownandcastlehotel@hotmail.com
Website www.crownandcastlehotel.co.uk

An old hotel, recently given a new lease of life, in the market square of a quiet and charming seaside village on the river Ore, north of Ipswich. It was taken over in early 1999 by the cookery writer Ruth Watson and her husband, David. Informally run, it is a far cry from their previous hotel, the luxurious *Hintlesham Hall*, Hintlesham. Here, the accent is on the restaurant, *The Trinity. Michelin* awards a *Bib Gourmand* to the chef, Brendan Ansbro, for such main courses as fresh crab cake; braised lamb; bourride of local cod, and traditional desserts, eg, plum pudding with eggnog custard tart; home-made ice creams. Local oysters and scallops are a speciality. The bedrooms are gradually being upgraded – with their William Morris fabrics and wallpaper, old furniture, potted plants, they are quite simple; many look over the estuary and Orford Ness. Some early hiccoughs ('breakfast arrangements a little chaotic'; 'garden room in need of a revamp') were reported this year. But the food is admired: 'Thoughtfully prepared menus with unusual, well-cooked dishes' are accompanied by 'eminently quaffable' house wines. Service is 'good and willing' if 'sometimes a little forgetful'. Teas and light meals (soups, omelettes, salads, etc) are served in the bar, and outdoors in summer. 'A rather dull-looking, pseudo-Tudor building,' says an inspector; she liked the 'jolly reception', but regretted the absence of a residents' lounge. There are cots, high chairs and special menus for children, and no restrictions on dogs. Orford's Norman castle and the sea are close by; Aldeburgh is a short drive north. (*HJM Tucker, and others*)

Open All year.
Rooms 18 double. 10 in garden wing, 1 in courtyard. 1 on ground floor.
Facilities Ramp. Lounge bar, bar, restaurant, private dining room. No background music. Small garden. Sea 500 yds.
Location Market square of village 9 miles E of Woodbridge. Parking.
Restrictions No smoking in some bedrooms.

Credit cards MasterCard, Visa.
Terms B&B: single £60–£110, double £90–£120; D,B&B: single £90–£130, double £120–£180. Full alc £31.50. Special breaks: D,B&B from £50 per person. Christmas package. 1-night bookings refused Sat.

OXFORD Oxfordshire — Map 2:C2

Cotswold House
363 Banbury Road
Oxford OX2 7PL

Tel/Fax 01865-310558
Email d.r.walker@talk21.com
Website www.housc363.freeserve.co.uk

Good value B&B in North Oxford is offered at this flower-festooned modern Cotswold stone house – 'a real gem,' says a visitor in 2001. Buses pass the front door every six minutes on a busy road into a city centre noted for its parking problems (double glazing mitigates the noise). Alan Clarke is the 'charming manager'. The bedrooms are modern and immaculately kept, with pastel linens and flounces, pink dolls, pot-pourri, chocolates, TV, a fridge; fresh milk on request for tea-making. Duvet or blankets according to preference. One single is small. Shower rooms have ample towels and plenty of hot water. Breakfast, traditional or vegetarian, is 'exceptionally well cooked, with plenty of everything, even a massive bowl of fruit'. *Blue Palms*, *Xian* and the *Greek Taverna* in Summertown, close by, are recommended for an evening meal. (*Tim Moorey*)

Open All year.
Rooms 2 family, 3 double, 2 single, all with shower. 1 on ground floor. Payphone in hall.
Facilities Lounge, breakfast room (classical backg ınd music). Unsuitable for ♿.
Location 1½ miles N of centre, just inside ring road (A40), on W side of Banbury Rd (A4165) between Apsley Rd and Squitchey La. Car park. Frequent buses to centre.
Restrictions No smoking. No children under 6. No dogs.
Credit cards MasterCard, Visa.
Terms [2001] B&B: single £42–£46, double £68–£74.

Old Bank NEW
92–94 High Street
Oxford OX1 4BN

Tel 01865-799599
Fax 01865-799598
Email info@oldbank-hotel.co.uk
Website www.oxford-hotels-restaurants.co.uk

With historic Oxford on the doorstep, this is Jeremy Mogford's second hotel in the city (see also *Old Parsonage*). 'The vaults are now full of wine, a much better idea,' says one correspondent (formerly, it was his bank). He found it 'beautifully converted, stylish and comfortable'. 'Wow! Superb location!' is another comment – it is on 'The High' opposite All Souls, and St Mary's church. An inspector enjoyed his attic room with its clean modern design, Stanley Spencer prints and views of dreaming spires. The old banking hall is now *Quod,* a bar/grill, hung with large contemporary oil paintings, many bought at graduate shows – 'very covetable'. Here breakfast and Italian-influenced meals are served. Last year, the restaurant management was criticised, but recent reports are favourable, though service can be slow on busy Saturday nights when 'lively can mean noisy' (tables are close together). Braised lamb shank with lentils, and confit of duck have been enjoyed, there is a range of pasta dishes at around £7, and a good breakfast buffet. Service is by 'friendly young staff'. Drinks and meals are served in an attractive courtyard in fine weather. From a rooftop viewing platform, the Oxford skyline can be admired; the best bedrooms share this view. Some rooms are small, but all have two telephone lines and voicemail. There can be noise from courtyard, kitchen or road, but one couple found their room 'amazingly quiet; all we could hear in the morning wcrc birds'. (*Humphrey Norrington, and others*)

Open All year, except 25/26 Dec.
Rooms 2 suites, 39 double, 2 single. 1 equipped for ♿. Air-conditioning.
Facilities Lift. Lounge, bar/grill (background music), 2 meeting/private dining rooms. Terrace, small garden.
Location Central (rooms facing High St double-glazed). From Magdalen Bridge into High St; 500 yds on left. Access to rear car park via Merton St, Magpie La.
Restrictions No smoking in some bedrooms. Guide dogs only.
Credit cards All major cards accepted.
Terms [2001] Room: single £135, double £155–£225, suite £255–£300. Breakfast: continental £8, English £11. 3-course Express menu, noon–7 pm £8.75; full alc £25. 50% Sun night discount for guests who stay Sat. *V*

Old Parsonage
1 Banbury Road
Oxford OX2 6NN

Tel 01865-310210
Fax 01865-311262
Email info@oldparsonage-hotel.co.uk
Website www.oxford-hotels-restaurants.co.uk

Jeremy Mogford's brasseries, with smart young staff and an imaginative modern English menu, have flourished in Oxford. The success of the *Old Parsonage* has spawned the even more stylish *Quod* at the *Old Bank* (*qv*); they attract locals and overnight visitors to the city alike. This is both a strength and a weakness of this hotel, and some recent reports tell of disorganised management and slow service. The food is still generally praised, but some hotel guests this year felt that 'catering to non-residents was the priority'. 'Locals fill the residents' limited space all day, including the breakfast room,' one wrote. The road on which the wisteria-clad 17th-century building stands 'is less busy now, due to traffic restrictions', the hotel tells us. You enter through an ancient door from a small courtyard into a large room where drinks and informal meals (eg, twice-baked spinach and Parmesan soufflé; chicken with 20 cloves of garlic; chargrilled quail on a potato rösti) are served all day by young waiters wearing dark green aprons. The walls are crammed with pictures; there is often background music. The bedrooms are mostly small but 'well designed', though rooms on the ground floor may be dark, and upstairs ones are reached up steep steps. A few rooms face the road, and some overlook the car park, but some are 'blissfully quiet'. The suites have a 'small, pretty sitting room'. In fine weather, residents may sit in the roof garden, and alfresco meals, including breakfast ('with plenty of choice, including nice fruity options'), are served in the courtyard. More reports, please.

Open All year, except 25–28 Dec.
Rooms 4 suites, 25 double, 1 single. 10 on ground floor.
Facilities Small lounge, bar/restaurant (jazz/classical background music 'when appropriate'). Terrace, roof garden, small walled garden. Unsuitable for ♿.
Location NE end of St Giles (some traffic noise; rooms double-glazed).
Restriction No dogs.
Credit cards All major cards accepted.
Terms [2001] B&B: single £135, double £155–£190, suite £200. Full alc £30. 2-night breaks.

See also SHORTLIST

PADSTOW Cornwall **Map 1:D2**

The Seafood Restaurant
Riverside
Padstow PL28 8BY

Tel 01841-532700
Fax 01841-532942
Email reservations@rickstein.com
Website www.rickstein.com

César award in 1995

'Sheer heaven. Luxurious accommodation, spacious and comfortable. Food divine as always; breakfast a special treat.' 'It cost an arm and a leg, but it was wonderful. The food could not be faulted. One night I tried the fish and chips; they were done to perfection.' This year's enthusiasm for Rick Stein's famous waterfront restaurant, with bedrooms in a series of houses in the village. But it should be emphasised that staying here is not a 'hotel experience'. The rooms, which vary greatly; are priced according to size and view. Some are in *St Petroc's House*, one of the oldest buildings in Padstow, which also houses a bistro. Some rooms are 'cramped', some look across the municipal car park. 'Ours had a fridge full of goodies, a galleried ceiling, a sitting area looking over a pretty courtyard with a fountain to the estuary, a huge bathroom with a double shower cubicle.' Most readers write of 'courteous staff', though some may be young and inexperienced, one couple 'would have liked someone acting as host or hostess', and a visitor in 2001 wrote of a disorganised breakfast. In the busy restaurant (book well in advance), dinner is in two sittings (7.30 and 9.30). 'The fish tastes as it does nowhere else in the country' and 'service is good and unfussy'. 'We loved the simplicity, the relaxed atmosphere. It would not appeal to those in search of luxury, but you get everything you need.' Also in Padstow are shops selling Stein jams, pickles, aprons, recipe books and TV cassettes, and Stein's cooking school, offering courses of all levels. (*ER Penny, Graham and Peta Snowdon, Mrs EJ Gleeson*)

Open All year, except 16–26 Dec, 31 Dec, 1 May.
Rooms 34 double, 1 single. 6 above restaurant, 13 in *St Petroc's* hotel, 6 in *St Edmund's House*, 3 above *Rick Stein's Café*.
Facilities *Seafood*: conservatory bar, restaurant. *St Petroc's*: lounge, reading room, bar, bistro. No background music. Sandy beaches ¼ mile. Unsuitable for ♿.

Location Restaurant on harbour; other buildings nearby. Garage, parking. Train: Bodmin Parkway, 15 miles; bus (infrequent) or taxi.
Restriction No children under 3 in main restaurant.
Credit cards MasterCard, Visa.
Terms [2001] B&B: single £35–£50, double £50–£170. D,B&B: single from £67, double £90–£115. Café meals. Full alc £40–£50. 2-day breaks in low season.

PAINSWICK Gloucestershire — Map 3:D5

Painswick Hotel
Kemps Lane
Painswick
GL6 6YB

Tel 01452-812160
Fax 01452-814059
Email reservations@painswickhotel.com
Website www.painswickhotel.com

César award: Country house hotel of the year

'As sympathetic and unstuffy a hotel as I have come across in a long while,' writes our most experienced inspector. It was a pleasure to see plenty of young couples dining in casual wear instead of the ranks of old farts so often found in the heavier kind of country house establishment.' The owners, Helen and Gareth Pugh, 'are hands-on hosts, thoroughly comfortable in their role, keen to help with luggage, telephoning to find out whether Painswick Hall's rococo garden was open.' The Pughs write: 'Our policy is not to impose rules on our guests. We welcome children of all ages, we have no dress code, and we attempt to employ staff with personality, not technically skilled robots.' The Palladian-style late 18th-century former home of wealthy rectors is in a 'gem of a town' near Stroud and Gloucester – its main street is lined with magnificent mansions, and the small lanes on either side are chock-a-block with absurdly picturesque cottages. Not on the main coach circuit, and all the better for that.' A standard double room, in the 1920s purpose-built garden wing, 'was unpretentiously congenial, with a fine view to hills beyond. Bathroom a bit dated, but we liked the many small touches: yellow plastic ducks, Scrabble, 18th-century satirical prints, daily internet weather report.' The grander rooms and suites are in the main building. The spacious lounge is 'dramatic in purple, with cosy settees and antiques'; the 'very agreeable' restaurant covers two rooms, one the panelled former chapel. It has an 'elegant, restrained decor and impeccably set tables'. Chef Kevin Barron favours a simple French style, using fresh local produce and light sauces. Main courses of organic chicken with asparagus and potatoes foie gras, and turbot with lobster ravioli were enjoyed. The wine list is 'reasonably priced, with a large selection of half bottles'. Breakfast 'maintained the form, with generous choice for the serious breakfast-eater, decent croissants, excellent marmalade, OK coffee'. The pretty garden has a croquet lawn, and a grotto where a vicar once rehearsed his sermons. Painswick's churchyard is 'a real curiosity'. (*Warmly endorsed by Gordon Hands*)

Open All year.
Rooms 17 double, 2 single.
Facilities 2 lounges, bar, restaurant (occasional background music), private dining/meeting room. ¾-acre garden. Unsuitable for ♿. Civil wedding licence.

Location In village off A46. Turn down by church; follow road round; right at cross. Hotel down hill on right. Train: Stroud, 5 miles.
Restriction No smoking in restaurant.
Credit cards Amex, MasterCard, Visa.
Terms B&B: single £85, double £120–£185; D,B&B: single £95, double £160–£210. Set lunch £18, dinner £28.50; full alc £40. Winter and summer breaks. Christmas package. 1-night bookings refused weekends.

PENZANCE Cornwall — Map 1:E1

The Abbey Hotel
Abbey Street
Penzance TR18 4AR

Tel 01736-366906
Fax 01736-351163
Email glyn@abbeyhotel.fsnet.co.uk
Website www.abbey-hotel.co.uk

César award in 1985

A 17th-century house, painted bright blue and with Gothic windows, in a narrow street that runs down to the sea. It is run informally, with more than a touch of eccentricity, by Jean and Michael Cox. When they are not there, visitors are ably looked after by the long-serving manager/chef/factotum, Glyn Green. The decor is distinctive: brightly coloured walls set off curios, oriental rugs, paintings and flowers, and there is a large choice of books and audio tapes. The drawing room, with flowered sofas and a chandelier, looks on to the walled garden. 'The service provided is limited, especially room service,' one visitor wrote. Others told of 'lovely treatment by the staff'; 'the friendliest of welcomes'. Meals are served by an open fire in the white-panelled dining room. The menu has three choices at each stage, of eclectic dishes, eg, lamb chump steaks on a lemon and rosemary jus, or salmon with crab enclosed and a tarragon cream sauce; pears in Burgundy, or geranium cream with berries steeped in sugar, with a lemon and passion fruit cordon. There is always a vegetarian main course. Some bedrooms overlook the garden; others face the harbour (some get street noise); some are small, with a small shower room. Room 1 is huge, with antiques and a working fireplace, and a wood-surrounded bath in its large bathroom. The suite, which looks over the harbour and St Michael's Mount, is airy and 'very comfortable'. The Coxes now run a seafood restaurant next door, in a former nightclub (this purchase has made the hotel much quieter at night, they write). They are creating a small cinema, which will run 'short seasons of unusual and classic films'. (*JFB*)

Open All year, except 1 week Christmas/New Year.
Rooms 1 2-bedroom suite (in adjoining building), 4 double, 2 single. No telephone.
Facilities Drawing room, dining room (classical background music evenings). Small walled garden. Sandy beach ¼ mile. Unsuitable for ♿.
Location Take road marked Sea Front; pass car park on left; right after 300 yds, just before bridge, then left, up slipway, to hotel. Courtyard parking for 7 cars.
Restrictions No smoking: dining room, 1 bedroom. No dogs in public rooms.
Credit cards Amex, MasterCard, Visa.
Terms [2001] B&B: single £60–£75, double £90–£155, suite £155–£215. Set dinner £24. Weekend breaks. Winter rates. 1-night bookings refused bank holidays.

The Summer House
Cornwall Terrace
Penzance TR18 4HL

Tel 01736-363744
Fax 01736-360959
Email summerhouse@dial.pipex.com
Website www.cornwall-online.co.uk/summer-house

César award in 2001

A higgledy-piggledy listed Regency house, in a 'quiet, elegant' mews near the seafront: it is a much-admired restaurant-with-rooms. The Neapolitan *patron*/chef, Ciro Zaino, has worked at some of London's most distinguished restaurants, including *The Halkin* and *The Capital* (*qqv*). His wife, Linda, is the 'endearingly enthusiastic' front-of-house manager. 'A peaceful oasis in a busy town,' said one visitor. 'It has none of the formality of a five-star hotel, but all the essentials of good living,' wrote another. A curving glass tower lights the house, and the decor is charming', with lots of bright yellow and green, polished wood, fresh flowers. 'The hospitality is warm. They offer genuine value.' There was one report this year of a misunderstanding over a booking for dinner, but most find the owners and staff 'very helpful', and the bedrooms 'lovely' (they have strong colours, white linen). The Mediterranean-style cooking is thought 'excellent', eg, seared scallops with fennel velouté, or duck breast with marinated peppers; sea bream with asparagus and citrus dressing, or rack of lamb with aromatic herbs; tiramisu, or glazed lemon tart with a coulis of berries. Wines are predominantly Italian. Breakfasts, too, 'are varied and excellent'. The restaurant, which has new wall paintings this year, leads on to a walled garden with terracotta pots and palm trees; teas are served here at bright blue tables. The bedrooms (some are spacious) have antique furniture, Victorian-style lights, fresh flowers. Step out to the waterfront for views of St Michael's Mount to the left, Newlyn to the right. (*Mary Tilden-Smith, Bill Bennett, and others*)

Open All year, except Jan/part Feb. Restaurant closed Sun/Mon.
Rooms 5 double. No telephone.
Facilities Lounge, restaurant (classical/Celtic background music at dinner). Small walled garden. Sea, beach, coastal path nearby. Unsuitable for ♿.
Location 5 mins' walk from centre. Drive along harbour; pass open-air swimming pool; follow promenade; right immediately after *Queen's Hotel*. Hotel on left. Car park. Train/bus/helicopter to Penzance.
Restrictions No smoking: in restaurant until 10 pm, all bedrooms. No children under 13. No dogs.
Credit cards MasterCard, Visa.
Terms [2001] B&B: single from £50, double £55–£80. Dinner £21.50. Off-season breaks. Christmas package. 1-night bookings refused bank holidays.

PICKERING North Yorkshire **Map 4:D4**

The White Swan NEW
Market Place
Pickering YO18 7AA

Tel 01751-472288
Fax 01751-475554
Email welcome@white-swan.co.uk
Website www.white-swan.co.uk

'I love it for the atmosphere, and the totally professional yet utterly human service, by people of warmth and humour. They never say no.

Astonishingly good value.' So writes the nominator of the Buchanan family's hotel in an old-fashioned market town in the North Yorkshire moors. The old grey stone building underwent a major refurbishment in 1999. 'Public rooms are small, comfortable and cosy – there is a lovely Georgian panelled "snug". Bedrooms are elegant and well equipped: good, deep baths, good showers. The food is modern Yorkshire (eg, mushrooms with polenta and rocket; braised shank of lamb; risotto of leek and saffron), competently done and getting better; the wine list is superb. Breakfast is a treat' (it includes kedgeree and eggs Benedict). 'No wrapped butter portions or puff pastry pie crusts,' writes the manager, Victor Buchanan, who is proud of his large selection of Bordeaux wines. The restaurant is red-walled and candlelit; the bar has a log fire, and a blackboard menu for informal eating. No piped music, and the bedrooms are 'strictly non-smoking' (offenders must pay £50). Children are promised 'care and attention', and 'well-behaved dogs' are welcomed. From Pickering you can take a steam train to walk on the moors. (*Carole Taylor; also Graham Snowdon,* Good Pub Guide)

Open All year.
Rooms 2 suites, 10 double.
Facilities Ramps. Lounge, bar, bistro, restaurant. No background music. Small garden.
Location Central, opposite Boots the chemist. Parking.
Restrictions No smoking: restaurant, bedrooms.
Credit cards Amex, MasterCard, Visa.
Terms [2001] B&B: single £70–£80, double £100–£110, suite £130–£150; D,B&B: single £90, double £140, suite £170. Full alc £28. Child in parents' room: under 5, free. Christmas package. 1-night bookings refused weekends.

PLYMOUTH Devon *See SHORTLIST* — Map 1:D4

POOLE Dorset *See SHORTLIST* — Map 2:E1

PORLOCK Somerset — Map 1:B5

The Oaks
Porlock TA24 8ES

Tel 01643-862265
Fax 01643-863131
Email oakshotel@aol.com
Website www.oakeshotel.co.uk

There are views across the Bristol Channel from this gabled Edwardian pebble-dashed house. It stands amid lawns and oak trees, in an elevated position above the tiny fishing village with its narrow main street and old buildings. A nearby weir is within earshot, and Exmoor lies behind. The 'really kind' owners, Tim and Anne Riley, provide a friendly welcome', say regular visitors who like the 'quite old-fashioned' atmosphere and the courtesies: help with suitcases, complimentary tea on arrival, etc. The newly decorated public rooms have chintzes, open fires, oil paintings and prints; flowery wallpaper and fabrics brighten the bedrooms. Meals are as traditional as the rest.

A typical four-course dinner menu includes cream of pear and watercress soup; Arbroath smokie bake; tenderloin of pork with mushrooms and sherry; hot apple pie with Bramley apple ice cream. Breakfast is good, 'but to give a choice of fruit juice or cereal seemed somewhat mean', one visitor thought. One warning: 'The hotel's entrance is at a sharp angle of the main road.' One of the smallest churches in England is at Culbone, three miles away. (*JW, and others; also Andrew Long*)

Open Mar–Nov, Christmas.
Rooms 9 double.
Facilities 2 lounges, bar, restaurant (classical background music at night). 1-acre garden. Sea, pebble beach 1 mile. Unsuitable for ♿.
Location ¼ mile from village 6 miles W of Minehead.
Restrictions Smoking in bar only. No children under 8. No dogs in public rooms.
Credit cards MasterCard, Visa.
Terms B&B: single £60, double £100; D,B&B (min. 2 nights): single £80, double £140. Set dinner £25. Christmas package.

PORLOCK WEIR Somerset — Map 1:B4

Porlock Vale House BUDGET
Porlock Weir TA24 8NY

Tel 01643-862338
Fax 01643-863338
Email info@porlockvale.co.uk
Website www.porlockvale.co.uk

'The welcome is second to none,' says a visitor this year, who enjoyed the 'relaxed atmosphere and creative cuisine' at one of Britain's leading riding hotels. Others wrote: 'The staff were exceptionally kind and helpful at all times.' 'Good value for money.' Although horse riding is an essential feature, with instruction and escorted riding on Exmoor, non-riders are welcome too. The setting is 'splendid, quiet' – in ancient oak woodlands on the lower slopes of Exmoor, and with superb views over the Bristol Channel to Wales. The public rooms 'are excellent' (deep chintz sofas, antique and period furniture, sporting prints and antlers). The panelled hall has a huge open fireplace, and there is a separate bar. In summer, the dining room opens on to a flower-filled terrace. The owners, Kim and Helen Youd, have undertaken five years of improvements of the former hunting lodge – 12 out of 15 bedrooms have been completed this year. Most rooms, particularly the larger rear ones, have a peaceful view over garden and paddocks to a wide sweep of beach and headland. Dinner is at 7.30 pm. Menus are available in the morning and guests are asked to choose by 6 pm, from dishes like braised scrumpy pork casserole with a black pudding crust; ragout of salmon with scallops, prawns, leeks and Noilly Prat; treacle and whisky steamed sponge pudding and custard. There are always vegetarian choices. Local cheeses are served with home-made chutneys. Bar lunches (home-made soup and sandwiches) are available. Breakfast, cooked to order, includes dry-cured bacon, free-range eggs, home-made marmalade. A drawback for some: 'TV reception is poor, unless you are fluent in Welsh.' The remote farmhouse where Coleridge 'is reliably said to have written *Kubla Khan*' is close by. (*A Pilkington, JD, and others*)

Open All year, except midweek in Jan.
Rooms 1 junior suite, 13 double, 1 single.
Facilities 3 lounges, bar, dining room (occasional classical background music at dinner); meeting room. 25-acre grounds leading to sea: gardens, riding stables. Only restaurant accessible for ♿.
Location Leave A39 at Porlock; drive through village; hotel is 1½ miles to NW by lower Porlock Weir coast road. Train: Taunton, 28 miles.
Restrictions No smoking: restaurant, 2 lounges, bedrooms. No children under 10 (under 16 for riding). No dogs in house (kennels available).
Credit cards Amex, MasterCard, Visa.
Terms B&B: £25–£55; D,B&B £44–£90. Bar lunches. Set dinner £20. 3-day breaks. Christmas, New Year packages. 1-night bookings sometimes refused weekends.

PORT ISAAC Cornwall — Map 1:D2

Port Gaverne Hotel
Port Gaverne
nr Port Isaac
PL29 3SQ

Tel 01208-880244
Fax 01208-880151
Email pghotel@telinco.co.uk
Website www.chycor.co.uk/hotels/port-gaverne

Families with children and dogs are welcomed at this traditional hotel, which has been in the hands of the same family for 32 years. Mrs Marjorie (Midge) Ross runs a 'relaxed' establishment (sometimes dubbed 'marginally chaotic'), which is liked for its wonderful location and simple English food. The low, white-walled old inn stands in a secluded cove, near the 'quintessential fishing village' of Port Isaac. 'In the dining room, warm fish salad and mussels were memorable starters, followed by delicious fresh fish dishes,' wrote one visitor. 'At lunch I had the best-ever crab sandwich with home-made brown bread. The wine list included some amazingly reasonable bottles, and a most unusual plummy Cabernet Sauvignon from Israel.' Other reports spoke of the 'delicious soups', 'great puds', also provided by the chef, Ian Brodey. Vegetarians are well catered for. 'The hotel copes brilliantly with visitors on a few days' stay, and also with clients who see it as their lovely local pub. My room was beautifully furnished, and warm.' Most of the bedrooms are large, with a 'proper bathroom'. Close by is a small beach, with sand, rocks, safe bathing. 'Fantastic walks on National Trust coastal paths, where wildlife and wild flowers are magnificent, thanks to the absence of pesticides.' Bicycles can be hired locally. (*JG*)

Open All year, except early Jan–mid-Feb.
Rooms 15 double, 1 single. Also self-catering cottages.
Facilities Lounge, 2 bars, restaurant. No background music. Small garden. Rock cove 60 yds; golf, fishing, surfing, sailing, riding nearby. Unsuitable for ♿.
Location ½ mile N of Port Isaac (signposted off B3314).
Restriction No smoking in restaurant. No children under 7 in restaurant.
Credit cards All major cards accepted.
Terms B&B £35–£45; D,B&B £50–£60. Full alc £30. Off-season breaks: 3 nights for the price of 2. *V*

For details of the Voucher scheme see page xxx.

PORTSCATHO Cornwall Map 1:E2

Roseland House NEW
Rosevine
nr Portscatho TR2 5EW

Tel 01872-580644
Fax 01872-580801
Email anthony.hindley@btinternet.com

'A friendly, uncomplicated place,' writes an inspector in 2001, restoring to the *Guide* Mr and Mrs Hindley's large white cliff-top house. 'Excellent', 'good value', 'a hotel for all tastes', others wrote. 'The owners really care about their guests.' The position is 'exceptional', above Gerran's Bay in the Roseland peninsula. 'Not for lovers of minimalist design. The interiors are cosy rather than smart (family photos, doilies, pot plants, two cats, in the lounge), and well maintained. All bedrooms have been newly decorated in oatmeal, cream and terracotta. Ours was spacious, with chunky new pine furniture, a chandelier, a brand new bathroom.' Almost all the rooms have a 'stunning sea view' (though some also look over a flat roof). In the conservatory dining room, 'tables are impeccably set, delicious smells emanate from the kitchen'. 'We enjoyed English cooking at its best: beef Wellington; pork tenderloin with a plum and prune sauce; abundant fresh vegetables, separately served and correctly cooked; "Eve's pudding" was feather-light, in a delicious sauce; strawberry sundae was equally tasty.' Cheese and biscuits come with a glass of port. Bread is home made; wines are reasonably priced. Breakfast includes locally smoked haddock and kippers. Picnic lunches and cream teas are available. A wooded path leads through the terraced gardens ('picturesque, not manicured') to a safe sandy beach. The South Cornish Coastal Path is close by; so are the Fal estuary (sailing and boating), several National Trust properties, the Heligan Gardens and the Eden Project. (*Ken and Mildred Evans, A Bruce, Frau Beugre, and others*)

Open Feb–end Oct.
Rooms 10 double. 1 on ground floor.
Facilities Sitting room, lounge, bar, restaurant, conservatory (classical background music at night). 6½-acre grounds: terraced gardens, private beach, safe bathing. Sailing, golf nearby.
Location N side of Portscatho. On A3078 to St Mawes, hotel sign on right, 2 miles after Ruan High Lanes. Train: Truro/St Austell, both 15 miles; hotel will meet.
Restrictions No smoking. No dogs in house (must be on a lead in grounds).
Credit cards Amex, MasterCard, Visa.
Terms [2001] B&B £35–£55; D,B&B £55–£70. Full alc £33. Child in parents' room: under 13, half price. Short breaks; weekly rates.

PORTSMOUTH Hampshire *See SHORTLIST* Map 2:E3

Readers with mobility problems might like to know of the *Smooth Ride Guides,* which publish information about many hotels with facilities for the disabled. *Tel* 01279-777966, *fax* 01279-777995, *email* july.ramsey@virgin.net, *website* www.easyspace.com/banner.

PRESTBURY Cheshire **Map 3:A5**

The White House Manor and Restaurant
New Road
Prestbury SK10 4HP

Tel 01625-829376
Fax 01625-828627
Email info@thewhitehouse.uk.com
Website www.thewhitehouse.uk.com

Appearances deceive at Ryland and Judith Wakeham's Georgian manor house. The sober red brick exterior conceals an extraordinary set of themed bedrooms, designed with humour, even fantasy. The central feature of the most recent creation – the Millennium suite – is an ultra-modern glass bed. The Studio has paintings, art books, lavish fabrics, a dramatic green-and-black bathroom. Glyndebourne, redecorated this year, has a sophisticated music centre and a collection of discs. Trafalgar is decorated with naval artefacts, burgundy drapes and gold braid, and has a power shower with body jets. The Crystal Room has a four-poster bed, a crystal chandelier and a whirlpool bath. Minerva, also redecorated, with a Turkish steam room and a collection of antique sporting equipment, is all about sport and health. All the rooms 'give a feeling of luxury', said a recent visitor. Travelling on her own, she appreciated being able to dine and breakfast at a large table in her bedroom – the restaurant is in a white-painted building five minutes' walk away. Here, Mr Wakeham and Mark Cunniffe serve 'contemporary British dishes' to a smart local clientele, eg, pressed ham hock terrine on a crush of peas, horseradish and mushrooms; calf's liver and bacon with hickory apple mash; warm plum and almond frangipane pie. 'Delicious breakfasts' can be continental, 'healthy' or 'full Cheshire'; all include fresh orange juice, thick brown toast, good coffee. Prestbury is a pretty village on the river Bollin. It has easy access to the ring of motorways reaching into Lancashire and across the Pennines, and Manchester airport is a short drive away. (*SD, and others*)

Open All year, except 25–26 Dec.
Rooms 8 double, 3 single. Some in coach house annexe.
Facilities Lounge, conservatory with honesty bar, restaurant (background jazz); function facilities. ½-acre garden. Unsuitable for ♿.
Location Edge of village on A538, 2 miles N of Macclesfield. Some traffic noise.
Restrictions No smoking: restaurant before 10 pm, bedrooms. No children under 10. No dogs.
Credit cards All major cards accepted.
Terms [2001] Room: single £40–£95, double £70–£120. Breakfast £6.50–£9.50. Set lunch £14.50, dinner from £15.50; full alc £33.50.

> Hotels often book you into their most expensive rooms or suites unless you specify otherwise. Even if all room prices are the same, hotels may give you a less good room in the hope of selling their better rooms to late customers. It always pays to discuss accommodation in detail when making a reservation, and to ask for a free upgrade on arrival if the hotel isn't full.

PURTON Wiltshire **Map 3:E5**

The Pear Tree at Purton
Church End
Purton, nr Swindon SN5 4ED

Tel 01793-772100
Fax 01793-772369
Email stay@peartreepurton.co.uk
Website www.peartreepurton.co.uk

'The staff make you feel you are the most important person in the hotel,' says a visitor this year to Francis and Anne Young's old stone house (Pride of Britain), on the edge of this Saxon village (the name means 'pear tree enclosure'). Other comments: 'Deserves all accolades. Offers value for money.' 'It was more than a year since my last visit, but the head waiter asked where I had been for so long and remembered my favourite table for dinner.' Given the location, only a few miles off the M4, the hotel is frequented by business travellers, and often used for weddings on Saturdays. But it is 'unintimidating'. 'Whatever you ask is promptly attended to. Meals are well cooked, nicely presented, with first-class, unhurried service.' But one visitor felt that vegetarians were not very well catered for, 'and the menu was the same three nights running'. In the green-and-white conservatory restaurant, candlelit at night, and with views of well-maintained gardens, chef Alan Postill serves ambitious modern dishes at dinner, eg, timbale of crab, avocado and sweet potato; griddled duck breast with spiked oriental sauce, sesame and coriander ratatouille; marbled chocolate terrine with sharp raspberry jelly. At lunch, simpler offerings include bubble and squeak with mild goat's cheese; braised lamb shank; always a traditional hot pudding. 'Early morning tea was brought with fresh flowers. Lovely yogurt with roast nuts at breakfast.' The bedrooms 'are well furnished, spotless', with fresh flowers that match the colour scheme, fresh fruit, sweets, biscuits, etc. 'The suite is perfect, with a balcony looking over the courtyard.' Bathrooms are 'impeccable'; many have a spa bath. Much redecoration has taken place this year. Purton is well placed for visiting Avebury, Rosemary Verey's gardens at Barnsley House, Dyrham Park, Bowood House, and STEAM, the museum of the Great Western Railway in Swindon. (*Sue Davies, GSB, TB*)

Open All year, except 26–30 Dec. Restaurant closed Sat midday.
Rooms 2 suites, 15 double, 1 single. Some on ground floor.
Facilities Ramps. Lounge/bar, library, restaurant; function facilities. No background music. 7½-acre grounds: croquet, jogging route. Civil wedding licence.
Location 5 miles NW of Swindon. From M4 exit 16 follow signs to Wootton Bassett/Purton; through Purton village, right at Spar grocer. Train: Swindon; taxi.
Restriction No dogs in public rooms, unattended in bedrooms.
Credit cards All major cards accepted.
Terms B&B: single/double £105–£125, suite £135–£155. Set lunch £17.50, dinner £29.50. Weekend breaks. *V*

Don't let old favourites down. Hotels are dropped when there is no endorsement.

RAMSEY, Isle of Man — Map 4:D1

Hillcrest House NEW/BUDGET
May Hill, Ramsey IM8 2HG

Tel 01624-817215
Email Admin@HillcrestHouse.co.uk
Website www.HillcrestHouse.co.uk

A maverick entry for the *Guide*, since the Isle of Man belongs neither to the UK nor the EU. Aurea and Anthony Greenhalgh received many plaudits from our readers when they presided over *The Archway*, Windermere. Now they are running an 'idyllic' little no-smoking guest house in a bay-windowed Victorian building in an old town on the north-east coast of this 'beautiful, magical' island. Organic ingredients are much in evidence at mealtimes ('we try to stress healthy eating without dogma,' writes the hostess), vegetarians have their own menu, and an added attraction could be acupuncture treatment by the host, a qualified practitioner. 'Rest, comfort and peace, what more can you want?' writes the nominator, who knew the Greenhalghs in their previous incarnation. 'Excellence in every way. Beauty and warmth in every room, dreamy '30s patchwork quilts; the rest romantically Victorian. Food to die for, prepared with love. Even better than home – you don't have to do a thing.' The no-choice evening meal might consist of butterbean, celeriac and wild garlic soup; roast cod with a herb crust; cider-poached pears with elderberry compote. The Greenhalghs promise 'wonderful walks in the glens and along the coast', and 'nearly traffic-free roads'; sandy beaches are within half a mile. (*Natalie Bown*)

Open All year.
Rooms 3 double. No telephone.
Facilities Lounge, dining room. No background music. Front garden. Unsuitable for ♿.
Location ¼-mile walk from centre. Parking. Ramsey is *c.* 10 miles NE of Douglas.
Restrictions No smoking. No dogs.
Credit cards None accepted.
Terms B&B £22–£29; D,B&B £37–£44. Christmas package. *V*

RAMSGILL-IN-NIDDERDALE North Yorkshire — Map 4:D3

The Yorke Arms
Ramsgill-in-Nidderdale
nr Harrogate HG3 5RL

Tel 01423-755243
Fax 01423-755330
Email enquiries@yorke-arms.co.uk
Website www.yorke-arms.co.uk

César award in 2000

Bill Atkins is 'an exemplary mine host' at this creeper-covered former shooting lodge on the green of a Dales village, but the cooking of his wife, Frances, wins even greater plaudits. The sophisticated food served from her all-female kitchen has a *Michelin Bib Gourmand* for quality at moderate prices, and 'the evening meals are worth the visit alone'. But the place retains the feel of a country inn (flagstone floors, log fires, oak beams, wooden tables), and it welcomes walkers who call in for a drink or a snack. Public rooms – 'with an abundance of rich colours and dark woods' – are 'quite opulent'. The lounge – 'where you would be happy to stay all day if the weather was poor' – has magazines and games. The bedrooms vary in size; all were refurbished this year. 'Gouthwaite, very large, has a sparkling bathroom and a view over the green through a picture window.' Grouse is 'comfortable if a little small'. A new cottage suite has its own kitchen and garden. Mrs Atkins's dishes are based on local lamb and game, eg, crispy duck with citrus and fennel, or black pudding in brioche with haddock and mustard sauce; roast grouse with bacon on rösti, or hake and langoustine risotto. 'A three-course dinner rapidly escalated into a feast' with *amuse-bouches* over aperitifs, tempting petits fours after dessert. Breakfast super: fresh orange juice, home-made marmalade, crunchy toast, really tasty bacon.' Imaginative bar lunches include home-made soup, and 'tuna seared to perfection'. The staff 'were very helpful; the knowledgeable wine waiter stood out'. Restaurant service 'can be stretched at busy times'. Good walking from the door; the Gouthwaite reservoir bird sanctuary is close by. You need a car to visit Ripon Cathedral, Harewood House and Fountains Abbey. (*Ffion Griffith, Philip and Eileen Hall, Mrs Lynn Wildgoose, Mr and Mrs Nigel Primrose, Trevor Lockwood; also* Good Pub Guide)

Open All year.
Rooms 1 suite (in cottage), 10 double, 3 single.
Facilities Lounge, 2 bars, restaurant (classical background music); function facilities. 2-acre grounds. Unsuitable for ♿.
Location Centre of village. B6265 from Ripon, B6165 Ripley to Pateley Bridge, Low Wath road to Ramsgill. Train: Harrogate; bus/taxi.
Restrictions No smoking: restaurant, bedrooms. No children under 9. Dogs in bar and suite only.
Credit cards All major cards accepted.
Terms D,B&B £80–£150. Full alc £33. Reductions for 3 nights or more; weekend breaks; walking weekends. Cookery courses. Christmas, New Year packages. ***V***

REETH North Yorkshire — Map 4:C3

Arkleside
Reeth, nr Richmond
DL11 6SG

Tel/Fax 01748-884200
Email info@arklesidehotel.co.uk
Website www.arklesidehotel.co.uk

First impressions count, and at Dorothy Kendall and Richard Beal's small hotel they are 'very good': 'Arriving at 9 am, I asked if I could leave my car in the tiny car park for the day, before checking in at teatime. "Delighted," was the response, "and do have a cup of tea." My day-long walk was all the more pleasurable.' This converted row of 17th-century miners' cottages stands near the green of the picturesque village. The decor is 'home-like'. A 'snug' area has been added to the bar, and a new large conservatory has 'astounding views' down the Swale valley. So does the new suite (with lounge and king-size bed). The suites have a bathroom, other rooms have a shower, but there is a shared bathroom. Bedroom 5 'has a comfortable bed but is decidedly compact and has a limited view towards Reeth Green'. Meals, prepared by Ms Kendall, are 'unpretentious, but unfailingly tasty'. Tomato and cream soup was 'excellent'; lamb noisettes came with interesting vegetables'; strawberry pavlova was 'brilliant'. A selection of at least five Dales cheeses is included in the dinner price. As guests gather in the bar before dinner 'there is a sense of intimacy, conversations carrying on all around'. This spills over into the restaurant where, although each party has its own table, there is a sense of community'. The muzak continues to grate for some: 'The tapes were awful but such was the happy ambience, they became more of a conversation subject than an irritation.' Ms Kendall and Mr Beal explain: 'We are trying to get away from it, but some guests like it.' The young staff are 'bright, friendly, very efficient'. A good base for visiting Barnard Castle, Teesdale and Wensleydale. 'After three days of extreme good value, I felt I was leaving friends.' (*Trevor Lockwood, LG; also John Thorpe*)

Open 10 Feb–31 Dec, except Christmas. Restaurant closed midday.
Rooms 2 suites (with bath, 1 in mews cottage), 8 double (with shower). No telephone.
Facilities Lounge, conservatory, bar, dining room (background tapes/CDs/radio most of the day). Small grounds. Trout-fishing rights on river Swale ½ mile. Unsuitable for ♿.
Location 10 miles W of Richmond (limited bus service). Off top right corner of village green. Parking.
Restrictions Smoking in bar only. No children under 10. No dogs in public rooms.
Credit cards MasterCard, Visa.
Terms B&B: single £45, double £70–£80. Set dinner £21. Walking, gourmet, Valentine, dinner party weekends. 3-day breaks, Christmas, New Year packages. 1-night bookings refused bank holidays.

The Burgoyne
On the Green
Reeth, nr Richmond
DL11 6SN

Tel/Fax 01748-884292
Email enquiries@theburgoyne.co.uk
Website www.theburgoyne.co.uk

César award: Yorkshire hotel of the year

'The combination of the friendly welcome and service of Derek Hickson (host), and Peter Carwardine's superb cooking, with the impeccable bedrooms and the comfortably furnished reception rooms would be enough in itself; but the setting in the Yorkshire Dales makes this an especially delightful and restful place to stay.' 'A very happy atmosphere. The service was impeccable.' 'The hosts do everything possible to see that all guests enjoy their stay.' The praise continues to roll in for this Grade II listed Regency house, which looks across a small front lawn to the village green. The house is a delight, dining is a pleasure and the surroundings are outstanding.' There are antiques, a log fire, books and magazines in the spacious lounge (where drinks are served), and a pink-and-green decor in the restaurant, where dinner is impeccably presented. It starts promptly at 8 pm. Some of the starters – mango and paw paw with prawns in a light curried mayonnaise; chicken livers in a sherry and grape sauce – 'will long be remembered'. A main course might be roast duckling with apple tartlet, or grilled sirloin steak with mushrooms and tomatoes. The desserts were luscious.' The wine list has a good choice of half bottles, and if you order a full bottle of the house wine, you pay only for what is consumed. The bedrooms are named after local hamlets; most are large, with a view of the green and the hills beyond (the rear view is less attractive). 'Gunnerside had just been tastefully and beautifully redecorated.' Three rooms have their bathroom across a corridor (a bathrobe and slippers are provided). Breakfast is admired, too, 'with hot strong coffee, decent helpings of butter and marmalade and a huge mixed grill'. (*Sally Burt, Moira Jarrett, Mr and Mrs GA Lilley, and others*)

Open 14 Feb–2 Jan. Restaurant closed midday.
Rooms 1 suite, 7 double. 1 adapted for ♿.
Facilities 2 lounges, dining room (jazz/classical background music as required). ½-acre garden. Trout-fishing rights on river Swale.
Location Centre of village, 10 miles W of Richmond. Parking.
Restrictions No smoking: dining room, 1 lounge, bedrooms. No children under 10. No dogs in dining room or unattended in bedrooms.
Credit cards MasterCard, Visa.
Terms [2001] B&B: single from £80, double £90–£110, suite £140. Set dinner £24.50. Off-season breaks, grouse-shooting parties. Christmas, New Year packages. 1-night bookings sometimes refused Sat.

REIGATE Surrey *See SHORTLIST* — Map 2:D4

RHYDYCROESAU Shropshire — Map 3:B4

Pen-y-Dyffryn
Rhydycroesau
nr Oswestry SY10 7JD

Tel 01691-653700
Fax 01691-650066
Email stay@peny.co.uk
Website www.peny.co.uk

'A good find,' says a visitor this year. The name may be Welsh, and the views westwards are towards the Welsh mountains, but this listed Georgian stone rectory is just in England, set on a Shropshire hill above the river Cynllaith, which marks the border. Lake Vyrnwy is nearby, and there are 'wonderful sunsets'. Visitors appreciate the setting – 'one of the most beautiful of any inland hotel we know' – and the 'relaxed atmosphere'. The owners, Miles and Audrey Hunter, set an informal tone, and children are welcome (so are 'well-behaved dogs'). 'A delightful haven; just the place to retreat to the silence of Shropshire,' says one guest. The Hunters have been busy redecorating. The bathrooms have been upgraded, contemporary fabrics have been introduced in the public rooms, and the restaurant and lounge have a new carpet. The bedrooms are not large, but most have a view; one has a double spa bath. Two rooms, each with a private patio, are in a converted coach house. The chef, David Morris, favours a modern British style with a green touch, using organic local produce where possible. Most of the vegetables are grown in the hotel's garden. Dishes include terrine of guineafowl and Gressingham duck breast; rack of Welsh March lamb with braised leeks and a redcurrant and rosemary jus; there is always a vegetarian main course. Guests may fish for trout in pools in front of the house, and there is good walking from the door, including the Offa's Dyke circular path. Golf, climbing, and stately homes and Welsh castles are nearby. (*Sir John Johnson*)

Open 20 Jan–20 Dec.
Rooms 10 double. 2, each with private patio, in coach house. 1 on ground floor.
Facilities 2 lounges, cocktail bar, restaurant; quiet classical background music evenings. 5-acre grounds: exercise area for dogs; trout fishing. Golf nearby.
Location 3 miles W of Oswestry by B4580. Follow signs to Llansilin. Train: Oswestry.
Restrictions No smoking: restaurant, main lounge, bedrooms. No dogs in public rooms.
Credit cards Amex, MasterCard, Visa.
Terms B&B £42–£66; D,B&B £57–£84. Set dinner £23. Child in parents' room: B&B £15–£20. 1-night bookings sometimes refused weekends. *V*

RIPLEY North Yorkshire — Map 4:D4

The Boar's Head
Ripley Castle Estate
Harrogate HG3 3AY

Tel 01423-771888
Fax 01423-771509
Email reservations@boarsheadripley.co.uk
Website www.ripleycastle.co.uk

César award in 1999

'The whole experience from the check-in to departure was wonderful. Breakfast, a disappointing experience in some hotels, was memorable.' A verdict this year on this 'comfortable hotel with the feel of an upmarket village pub'. It was converted from an earlier inn by Sir Thomas and Lady Ingilby (his family have lived in the castle on the estate for 650 years). Steve Chesnutt, who has been running the kitchen for six years, has been promoted to 'chef/*patron*'. Jason Main, four years at the hotel, works with him in the kitchen. They serve modern dishes, eg, warm salad of crispy duck on plum and blackberry dressing; jambonette of corn-fed chicken with black pudding and veal sweetbreads; sticky toffee pudding. Or you can eat in the bar/bistro, where there is a simpler but interesting menu (eg, Cumberland sausage ring with black olive potato) and a 'cheerful atmosphere' – it is popular with locals. It serves good beers, including Crackshot, brewed to the inn's own 17th-century recipe. The 'superior' bedrooms in *Birchwood House*, across a courtyard, are liked, with their fresh flowers, books, and daily carafe of sherry. But some other rooms are small and less well furnished, and some look over the beer garden, busy in fine weather. The lounges have antique and period furniture, portraits and paintings. Ripley Castle is a popular tourist attraction, and hotel guests have access to the grounds, its deer park, lake,

Victorian gardens and greenhouses. A Super Sleuth weekend break includes a black-tie banquet in the castle. One reader this year reported a booking muddle. Fountains Abbey is 15 minutes' drive away; York is 40 minutes. Plenty of castles, stately homes and gardens to visit. (*Mr and Mrs C Astley,* Good Pub Guide*, and others*)

Open All year.
Rooms 25 double. 10 in courtyard, 6 in *Birchwood House* opposite. Some on ground floor.
Facilities 2 drawing rooms, bar/bistro, restaurant; background music. 20-acre grounds: garden; access to 500-acre castle estate with deer park, lakes, fishing. Civil wedding licence.
Location 3 miles N of Harrogate on A61 Harrogate–Ripon. Bus from Ripon.
Restrictions No smoking in 3 bedrooms. No dogs in public rooms, castle grounds.
Credit cards All major cards accepted.
Terms [2001] (*Non-refundable deposit of £50 required*) B&B: single £99, double £120. Set lunch £14, dinner £23.50; full alc £30. Child in parents' room: under 15, B&B £20. Cookery demonstrations. Yorkshire breaks (D,B&B £80 per person per night, min. 2-night stay). Super Sleuth weekends. Christmas package.

ROCK Cornwall — Map 1:D2

St Enodoc
Rock, nr Wadebridge
PL27 6LA

Tel 01208-863394
Fax 01208-863970
Email enodoc@aol.com
Website www.enodoc-hotel.co.uk

César award in 2000

A seaside cousin of the admired *Knightsbridge Green Hotel* in London (*qv,* also owned by the Marler family), this attractive hotel is family-friendly. It sits in a cluster of houses along a small road running parallel to the beach above the Camel estuary. It has a light, Mediterranean-type decor by Emily Todhunter, and the effect is 'one of simple, modern comfort with an eye on tradition': 'marvellous paintings' on gleaming white walls; distressed-effect furniture in vivid turquoise or blue; high-quality furniture and fittings. 'The bedlinen is crisp; the towels are fluffy; the lighting is excellent and the views are stunning.' Meals are served at wooden tables in the large, split-level *Porthilly Bar*, which has panoramic views and a terrace for summer eating. Its informal style, and the food, were enjoyed this year. A Pacific Rim menu is served – 'with a choice of four starters and four main courses. It might include seared scallops and chorizo sausage with creamed leeks; fillet of salmon steamed in nori leaves with soba noodles and Japanese master stock. The wine list 'is interesting'. If you wish to dine elsewhere (Padstow is a short ferry ride across the estuary), they will help with ferries, bookings, etc. 'Very good breakfast, with croissants and bread baked on the premises, and daily papers.' There is a gym, a sauna and a billiard room, and a heated swimming pool in the large garden. The manager, Mark Gregory, and his staff are 'young, sophisticated, helpful at all times'. The tiny church recovered from the dunes, where John Betjeman is buried, is on the adjacent St Enodoc golf course.

Open Feb–mid-Dec.
Rooms 4 family suites, 15 double.
Facilities Ramp. Drawing room, library, bar/grill (modern background music 12–2 pm, 6–11 pm); gym, sauna, squash, billiards. 2-acre grounds: swimming pool (heated Apr–Sept). Sandy beach, water sports, 3 mins' walk. Only restaurant suitable for ♿.
Location NW of Wadebridge. Take A30 to Bodmin, A389 to Wadebridge, B3314 to Rock. Train to Bodmin.
Restrictions Smoking in bar/grill only. No dogs.
Credit cards All major cards accepted.
Terms B&B: single £55–£100, double £80–£155, suite £105–£210. English breakfast £6.50. Full alc: lunch £25–£27, dinner £35–£38. Child in parents' room: 3 years and over, £10. Golf, midweek, off-season breaks. *V*

ROGATE Hampshire — Map 2:E3

Mizzards Farm BUDGET

Rogate
Petersfield GU31 5HS
Tel 01730-821656
Fax 01730-821655
Email julian.francis@hemscott.net

'A reminder of how rural life must have been' is given by this 16th-century farmhouse, by the river Rother, in a designated area of outstanding natural beauty. Julian and Harriet Francis run an informal, upmarket B&B, which the guests 'are encouraged to regard as a temporary home', free to stroll around the landscaped gardens and lake and to swim in the covered pool. Residents have their own drawing room. There is much hewn woodwork. The 'well-proportioned bedrooms' have a good-size bathroom 'with interesting exhortations to visitors'. One room has a four-poster. Breakfast, which includes eggs Rubens, kippers, and home-produced honey and jam, is served in a vaulted dining room, from which a staircase rises to a gallery. No evening meal, but plenty of pubs and restaurants are nearby. There is good walking on the South Downs and in the Wealden country. Petworth, Goodwood, Uppark and Arundel are among the nearby houses to visit. (*Endorsed this year by Stuart G Pratt*)

Open All year, except Christmas, New Year.
Rooms 3 double. No telephone.
Facilities Lounge, breakfast room. No background music. 2-acre grounds: covered swimming pool (open May–end Sept), croquet, chess, lake, river. Golf, riding, polo nearby. Unsuitable for ♿.
Location From centre of Rogate go S ½ mile, cross river, take 1st turning on right.
Restrictions No smoking. No children under 7. No dogs.
Credit cards None accepted.
Terms B&B: single £34–£45, double £60–£72. 1-night bookings refused weekends in season.

> Many people are upset when they cancel a booking and discover that they have lost a deposit or been charged the full rate of the room. Do remember that when making a booking you are entering into a contract with the hotel. Always make sure you know what the hotel's policy about cancellations is.

ROMALDKIRK Co. Durham — Map 4:C3

The Rose and Crown
Romaldkirk
nr Barnard Castle DL12 9EB

Tel 01833-650213
Fax 01833-650828
Email hotel@rose-and-crown.co.uk
Website www.rose-and-crown.co.uk

'What a pleasure to find a hotel with such attention to detail (eg, umbrellas in the Steading accommodation), and where the pursuit of excellence is practised in all aspects.' A glowing report on this old favourite, in an unspoilt village on the edge of Teesdale, is balanced this year by a visitor who detected a 'take it or leave it' attitude (things may run less smoothly in the owners' absence). The food, however, won general praise. The 18th-century coaching inn faces an oak-shaded green, with stocks, a water pump, cows grazing, and a Norman church (its bells strike the hour). Christopher and Alison Davy have completed a four-year programme of redecoration, renovating the second-floor suite, and even eliminating the last creaking floorboards. The public rooms have log fires, panelling, brass and copper, old farming implements, prints, maps and etchings, fresh flowers; the small lounge is equipped with magazines. Good meals are served in the beamed, traditional bar, where old-fashioned seats face a log fire The oak-panelled restaurant serves a combination of modern and regional cooking, eg, halibut with Cotherstone cheese and cream and red onion marmalade; Teesdale Fell Lamb with potato and woodland mushroom broth and béarnaise sauce; apple and sultana pie. 'Breakfast porridge and full English were very good.' The purpose-built courtyard bedrooms, which open on to the car park, are good for walkers, dog-owners and business people. Rooms in the main house have a modern bathroom; suites have a hi-fi system. The Davys have written a guide-book to local attractions (including Durham cathedral and castle, the Bowes Museum, and some of Britain's finest grouse moors). (*Hamish Horsburgh; also* Good Pub Guide*, CH, and others*)

Open All year, except Christmas. Restaurant closed to non-residents Sun evening.
Rooms 2 suites, 10 double. 5 in rear courtyard annexe. Some on ground floor.
Facilities Residents' lounge, lounge bar, Crown Room (bar meals), restaurant. No background music. Fishing, grouse shooting, birdwatching nearby.
Location Centre of village, 6 miles NW of Barnard Castle on B6277. Ample parking. Hourly bus from Barnard Castle. Rail services to Darlington.
Restrictions No smoking in restaurant. No dogs in main lounge, restaurant.
Credit cards MasterCard, Visa.
Terms [2001] B&B: single £62, double £86, suite £100. Bar lunches. Set lunch £13.95, dinner £25. Special breaks all year. Walking, wine weekends. *V*

> The *V* sign at the end of an entry indicates a hotel that has agreed to take part in our Voucher scheme and to give *Guide* readers a 25 per cent discount on their room rates, subject to the conditions explained in *How to read the entries*, and listed on the back of the vouchers.

ROSS-ON-WYE Herefordshire — Map 3:D5

Pengethley Manor NEW
Pengethley Park, nr Ross-on-Wye
HR9 6LL
Tel 01989-730211
Fax 01989-730238
Email reservations@pengethleymanor.co.uk
Website www.pengethleymanor.co.uk

'Very elegant, with well-furnished bedrooms, wonderful views, excellent food, efficiently served.' Near an old market town on the river Wye, Mr and Mrs Wisker's Georgian manor house (Best Western) stands in a large park, with a golf course, a trout lake, a vineyard and 'designer walks' through fields – 'these require tough shoes,' says the nominator. The Dutch chef (for 12 years), Fred van der Knaap, produces 'wonderful soups'; fresh local salmon, and roast beef carved at the table are specialities; vegetarians are catered for; service is by white-gloved staff. 'Breakfast in our bedroom arrived punctually, an exercise requiring stamina on the part of the staff as we were on the top of the stable block. This could be unpleasant in poor weather, but we were lucky. All very peaceful.' But there is a conference centre, and weddings are held. 'The exit is on the bend of a busy road.' Some rooms have a four-poster and a spa bath. 'Children are catered for and pets are welcomed,' says the brochure. (*Mrs EB Schaffer*)

Open All year.
Rooms 4 suites, 24 double. 12 in annexes. Some on ground floor; 1 equipped for ♿.
Facilities Ramp. Lounge, bar, library, restaurant; background music; conference facilities. 15-acre grounds: 9-hole par 3 golf improvement course, swimming pool, croquet. Civil wedding licence.
Location 4 miles NW of Ross-on-Wye, on A49. Hourly bus between Ross-on-Wye and Hereford.
Restrictions No smoking in restaurant. No dogs in public rooms.
Credit cards All major cards accepted.
Terms B&B: single £60–£95, double £80–£150, suite £95–£150; D,B&B: single £75–£110, double £120–£180; suite £140–£190. Full alc £30. Child in parents' room: under 16, free. Christmas package. *V*

ROSTHWAITE Cumbria — Map 4: inset C2

Hazel Bank BUDGET
Rosthwaite
nr Keswick CA12 5XB
Tel 017687-77248
Fax 017687-77373
Email enquiries@hazelbankhotel.co.uk
Website www.hazelbankhotel.co.uk

'A special place for us – not just because of the comfort and the superb view of Borrowdale from the lounge. The personal attention to detail by Glen and Brenda Davies make it a home from home. On our daughter's birthday they gave her a huge bouquet and baked a superb gateau.' A plaudit this year from regular visitors to this small guest house. The site of the Victorian-style building (with Gothic and Moorish influences) so impressed Hugh Walpole that he used it in two of his novels. It stands in landscaped grounds and woodland in one of the loveliest valleys in the Lake District. After three years here, the welcoming hosts 'have really got into their stride', according to another regular. 'They take a personal interest in visitors, and create a happy atmosphere. Guests who come on their own are not left out. Every care is taken to present attractive meals for people who have spent the day exploring this magnificent area. Everywhere is spotless.' Smoking is banned throughout the hotel *and* the grounds. Mrs Davies cooks dinner, which has a daily-changing four-course menu. No choice for the first two courses – they might be roasted mushroom soup with tarragon; seared breast of duckling with a blueberry, port and red wine sauce. Then come traditional puddings and local cheeses. 'Terrific breakfast': a wide range of fruit, cereals, yogurt and juices followed by 'a perfectly cooked hot dish'. The pretty village of Rosthwaite is largely owned by the National Trust, and this is a good area for walking and hiking. (*Alex and Vera Robinson, Mrs Pat Harman*)

Open All year, except Christmas.
Rooms 1 suite (in cottage, can be self-catering), 8 double. 2 on ground floor. No telephone.
Facilities Lounge, honesty bar, dining room; drying room. No background music. 4-acre grounds: croquet, woods, becks. Derwent Water 3 miles.
Location About 6 miles S of Keswick on B5289 to Borrowdale. Just before Rosthwaite village turn left over small humpbacked bridge. Bus: 79 Keswick–Borrowdale.
Restrictions No smoking (house and garden). No children under 10. No pets.
Credit cards MasterCard, Visa.
Terms [2001] D,B&B £47.50–£64.50. Set dinner £17.95. Painting course in July. 1-night bookings sometimes refused, if far in advance.

RUSHLAKE GREEN East Sussex — Map 2:E4

Stone House — *Tel* 01435-830553
Rushlake Green — *Fax* 01435-830726
Heathfield TN21 9QJ — *Website* www.stonehousesussex.co.uk

'Like visiting friends, not hotel-like at all,' says one of this year's enthusiastic reports on this magnificent house, which has been the family home of the Dunns since it was built in about 1495 (later, a Georgian wing was added). It stands peacefully in a vast estate in unspoilt countryside on the Kent/Sussex border, in a 'wonderful garden', with an ornamental lake, gazebos, nooks and crannies for sheltering from the wind, and a 100-foot herbaceous border. Jane and Peter Dunn run it on house-party lines. Family portraits hang on the walls, and the public rooms are filled with antiques, heirlooms and family photographs. There are log fires, and a mahogany-panelled billiard room with a full-sized antique table. The two grandest bedrooms, up a sweeping staircase, have a four-poster and lavish furnishings. The rooms in the Tudor wing have less space but lots of character (beams and sloping ceilings). The septuagenarian host greets guests 'with old-world charm'. Mrs Dunn, a Master Chef of Great Britain, has a *Michelin Bib Gourmand* for her 'French- and Thai-influenced cooking'. Dinner (residents only) is elegantly served in the panelled dining room. Five choices for each course including, eg, yellow courgette flower soup; roast breast of duck marinated with honey, ginger and mustard, with a plum and spring onion salsa; layered ginger cream with crystallised ginger. There is a vegetarian menu and an extensive wine list. Vegetables and herbs are home grown; game comes from the estate. A simple continental breakfast is brought to the bedroom; a traditional one, with a 'superb buffet', is served downstairs. Plenty of outdoor activities (see below); pheasant shoots and corporate entertainment activities are arranged. A picnic can be ordered, complete with a table and chairs, for nearby Glyndebourne. Local sights include Battle, Bateman's, Sissinghurst and Leonardslee, a long stretch of Sussex coast. Gatwick is 35 miles away. (*Barry Rogers, and others*)

Open 3 Jan–24 Dec.
Rooms 1 suite, 2 junior suites, 3 double, 1 single.
Facilities Hall, drawing room, library, billiard room, dining room. No background music. 1,000-acre estate: 5½-acre garden, farm, woodland, croquet, archery, off-road driving, shooting, ballooning, pheasant/clay-pigeon shooting, 2 lakes, rowing, fishing. Unsuitable for ♿.
Location 4 miles SE of Heathfield. B2096 towards Battle; 4th right to Rushlake Green. Left at green; keep green on right; entrance far left at crossroads. Train: Stonegate; pre-booked taxi.
Restrictions No children under 9. No dogs in public rooms.
Credit cards MasterCard, Visa.
Terms (*Not VAT-rated*) B&B: single £65–£80, double £90–£225, suite £155–£225. Set meals (advance booking for lunch necessary) £24.95; Glyndebourne hamper £27.50. Weekend house parties, winter breaks. 1-night bookings sometimes refused. *V* (1 Nov–31 Mar; not Fri, Sat)

RYE East Sussex — Map 2:E5

Jeake's House BUDGET
Mermaid Street
Rye TN31 7ET

Tel 01797-222828
Fax 01797-222623
Email jeakeshouse@btinternet.com
Website www.jeakeshouse.com

César award in 1992

Jenny Hadfield runs a civilised B&B in one of Rye's picturesque, sloping, cobbled streets. It has been created from three old converted buildings: Jeake's storehouse, once a wool house, a Baptist school and then the home of the American poet Conrad Aiken; a chapel which became a men's club; and the neighbouring Elders House. It is filled with books, antiques, old pictures and samplers. The bedrooms and bathrooms are 'spotless and lovely', each with a different colour scheme and a brass or mahogany bed; some furniture is at odd angles, due to the sloping floors. 'Quite superb: historic, homely, luxurious and friendly all at once; firmly stamped with the personality of the attentive hostess. We particularly appreciated the vegetarian breakfast, and Yum Yum, the Siamese cat,' said one visitor. Whisper this, so as not upset the 'veteran resident moggie, Sam'. Some rooms look over the courtyard garden (with a pond and fountain) across rooftops to fields beyond; others are above the street (not noisy). One room is small. Some bathrooms are shared (bathrobes are provided). The parlour, which has an upright piano, has been extended to include a fireplace; the sitting room has a bar. Breakfast is served from 8 am in the large, galleried chapel with deep red walls, high windows, good paintings and china, and plants. There is a buffet with fresh fruit; well-cooked hot dishes, home-made marmalade, etc. Rye, perched above a plain between the rivers Rother and Tillingham, has many literary connections: EF Benson immortalised it as 'Tilling' in his Mapp and Lucia novels; both Henry James and Rumer Godden lived in Lamb House, now owned by the National Trust. (*AE*)

Open All year.
Rooms 1 suite, 10 double, 1 single. 10 with *en suite* facilities.
Facilities Parlour, bar/lounge, breakfast room (classical background music). Unsuitable for ♿.
Location Central. Private car park (£3 daily). Train/bus station 5 mins' walk.
Restrictions No smoking in breakfast room. No children under 11. No dogs in breakfast room.
Credit cards MasterCard, Visa.
Terms B&B £30.50–£65. Child in parents' room: 50% of adult rate. Reductions for 4 days or more; 15% midweek reduction Nov–Feb, except Christmas, New Year. Christmas package. 1-night bookings usually refused weekends.

The Old Vicarage BUDGET
66 Church Square
Rye TN31 7HF

Tel 01797-222119
Fax 01797-227466
Email oldvicaragerye@tesco.net
Website www.oldvicaragerye.co.uk

Unmissably pink, this unpretentious little B&B, an 18th-century ex-vicarage, stands by the 15th-century church on a lovely traffic-free square. Like so many Rye houses, it has literary connections: Henry James wrote *The Spoils of Poynton* here before moving to Lamb House, close by. 'Early evening was enlivened by bell-ringing practice in the church, but after 9 all was blissfully quiet,' says an inspector in 2001. The owners, Paul and Julia Masters, whose family home this is, 'have thought of everything one could need', and much is included in the price. Tea is offered on arrival; at 6 pm, sherry decanters are placed in the small sitting room for help-yourself drinks. 'Breakfast, in a small bay-windowed room overlooking the garden, puts many posh places to shame: a basket full of packets of cereals stands on each table; warm scones and soda bread are brought as you decide what else you can manage. The home-made marmalade was so delicious I scoffed the lot; Mrs Masters noticed and gave me a pot of it to take home.' The menu includes leaf tea, freshly ground coffee, home-made yogurt, free-range eggs, award-winning sausages and a copy of *The Times*. The cheerful bedrooms have flowery fabrics, a hot drinks tray, TV, masses of local information, and views of the walled garden, the church, or Rye rooftops. The top floor was recently converted into a two-bedroomed suite with a lounge and shower room. Rye has a number of expensive restaurants, but *The Copper Kettle* 'serves good food at reasonable prices', or you could try the restaurant at the back of *The Fish Shop*: fresh fish daily, speciality cod, chips and mushy peas with tea, bread and butter (£3.95).

Note: This old vicarage is not to be confused with *The Old Vicarage Hotel* in East Street.

Open All year, except Christmas.
Rooms 1 suite, 4 double. No telephone (payphone available).
Facilities Lounge, small library/TV room, breakfast room. No background music. Small walled garden. Tennis, bowling, putting nearby; beach (safe bathing) 2 miles. Unsuitable for ♿.
Location By St Mary's church. Follow signs to town centre. Through Landgate Arch to High St, 3rd left into West St. Private parking nearby.
Restrictions No smoking. No children under 8. Guide dogs only.
Credit cards None accepted.
Terms B&B £29–£60. Winter breaks Nov–Jan; weekly discounts. 1-night bookings refused weekends.

See also SHORTLIST

ST ALBANS Hertfordshire ***See SHORTLIST*** **Map 2:C3**

ST AUSTELL Cornwall Map 1:D2

Boscundle Manor
Tregrehan
St Austell PL25 3RL

Tel 01726-813557
Fax 01726-814997
Email stay@boscundlemanor.co.uk
Website boscundlemanor.co.uk

Andrew and Mary Flint run their restaurant-with-rooms in hands-on style. 'We are small enough to give personal help to guests; we would not be ideal for anyone looking for a formal hotel atmosphere,' they write. Their 18th-century stone manor house stands in large wooded grounds with terraced gardens, and the remains of a tin mine, now converted to make a pond, a lake, and a 'spectacular two-hole golf course'. You can still see the remains of the engine house and the main shaft, and old mine buildings have been converted to house a games room (it has new gymnasium equipment this year) and a swimming pool, 'mainly for adult exercise'. There is an open-air swimming pool, too. 'The cuisine was superb, the accommodation excellent,' says one visitor. Others wrote of the 'charming house, hospitable hosts, great breakfasts'. Inspectors liked the 'domestic ambience'. 'The interior is cosy, done with taste: lovely old china, antique bits, oil paintings by a local artist, beautiful old Cornish watercolours. Our bedroom, simple but comfortable, had William Morris textiles, frilly lampshades, knick-knacks, magazines, fresh flowers, a compact bathroom.' At dinner, the Flints eat at the same time as their guests, and they join them for conversation over coffee. Service is by 'unobtrusive but pleasant' staff. Mrs Flint has returned to the kitchen ('I was getting bored just floating around the place'). She provides three choices of starter, and canvasses guests on their preferences for the single main course, offering alternatives (including vegetarian ones). The menu might include crab mayonnaise; baked salmon with hollandaise sauce; cheesecake with raspberry topping. There is a cheeseboard to end, and 'the wine list is fantastic, with over 40 clarets'. Some noise is audible from surrounding roads. The Eden Project is 'almost next door', and other famous gardens are not far. Carlyon Bay is half a mile away. (*HJM, and others*)

Open Apr–Oct inclusive. Dining room closed to non-residents Sun.
Rooms 2 suites, 6 double, 2 single. 2 in cottage, 2 in garden.
Facilities Sitting room, conservatory, bar, dining room; private dining room. No background music. 14-acre grounds: old mine shaft; games room (gym, etc), 2 swimming pools (1 indoors); golf practice area. Riding, sailing, fishing, golf nearby. Unsuitable for ♿.
Location 2 miles E of St Austell. From A390 to Truro follow signs to Tregrehan.
Restrictions No smoking in dining room. No dogs in public rooms.
Credit cards Amex, MasterCard, Visa.
Terms B&B: single £70–£90, double £120–£140, suite £180–£200; D,B&B £75–£120 per person. Set dinner £20. Reductions for 3 or more days; and B&B stays of 6 or more days.

ST BLAZEY Cornwall — Map 1:D3

Nanscawen House BUDGET
Prideaux Road
nr St Blazey PL24 2SR

Tel/Fax 01726-814488
Email keith@nanscawen.com
Website www.nanscawen.com

'This impeccably run and very welcoming B&B continues to give outstanding value for money,' says a visitor to Keith and Fiona Martin's wisteria-covered home, the 16th-century seat of the Nanscawen family, in the 'bosky hillside setting' of the Luxulyan valley. The three bedrooms are large: Rashleigh 'is delightful', with flowery fabrics, lots of pink and blue, a garden view and a bathroom with a spa bath; Prideaux has a four-poster bed. In the large drawing room, a small honesty bar has a selection of wines, liqueurs and brandies. Breakfast, in a conservatory, includes freshly squeezed orange juice, local smoked salmon with scrambled eggs; also fruit and yogurt. Cream teas are served. There is a large, secluded garden with a heated swimming pool, and a spa bath heated to 97°. Hospitality is 'unobtrusive and cordial'. For an evening meal, the Martins will advise about the many restaurants nearby. The Eden Project is just two miles away; Lanhydrock is ten minutes' drive; St Austell is four miles, Fowey is five. Plenty of beaches are within easy reach. (*John Naylor*)

Open All year.
Rooms 2 double, 1 single.
Facilities Drawing room with honesty bar. Breakfast room. No background music. 5-acre grounds: gardens, swimming pool (heated Apr–Sept), spa bath. Golf, riding, beaches, fishing. Unsuitable for ♿.
Location 4 miles NE of St Austell. After level-crossing in St Blazey, from A390, turn right opposite Texaco garage. *Nanscawen* ¾ mile on right (row of trees marks foot of drive). Parking.
Restrictions No smoking. No children under 12. No pets.
Credit cards MasterCard, Visa (*3% surcharge, except on deposits*).
Terms B&B double £60–£84. Special breaks Oct–Mar.

> The 'Budget' label by a hotel's name indicates an establishment where dinner, bed and breakfast cost around £50 per person, or B&B about £30 and an evening meal about £20. These are only a rough guide, and do not always apply to single accommodation, nor do they necessarily apply in high season.

ST HILARY Cornwall — Map 1:E1

Ennys
Trewhella Lane, St Hilary
nr Penzance TR20 9BZ

Tel 01736-740262
Fax 01736-740055
Email ennys@zetnet.co.uk
Website www.ennys.co.uk

A 'really well-run and welcoming' B&B, owned by Gill Charlton, former travel editor of the *Daily Telegraph*. She writes: 'At night it is truly dark here, and the only sound is the hooting of owls in the woods.' The Grade II listed 17th-century manor house stands at the end of a mile-long single-track drive, surrounded by fields that lead down to the river Hayle (good for walks and picnics). Roses and creepers surround the front door; exotic plants grow in sheltered gardens where there are a grass tennis court and a good-sized heated swimming pool (not available to guests between 12.30 and 4.30 pm). The large sitting room has books, a log fire, and souvenirs of the owner's travels (eg, the odd Buddha and fertility symbol). Three bedrooms, furnished in modern style and with a window seat overlooking the garden or countryside, are in the main building. Two family suites and three self-catering apartments (sometimes offered on a B&B basis in low season) are in converted barns opening on to a courtyard. Guests help themselves to afternoon tea with home-baked scones and cakes (included in the B&B rates) in the kitchen. Breakfast includes home-laid eggs. For meals, Ms Charlton can recommend the best pubs and restaurants in the area. St Hilary is a hamlet in the narrow end of Cornwall where the sea is visible to the north and the south. There is plenty to see and do nearby: sandy surfing beaches, the Land's End and Lizard peninsulas, St Michael's Mount and famous gardens (Trelissick, Trebah, Trengwainton). (*Wendy Broer*)

Open 12 Feb–1 Nov.
Rooms 2 family suites in converted barn, 3 double. Also 3 self-catering apartments (can be let for B&B off season). No telephone.
Facilities Sitting room, breakfast room. No background music. 20-acre grounds: swimming pool (not available 12.30–4.30 pm), tennis. Sandy beach 3 miles; fishing, sailing, windsurfing, riding, golf nearby. Unsuitable for ♿.
Location 5 miles E of Penzance, off B3280 between St Hilary and Relubbus. Train to Penzance; taxi.
Restrictions No smoking: breakfast room, bedrooms. No children under 2. No dogs.
Credit cards MasterCard, Visa.
Terms B&B: single £40–£50, double £65–£75, suite £90–£110. 1-night bookings refused high season weekends/bank holidays.

ST IVES Cornwall — Map 1:D1

The Garrack
Burthallan Lane
St Ives TR26 3AA

Tel 01736-796199
Fax 01736-798955
Email garrack@accuk.co.uk
Website www.garrack.com

A traditional hotel, which the Kilby family has run for over 30 years: Michael and Stephen Kilby are now in charge. The creeper-clad stone building, a Relais du Silence, stands on a hill above Porthmeor beach (European Blue Flag for cleanness, popular with surfers), and the town is a short but steep walk away. *The Garrack* is 'very homely, in a 1950s way, with most hospitable staff', and it offers 'excellent value for money'. It has wide beach and sea views, and is good for a family holiday: it has bedrooms with bunk beds; also children's menus, baby-listening, etc. 'Straightforward, good meals' are served in the restaurant. With its conservatory extension, and storage tank for live lobsters, it is popular with outside diners. Local lamb, organic beef, venison and home-grown vegetables are also served; there is always a vegetarian option. The wine list numbers over 80 vintages, including plenty of half bottles. The bedrooms are well appointed; some have a four-poster and a spa bath. The more traditional ones are in the old house; more modern ones are in an extension. Two rooms are in a cottage annexe, some way from the main building. The small leisure centre has a swimming pool ('small but adequate', with a counter-current swim jet), and an all-day snack bar. Loungers and palm trees stand on the lawn. Nearby are the Tate, the Barbara Hepworth museum and garden, numerous private art galleries. The coastal footpath passes close by. (*P and MD*)

Open All year.
Rooms 16 double, 2 single. 1 designed for ♿. 2 in cottage.
Facilities 2 lounges, TV lounge, restaurant (mixed background music at night); conference facilities. 2-acre grounds: garden, leisure centre: small swimming pool, sauna, whirlpool, solarium, fitness room, coffee shop, bar. Beaches 5–10 mins' walk.
Location 1 mile from centre. From Penzance on B3311, turn right on to B3306 towards St Ives. Hotel off this, to left.
Restrictions No smoking: restaurant, leisure centre. Dogs in designated bedrooms; not in public rooms.
Credit cards All major cards accepted.
Terms B&B: single £62–£63.50, double £104–£151; D,B&B: single £80–£82, double £140–£189. Snack lunches. Set dinner £24; full alc £35. Child in parents' room: 5% to 20% of adult rate, according to age. Off-season breaks. Christmas programme.

ST KEYNE Cornwall — Map 1:D3

The Well House NEW

St Keyne
Liskeard PL14 4RN

Tel 01579-342001
Fax 01579-343891
Email enquiries@wellhouse.co.uk
Website www.wellhouse.co.uk

In a 'wonderful setting' in a small wooded valley near Liskeard, Nick Wainford runs 'with just the right mixture of informality and efficiency', this 'enchanting' Victorian tea magnate's stone house (he owns it with Ione Nurdin). In the grounds are duck ponds, an all-weather tennis court and a swimming pool; you enter through an arch of greenery. 'One of the most characterful places we have stayed in,' say inspectors in 2001. 'As near perfection as we have found. Taste is impeccable throughout. Beautiful paintings abound, also wonderful flower and plant arrangements. Everything is smart and well maintained. The small lounge has a spectacular marble fireplace, good antiques, classy furniture. No reception desk, no signing in. Mr Wainsford, who is omnipresent, welcomed us as if we were personal friends, and later bade us a fond farewell. With his half-moon spectacles, he reminded us of a benevolent parson in a Jane Austen novel. The manager, Denise Manning, is charming. A striking staircase leads to bedrooms with double doors to ensure privacy. Our room was palatial, well lit; its furniture exuded elegance; large sash windows overlooked the slopes of the well-maintained garden descending towards trees and valley below.' A new chef, Mathew Corner, runs the bay-windowed restaurant, popular with locals. 'Our superb dinner included excellent smoked salmon with seared scallops; perfect bream on a mound of salsify; assiette of rhubarb – a masterpiece. Tables are well spaced, and dining is a relaxing experience. Breakfast was enjoyable too: home-made muesli, compote of fruit, Greek yogurt with local honey; perfect scrambled egg; smoked haddock a treat.' Each bedroom has a different colour scheme: terracotta, yellow, lavender, etc; two have a private terrace. Bathrooms are 'state-of-the-art modern, all white, with large towels'. Tea and coffee, with 'superlative home-made biscuits', are freely offered. Mr Wainford is often accompanied by Jester, a Staffordshire bull terrier – 'the guests find him very amusing,' he says. He is a claret enthusiast, and 'the extensive wine list is reasonably priced'. The Eden Project is close by.

Open All year.
Rooms 9 double.
Facilities Lounge, bar, restaurant. No background music. 4-acre grounds: tennis, swimming pool. Fishing, riding, golf nearby; coast 4 miles. Unsuitable for ♿.
Location 3 miles S of Liskeard by B3254. At church, fork left to St Keyne Well; hotel ½ mile on left.
Restrictions No smoking in restaurant. No children under 8 at dinner (high tea provided). No dogs in restaurant.
Credit cards MasterCard, Visa.
Terms B&B: single £75–£95, double £110–£160. Set lunch/dinner (2 to 4 courses) £25.50–£33.50. Autumn/winter breaks. Christmas package. 1-night bookings sometimes refused.

ST MARTIN'S Isles of Scilly — Map 1:C1

St Martin's on the Isle
St Martin's, Isles of Scilly
Cornwall TR25 0QW

Tel 01720-422092
Fax 01720-422298
Email stay@stmartinshotel.co.uk
Website www.stmartinshotel.co.uk

Set on the shore of this 'idyllic' car-free island, this Pride of Britain member was purpose-built in the 1980s in the style of a row of traditional stone fishermen's cottages. It looks across to Tresco and Teän ('stunning views; spectacular sunsets') – but the west-facing garden 'sometimes gets the full force of prevailing winds'. The lawns are dotted with tables, chairs and parasols, and the island, an area of outstanding beauty and a marine park, has white beaches with 'perfect castle-building sand'. In school holidays, the hotel is busy with families (it provides buckets and spades, games, videos and baby-listening); at other times it is a peaceful place to stay. 'Our family of four enjoyed it very much,' says a report this year. 'The food was superb, beautifully presented; very good breakfasts; decent high tea for children under 12 (proper food, not child muck), and a nice little wine list. Very helpful staff; the hands-on manager, Keith Bradford, is friendly and informal' – he meets arriving guests off the launch, and runs the hotel with 'constant attention to detail'. 'Everybody is addressed by name.' The split-level public rooms have stone walls, 'extravagant flowers everywhere'. Bedrooms have a 'good but plain' decor (modern furniture, striped fabrics); they vary in size; many have a sea view. The new chef, Stewart Eddy, cooks 'light modern dishes with an emphasis on seafood'. In the main restaurant (where modern paintings hang on yellow walls) you might choose from the *prix-fixe* menu: crab cappuccino soup; roast turbot on saffron risotto; hot plum tart with vanilla pod ice cream. 'Tables are rotated so everyone gets the view.' Light meals are served in the bar/grill. Trips by launch, with a picnic, to other islands are arranged; birdwatching walks are organised, and guests can go fishing on a Cornish crabber (their catch will be cooked for breakfast). 'A wonderful spot.' 'A gem, albeit an expensive one.' But an off-season package includes all drinks. 'If you choose to travel by helicopter (great fun), book your flight well in advance.' (*Fiona Stapley, A and PT*)

Open Apr–Oct.
Rooms 2 suites, 28 double. Some on ground floor.
Facilities Ramps. Lounge, lounge bar/grill, restaurant; snooker room, small indoor swimming pool. No background music. 1-acre garden on beach, jetty, boating, diving, water sports. Civil wedding licence.
Location North end of island. Boat or helicopter from St Mary's; hotel will arrange all-in travel package. No cars on island.
Restrictions No smoking in restaurant. No children under 12 at dinner. No dogs in public rooms.
Credit cards All major cards accepted.
Terms [2001] B&B £75–£125; D,B&B £85–£320. Bar lunch £10, set dinner £35. Light meals available. Up to 2 children under 16 free in parents' room. 3-day off-season package. 1-night bookings refused in season.

ST MARY'S Isles of Scilly — Map 1:C1

Star Castle
The Garrison, St Mary's
Isles of Scilly
Cornwall TR21 0JA

Tel 01720-422317
Fax 01720-422343
Email recept@starcastlescilly.demon.co.uk
Website www.starcastlescilly.demon.co.uk

John and Mary Nicholls's unostentatious hotel is an old fortress that was built in the form of an eight-pointed star as a defence against the Spanish Armada. Surrounded by a dry moat and 18-foot ramparts, it stands above the town and has views of sea and islands in all directions ('wonderful sunsets'). The Prince of Wales, later King Charles II, took refuge here before fleeing to France in 1646; another Prince of Wales, the future Edward VIII, inaugurated the hotel in 1933. Mr Nicholls is a 'hands-on' host, greeting guests at mealtimes, and remembering names (he is also head of the lifeboat service, and a pilot for visiting ships). 'The staff are friendly, but not intrusive,' says a visitor this year, who enjoyed the variety of food in the conservatory fish restaurant in the garden. It serves, eg, Mediterranean vegetable terrine; monkfish and lobster St Jacques; Scillonian fish stew (but one visitor who ordered Dover sole was surprised to get lemon sole with the comment: 'It's just as nice'). The dining room, in the former officers' mess, serves more traditional dishes, like fried whitebait, or avocado and tomato salad; roast beef with stuffed artichokes, or Moroccan lamb. Both restaurants always offer a vegetarian dish. Wines are reasonably priced, with a good selection of half bottles. The most characterful bedrooms are in the main house; three singles are in guardrooms on the battlements. Two modern blocks in the grounds have large bedrooms and suites, suitable for a family. Some have a private garden or a veranda. These rooms are well appointed, but sound-proofing may not be perfect. There is a small lounge, and a small bar in the former dungeon, but most visitors take advantage of the sun-trap lawns, enclosed by high hedges, in the subtropical gardens (there is also a covered swimming pool). Guests can go island-hopping in the hotel's 32-foot launch (Tim the boatman is commended for his 'wit and repartee'). (*Bob Black, JK*)

Open Mar–end Oct.
Rooms 5 suites, 25 double, 4 single (3 in ramparts). 22 in 2 garden annexes.
Facilities Lounge, games room, bar, 2 restaurants (classical background music at night). 4½-acre grounds: covered swimming pool, tennis; private motor launch. Beach nearby. Golf, cycle hire, riding, sailing, diving, fishing available. Unsuitable for ♿.
Location ¼ mile from town centre. Boat (2¾ hours), helicopter (20 mins) from Penzance; Skybus (15 mins) from Land's End (except Sun); hotel will meet.
Restrictions No smoking in restaurants. No children under 5 in restaurants at night. No dogs in public rooms, except bar.
Credit cards MasterCard, Visa (*surcharge*).
Terms [2001] B&B £53–£84; D,B&B £63–£108. Bar lunch from £4. Set dinner £28; full alc £38. Child in parents' room: 5–55% of adult rate. Inclusive breaks (including travel) Mar–Oct. *V* (low season only)

ST MAWES Cornwall **Map 1:E2**

Tresanton
Lower Castle Road
St Mawes TR2 5DR

Tel 01326-270055
Fax 01326-270053
Email info@tresanton.com
Website www.tresanton.com

'Lovely as ever.' 'A very attractive hotel. The staff were extremely willing.' Enthusiasm this year for this 'smart, modern, yet unpretentious' hotel owned by Olga Polizzi of the Forte dynasty. She and her husband, the journalist William Shawcross, are often to be seen; her two daughters are also involved in the running. 'It is beautifully done, with lots of linen in sand and sea colours, simple and unchintzy.' With wooden, tiled and mosaic floors and Riviera-like views, it has a Mediterranean feel (apart from 'a rack of Wellington boots of all sizes, for guests to borrow'). Service is 'informal, mainly young', if sometimes disorganised, and some visitors wrote of a mixed experience that didn't justify the high cost. But the setting on the Roseland peninsula is 'brilliant'. The collection of white buildings stands in terraced sub-tropical gardens above the fishing village, overlooking the Fal estuary. Nearby is a castle built by Henry VIII. The best bedrooms are big, with 'a huge bed with good sheets, and a nice bathroom'. But again this year we had a report of a small, poorly furnished room at the top. In the 'stunning restaurant', with its white marble floor, white-clothed tables close together in rows, and large white plates, 'the food is very good, quite sophisticated'. Peter Robinson's modern *prix-fixe* menu includes, eg, crab and radicchio risotto; turbot with warm olive sauce; steamed pear pudding. The wine list, 'with stiff mark-ups', is 'reasonably good, if eccentric'. The young are welcomed: boxes of toys and games are in the lounge, and there is a children's menu. A small sand/rock beach is close by. *Tresanton* has a little cinema and a film library; it owns an eight-metre racing yacht, the *Pinuccia*. Nearby are coastal walks, Cornish gardens, St Ives, St Michael's Mount. (*Dione and Pat Gibson, Emily Read, Anne and Denis Tate, and others*)

Open All year.
Rooms 2 suites, 24 double. In 3 buildings.
Facilities 2 lounges, bar, restaurant; cinema, conference facilities. No background music. Terraced garden. Near sea, sand, rock beaches, safe bathing; 8-metre yacht. Unsuitable for ♿. Civil wedding licence.
Location On cliff road, near castle. From A3078, follow signs to St Mawes. *Do not take road to castle.* Carry on along Polvarth Rd, into village, along seafront. Hotel on right. Train: Truro; bus/taxi.
Restriction No dogs.
Credit cards Amex, MasterCard, Visa.
Terms B&B: single £170–£187, double £215–£235, suite £315–£365. Extra bed £30. Set lunch (2 to 3 courses) £15–£20; dinner £33. Christmas package.

SALISBURY Wiltshire ***See SHORTLIST*** **Map 2:D2**

SANDGATE Kent **Map 2:E5**

Sandgate Hotel and Restaurant La Terrasse
The Esplanade
Sandgate, Folkestone CT20 3DY

Tel 01303-220444
Fax 01303-220496
Website www.sandgatehotel.com

César award in 1999

You can see the lights of France from this conversion of two Victorian houses, which stands across a sometimes noisy road from the wide beach of a village on the smart side of Folkestone. And the accent inside this French restaurant-with-rooms is distinctly French. Zara Gicqueau, who runs front-of-house, is a local, but her husband, Samuel, is from the Loire. He is the chef of the *Michelin*-starred restaurant, *La Terrasse*, and he and the restaurant manager, Joël Fricoteaux, have worked at *Le Manoir aux Quat'Saisons*, Great

Milton (*qv*). 'The restaurant was immaculate, with attentive service from the French staff who spoke excellent English. Chair pulled out, napkin placed on lap, nothing too much trouble,' reports one visitor. Others wrote: 'The staff were friendly. The bedrooms though small, are a delight, comfortable and impeccably clean.' 'Rather expensive, but a special treat.' The smart public rooms have floor-to-ceiling windows overlooking the sea. The small restaurant is yellow and blue, with French silver and porcelain, and paintings of Loire vineyards. It opens on to a terrace that has sunshades in summer. Tables must be booked in advance (residents are not guaranteed a place). The cooking is 'classical French with a modern interpretation', eg, carpaccio of scallops and caviar; steamed sea bass with braised chicory and a Noilly sauce; roast William pear with a ginger-scented caramel sauce. The 'beautiful continental breakfast' has freshly squeezed orange juice, home-made croissants and jams, and an English fry-up is also available. Day trips by superseacats to Calais and Ostend are organised. Sandgate has many antique shops and a well-restored Tudor castle. The Channel Tunnel is ten minutes' drive; Dover is eight miles away. (*John Biesmans, Janice Carrera, HS, and others*)

Open All year, except 1 week Oct, 4 weeks Jan. Restaurant closed Sun evening, all Mon, Tues midday, except bank holidays.
Rooms 12 double, 2 single.
Facilities Lift. Lounge/bar, restaurant (classical background music); terrace. Pebble beach, safe bathing, opposite. Not really suitable for ♿.
Location On seafront. 3 miles W of centre of Folkestone, on A259 coastal road to Hythe (some traffic noise). Train: Folkestone; bus/taxi.
Restrictions No smoking in restaurant. No dogs.
Credit cards All major cards accepted.
Terms B&B: single £45–£71, double £58–£76. Set lunch/dinner £22–£31; full alc £50. Weekend, midweek breaks.

SCARBOROUGH North Yorkshire — Map 4:C5

Interludes NEW/BUDGET
32 Princess Street
Scarborough YO11 1QR

Tel 01723-360513
Fax 01723-368597
Email interludes@ntlworld.com
Website homepage.ntlworld.com/interludes

Theatre buffs, Ian Grundy and Bob Harris, this year celebrate a decade of running their small guest house in the old town, below Scarborough's castle and above its harbour. They offer a variety of breaks associated with the Stephen Joseph Theatre, which regularly stages Alan Ayckbourn's plays. 'Behind the rather plain exterior and an ugly garage next door, is a beautifully decorated interior,' say the nominators, who liked also the smoke-free, child-free ambience. The bedrooms, named after theatres, Wyndham, Odeon, etc, have lush drapes, ornate mirrors, bold colours. In this tall and narrow building 'the less able-bodied might have a problem with the stairs'. Meals are communally served around two tables. Dinner is 'excellent value' at £12.50 – a typical menu: melon with raspberry coulis; salmon poached in wine, or baked chicken breast; apple and blackberry crumble with custard. Coffee and mints are included.

Breakfast can be continental, or light or full English. (*Andy and Sue Hetherington*)

Open All year, except owners' holidays. Restaurant closed 1 night a week.
Rooms 5 double. 1 with bath and shower, 3 with shower.
Facilities Lounge, dining room (theatrical background music during meals). Small patio. Unsuitable for ♿.
Location From harbour: narrow road between *Newcastle Packet* pub and *Princess* café. Princess St is 2nd on left; hotel halfway along. Parking.
Restrictions No smoking. No children under 16. No dogs.
Credit cards MasterCard, Visa.
Terms [2001] (*Not VAT-rated*) B&B. single £32, double £55. Set dinner £12.50. Discounts for 3 or more nights.

See also SHORTLIST

SEATON CAREW Co. Durham — Map 4:C4

The Staincliffe Hotel BUDGET — *Tel* 01429-264301
The Cliff — *Fax* 01429-421366
Seaton Carew TS25 1AB

Seaton Carew, 'founded by Quakers from Darlington whose influence on the local architecture is clearly visible', is an old holiday resort on the North Sea coast – it still has a substantial day-trip trade. Here, Jeff and Lynn Hind have given this pre-Victorian hotel 'the mother of all make-overs'. They employed two local designers with 'astounding results', said the nominator. Each room is hand-decorated in a different style, with much use of stencils. The Gothic Turret has walls stippled red with gold motifs; the Napoleon Campaign Tent suite has a four-poster bed; in Wisteria you might wake to the scent of orange groves; The Architectural Room is 'postmodern minimalist' in style. The bar is done with nautical bric-a-brac. 'The function room could be described as Art Deco massive, and the restaurant/bistro as Art Nouveau Baroque. The menu, if not entirely original, was interesting: Thai-style fish-cakes and nicely succulent medallions of beef made for a more exciting meal than expected. Fried fish, chips and mushy peas, the traditional northern seaside fare, is also available, and a note in the bedroom says that if you specify in advance what sort of fish you want, the chef will get it from the morning market and cook it to order.' There is a good choice of vegetarian dishes. The town is home to Teesside's chemical works, but 'once inside the hotel, you quickly forget them, such is the effort that has been put into the decor'. 'Good value.' Weddings and conferences are often held. (*PJ*)

Open All year.
Rooms 5 suites, 13 double, 2 single.
Facilities Foyer, lounge bar, cocktail bar, restaurant; background music throughout; ballroom (various entertainments: murder and mystery, etc); conference facilities. 2-acre garden overlooking sea. Unsuitable for ♿. Civil wedding licence.
Location On A178, W of Hartlepool marina, in resort 2 miles S of Hartlepool. From Hartlepool, on A689, turn right at *Owton Lodge* pub and roundabout. Follow road to sea; turn left; hotel ½ mile on left.

Restrictions No smoking in bedrooms. No dogs.
Credit cards All major cards accepted.
Terms [2001] B&B: single £48–£58, double £58–£68. Full alc £20. Christmas package.

SEAVIEW Isle of Wight — Map 2:E3

The Priory Bay Hotel
Priory Drive
Seaview PO34 5BU

Tel 01983-613146
Fax 01983-616539
Email enquiries@priorybay.co.uk
Website www.priorybay.co.uk

'Charming, well run, unpretentious.' 'Our deluxe room was large, nicely decorated, with two windows overlooking the sea – wonderful! The hotel is very comfortable, not lavish. Staff very friendly, though some were inexperienced. Both the *à la carte* and fixed-price menus were excellent, varied, and we could mix and match between the two. The standard of cooking was high. Lovely fresh-baked rolls were in plentiful supply; the wine list is fairly priced. Full marks for giving us the two-night Easter stay we wanted, unlike many of the local hotels that insisted on three.' Enthusiasm in 2001 for this informal hotel, both child- and dog-friendly, in an 'idyllic setting'. The remarkable building, renovated by Andrew Palmer, founder of the New Covent Garden Soup Company, and his brother James, is a Tudor farmhouse with Georgian, Victorian and modern additions, on the site of a Cluniac priory. The huge grounds contain a nine-hole par three golf course, and a track leads through bluebell woods to a lovely beach, with sand, rock pools, safe bathing, and a 'very good' seafood café. The 'magnificent public rooms' are admired, in particular the huge salon, with its octagonal window over the fireplace, luxurious sofas, coffee-table books and magazines. In the restaurant (with elaborate plasterwork and giant murals of local views of yesteryear), Amanda Webb cooks a modern European menu, eg, crab ravioli seasoned with ginger, coriander and chilli; rack of lamb on sweet garlic potatoes; sea bass with star anise and saffron sauce. The bedrooms vary from 'spacious and lovely' to 'pleasant, simply but adequately furnished, with good lighting'; a room in the eaves was thought 'delightful'. Cottages in the grounds, some 'attractive and thatched', some 'hideous', provide suites that are good for families and dog-owners (some are self-catering) 'but these rooms are not of the same standard as the rest'. *(Jean Taylor, John A Jenkins, LE)*

Open All year.
Rooms 4 suites, 24 double. Also 10 cottages. 2 ground-floor rooms.
Facilities Ramps. 2 lounges, bar, restaurant; classical background music all day; function facilities. 70-acre grounds: unheated outdoor pool; 9-hole par 3 golf course, tennis, beach: café, sailing, fishing, windsurfing. Riding, gliding nearby. Unsuitable for ♿. Civil wedding licence.
Location S of Seaview, between St Helens and Nettlestone. Bus/taxi from Ryde, 3 miles.
Restrictions Smoking discouraged in restaurant. No dogs in main hotel.
Credit cards Amex, MasterCard, Visa.
Terms [2001] B&B: single £49–£139, double £90–£248; D,B&B £69–£144 per person. Bar meals. Set dinner £25; full alc £34. 3-day midweek breaks. Christmas package. 1-night bookings sometimes refused Sat. ***V***

Seaview Hotel & Restaurant
High Street
Seaview PO34 5EX

Tel 01983-612711
Fax 01983-613729
Email reception@seaviewhotel.co.uk
Website www.seaviewhotel.co.uk

César award in 1988

Nicholas and Nicola Haywards' small hotel/restaurant 'of character' stands on the main road, leading down to the sea, of an old sailing village on the north-east shore of the island. It houses a large collection of clocks and things nautical. Lots of bright colours in the decor: 'Our room was mustard yellow and bottle green, spotless, but with a cramped bathroom,' one visitor wrote. Another enjoyed a 'large and pleasant' front room, with bay window and sea view. The 'helpfulness and friendliness of the staff' are praised – 'and they do their jobs very professionally'. 'Service was attentive without being fussy.' 'The owners are omnipresent.' Children are 'welcomed rather than merely tolerated'. With two restaurants, a pub and lounge bar on the ground floor, and in summer a pavement café, things can get very crowded (food is sometimes also served in the residents' lounge). In low season, the hotel is popular with retired people. It is too small to offer many facilities for children, but the adjacent two-bedroom cottage is good for a family. The rooms vary in size; rear ones arc quietest. Some overlook the car park, and one above the kitchens can be noisy until late. The cooking is mostly thought 'very good'. Plenty of choice on the menus, eg, herring roes on toasted muffin with lemon and capers; loin of pork with black pudding stuffing and cider sauce; brandy snap basket with blackcurrant sorbet. Or you could order fish and chips in the bar. At breakfast there is freshly squeezed orange juice, porridge and kippers; 'no horrid little packets; you are waited on from start to finish'. Dogs are welcomed. Guests have access to a new sports club nearby. (*JC, John Astle-Fletcher, HJM Tucker, and others*)

Open All year, except 3 days over Christmas. Restaurant closed Sun night, except bank holidays.
Rooms 2 suites, 14 double. 2 in annexe, with balcony. 2 on ground floor.
Facilities Lounge, 2 bars (background 'easy listening' music), restaurant; function room; patio. Access to local sports club (swimming pool, gym, tennis, etc). Sea, sandy beach 50 yds: sailing, windsurfing. Unsuitable for ♿.
Location Village centre. Follow signs for seafront. Small car park. Bus/taxi from Ryde 3 miles, Cowes 10 miles.
Restrictions No smoking: 1 dining room, lounge, 2 bedrooms. No children under 5 in restaurant after 7.30 pm. No dogs in public rooms.
Credit cards All major cards accepted.
Terms B&B: single from £55, double from £70, suite from £125. Bar meals. Set Sun lunch £15.95; full alc from £28. Child in parents' room: under 12, £2.50–£10.50. Weekend, midweek, painting breaks. New Year package. 1-night bookings refused weekends. *V*

SHEFFIELD South Yorkshire ***See SHORTLIST*** **Map 4:E4**

If you find details of a hotel's location inadequate, please tell us.

SHEPTON MALLET Somerset — Map 1:B6

Charlton House and Mulberry Restaurant
Charlton Road
Shepton Mallet BA4 4PR

Tel 01749-342008
Fax 01749-346362
Email enquiry@charltonhouse.com
Website www.charltonhouse.com

'You are always welcomed at your car and accompanied into the hotel.' The service – 'friendly, informal but highly professional' – makes this Domesday manor house a favourite with visitors. It was transformed into a small hotel in 1997 by Roger and Monty Saul, founders of the Mulberry label. The interior is a showcase for their products, and the decor is lavish and theatrical, with silks and velvets, bright colours, prints and paintings, knick-knacks, fresh flowers. Wellington boots, lacrosse sticks and fishing tackle are displayed at the entrance to give a country house feel. 'What we loved most was the individuality of the bedrooms: we've stayed in four so far and all are beautiful. Special mention should go to Adam and Eve (with a headboard depicting the naked couple with the serpent and docile lion) and Folly, which is huge and has an enormous freestanding cast iron bath,' writes one enthusiast. The restaurant, with its hooded kaftan chairs, has a *Michelin* star for Adam Fellows's modern cooking, eg, layers of feta cheese and red pepper confit; roast loin of venison with parsnip purée and port and black pepper reduction; warm pineapple Tatin with an orange and chilli caramel. Staff are 'young, intelligent, impeccably dressed'. Children are welcomed. The river Sheppey, with fishing rights, runs through the grounds, which get some noise from the busy road nearby. Wells is six miles away; Bath is 19 miles: other local sights include Glastonbury, Longleat, the Cheddar Gorge. (*Sophie Lutz and John Holborow, IE, and others*)

Open All year.
Rooms 3 suites, 13 double. 3 in lodge, 1 in coach house.
Facilities Ramps. Drawing room, bar, restaurant (light jazz/classical background music all day); conference/function facilities; sauna, plunge pool. 8-acre grounds: gardens, tennis, croquet, trout lake, river (fishing), helipad. Riding, golf nearby. Civil wedding licence.
Location On A361, 1 mile E of Shepton Mallet, towards Frome (on right). Train: Castle Cary, 4 miles.
Restrictions No smoking in restaurant. Dogs in 1 bedroom only, not in public rooms.
Credit cards All major cards accepted.
Terms B&B: double £155–£250, suite £250–£355. Set lunch £12.50–£16.50, dinner £38.50; full alc £50. Autumn/winter weekend, midweek breaks. Christmas package. 1-night bookings refused Fri/Sat.

****

Traveller's tale Hotel in Scotland. The owners of this hotel are much in evidence and are considerate hosts, but they tend to express trenchant views on such subjects as Thatcherism and fox-hunting. This puts the guest who disagrees in something of a quandary – although observation suggests that such guests are few and far between.

****

SHERINGHAM Norfolk — Map 2:A5

The Beaumaris NEW
15 South Street
Sheringham NR26 8LL

Tel 01263-822370
Fax 01263-821421
Email beauhotel@aol.com
Website www.ecn.co.uk/beaumaris

Owned by Stevens family since 1947, now run by 3rd generation, Alan and Hilary Stevens: traditional, reasonably priced hotel, with white walls and steep roof, in cul-de-sac in north Norfolk seaside town. Traditional decor: patterned carpets and chairs. No background music; straightforward cooking. 'Very relaxing atmosphere,' says nominator. Open 1 Mar–15 Dec. 21 bedrooms, some family, some on ground floor with wheelchair access. Lounge, bar/lounge, restaurant (no smoking); ramps. Garden with steam train alongside. Blue Flag beach 5 mins' walk; 18-hole golf course nearby. All major credit cards accepted. B&B £38–£42; D,B&B £52–£55. Snack lunches. Set dinner £14.95. More reports, please.

SHIPTON GORGE Dorset — Map 1:C6

Innsacre Farmhouse
Shipton Gorge
nr Bridport DT6 4LJ

Tel/Fax 01308-456137

'Seldom have we stayed in a more relaxed home. Sydney and Jayne Davies are friendly, amusing, wonderfully tolerant. They fall over themselves to make you happy.' 'Great hospitality.' More accolades this year for this 17th-century farm guest house. 'It is an interesting building, old, well loved, very Provençal in style, from wall colours and furniture to the huge French cups at breakfast.' One couple's first impression of the large, low-ceilinged sitting/dining room on a wet October evening was 'of gloom', but 'with a fire burning merrily and all the lights on, it was very cosy'. The position, in large, hilly grounds, 'is wonderful'. Free tea and home-made biscuits are provided for arriving guests. Mrs Davies's 'imaginative home cooking' is also admired. A three-course no-choice supper is served by arrangement, at 8 pm. Specialities include roast wild boar; ham hock and beans; baked pears with hot toffee sauce; apple tart. *Innsacre,* reached up a cobbled drive through large grounds, has a flowery terrace, gardens and an orchard. The large downstairs room is divided by screens to form a lounge with a huge inglenook fireplace, and a beamed, stone-walled dining area with oak tables and chairs. 'Unusual antiques, interesting paintings and prints, good fabrics, fresh flowers, all reflect the owners' taste.' The bedrooms (all were redecorated this year and given new towels) are furnished in French country style: oak beds, Egyptian cotton sheets, blue and white duvets. The hayloft is suitable for a family. The 'seriously addictive' cooked breakfast, at 8.45 am, includes fresh orange juice, a choice of English grill, continental brioche and pastries or American pancakes with yogurt, fruit and syrup. Dogs are welcomed (for a charge of £5 whatever the length of stay). House parties are catered for. The sea and the National Trust coastal path are three miles away. (*Ann Evans, RJ Endicott, Philip and Eileen Hall, and others*)

Open All year, except Christmas. Dining room closed midday, and Sat evening Easter–Oct.
Rooms 4 double, all with bath with shower attachment. No telephone.
Facilities Lounge/bar, dining area. No background music. 10-acre grounds. Fishing, shingle/sand beach nearby. Unsuitable for ♿.
Location 2½ miles SE of Bridport. Take A35 west from Dorchester. After *c.* 12 miles, 2nd left to Shipton Gorge; go round hill; entrance on left after *c.* ⅓ mile. Train: Dorchester; then taxi.
Restrictions Smoking in bar only (in evening only). No children under 9. No dogs in restaurant.
Credit cards MasterCard, Visa.
Terms B&B: single £50–£80, double £65–£80. Evening meal (by arrangement) £17.50. 10% reduction for 5 or more nights. Child in parents' room: £15. 1-night bookings refused Sat, bank holidays.

SHREWSBURY Shropshire *See SHORTLIST* — Map 3:B4

SHURDINGTON Gloucestershire — Map 3:D5

The Greenway
Shurdington,
nr Cheltenham GL51 5UG

Tel 01242-862352
Fax 01242-862780
Email greenway@btconnect.com

Creeper-clad mansion (Pride of Britain), Elizabethan in origin, 2½ miles SW of Cheltenham, set well back from the A46 in 8-acre grounds (croquet). Recently refurbished; 'lovely and peaceful'. New manager, Andrew MacKay, leads 'cheerful staff'. Traditional decor: antique furniture, formal flower arrangements; occasional classical background music. 'Public rooms confidently furnished'; large bedrooms in country house style. Modern English cooking, quite elaborate, by new chef, Dean Selby, served in formal restaurant (residents should book). Conservatory overlooks terrace and sunken garden with lily pond. No smoking: restaurant, 8 bedrooms. No children under 7. Guide dogs only. All major credit cards accepted. 21 bedrooms (some on ground floor). B&B £69.50–£107.50; D,B&B (min. 2 nights) £89.50–£132.50. Set lunch £18.50, dinner £38.50. More reports, please.

SIDMOUTH Devon *See SHORTLIST* — Map 1:C5

> 'Set meals' indicates fixed-price meals, with ample, limited or no choice on the menu. 'Full alc' is the hotel's estimated price per person of a 3-course *à la carte* meal, with a half bottle of house wine. 'Alc' is the price of an *à la carte* meal excluding the cost of wine.

SOAR MILL COVE Devon — Map 1:E4

Soar Mill Cove Hotel
Soar Mill Cove
nr Salcombe TQ7 3DS

Tel 01548-561566
Fax 01548-561223
Email info@makepeacehotels.co.uk
Website www.makepeacehotels.co.uk

'A welcoming atmosphere; delightful staff. The walks down to the beach, and the sunsets, are fabulous.' Praise this year for the Makepeace family's purpose-built hotel which stands at the head of an isolated cove near Salcombe. 'Nicely run [by chef/*patron* Keith Makepeace], in ravishing surroundings; expensive, but hard to fault in essentials,' wrote another visitor. Its most devoted fan found it 'as always supremely comfortable'. National Trust land is all around, and a beautiful bay, with a wide sandy beach, is a short distance away, down a hill. All the bedrooms are on the ground floor, and have patio doors opening on to a private terrace (one visitor found his 'a bit cheek-by-jowl with the neighbours'). All beds are new this year, and new thermostatic showers have been fitted in the bathrooms. Dinner orders are taken in the early evening, and opinions on the cooking vary from 'imaginative and good', 'fish is always excellent', to 'fussy'. The menu includes, eg, poached fillet of plaice stuffed with grapes, with a saffron stamen sauce; pan-fried breaded escalope of veal, glazed with a topping of Cornish Yarg and English mustard. The hotel bills itself as child-friendly, and parents appreciate the safe, small outdoor and indoor swimming pools, the play areas and acres of grass. Off-season it is popular with retired people. Beauty treatments, aromatherapy and cooking lessons are available. A car is essential if you want to explore, but be warned of 'very narrow lanes'. The Makepeaces also own the *Rosevine Hotel*, Portscatho, Cornwall. (*Val Hennessy, Phyllida Flint, Margaret Box, D Barnett, and others*)

Open Feb–end Dec.
Rooms 3 family suites, 18 double. All on ground floor.
Facilities Lounge (pianist twice weekly), bar, restaurant; small indoor swimming pool; treatment room (hairdressing, reflexology, aromatherapy, etc). 10-acre grounds: small swimming pool, tennis, putting, pet donkey, miniature pony, children's play area, jogging trail. Sea, sandy beach, 600 yds.
Location 3 miles W of Salcombe. From A381 turn right through Marlborough; follow signs for Soar, then Soar Mill Cove. Train: Totnes; bus: Malborough, 3½ miles; hotel will meet.
Restrictions No smoking: restaurant, bedrooms. No dogs in public rooms.
Credit cards Amex, MasterCard, Visa.
Terms B&B £75–£140; D,B&B £75–£180. Set lunch £25, dinner £34. 3-day packages. Cookery weekends. Christmas break.

SOMERTON Somerset — Map 1:C6

The Lynch BUDGET
4 Behind Berry
Somerton TA11 7PD

Tel 01458-272316
Fax 01458-272590
Email the_lynch@talk21.com
Website www.thelynchcountryhouse.co.uk

'A modest entrance from a village street leads into immaculate gardens, and at once you feel you're in the depths of the rolling Somerset countryside, with rustic views into the valley of the river Cary.' The owner, Roy Copeland, with his black poodle, Lotti, 'is a thoughtful host'. He carries your bags to your room in the Grade II listed Georgian building, with oatmeal walls and a grey slate roof, that he runs as an upmarket B&B. His staff are 'unobtrusive and friendly', and the bedrooms are well supplied with local information. The best rooms are on the first floor; the honeymoon suite overlooks herbaceous borders in front of the house, and has 'a wonderful Georgian four-poster'. Simpler, but still pretty, rooms are on the top floor. A glass lantern on the roof provides a panoramic view of the surroundings. There is a small sitting area for residents. Breakfast 'is a leisurely event', served in a room that overlooks a lake with black swans, exotic ducks and fish. There is a good choice of fruit, yogurt and cereals, and 'the best muesli I've ever tasted'. Mr Copeland has been known to forget the orders as he chats amiably among the tables. 'But I would sooner have a warmer, slightly haphazard atmosphere than a cool efficient one. Mr Copeland was a professional jazz musician; I would like my next visit to coincide with one of his jazz evenings.' No dinners, but advice is given, with menus, on where to eat in the village; a fireside dinner in the *Globe* pub, in the market place, was recently enjoyed. Somerton has a lovely church; Glastonbury and the Cheddar Gorge are nearby. (*Trevor Lockwood, CR*)

Open All year, except Christmas/New Year.
Rooms 5 double. Also 3-bedroomed cottage.
Facilities Breakfast room, small sitting area. No background music. 2½-acre grounds: lake. Unsuitable for ♿.
Location N edge of village (5 mins' walk to centre). Train: Castle Cary. Parking.
Restrictions No smoking. No dogs in public rooms.
Credit cards All major cards accepted.
Terms [2001] B&B: single £45–£53, double £49–£85.

SOUTHAMPTON Hampshire ***See SHORTLIST*** **Map 2:E2**

SOUTHWOLD Suffolk **Map 2:B6**

The Swan
Market Place
Southwold IP18 6EG

Tel 01502-722186
Fax 01502-724800
Email swan.hotel@adnams.co.uk
Website www.adnams.co.uk

A 300-year-old building, the premier hotel in this charming Suffolk town which 'has the feel of a real community, rather than a seaside resort'. Like most hotels round here, it is owned by Adnams the brewer and wine merchant. Carole Ladd is the manager. With white-framed windows, iron balconies, Union flag flying, it stands in the market place by the town hall. Its 'old-fashioned style' is liked. 'Service is excellent,' say visitors this year (it can be pressed at times). Other guests wrote of 'charming staff, polite management. 'Our bedroom's floor creaked, but its bathroom had been updated.' The public areas, often busy with outside guests taking tea and meals, are smart and traditional: a flagstoned hall, a spacious lounge with deep chairs and an open fire, a staircase with wrought iron banisters. A new chef, Ian Howell, supervises both bar and restaurant. His *table d'hôte* menu might include dressed crabs; roast chump of lamb with pease pudding, haricot beans and rosemary jus; calf's liver with bacon and black pudding. One couple wrote in 2001 of 'tough lamb and over-crisp vegetables', but the bar snacks are 'very good' and the wines as good and reasonable as ever'. Breakfast includes 'wonderful bacon and sausages', haddock and kippers. The best bedrooms are in the main house. The four-poster suite 'is luxurious'; a spacious double has a 'curved window on one side with a view of the sea, and a large main window overlooking the square'. A room under the eaves has 'a feeling of faded gentility'. The purpose-built bedrooms at the rear, round what was once a bowling green, are good for dog-owners. Southwold's long shingle beach is a short walk away. A special break, with tours of local gardens, is sometimes offered. (*Anne and Denis Tate, and others*)

Open All year. Restaurant closed midday Jan–Easter, except Christmas.
Rooms 2 suites, 37 double, 4 single. 17 in garden annexe (all on ground floor).
Facilities Lift. Drawing room, bar, restaurant; function facilities. No background music. ½-acre garden: croquet. Sea close by.
Location Central. Rear parking. Train: Halesworth, 9 miles, Darsham, 11 miles; taxi.
Restrictions No smoking in restaurant. No children under 5 in restaurant after 7 pm. Dogs in annexe rooms only; not in public rooms.
Credit cards All major cards accepted.
Terms [2001] B&B: single £65–£70, double £100–£140, suite £170–£180. Bar lunches. Set lunch £20, dinner £24.50; full alc £44.50. Christmas package.

STADDLEBRIDGE North Yorkshire — Map 4:C4

McCoy's
The Cleveland Tontine
Staddlebridge
Northallerton DL6 3JB

Tel 01609-882671
Fax 01609-882660
Email enquiries@mccoysatthetontine.co.uk
Website www.mccoysatthetontine.co.uk

César award in 1989

The McCoy brothers – Peter, Tom and Eugene – have become a northern institution at their quirky restaurant-with-rooms which they run with 'laid-back professionalism'. They pride themselves on their lack of formality, and describe the decor as 'a comfortable mismatch of colour, a pastiche of style and accent, born more out of penury than design'. The place may be slightly less eccentric after two decades, and they now employ a chef, Marcus Bennett, but *Guide* readers relish its exuberant style and the 'technically proficient, stylishly presented cooking that concentrates on flavour'. The Victorian stone house stands at the Cleveland Tontine, where two busy roads converge on the edge of the North Yorkshire moors. The furniture is a higgledy-piggledy mix: 'Comfy sofas and chairs from junk shops', potted plants and the odd cat in the lounges, while the bedrooms are cheerful, with contrasting wallpapers, good lighting, effective double glazing, plenty of storage space and a straightforward bathroom. The restaurant, dimly lit and with bare floorboards, potted palms, good napery and cutlery, opens for dinner on Friday and Saturday. Its eclectic fixed-price menus include dishes like black pudding with olive and basil focaccia and tomato jam; sea bass with deep-fried mussels and cous-cous; chocolate brioche bread-and-butter pudding. The downstairs bistro, open all week, serves similar dishes from a blackboard menu to loud '40s music; tables are closely packed. There is an 'early grazing' menu between 7 and 8 pm. The 70-item wine list is as cosmopolitan as the food, and has plenty of half bottles. The 'great breakfast', served until late in a 'lovely bright room', includes anything you want, even a newspaper. 'We had a gorgeous plate of exotic fruits, excellent scrambled eggs on toast made from home-made bread. The friendly young staff are efficient.' The McCoys now provide the catering on GNER's London-to-Edinburgh service. More reports, please.

Open All year, except 25/26 Dec, 1 Jan. Restaurant open Fri, Sat; bistro daily.
Rooms 6 double.
Facilities 2 lounges (residents only), breakfast room, bar, bistro, restaurant; background music 'as the mood takes us'. Garden. Unsuitable for ♿.
Location 6 miles NE of Northallerton, at junction of A19/A172 (rooms double-glazed); enter via southbound lane of A172.
Restriction No dogs in public rooms.
Credit cards All major cards accepted.
Terms [2001] B&B: single £75, double £95. Set lunch £9.95–£11.95, dinner £14.95–£16.95; full alc £37.

STAMFORD Lincolnshire — Map 2:B3

The George
71 St Martins
Stamford PE9 2LB

Tel 01780-750750
Fax 01780-750701
Email reservations@georgehotelofstamford.com
Website www.georgehotelofstamford.com

César award in 1986

Built in 1597, this 'very civilised' coaching inn has had many famous guests, including Charles I (1641), William III (1696) and the Duke of Cumberland returning from victory at Culloden (1745). With its mullioned windows, flagstoned entrance hall, old panelling and creaking floorboards, it is full of character and 'extremely comfortable'. It has an array of attractive public rooms and bars, and a 'lovely cobbled courtyard', flowery in summer with tubs and hanging baskets, where drinks are served. The London Room and the York Bar (with 'excellent Ruddles County direct from the barrel') were once waiting rooms for stagecoach passengers. 'Not cheap, but lives up to its reputation,' said a 2001 visitor who enjoyed his 'very pleasant room, excellently furnished'. Another wrote: 'It is often busy, but service does not suffer. The staff are exceptionally skilled; food, service and decor are of high quality.' Meals in the restaurant, candlelit at night, are traditional, eg, grilled Dover sole; calf's liver and bacon; roasts on a carving wagon; cheeses and puddings on trolleys. 'One of the few places where we regularly order good wine, due to their excellent pricing policy.' On busy Saturdays, dinner is sometimes in two shifts. Bedrooms vary greatly, and some are quite a walk from reception. Some have a four-poster, some have antiques. Roadside rooms get traffic noise. Some are ‘a bit basic’, and can be hot in summer. Unusually, a room-service cooked breakfast is available; otherwise it is taken among tropical plants in the garden room, where light meals and teas are also served. There is an ancient crypt under the cocktail bar, and a walled, monastic rear garden with a sunken lawn for croquet. Stamford is an unspoilt old market town. On its outskirts is Burghley House, a magnificent stately home with a 300-acre deer park. (Good Pub Guide, *David Barnett, and others*)

Open All year.
Rooms 1 suite, 36 double, 10 single.
Facilities Ramps. 2 lounges, 2 bars, 2 restaurants; 4 private dining rooms, business centre. No background music. 2-acre grounds: courtyard, monastery garden, croquet. Rutland Water 6 miles. Civil wedding licence.
Location ½ mile from centre (front rooms double-glazed; quietest overlook courtyard). From A1, turn at roundabout signposted Stamford B1081. Hotel at bottom of hill by traffic lights. Large car park. Railway station 100 yds.
Restrictions No smoking in main restaurant until after 10 pm. No dogs in restaurants.
Credit cards All major cards accepted.
Terms [2001] B&B: single £78–£110, double £105–£220, suite £145–£150. Light meals available. Set lunch £16.50–£17.50; full alc £44. Weekend rates. Special breaks Easter, Aug.

See also SHORTLIST

STAVERTON Devon — Map 1:D4

Kingston House

Staverton
nr Totnes TQ9 6AR

Tel 01803-762235
Fax 01803-762444
Email info@kingston-estate.net
Website www.kingston-estate.net

Michael and Elizabeth Corfield have restored their 18th-century wool merchant’s house in the lovely countryside of the South Hams near the Tudor town of Totnes, ‘with great care and attention’. ‘Fine features are to be found at every turn’, including ancient panelling, partially exposed murals and a magnificent marquetry staircase. ‘Entering the house is like stepping back into another century,’ one guest wrote. The three large bedrooms are full of authentic details (one bathroom is not *en suite*). ‘Magnificent antique four-poster beds, drapes, lovely rugs, valuable knick-knacks trustingly displayed, quality white linen, comfortable, non-creaky beds. No TV – hurrah!’ The Blue Bathroom has faux marble wall paintings, a huge 1830s bath, a view over the walled garden, the sound of rooks. Guests appreciate the welcome by the ‘sweet and caring’ hostess, the fires burning in the hall and lounge, the Great Danes, Apollo and Juno, dozing on the carpet. The public rooms are ‘lovely, large and comfortable’, but the piped classical music was less appreciated. In the pretty dining room, with only three tables, the no-choice dinner is based on 18th-century menus, eg, fillet of beef in red wine with oranges and mace; chicken supreme cooked in fruit juices with ginger and marmalade. But again this year a visitor thought it overpriced. When the house is full, guests can be accommodated in cottages (they have just been refurbished) which are otherwise let on a self-catering basis. More reports, please.

Open All year, except Christmas; dining room closed Christmas/New Year, and to non-residents.
Rooms 3 double (1 bathroom not *en suite*). Also 18 in 9 cottages (can be self-catering; 2 suitable for ♿). No TV.
Facilities Hall (classical background music), drawing room, sitting room with TV, dining room. 13-acre grounds. Golf, fishing nearby. Civil wedding licence.
Location 4 miles N of Totnes. From A38 at Buckfastleigh, 22 miles S of Exeter: A384 towards Totnes for 2½ miles. At Staverton, bear left at *Sea Trout* inn; follow Kingston signs 1 mile. Train: Totnes; taxi.
Restrictions No smoking: dining room, main house bedrooms. Children and dogs in cottages only.
Credit cards All major cards accepted.
Terms [2001] B&B: single £85, double £130, suite £140–£150; D,B&B £99.50–£119.50 per person. Set dinner £32.40–£34.50. *V*

STOCKCROSS Berkshire — Map 2:D2

The Vineyard
Stockcross, Newbury
RG20 8JU

Tel 01635-528770
Fax 01635-528398
Email general@the-vineyard.co.uk
Website www.the-vineyard.co.uk

Tall metal sculptures welcome visitors to the car park, and tongues of flame leap from the surface of a large pool in front of this extravagantly renovated old hunting lodge in a moneyed, if not particularly attractive, area near Newbury. It is owned by Sir Peter Michael, founder of Classic FM, and named in honour of his Californian winery. Our inspectors reported: 'The decor is stunning, in lush country house style, based on good antiques and Sir Peter's eclectic art collection: colourful and expensive oriental rugs, sofas piled with large buttoned cushions, chess sets, artistic flower arrangements, plants, magazines, newspapers and books give a welcoming air. Our bedroom, designed by Emily Todhunter, was huge, with views of the garden, bouffant drapes, antiques, paintings (mostly of naked women), a four-poster, poor reading lights, a well-designed bathroom. But we heard the traffic on the busy road by the hotel, and also the noise of a pump.' A visitor this year was disappointed by his bedroom (Caymus) which was 'too dark' though its bathroom was 'large and splendid'. In the *Michelin*-starred restaurant, where a pianist sometimes plays, the wine list is either 'a dream' or 'ludicrously long', depending on your taste, with 1,400 wines (500 are Californian). The chef, Billy Reid, who formerly worked at *L'Escargot*, in London, serves 'beautifully presented and well-executed' dishes, eg, breast of guineafowl with prunes, baby carrots and turnips; loin of lamb with Madeira and rosemary jus. There is a separate vegetarian menu. This year's visitor did not particularly warm to the place ('there was no comment card, nor did reception ask: "Was everything all right?"'), but he found dinner 'excellent', the staff 'delightful' and breakfast 'perfectly satisfactory'. Conferences and functions are catered for. (*John Gibbon, and others*)

Open All year, except Christmas.
Rooms 15 suites, 10 double, 6 single. Some on ground floor.
Facilities Lift, ramps. Lounge, bar, conservatory, restaurant (pianist or classical background music); private dining room; function rooms, spa: swimming pool, whirlpool, gym. Garden: patio. Civil wedding licence.
Location 3 miles NW of Newbury. A4 to Hungerford; join B4000 at bypass junction; *Vineyard* is signposted. Train: Newbury; taxi.
Restrictions No smoking in some bedrooms. No dogs.
Credit cards All major cards accepted.
Terms [2001] (*Excluding VAT*) B&B: single from £149, double from £209, suite from £249; D,B&B (Fri–Sun) £125–£165 per person. Set lunch £17, dinner £47; full alc £48. Spa, golf weekends.

STOKE GABRIEL Devon — Map 1:D4

Gabriel Court
Stoke Gabriel
nr Totnes TQ9 6SF

Tel 01803-782206
Fax 01803-782333
Email obeacom@aol.com
Website www.gabrielcourthotel.co.uk

'The sort of hotel we had been hoping to find,' says a report this year on the Beacom family's unpretentious white-painted manor house in an old village on an inlet of the river Dart. Another told of 'ideal owner/hosts – ready to chat when you want and they have time, happy not to, when you or they don't'. A regular visitor wrote: 'It suits you or it doesn't, but for sheer reliability it is difficult to beat.' Some find it 'dated'; admirers think it 'very well run'. The 14th-century building, tower topped with a weather vane, was occupied by one family from 1487 until 1928; bedrooms are in a modern extension. In the terraced Elizabethan-style gardens are clipped yew arches, box hedges, magnolia trees, a swimming pool and a grass tennis court. One of the Beacoms is always around; the owner or his son comes out to greet arriving guests and carry their luggage along the brightly carpeted corridor. Most bedrooms face south. The food ('properly hot') is English traditional (main courses like roast beef, or grilled lemon sole; old-time puddings and a cheese trolley to end). Vegetables are plainly served ('overcooked' for some tastes). Some visitors would like a lighter option to the five-course (£28) set dinner menu. The half-board price includes afternoon tea and a traditional breakfast. Children are welcomed; so are dogs. Trips on the Dart can be organised. Paignton and the coast (safe beaches) are near. Greenway House, the home of Agatha Christie, is three miles away. (*Mrs A Pantin, Stephen Hugh-Jones, Richard Creed, and others*)

Open All year. Dining room closed midday, except Sun.
Rooms 3 family, 14 double, 2 single. 1 chalet.
Facilities Lounge, bar lounge, TV/meeting room, dining room. No background music. 2½-acre garden: heated swimming pool, tennis, children's playground. River Dart, fishing 300 yds. Golf, riding nearby. Beach 3 miles. Unsuitable for ♿.
Location In village 3 miles SW of Paignton; turn S off A385 to Totnes. Train: Totnes/Paignton; taxi.

Restrictions No smoking in dining room. Dogs must be on a lead in public rooms.
Credit cards All major cards accepted.
Terms [2001] B&B: single £49–£59, double £80; D,B&B: single £80–£85, double £130–£135. Packed lunches available. Set Sun lunch £13.50, dinner £28. Christmas package.

STOKE-ON-TRENT Staffordshire ***See SHORTLIST*** **Map 3:B5**

STON EASTON Somerset — Map 2:D1

Ston Easton Park NEW
Ston Easton, nr Bath
BA3 4DF

Tel 01761-241631
Fax 01761-241377
Email stoneastonpark@stoneaston.co.uk
Website www.stoneaston.co.uk

A magnificent Palladian mansion in a large park between Bath and Wells. Its gardens were designed by Humphry Repton in the 18th century; the river Norr flows over his flight of shallow cascades; ancient trees stand on green lawns; there is a large herb and vegetable garden. The sitting rooms and library are grand, with antiques, fine paintings, comfortable sofas, elegant flower arrangements. The dining room has a modern decor of white-painted panelling, bamboo chairs, flowers and candles. There are three spacious, air-conditioned suites in a garden cottage. The bedrooms have antiques, paintings, ornaments, etc. Those on the first floor have huge windows and fine proportions; smaller ones are on the floor above, and inspectors thought theirs expensive (£255 B&B) for its size, and the four-poster poorly lit for reading. 'The young staff were friendly, if sometimes amateurish,' they wrote, 'but we never saw the manager; we thought he should have come to apologise after we complained about a noisy extractor fan (but we did get a price reduction). The dinner was good in the modern manner – very pretty artichoke starter and crayfish risotto, but a scarcity of vegetables, and we found the restaurant atmosphere a bit staid. Breakfast was all right. We enjoyed walks in the garden with the house spaniel.' Ston Easton's new owners, Von Essen Hotels, also own *Congham Hall*, Grimston, and *The Mount Somerset*, Lower Henlade (*qqv*), and they recently bought *Thornbury Castle*, Thornbury, on which we'd like reports, please.

Open All year.
Rooms 3 suites (in cottage, 75 yds), 18 double, 1 single.
Facilities Drawing room, salon, library, restaurant, 2 private dining rooms; terrace. 30-acre grounds: tennis, river. Only restaurant suitable for ♿. Civil wedding licence.
Location On A37 Bristol–Shepton Mallet. Train: Bath, etc; then taxi.
Restrictions No smoking in restaurant. No children under 7, except babies. No dogs in house (kennelling in basement).
Credit cards All major cards accepted.
Terms B&B: single £105–£130, double £170–£390, suite £290–£390. English breakfast £5 added. D,B&B £120–£235 per person. Set lunch (2–3 courses) £11–£16, dinner £39.50; full alc £52. Christmas package. *V*

STONOR Oxfordshire — Map 2:C3

The Stonor Arms
Stonor
nr Henley-on-Thames
RG9 6HE

Tel 01491-638866
Fax 01491-638863
Email stonorarms.hotel@virgin.net
Website www.stonor-arms.co.uk

Smart restaurant/hotel, managed by Sophia Williams, in 18th-century inn in centre of village on B480, 5 miles NW of Henley. Cosy lounge with open fire; bar with 'very Henley decor'. Formal restaurant (no smoking) and small conservatory serve modern English cooking. Good breakfast. No background music. Civil wedding licence. 2-acre walled garden. Car park. 10 bedrooms (with antiques, good fabrics; 4 no-smoking, 1 adapted for ♿) in converted barn at rear, well away from road. No children under 13 at dinner. No dogs in public rooms, except bar. Amex, MasterCard, Visa accepted. B&B: single £120, double £145–£175. Bar meals; full alc £35. A new chef this year, and recent reports mixed; we'd like more, please. *V*

STOW-ON-THE-WOLD Gloucestershire — Map 3:D6

Grapevine Hotel NEW
Sheep Street
Stow-on-the-Wold GL54 1AU

Tel 01451-830344
Fax 01451-832278
Email enquiries@vines.co.uk
Website www.vines.co.uk

In centre of old Cotswold market town: Sandra Elliott's hotel (Best Western), managed by John Fraser. Good food in lovely conservatory canopied by ancient vine. Lounge, bar (snacks served); background CDs. Weddings, functions catered for. Car park. No smoking: restaurant, bedrooms. 22 rooms – nominators admired theirs ('chintzy, well lit, warm') in garden annexe. All major credit cards accepted. B&B: single £77–£97, double £115–£135. Set lunch £13, dinner £27.50. More reports, please. *V*

The Royalist NEW
Digbeth Street
Stow-on-the-Wold GL54 1BN

Tel 01451-830670
Fax 01451-870048
Email info@theroyalisthotel.co.uk
Website www.theroyalisthotel.co.uk

Said to be the oldest inn in England, *The Royalist* was taken over in 2000 by Alan and Georgina Thompson, formerly of *755* restaurant in London (he is a member of the Slow Food Movement). 'Our twin-bedded room was the smallest we have ever stayed in,' one couple wrote in 2001. But they liked the mix of old prints and striking modern art in the corridors, and the 'immaculate housekeeping'. 'They have made a fine job of restoring it,' says an inspector. 'Its unique antiquity is agreeably understated.' He admired the 'tasteful decor' of his attic bedroom, Saxon (with vaulted ceiling and beams), and its good lighting, but thought it expensive (it is small, with only one window). 'In the elegant *947AD* restaurant, our starter was a brilliantly conceived dish of seared scallops with aubergine crisps and caramelised apples and onions, definitely of *Michelin*-star quality. A main course of sea bream with spicy Puy lentils was also very good, as was the apple tarte Tatin with ginger and honey ice cream. Mrs Thompson made an agreeable impression as she chatted around the tables.' 'Service can be disorganised at meals', and another report mentioned a lack of 'nice touches' in the bedroom. The general verdict: 'With the problems ironed out, this could be a class act.' Alfresco meals are served in the inn's small landscaped garden, and a conservatory is planned. The Thompsons also own the adjacent *Eagle and Child*, where they plan to serve 'jolly good pub food' seven days a week. They also hope to serve a traditional spit roast (a baron of local beef) on the first Sunday of each month.

Open All year.
Rooms 1 suite, 7 double. 4 more (2 on ground floor) planned for 2002.
Facilities 2 lounges, pub (background music sometimes), restaurant. Patio.
Location Central, set back from main road and green. A424 Burford–Stow. Turn right at top of hill by traffic lights; 200 yds on left. Parking.
Restrictions No smoking: restaurant, bedrooms. No children under 5 in restaurant. Dogs in bar only.
Credit cards Amex, MasterCard, Visa.
Terms B&B: single £52.50–£90, double £67.50–£130, suite £127.50–£170. Set lunch £9.50–£20; full alc £30. Christmas package. ***V***

STRATFORD-UPON-AVON Warwickshire — Map 3:D6

Caterham House
58/59 Rother Street
Stratford-upon-Avon CV37 6LT
Tel 01789-267309
Fax 01789-414836

César award in 1998

A theatre-goer arriving from a nine-hour Royal Shakespeare Company marathon (all three parts of *Henry VI* in one day) was impressed to find that Dominique Maury, the Anglophile French owner of this B&B, had already sat through the same epic. 'Conversation for theatre-goers is easy and informed, as M. Maury appears to have seen all the RSC productions in the last 20 years.' Another visitor liked the 'nice combination of privacy and intimacy'. This coral-pink Georgian House, a short walk from the theatre, is popular with theatre-goers and actors. M. Maury runs it with his English wife, Olive, who is responsible for the idiosyncratic decor: 'beautiful hall, landings and stairs; gleaming paintwork; unusual pictures, painted furniture, English and French antiques'. Each bedroom has its own character; some have a brass bedstead (some beds are king-size, others may be narrow). The rooms have plants and flowers, but one reporter 'wished for a bedside table'. 'The cooked breakfasts are superb, and the croissants, needless to say, are the best. Very good value.' Dominique Maury presides over the 'excellent' bar in the lounge, which opens on to a small flowery patio. Plenty of restaurants nearby. Close to shops and market. (*Andrew and Christine McManus, Jim and Lucy Bowers, and others*)

Open All year, except Christmas Day.
Rooms 14 double. 2 in annexe, 2 in cottage. No telephone (payphone available).
Facilities Lounge with TV, bar, breakfast room; no background music; small patio. Unsuitable for ♿.
Location Central, opposite police station (some traffic noise). Car park.
Restriction Dogs by arrangement; not in public rooms or unattended in bedrooms.
Credit cards MasterCard, Visa.
Terms B&B: single £60–£70, double £80–£90. Child in parents' room: babies free; under 10, 50% of adult rate.

STRETTON Rutland — Map 2:A3

Ram Jam Inn
Great North Road
Stretton LE15 7QX

Tel 01780-410776
Fax 01780-410361
Email rji@rutnet.co.uk
Website www.ramjaminn.co.uk

An unusual name, and an unusual entry for the *Guide*: Mike Littlemore and Margaret Cox's inn on the Great North Road between Grantham and Stamford is more like a motel with attitude – an interesting stopping place for travellers on the A1(M). Some redecoration has taken place this year. It has wooden floors, terracotta tiles, cheerful colours, an open-plan kitchen, a bar, café and bistro, decorated with old copper pans, stone cider jars and the like. Eating arrangements are flexible (no fixed menus). In the bar area, visitors perch on stools; tables are dotted around. Food is 'simple and good': steak-and-kidney pudding; fish and chips; polenta cakes; always a dish of the day; calorific puddings like raspberry cranachan; jam roly poly. Bread and teatime scones are home-baked. Drinks range from tea, coffee, freshly squeezed orange juice to beers and a serviceable list of wines. The bedrooms, upstairs, are bright, with patterned wallpaper, wicker chairs, an efficient bathroom; all but one overlook the garden and orchard, so traffic noise is not too much of a problem. Breakfast includes hearty cooked dishes and the morning newspapers. More reports, please.

Open All year, except 25 Dec.
Rooms 1 family, 6 double.
Facilities Ramp. Open-plan bar/café/bistro; light background music all day; conference room. 3-acre grounds: patio, sunken garden. Only eating/sitting areas suitable for ♿.
Location W side of A1, 9 miles NW of Stamford. Travelling S leave A1 on B668 to Oakham; travelling N leave A1 through Texaco garage just past B668 turn-off. Large car park.
Restrictions No smoking in eating areas. Dogs outside only.
Credit cards Amex, MasterCard, Visa.
Terms [2001] Room: single £46, double £56–£66, family £72. Breakfast £5.75. Full alc £28.10.

> Don't let old favourites down. Hotels are dropped when there is no endorsement.

STURMINSTER NEWTON Dorset — Map 2:E1

Plumber Manor
Sturminster Newton DT10 2AF

Tel 01258-472507
Fax 01258-473370
Email book@plumbermanor.com
Website www.plumbermanor.com

César award in 1987

'Richard Prideaux-Brune never changes. He is always most charming and quite a wag. Fortunately, the character of his country hotel has not changed either; ie, it is un-plush, in places pleasantly old-fashioned.' This is a family concern, run, with his wife Alison, by Mr Prideaux-Brune, in the Jacobean house which has been in his family since the early 17th century. His brother Brian presides over the kitchen. Two black Labradors 'add a special charm'. Some bedrooms in the main house may be in need of decoration (they lead off a gallery hung with family portraits). The best rooms, in a converted barn, are spacious and well equipped, though their bathrooms are 'rather dated'. 'The quality of the food and service is quite exceptional,' says a new visitor. Another guest writes of 'the very best of home cooking'. The English/French dishes might include Thai mussels with coconut milk; fillet of beef rolled in herbs and porcini, wrapped in Denhay ham. The dessert trolley, 'not for the faint-hearted', is laden with dishes like chocolate truffle torte, and lemon and ginger crunch. 'No hint of pretentiousness, as reflected in a reasonable and practical house wine list.' Two marked walks lead from the grounds. Local attractions include the lovely old town of Sherborne; the sights of Hardy country; Cerne Abbas, Old Wardour Castle and Kingston Lacy. (*NM Mackintosh*, *SF Riddell, and others*)

Open All year, except Feb. Restaurant closed midday, except Sun.
Rooms 16 double. 10 in stable courtyard (2 on ground floor).
Facilities 2 lounges (1 with bar), gallery, restaurant. No background music. 7-acre grounds: garden, tennis, croquet, trout stream; stabling for visiting horses. Golf, swimming, fishing, clay-pigeon shooting nearby.
Location 2 miles SW of Sturminster Newton; turn off A357 towards Hazelbury Bryan. Train: Gillingham, Dorset; then taxi.
Restrictions Children and dogs by prior arrangement. No dogs (except owners') in public rooms.
Credit cards All major cards accepted.
Terms B&B: single £85–£100, double £100–£155. Set lunch (Sun) £17.50, dinner £23. Child in parents' room: £10. Short breaks Nov–Mar. 10% discount on 2-night stay Oct–Apr.

> Always let a hotel know if you have to cancel a booking, whether you have paid a deposit or not. Hotels sustain huge losses due to 'no-shows'.

Stourcastle Lodge
Gough's Close
Sturminster Newton DT10 1BU

Tel 01258-472320
Fax 01258-473381
Email enquiries@stourcastle-lodge.co.uk
Website www.stourcastle-lodge.co.uk

Ken and Jill Hookham-Bassett's 300-year-old house, with a slate roof and tall white chimneys, stands in a traffic-free close off the high street of this small market town. They are 'welcoming and hard-working hosts', who offer 'good value for money', say *Guide* readers. Dinners are 'imaginative, and of a consistently high standard'. Works by local artists hang on the walls; in the cottage-style garden, humorous sculptures, eg, Henrietta and her seven piglets, are scattered around. All the bedrooms overlook the garden, and are named after members of the Dashwood family, who owned the lodge in the 18th century. They are decorated with stencils, and all but one have an antique brass bed; two have a whirlpool bath. A collection of antique kitchen implements is displayed in the dining room, where Mrs Hookham-Bassett's Aga-cooked meals are served. Coq au vin; breast of duck on a pea and mint sauce; queen of puddings; whisky and lemon bread-and-butter pudding are some of the traditional dishes on her menus (no choice until dessert). Herbs and vegetables come from the garden. No licence; bring your own wine. 'Very good breakfasts' (with home-made muesli, bread and preserves, and free-range eggs). The river Stour, with fishing, is 300 yards away. Stourhead is nearby. Bath, Glastonbury, Salisbury and Dorchester all in striking distance. More reports, please.

Open All year. Lunch not served.
Rooms 5 double.
Facilities Lounge, dining room. No background music. ¼-acre garden. River with coarse fishing 100 yds. Unsuitable for ♿.
Location 25 yds from centre.
Restrictions No smoking: restaurant, bedrooms. No dogs.
Credit cards MasterCard, Visa.
Terms B&B: single £41–£48, double £63–£77. Set dinner £19.50. Child in parents' room: 50% of adult rate. Reductions for long stays. Christmas package.

SUTTON COLDFIELD West Midlands — Map 3:C6

New Hall
Walmley Rd
Walmley, Sutton Coldfield
B76 1QX

Tel 0121-3782442
Fax 0121-3784637
Email newhall@thistle.co.uk
Website www.newhallhotel.net

The oldest inhabited moated manor house in England is an exception to the *Guide*'s practice of eschewing large chains. It belongs to the Thistle Group but 'the general set-up and attention to detail are atypical of a chain hotel', according to a regular visitor. 'The manager, Caroline Parkes, sets high personal standards and demands equally high standards of the staff.' The magnificent 12th-century building has mullioned windows, stained glass, much panelling and carved oak. Terraced gardens, designed in the 16th and 17th centuries, lead to wooded areas, walks, and outdoor entertainments (see below). Some of the impressive public rooms are given over to functions and conferences: 'The Great Chamber is quite stunning.' The meals served in the formal dining room (with stained-glass windows) have been admired too. There is a new chef again this year, Simon Malin, who has an 'eclectic' style, eg, fresh herb and lemon risotto with a rosette of seared scallops; braised belly of pork with a potato, chorizo and bean cassoulet; iced cinnamon and apple parfait with hot apple fritters. A light breakfast can be served in the bedrooms, a generous cooked one is available in the restaurant. The best bedrooms, in the main house, are 'sumptuous', with heavily festooned curtains, a four-poster bed, a decanter of sherry, home-made biscuits. Each is named after a type of lily (Lucinda, Dawn, etc). The rooms in a purpose-built wing are good too, if 'less interesting'. The new leisure spa has an indoor swimming pool, gym, sauna and steam room – guests may use it free of charge. Prices have risen considerably. The Snow Dome indoor ski slope at Tamworth is 10 minutes' drive away; Birmingham's airport is nearby; the city centre is 20 minutes' drive away. (*PR*)

Open All year.
Rooms 10 suites, 50 double. Some on ground floor, 1 adapted for ♿.
Facilities 2 drawing rooms, cocktail bar, restaurant; function facilities. Background music. 26-acre grounds: gardens, woodland walks, putting green, 9-hole par 3 golf course, croquet, floodlit tennis, trout lake; spa: indoor swimming pool, sauna and steam room. Civil wedding licence.
Location 8 miles from Birmingham centre. On B4148, near Walmley village; close to M42 and M6 motorways (hotel will send directions).
Restrictions No smoking: restaurant, most bedrooms. No children under 8. No dogs.
Credit cards All major cards accepted.
Terms [2001] Room: single from £156, double from £189, suite from £325. Breakfast £15.75. Set meals £29.50–£39.50. Child in parents' room: under 16, free. Weekend, champagne, theatre breaks. Christmas, New Year packages.

SWAFFHAM Norfolk — Map 2:B5

Strattons
4 Ash Close
Swaffham PE37 7NH

Tel 01760-723845
Fax 01760-720458
Email strattonshotel@btinternet.com
Website www.strattons-hotel.co.uk

'An eccentric and most enjoyable stay, as if one was in a very pleasant time warp. A splendid, varied and innovative meal.' Praise this year for Les and Vanessa Scott's informally run Grade II listed Palladian-style villa. Former art students, they combine vivid design with a 'green' philosophy: they took part in a government project to minimise waste, and have won a clutch of awards, including the British Airways Tourism for Tomorrow UK award. Other compliments: 'Considerate, charming hosts.' 'A singular place, run by a couple who care.' 'Both romantic *and* child-friendly.' Though near the centre of the old market town, *Strattons* has a rural feel: bantams, guineafowl and ducks peck under old trees in the garden. It is the Scotts' family home, inhabited also by their two children and their pets. The decor is found 'cluttered' by some, 'inspiring, invigorating' by others. In the public rooms, 'every surface is covered': cats – both real and artificial – abound; collector's items include an old sewing machine, a marble phrenological bust. Exotic bedrooms include the Venetian Room, vivid blue, with a mural of Botticelli's Venus in the bathroom; the Tuscan Room (Mediterranean decor). The Moroccan-style room, painted red throughout, has red plush, 'splendid quirky' details, a bathroom like a tent, a huge bath. The Sea Room is new this year. Vanessa Scott's daily-changing four-course dinner menu uses locally grown vegetables, and home-grown herbs and edible flowers. 'Starters like poached garlic and cheese custard; a fragrant soup each night; roast pork with caramelised apples and a mustard and Calvados sauce; wonderful wild mushroom risotto; stunning steamed apricot pudding. Wines come from an extensive cellar – most evenings we left the choice to Les Scott' (his hand-written list offers plenty by the glass). 'Great breakfasts' have home-blended muesli, kedgeree, oyster mushrooms on toast, goat's cheese omelette. 'Slightly expensive but the peace and hospitality eased the path.' Dogs are welcomed. Swaffham has elegant 18th-century buildings, and a traditional market on Saturday. Houghton village (National Trust) and many medieval churches are nearby; the North Norfolk Heritage Coast is 30 minutes' drive. (*John Townsend, Sheena Canham*)

Open All year, except Christmas. Lunch by arrangement.
Rooms 1 suite, 5 double.
Facilities Drawing room, TV room, restaurant (occasional background music); terrace. 1-acre garden. Unsuitable for ♿.
Location Enter Ash Close at N end of Market Place, between estate agent and Express Cleaners. Ample private parking. Train/bus: King's Lynn/Downham Market; then taxi or coach.
Restrictions No smoking. No dogs unaccompanied in bedrooms.
Credit cards Amex, MasterCard, Visa.
Terms [2001] B&B: single from £80, double from £90, suite from £150. Set dinner £32. 3-night midweek rates. 1-night bookings sometimes refused.

SWINBURNE Northumberland — Map 4:B3

The Hermitage BUDGET — *Tel* 01434-681248
Swinburne — *Fax* 01434-681110
nr Hexham NE48 4DG — *Email* stewart@thehermitagenow.freeserve.co.uk

'No nonsense is the key to this most attractive house in large and delightful grounds,' says a recent visitor. It is the family home of Katie and Simon Stewart, just four miles from Hadrian's Wall. They are 'warm-hearted hosts' though, as is often the way with a family-run B&B, guests are expected to be out of the house between 10.30 am and 5 pm. No signs proclaim its existence, but careful instructions are given. You approach through a grand arch and up a long private drive, bordered in spring by daffodils. The public rooms are 'superb, restful', with a 'true country house feel', family portraits and good antiques. Bedrooms are 'large and comfortable'; bathrooms are 'well equipped, with constantly hot towel rails'. One room, 'reached up a staircase, round corners and along halls', has views over the garden and woodland beyond from one window, and the large vegetable patch from the other. Period furniture and appropriate decor combine with practicalities like two suitcase stands. Breakfast is a hearty affair with lots of thick toast', though one visitor found six days' of canned grapefruit and a choice of three cereals from family-sized packets a little tiresome'. In fine weather, it is served on a terrace. Several good pubs are within 15 minutes' drive of this hamlet close to Hexham. Swinburne has a large reservoir and a 17th-century house on the site of an old castle. Many of Northumberland's castles, mansions and gardens are within easy reach. (*RO, and others*)

Open Mar–Sept inclusive.
Rooms 2 suites, 1 double. No telephone, TV.
Facilities Drawing room with TV, breakfast room. No background music. 2-acre garden: tennis. Unsuitable for ♿.
Location A68 for 7 miles N of Corbridge; turn left on to A6079. Lodge gates 1 mile on right. Follow drive for ½ mile.
Restrictions No smoking upstairs. No children under 10. No dogs.
Credit cards None accepted.
Terms [2001] B&B £30–£50.

TALLAND-BY-LOOE Cornwall — Map 1:D3

Talland Bay Hotel
Talland-by-Looe PL13 2JB

Tel 01503-272667
Fax 01503-272940
Email tallandbay@aol.com
Website www.smoothhound.co.uk/hotels/tallandb

César award in 1996

'A quiet, comfortable hotel; stunning views,' says a visitor this year to this 'lovely old house' owned by Barry and Annie Rosier. It stands in sheltered subtropical gardens, 150 feet above a wide bay. The 16th-century building has been much extended over the years, creating 'a harmonious whole', write inspectors in 2001. 'Even in the owners' absence, this is a smooth operation.' The style is not fulsome: some reports tell of an 'aloof welcome' – 'reception isn't warm, but you get used to it'. But others called the hotel 'delightful', the staff 'competent', and front-of-house 'extremely pleasant'. 'Food has improved' since the arrival last year of the chef Mathew Read. The wood-panelled dining room 'is extremely attractive, with small-paned windows, antique china in alcoves; fresh flowers'; the best tables have good views. 'Delicious *amuse-gueules* come with pre-dinner drinks. The menus are well balanced, nicely cooked, with a wide choice; desserts the weakest point.' Typical main courses: confit of duck on a white bean casserole with smoked bacon and thyme; seared scallops with basil linguine, tomato sauce and Parma ham; always a vegetarian choice. The bedrooms vary greatly; the best have 'smart draperies and great views'. Some, in the oldest part, have walls three feet thick. Some have a private garden. Some are quite small, and some bathrooms may be 'cramped'. Five rooms are in cottages – one, near the car park and kitchen, suffers from noise and overheating; there are two family suites. Light lunches are served in the bar or on the terrace. Breakfasts have fresh orange juice, 'nice scrambled eggs', a copious mixed grill. Afternoon tea, with 'luscious cakes', is included in the room rate. There is easy access to the coastal path. The Heligan Gardens, the Eden Project, and several National Trust properties are nearby. (*John and Pat Woodliffe, Stephen Cooper; also Barry Rennick, and others*)

Open Feb–end Dec.
Rooms 1 suite, 2 family, 16 double, 3 single. 5 in cottages.
Facilities Lounge, library, bar, restaurant; patio. No background music. 2½-acre garden: swimming pool, badminton, putting, croquet. Beach 5 mins' walk. Golf nearby. Unsuitable for ♿.
Location 2½ miles SW of Looe. Left at hotel sign on Looe–Polperro road. Train: Liskeard, 5 miles; taxi/branch line to Looe.
Restrictions No smoking in restaurant. No children under 5 at dinner. Dogs by arrangement in some bedrooms; not in public rooms.
Credit cards All major cards accepted.
Terms [2001] B&B £47–£79; D,B&B £67–£99. Snack lunches. Set lunch £12.50, dinner £23; full alc £39.50. Reductions for children, according to age. Off-season breaks. Christmas, New Year packages.

TAPLOW Buckinghamshire — Map 2:D3

Cliveden
Taplow SL6 0JF

Tel 01628-668561 (*in UK* 0800 454063)
Fax 01628-661837 (*in UK* 0800 454064)
Email reservations@clivedenhouse.co.uk
Website www.clivedenhouse.co.uk

A magnificent stately home, set above the Thames in large National Trust grounds. Its history is long and colourful: three dukes lived here; so did the Astor family, for four generations, when they entertained politicians and royalty, and Christine Keeler famously frolicked in the swimming pool. It is now an expensive hotel, owned by an American-based company, and run in the style of an Edwardian house party: guests' names on hand-written cards on bedroom doors, butlers and footmen at the ready, maids in pinafores. There have been many changes in the past year. Vivien Sirotkin is now manager, and a new head chef was due to be appointed as we went to press: he will supervise the two restaurants, *The Terrace*, and *Waldo's* (currently *Michelin*-starred). We'd like reports on these developments, please. Last year, inspectors liked the 'trappings of a grand country house', the informal staff, the copious breakfast buffet, the swimming pools. 'Dining and breakfasting overlooking the gardens is a real pleasure.' Residents can enjoy the magnificent grounds (open to the public) when the sightseers have left, and the spectacular public rooms (with tapestries, suits of armour, fine paintings), when they are free of the functions held during the day. Many sporting facilities (see below) are included in the room price. Children and dogs are welcomed. The bedrooms are named for previous owners and visitors. In the main house, Nancy Astor, Buckingham, etc, are as splendid as the public rooms; in the garden wing, Gladstone, Grenfell, etc, are attractive but less characterful. One suite is a cottage by the river. The *Royal Crescent Hotel*, Bath (*qv*), is under the same management. More reports, please.

Open All year. *Waldo's* probably closed Jan.
Rooms 15 suites (1 in cottage), 23 double. 12 in wings. 9 on ground floor. 13 air-conditioned.
Facilities Lift, ramp. Great Hall, library, boudoir, billiard room, breakfast room, 2 restaurants, conservatory; function facilities; crèche; club: indoor and outdoor swimming pools, sauna, spa bath, gym, health/beauty treatments. No background music. In 376-acre National Trust grounds on river Thames; tennis, squash, riding, practice golf, fishing, jogging; 3 vintage boats for river trips. Civil wedding licence.
Location 10 miles NW of Windsor. M4 exit 7. On B476 opposite *Feathers* pub. Train: Burnham, 2 miles.
Restriction No smoking: restaurants, 7 bedrooms. No dogs in public rooms.
Credit cards All major cards accepted.
Terms [2001] (*Excluding VAT on meals, £3 donation to National Trust*) Room: double £320–£460, suite £485–£875. Breakfast £12–£17. *Terrace*: set lunch £38; full alc dinner £58.50; *Waldo's*: set dinner £58 and £84. Fitness, Christmas, New Year packages. 1-night bookings often refused weekends.

TAUNTON Somerset — Map 1:C5

The Castle
Castle Green
Taunton TA1 1NF

Tel 01823-272671
Fax 01823-336066
Email reception@the-castle-hotel.com
Website www.the-castle-hotel.com

César award in 1987

There is something essentially British about this 'really splendid hotel', wisteria-covered and castellated, which the Chapman family has owned for half a century. It has welcomed royalty from Queen Victoria to Queen Elizabeth II. Kit Chapman, who now presides, grew up here – his autobiography acknowledges that hotel-keeping has developed from being a 'trade' to a respectable occupation. Food is a key element: the *Castle*'s restaurant established the careers of TV chefs Gary Rhodes and Phil Vickery. Now Richard Guest, who has worked with Anton Edelmann at *The Savoy*, London, 'is making his mark' in the kitchen, aiming to regain its *Michelin* star. He continues the modern style of cooking using local produce (suppliers get a credit on the menu). Dishes include jellied tomato consommé with crab; steamed mutton and caper pudding; glazed apple custard. Readers report food 'of the highest quality' that is 'beautifully cooked and presented', with 'excellent service'. The wine list 'is wide ranging and reasonably priced'. Light meals are available in *Brazz,* the lively café/restaurant adjacent. A continental breakfast can be brought to the bedroom; a substantial cooked one is served in the dining room. The public rooms are elegant, with old oak furniture, tapestries, paintings, elaborate flower arrangements. A fine wrought iron staircase leads to the bedrooms, which vary in size and style. 'Mine was spacious, quiet, with a good bathroom.' Front rooms are triple-glazed against local noise; the quietest rooms overlook the garden. The penthouse suite and roof garden have views of the Quantock and Blackdown hills. In low season, musical weekends are held. (*Brian and Eve Webb, SP Edwards*)

Open All year.
Rooms 5 suites, 27 double, 12 single.
Facilities Lift, ramps. Lounge, lounge bar, restaurant, brasserie (background music); private dining/meeting rooms; roof garden. ¼-acre garden.
Location Central (follow signs for castle). Garages (£10 per night), parking. Bus station 2 mins; railway station 5 mins.
Restrictions No smoking: restaurant, some bedrooms. Small dogs only, not in public rooms.
Credit cards All major cards accepted.
Terms [2001] B&B: single £105, double £170, suite £250. D,B&B £90 per person. Set lunch £20; full alc £50. 2-day breaks, musical weekends, Christmas, New Year packages. Special rates for honeymooners, old boys/parents from local schools.

TEFFONT EVIAS Wiltshire — Map 2:D1

Howard's House
Teffont Evias
nr Salisbury SP3 5RJ

Tel 01722-716392
Fax 01722-716820
Email enq@howardshousehotel.com
Website www.howardshousehotel.com

César award in 1993

'Perfect, picturesque location, beautiful gardens. Nothing too much trouble.' 'Excellent welcome, owner/chef very helpful.' Paul Firmin continues to gather plaudits for his 'extremely civilised' hotel and restaurant (*Michelin Bib Gourmand*) in a pretty Wiltshire village. The house, which stands near the little river Teff, was built in 1623, and extended and renovated in 1837, following the then owner's visit to Switzerland during his Grand Tour – hence the steeply pitched, broad-eaved roof. The style is relaxed: children and dogs are welcomed; there is no dress code. The smallish bedrooms, done in pastel shades, have 'exquisite biscuits, and real milk in a thermos for early morning tea'. But the four-poster room 'wasn't worth the extra expense', one visitor thought, because of 'noise from the kitchen'. The lounge is decorated in warm yellows that complement an old stone fireplace and exposed beams. It can get busy in peak periods, thanks to the popularity of the green-and-white restaurant. Mr Firmin, with Boyd McIntosh, serves modern British cooking, eg, pan-seared king scallops with spicy rocket salad, lemongrass and couscous; marinated loin of lamb with braised Savoy cabbage, sautéed wild mushrooms and a rosemary and redcurrant glaze; almond and raspberry tart with honey and cinnamon ice cream. An 'excellent wine list' includes some reasonably priced bottles. 'Breakfast is very good, best orange juice ever.' There are two acres of romantic gardens with ancient box hedges and secret corners. Stonehenge and Wilton House are within 20 minutes' drive. (*A Bruce, Mrs Denise Chubb, and others*)

Open All year, except Christmas. Restaurant closed midday, except Sun.
Rooms 9 double.
Facilities Lounge, restaurant (occasional classical background music). 2-acre grounds: croquet. River, fishing nearby. Unsuitable for ♿. Parking.
Location On B3089, 9½ miles W of Salisbury. In Teffont Magna, follow signs to hotel. Train: Tisbury, 3 miles; then taxi.
Restrictions No smoking in restaurant. No dogs in restaurant.

Credit cards All major cards accepted.
Terms B&B: single £85, double £135–£155. Set lunch (Sun) £18.50, dinner £19.95; full alc £37. 2-night breaks. *V*

TEIGNMOUTH Devon Map 1:D5

Thomas Luny House
Teign Street
Teignmouth TQ14 8EG

Tel 01626-772976
Email alisonandjohn@thomas-luny-house.co.uk
Website www.thomas-luny-house.co.uk

'The standards are high, and it is excellent value, particularly for the single traveller,' writes a regular visitor to John and Alison Allan's 'excellent B&B'. Other visitors praised the 'charming, friendly hosts'. Named for the marine artist who built it, the small Georgian house is near the fish quay, in the old part of town. You enter via an archway ('which needs a bit of thought before you drive through') in a high whitewashed wall. The double drawing room and breakfast room, both with an open fire, lead through French windows on to a small garden. Three bedrooms are spacious and comfortable, the fourth is small; all have fresh flowers, Malvern water, books and magazines. Guests may choose between a hospitality tray and a delivery to the room of early morning tea. 'Some choose both,' write the Allans. Breakfast, now served at separate tables, includes freshly squeezed orange juice, home-made yogurt, 'the best scrambled eggs I've ever had', 'lovely home-baked fruit bread' and leaf tea. Tea and cake on arrival, and a morning newspaper are included in the rates. Teignmouth's days as an elegant bathing resort are long gone, but 'the countryside around is full of delights', including good birdwatching on the Exe estuary. (*John Fenn, MF*)

Open All year.
Rooms 4 double.
Facilities 2 lounges, breakfast room. No background music. Small walled garden. Sea, sandy beach 5 mins' walk. Unsuitable for ♿.
Location Central. From A380 take B3192 to Teignmouth. Left at traffic lights; right at next lights; 1st left into Teign St. Courtyard parking.
Restrictions No smoking. No children under 12. No dogs.
Credit cards MasterCard, Visa.
Terms (*Not VAT-rated*) B&B: single £30–£40, double £55–£75. Winter breaks.

TEMPLE SOWERBY Cumbria Map 4: inset C3

Temple Sowerby House NEW
Temple Sowerby
nr Penrith CA10 1RZ

Tel 017683-61578
Fax 017683-61958
Email stay@temple-sowerby.com
Website www. temple-sowerby.com

In old village in Eden valley 6 miles NW of Appleby: extended Cumbrian farmhouse on A66, opposite Temple Sowerby's green. Thick walls, fine views towards Cross Fell (highest peak in Pennines), 2-acre formal walled garden. New owners in 2000, Paul and Julie Evans, 'very welcoming'; new chef too, Richard Axford ('classical cooking with contemporary presentation' served à la carte*). Closed Christmas. 13 bedrooms (some family, 2 suitable for* ♿*). 2 lounges, bar, restaurant (classical background music), conservatory; conference/function facilities. No smoking in restaurant. No dogs in public rooms. Amex, MasterCard, Visa accepted. B&B: single £68–£75, double £98–£120; D,B&B (min. 2 nights) £67.50. Full alc £30 [2001]. More reports, please.* *V*

TETBURY Gloucestershire — Map 3:E5

Calcot Manor
nr Tetbury GL8 8YJ

Tel 01666-890391
Fax 01666-890394
Email reception@calcotmanor.co.uk
Website www.calcotmanor.co.uk

César award in 2001

The needs of adults and children are thoughtfully balanced at Richard Ball's family-friendly Cotswold country hotel, which combines a welcome for children with unstuffy sophistication. Family rooms are in a barn a short walk from the main house. They have a double bedroom, a sitting room with bunk beds or sofa beds, TV with video, baby-listening, etc. There is a small heated outdoor pool, a supervised playroom, the 'Playzone' (with a qualified nanny), for children over three, and a collection of toys and games. Adults on their own are assigned a bedroom in the main house or converted stables ('we loved the privacy'). Some rooms have a six-foot bed; some have a whirlpool bath; all are stocked with shortbread, fruit, toiletries, etc. 'We had a good room, well-appointed, bed turned down nicely; an even better bathroom,' says one visitor this year, who thought the public rooms were 'comfortable and old-fashioned, ie, as they should be'. Children are fed in the nursery or the *Gumstool* pub. Real ale is available here, and an interesting menu – eg, rocket, spinach and ricotta ravioli; Stilton and port rarebit – as well as fish and chips and shepherd's pie, and they will produce peanut-butter sandwiches on demand. Dishes come in 'ample' or 'generous' portions. In the conservatory restaurant Michael Croft serves dishes like slow-roasted Gloucester Old Spot pork confit; seafood risotto with lemon and herbs; caramelised fig tarte Tatin. Breakfasts include fresh orange juice and local sausages. Conferences and functions are held. Tetbury has a market place with lovely old houses, and the 600-acre Westonbirt Arboretum. A good base for exploring Laurie Lee country. (*RC, KJB,* Good Pub Guide*; also VH*)

Open All year.
Rooms 4 suites, 24 double. 19 in barns and stables. 11 on ground floor.
Facilities Ramps. 2 lounges, restaurant, bistro (background light jazz); private dining room, conference facilities; children's playroom with nanny (open 4 hrs daily). 9-acre grounds: heated swimming pool, tennis, children's play area, croquet; bicycles. Golf, fishing, riding nearby. Bicycles provided. Civil wedding licence.
Location 4 miles W of Tetbury, on intersection of A4135/A46. Train: Kemble, 6 miles; taxi.
Restrictions No smoking in main restaurant. No dogs.
Credit cards All major cards accepted.

Terms B&B: single £125, double £140–£180, suite £190. Set lunch £15; full alc £30. Child in family suite: under 1, free; 1–12, £15; over 12, £25 (incl. English breakfast and high tea). 2-day breaks. Christmas package. 1-night bookings refused peak season Sat.

The Close
8 Long Street
Tetbury GL8 8AQ

Tel 01666-502272
Fax 01666-504401
Email reception@theclosehotel.co.uk
Website www.theclosehotel.co.uk

'This has to be my find of the year. I was welcomed and cosseted throughout.' 'A good welcome from a willing and enthusiastic young staff.' 'They all give the impression that they enjoy doing their job.' Praise continues for this 16th-century town house close to the market square in the mellow Cotswold town. The hotel is owned by Old English Inns, but is managed in a 'relaxed personal style' by Louise and Daren Bale – he is also the chef. 'They work so hard; they deserve a fanfare,' says one regular. The thoughtful extras' in the bedrooms – Madeira, plastic ducks, a 'personal cuddly guard dog', and a little tree at Christmas – are enjoyed. The rooms vary in size, and the lighting can be dim (an extra table lamp was brought on request); most look on to the walled garden at the rear. There are open fires, polished furniture and floorboards, fresh flowers and board games in the public rooms. Mr Bale 'obviously loves cooking and is good at it – the food was excellent'. His menu might include smoked Parmesan risotto; ballotine of chicken with parsley mash, smoked bacon cabbage and potato confit; banoffee parfait. The hotel opens on to Tetbury's busy high street; entry by car is at the back. Weddings and other functions are extensively catered for. Not ideal for disabled visitors – 'we do help them, but there are steps all over,' says the hotel. (*Gordon Hands, Brian and Eve Webb, JM, and others*)

Open All year.
Rooms 15 double. Some on ground floor.
Facilities Ramps. 2 lounges (pianist most weekends), restaurant; classical background music; 3 function rooms. 1-acre grounds: croquet. Unsuitable for ♿. Civil wedding licence.
Location Centre of Tetbury (rear rooms quietest). Car park.
Restrictions No smoking in restaurant. No children under 12 in restaurant. No dogs in public rooms.
Credit cards Amex, MasterCard, Visa.
Terms B&B: single £60–£75, double £70–£100; D,B&B: single £85–£100, double £130–£180. Set lunch £16.50, dinner £32.50; full alc £50. Midweek breaks. Christmas package. 1-night bookings occasionally refused Sat.

THIRSK North Yorkshire — Map 4:C4

Sheppard's Hotel & Restaurant BUDGET
Front Street, Sowerby
Thirsk YO7 1JF

Tel 01845-523655
Fax 01845-524720
Email sheppards@thirskny.freeserve.co.uk

Sheppard family's restaurant-with-room, 'a gem', in picturesquely converted farm buildings round cobbled courtyard, ½ mile from centre. 'Delightful, quiet room, almost a suite, in old stables,' say returning visitors this year. Good, quite modern cooking (eg, pork loin with wild mushroom cream; bangers and mash with caramelised onion); background music. Closed 1st week Jan, Sun/Mon midday. 8 bedrooms (3 above restaurant, 5 in granary). No smoking: restaurant, bedrooms. MasterCard, Visa accepted. B&B £32–£62. Full alc £29.15 [2001]. *V*

THORNHAM Norfolk — Map 2:A5

Lifeboat Inn NEW
Ship Lane
Thornham PE36 6LT

Tel 01485-512236
Fax 01485-512323
Email reception@lifeboatinn.co.uk
Website www.lifeboatinn.co.uk

'A rambling old white-painted pub, very popular, in a good position.' It is an extended 16th-century smugglers' ale house, in a village on the north-west Norfolk coast. 'We'll go again,' say the nominators. They liked the 'attractive beamed and candlelit dining room, with interesting, well-presented food, competent and friendly service'. You can take two or three courses on a *table d'hôte* menu, eg, asparagus with sweet chilli sauce; grilled marlin on marinated new potatoes; warm carrot and orange cake with rosemary cream. 'The picturesque bar, with antique paraffin lamps, pews, carved oak tables, and rugs on a tiled floor, has a different menu, also interesting': mussels are a speciality, poached in white wine, garlic and cream. Or you could try Lifeboat fish pie, or spiced crab and ginger fish-cakes. There is a large old fireplace in reception. 'Excellent breakfasts' include make-your-own muesli, local spicy sausage, scrambled eggs with smoked salmon. Bedrooms are in the pub (most have a view over the harbour to the sea) or in another old inn, the *Old Coach House*, a short walk away (it has a bar, and a café that serves teas, and pizzas and pasta in the evening). 'Our room was adequate in size, with pine furniture, but lamps too dim for reading in bed.' An ancient vine grows in the conservatory; in summer (when the pub gets very busy) guests can sit in the walled patio garden. 'We welcome reasonably well-behaved dogs and all children,' write the owners, Charles and Angela Coker. Thornham's sandy beach is a short walk away. The Titchwell Marsh nature reserve is a two-mile drive. (Good Pub Guide, *Derrick and Margaret Elliott*)

Open All year.
Rooms 13 double in inn, 9 in *Old Coach House*, 5–10 mins' walk. 1 ground-floor room.
Facilities Reception lounge, conservatory, 3 bars, 2 dining rooms. ¼-acre patio garden. Sea 20 mins' walk. Golf nearby. Unsuitable for ♿.
Location Turn off A149 by *King's Head*; take 1st left turn. Parking. 1 bus a day from Hunstanton.
Restrictions No smoking in bedrooms, or in restaurant until other diners have finished. No dogs in restaurant.
Credit cards MasterCard, Visa.
Terms B&B: single £47–£60, double £64–£90; D,B&B: single £69–£82, double £108–£134. Bar meals. Set dinner £24. Christmas package.

TINTAGEL Cornwall **Map 1:C3**

Trebrea Lodge
Trenale
Tintagel PL34 0HR

Tel 01840-770410
Fax 01840-770092
Email trebrea-lodge@supanet.com

John Charlick and Sean Devlin combine 'courtesy with professionalism' as they run their Grade II* listed grey stone manor house in relaxed style. With a Georgian facade but 14th-century origins, it stands on a wooded hillside with uninterrupted views across open fields to the Atlantic. Because it is only one room deep, the rooms have windows on both sides. 'Lying in bed looking towards the sea must be the nearest one gets to heaven on earth,' said one visitor. There is a smart upstairs drawing room with antique furniture, and a cosier sitting/smoking room, with an honesty bar and a log fire, on the ground floor. The bedrooms vary in shape and size; they have antiques, interesting pictures, and everything you could want' – sherry, fresh milk, mineral water, etc. One room has a carved wooden four-poster; a small one with beamed ceiling is reached up a steep stairway; one, in the old washhouse, has a separate entrance (an umbrella is provided). You should reserve your table when booking a bedroom, for the restaurant is often busy. Dinner is at 8 pm. Mr Devlin's menu appears at breakfast; it is a no-choice meal, but alternatives can be requested. It might consist of celery and almond soup; spiced orange breast of chicken; crème brûlée; local cheeses (Cornish Yarg, Devon Sharpham). There's a small, well-chosen wine list. The breakfast, with fresh orange juice, and a buffet on a sideboard, 'is excellent'. Tintagel's romantic ruin should be seen even if the village is touristy. The old fishing villages of Boscastle and Port Isaac are within easy reach, as is Lanhydrock house and gardens. Excellent walking nearby, along National Trust coastline or on Bodmin Moor. More reports, please.

Open 1 Feb–31 Dec. Dining room closed midday.
Rooms 7 double. 1 in annexe.
Facilities 2 lounges, dining room. 4½-acre grounds. Sand/rock beach ¾ mile. Unsuitable for ♿.
Location ½ mile SE of Tintagel. From Boscastle road, right by modern RC church on edge of village, right at top of lane. House 300 yds on left. Train: Bodmin Parkway; then taxi.
Restrictions Smoking in lounge bar only. No children under 12. 'Well-behaved dogs' by arrangement (£3.75 daily).
Credit cards Amex, MasterCard, Visa.
Terms [2001] B&B: single £62–£67.50, double £86–£96; D,B&B: single £86–£91.50, double £134–£144. Set dinner £24. 2- to 7-day breaks. Christmas package. 1-night bookings sometimes refused.

****

Traveller's tale Hotel in Liverpool. In the restaurant, the service was careful, the food flashy and uninteresting. I looked at a vacuum cleaner during dinner, and later watched a team of young staff moving furniture about me. Breakfast was hotel hotplate style.

****

TITCHWELL Norfolk **Map 2:A5**

Titchwell Manor
Titchwell, nr Brancaster
PE31 8BB

Tel 01485-210221
Fax 01485-210104
Email margaret@titchwellmanor.co.uk
Website www.titchwellmanor.co.uk

'Enthusiastic staff', 'good attention to detail' and 'very welcoming owners' distinguish Margaret and Ian Snaith's small hotel, a 'comfortable place to stay', which has 'wonderful views over salt marshes to the sea'. Special packages are offered in winter to RSPB members visiting the Titchwell Manor bird reserve. The 'substantial Victorian building with additions' is on a main road, but winter visitors were not troubled by traffic noise. The decor is simple and colourful, with stencilled walls and patterned fabrics. 'Our well-equipped bedroom looked over a neat garden.' 'The pretty restaurant leads into a conservatory, which opens on to the sheltered, neatly kept walled garden.' The food is thought 'excellent, with a good selection at dinner, and generous breakfasts'. Two eating places: a seafood bar, and a semi-formal dining room where the three-course set-price menu might include fresh Cromer crab; grilled sea bass with toasted sesame seeds; butterscotch baked cheesecake. 'In this beautiful part of the world, the sky seems to take on an extra dimension.' Two championship golf courses are nearby. (Good Pub Guide)

Open All year, except last 2 weeks Jan.
Rooms 8 suites, 8 double. 4 in stable annexe. Some on ground floor.
Facilities Lounge, seafood bar (classical background music), restaurant. ½-acre garden. Beaches, golf nearby.
Location 5 miles E of Hunstanton. On A149 coast road between Brancaster and Thornham. Nearest station: King's Lynn.
Restrictions No smoking: restaurants, 5 bedrooms. No children in restaurant after 7 pm. No dogs in public rooms.
Credit cards Amex, MasterCard, Visa.
Terms B&B: double £50–£90, suite £50–£110. Set lunch £15, dinner £23; full alc £30. 2-day breaks: D,B&B from £50 per person. *V*

TORQUAY Devon *See SHORTLIST* **Map 1:D5**

TREBARWITH STRAND Cornwall **Map 1:C3**

The Old Millfloor BUDGET
Trebarwith Strand
Tintagel PL34 0HB

Tel/Fax 01840-770234

Run in 'laid-back, but pleasantly efficient' style by its 'slightly eccentric' owner, Janice Waddon-Martyn, this small white 16th-century guest house stands in a large garden with a millstream. The beach is a ten-minute stroll away, and there is good cliff walking in this beautiful area of north Cornwall. Children are welcomed here. Breakfast ('especially good and lavish') is between 8 and 10 am, and guests are encouraged to ask for tea and coffee whenever they please. The interior is airy, with plenty of colour, gleaming wood, fresh flowers. No TV or piped music in the lounge, where log fires burn, even in summer if it is cold. Bedrooms have white walls, pure white linen, lots of lace, big feather pillows, a hand-basin and TV. There is one large shared bathroom (queues sometimes build up). The home-cooked supper, with limited choice, is served by candlelight between 7 and 8 pm in the small beamed dining room. 'The very simple cooking is good, and portions are generous.' A sample menu: twice-baked cheese soufflé, or leek and potato soup; grilled steak, or vegetables en croûte; treacle tart with Cornish cream, or home-made ice cream with chocolate sauce. No licence; bring your own wine. Organic meat and local vegetables are used when possible, rolls are freshly baked, as are the scones for tea (no charge). Not for the disabled or infirm, as the house is reached by a steep path down from the road. Best take the minimum of luggage. Tintagel is two miles away. More reports, please.

Open Easter–Nov.
Rooms 3 double, with wash-basin. TV; no telephone.
Facilities Lounge/dining room. No background music. 10-acre grounds: garden, orchard, paddocks, stream. Beach 10 mins' walk down, 20 mins up. Riding centre 2½ miles. Unsuitable for ♿.
Location 2 miles S of Tintagel by B3263. Train: Bodmin Parkway; then taxi/bus.
Restrictions No smoking. No dogs.
Credit cards None accepted.
Terms [2001] (*Not VAT-rated*) B&B £20–£22. Set dinner £13.50. Unlicensed: bring your own wine. Child in parents' room: free; in separate room: 50% of adult rate.

TRESCO Isles of Scilly — Map 1:C1

The Island Hotel
Tresco, Isles of Scilly
Cornwall TR24 0PU

Tel 01720-422883
Fax 01720-423008
Email islandhotel@tresco.co.uk
Website www.tresco.co.uk

'Tresco has one of the most beautiful settings in the British Isles,' writes a correspondent this year, visiting this 'comfortable and, on the whole, well-run' hotel, 'a place for the well heeled to recharge their batteries'. She loves the 'gentle climate, the moonlit walks, and the subtropical Abbey Gardens of this tiny private island, warmed by the Gulf Stream, which Robert Dorrien Smith leases from the Duchy of Cornwall. This modern building stands by a beach (a tractor and trailer convey guests from the quay or heliport). Its decor may be conventional, but public areas are spacious. A floor-to-ceiling glass wall in the sitting room gives dramatic views of the rocky coastline and other islands.' Other guests wrote of 'food of the highest standard'; service by 'enthusiastic, if sometimes slightly amateurish, students', but at breakfast, it 'can be haphazard'. Some visitors in 2000 felt the place was 'trading on its reputation', but since then a new manager, Jamie Le-Friec, has arrived. Children are well looked after – they can play in safety, and bicycle to deserted beaches. During the school term, 'nothing disturbs the peace', though at lunch, when visitors from neighbouring islands come, the place is lively, 'everyone having fun'. The chef, Peter Hingston, serves main courses like brill with saffron creamed potatoes and a fresh beetroot sauce; lemon sole with steamed baby vegetables and a lemon beurre blanc. Local lobsters can be ordered for a supplement. Tables are rotated, so everyone gets a window table. Suites have a balcony, and the best bedrooms have picture windows opening on to a private patio. Bar lunches, snacks, tea, coffee and drinks are served. Breakfast includes plenty of fruit 'and scrummy Abbey Platter (the works)'. There is a collection of buckets, spades and pushchairs for general use. In October, Tresco is visited by rare migrant birds from Asia and America. There are ruined castles, civil war battle sites and prehistoric burial sites to be explored. (*Pat Harman, Rosemary Wright, and others*)

Open Mar–end Oct.
Rooms 3 suites, 37 double, 8 single. Some in 2 annexes. 2 on ground floor.
Facilities Lounge, bar, restaurant, games room. No background music. 2¾-acre grounds: tennis, croquet, bowls, swimming pool (open May–30 Sept); beach: safe bathing, diving, snorkelling. Bicycle hire (book in advance). Tresco unsuitable for ♿.
Location NE side of island. Boat/helicopter from Penzance. Hotel will make travel arrangements and meet guests.
Restrictions No smoking in restaurant. No dogs allowed on Tresco.
Credit cards All major cards accepted.
Terms [2001] D,B&B £93–£128. Snack/packed lunches. Set dinner £37; full alc £43. Reductions for 5 or more days.

See also SHORTLIST

TUNBRIDGE WELLS Kent — Map 2:D4

Hotel du Vin & Bistro
Crescent Road
Tunbridge Wells
TN1 2LY

Tel 01892-526455
Fax 01892-512044
Email reception@tunbridgewells.hotelduvin.com
Website www.hotelduvin.com

Appropriately for a hotel belonging to a small group devoted to serving superior wines with informal food at reasonable prices, there is much praise for the 'extremely knowledgeable and unimposing' young French *sommelier*, Dimitri Mesnard. The highlight of one couple's visit was time spent 'chatting to this interesting and interested guy' in the snooker room, which is devoted to Havana cigars ('you could be in Cuba'). Another couple had stopped only for Sunday lunch: they lingered over champagne in the stylish Burgundy bar, full of comfy sofas and chairs. 'We liked the place so much we decided to stay the night and were most impressed with the bedroom and its facilities' (they had negotiated a 'great rate because it was Sunday night'). The 18th-century Grade II listed sandstone building overlooking Calverley Park was extended in the 1830s by Decimus Burton, known for the Palm House at Kew Gardens. Now part of Gerard Basset and Robin Hutson's Hotel du Vin Limited Group (see also Birmingham, Bristol and Winchester), it is managed by Matthew Callard. The bedrooms ('large and light, minimally but well furnished') are sponsored by wine and champagne

THE 2002 GOOD HOTEL GUIDE

Use this voucher to claim a 25% discount off the normal price for bed and breakfast at hotels with a *V* sign at the end of their entry. **You must request a voucher discount at the time of booking and present this voucher on arrival. Further details and conditions overleaf.** Valid to 5th September, 2002.

THE 2002 GOOD HOTEL GUIDE

Use this voucher to claim a 25% discount off the normal price for bed and breakfast at hotels with a *V* sign at the end of their entry. **You must request a voucher discount at the time of booking and present this voucher on arrival. Further details and conditions overleaf.** Valid to 5th September, 2002.

THE 2002 GOOD HOTEL GUIDE

Use this voucher to claim a 25% discount off the normal price for bed and breakfast at hotels with a *V* sign at the end of their entry. **You must request a voucher discount at the time of booking and present this voucher on arrival. Further details and conditions overleaf.** Valid to 5th September, 2002.

THE 2002 GOOD HOTEL GUIDE

Use this voucher to claim a 25% discount off the normal price for bed and breakfast at hotels with a *V* sign at the end of their entry. **You must request a voucher discount at the time of booking and present this voucher on arrival. Further details and conditions overleaf.** Valid to 5th September, 2002.

THE 2002 GOOD HOTEL GUIDE

Use this voucher to claim a 25% discount off the normal price for bed and breakfast at hotels with a *V* sign at the end of their entry. **You must request a voucher discount at the time of booking and present this voucher on arrival. Further details and conditions overleaf.** Valid to 5th September, 2002.

THE 2002 GOOD HOTEL GUIDE

Use this voucher to claim a 25% discount off the normal price for bed and breakfast at hotels with a *V* sign at the end of their entry. **You must request a voucher discount at the time of booking and present this voucher on arrival. Further details and conditions overleaf.** Valid to 5th September, 2002.

CONDITIONS

1. Hotels with a ***V*** have undertaken to give readers a discount of 25% off their normal bed-and-breakfast rate (or their room rate if breakfast is charged separately). You will be expected to pay full prices for other meals and all other services.
2. You may use one voucher for a single-night stay or for a longer visit, and for yourself alone or for a partner sharing your room. But you will need two vouchers if you are booking more than one room.
3. Participating hotels may refuse a voucher reservation if they expect to be fully booked at the full room price nearer the time, or accept a voucher for one night only.

CONDITIONS

1. Hotels with a ***V*** have undertaken to give readers a discount of 25% off their normal bed-and-breakfast rate (or their room rate if breakfast is charged separately). You will be expected to pay full prices for other meals and all other services.
2. You may use one voucher for a single-night stay or for a longer visit, and for yourself alone or for a partner sharing your room. But you will need two vouchers if you are booking more than one room.
3. Participating hotels may refuse a voucher reservation if they expect to be fully booked at the full room price nearer the time, or accept a voucher for one night only.

CONDITIONS

1. Hotels with a ***V*** have undertaken to give readers a discount of 25% off their normal bed-and-breakfast rate (or their room rate if breakfast is charged separately). You will be expected to pay full prices for other meals and all other services.
2. You may use one voucher for a single-night stay or for a longer visit, and for yourself alone or for a partner sharing your room. But you will need two vouchers if you are booking more than one room.
3. Participating hotels may refuse a voucher reservation if they expect to be fully booked at the full room price nearer the time, or accept a voucher for one night only.

CONDITIONS

1. Hotels with a ***V*** have undertaken to give readers a discount of 25% off their normal bed-and-breakfast rate (or their room rate if breakfast is charged separately). You will be expected to pay full prices for other meals and all other services.
2. You may use one voucher for a single-night stay or for a longer visit, and for yourself alone or for a partner sharing your room. But you will need two vouchers if you are booking more than one room.
3. Participating hotels may refuse a voucher reservation if they expect to be fully booked at the full room price nearer the time, or accept a voucher for one night only.

CONDITIONS

1. Hotels with a ***V*** have undertaken to give readers a discount of 25% off their normal bed-and-breakfast rate (or their room rate if breakfast is charged separately). You will be expected to pay full prices for other meals and all other services.
2. You may use one voucher for a single-night stay or for a longer visit, and for yourself alone or for a partner sharing your room. But you will need two vouchers if you are booking more than one room.
3. Participating hotels may refuse a voucher reservation if they expect to be fully booked at the full room price nearer the time, or accept a voucher for one night only.

CONDITIONS

1. Hotels with a ***V*** have undertaken to give readers a discount of 25% off their normal bed-and-breakfast rate (or their room rate if breakfast is charged separately). You will be expected to pay full prices for other meals and all other services.
2. You may use one voucher for a single-night stay or for a longer visit, and for yourself alone or for a partner sharing your room. But you will need two vouchers if you are booking more than one room.
3. Participating hotels may refuse a voucher reservation if they expect to be fully booked at the full room price nearer the time, or accept a voucher for one night only.

companies. 'The sheets are fantastic and the bath brilliant; CD-players mean you can bring your favourite music with you.' Some bathrooms have a freestanding Edwardian-style bath and a cubicle with a power shower. The quietest rooms, at the back, overlook the park (at the front is a busy road on a steep hill). The public rooms, decorated with copies of paintings by Modigliani, Picasso, etc, are candlelit at night, but dimmer switches enable you to turn up the lighting if you wish to read. The busy bistro (you must reserve a table) serves modern dishes, eg, monkfish and skate terrine with crispy whitebait; roast cod with olive oil mash and gremolata; fig tart with honey ice cream. 'The Mediterranean-style cooking would grace any bistro anywhere,' said a lunchtime visitor. 'It was delightful, with great food, great service,' wrote another. 'John Gielgud used to stay here in olden days. How he would have loved it now.' (*Sophie Lutz and John Holborow, John Townsend, and others*)

Open All year.
Rooms 1 suite, 32 double.
Facilities Lift. Lounge, bar, snooker lounge, bistro. No background music. 1-acre grounds.
Location Central, by intersection of Mount Pleasant Rd and Crescent Rd/Church Rd (opposite Assembly Hall, police station). Private car park.
Restriction No dogs.
Credit cards All major cards accepted.
Terms [2001] Room: single/double £80–£150, suite £130–£150. Extra bed £10. Breakfast: continental £8.50, English £11.50. Full alc £30.

TWO BRIDGES Devon — Map 1:D4

Prince Hall
nr Two Bridges
Yelverton PL20 6SA

Tel 01822-890403
Fax 01822-890676
Email info@princehall.co.uk
Website www.princehall.co.uk

Harvey and Rosie, the friendly house dogs, welcome visitors to this late 18th-century house, which has panoramic views over the West Dart valley. 'They know their place', and equally well-behaved visiting dogs are welcome at no extra charge. Not a place to visit if you don't like dogs: one visitor with an aversion was not impressed with other guests feeding their pets after-dinner mints in the bar. Carrie and Adam Southwell are 'attentive' owners with a thoughtful staff who run their small hotel with 'an atmosphere of a private house party'. The decor 'is that of a comfortable country home, not over-fancy'. Many of the bedrooms are spacious; the best, like the bar and restaurant, have 'fantastic views' over the moors; standard ones overlook a courtyard. The menus (with choice) are based on local meat and game and locally caught fish, eg, Devon crab mornay; peppered Brixton monkfish on a bed of crab and smoked salmon pâté; Chagford pork with caramelised apples in a Calvados sauce. 'Excellent home-baked rolls; portions adequate to large; everything properly hot.' The wine list is strong on New World bottles, and reasonably priced. Again a visitor found the piped music annoying, though guests sometimes choose the classical CDs that are played. 'Breakfast is served with a smile between 8.30 and 9.30 am, after that you just get the smile,' say the Southwells. Cream teas are served, in the garden in summer. You can walk from the grounds straight on to the moor. The dramatic landscape is said to have inspired Sir Arthur Conan Doyle, a visitor in the late 19th century, to write *The Hound of the Baskervilles*. (*CR Head, and others*)

Open Mid-Feb–mid-Dec. Restaurant closed midday (packed lunch available).
Rooms 8 double, 1 single.
Facilities Sitting room, lounge/bar, restaurant; jazz/classical background music at night. 6-acre grounds. River Dart, fishing 3 mins' walk; riding, shooting, golf nearby. Only restaurant and bar suitable for ♿.
Location 1 mile E of Two Bridges, on B3357 to Ashburton. Train: Plymouth, 17 miles; taxi.
Restrictions No smoking in restaurant. No children under 10 at dinner.
Credit cards All major cards accepted.
Terms [2001] B&B £45–£60; D,B&B £65–£80. Set dinner £29. Reductions for 3 or more nights. 1-night bookings refused Sat in high season, bank holidays.

ULLSWATER Cumbria — Map 4: inset C2

Howtown Hotel BUDGET — *Tel* 017684-86514
Ullswater, nr Penrith CA10 2ND

César award in 1991

An unsophisticated guest house, 102 years old this year, set back from the road in a 'beautiful, well-kept garden', on the eastern shore of the second largest lake in the Lake District. 'The situation is outstanding,' say aficionados. It is a 'marvellous retreat', 'a very nice old country house', with solid furniture, a 'remarkable collection of pewter', 'magnificent flowers' in the entrance lounge, 'super furniture and paintings, good dinners and a good wine list'. 'The staff are knowledgeable and polite,' a guest writes this year. 'Most visitors are on friendly terms with the management. Everything is efficiently supervised by a small Lakeland terrier. A delicious "cold" lunch consisted of soup with lovely little home-made rolls and perfect butter pats; cold salmon (not farmed) with tiny new potatoes; beautiful, fresh lemon mousse.' The owner, Jacquie Baldry, and her son, David, are the third and fourth generation to be involved; service is by young women, many from the south of England. Many bedrooms now have a bathroom, either *en suite*, or across a corridor. The large best room, to the right of the upstairs sitting room, has a view on to the lake. In the main house, early morning tea is brought to the room, and rooms are serviced during dinner. The bar carries 'an admirable selection of malt whiskies'. In the dining room, with tables close together, the no-choice dinner is at 7 pm. No written menu; cooking is traditional, often with a roast for the main course. On Sunday there is a *table d'hôte* lunch and a cold supper. Substantial picnics are provided. Generous breakfasts have stewed and fresh fruit, eggs as you wish. Cream teas ('amazingly cheap at £2.50') come with fresh-baked scones, good jams, and a silver teapot. *Howtown* is well placed for yachting, windsurfing and other water sports, and is a favourite of walkers and climbers. Very popular; book well ahead. (*Stephanie Sowerby*)

Open End Mar–1 Nov.
Rooms 10 double, 2 single. 10 with bath/shower. 2 in annexe. 4 self-catering cottages. No telephone/TV.
Facilities 4 lounges, TV room, 2 bars, dining room. No background music. 2-acre grounds. 200 yds from lake: private foreshore, fishing. Walking, sailing, climbing, riding, golf nearby. Unsuitable for ♿.
Location E shore of lake, 4 miles S of Pooley Bridge. Bus from Penrith station, 9 miles.
Restrictions No children under 7. Dogs by arrangement; not in public rooms.
Credit cards None accepted.
Terms [2001] D,B&B £45.50–£51. Set lunch: weekday from £7.50, Sun from £9.25, packed £3.75. Set dinner from £15.50; cold Sun supper from £10. 1-night bookings sometimes refused.

Sharrow Bay
Ullswater
nr Penrith CA10 2LZ

Tel 017684-86301
Fax 017684-86349
Email enquiries@sharrow-bay.com
Website www.sharrow-bay.com

César award in 1985 and 1999

One of the seven original *Guide* entries, *Sharrow Bay* (Relais & Châteaux) 'continues in its own inimitable way', pampering its guests in a spectacular setting on the eastern shore of Ullswater, looking to jagged fells. With managing director Nigel Lightburn and a long-serving staff, the founder, Brian Sack, still presides. Reminders of his late partner, Francis Coulson, are everywhere: his large tombstone in the garden; his name on the bedroom welcoming cards and the menus. This is the original English country house hotel, 53 years old. Mr Sack says its success is due to 'a personal touch, and a genuine love of people'. Tipping is not allowed, 'so there is no servility'. In the pink-and-gold public rooms, 'now rather dated', antiques and ornaments fill every corner, cherubs peek from curtains and hang from ceilings. The opulent bedrooms have a fridge, games, glossy books, countless ornaments. Some rooms in the main building are small, but the new garden ones are spacious; so are those in *Bank House*, a mile away (a 'people carrier' transports guests). Fittings are 'of high quality'; housekeeping and maintenance are 'impeccable'. In the *Michelin*-starred restaurant, 'it is difficult not to keep eating the vast quantities of delicious food'. The six-course dinner, at 8, has a huge choice, with main courses like medallion of veal with veal sweetbreads and wild mushroom sauce; noisette of venison with celeriac purée and brandy and port sauce, all elaborately garnished. A queue builds up to choose from the desserts. Teas are lavish, and at breakfast 'the waiters seem to compete to see how much they can persuade you to eat'. 'The wonderful picnic for our homeward journey lasted for ever.' The public areas are sometimes crowded, the whole experience is too much for some tastes, and one reporter found the staff 'slightly severe'. But the fans (many are regulars) lap up the 'superlative comfort'. (*James L Clarke, Ruth West, Conrad and Marilyn Dehn; also Mabel Kathleen Stafford, Sir Timothy Harford*)

Open Early Mar–end Nov.
Rooms 5 suites, 19 double, 2 single. 6 in garden, 4 in lodge, 7 at *Bank House* (1 mile). 1 on ground floor 'for people with mobility problems'.
Facilities Main house: 2 lounges, conservatory, 2 dining rooms; *Bank House*: 2 lounges, breakfast room. No background music. 6-acre grounds: gardens, woodland; ½-mile lake shore, safe (cold) bathing, private jetty, boathouse. Civil wedding licence.
Location E shore of Ullswater, 2 miles S of Pooley Bridge. M6 exit 40. Turn on to Howtown La by small church in Pooley Bridge.
Restrictions No smoking in restaurant. No children under 13. No dogs.
Credit cards MasterCard, Visa.
Terms D,B&B £115–£210. Set lunch £36.25, dinner £47.25. 20% midweek reduction off-season. 1-night bookings sometimes refused weekends.

UPPER SLAUGHTER Gloucestershire — Map 3:D6

Lords of the Manor
Upper Slaughter, nr Bourton-on-the-Water
GL54 2JD

Tel 01451-820243
Fax 01451-820696
Email lordsofthemanor@btinternet.com
Website www.lordsofthemanor.com

A classic Cotswold setting in a picture-postcard village attracts American and Japanese visitors to this former 17th-century rectory, now a smart modern hotel whose restaurant commands a *Michelin* star. The lovely house sits in eight acres of lake and parkland with walled gardens to the rear. One visitor, ignored by a porter on a rainy December day, felt the hotel was caught off-guard by a 3.30 pm arrival. But recovery was swift over excellent home-made biscuits in a long L-shaped suite, furnished with antiques, in the eaves, though limited headroom forced this six-foot guest to 'walk with a constant crouch'. Bedrooms in the main house are excellent, and there are good ones in converted stables. The situation is charming, with views down the lawns to a willow-flanked lake,' said another visitor. 'The dining room is an enchanting place with well-spaced tables, plentiful flowers and a pleasant atmosphere – not too hushed but also not anonymous.' But one couple were put out when they were relegated to the 'smoky' bar for tea and drinks due to weekend parties. John Campbell's modern European cooking, 'ideal for a real spoil', is 'very good – light, well executed, not over-ambitious'. The 'little extra courses' are enjoyed, also dishes like risotto of smoked haddock; mustard sherbet; wild salmon with spiced lentils and foie gras; mandarin brûlée with cappuccino ice cream. With open fires, strong colours, fresh flowers, antiques and family portraits, the public rooms have a country house air. The restaurant overlooks the walled garden. Some bedrooms look on to the old courtyard, where the village dining hall once stood. Sister hotel to *The Feathers*, Woodstock (see Shortlist). (*Paul Hingston, and others*)

Open All year.
Rooms 3 suites, 22 double, 2 single.
Facilities Drawing room, library, writing room, bar, restaurant. No background music. 8-acre grounds: carp lake. Unsuitable for ♿.
Location Edge of village, 3 miles SW of Stow-on-the-Wold.
Restrictions No smoking in restaurant. No young children at dinner. No dogs.
Credit cards All major cards accepted.
Terms B&B: single £99, double from £149, suite £299. Set lunch £21; full alc £80. Summer and winter breaks. Christmas, New Year rates.

VERYAN Cornwall — Map 1:D2

The Nare
Carne Beach
Veryan
nr Truro TR2 5PF

Tel 01872-501111
Fax 01872-501856
Email office@narehotel.co.uk
Website www.narehotel.co.uk

'A very good hotel. Courtesy is paramount.' 'Difficult to fault: excellent staff, beautiful rooms, top-class wine and food, wonderful views and facilities for children.' 'A blissful hideaway. Proudly old-fashioned in a very modern and efficient way. Atmosphere of peace. Lovely flowers everywhere. We were happy and cosseted.' The praise continues for this traditional family hotel, owned and run by Mrs Bettye Gray, and her grandson, Toby Ashworth (the fourth generation of a hotel-keeping family). Andrew Law is the new manager. Set in extensive grounds on the Roseland peninsula above Carne Beach, *The Nare* is surrounded by National Trust land. In its subtropical gardens are a swimming pool, a tennis court, secluded corners for sunbathing. There is direct access to the beach and safe bathing. The interior has a country house feel, with antiques, oriental rugs, ornaments. The bedrooms vary in size; the best ones have a sea view; many have a balcony. Deluxe doubles have a large bedroom-cum-lounge with a full-length patio, a huge bathroom, a walk-in wardrobe. There are inter-communicating rooms for families. Old-fashioned services (shoe-cleaning, evening room-tidying, hot-water bottles in beds, etc) are appreciated. The varied menu includes vegetarian options and local fish and seafood, and ends with a dessert trolley, and coffee and petits fours in the lounge. 'Lovely fresh fruit and exceptional smoked haddock at breakfast. Tempting home-made cakes and scones for tea.' Light suppers and lunches, and a high tea for under-sevens, are served in the Gwendra Room. The hotel's 22-foot boat, the *Maggie O'Nare*, is available for charter. Veryan's name is a corruption of St Symphorien, to whom the village church is dedicated. (*Ken and Mildred Edwards, Freddie Stockdale, Eve and Brian Webb; also D Barnett*)

Open All year.
Rooms 3 suites, 30 double, 6 single. Some on ground floor. 1 adapted for ♿.
Facilities Lift, ramps. Lounge, drawing room, 2 bars, billiard room, light lunch/supper room, restaurant, conservatory; drying room; indoor swimming pool, spa bath, sauna, gym. No background music. 5-acre grounds: gardens, heated indoor and outdoor swimming pools, tennis, children's play area, safe sandy beach, sailboarding, fishing. Concessionary golf at Truro Golf Club.

Location From A390: B3287 towards Tregony; A3078 towards St Mawes *c.* 1½ miles. 1st left to Veryan; through village (*New Inn* on left); 1 mile straight towards sea. Signposted from main road.
Restriction No smoking: restaurant, drawing room. No dogs in public rooms.
Credit cards MasterCard, Visa.
Terms D,B&B £86–£245. Set lunch £15, dinner £35; full alc £41. Special breaks: bridge, etc. Christmas package.

WAREHAM Dorset — Map 2:E1

The Priory
Church Green
Wareham BH20 4ND

Tel 01929-551666
Fax 01929-554519
Email reception@theprioryhotel.co.uk
Website www.theprioryhotel.co.uk

César award in 1996

'The setting is superb, the building is beautiful and the gardens are a joy to be in,' says a visitor this year to John and Stuart Turner's luxurious hotel. Other reporters wrote of 'a personal welcome'; 'service that is attentive, but never overpowering'. Formerly the Priory of Lady St Mary, it stands in 'immaculately maintained grounds, full of hidden corners and interesting plants', that slope down to the river Frome. The approach is across a green, 'a coloured oasis of Georgian houses', via a flagstoned courtyard, colourful in summer with busy lizzies, petunias and geraniums. The 'country house atmosphere' is admired (background music is no longer played). Breakfast ('with excellent toast and real orange juice') is served in the 'light and airy' Garden Room; so is lunch (it can be alfresco in summer). 'Delicious nibbles with pre-dinner drinks in the comfortable beamed drawing room' precede dinner in the stone-vaulted cellars, which several visitors this year thought 'a bit gloomy'. 'Dinners were enjoyable', but some of the young restaurant staff may be 'inexperienced'. The chef, Stephen Astley, cooks modern dishes (main courses like halibut with baby vegetables, asparagus and a champagne sauce; breast of chicken filled with a wild mushroom mousse on creamed leeks). The bedrooms vary greatly (some are small), but all have fruit and books; many have views of the Purbeck hills. 'Our double in the main house was charming and peaceful, with a lovely view downriver.' The best rooms (one has a four-poster bed) are in the Boathouse, a converted barn on the riverbank. There can be noise from the main road out of Wareham. The Turner family also own the *Casterbridge Hotel*, Dorchester (*qv*). Corfe Castle is near; so is good walking in the Purbeck countryside and on the South West Coast Path. (*JC, SP*)

Open All year.
Rooms 2 suites, 14 double, 3 single. 4 in boathouse. Some on ground floor.
Facilities 2 lounges (1 with pianist Sat evenings), bar, 2 dining rooms. 4-acre gardens: croquet; river frontage: mooring, fishing; bicycle hire. Sea 4 miles. Unsuitable for ♿.
Location From A351 bypass at station roundabout, take North Causeway/North St to centre. At traffic lights, left into East St, 1st right into Church St; hotel between church and river.

Restrictions No smoking in dining rooms. No children under 8. Guide dogs only.
Credit cards All major cards accepted.
Terms [2001] B&B: single £85–£140, double £110–£230, suite £265. Light lunches. Set lunch £21, dinner £27.50–£32.50; full alc £51. Off-season breaks. Christmas package.

WARMINSTER Wiltshire — Map 2:D1

Bishopstrow House
Boreham Road
Warminster BA12 9HH

Tel 01985-212312
Fax 01985-216769
Email enquiries@bishopstrow.co.uk
Website www.slh.com/bishopst

'Atmosphere of comfort, elegance; seemingly effortless attention to detail. Service is welcoming, professional and discreet. It is the rarest of combinations: everything adults could want, and good for children too – they are treated like valued guests.' 'We return often; the facilities provide constant amusement for teenagers and dog; the spa is a joy.' A late Georgian country house, liked for its 'easy feel'; one guest thought it resembled 'a family hotel such as you would find in southern France or Italy'. Its large grounds (mostly reached through a tunnel under a road) include a lovely stretch of the river Wylye, ancient trees, temples, quiet spots for 'soaking up the sun'. The spa, with a 'very pretty, good-sized swimming pool', beauty treatments, etc, brings a 'real mix of guests: families, young and old romantics, celebrities'. The manager, David Dowden, heads an 'enthusiastic staff'. Public rooms have strong colours, tartan carpets, huge mirrors, heraldic motifs. One couple thought the picture-hanging 'extraordinary', and lighting may be dim in some bedrooms and bathrooms – 'next time we'll take strong light bulbs'. The rooms vary greatly. Some are spacious and luxurious; smaller ones, up steep stairs, are 'full of character'. Some bathrooms, and a suite, may need updating ('useless showers' is one comment). Front rooms can get noise from cars and delivery trucks. In the elegant dining room, overlooking the garden, Chris Suter's modern cooking 'is superb'. Plenty of choice, eg, crostini of chargrilled scallops and asparagus; braised lamb shank with haricots blancs; chocolate sponge with cappuccino ice cream. 'The wine list is interesting, the *sommelier* very helpful.' 'Children's meals are superior.' Snacks are available all day. 'Breakfast a treat: fresh orange juice, thick yogurt, home-made preserves.' Local attractions: Longleat, Stourhead, Stonehenge, Bath and Salisbury. (*Robin McKie and Sarah Mitchell, Jan and Michael Moore; also V Elden*)

Open All year.
Rooms 2 family, 6 suites, 24 double.
Facilities Hall, drawing room, library, bar, conservatory, restaurant (pianist or jazz/classical background music during meals); children's games room; function/conference facilities; health spa (gym, hairdresser, swimming pool, sauna, solarium). 28-acre grounds: swimming pool, indoor/outdoor tennis; river, fishing rights (15 Apr–15 Oct), shooting. Golf nearby. Unsuitable for ♿. Civil wedding licence.
Location B3414, 1½ miles E of Warminster. Train: Westbury, 8 miles; taxi.
Restriction No smoking: restaurant, 1 bedroom.

Credit cards All major cards accepted.
Terms (*Excluding 'voluntary' 15% service charge on meals*) B&B: single from £99, double £190–£245, suite £305–£330. English breakfast £7. Bar meals. Set lunch/dinner £35. Child in parents' room: B&B £25. Christmas package. 1-night bookings refused Fri, Sat.

WARTLING East Sussex — Map 2:E4

Wartling Place NEW

Wartling, nr Herstmonceux
BN27 1RY

Tel 01323-832590
Fax 01323-831558
Email accom@wartlingplace.prestel.co.uk
Website www.countryhouseaccommodation.co.uk

A 17th-century ex-rectory set in mature gardens, opposite the 13th-century church of this pretty Sussex village. The owners, Barry and Rowena Gittoes, offer 'country house accommodation': B&B and an evening meal by arrangement. 'They are extremely pleasant,' says an inspector. 'And really seemed to care if we had enjoyed our stay. Our bedroom had solid pine furniture, understated colours and, joy, a *plain* carpet. The bed was very comfortable, and we slept well despite slight road noise. A page of dos and don'ts indicated that guests were expected to be out during the day, until evening. Public areas were attractive, with fresh flowers. An honesty bar and a large communal dining table are in a huge but quite cosy room. Breakfast, ordered the night before, and served between 8.30 and 9 am, included a large choice of cereals and juices, lovely yogurt. The cooked plateful was generous. There was thick wholemeal toast; butter and jams were in china dishes. We enjoyed breakfasting with our fellow guests, including an impeccably behaved baby; the family spaniel was in attendance. The gardens are most attractive, and filled with birdsong. Remarkable value by any standards.' The beds are king-size; two are four-posters. The house was once a rest home; staircases have short, wide flights. Though the village is off the beaten track, there is a wealth of places to visit nearby.

Open All year.
Rooms 4 double. Also self-catering cottage. No telephone.
Facilities Lounge (classical background music), dining room. 3-acre garden. Sea, rock/sand beach 5 mins' drive.
Location 3 miles N of Pevensey. From Herstmonceux follow signs to Wartling. House on right, opposite church.
Restrictions No smoking. No dogs.
Credit cards Amex, MasterCard, Visa.
Terms B&B: single £55–£65, double £70–£95. Evening meal by arrangement £25. Champagne package. 1-night bookings refused weekends July/Aug.

****

Traveller's tale Hotel in Devon. Dinner was good, but breakfast was poor. It included cheap orange juice and undercooked toast. My scrambled eggs needed carving; my husband's bacon and eggs were greasy. Coffee was diabolical. The room was unheated.

****

WASDALE HEAD Cumbria — Map 4: inset C2

Wasdale Head Inn
Wasdale Head
nr Gosforth CA20 1EX

Tel 019467-26229
Fax 019467-26334
Email wasdaleheadinn@msn.com
Website www.wasdale.com

An old three-gabled building in an isolated position, seven miles up a dead-end road at the head of Wasdale, England's deepest lake. It has had a *Guide* entry for 20 years. Howard and Kate Christie run it informally, with their border collie, Sam. 'A super place, with helpful, hard-working staff,' says one report. One correspondent, who toured the Lakes walking from pub to pub/hotel, wrote that this was one of the best places on the trip – 'simple, very comfortable, in a stunning setting'. The decor is traditional, with solid old furniture, wood panelling, and a collection of climbing photographs; the 'comfortably old-fashioned' residents' lounge has books and games. The main bar, which has an open fire, is named after the inn's first landlord, Will Ritson, reputed to be the world's biggest liar – lying competitions are held in the village once a year in his memory. The inn runs beer festivals (it now has its own brewery, making real ales, 'Wasd'ale' and 'Great Gable') and mountaineering-related courses, including women's courses with female instructors. At Christmas, it offers a 'Bah Humbug' package – 'no crackers, no silly hats, no Santa' – with a picnic lunch of sandwiches, a Mars bar and crisps, to be eaten in the hills. Howard Christie is co-chef with Mike Nixon, using local produce when possible, in dishes like venison steak with beer and berry gravy; fillet of port on a bed of sautéed potatoes with apple dressing; calorific puddings include sticky toffee pudding with butterscotch sauce. Portions are 'designed for people who have been on the fells all day'. Breakfasts are equally hearty, with a buffet of fruit, cheeses, etc, and porridge, local bacon, free-range eggs; devilled kidneys or kedgeree by arrangement. Bar meals, packed lunches and cream teas are available. Three suites have a small dining room and kitchenette. There is a large drying room, and a full laundry service. A Lakeland package is offered with two other hotels. (*PW; also* Good Pub Guide)

Open All year. Restaurant closed midweek in winter.
Rooms 1 family, 3 suites (with kitchenette) in annexe 20 yds; 8 double, 2 single. 2 on ground floor. Also self-catering apartments. No TV (poor reception).
Facilities Lounge, residents' bar, public bar, restaurant; steam room; drying room; beer garden. No background music. 3-acre grounds: stream, pond, fitness trail. Wastwater 1 mile, sea 12 miles. Unsuitable for ♿.
Location 10 miles from Gosforth, Holmrook. Follow signs from A595. Train: Seascale; hotel will meet.
Restrictions No smoking: restaurant, lounge, 6 bedrooms. 'Well-behaved dogs accepted subject to Sam's approval.'
Credit cards Amex, MasterCard, Visa.
Terms B&B £35–£45. Bar/picnic lunches. Set dinner £22. Special breaks. Courses: rock-climbing, fell walking, cooking, etc, all year. Christmas package.

WATER YEAT Cumbria — Map 4: inset C2

Water Yeat Guest House BUDGET *Tel/Fax* 01229-885306
Water Yeat
nr Coniston LA12 8DJ

'The welcome was friendly, the rooms comfortable; they were without television and radio, making this a very tranquil stop. We could have stayed a week.' Praise this year for Ursula Walsh's inexpensive country guest accommodation in her 17th-century farmhouse, half a mile from the southern tip of Coniston Water. There are five simple bedrooms (one for families), with floral fabrics, and lovely views over the woodland gardens. Meals are served communally in the beamed dining room: 'Dinner was excellent with generous portions' (main courses like lamb noisettes with asparagus and flageolet beans; trout fillets with lemon butter and capers). 'Good hearty Cumbrian breakfasts.' 'Generous, interesting hosts, excellent value,' say visitors. (*Dr JDL Bell*)

Open Mid-Feb–end Nov. Dining room closed Sun night, except bank holidays.
Rooms 5 double. No telephone/TV.
Facilities Lounge, dining room. No background music. 4-acre grounds. 10-mins' walk to lake. Unsuitable for ♿.
Location On A5084, 2½ miles from Coniston Water. Bus-stop close to house.
Restrictions No smoking. No children under 4 except with full house booking. No dogs.
Credit cards None accepted.
Terms B&B £28.50–£38.50; D,B&B £47–£57. Set dinner £18.50. Reductions for more than one night. 1-night bookings refused bank holidays. *V*

****

Traveller's tale Hotel in Norfolk. Our bedroom gave the initial impression of being attractive, but when my wife took off the bedcover we were worried because this thin and pimpled item was badly stained (I would not even give it to Oxfam if it was mine). We telephoned Reception and asked for it to be changed. While we were out for a walk, a replacement was dumped on the bed. We opened it out to find that someone had been sick on it at some stage. We called Reception again, and a third replacement was sent up. When it was unfolded, a huge stain was revealed. This incident made us look more carefully at the room: we found biscuit crumbs in the drawers, a dirty bed valance and extensive high-level dust. The underside of the loo seat was disgusting. When we brought the above to the attention of the receptionist she did not seem much bothered, though she did offer to take £20 off the bill. Later, the owner telephoned me at home but he only complained about shortage of staff, offering no compensation.

****

WATERHOUSES Staffordshire — Map 3:B6

The Old Beams
Leek Road
Waterhouses ST10 3HW

Tel 01538-308254
Fax 01538-308157

A restaurant-with-rooms, very French in style and with a *Michelin* star, in a hamlet on the edge of the Peak District. An old cottage houses the large reception lounge/bar, and the beamed, low-ceilinged dining room and its conservatory extension, which has Italian-style frescoes and luxuriant plants, and overlooks the sloping garden. The small bedrooms, each named after a local pottery (Royal Doulton, etc), are across a major road in an old smithy – ask for one on the quieter side, by a millstream. They have bright flowery fabrics, hand-embroidered sheets, fruit, flowers, home-made biscuits and fudge, books, glossy magazines, a marble bathroom with thick towels, an umbrella. 'A nice touch is that the crockery used in each room reflects its name. The food was excellent. Nothing was too much trouble; even in pouring rain, a tea tray was delivered to my room,' says one visitor this year. 'Expensive but very good', is another verdict. The owner/chef (for 21 years), Nigel Wallis, serves modern dishes on an *à la carte* menu (eg, tart of sweetbreads in Madeira sauce; braised shank of lamb in red wine sauce; tart of burnt limes with vanilla ice cream). His wife, Ann, is 'wonderful at front-of-house', 'full of warmth'. Their son, Simon, is the wine waiter, 'accomplished in his art' – the house wines are 'reasonably priced', and there is a good selection of half bottles. Coffee comes with 'excellent petits fours'. A continental breakfast ('delicious tiny buttery croissants; toast made from home-made bread') is included in the room rate. A cooked breakfast costs extra. Alton Towers is nearby. (*Sue Davies, JT, and others*)

Open Feb–31 Dec. Closed Sun evening/Mon; restaurant closed midday, except Fri and Sun.
Rooms 5 double. All in annexe across road. 1 on ground floor.
Facilities Reception/lounge/bar, restaurant (occasional background music). ½-acre garden. Unsuitable for ♿.
Location On A523 Ashbourne–Leek (all rooms double-glazed). Bus from Derby/Manchester.
Restrictions No smoking: restaurant, bedrooms. No dogs.
Credit cards All major cards accepted.
Terms B&B: single £70, double £80–£120. Cooked breakfast £5–£6.50. Set lunch £23.50; full alc £50.

****

Traveller's tale Hotel in Ireland. A shrill ringing, reminiscent of an old-fashioned shop bell, heralded our arrival. We entered a small, dark space, containing a few ancient dried flowers wilting under a load of dust, and a coolie hat which had seen better days. The owner appeared, affable but not effusive. No queries about how our journey had been; no offer of a cup of tea.

****

WATERMILLOCK Cumbria — Map 4: inset C2

Leeming House
Watermillock
Penrith CA11 0JJ

Tel 017684-86622
Fax 017684-86443
Email heritagehotels_ullswater.leeming_house@forte-hotels.com
Website www.heritage-hotels.com

'The weather was superb, but the hotel made the holiday,' says one of many enthusiastic reports this year, but one couple detected a 'chain feeling'. It is owned by Forte Heritage Hotels; Christopher Curry is the much-admired 'hands-on manager'. Other visitors called it 'a proper hotel, aiming to reach the highest standards (and succeeding, apart from a few anomalies)', and wrote of 'personable young staff' and immaculate rooms. 'Warm and welcoming', 'beautiful and serene, with extensions that have mellowed well', the Regency house stands in a lovely *jardin à l'anglaise* that slopes gently towards Ullswater. 'The trees are handsome and varied, and a well-documented tree trail makes for an interesting walk. The view to the lake from the public rooms is over steep steps, a fountain, a meadow. Red squirrels and birds come to the wooden feeding boxes opposite the dining room windows.' Good fabrics and 'classy paintings' abound. 'Exquisite fresh flowers' are everywhere. In the elegant restaurant, Adam Marks's cooking, 'a blend of traditional and modern', with a wide choice, 'goes from strength to strength'. 'The venison was faultless, and served on a properly hot plate (unusual these days).' Scallops with avocado slices and onion bahji were also enjoyed. Puddings include 'original ticky tacky toffee pudding'; brandy cheesecake with raspberry coulis. Some upstairs bedrooms in the original house, notably the mini-suite, have 'spectacular views' from their balcony. Newer rooms 'have less character, but are equally well equipped'. Breakfast ranges from fresh fruit salad and porridge to a traditional Cumberland platter; but one visitor thought the 'commercial toast and marmalade' inappropriate. A good base for visiting the Eden valley, Hadrian's Wall, etc. (*KV Sutton, Chris H Hay, David Sulkin, Francine and Ian Walsh*)

Open All year.
Rooms 35 double, 5 single. 10 on ground floor. 1 designed for ♿.
Facilities Ramp. Drawing room, sitting room, library, bar, conservatory, restaurant, private dining room; function/conference facilities. No background music. 22-acre grounds on lake shore: croquet, tree trail. Civil wedding licence.
Location W shore of Ullswater, on A592. 8 miles from M6 exit 40. Train: Penrith; bus/taxi.
Restrictions No smoking: restaurant, library, 11 bedrooms. No dogs in public rooms.
Credit cards All major cards accepted.
Terms B&B £59–£114; D,B&B £74–£129. Lunch alc. Set dinner £29.50. Christmas package. *V* (Nov–Mar)

> The length of an entry need not reflect the merit of a hotel. The more interesting the report, or the more unusual or controversial the hotel, the longer the entry.

Old Church Hotel
Old Church Bay
Watermillock
Penrith CA11 0JN

Tel 017684-86204
Fax 017684-86368
Email info@oldchurch.co.uk
Website www.oldchurch.co.uk

Four acres of grounds on the shore of Ullswater, England's second largest lake, give a peaceful aspect to this small hotel, originally an 18th-century country house built on the site of a 12th-century church. The owner, Kevin Whitemore, runs 'a calm and relaxed place to unwind in' with his daughters. Decorated in warm colours, the house is filled with lavish soft furnishings, flowers, pot plants, books and magazines. The hall has a carved oak Victorian Gothic fireplace; the lounge has pink wallpaper, pink built-in dressers, pink upholstered chairs. The bedrooms, with lake or fell views, vary in size and style. One with a lake view was liked this year: 'large and well-furnished, with a small but spotless bathroom'. Some tables in the dining room look over the lake. The home-cooked dinner is modern English, eg, courgette and fennel soup; fillet of salmon with a dill and Cumberland mustard glaze; breast of Gressingham duckling with sweet and sour sauce. Rich desserts include clotted cream fudge torte; white chocolate, rum and raisin truffle cake. Breakfasts are generous, but the full English variety is available only after 9 am. Children are welcomed (games, etc, are provided). 'Good value, and no service charge. The price quoted is what you are expected to pay.' Good walking in the area, but a car is needed. (*Mrs M Watson*)

Open Mar–Nov. Restaurant closed midday, Sun evening, also Sun in Mar and Nov.
Rooms 10 double.
Facilities Lounge, bar, dining room (background music sometimes). 4-acre grounds on lake: mooring, fishing, rowing boat. Unsuitable for ♿.
Location Off A592, 3 miles S of Pooley Bridge; 7 miles from M6 exit 40. Train: Penrith; bus 108.
Restrictions No smoking: dining room, 1 lounge, bedrooms. No dogs in house.
Credit cards Amex, MasterCard, Visa.
Terms B&B £45–£85; D,B&B £75–£100. Set dinner £30. 3-night breaks. 1-night bookings sometimes refused Sat, bank holidays.

Rampsbeck
Watermillock
Penrith CA11 0LP

Tel 017684-86442
Fax 017684-86688
Email enquiries@rampsbeck.fsnet.co.uk
Website www.rampsbeck.fsnet.co.uk

The imposing entrance to this white-walled 18th-century country house opens to a sweeping staircase and rooms with large bay windows, high ceilings and elaborate mouldings, and a traditional decor (patterned carpets, flowery curtains and wallpaper). The views over 18 acres of manicured gardens and paths leading down to Ullswater 'are breathtaking'. There is a 'homely welcome from Marion Gibb and her smartly attired staff of friendly girls'. She runs the hotel with her husband, Thomas, and her mother, Marguerite MacDowall. The lounge has a large marble fireplace, Victorian furniture, current newspapers, plants and flowers. The bedrooms are spacious, with an old-fashioned look; some have lake views and a balcony with table and chairs where afternoon tea or continental breakfast can be taken. Andrew McGeorge's cooking, served in the spacious, candlelit dining room, mixes modern French and English characteristics. His daily-changing *table d'hôte* menu gives three or four choices of each course: eg, roasted fillet of mackerel with ratatouille and crispy onions; Barbary duck with mushroom risotto; banana tarte Tatin with rum-and-raisin ice cream. The wine list is wide ranging and moderately priced. The breakfasts are 'out of this world, particularly the scrambled eggs', say recent guests. The market town of Penrith is nearby; so is the remote valley of Martindale with its 1,300-year-old yew tree. More reports, please.

Open Mid-Feb–1st week Jan.
Rooms 1 suite, 17 double, 2 single.
Facilities Hall, 3 lounges, bar, restaurant. No background music. 18-acre grounds: croquet, lake frontage: fishing, sailing, windsurfing, etc. Golf, clay-pigeon shooting, archery nearby. Unsuitable for ♿.
Location 5½ miles SW of Penrith. From M6 exit 40, follow signs for A592 to Ullswater. At T-junction on lake shore turn right. Hotel 1¼ miles. Train: Penrith, 5½ miles; bus/taxi.
Restrictions No smoking: restaurant, 1 lounge, 2 bedrooms. No small children in restaurant at night. Dogs by prior arrangement, not in public rooms, except hall.
Credit cards MasterCard, Visa.
Terms [2001] B&B £50–£100; D,B&B £69–£130. Set lunch £27.50, dinner £30–£42. Special breaks. Christmas package. 1-night bookings occasionally refused.

WATH-IN-NIDDERDALE North Yorkshire — Map 4:D3

The Sportsman's Arms BUDGET

Wath-in-Nidderdale, Pateley Bridge
nr Harrogate HG3 5PP
Tel 01423-711306
Fax 01423-712524

In peaceful conservation village, 2¼ miles NW of Pateley Bridge: Ray and Jane Carter's 'civilised restaurant-with-rooms' (says Good Pub Guide*) in 17th-century sandstone building reached by old packhorse bridge across river Nidd. 'High standards, agreeable staff'; good English/French meals (Mr Carter has worked in France) in bar and dining room. 'Sensible, extensive' wine list, with some reasonably priced bottles. Good breakfasts. 2 lounges. Open fires in public rooms. No background music. Functions catered for. Unsuitable for ♿. 1-acre garden. River 100 yds (fishing rights). Birdwatching, abbeys, castles nearby. Closed Christmas. 13 bedrooms, some large; 6 in converted barn and stables around courtyard, 25 yds; 1 on ground floor. No smoking: dining room, bedrooms. No dogs in public rooms, except bar. MasterCard, Visa accepted. B&B £35–£45; D,B&B £42.50–£70; full alc £35 [2001]. More reports, please.*

WELLS Somerset *See SHORTLIST* — Map 1:B6

WENLOCK EDGE Shropshire Map 3:C5

Wenlock Edge Inn BUDGET
Hilltop, Wenlock Edge
nr Much Wenlock TF13 6DJ

Tel 01746-785678
Fax 01746-785285
Email info@wenlockedgeinn.co.uk
Website www.wenlockedgeinn.co.uk

'A fine example of an honest, old-fashioned inn', on a minor road near one of the highest points of the dramatic wooded ridge made famous by AE Housman and Mary Webb. Run by two generations of the Waring family, Harry, Joan, Diane, Jonathan and Stephen, it 'scores top marks for its good country cooking and genuinely warm welcome'. There are 'stunning views' to the west and south in this designated area of outstanding natural beauty, largely owned by the National Trust. 'As a stranger on my own, I was made genuinely at home,' one visitor wrote. 'After a very good dinner and a convivial evening, all was quiet by midnight.' The large menu includes, eg, warm pasta and spring vegetable salad; venison and red wine pie; a wide choice of tarts, sponges and crumbles. The inn also has 'a decent wine list, well-kept local ales and interesting whiskies'. One bar has wooden pews, an old oak counter and an open fire; the other has an inglenook fireplace with a wood-burning stove. Tables on the terrace are set amid tubs of colourful flowers. 'The locals are friendly', especially on the second Monday of the month, when a story-telling club meets. A residents' lounge is upstairs. The three 'cosy bedrooms' have beams, a sloping ceiling, smallish windows with a padded window seat, TV, books, magazines, knick-knacks, 'lots of goodies', and a shower room with water from the inn's own well. 'Breakfast was copious and tasty, with some of the best bacon I've encountered.' There is a wildlife pond in the small side garden. (Good Pub Guide, *TL*)

Open All year, except 24–26 Dec. Dining room closed Mon midday, to non-residents Mon.
Rooms 3 double. 1, on ground floor, in adjacent cottage. No telephone.
Facilities Residents' lounge, lounge bar, public bar, dining room. No background music. Patio; small garden; paddock opposite. Walking, riding, fishing, mountain biking nearby. Unsuitable for ♿.
Location On B4371, 4 miles W of Much Wenlock.
Restrictions No smoking in dining room. Children under 8 not accommodated (no under-14s in bar). Dogs in cottage room, bar area only.
Credit cards Amex, MasterCard, Visa.
Terms B&B: single £45, double £75. Full alc £20. *V*

****

Traveller's tale Hotel in Yorkshire. We were seen to our bedroom, up a long flight of steep steps, by a genteel lady, not of an age that we could have asked her for help with luggage. Various young men lounged about without inclination to help. The staff were clearly not being paid much. They were either young or very old; all were useless. Nobody seemed to know what was going on.

****

WEST PORLOCK Somerset — Map 1:B5

Bales Mead
West Porlock TA24 8NX
Tel 01643-862565
Fax 01643-862544
Email balesmead@btinternet.com

'A special place. They made our honeymoon unforgettable.' 'The hosts were attentive and helpful in countless ways.' 'They are charming company, masters of the art of conversation. From the moment we arrived we felt like welcome guests.' 'The house and garden are extremely pretty.' Praise again for Stephen Blue and Peter Clover's small B&B, an Edwardian house in a hamlet between Porlock and Porlock Weir, in the Exmoor National Park. It looks over the 'stunning coastline' and is surrounded by wild moors and rolling hills. The decor is eclectic – the owners describe it as 'ranging from Victorian to contemporary designer chic' – 'with enough quirks to make it feel homely'. The bedrooms have hand-stencilled wall borders and good fabrics, a hot-water bottle and crystal decanters containing bath oils and salts). A third room is available if guests are willing to share a bathroom. Breakfast, at 9 am sharp, is served communally or at separate tables by candlelight. It includes freshly squeezed orange juice, fresh fruit salad, yogurt, cooked dishes garnished with flowers, all on Royal Doulton china with silver cutlery, lace tablecloths, proper table napkins. On special occasions, Stephen Blue will play the piano. No evening meal, 'but their recommendations for where to go were spot on'. Porlock Weir has a picturesque, tiny harbour. Local attractions include Dunster Castle, Arlington Court, National Trust villages, gardens, etc. (*Adam Newey, Melanie and Brian Davy, David Stevens*)

Open All year, except Christmas/New Year.
Rooms 3 double, 2 with private facilities. No telephone.
Facilities Lounge, breakfast room (classical background music). ½-acre garden. Shingle beach, harbour ½ mile; bathing, fishing, boating. Unsuitable for ♿.
Location Off A39, between Porlock village and harbour at Porlock Weir.
Restrictions No smoking. No children under 14. No dogs.
Credit cards None accepted.
Terms B&B: single £50–£70, double £70. 1-night bookings sometimes refused.

WESTDEAN East Sussex — Map 2:E4

The Old Parsonage
West Dean
nr Seaford BN25 4AL
Tel/Fax 01323-870432
Email raymondj.woodhams@virgin.net

A 'delightful B&B', with 'hospitable owners', Raymond and Angela Woodhams, who provide 'good value'. One visitor thought it 'perfect, like a smaller version of an Oxford senior common room'. With thick stone walls, mullioned windows, old timbers, a sympathetic Victorian extension, the atmospheric medieval building stands by a 12th-century church in a conservation village by Friston Forest. One couple's bedroom was the former baronial hall, with a four-poster bed, tiny casement windows (looking over gravestones), great beams, medieval works of art, 'even a processional cross propped up in one corner'. Its private bathroom, across the hallway, had 'all manner of herbal and visual delights, including botanical prints'. The other two bedrooms are in the Victorian wing. The breakfast room, reached via a spiral stone staircase, has 'superb antique furniture' and orchids, and breakfast is 'a feast, with fresh fruit juice, home-made preserves and muesli, an enormous traditional English breakfast, like a mixed grill, designed to last until dinner time'. No restaurant; *The Hungry Monk* at Jevington is warmly recommended, or you could try *The Tiger*, an old pub at Eastdean. Beautiful gardens and old stone walls surround the house; sheep graze in a pasture opposite. The sea is reached by a country path through a designated area of outstanding natural beauty. Beachy Head is 20 minutes' drive away. (*MB*)

Open All year, except Christmas, New Year.
Rooms 3 double. No telephone/TV, etc.
Facilities Sitting room, breakfast room. No background music. 2-acre grounds surrounded by forest. Sea, safe bathing, fishing 1 mile; golf, racing nearby. Unsuitable for ♿.
Location 5 miles W of Eastbourne. Off A259 Brighton–Hastings coast road, E of Seaford. Train: Seaford; then taxi (5 mins).
Restrictions No smoking. No children under 12. No dogs.
Credit cards None accepted.
Terms B&B: double £70–£80. 1-night bookings sometimes refused weekends.

WHEELOCK Cheshire — Map 3:A5

The Grove House BUDGET — *Tel* 01270-762582
Mill Lane, Wheelock — *Fax* 01270-759465
nr Sandbach CW11 4RD

Owned by Katherine and Richard Shaw with Mrs Brenda Curtis, this restaurant-with-rooms is liked for its 'feeling of a private home'. Flowers, potted plants, knick-knacks, books and family photographs fill the Georgian house in what was once an old village on the Trent and Mersey Canal – it is now a continuation of Sandbach. Mr Shaw is the chef, providing ambitious modern cooking on a long daily-changing menu, eg, cod topped with crushed prawns and smoked salmon, bound in cream cheese; calf's liver on a bacon, baby onion and oyster mushroom stew. Some visitors have found the food 'superb', but one reporter this year wrote of 'a strange sauce' on the vegetables. The wine list 'demonstrates genuine expertise'. Vegetarians are well catered for. An 'Early Bird' dinner (£9.50–£12.50) is offered on Wednesday to Friday evenings; tables must be vacated by 8.15. 'Service at both dinner and breakfast was friendly and efficient,' one visitor wrote this year. But some have disliked the background music. Most bedrooms are spacious and light, with 'a good bathroom' and 'real attention to detail', including a complimentary bottle of wine, replaced each day. One couple disliked their twin-bedded room, but others wrote: 'Decor slightly OTT but fun.' Jodrell Bank, Little Moreton Hall and Crewe railway station are nearby. 'A lovely spot; very useful for walkers of the Cheshire canal ring.' (*KB, and others*)

Open All year. Only restaurant open 27–30 Dec.
Rooms 1 suite, 6 double, 1 single.
Facilities Lounge, bar, restaurant, private dining/meeting room, patio restaurant; jazz/classical background music. ½-acre garden. Golf, fishing, riding nearby. Only restaurant suitable for ♿.
Location Off A534 2 miles S of Sandbach; near M6 exit 17. Straight across roundabout with Safeway supermarket on right. Left at next roundabout; follow signs to Wheelock. Hotel is on left, immediately after *Nag's Head*. Train: Crewe; local bus.
Restrictions No smoking: restaurant, 2 bedrooms. Dogs by arrangement; not in public rooms.
Credit cards Amex, MasterCard, Visa.
Terms B&B: single £30–£50, double £60–£75, suite £70–£85. Set Sun lunch £13, dinner £9.50–£14.50; full alc £20. Weekend rates.

WHITBY North Yorkshire *See SHORTLIST* Map 4:C5

WHITEWELL Lancashire Map 4:D3

The Inn at Whitewell

Forest of Bowland
nr Clitheroe BB7 3AT
Tel 01200-448222
Fax 01200-448298

'A good retreat for those seeking a romantic weekend away,' says the *Good Pub Guide*. 'Small, quirky, comfortable, in a beautiful area' – deep in the forest, and reached via narrow lanes, it is a civilised place, run with humour by Richard Bowman, a former Lancashire county cricketer, who leases it from the Duchy of Lancaster. 'The willing and informal staff provide relaxing hospitality.' Food is 'excellent', and the wine list is 'remarkable in quality, value and length' (Mr Bowman is also a wine merchant). Antiques and old paintings abound (there is also an art gallery), and log fires warm the public rooms. Bedrooms are 'fabulous', with a CD-player, a luxurious bathroom. Some (at the back) look over 'a beautiful wilderness'; some have a peat fire. 'The bar, very attractive, if a bit huntin', shootin' and fishin', buzzes with young folk.' 'Soups are regarded here as serious food,' says a note on the restaurant's menu; main courses included roast loin of venison with artichoke purée; lamb's kidneys with black pudding; 'traditional, sometimes nursery-like' puddings follow. Bar lunches and suppers might include goat's cheese baked in flaky pastry; Whitewell fish pie. Set on the river Hodder, the inn has seven miles of fishing for salmon, trout, grayling, etc. 'Many dogs are regular customers,' says Mr Bowman, warning that 'the odd cat might therefore prove a problem in the public rooms'. Children are welcomed too.

Open All year.
Rooms 1 suite, 16 double. 4 (2 on ground floor) in coach house 150 yds.
Facilities 2 bars, 3 dining rooms. No background music. 3-acre garden, riverside lawn, 7 miles fishing. Unsuitable for ♿. Civil wedding licence.
Location 6 miles NW of Clitheroe. Take B6246 from Whalley, or road through Dunsop Bridge from B64778.

Restriction Only 'frightening dogs' banned from public rooms.
Credit cards All major cards accepted.
Terms B&B: single £62, double £87, suite £118. Bar meals. Full alc £33.

WHITSTABLE Kent — Map 2:D5

Hotel Continental
29 Beach Walk
Whitstable CT5 2BP

Tel 01227-280280
Fax 01227-280257
Website www.oysterfishery.co.uk

Whitstable has become fashionable with funky young Londoners seeking seaside pleasures within an hour of the city. As a result this 1930s hotel, decorated in simple Art Deco style and set across the road from the beach at the end of the seafront, is often busy and, while some reports write of 'very friendly staff; nice atmosphere' and a 'clean and warm room', others indicate that service sometimes suffers. The hotel is owned by the Whitstable Oyster Fishery Company, which also runs the town's popular seafood restaurant (oysters have been a reason to visit Whitstable since Roman times). It is quite a hike away, and the *Continental*'s brasserie-style restaurant makes an attractive alternative. 'Very French in feel', it has sea views ('lovely sunsets'), and it offers 'good value', and 'good cooking', eg, moules marinière; roast sea bass with red pepper, tomato and anchovy; 'rather original' puddings, such as fruit jellies, panna cotta with raspberry sauce. Children's menus and vegetarian dishes are offered too. But this hotel will not suit all tastes. 'The old building has been renovated to maintain its character,' says its brochure. 'This means that there is limited storage in some rooms.' Nor is the accommodation luxurious: some rooms are extremely small. But the best are good-sized, with a balcony overlooking the sea. The place 'has a strange charm', one visitor thought. It also has modern bathrooms, 'a wonderful view across the estuary', and good walking from the door. The breakfast, accompanied by newspapers, has freshly squeezed orange juice and a buffet with cooked dishes. There is also accommodation in six fisherman's huts on the beach. Nearby are the Imperial Oyster Cinema (under the same ownership), ten-pin bowling and water sports. (*JC Ford, E Marsh, and others*)

Open All year, except Christmas.
Rooms 23 double. Also 6 huts.
Facilities Lounge, bar, restaurant; background jazz at night. Shingle beach opposite; windsurfing, etc. Unsuitable for ♿.
Location Central, on waterfront. 2 car parks.
Restrictions No smoking: part of restaurant, all bedrooms. No dogs.
Credit cards All major cards accepted.
Terms B&B: single £47.50–£65, double £55–£125. Full alc £20. Stay Fri/Sat, get Sun free.

> We quote either prices per room, or else the range of prices per person – the lowest is likely to be for one person sharing a double room out of season, the highest for a single room in the high season.

WICKHAM Hampshire Map 2:E2

Old House NEW

The Square
Wickham PO17 5JG
Tel 01329-833049
Fax 01329-833672
Email enq@theoldhouse.co.uk

This old village in the Meon valley is said to be one of the finest in southern England. Its huge square is a conservation area, lined by a striking variety of old buildings including this red brick, creeper-covered Grade II listed early-Georgian town house, which has been a hotel/restaurant for many years. It returns to the *Guide* with new owners, John and Gloria Goodacre, praised by a visitor who arrived unexpectedly, 'thanks to my air-headed approach to reservations', with her husband and nine-month-old daughter. 'The welcome was warm, the service obliging, the value for money very good. Our room, hastily made available, was spacious and bright. They warmed the baby's meal, and once she was asleep we descended to a delicious dinner, accompanied by a St-Émilion from a well-chosen list. We had to leave early for the ferry, but a late-night tap at the door signalled the arrival of a breakfast tray generously stocked with croissants, flasks of milk and fresh orange juice.' Since that report, a new chef, Peter Howard, has arrived, so we'd like to hear from diners in the beamed, high-ceilinged *Pêches au Vin* restaurant. It serves starters such as smoked halibut and salmon roulade, or baked avocado with cream cheese and pepper coulis; main courses include scallops wrapped in bacon; breast of guineafowl stuffed with wild mushrooms. Vegetarians are catered for. In summer, you can lunch in the walled garden. Most bedrooms are large, and those on the second floor have beams and a sloping ceiling. From Wickham there is a walk down a disused railway line to Alton. The New Forest and Beaulieu Abbey are close by. (*Amanda Forsyth*)

Open All year, except 10 days from afternoon of 25 Dec.
Rooms 2 suites, 5 double, 2 single.
Facilities Lounge, bar (background music), restaurant; private dining/conference room. ¼-acre garden. Only restaurant suitable for ♿.
Location Centre of village at junction of A32 and B2177, 3 miles N of Fareham (front rooms double-glazed). Car park. Train: Fareham; then bus.
Restrictions No smoking: restaurant, bedrooms. No dogs.
Credit cards All major cards accepted.
Terms B&B: single £65, double £80, suite £85. English breakfast £5 added. Set lunch £15, dinner £18.50; full alc £35. 2/3-day breaks. 1-night bookings refused Sat. *V*

WILLITON Somerset Map 1:B5

The White House

Williton TA4 4QW
Tel 01984-632306 and 632777

César award in 1988

Two summer visits confirm decades of excellence by Dick and Kay Smith in their modest Georgian house, which they have been running for 31 years as a restaurant-with-rooms (they take a long winter break to recharge their batteries). A regular guest, since the first edition of the *Guide*, reports that 'excellent all-round standards have been maintained'. New visitors were briefly worried by decor – 'like the faded set for a 1970s play' – but soon decided that 'this is a wonderful place to stay'. 'The welcome is exceptionally warm and kindly. No cloying over-attentiveness, just a gentle and very genuine desire to ensure that you feel at home.' The house stands on a busy road, but it has a courtyard garden, with shingle, palms, fig trees and trailing geraniums, and is filled with antiques, paintings, prints and ceramics. Old wine auction prints hang on the cork walls in the bar. Bedrooms in the main house are spacious, and thoughtfully equipped; the smaller, quieter rooms, in converted stables and a coach house, are also thought excellent. The Smiths ('lovely people') work together, unaided, in the kitchen, and produce 'unfussy dishes, based on good local ingredients, cooked with skill and care'. 'The food is simply sensational. Everything tastes fresh and wholesome.' The four-course dinner, with choice, might consist of smoked haddock and yellow pepper soup; steamed asparagus with hollandaise sauce; lightly roasted loin of spring lamb; hazelnut meringue cake with apricots, or West Country cheeses with home-made oatcakes. The Smiths take wine seriously – they have won a 'house wine of the year' award on several occasions. Breakfast has freshly squeezed orange juice, 'splendid poached eggs', good coffee. Williton is well placed for visiting Exmoor and the Quantock hills. Dunster Castle and Cleeve Abbey – an impressive monastic site – are within striking distance. (*John Astle-Fletcher, Paul Carter*)

Open Mid-May–Nov. Restaurant closed midday.
Rooms 10 double. 4 in annexe around courtyard. 1 on ground floor.
Facilities Lounge, bar, restaurant. No background music. Sea, shingle beaches 2 miles; sandy beach 8 miles.
Location Centre of village on A39 (rear rooms quietest). Forecourt parking. Train: Taunton, 15½ miles; bus/taxi.
Restrictions No smoking in restaurant. Dogs by arrangement (annexe rooms only).
Credit cards None accepted.
Terms B&B £42–£66. Set dinner £34. 2/3-day breaks. ***V***

WILMINGTON East Sussex — Map 2:E4

Crossways Hotel
Lewes Road
Wilmington BN26 5SG

Tel 01323-482455
Fax 01323-487811
Email stay@crosswayshotel.co.uk
Website www.crosswayshotel.co.uk

'A nice place, with good food.' David Stott and Clive James are the 'exuberant owners' of this restaurant-with-rooms 15 minutes' drive from Glyndebourne, in the Cuckmere valley. The 'Long Man of Wilmington' is said to be the largest chalk-cut figure in Europe, and the affluent village has a ruined 13th-century Benedictine priory, and lots of old cottages. This handsome rectangular house, white-painted and green-shuttered, is on the Eastbourne to Lewes main road, but windows are double-glazed, and the large garden, with a pond, rabbits and a herb garden, provides a buffer zone. 'If our ducks don't give you a friendly welcome, we will,' the owners promise. A collection of cheese dishes fills the dining and breakfast rooms. No guest lounge, but the bedrooms contain 'every appliance imaginable – fridge, TV, clock, etc, knick-knacks galore'. Some rooms have a sofa; one has a balcony. 'Our small bedroom had a pleasant view over the garden; the shower room was small and narrow but it worked well,' one couple wrote. The cooking is 'dinner-party type', 'generous and rich without being sophisticated' (main courses like poussin with Madeira; duck with cranberries, kumquats and ginger), and the atmosphere in the small dining room is intimate. Plenty of choice on the monthly-changing, four-course menu, ending with 'exceedingly good desserts', eg, strawberries in muscat wine; lemon and gooseberry sorbet. Some English wines, including Breaky Bottom and Sussex Sunset, are available. 'Breakfast had good marmalade.' Good walking on the South Downs Way and the Weald Way, close by. (*HS, and others*)

Open 24 Jan–24 Dec. Restaurant closed midday, Sun, Mon.
Rooms 5 double, 2 single.
Facilities Breakfast room, restaurant (occasional classical background music). 2-acre grounds. Sea 4 miles. Unsuitable for ♿.
Location 6 miles N of Eastbourne on A27 (some rooms double-glazed). Large car park. Train: Polegate, 2 miles; taxi.
Restrictions No smoking in restaurant. No children under 12. No dogs.
Credit cards Amex, MasterCard, Visa.
Terms B&B: single £51–£52, double £78–£82; D,B&B (min. 2 nights) £66 per person. Set dinner £29.95. Gourmet, Glyndebourne breaks.

WIMBORNE MINSTER Dorset — Map 2:E1

Beechleas
17 Poole Road
Wimborne Minster BH21 1QA

Tel 01202-841684
Fax 01202-849344
Email beechleas@hotmail.com
Website www.beechleas.com

Josephine McQuillan's small hotel/restaurant, a Grade II listed red brick Georgian town house, is 'unstuffy and unpretentious'. 'We found the friendly young staff efficient,' says a visitor this year. Others wrote: 'Attention to small details sets *Beechleas* apart.' A first-floor bedroom was admired: 'It was pretty, large and comfortable, with good-quality furnishings.' But some rooms have been thought 'poky', with over-heavy duvets, and some get traffic noise from the busy road to Poole. Both the small drawing room and the restaurant have an open fire. Richard Medley has been promoted to head chef, and we would welcome reports on his 'Anglo-French modern' cooking. One couple this year found the *nouvelle cuisine* not to their taste, and the service slow, but another reported that booking was essential, as the restaurant 'is excellent and is gaining quite a reputation locally'. The lengthy menu might include sautéed king scallops flambéed with Pernod on a bed of leeks; supreme of chicken with mozzarella, wrapped in smoked bacon on roasted vegetables with a garlic and thyme-scented mash. 'Breakfast, in the conservatory overlooking the garden, was pleasant. Good coffee, warm rolls, but the jams were indifferent.' Wimborne is a delightful market town, with an impressive minster and a large Friday market, 'lots of proper shops, little alleys, and a feeling of space'. The surrounding countryside is 'gentle and varied'. A local guide will take hotel guests on a Thomas Hardy tour. Kingston Lacy, a National Trust house with an outstanding collection of paintings, is just west of town. (*Mr and Mrs Nigel Primrose, A and DW, and others*)

Open All year, except 24 Dec–12 Jan. Lunch by arrangement.
Rooms 9 double. 2 in coach house, 2 in lodge. 2 on ground floor.
Facilities Lounge/bar, restaurant (background music 'when appropriate' during meals). Small walled garden. Coast 6 miles.
Location 5 mins from centre, on road (some rooms get traffic noise). Parking.
Restrictions No smoking: restaurant, bedrooms. Dogs in ground-floor bedroom only; not in public rooms.
Credit cards All major cards accepted.
Terms B&B: single £69–£89, double £79–£109. Lunch (by arrangement) £19.75. Set dinner (2 to 3 courses) £19.75–£23.75. Child in parents' room: from £10. Weekend breaks from £60 per person D,B&B.

WINCHCOMBE Gloucestershire — Map 3:D5

Wesley House
High Street
Winchcombe GL54 5LJ

Tel 01242-602366
Fax 01242-609046
Email enquiries@wesleyhouse.co.uk
Website www.wesleyhouse.co.uk

The Methodist preacher John Wesley is believed to have stayed in this 15th-century half-timbered building in 1779; hence its name. Today, Matthew Brown ('a natural host, with a mischievous manner') runs it as a restaurant-with-rooms. 'Small, inviting, higgledy-piggledy', with 'a warm welcome, pleasant service', it stands on the busy main street of this ancient town. You step inside to a lounge with a log fire; beyond is the two-tier restaurant. A steep beamed staircase leads to the bedrooms. All but one are very small, but they are stylish, with black beams, rich fabrics, antiques, *objets d'art*; some get street noise; most bathrooms are minute, 'but fresh fruit on a landing, and milk in a thermos flask make all the difference'. The best bedroom, The Terrace, has panoramic views across the North Cotswold edge and the fields surrounding Sudeley Castle (once the home of Henry VIII's last wife, Catherine Parr). We'd be grateful for reports on the meals: the chef (since October 2000), Alex Breach, serves main courses like grilled sea bass with chervil beurre blanc; calf's liver with bacon and a piquant sauce. Puddings include honey mousse with a mango coulis; steamed prune and Armagnac sponge. The wine list includes some interesting South African bottles. Breakfast has freshly squeezed orange juice, warm rolls and croissants, butter and jams in little bowls, 'excellent cooked dishes ranging from smoked haddock to home-made sausages'. Winchcombe, in the Isbourne valley, a designated area of outstanding natural beauty, was a prosperous wool trading centre in the Middle Ages; its grand church and fine old half-timbered buildings recall this period.

Open All year. Restaurant closed Sun evening.
Rooms 5 double (1 with terrace), 1 single.

Facilities Lounge/bar, restaurant with terrace; classical background music at night; function facilities; roof terrace. Horse racing, riding, golf nearby. Unsuitable for ♿.
Location High street of town 6 miles NE of Cheltenham (4 rear/side rooms quietest). Street parking. Bus from Cheltenham.
Restrictions No smoking: restaurant, bedrooms. No small children, except babies. No dogs.
Credit cards Amex, MasterCard, Visa.
Terms B&B: single £40–£45, double £60–£75. Set lunch £14.50, dinner £21.50–£31. 1-night bookings sometimes refused weekends. *V*

WINCHESTER Hampshire — Map 2:D2

Hotel du Vin & Bistro
14 Southgate Street
Winchester SO23 9EF

Tel 01962-841414
Fax 01962-842458
Email info@winchester.hotelduvin.com
Website www.hotelduvin.com

César award in 1998

As the name implies, a wide range of wines without a large mark-up, served with affordable food, is the order of the day at this Georgian red brick town house near the cathedral. It was the first of a small group owned by Gerard Basset and Robin Hutson – there are now sister hotels of the same name in Tunbridge Wells, Bristol and Birmingham (*qqv*). They are liked for their unpretentious air (no dress code, etc), 'appealing bedrooms' and child-friendly attitude. The Winchester operation, managed by Michael Worren, has a decor dedicated to wine: walls are densely hung with vinous pictures, labels, menus and old photographs. Each bedroom is sponsored by a wine company and done in its colours, in uncluttered modern style. All have a CD-player, Egyptian cotton sheets, an efficient bathroom with a power shower. Some rooms are in the main house; others in a purpose-built building; garden-facing rooms are the quietest. Housekeeping may not always be perfect. 'Brown Brothers, stylish in black and white checks and ticking, was comfortable, but lighting could have been better.' Courvoisier (cream and white) is large and quiet; Durney Vineyards is a 'sensuous' suite, with a four-poster draped in maroon velvet and murals that reproduce celebrated nudes. The high-ceilinged sitting room has a *trompe l'oeil* painting, huge sofas and squashy armchairs. In the lively bistro, pale yellow, softly lit and music-free, with wooden floors, small polished mahogany tables, and a 'willing young staff', the new chef, Gareth Longhurst, serves modern 'unfussy' cooking in generous portions, eg, seared tuna with red onion and potato salad; tempura of haddock with pea purée. (*Gillian Pinder, JFH, and others*)

Open All year.
Rooms 1 suite, 22 double. 4 in garden. 1 on ground floor with ♿ access.
Facilities Drawing room, bar, restaurant. No background music. Small walled garden.
Location Central (back rooms quietest). Hotel will send directions. Car park. Station 10 mins' walk.
Restriction Guide dogs only.

Credit cards All major cards accepted.
Terms Room: single/double from £95, suite £185. Breakfast £8.50–£11.50. Full alc £40. Extra bed for child: £10. Christmas package.

The Wykeham Arms
75 Kingsgate Street
Winchester SO23 9PE

Tel 01962-853834
Fax 01962-854411
Email doreen@wykehamarms.fsnet.com

César award in 1996

'This was the tops; lively, informal, unpretentious, with very good food,' writes an inspector in 2001, after visiting this 250-year-old building. A Winchester institution, named after the college's founder, William of Wykeham, and fondly known by locals as *The Wyke*, it stands between the cathedral and the college. Graeme Jameson, the landlord who gave it a characterful decor of memorabilia (cigarette cards, hats, pictures of royalty, schoolboys' oak desks, walking sticks arranged in rows, about 1,600 tankards), now only advises about the wines. The new young managers, Peter and Kate Miller, are 'affable and hands-on'. The staff, mostly girls, all English, 'are friendly, informal, efficient'. You enter straight into the bar (no reception desk), off which radiates a series of eating areas. Some smallish bedrooms, reached up narrow stairs, are above the pub (some might get noise until closing time). 'Mine was genuinely cosy, inviting, with pale wooden furniture, small pictures on walls, a teddy bear on the bed ("she will look after you, as your wife is not here," said the receptionist).' Smarter rooms are in the annexe, the *St George*, a 16th-century building opposite – it has a suite on two floors, a courtyard garden, a sitting room (also a post office/store and a wine merchant). The lunchtime menu ranges from toasted sandwiches to smoked haddock and bacon chowder. 'My dinner was excellent: duck breast in oriental jus, with warm potato salad; "chocolate nemesis" (a rich, gooey cake); lovely brown bread in great chunks.' Wines are taken seriously, and many good ones are available by the glass. 'Breakfast, served by Mr Miller, very friendly, in a small upstairs room, was good, though orange juice was packaged: delicious scrambled eggs and mushrooms; haddock, etc.' Frequent concerts in the college, and Evensong in the cathedral provide culture on the doorstep. Difficult to find if you arrive by car, but detailed instructions accompany booking confirmations. (Good Pub Guide*, and others*)

Open All year, except 25 Dec. Closed for accommodation New Year.
Rooms Pub: 7 double; *St George*: 1 suite, 5 double, 1 single.
Facilities Pub: 2 bars, 4 eating areas, breakfast room; sauna; small garden. *St George*: sitting room, kitchen; garden. No background music. Unsuitable for ♿.
Location By Kingsgate arch, between college and cathedral; hotel will send directions. Car park.
Restrictions No smoking: 3 eating areas, breakfast room, *St George* bedrooms. No children under 14. No dogs in *St George* bedrooms.
Credit cards All major cards accepted.
Terms B&B: single £45, double £79.50, suite £117.50. Full alc £30–£35.

WINDERMERE Cumbria — Map 4: inset C2

Gilpin Lodge
Crook Road
nr Windermere LA23 3NE

Tel 015394-88818
Fax 015394-88058
Email hotel@gilpin-lodge.co.uk
Website www.gilpin-lodge.co.uk

César award in 2000

'Our preferred night stop in the Lakes.' 'Beautifully decorated; most comfortably furnished; extremely well managed.' 'Great attention to detail. Excellent housekeeping, imaginative food.' 'They have got everything right, from the staff (always around when you need them) to our fabulous bedroom and bathroom (Buttermere).' Some tributes this year to John and Christine Cunliffe's white house (Pride of Britain), dating from 1901 with carefully grafted extensions. Fronted by a flagstaff and a dovecote, it stands well back from a road, in large grounds with 'charming gardens', ponds, woodlands and moor. It is run on country house lines (no reception, no formal bar). 'Neither grand nor stylish, it has a comfortable feel.' Service 'is friendly without formality'. In winter, fires blaze in large sitting rooms decorated with bright colours, good fabrics, antiques, china ornaments, fresh flowers. Many bedrooms are spacious, with a sitting area and good views. 'The guest pack is amusingly and warmly written.' The chef, Grant Tomkins, serves modern dishes, eg, monkfish collops with saffron noodles and pesto; guineafowl with a thyme and pancetta risotto; Irish whiskey and chocolate marquise with warm compote of berries. Portions may be a bit large for some tastes, but 'raw materials are first class and well handled'. Lunches range from a full meal in the restaurant to a light one in the lounge. Afternoon teas are 'a work of art'. Breakfast includes fresh orange juice, porridge, home-baked breads, strawberry sorbet in pink champagne, all manner of cooked dishes. Golfing breaks are offered at Windermere golf course across the road. (*Sir John Johnson, Prof. Wolfgang Stroebe, Hannah Cotton, Sophie Lutz and John Holborow, DW*)

Open All year.
Rooms 14 double. Some on ground floor.
Facilities Ramps, 2 lounges, 3 dining rooms ('easy listening' background music during lunch and dinner). 20-acre grounds: ponds, croquet. Lake Windermere, fishing, boating, etc, 2 miles. Free access to nearby country club: swimming pool, sauna, squash, etc.
Location On B5284 Kendal–Bowness. M6 exit 36. Train: Windermere, 2 miles; then taxi.
Restrictions No smoking in restaurant. No children under 7. No dogs.
Credit cards All major cards accepted.
Terms B&B £45–£105; D,B&B £65–£125. Alc lunch £30. Set dinner £35. Off-season reductions. Christmas, New Year packages. 1-night bookings sometimes refused weekends.

Report forms (Freepost in UK) will be found at the end of the *Guide*. If you need more, please ask. But it is not essential that you use them for your reports.

Holbeck Ghyll
Holbeck Lane
Windermere LA23 1LU

Tel 015394-32375
Fax 015394-34743
Email stay@holbeckghyll.com
Website www.holbeckghyll.com

'What a treat. David and Patricia Nicholson have created a haven of comfort. Service was excellent, and not pretentious,' says a visitor this year to this luxurious hotel (Pride of Britain). Others called it 'expensive, but excellent'. The former hunting lodge of Lord Lonsdale, first president of the Automobile Association and donor of the Lonsdale Belt for boxing, is reached up a steep drive off the road to Ambleside. It has 'stunning views' across Lake Windermere to Langdale Falls. In the large grounds are streams, wildlife, tennis, croquet and a jogging trail. A small spa provides health and beauty treatments. Public rooms have stained glass, open fires, wood panelling, large pieces of antique furniture, strong colours. Bedrooms in the main building are well appointed, but the best (newer) rooms are in the lodge; these have a balcony or patio with lake views; four have a kitchenette. Two dining rooms: the older, oak-panelled one is the more opulent; the *Terrace Restaurant* has French windows leading on to a patio for alfresco lunches and early evening meals in summer. 'The dinners were delightful, beautifully presented, with irresistible desserts.' David McLaughlin took over as chef in June 2000 in the *Michelin*-starred restaurant. His style is 'traditional British with French influence', eg, roast quail with onion compote, truffle jus; sea bass with sweet pepper and fennel bouillon; biscuit glacée with exotic fruit. Simpler dishes and vegetarian options can be provided. 'Good breakfasts, especially the croissants on Sunday' (but one visitor disliked the £5 room-service charge). Children are welcomed, though there are few special facilities for them. The homes of Wordsworth and Beatrix Potter are nearby. (*Barbara Wood*)

Open All year.
Rooms 5 suites, 15 double. 6 (4 with kitchenette) in lodge in grounds. Some on ground floor.
Facilities Ramps. 2 lounges ('relaxing' background music in 1), bar, restaurant; function facilities; small spa: sauna, steam room, etc. 7-acre grounds: streams, ponds, woods to lake shore (800 yds), tennis, putting, croquet, jogging track. Civil wedding licence.
Location 3 miles N of Windermere off road to Ambleside. Pass Brockhole Visitor Centre on left, right turn (Holbeck La) towards Troutbeck. Drive ½ mile on left. Station 3 miles.
Restrictions No smoking: restaurant, lodge bedrooms. No dogs in public rooms.
Credit cards All major cards accepted.
Terms B&B: single £110–£130, double £140–£220, suite £200–£240; D,B&B £80–£160 per person. Set lunch £27.50, dinner £45. 10% reduction for 5 or more nights. Off-season, Christmas, New Year breaks. 1-night bookings sometimes refused Sat. ***V***

Before making a long detour to a small hotel, do check that it is open. Some are known to close on impulse.

Storrs Hall
Windermere LA23 3LG

Tel 015394-47111
Fax 015394-47555
Email reception@storrshall.co.uk
Website www.storrshall.co.uk

'It's just beautiful.' 'The location is perfect.' Rave reports came for this Grade II listed Georgian mansion, built by John Gandy, an associate of Sir John Soane, in the style of a villa on Lake Como (but it has a 'rather institutional' extension). It stands in wooded grounds on a peninsula, with views to the south down the lake (not another building in sight) and to the north towards Bowness. Wooded pathways lead to two jetties; boats bob in a small bay, and a small temple rises from the water. Richard Livock, co-owner with Les Hindle, is an antiques dealer, and the house is 'a treasure trove of furniture and art'. In the large entrance hall, lit by a cupola, huge flower arrangements stand on tables and pedestals. The high-ceilinged drawing room has an open fire, rare books, a grand piano. The library contains 'every imaginable board game'. The bar is sporty (stuffed fish and animals, and antlers). Some find the atmosphere 'a bit starchy' and the Victorian furniture 'rather heavy'. But the large best bedrooms have 'a magnificent bed, huge wardrobe, spacious bathroom with a freestanding, claw-footed bath and separate shower'; 'everything you could want, including the view: two white swans drifted across the still water'. 'The personal attention you receive is never flagging.' The manager, Nigel Lawrence, 'a gem of the old school', is 'assiduously deferential'. The restaurant/conservatory looks over lawns that are sometimes visited by fawns. The chef, Michael Dodds, serves 'modern/traditional' cuisine: traditional roasts at Sunday lunch; main courses like pan-fried calf's liver with red wine sauce, or roast breast of Gressingham duck with Madeira jus at dinner. 'Service was attentive and good-humoured. Breakfast very good – fresh orange juice, excellent porridge, fruit, etc.' 'Lovely home-baked cakes for tea.' (*RW, and others*)

Open Feb–Dec.
Rooms 3 suites, 20 double, 3 single.
Facilities Drawing room, library, bar, restaurant; light classical background music. 17-acre grounds: lake frontage, fishing, boating, etc. Unsuitable for ♿. Civil wedding licence.
Location 4 miles S of Windermere, on A592. Train: Windermere, Oxenholme; taxi.
Restrictions Smoking banned in restaurant, discouraged in bedrooms. Children under 12 by arrangement. No dogs in public rooms.
Credit cards Amex, MasterCard, Visa.
Terms B&B: single £100–£135, double £165–£200, suite £250–£315. Set lunch £17.50, dinner £37.50. Spring and autumn breaks. Christmas package. *V*

WINDSOR Berkshire ***See SHORTLIST*** **Map 2:D3**

Always let a hotel know if you have to cancel a booking, whether you have paid a deposit or not. Hotels sustain huge losses due to 'no-shows'.

WINTERINGHAM Lincolnshire — Map 4:E5

Winteringham Fields
Winteringham DN15 9PF

Tel 01724-733096
Fax 01724-733898
Email wintfields@aol.com
Website www.winteringhamfields.com

César award in 1996

Michelin inspectors are said to know instinctively when a chef strays from his kitchen. This may be one reason why Germain Schwab retains his coveted two stars. The Swiss-born chef is always at his stoves at the restaurant-with-rooms he runs with his wife, Annie, in a quiet village on the south bank of the Humber. 'It is beautifully run with good service and an unobtrusiveness that is ideal if you arrive tired,' says a reporter this year. Meals begin with an array of appetisers and are punctuated by 'interesting titbits'. The *à la carte* menu might include paupictte of wood pigeon with spicy beetroot tortellini and parsnip purée; tournedos of monkfish with purée of fennel and orange and rosemary jus. Fish arrives daily from Grimsby; game is served in season. Desserts such as chocolate and hazelnut pavé with praline anglaise, and Granny Smith sorbet in chilled blackberry soup are equally spectacular; the cheese trolley 'is a revelation'. A simpler, three-course no-choice *menu du jour* is also available. The 16th-century house has exposed beams, low doorways and ceilings, oak panelling, narrow corridors and Victorian furniture. In the bedrooms 'no detail has been overlooked: good lighting, fresh flowers, up-to-date magazines, etc'. The rooms in the main building have uneven floors and chintzy fabrics (one has a four-poster and a bathroom down a tiny flight of steps). More spacious ones are in converted stables across the courtyard. A new conservatory behind the restaurant overlooks the landscaped vegetable garden. 'Unsurpassed breakfasts with lovely marmalade, ambrosial lemon curd in swan-shaped dishes, fresh orange juice on the table, lightest-ever brioches, croissants, etc, and the immediate arrival of coffee.' But one couple was surprised that scrambled eggs cost extra. Annie Schwab (who has an MBE for services to tourism) runs the place with a 'marvellous staff' – 'efficient and enthusiastic, yet also informal and friendly'. A marked path leads to a birdwatchers' hide. 'A perfect treat'; 'expensive, but worth every penny' are typical comments. (*John Townsend, and many others*)

Open All year, except Sun, Mon, 2 weeks Christmas/New Year, last week Mar, 1st week Aug, last week Oct.
Rooms 2 suites, 8 double, 3 in courtyard, 200 yds. 3 on ground floor.
Facilities Lounge, bar, restaurant, conservatory, private dining room. No background music. ½-acre grounds; pond. Unsuitable for ♿.
Location Centre of village 4 miles SW of Humber Bridge. Train: Scunthorpe; bus. Parking.
Restrictions No smoking: restaurant, bedrooms. No children under 8, except babies. Dogs at proprietors' discretion, not in public rooms.
Credit cards Amex, MasterCard, Visa.
Terms B&B: single £75, double £100–£160, suite £120–£170. English breakfast £10. Set lunch £28, dinner £36; full alc £85.

WITHERSLACK Cumbria — Map 4: inset C2

The Old Vicarage NEW

Church Road, Witherslack
nr Grange-over-Sands
LA11 6RS

Tel 015395-52381
Fax 015395-52373
Email hotel@oldvicarage.com
Website www.oldvicarage.com

Jill and Roger Brown and Irene and Stanley Reeve have for 24 years run this civilised hotel/restaurant which stands by the church in a hamlet with views over Morecambe Bay. It returns to the *Guide* with several positive reports this year. Some rooms are in the Georgian main house. The 'less than private *en suite* arrangements' in Room 5 are not to everyone's taste, 'but many of our regular guests specifically ask for it,' writes Mrs Brown. Larger rooms are in a newer building in a damson orchard. 'It is that rarity, a top-quality hotel that will take dogs,' writes a regular visitor. 'Our orchard room was large, comfortable, with its own patio overlooking the little forest. We watched the birds through the window, where there are thoughtfully placed bird feeders. Total tranquillity at night – it is well off the beaten track. Not cheap; but worth paying for quality. The Browns' son, James, is the chef and he knows his stuff. Breakfasts are a dream, so large that lunch is not needed.' 'The bedroom decor is quintessentially English,' add inspectors: 'Flowered wallpaper, flowery fabrics, pine furniture. Lighting was well placed for reading; all was spotless. The orchard rooms have a CD-player, a questionable extra, as soundproofing is imperfect – we were treated to our neighbours' collection of Country and Western. The restaurant seeks out the best local suppliers. Dishes are elaborate, but they offer to cook them more plainly if you ask. My guineafowl was excellent, moist and full of flavour, and the vegetarian lemon mascarpone on a rösti with Parmesan-crusted plum tomatoes and a chiffonade of basil had robust flavours and elegant presentation. Breads are home-baked, and wines provide high quality at a range of prices. The breakfast buffet had fresh orange juice; bacon and eggs were perfect, scrambled eggs not so good. A comfortable place, with pleasant staff. The location is wonderful, surrounded by woods, hedges, wild flowers.' (*Susan Chait, and others*)

Open All year.
Rooms 15 double, 1 single. 5, on ground floor, in *Orchard House* 100 yds.
Facilities 2 lounges, 2 dining rooms (classical background music at night). 5½-acre grounds: tennis. River fishing 5 miles. Unsuitable for ♿.
Location 4 miles N of Lindale. From M6 exit 36, follow signs for Barrow (A590). 1st left in Witherslack (signposted: church).
Restrictions No smoking in restaurant. No dogs in public rooms.
Credit cards Amex, MasterCard, Visa.
Terms B&B: single £65, double £100; D,B&B: single £90, double £150. Set lunch/dinner (before 7 pm) £12.50–£15.50; full alc £36. Christmas package. Child in parents' room: B&B £20–£30. *V*

> We need feedback on all entries. People often fail to send in reports on the better-known hotels, assuming that 'someone else is sure to'.

WOLVERHAMPTON West Midlands ***See SHORTLIST*** **Map 3:C5**

WOOLACOMBE Devon Map 1:B4

Watersmeet
Mortehoe
Woolacombe EX34 7EB

Tel 01271-870333
Fax 01271-870890
Email watersmeethotel@compuserve.com
Website www.watersmeethotel.co.uk

'A rare quiet spot in Devon' – on a cliff above the rocky coast, with views from Woolacombe Bay past Hartland Point to Lundy Island – is the setting for 'a comfortable hotel' whose staff 'are relaxed and helpful'. National Trust land is all around, and there is good walking at Morte Point close by. The owners, Mr and Mrs Wickman, marked their first year in charge by remodelling the entrance and creating five premier sea-view bedrooms. The manager, Neil Bradley, and senior staff have remained. Good for a family holiday, *Watersmeet* has a heated outdoor pool and an indoor one with a wave machine; a wide beach with sand and rock pools is a short walk down steps from the large garden; many activities are available (see below). Children's teas 'are appealing to them, and also healthy'. Breakfasts were thought good and promptly served' this year. One visitor (in the summer) felt the hotel needed a spring clean; another thought the housekeeping 'very good', and the dinners 'excellent' though the 'chef has a tendency to cook some dishes in an unexpected way, eg, monkfish with a highly flavoured dark sauce which somehow did not go with the white fish'. The dining room is 'very elegant, with well-trained and speedy service', and there is plenty of choice on the menu, eg, scallops with white wine sauce; lemon sole with prawns and a coconut and chilli sauce; lemon and cream torte with honey ice cream. Interconnecting lounges overlook the view. In low season there are bridge, golfing and painting holidays. 'Not cheap but enjoyable.' (*Evelyn Schaffer, and others*)

Open Feb–Jan.
Rooms 21 double, 1 single. Some on ground floor.
Facilities Lounge, 2 bars, restaurant (classical background music; pianist twice weekly); indoor swimming pool, games room. 3-acre grounds: tennis, swimming pool, croquet, golf practice; by sandy beach: sea bathing, rock pools, surfing. Golf, clay-pigeon shooting, riding arranged.
Location On coast. Mortehoe is 4 miles SW of Ilfracombe. Train: Barnstaple, 16 miles. Parking.
Restrictions No smoking in restaurant. No children under 8 at dinner. No dogs.
Credit cards Amex, MasterCard, Visa.
Terms [2001] B&B £61–£127; D,B&B £74–£140. Light lunch from £2.95; set dinner £28. Christmas package.

We asked hotels to estimate their 2002 tariffs, but many preferred not to think so far ahead and gave their 2001 tariffs. Prices should always be checked on booking.

WORCESTER Worcestershire *See SHORTLIST* Map 3:C5

YARMOUTH Isle of Wight Map 2:E2

The George
Quay Street
Yarmouth PO41 0PE

Tel 01983-760331
Fax 01983-760425
Email res@thegeorge.co.uk
Website www.thegeorge.co.uk

Built as a residence for Admiral Sir Robert Holmes, then Governor of the island, and visited by Charles II in 1651, this is now a stylish hotel, owned by Jeremy and Amy Willcock and John Illsley (of Dire Straits fame). The manager, Jacki Everest, runs it with a large staff. It stands between the pier and a fortress, built by Henry VIII as a defence against the French. The building is lovely, with its flagstoned hall, wide wooden staircase, panelled residents' lounge with an open fire, and 'beautiful bedrooms' on the two upper floors – many have their original wood panelling; two lead on to a balcony. 'No. 20 was one of the best hotel rooms we have ever experienced,' one couple wrote. 'It overlooked the small, immaculate garden, the minute shingle beach, the sails in the Solent and the constant movement of the ferries; the bathroom was particularly nice, with a "loo with a view".' But two singles above the street are described as 'noisy and poky'. The yellow-walled brasserie is popular with locals and yachties (dishes like guineafowl with foie gras; black pudding and a wild mushroom risotto; duck toad in the hole with a vegetable sauce. *The Restaurant*, formal and red walled, has a *Michelin* star for the cooking of Kevin Mangeolles, eg, crab salad with peanut brittle and guacamole; sea bass with poached oyster, girolles and polenta crisps (a note on the menu says that you can ask for ingredients to be more plainly cooked). Some visitors have complained of 'a scarcity of vegetables' and 'not all the items on the breakfast menu were available'. The hotel can be taken over for a house party; its yacht, the *Master George*, is available for hire. The ferry from Lymington docks close by; unless you want to drive round the island, you should park on the mainland and travel as a foot passenger, thereby halving the exorbitant price of the crossing (the hotel has no car park). The *Master Builder's House*, Beaulieu (*qv*), is under the same ownership. More reports, please.

Open All year; restaurant open Tues–Sat dinner only.
Rooms 1 suite, 14 double, 2 single.
Facilities Lounge, bar, brasserie, restaurant; conference room. No background music. ¼-acre garden on pebble beach (no bathing). Sailing, riding, golf, clay-pigeon shooting, walking nearby. Unsuitable for ♿. Civil wedding licence.
Location Waterfront, by ferry port. Train/car: Lymington Pier; then ferry.
Restrictions No smoking in 4 bedrooms. No children under 10. Dogs by arrangement; not in public rooms, except bar.
Credit cards Amex, MasterCard, Visa.
Terms B&B: single £115, double £155, suite £175–£205. Set lunch £17.95, dinner £45.50; full alc £37. 2-night D,B&B rates: 1 dinner free each night. Christmas package. 1-night bookings refused weekends.

YORK North Yorkshire Map 4:D4

The Grange
1 Clifton
York YO30 6AA

Tel 01904-644744
Fax 01904-612453
Email info@grangehotel.co.uk
Website www.grangehotel.co.uk

The staff are 'very friendly, very courteous' at Jeremy Cassel's Regency town house, close to the ancient city walls and within walking distance of the minster. Returning visitors this year had a 'very enjoyable' meal in the hotel's red-walled *à la carte Ivy Restaurant.* Here, the chef, Michael Whiteley, cooks modern dishes like foie gras and quail in a duck and Madeira jelly; roast wild duck with sweet potato cake and spinach purée. The brasserie, in a vaulted cellar (open at midday and in the early evening), serves more robust fare (eg, onion and Bayonne ham tart; braised beef with root vegetables; Moroccan spiced chickpeas with couscous; chocolate and prune pudding). The cooking here was thought less good this year. There is also a seafood bar, where fish dishes can be accompanied by a glass of Dom Ruinart champagne. The bedrooms have fine fabrics, antiques, good lighting, a smart bathroom. A four-poster room was liked: 'well equipped, very romantic'. A 'superior king-size' room, though not large, and with limited drawer/shelving space, 'was very comfortable'. The public rooms, decorated in keeping with the age of the house, have panelling, smart wallpapers, family portraits, open fires, and there is a grand staircase. But one couple, who had hoped to take tea in the drawing room, found it 'taken over by a small conference'. A busy road passes the building, but front windows are double-glazed. (*P and EH, and others*)

Open All year.
Rooms 1 suite, 26 double, 3 single. 6 on ground floor, 1 adapted for ♿.
Facilities Ramps. Drawing room, morning room, library, restaurant, brasserie, seafood bar; jazz/popular background music; conference facilities. Civil wedding licence.
Location 500 yds from city wall, on A19 N to Thirsk (front rooms double-glazed). Car park.
Restrictions No smoking in restaurant. Small dogs only, not in public rooms.
Credit cards All major cards accepted.
Terms [*Until Apr 2002*] B&B: single £100, double £118–£190, suite £220; D,B&B £65–£123 per person. Set Sun lunch £12.50, dinner £26; full alc £25–£32. 2-day breaks. Christmas, New Year packages. 1-night bookings sometimes refused.

Middlethorpe Hall
Bishopthorpe Road
York YO23 2GB

Tel 01904-641241
Fax 01904-620176
E-mail info@middlethorpe.com
Website www.middlethorpe.com

A handsome Grade-II listed William and Mary mansion, formal perhaps – jackets and ties are required in the main dining room – but 'the staff are very friendly, particularly porters, who remember your name'. The facade is matched by an imposing interior: a black-and-white marble-floored hall, an intricately carved staircase; antiques, oil paintings, *objets d'art*, chandeliers in the 'relaxing public rooms' (where mobile phones and laptop computers are banned). Once the home of the diarist Lady Mary Wortley Montagu, *Middlethorpe Hall* (Relais & Châteaux) has been restored by Historic House Hotels Ltd (see also *Hartwell House*, Aylesbury, *The Cadogan*, London, *Bodysgallen Hall*, Llandudno, Wales). 'The restful decor, and the tranquillity of the gardens restore the most jaded spirits,' writes one enthusiast, though the hum of traffic from the busy nearby road is audible. The best bedrooms, in the main house, are enormous and grand. Some have a large sitting room; some have two bathrooms. But one visitor complained of a poorly designed bathroom. The cheaper rooms, in converted stables, are 'pretty, and well provided with pampering'. One guest thought the dining room inadequately staffed for the visit of a large group and breakfast service can be disorganised. But Martin Barker's traditional English cooking was found 'interesting and good', particularly the sweetbread sausage (black pudding, and cauliflower soup are other starters); main courses include poached guineafowl with truffled potatoes; pigeon wrapped in prosciutto. 'Super puds.' Vegetarians are catered for. There is also a simpler grill room. 'The lift is tiny, and stairs are steep.' The attractive spa, with pool, gym and beauty treatments, is concealed behind the cottages. Castle Howard, Newby Hall and the Harlow Carr Botanical Gardens are nearby. (*IGC Farman, Jane and Martin Bailey, and others*)

Open All year. Closed to non-residents Christmas Day, 31 Dec.
Rooms 7 suites, 19 double, 4 single. 19 in courtyard.
Facilities Drawing room, sitting room, library, bar, restaurant, grill room, private dining rooms; function facilities. No background music. 20-acre grounds: walled garden, croquet, lake, spa: health and beauty facilities, swimming pool. Unsuitable for ♿.
Location 1½ miles S of centre, by racecourse. From A64 follow signs to York, then A1036 and signs to Bishopthorpe, then Middlethorpe. Train: York; then taxi.
Restrictions No smoking in restaurant. No children under 8. No dogs.
Credit cards MasterCard, Visa.
Terms [2001] Room: single £109–£140, double £160–£250, suite £220–£325. Breakfast £14.50. Set lunch £19, dinner £36. 2-night breaks. Christmas, New Year packages.

Mount Royale
The Mount
York YO24 1GU

Tel 01904-628856
Fax 01904-611171
Email reservations@mountroyale.co.uk
Website www.mountroyale.co.uk

'We were made very welcome. The staff were extremely friendly.' 'An excellent place.' 'Good value. Very '70s. Very Yorkshire.' This 'dependable, traditional' hotel is near the racecourse and Micklegate Bar, and three-quarters of a mile from the minster. It has been run for many years by the Oxtoby family; Stuart Oxtoby is now in charge, with a long-serving staff. The building is William IV with modern extensions; in the mature garden at the back there is a heated swimming pool. The best bedrooms, with a sitting area and a private veranda, are in the garden annexe, connected to the main building by a covered walkway filled with orange, lemon and fig trees, bougainvillaea and subtropical plants. Some rooms in the main house are quite small and old-fashioned; front ones have double glazing to cut out the noise from the busy road outside. Public rooms include a small bar, a lounge with antiques, a conservatory; there is also a beauty centre, and a full-sized snooker table. A pianist plays at night in the restaurant (it consists of several rooms, most of which overlook the garden). Here, the food is traditional, eg, salmon and haddock fish-cakes; medallions of pork fillet with a whisky and mustard sauce. A brasserie, *Oxos*, offers lighter dishes, like asparagus with Parmesan shavings; smoked haddock Florentine. Vegetarian dishes are served, and 'plenty of bargains' are to be found on the wine list. Breakfast has a buffet with lots of choice, and cooked dishes such as kedgeree. (*SF Riddell, Linda Beckwith*)

Open All year, except 24 Dec–2 Jan. Brasserie open Sun–Fri; restaurant open Mon–Sat.
Rooms 6 suites (4 in garden annexe), 16 double, 1 single. 6 on ground floor.
Facilities Lounges, TV room, bar, brasserie, restaurant (pianist in restaurant at night); background CDs in public rooms; function/meeting room; beauty centre. ½-acre grounds: swimming pool (heated May–Sept). Wishing well. Unsuitable for ♿.
Location Past racecourse on A1036 from Tadcaster, at junction with Albemarle Rd (front rooms double-glazed). Parking. 10 mins' walk or bus from centre.
Restrictions No smoking in restaurant. Dogs not to be left alone in bedrooms.
Credit cards All major cards accepted.
Terms [2001] B&B: single from £85, double from £105, suite £140. Full alc from £25. 2-day breaks.

See also SHORTLIST

****

Traveller's tale Hotel in Hertfordshire The dining room was of such stygian gloom that the candles on each table were necessary so that diners could see the food. Unfortunately they were of a height that made seeing one's dining companion an impossibility. There were about 20 people in the dining room, and the menu consisted of 10 starters and 10 main course choices! My main course was a disaster, which went back to the kitchen practically untasted. No one took the trouble to find why I had not eaten anything. Puddings each night were fresh from the chiller cabinet. Breakfast was equally dreadful. How difficult is it to make toast? Here, they open a plastic bag and put slices in a toaster and guests then spread poor-quality jam on the resulting 'toast'. After breakfast on Sunday, we retired to the lounge to read the papers but were joined by the housekeeper and her vacuum cleaner. We paid the bill and left.

****

Scotland

Seven Danube Street, Edinburgh

Fortunately, the days have passed in rural Scotland when high tea was served up to 6 pm, after which it was impossible to find anything to eat other than fish and chips, or crisps combined with whisky in a pub. While some say there are still dark corners in the Scottish hospitality industry, we list in this chapter nearly 100 hotels where you can find accommodation ranging from simple to luxurious, often with good food too. Glasgow and Edinburgh both have examples of modern, stylish hotels, and Edinburgh has a number of special B&Bs, including one of this year's *César* winners. We have a strong presence along the west coast, a popular route for touring motorists, and have some excellent island listings, including no fewer than four on Skye and three on Harris. We are pleased to include 17 new hotels this year, several of them welcome returnees to the *Guide*. These include a fairy-tale castle overlooking the Irish Sea; a Borders mansion with views of the Cheviot Hills; a new hotel in Edinburgh with a contemporary style and a lively bar/restaurant; a restored Islay hotel with splendid seascapes; and a simple, welcoming place on the holy island of Iona.

ABERDEEN *See SHORTLIST* Map 5:C3

ACHILTIBUIE Highland Map 5:B1

Summer Isles Hotel
Achiltibuie
by Ullapool IV26 2YG

Tel 01854-622282
Fax 01854-622251
Email summerisleshotel@aol.com
Website www.summerisleshotel.co.uk

César award in 1993

'As near perfection as one could wish.' 'Excellent in every way.' Eulogies continue for Mark and Geraldine Irvine's 'deceptively modest-looking' hotel, set up a single-track road off the road north from Ullapool. Achiltibuie itself 'lacks beauty', but all around is 'unrivalled scenery'. From the small, glassed-in public rooms in the front, where fires burn even in summer, there are views across to the Summer Isles and the Hebrides beyond. 'Many hotels offer more obvious attractions, but *Summer Isles* provides the infinitely rarer combination of comfort, efficiency, first-class food, with a genuine concern for guests' well-being. The Irvines are actually reducing the number of bedrooms to avoid overcrowding in the dining room.' Accommodation varies from 'quite basic' rooms in a log cabin or cottage to lavish suites; some rooms overlook the car park; the Boat House suite is by the road. In this 'very friendly' place, guests tend to socialise over pre-dinner drinks. The five-course dinner, served at 8, at well-spaced tables, is 'the highlight of the day'. No choice; portions are substantial. The chef, Chris Firth-Bernard, has a *Michelin* star for his modern British cooking: 'Starters like fish soup, Stilton and hazelnut roulade, or langoustines and spiny lobsters, the dissection of which reduces the dining room to unnatural silence. Main courses alternate fish and meat, cooked so that the excellence of the ingredients is enhanced. The pudding trolley provokes unbridled greed – guests are encouraged to try more than one. Then comes a magnificent selection of cheeses.' There is an 'immensely long' wine list. 'Excellent breakfasts' have home-made bread and rolls, muesli, fruit, and cooked dishes. Bar lunches are served. 'The weather can range from Arctic to Aegean within a week,' say the Irvines. 'Bring wellingtons, comfortable old clothes, your dog, binoculars, paintboxes and midge cream.' Underwater scenery can be explored with the local diving school. (*Margaret Box, Carol Jackson, HJM Tucker, William Goodhart, Don Lupton, Conrad and Marilyn Dehn*)

Open Easter–mid-Oct.
Rooms 4 suites, 8 double. Some in annexes. Some on ground floor. 5 with TV.
Facilities Lounge, study/TV room, residents' bar, public bar/restaurant. No background music. Small garden. Sea 100 yds; bathing 3 miles. Lochs, fly-fishing nearby. Unsuitable for ♿.
Location NW of Ullapool; after 10 miles turn off A835 on to single-track road skirting lochs Lurgain, Bad a Ghaill and Osgaig. Hotel just past village post office. Bus from Ullapool twice daily.
Restrictions Smoking banned in dining room, discouraged in bedrooms. No children under 6. No dogs in public rooms or unaccompanied in bedrooms.

Credit cards MasterCard, Visa.
Terms [2001] B&B: single £69–£150, double £104–£130, suite £180–£220. Bar lunches. Set dinner £41. 10% discount for 6 or more nights.

ANNAN Dumfries and Galloway ***See SHORTLIST*** **Map 5:E2**

ARDVOURLIE Western Isles Map 5:B1

Ardvourlie Castle
Aird a Mhulaidh
Isle of Harris HS3 3AB

Tel 01859-502307
Fax 01859-502348

On the rocky foreshore of Loch Seaforth (*Aird a Mhulaidh* is Gaelic for 'the headland below the high peak') stands this handsome white Victorian lodge which brother and sister Derek and Pamela Martin resurrected from near ruin. Its position, in the centre of the island, makes it a good base for exploring Lewis and the mountains and lochs of north Harris. Antiques and Victorian furnishings re-create a 19th-century atmosphere: oil and gas lights in the dining room, open fires in the lounge and library; oak panelling and Victorian or Edwardian beds in the bedrooms. But there are modern comforts too: eg, lots of hot water. Meals are served in style, matching the grandeur of the house. Derek Martin's cooking is traditional, and benefits from superb local produce, particularly lamb and fish. The no-choice menu features such dishes as king prawn and orange cocktail; halibut poached with mushrooms, onion and cream; blueberry pancakes with cream and yoghurt; and there are unusual Scottish cheeses. 'The helpings were so substantial that neither of us ever finished a main course,' one couple wrote – they are aimed at appetites whetted by walking, birdwatching and flower-spotting. Breakfasts include locally smoked fish, traditionally produced bacon, home-baked bread, home-made marmalade and preserves, and there are home-baked scones and cakes at teatime. Mr Martin's son and daughter-in-law now sometimes assist. (*C and MD*)

Open Apr– Oct. Dining room closed to non-residents.
Rooms 4 double. 3 with bath and hand-held shower. 1 on ground floor. No telephone/TV.
Facilities Lounge with honesty bar, library with piano, dining room. No background music. 13-acre grounds on loch. Unsuitable for ♿.
Location Off A859 12 miles NE of Tarbert, 25 miles S of Stornoway, both reached by ferry. Occasional buses from both.
Restrictions Smoking banned in restaurant; by agreement with other guests in lounges. Children must be old enough to dine with parents. No dogs.
Credit cards None accepted.
Terms D,B&B £95–£115. Packed lunch available. Set dinner (residents only) £25. Single supplement £20. Reductions for 5 or more nights. 1-night bookings refused early in year.

> Important: terms printed in the *Guide* are only a rough indication of the size of the bill to be expected at the end of your stay. It is vital that you check the tariffs when booking.

ARISAIG Highland — Map 5:C1

Arisaig Hotel BUDGET
Arisaig PH39 4NH

Tel 01687-450210
Fax 01687-450310
Email arisaighotel@dial.pipex.com
Website www.arisaighotel.co.uk

Mr and Mrs Ross's modest hotel, dating from 1720, on Loch Nan Ceall, near pier. 13 well-appointed bedrooms; front ones with lovely views. Smart residents' lounge, 3 bars (live music at weekends). Bar meals, teas with home-made scones available. Local fish, langoustines, etc, also haggis, Aberdeen Angus steaks, served in no-smoking restaurant ('easy listening' background music at night). Families welcomed (playroom has toys and games). Closed Christmas. Unsuitable for ♿. MasterCard, Visa accepted. B&B £32–£36. Full alc £22. More reports, please.

Arisaig House
Beasdale
by Arisaig PH39 4NR

Tel 01687-450622
Fax 01687-450626
Email ArisaiGHse@aol.com
Website www.ArisaigHouse.co.uk

'In a word, paradise. We had our wedding breakfast there in 1996, and have returned regularly since. The setting is magnificent, whatever the time of year. Service, food and accommodation are consistently excellent.' Renewed praise for the Smither family's handsome Victorian mansion (Relais & Châteaux) on a large estate with giant redwoods, west of Fort William, by the Road to the Isles. 'Excellent in all departments,' was another compliment this year. 'The urbane new manager, Vincent Gullon, has settled in well.' Tall windows fill the grey brick house with light. It has a carved oak staircase; a drawing room with vaulted ceiling and log fire. The billiard room has college oars and an antique billiard table. The bedrooms, priced according to size and view, are 'charming and traditional, if expensive'; most are spacious. In summer, light lunches and teas are served on a terrace amid roses and begonias. In the 'splendid grounds', you can walk through rhododendrons, azaleas and conifers to a crescent of beach, and rocky promontories with 'wonderful views' across the water. The walled kitchen garden provides some of the ingredients used in Duncan Gibson's 'imaginative cooking' ('Scottish with French influence'). Typical dishes on the four-course menu: navarin of seafood in a saffron-infused prawn consommé, or beef carpaccio with oyster cream and Parmesan; breast of duck with sweet potato purée and bitter orange sauce, or poached sea trout in a lime and dill butter. There are always vegetarian choices, and you can ask for a dish to be simply prepared. Breakfast, personally served, rather than self-help, has a wide choice of fruit, yogurt, etc, as well as a cooked Scottish affair. A good base for exploring the jagged Highland coast, Skye and the Hebrides. (*Angela Taylor, Mr and Mrs JE Rednall*)

Open Mar–Nov. Closed Tues/Wed Mar and Oct.
Rooms 12 double.
Facilities 2 lounges, bar (classical background music), billiard room, dining

room; meeting room. 20-acre grounds: croquet, helipad. Sea loch 15 mins' walk. Unsuitable for ♿.
Location On A830 Fort William–Mallaig, 3 miles E of Arisaig village. Train: Beasdale, 1 mile; hotel will meet.
Restrictions No smoking: dining room, bedrooms. No children under 8, except babies up to 9 months. Guide dogs only.
Credit cards MasterCard, Visa.
Terms [2001] B&B: single £130, double £175–£295. Set lunch £25, dinner £32.50–£39.50. Reductions for 5 or more nights May, June, July, Sept.

The Old Library Lodge BUDGET
Arisaig PH39 4NH

Tel 01687-450651
Fax 01687-450219
Email reception@oldlibrary.co.uk
Website www.oldlibrary.co.uk

'We thoroughly enjoyed our stay,' says an endorsement this year for this former library, built as stables 200 years ago, and converted into a bistro-style restaurant-with-rooms by Alan and Angela Broadhurst. It stands on the waterfront of the old village, looking across Loch Nan Ceall, where *Local Hero* was set, to the Inner Hebrides (reached by ferry). All around is beautiful Highland scenery. The cooking is 'modern Scottish with French touches'. Plenty of choice on the dinner menu, eg, shellfish bisque with home-made bread; grilled duck breast marinated in honey and soy sauce; rum-flavoured chocolate pot. Lunches of soups, salads, fish-cakes, omelettes and casseroles are served, on the front patio in fine weather. There is a residents' lounge upstairs. Two bedrooms are in the main house (one is small); the others are in an extension at the rear. These have a little balcony with a table and chairs, overlooking the small terraced garden. Some walls may be thin. On display are watercolours by a local artist (some are for sale). Guests arriving by train can be met at the station. (*Michael Williamson, RH*)

Open Mar–Nov. Restaurant closed midday Tues.
Rooms 6 double.
Facilities Lounge, restaurant (low-key jazz during dinner). Small garden, patio. Loch foreshore across road (shingle beach; no bathing). Unsuitable for ♿.
Location Village centre, on waterfront (quiet at night). Public parking.
Restrictions No smoking: restaurant, bedrooms. No dogs.
Credit cards Amex, MasterCard, Visa.
Terms B&B £38–£45. Full alc lunch £12.50, dinner £28. 10% reduction for 3 or more nights. *V*

AUCHENCAIRN Dumfries and Galloway Map 5:E2

Balcary Bay Hotel NEW
Shore Road, Auchencairn
nr Castle Douglas
DG7 1QZ

Tel 01556-640217 and 640311
Fax 01556-640272
Email reservations@balcary-bay-hotel.co.uk
Website www.balcary-bay-hotel.co.uk

A 'very pleasant family hotel' in an 'idyllic and peaceful setting' right on the shore of the Balcary Bay. 'You can't get much closer to the water,' one guest wrote. It returns to the *Guide* this year, with many enthusiastic reports backed by a positive inspection. 'A superb position; at high tide you hear the waves lapping as you go to sleep. The quality of evening light is breathtaking.' The 'comfort, excellent food and careful personal attention' are praised. The large white building is gabled and turreted, with window surrounds picked out in blue and corner brickwork in cream; inside are 'charming public rooms and well-furnished bedrooms'. The residents' lounge is 'hospitable', and there is a pretty conservatory, 'perfect for summer lunches', overlooking the water. Bedrooms range from spacious to smallish; one guest had a minor quibble that the bathroom shelf sloped, leading to an eventual avalanche of toiletries, but she loved her 'cosy room'. Three 'fabulous' new rooms on the ground floor, with a patio, huge plate-glass windows and direct access to the beach, are a 'birdwatcher's dream'. Graeme Lamb owns and runs the hotel with his wife, Clare, having taken over from his parents, Ron and Joan, who still come in to help. He and his plaid-wearing staff come in for generous praise from guests, especially from parents of children: 'They were the most welcoming staff we have ever met. The chefs carried our disabled 11-year-old son up and down stairs, with only two minutes' notice, whenever he needed to be moved; cots were quickly found for our baby, extra towels were never a problem, and a teddy was already placed on our four-year-old daughter's bed. There were children's portions of any dish they wanted, and the waitresses always had time to chat with them.' In the restaurant, which looks over the bay, the chef, Charles Kelly, produces imaginative food on a daily menu: 'Memorable tastes were salmon with cucumber spaghetti; scallop and chorizo gateau; wonderful sticky toffee pudding.' Vegetables are 'fresh and beautifully cooked'. There is a vegetarian menu, and a good wine list. (*John Knighton, Deborah Zachary, Eric Dodson, and others*)

Open Approx 1 Mar–26 Nov.
Rooms 17 double, 3 single. 3, on ground floor, with access for ♿.
Facilities 2 lounges, cocktail bar, and conservatory, restaurant. No background music. 3½-acre grounds: by pebble beach. Direct access to beach, safe bathing.
Location From A711 Dumfries–Kirkcudbright, follow signs to Auchencairn; turn left over bridge on entering village, and follow shore road for 2 miles.
Restrictions No smoking: restaurant, 1 lounge, conservatory. No dogs in public rooms.
Credit cards Amex, MasterCard, Visa.
Terms B&B: £54–£61; D,B&B £60–£82. Bar lunches from £5.75. Set Sun lunch £11.50, dinner £25.75; full alc £32. Autumn/spring breaks. 1-night bookings sometimes refused.

AUCHTERHOUSE Highland — Map 5:D2

Old Mansion House
by Dundee
DD3 0QN

Tel 01382-320366
Fax 01382-320400
Email oldmansionhouse@netscapeonline.co.uk
Website www.visitscotland.com/oldmansionhouse

'A beautiful house, a beautiful room and a wonderful welcome, immediately making me feel relaxed and valued' – one visitor's impressions in 2001 of this handsome white mansion. It stands on a knoll in large wooded grounds near Dundee, on the site of a medieval castle – it was rebuilt as a mansion in the 17th/18th centuries, and was home to the Earls of Strathmore, the Buchans, Ogilvies and others. It is now a stylish and sumptuous small hotel, owned and run by Maxine and Jannick Bertschy (they are Scottish; he is of Swiss extraction). 'The bedroom, with amazing ceiling plasterwork, was, for me, the best part: quiet, tastefully decorated, with terrific views over the extensive gardens … and a glass of Chardonnay brought up to accompany my bath!' The rooms vary in size; some are large, with a four-poster. In the Vaulted Room (*c.* 1245) you can play chess or listen to music. 'Nice touches' include sherry and books; bathrooms have plenty of toiletries. The dining room, 'wonderfully surreal', has an ornate plasterwork ceiling (Jacobean) 'like stalactite deposits in a fairyland castle', and an impressive mantel with heraldic emblems. Chef Tim Cribben provides Scottish and European cooking, with some choice on the *prix-fixe* menu, and plenty on the *carte*. 'The evening meal was of a high quality: smoked salmon terrine, lamb with berry jus and roasted vegetables; a great selection of home-made chocolates and sweets to go with my coffee (in the library/bar by the fire).' There is also a bistro. 'Breakfast was fine, with venison sauces, but without special touches like home-made preserves.' Children are welcomed. (*Val Juneman*)

Open All year.
Rooms 2 suites (1, for 4, on ground floor, in *Lodge House*), 5 double.
Facilities Lounge, library/bar (classical/Scottish background music), courtyard bar/bistro, dining room, private dining room. 14 acre grounds: tennis, croquet, squash, swimming pool, river. Clay-pigeon shooting, horse riding, off-road driving, golf nearby.
Location 5 miles NW of Dundee. Take A923 (Coupar Angus) off Kingsway; through Birkhill village, join B954. House 2 miles on left, outside Auchterhouse.
Restrictions No smoking: restaurant, some other public areas, bedrooms. Dogs by arrangement (*Lodge House* only).
Credit cards All major cards accepted.
Terms B&B: single £80–£85, double £110–£120, suite £140–£150; D,B&B from £75 per person. Set lunch £20, dinner £30; full alc £35. Christmas/Easter packages. *V*

AVIEMORE Highland — Map 5:C2

Corrour House BUDGET
Inverdruie, by Aviemore
PH22 1QH

Tel 01479-810220
Fax 01479-811500
Website www.corrourhouse.co.uk

Originally a dower house for the Rothiemurchus estate, this Victorian house, bay-windowed and gabled, is now a welcoming small hotel. It stands quietly in wooded grounds well away from busy Aviemore, with views over fields and forest to the Cairngorm mountains. The owners, David and Sheana Catto, are 'kind hosts', said the nominator, and the bedrooms are 'large, spotless and comfortable'. The 'very good' four-course dinner menu, based on locally produced ingredients and home-grown herbs and vegetables, has two choices at each course, eg, scallops and bacon on lemon cream sauce; carrot and orange soup with coriander; roast leg of lamb with red wine and herb gravy; strawberry and almond Pavlova roulade. During dinner, you might see deer stroll across the lawn. Breakfast is good, too, with unusual jams. 'Excellent value for money.' A good base for touring Strathspey, and the Rothiemurchus estate has many tourist activities – Land Rover safaris, etc. (*DP*)

Open 27 Dec–31 Oct.
Rooms 7 double, 1 single.
Facilities Lounge, bar, dining room; classical background music at night. 4-acre grounds. River, fishing, skiing, golf nearby. Unsuitable for ♿.
Location ½ mile S of Aviemore on B970, signposted Glenmore and Coylumbridge. Train/bus from Aviemore.
Restrictions No smoking: dining room, lounge, some bedrooms. No dogs in public rooms.
Credit cards MasterCard, Visa.
Terms B&B £30–£45; D,B&B £50–£70. Set dinner £25. Reductions for 2 or more days D,B&B. *V*

BALLANTRAE South Ayrshire — Map 5:E1

Glenapp Castle NEW
Ballantrae
KA26 0NZ

Tel 01465-831212
Fax 01465-831000
Email enquiries@glenappcastle.com
Website www.glenappcastle.com

'A shining new star on the Scottish hotel scene.' 'The best country hotel to open in Britain in the last ten years.' Two eminent *Guide* hoteliers commend this 19th-century fairy-tale castle, once the seat of the Earl of Inchcape. Reached up a drive behind locked wrought iron gates (you must telephone for admittance), and overlooking the Irish Sea, it stands in large wooded grounds, with a lake, a large walled garden, a magnificent Victorian glasshouse. Our inspectors were delighted: 'The charming young owners, Graham and Fay Cowan, have taken six years of loving restoration to create a unique place. Much of the interior has been preserved, including the Austrian oak-panelled entrance hall and staircase. Superb antiques, fine paintings, colourful rugs, vibrant paintwork, intricate plasterwork, create the feel of a luxurious country house. The main drawing room, though massive, feels cosy; in the parquet-floored library are floor-to-ceiling bookshelves, an intricately carved fireplace. The dining room has elegant napery, glassware and china, upholstered armchairs.' Spacious bedrooms have a wide bed, books, videos, a CD-player. 'Our huge bathroom had a deep, freestanding Victorian bath.' 'The owners seem to be there whenever needed, whisking away wet macs when we returned from a sodden walk, offering a late lunch, presiding over evening drinks.' They aim for a 'traditional country house party' atmosphere, accepting guests only by prior arrangement, and charging a flat rate (including all drinks, though alternative wines can be chosen from a list for an extra charge). Laurent Gueguen's cooking on a five-course no-choice menu (written in French) is thought 'good, not exceptional', 'perhaps over-ambitious – delicious *amuse-bouches*; parsnip soup with ginger was excellent, but beef tournedos was overcooked, and banana tarte Tatin didn't quite work'. Breakfast, in a lemon and green room, has fresh orange juice, plenty of choice, 'but service, though willing, was somewhat forgetful'. (*Michael Leonard, Paul Henderson, and others*)

Open Beginning Apr–end Oct. All year for private parties/conferences.
Rooms 2 suites, 15 double. Some on ground floor. 1 adapted for ♿.
Facilities Lift, ramp. Lounge, library, 2 dining rooms. No background music. 30-acre grounds: walled garden, tennis, croquet. Golf, fishing, shooting, boat trips arranged. Wedding facilities.
Location 1 mile from A77, near Ballantrae. Through village, cross river Stinchar. After 100 yds, 1st turning on right. At wrought iron gates use telephone entry system (on green pillar).
Restrictions Smoking in library only. No children under 5 at dinner. Dogs in ground floor rooms only (if accompanied), not in public rooms.
Credit cards Amex, MasterCard, Visa.
Terms [2001] Full board (with drinks): single £300, double £410, suite £450–£500. Child in parents' room: under 5, free; 5–15, £100.

BALLATER Aberdeenshire **Map 5:C3**

Balgonie Country House
Braemar Place
Ballater AB35 5NQ

Tel/Fax 013397-55482
Email balgoniech@aol.com
Website www.royaldeesidehotels.com

In peaceful 4-acre grounds looking over golf course to hills of Glen Muick: John and Priscilla Finnie's Edwardian country house. 1 mile from Ballater, off A93 Aberdeen–Perth. Sitting room, bar, dining room (no smoking, no background music). Good cooking, 'French with local Scottish produce', eg, terrine of partridge and chicken livers; sea bass with saffron risotto and sauce vierge; walnut and whisky cream. Salmon fishing on river Dee arranged. Open 10 Feb–5 Jan. Only dining room suitable for ♿. No dogs in public rooms. All major credit cards accepted. 9 double bedrooms. B&B £45–£72.50; D,B&B £77.50–£105. Set lunch £19, dinner £31.50. No recent reports; we'd like some, please. *V*

Darroch Learg
Braemar Road
Ballater AB35 5UX

Tel 013397-55443
Fax 013397-55252
Email nigel@darrochlearg.co.uk.

Two Victorian listed buildings constitute this hotel – the Gaelic name means 'an oak copse on a sunny hillside'. It looks over the Dee valley and Ballater's golf course to Lochnagar mountain. Owned by the Franks family for over 40 years, it is run by Nigel Franks, and is liked by *Guide* readers for its setting, food and country house ambience. The main house is baronial and turreted; the other, *Oakhall*, a pink and granite former hunting lodge, has cheaper bedrooms and is suitable for a group booking. 'This is almost our favourite hotel in Scotland,' one enthusiast comments. 'The views are superb, the cream, blue and yellow colour scheme of our quiet room was very pleasant. Breakfasts are great (delicious porridge).' Others wrote of 'friendly owners', 'charming staff'. Drinks are served in an attractive drawing room with a log fire, or in a 'smoke room'. The 'superb food' is admired too. In the conservatory restaurant, candlelit at night, the 'talented chef', David Mutter, cooks modern dishes on menus with plenty of choice, eg, ravioli of foie gras with onion jam, Parmesan cream and pesto; loin of lamb with ratatouille and red wine sauce; lemon tart with raspberry sauce. The 'excellent wine list' includes plenty of half bottles, and a fixed mark-up per bottle means that the higher quality wines are good value. The bedrooms vary; most have good views; they are supplied with bathrobes, flowers and fruit; some have antiques. Some upper rooms in *Oakhall* can be 'cramped'. Children are welcomed, though there are no special facilities for them. A good base for exploring Crathes and Drum, Corgarff Castle and the Speyside distilleries, and for a golfing or fishing holiday. (*FD, and others*)

Open All year, except Christmas, last 3 weeks Jan.
Rooms 17 double, 1 single. 5 in *Oakhall*. 1 on ground floor.
Facilities Ramp. 2 lounges, smoking room, conservatory restaurant. No background music. 4-acre grounds. River Dee, fishing ¼ mile (prior notice needed); tennis, golf nearby.
Location On A93, ½ mile W of Ballater. Bus from Aberdeen.
Restrictions No smoking: restaurant, 2 lounges, bedrooms. No dogs in public rooms.
Credit cards All major cards accepted.
Terms B&B £40–£77.50; D,B&B £61–£106.50. Set lunch £19.50, dinner £35. Child in parents' room: under 12, free. Autumn, spring breaks. New Year package. 1-night bookings refused 1st weekend Sept. *V* (Oct–Apr)

BALQUHIDDER Stirling — Map 5:D2

Monachyle Mhor
Balquhidder
Lochearnhead FK19 8PQ

Tel 01877-384622
Fax 01877-384305
Email info@monachylemhor.com
Website www.monachylemhor.com

'Somewhere to keep as a treasured secret,' said one correspondent, inconsistently but selflessly recommending this pretty pink farmhouse overlooking lochs Voil and Doine. Once the home of the family of Rob Roy MacGregor (he is buried in the village church four miles away), it is now owned by Jean and Rob Lewis and their son, Tom. It stands at the end of the narrow road 'breathtakingly beautiful, but treacherous in places', and mentioned in Stevenson's *Kidnapped*, that winds along Loch Voil through the Braes o' Balquhidder. All around is a vast estate with a working farm, two lakes with fishing, deerstalking and grouse shooting in season. The atmosphere is informal, the public rooms are small, and the lounge was thought 'dull' this year, but 'Jean is a superb host, the centre of social interaction before and after dinner'; 'go for the friendly service, fantastic location, outstanding food'. The eclectic cooking of Tom Lewis is served in a conservatory-style restaurant. 'Our menu included smoked haddock thermidor with garden spinach and free-range egg; pumpkin and rosemary soup with crème fraîche; fillet of pork with Toulouse sausage and mixed bean cassoulet; Pavlova with Drambuie cream.' Meat and fish are locally produced, Tom Lewis cures his own 'bresaola' and 'Parma ham', and the organic walled garden provides vegetables and herbs. The wines are fairly priced. One couple, less ecstatic about dinner, found breakfast 'delicious, with scrambled eggs and smoked salmon, freshly squeezed orange juice, home-baked bread, and scones just out of the oven'. There are good bar meals and sandwiches, too. Some bedrooms in the main house have been enlarged, and given better lighting and a bigger bathroom with a power shower. The newer rooms in the courtyard, though 'attractively appointed', are thought to 'lack ambience'. Additional rooms are in a four-bedroom Victorian house in Strathyre (eight miles away). (*Ffion Griffith, CC Schofield, and others*)

Open All year.
Rooms 4 suites, 6 double. 5 in courtyard. Self-catering cottages.
Facilities Lounge, bar, restaurant. No background music. 2,000-acre estate: garden, farm, loch, river, grouse moor; walking, salmon/trout fishing, deer-stalking. Unsuitable for ♿.
Location 11 miles NW of Callander. Turn right off A84 at *Kingshouse Hotel*; follow road 6 miles along glen.
Restrictions No smoking: restaurant, bedrooms. No children under 12. No dogs in house.
Credit cards MasterCard, Visa.
Terms [2001] B&B: single £50–£75, double £75–£95. Set lunch £18.50, dinner £32.50.

BLAIRGOWRIE Perth and Kinross — Map 5:D2

Kinloch House
by Blairgowrie PH10 6SG

Tel 01250-884237
Fax 01250-884333
Email info@kinlochhouse.com
Website www.kinlochhouse.com

A grand 19th-century Scottish mansion, run as a hotel by the Shentall family since 1981. It has 'the feel of a country house', with oak panelling, family portraits, *objets d'art* and books in the public rooms. In the large, peaceful wooded grounds are Highland cattle, a restored Victorian walled garden and a newly built health and fitness centre (for residents only). At dinner, Mr Shentall, 'resplendent in his kilt', is 'witty and welcoming'; other male staff wear tartan trews; male visitors are expected to wear a jacket and tie. 'Service cannot be faulted,' says a regular visitor, 'and the food is excellent, beautifully presented, with very good choice.' Bill McNicoll, the chef, comes into the dining room to carve the roasts from the trolley. His 'modern Scottish' menus, based on local produce, include Arbroath smokie soufflé; loin of roe deer wrapped in a partridge and herb mousse; Highland salmon marinated in whisky, honey and herbs. There is also a vegetarian menu. 'Everything is fresh and cooked to order. The young staff are willing. No background music, a pleasant change.' Many bedrooms are spacious; 'ours was warm, with lashings of hot water; housekeeping could not be faulted'. Some rooms have a four-poster and a large Victorian bath. At breakfast there is freshly squeezed orange juice and a huge selection of cooked dishes, including kedgeree. Popular with shooting parties (the house has a game larder, drying facilities and kennels for gun dogs), fishermen (plenty of lochs and rivers nearby), and golfers (30 courses within an hour's drive). (*Janice Carrera*)

Open All year, except 18–29 Dec.
Rooms 2 suites, 14 double, 4 single. 4 on ground floor.
Facilities Ramp. Drawing room, conservatory, lounge bar, 2 dining rooms, private dining room. No background music. 35-acre grounds: walled garden; health and fitness centre (sauna, steam room, spa, exercise pool, gym). Fishing, sailing, golf nearby.
Location 3 miles W of Blairgowrie, on A923 to Dunkeld. Train: Perth, 16 miles; then taxi.
Restrictions No smoking in restaurant. No children under 7 in restaurant, or under 12 in health and fitness centre. No dogs in public rooms.
Credit cards All major cards accepted.
Terms B&B: single £60–£85, double £99–£163, suite £140–£220; D,B&B: single £75–£108, double £110–£220, suite £220–£270. Set lunch £17, dinner £35. Winter and summer breaks. New Year package.

BRODICK North Ayrshire — Map 5:E1

Kilmichael Country House
Glen Cloy, by Brodick
Isle of Arran KA27 8BY

Tel 01770-302219
Fax 01770-302068
Email enquiries@kilmichael.com
Website www.kilmichael.com

'A wonderful three-day stay' was enjoyed by visitors this year to this late 17th-century listed building, said to be the oldest in Arran. It has a 'beautiful setting' at the end of an unmade road; its extensive grounds, patrolled by ducks and peacocks, have spectacular views of Arran's mountains. The owners, Geoffrey Botterill and Antony Butterworth, and their staff are 'very friendly' and the house contains a collection of Levantine and oriental antiques. The bedrooms, all different (Forest, Blue, the Garden and Fullerton suites, etc), are supplied with fresh flowers and fruit, an Ordnance Survey map, and 'a wee dram of whisky to welcome you on arrival'. Some are in converted stables in the landscaped garden. Bathrooms have 'wonderfully peaty brown water'. Log fires burn in the public rooms. The food, served with fine silver and crystal, is 'a blend of traditional and modern, with strong Mediterranean influences'. Two choices of each course on the four-course menu: eg, smoked salmon and prawn cheesecake with a flower and herb salad; lemon and lavender sorbet; rack of lamb with walnuts and pomegranates; damson gin fool, or 'Mr McClery's excellent cheeses'. There is always a vegetarian dish, and a light room-service meal can be requested. Reservations are for B&B; you must book a table for dinner. Breakfast eggs are supplied by *Kilmichael*'s free-range chickens. There is good walking from the door. Nearby Brodick is a large resort village; Brodick Castle, home of the Dukes of Hamilton, is open to the public. Arran, the most southerly and the most accessible of the Scottish islands, has seven golf courses and many interesting geological sites. (*Bill Strang and Stuart Pearson*)

Open Mar–Oct. Lunch not served.
Rooms 3 suites, 4 double. 3 in converted stables. 6 on ground floor. 2 self-catering cottages.
Facilities 2 drawing rooms, dining room ('classical/nostalgic' background music during meals). 4½-acre grounds: burn. Beach 1 mile; sailing, golf, walking nearby.
Location 1 mile from village. Ferry from Ardrossan; from ferry terminal, go N on A841; turn inland opposite golf club; follow signs to long drive leading to house. Bus to end of drive, or they will meet ferry.
Restrictions Smoking in 1 drawing room only. No children under 12. No dogs in public rooms.
Credit cards MasterCard, Visa.
Terms [2001] B&B £60–£75. Set dinner £29.50. Discounts for 3–7 nights; ferry-inclusive packages available. 1-night bookings occasionally refused Sat.

BUNCHREW Highland — Map 5:C2

Bunchrew House
Bunchrew
Inverness IV3 8TA

Tel 01463-234917
Fax 01463-710620
Email welcome@bunchrew-inverness.co.uk
Website www.bunchrew-inverness.co.uk

'In wonderful setting', silver-spired, castellated 17th-century mansion overlooking Black Isle, on shores of Beauly Firth, 2½ miles NW of Inverness. 'Helpful owners', Janet and Graham Cross (he tells stories of the house ghost); 'everything clean and welcoming'. Ambitious French-influenced Scottish food, using local ingredients, in spacious dining room overlooking Beauly Firth; 'comfortable bar'; Celtic/classical background music in public rooms. Conference/function/wedding facilities. 20-acre grounds: landscaped gardens, fishing. Golf, skiing, sailing nearby. Unsuitable for ♿. No smoking in restaurant. No dogs in public rooms. Closed Christmas. Amex, MasterCard, Visa accepted. 14 bedrooms. B&B: single £85–£150, double £115–£195; D,B&B £82.50–£175 per person. Set lunch £23, dinner £29.50. More reports, please.

CAMPTOWN Borders — Map 5:E3

Jedforest Hotel NEW
& Restaurant Bardoulet
Camptown, Jedburgh
TD8 6PJ

Tel 01835-840222
Fax 01835-840226
Email mail@jedforesthotel.freeserve.co.uk
Website jedforesthotel.freeserve.co.uk

New owners, since late 1999, Mr and Mrs Ferguson, have extensively refurbished the 'first and last hotel in Scotland', quietly set in 35-acre estate with riverside walk and fishing. 7 miles N of border. 3 miles S of Jedburgh (with impressive ruined abbey) on A68. 'Good decor, spacious bedroom, lovely breakfast toast,' say nominators. 'Very good nouvelle cuisine *by chef Patrick Bardoulet and his French team, but service can be slow, and we would have liked more vegetables.' No smoking: restaurant, bedrooms. No dogs in public rooms. All major credit cards accepted. 8 bedrooms (4 more, on ground floor, planned for 2002). B&B: single £57.50–£75, double £85–£115; D,B&B £62–£94.50 per person. Full alc £35 [2001]. More reports, please.* ***V***

CARDROSS Argyll and Bute **Map 5:D1**

Kirkton House BUDGET
Darleith Road
Cardross G82 5EZ

Tel 01389-841951
Fax 01389-841868
Email ghg@kirktonhouse.co.uk
Website www.kirktonhouse.co.uk

'Stewart and Gillian Macdonald give a really warm welcome to their 160-year-old converted farmhouse, which has generous views of the river Clyde and the hills beyond,' write an appreciative couple. 'The accommodation is not luxurious, but homely and comfortable.' Others, too, found the hosts 'charming', 'real professionals', the hotel 'delightful' and their bathroom 'worthy of a five-star hotel'. One lone visitor, late in the season, felt slightly neglected, especially at dinner when a large party took up a lot of attention. And the lounge gets crowded when the house is full. In general, though, there is high praise for the reasonably priced evening meal, ordered in the lounge at 7 and served by oil lamplight at 7.45. The traditional menus include mushrooms on toast; haggis 'n' neeps; Dover sole; beef and venison steaks. 'Gillian is an excellent cook of traditional fare. Her fruit crumble and custard is just how it should be – so much so that we had second helpings.' For breakfast there are Loch Fyne kippers; smoked haddock; large grills. Children are welcomed (babysitting can be arranged), and so are pets. A good base for touring: Glasgow is only 18 miles away. 'Quiet location, great welcome, great food. Great value for money.' Local attractions: Loch Lomond, Rennie Mackintosh's Hill House, Geilston Gardens (National Trust). (*Michael and Maureen Heath, Mary J Nicholson, HJM Tucker, and others*)

Open 1 Feb–30 Nov.
Rooms 6 double. 2 on ground floor. 1 suitable for ♿.
Facilities Lounge, dining rooms. No background music. 2-acre grounds: children's playground, paddock, stabling.
Location Turn N at W end of village, up Darleith Rd. Hotel ½ mile on right after 3 cottages.
Restrictions Smoking banned in restaurant, allowed in other public rooms 'if other guests agree'. Dogs in public rooms by arrangement.
Credit cards All major cards accepted.
Terms B&B £33.50–£45; D,B&B £49.75–£61.75. Set dinner £16.25–£20; full alc £24.50. Child in parents' room: baby, free; under 12, from £11.

If you are nominating a hotel, please tell us enough to convey its character and quality.

CHIRNSIDE Borders Map 5:E3

Chirnside Hall NEW
Chirnside, nr Dunns
TD11 3LD

Tel 01890-818219
Fax 01890-818231
Email chirnsidehall@globalnet.co.uk
Website www.chirnsidehallhotel.com

In 2000, Christian and Tessa Korsten took over this recently restored 1830s mansion near the Borders, now warmly recommended to the *Guide*. 'From the front windows there are views across rolling countryside to the Cheviot hills. The hostess, with a delightful mix of Dutch and Scottish accents, maintains a discreet presence in the public rooms. Our bedroom had a comfortable settee, and shortbread biscuits. The large double drawing room is sumptuously furnished with period settees and chairs.' The spacious dining room has white and blue linen, blue candles, high-backed upholstered chairs and well-apart tables ('ours, for two, would have been used by many other establishments to seat four or six'). 'Dinner was tastefully prepared and presented by the chef, Robert Taylor.' His traditional menus include asparagus and prawn salad; herb-crusted salmon with saffron pasta and lemon butter sauce; baked stuffed apple with toffee sauce and crème fraîche. Log fires warm the lounge and dining room; there is a billiard room and a fitness room. Edinburgh and Newcastle are both an hour's drive away. (*Maurice and Vera Hook, and others*)

Open All year.
Rooms 10 double.
Facilities 2 lounges, billiard room, fitness room, dining room; 'easy listening' background music all day; library (conference facilities). 5-acre grounds. Golf, walking, fishing, horse riding nearby. Unsuitable for ♿.
Location NE of Chirnside, off A6015 to Berwick-on-Tweed.
Restrictions No smoking in dining room. Children under 12 'negotiable'. No dogs in public rooms.
Credit cards MasterCard, Visa.
Terms B&B £60–£75; D,B&B £77.50–£92.50. Set dinner £23.50. 2/3-day breaks. Christmas package.

COLBOST Highland Map 5:C1

Three Chimneys Restaurant and House Over-by
Colbost, Dunvegan
Isle of Skye IV55 8ZT

Tel 01470-511258
Fax 01470-511358
Email eatandstay@threechimneys.co.uk
Website www.threechimneys.co.uk

César award in 2001

'A superlative experience. From the warmth of the welcome, the superb split-level, state-of-the-art suites, the exquisite food, everything was exemplary.' 'A high-quality operation. The owners and staff are charming.' 'They take pride and enjoyment in what they are doing, without pomp or ceremony.' In a 'supremely beautiful' setting by Loch Dunvegan, in the remote north-west of the Isle of Skye, Eddie and Shirley Spear run their restaurant-with-rooms in two crofters' cottages, 'with neat flowerbeds and lush grass'. The suites are across the courtyard from the restaurant ('over-by' is Scottish for 'next door'). Inside the traditional buildings is a modern decor of 'simple designer chic': wood, natural fabrics, soft colours, uncluttered lines. The suites' tall windows open on to wild scenery: 'We pulled back our curtains to see a flock of sheep strolling past, and the sparkling silver loch beyond.' 'Sublimely comfortable' large beds have excellent reading lamps. Bathrooms are luxurious. The restaurant – two 'cosy rooms' – has candles, dark beams, white walls, a fire in the adjoining bar. 'Couldn't fault the food', 'exquisite', are typical comments, though one writer thought it 'good but not "super gastronomic", with rather too many supplementary charges'. Lobster bisque is 'outstanding', 'to die for'. Diners choose between two and four courses, eg, crispy salmon fish-cakes with watercress crème fraîche; partan bree; venison collops and skirlie potato cake; chocolate tart. 'The charming eldest son of the house is enthusiastic about his father's excellent wines.' The 'light and airy' breakfast room contains a fine buffet; 'smoked salmon on toast spread with crowdie was the highlight'; there is porridge with thick cream, smoked duck and venison, home-made oatcakes and jams. The house contains a wide choice of videos and books. The position on the edge of a sea loch ensures a huge variety of wildlife – seals, golden eagles, gulls, cormorants, etc. (*Val Ferguson, Padi Howard, Peter Hutchinson; also Graham and Peta Snowdon, Bill Bennett*)

Open All year, except part of Jan. Restaurant closed midday in winter, Sun all year.
Rooms 6 suites, in separate building, all on ground floor.
Facilities Ramps. Reception/morning room, bar, breakfast room, restaurant. No background music. Garden on loch. Wedding/conference facilities.
Location 5 miles W of Dunvegan, by B884 (single track road), on shore of Loch Dunvegan.
Restrictions Smoking in bar only. No dogs.
Credit cards Amex, MasterCard, Visa.
Terms B&B: single £100–£130, double £107–£130. Set lunch (3 courses) £18, dinner (4 courses) £35; full alc £42.95. Child in parents' room: under 6, free. Autumn, winter breaks. Christmas, New Year packages. 1-night bookings sometimes refused weekends. ***V***

CRINAN Argyll and Bute — Map 5:D1

Crinan Hotel

Crinan PA31 8SR

Tel 0154-6830261
Fax 0154-6830292
Email nryan@crinanhotel.com
Website www.crinanhotel.com

'The rooms are very comfortable; the setting is superb,' writes a visitor this year to this large white building by the sea, owned for 25 years by Nick and Frances Ryan (the artist Frances Macdonald) – 'delightful, eccentric hosts'. The appointment this year of Iris Marhencke as manager gives them 'more time to spend with their guests'; they have opened a shop and a small gallery. 'One of the finest views in Britain,' said another report – the hotel looks over the Crinan Canal basin, the picturesque, tiny village and its harbour, the rugged coastline of Argyll and across to Mull and Jura. Mrs Ryan has created a garden full of azaleas, rhododendrons, roses and herbaceous plants. The bedrooms are simple; two are small (as are some bathrooms). Most were recently redecorated; they have good fabrics, pine furniture, fresh flowers; nine have a balcony. In the 'cheerful lounge' are antiques and good paintings – many by Mrs Macdonald. A new chef, Mark Wishart, joined in June 2000 (he has worked with Gordon Ramsay and Albert Roux); press reports of his cooking are positive, and we would like your views, please. Two restaurants: *Westward*, on the ground floor, and soon to be given a new 'seascape' decor, serves fish, local beef and game. In the pricier top-floor *Lock 16*, diners watch the sunset through picture windows as they eat very fresh fish (eg, wild Scottish salmon; Loch Crinan lobster with Loch Fyne princess clams). Two 'stylish bars': the rooftop one has a colonial-style decor; the public one serves light lunches. There is a coffee shop for snacks and teas. Some visitors have criticised the breakfasts, but the *Good Pub Guide* says they 'can be outstanding'. There is good walking from the doorstep, along the canal and in woods noted for wildlife. (*JL Marland*)

Open All year, except Christmas. *Lock 16* open 1 May–end Sept.
Rooms 1 suite, 19 double (2 usually let as singles).
Facilities Lift, ramp. 2 lounges, 3 bars, 2 restaurants. No background music. ½-acre garden. Safe, sandy beaches nearby; fishing. Boat trips.
Location In Lochgilphead, take A816 to Oban; left after 2 miles on to B841 to Crinan. Hotel pickup at Lochgilphead.
Restrictions No smoking in restaurants. No dogs in restaurants.
Credit cards Amex, MasterCard, Visa.
Terms D,B&B: single £70–£105, double £130–£250, suite £260–£500. Bar lunches from £10. Set dinner from £38.50. Winter rates. *V*

DAIRSIE Fife — Map 5:D2

Todhall House BUDGET
Dairsie
by Cupar KY15 4RQ

Tel 01334-656344
Fax 01334-650791
Email todhallhouse@ukgateway.net
Website www.todhallhouse.com

'We were just as impressed on our second visit,' say returning visitors to John and Gill Donald's 'good-value', handsome stone country house. It stands by a lily pond in its quiet garden outside a village near St Andrews. 'We are just a simple B&B,' say the Donalds, modestly, but the 'immaculately maintained house' has much comfort: 'Our room had a four-poster bed, a large bathroom with every extra, fine views to a distant castle over gardens, fields and valley. The furnishings are elegant and fresh; the lounge is full of original paintings, guidebooks, maps, etc. The dining room is a delight, with antique furniture, cut glass, Spode crockery, silver cutlery.' Breakfast 'is excellent (but carton orange juice)': fruit compote, fresh strawberries, good porridge, locally smoked haddock. A simple 'traditional' evening meal, by arrangement, is eaten communally (as is breakfast) and prepared using local produce, eg, smoked salmon salad; roast leg of lamb with garlic and rosemary; bread-and-butter pudding. No licence; bring your own drink (no corkage charge). 'The genuine friendliness shown by the owners and their dogs, Hanna and Bracken, make you feel immediately at home.' For dining out, you could try *The Grange*, or *The Doll's House* in St Andrews. Numerous golf courses are nearby, so are National Trust of Scotland properties, such as Hill of Tarvit, Kellie Castle and the East Neuk fishing villages. There is good walking on the coast and in the hills. (*Michael and Maureen Heath, AM MacKenzie, Dr C Shenton*)

Open Mar–end Oct.
Rooms 3 double. No telephone (payphone available).
Facilities Lounge, dining room. No background music. 2-acre garden: unheated swimming pool. River fishing 2 miles; sea 7 miles. Unsuitable for ♿.
Location Off A91, 2 miles E of Cupar, ½ mile before Dairsie village. House ½ mile from main road; look for sign at road end. Train: Cupar/Leuchars; they will meet.
Restrictions No smoking. No children under 12. No dogs.
Credit cards MasterCard, Visa.
Terms B&B £28–£40; D,B&B £46–£60. Set dinner (by arrangement) £18–£25. (Bring your own wine/drinks.) 10% discount for 7-day stay. 1-night bookings refused July/Aug.

DERVAIG Argyll and Bute — Map 5:D1

Druimard Country House
Dervaig, nr Tobermory
Isle of Mull PA75 6QW

Tel 01688-400291 and 400345
Fax 01688-400345
Email druimard@hotels.activebooking.com
Website www.druimard.co.uk

In a 'wonderful situation' this small, mellow Victorian house is on a hill just outside a pretty stone-built village in the north of Mull. It has lovely views over open countryside and the marshy estuary at the mouth of the Bellart river to the hills beyond. There is a comfortable lounge, and books, personal photos and memorabilia 'give the feel of a private home'. The bedrooms – some large, others rather small – are warm and comfortable, too, with knick-knacks, fruit, mineral water and good closet space; the 'very friendly hosts', Haydn and Wendy Hubbard, have added two on the ground floor, suitable for disabled visitors or, since they interconnect, for a family. Mr Hubbard presides over the small conservatory bar, and Mrs Hubbard cooks the 'excellent gourmet dinners', using local produce. Breakfasts are 'equally good', and there are 'wonderful packed lunches'. 'Responsibly behaved' children are welcomed, and they can have high tea at 5.30. A converted cow byre in the grounds houses the world's smallest professional theatre, the 43-seat Mull Little Theatre, which plays from April to October. Pre-theatre meals are served on performance nights. *Druimard* makes a good base for enjoying Mull's castles, wildlife and walking; it has ample drying facilities. Calgary beach, a wide expanse of white sand, is close by; boat trips can be arranged to see minke whales, puffins on Lunga, and Fingal's Cave on Staffa. Tobermory, the island's capital, is eight miles away. (*Prof. John Hearle, and others*)

Open 1 Apr–end Oct. Restaurant closed midday to non-residents (snack meals available for residents).

Rooms 7 double. 2, on ground floor, suitable for ♿.
Facilities Ramp. Lounge, conservatory/bar, restaurant (classical background music at night). 1-acre grounds: theatre. Golf, beaches, fishing (ghillie available) nearby.
Location From Craignure ferry, A849 W through Salen. Left to Dervaig after 1½ miles. Hotel on right before village.
Restrictions Smoking banned in restaurant, discouraged in bedrooms. No dogs in public rooms.
Credit cards MasterCard, Visa.
Terms [2001] D,B&B £62.50–£85. Set dinner £29.50. Child in parents' room: under 14, £25. Spring and autumn breaks: 3 nights for price of 2.

DOUNE Perth and Kinross — Map 5:D2

Mackeanston House
Doune FK16 6AX

Tel 01786-850213
Fax 01786-850414
Email mackean.house@cwcom.net
Website www.aboutscotland.com/stirling/mackeanston

In the very middle of Scotland – nearby is an ancient tower marking the centre on the east/west axis – is this Wolsey Lodge. Set amid the lochs and mountains of the Trossachs (*Braveheart* and *Rob Roy* country), it is the family home of Colin and Fiona Graham and their two sons. He belongs to a port-importing family and may play the bagpipes before dinner, she is a 'talented chef', and both are very knowledgeable about wine. Two energetic spaniels, Whinnie and Bramble, welcome visiting children. Two bedrooms are in the main house; they have antique furniture, and watercolours painted by members of the family. Two more rooms are in a traditional cottage about five minutes' walk away, which can also be let on a self-catering basis. There is a large lounge/conservatory/dining room for guests; it has 'marvellous views' across the garden to the Gargunnock hills, Stirling Castle and the Wallace Monument. Home-cooked meals use free-range eggs, local smoked fish, fresh vegetables from the garden, home-made bread and preserves; menus are decided on in discussion with guests, eg, tomato and basil soup; pan-fried wild venison with garden herbs; home-made home-grown strawberry ice cream. Doune, a small, winding village, has one of Scotland's best-preserved medieval castle ruins. More reports, please.

Open All year, except Christmas.
Rooms 4 double. 2, on ground floor, in cottage (can be self-catering). No telephone.
Facilities Conservatory/sitting/dining room. No background music. 1-acre garden: tennis. Fishing in river Teith nearby. Unsuitable for ♿.
Location From M9 Stirling–Perth, exit 10 to A84. After 5 miles, B826 to Thornhill; after 2 miles, take driveway on left. Right at end of farm road.
Restrictions No smoking. No dogs in public rooms.
Credit cards MasterCard, Visa.
Terms B&B £35–£50; D,B&B £47.50–£75. Set dinner £25. Babies in cots: no charge.

Make sure that the hotel has included VAT in the prices it quotes.

DULNAIN BRIDGE Highland — Map 5:C2

Auchendean Lodge
Dulnain Bridge
Grantown-on-Spey PH26 3LU

Tel/Fax 01479-851347
Email hotel@auchendean.com
Website www.auchendean.com

'A glorious break' was spent this year at this white hunting lodge, set on a hillside with wide views over the Spey valley to the Cairngorm mountains. Arts and Crafts features of the Edwardian building have been preserved, and the decor is traditional. The 'truly welcoming hosts', Ian Kirk and Eric Hart, encourage a sociable atmosphere in the public rooms, which are crammed with 'unusual knick-knacks'. Guests are introduced to each other, and they may play the piano. Some bedrooms are a bit small, with large pictures and pieces of furniture, but many have 'a superb view', and beds are 'properly made', with good linen. The food, which won the Macallan Taste of Scotland award in 2000, 'is memorable', says a guest this year. Eric Hart is the chef and a mycologist: he takes guests foraging for wild mushrooms, which appear on the four-course menu in dishes like wild mushroom and walnut soup; ceps and angel wings on toast. Main courses include baked monkfish with wholegrain mustard sauce; venison casserole with red wine, juniper and herbs. Ian Kirk, kilted in the evening, gives 'much appreciated' advice on wine. Breakfast is a 'tour de force', with home-made marmalade and jams, honey from the garden, haggis, locally made sausages, free-range eggs. Behind the house is a wooded hill with excellent walking, wild flowers, plenty of wildlife. Three cats and two ducks patrol the garden. The ageing Border collie, Jock ('he receives nearly as many Christmas cards as we do,' write the hosts), has been joined by another border collie, Bess. Visitors' dogs are welcomed. The RSPB Abernethy reserve is nearby. (*Diana Hall Hall*)

Open All year. Restaurant closed midday.
Rooms 4 double, 1 single. 1 self-catering flat. No telephone.
Facilities 2 lounges, restaurant. No background music. 2-acre garden: putting. 200-acre woodland adjacent; river Spey 300 yds, fishing. Golf, skiing, watersports, shooting nearby. Only restaurant suitable for ♿.
Location 1 mile S of Dulnain Bridge, on A95 to Aviemore (some rooms might get slight traffic noise). Train/bus: Aviemore, 10 miles; then taxi.
Restrictions No smoking: restaurant, 1 lounge. Dogs in bedrooms and 1 lounge only.
Credit cards All major cards accepted.
Terms B&B £37–£48; D,B&B £63–£75. Picnic lunches by arrangement. Set dinner £27. Discounts for 3 days or more. Christmas package.

****

Traveller's tale Hotel in Hampshire. The welcome was of the 'ring the bell for attention' variety and we felt guilty to be taking such a busy person away from important duties to show us to our bedroom. The room had a wonderful view, but seemed lacking in the housekeeping department – there was a broken shirt button on the bedside table on our arrival, and it was still there when we left.

****

DUNDEE *See SHORTLIST* Map 5:D3

DUNKELD Perth and Kinross Map 5:D2

Kinnaird
Kinnaird Estate
by Dunkeld PH8 0LB

Tel 01796-482440
Fax 01796-482289
Email enquiry@kinnairdestate.com
Website www.kinnairdestate.com

'As always, we were made to feel thoroughly at home in this beautiful hotel,' wrote a visitor on her fourth visit to this creeper-covered 18th-century Grade B listed house. It stands in a vast estate in Perthshire; the river Tay, one of Scotland's best fishing rivers, flows through the grounds. It is luxurious (Relais & Châteaux) 'and expensive, but you don't feel you are being overcharged'. The public rooms are much as they would have been 80 years ago, when the then dower house to Blair Castle was filled with house parties. They have family portraits, a grand piano, antiques, flowers, billiards, backgammon and bridge, and perpetually burning fires. The bedrooms, each with a gas log fire, are 'sumptuous'; most are large, with a view of the valley. The owner, Constance Ward, and many of her guests, are American, and the hotel is 'superbly managed' by Douglas Jack. His large staff 'strike the balance between professionalism and unstudied warmth'. Men wear a jacket and tie at dinner in the chandeliered and frescoed restaurant, where meals cooked by Trevor Brooks might include scallops wrapped in pancetta with celeriac velouté; roast poussin with pak choi, artichoke purée and truffle sauce; hot caramel soufflé with vanilla ice cream. The wine list has many half bottles. Guests may fish for salmon in the Tay, and for trout in *Kinnaird*'s lochs, and many other activities are available on the estate (see below). (*Margaret Watson*)

Open All year.
Rooms 1 suite, 8 double, 1 on ground floor. 8 self-catering cottages in grounds (2 can be let as suites).
Facilities Lift, ramp. Drawing room, morning room, study, billiard room, dining room; function facilities. No background music. 9,000-acre estate: gardens, bowling, tennis, croquet, shooting, walking, birdwatching, salmon fishing on river Tay, 3 trout lochs. Riding, golf, clay-pigeon shooting nearby.
Location NW of Dunkeld. From A9 Perth–Pitlochry, left on to B898 Dalguise–Balnaguard 2 miles after Dunkeld. *Kinnaird* 4½ miles on right.
Restrictions No smoking: dining rooms, bedrooms. No children under 12. Dogs by arrangement; not in house (heated kennels available).
Credit cards Amex, MasterCard, Visa.
Terms [2001] D,B&B £250–£515. Packed lunch available. Set lunch £30, dinner £45. 3-day packages Christmas, New Year. 1-night bookings refused bank holidays.

The second volume of the *Guide*, containing nearly 1,000 Continental hotels, will be published early in 2002. Deadline for reports on Continental hotels: 30 September 2001; for new nominations: 14 September 2001.

DUNOON Argyll and Bute Map 5:D1

The Enmore
Marine Parade, Kirn
Dunoon PA23 8HH

Tel 01369-702230
Fax 01369-702148
Email enmorehotel@btinternet.com
Website www.enmorehotel.co.uk

'Comfortable, spacious, well decorated. The owners could not have treated our family more hospitably if we had been close relatives.' One of several bouquets this year for this 'superbly situated' small hotel/guest house. It is on a seafront road along the Firth of Clyde, and has views across to Gourock (15 minutes away on the ferry). Recently upgraded and refurbished, the pretty, white-painted Victorian 'gentleman's retreat' is run by an exuberant hostess, Angela Wilson, and her husband David (he is the chef), with 'great attention to detail'. 'The public rooms are excellently furnished.' 'There is a lovely, large drawing room, with nice pictures and a big log fire.' 'The ambience is good' – introductions are made, to encourage a convivial atmosphere. 'Our bedroom was charming, light and bright, with much yellow, fresh flowers, a nice bright bathroom.' Some rooms have a four-poster bed and a spa bath. Reports on the food range from 'disappointing' to 'very good', 'excellent'. You can choose from two to four courses from the no-choice menu, eg, avocado and prawns; leek and potato soup; oven-baked whole Dover sole; desserts or Scottish cheeses. The *Enmore* owns the only squash courts in this part of Argyll (with video-replay facilities). Children and dogs are welcomed. (*Michael and Maureen Heath, Dr Jerry Asquith, John Ford, BFM Halliwell, and others*)

Open Mid-Feb–mid-Dec. Occasional closures Apr–June.
Rooms 2 suites, 7 double.
Facilities Lounge, bar, 2 dining rooms; background CDs as required; meeting rooms; squash court. 1½-acre garden. Shingle beach opposite. Only dining rooms suitable for ♿. Wedding facilities.
Location Seafront. 1 mile from centre. Parking.
Restriction No smoking in dining rooms.
Credit cards Amex, MasterCard, Visa.
Terms B&B: single £49–£59, double £60–£90, suite £100–£150; D,B&B: single £69–£79, double £110–£130, suite £130–£200. Set lunch £20, dinner £25; full alc £30. 'Luxury' breaks. *V*

EDINBURGH Map 5:D2

The Bonham
35 Drumsheugh Gardens
Edinburgh EH3 7RN

Tel 0131-226 6050
Fax 0131-226 6080
Email reserve@thebonham.com
Website www.thebonham.com

A 'posh hotel with fancy prices', made up of three Victorian buildings in a quiet square near the West End. Owned by Peter Taylor's Town House Company (see also *The Howard*, below, and *Channings*, Shortlist), and managed by Fiona Vernon, it is geared to the business trade, with 'pioneering communications technology' in all the bedrooms. The decor is chic, using rich colours; paintings by young Scottish artists hang throughout the building. Some of the spacious bedrooms have a huge bay window looking across town to the Firth of Forth; one has black bedspreads, gold cushions, lots of polished dark wood; another has a burgundy carpet and blue chairs. One suite has a huge sitting room with 12-foot-high ceiling, a neo-Adam chimney piece and an Arts and Crafts-style cabinet concealing the TV and minibar. One visitor considered *The Bonham* 'very cool'; another thought it 'smart, but a bit snobby', and was unimpressed by the minibar which automatically 'made a charge for any item that was removed for more than ten seconds'. The oak-panelled restaurant, open to the public, serves 'contemporary European' cooking by Michel Bouyer (formerly *sous-chef* at *The Howard* – its restaurant is now closed), eg, green asparagus soup with chervil; marinated rump of lamb with Puy lentil casserole and crushed sweet potato; hot orange and cardamom soufflé. More reports, please.

Open All year, except 3–6 Jan.
Rooms 2 suites, 36 double, 10 single. 1 room designed for ♿.
Facilities Lift, ramp, Reception lounge, restaurant (modern jazz during meals).
Location West End, 5 mins' walk from Princes Street, ½ mile from station. Street parking. Bus from centre.
Restriction No smoking: lounge, bedrooms. Guide dogs only.
Credit cards All major cards accepted.
Terms B&B: single from £135, double from £165, suite £295. Scottish breakfast £7.50. Set lunch £12.50–£15. Full alc £28. Various breaks. *V*

The Howard
34 Great King Street
Edinburgh EH3 6QH

Tel 0131-315 2220
Fax 0131-557 6515
Email reserve@thehoward.com
Website www.thehoward.com

A major change has occurred at this 'stylish and rather formal' small hotel owned by Peter Taylor's Town House Company. Its restaurant, *36*, has gone, in order to make way for three suites, each with a private terrace and separate entrance. Guests who want to dine are now referred to the restaurants at the sister hotels, *The Bonham*, see above, and *Channings*, see Shortlist. The changes were prompted, says the hotel, by the high demand for luxury accommodation in Edinburgh. Aiming 'to provide a personal atmosphere', and composed of three Georgian houses, *The Howard* stands on a cobbled New Town street (some traffic by day, but little at night). Drinks and tea are served by an open fire in the drawing room, which has brocade curtains, antiques and oil paintings, a large crystal chandelier. The pretty breakfast room has murals dating back to the 1800s. The bedrooms (many are spacious) have antiques, a period Bakelite telephone and a roll-top bath. 'The single rooms are unusually attractive,' one returning visitor wrote. More reports badly needed.

Open All year, except 23–27 Dec, 3–6 Jan.
Rooms 5 suites, 11 double, 2 single.
Facilities Lift. Drawing room (classical background music), writing room, breakfast room. Unsuitable for ♿.

Location New Town, 10 mins' walk from Princes Street. Car park. Bus from centre.
Restriction No smoking in bedrooms. Guide dogs only.
Credit cards Amex, MasterCard, Visa.
Terms B&B: single £155–£175, double £225–£280, suite £295–£365. *V*

Rick's NEW
55a Frederick Street
Edinburgh EH2 1LH

Tel 0131-622 7800
Fax 0131-622 7801
Email info@ricksedinburgh.co.uk
Website www.ricksedinburgh.co.uk

'A real find: a lively bar/restaurant with ten beautifully designed, sublimely comfortable, modern bedrooms,' says the well-travelled nominator of this small company-owned (Montpeliers Ltd) hotel in Georgian New Town. It opened in August 2000. 'Fortunately no *Casablanca* theme, despite the name. The decor is contemporary: lots of taupe suede, pale grey walls, slate and stone floors.' The bedrooms have a walnut headboard, designer fabrics, a modem point, cable TV, a CD- and a DVD-player; bathrooms are 'state-of-the-art'. The manager, Jamie McComb, and his staff are 'terrifically competent, friendly, and unstuffy'. Food is served all day. Breakfast, from 7 am until noon (all day on Saturday and Sunday), has freshly squeezed fruit juices, brioches, muffins, mixed grills, etc. The dinner menu, offered from 6 pm, includes all kinds of seafood, and dishes like herb- smoked chicken with potato cakes; grilled tuna with coriander mash and crispy onions; chocolate tart with pear purée. 'The bar/restaurant is lively and generally packed in the evenings, with a young clientele, but the rooms are in a separate building and remain undisturbed. Slightly self-consciously trendy; it wouldn't suit everyone, but it's by miles the nicest place I've stayed at in Edinburgh.' (*Claire Wrathall*)

Open All year.
Rooms 10 double.
Facilities Bar/restaurant ('contemporary/upbeat' background music all day), restaurant. Unsuitable for ♿.
Location In New Town, 5 mins' walk from city centre (Bus 80). Metered parking.
Restrictions No children in bar/restaurant after 8 pm. No dogs.
Credit cards Amex, MasterCard, Visa.
Terms Room: £105.75. Breakfast £3.50–£6.65. Alc £16–£26. Christmas package.

Saxe Coburg House
24 Saxe Coburg Place
Edinburgh EH3 5BP

Tel 0131-332 2717
Fax 0131-315 3375
Email birrell@zetnet.co.uk
Website www.saxe-coburg-house.co.uk

'One of those small gems you want to keep to yourself,' writes one visitor, altruistically, about George and Gillian Birrell's 'excellent' B&B in Stockbridge. The Birrells are 'very helpful', say others, and their 'wonderful' Georgian house is in 'a charming area' with plenty of restaurants and cafés, and only 15 minutes walk from the city centre. 'Our bedroom was comfortable, elegant, warm (important in

Edinburgh in November). It had everything we could have wanted; the bathroom was equally luxurious. The drawing room was charming and the breakfast first class.' Courses on Scottish history, literature and cooking are held, and golf and leisure tours of Scotland can be arranged. (*Nigel Fletcher, Andrew Palmer*)

Open All year, except Christmas.
Rooms 1 family suite, 3 double, 1 single.
Facilities Drawing room, library, breakfast room. Unsuitable for ♿.
Location Stockbridge: 15 mins' walk, or bus/taxi to centre.
Restrictions No smoking. No pets.
Credit cards Amex, MasterCard, Visa.
Terms B&B: single £45–£55, double £80–£98, suite £90–£120. Off-season midweek packages. *V*

Seven Danube Street
7 Danube Street
Edinburgh EH4 1NN

Tel 0131-332 2755
Fax 0131-343 3648
Email seven.danubestreet@virgin.net
Website www.aboutedinburgh.com/danube

César award: Scottish B&B of the year

'Possibly the best B&B in the whole of the UK?' wonders one delighted visitor to this 'wonderful period house' (New Town Georgian) in a 'lovely quiet position' in the Stockbridge area. 'Nothing seems too much trouble' for the 'charming owners', Fiona Mitchell-Rose and her husband, Colin. There is plenty of evidence that this is a family home – dog's cushions (belonging to George, 'a most adorable black pug') in the hallway; inherited pictures and tasteful furniture; there is a lovely cupolated staircase. The 'beautifully appointed' guest bedrooms are on the lower floor. All are well supplied with extras; beds have an electric blanket. Spick-and-span bathrooms have a power shower, lush Egyptian cotton bath towels, and various toiletries – even dental floss. One room has a king-size four-poster. 'Outstanding breakfasts', served at one large table, include home-made bread, scones, croissants, freshly squeezed juice, fresh fruit salad, cooked dishes if required. There are also two bedrooms in a 'delightful' flat around the corner (usually let as self-catering). Danube Street is a curved cobbled street in a quiet backwater away from the city noise, yet within walking distance of Princes Street, and Mrs Mitchell-Rose happily gives 'reliable advice on sightseeing and restaurants'. 'Altogether exceptional.' (*NM Mackintosh, Susan Hope, Wendy and Dr Michael Dods*)

Open All year, except Christmas.
Rooms 2 double, 1 single. Also 1 self-catering flat for 4–6 people, 50 yds.
Facilities Lounge, breakfast room. No background music. Small garden. Unsuitable for ♿.
Location *c.* 1 mile from centre. Metered parking. Bus at end of street.
Restriction No smoking.
Credit cards MasterCard, Visa.
Terms B&B: single £55–£65, double £90–£110. *V*

For details of the Voucher scheme see page xxx.

24 Northumberland Street
24 Northumberland Street
Edinburgh EH3 6LS

Tel 0131-556 8140
Fax 0131-556 4423
Email ingram@ednet.co.uk
Website www.ingrams.co.uk

In a 'perfect, quiet location', near Princes Street, David and Theresa Ingram run a B&B in their classic New Town house. With its four storeys leading off a stone staircase lit by an oval cupola, it is 'spacious, beautifully cared for', and 'preferable to most Edinburgh hotels', says a visitor this year. The goatee-bearded Mr Ingram, who is also an antique dealer, 'is an erudite man of clear opinions'; his wife is 'full of energy'. 'Excellent breakfasts', with 'the best fruit salad I have eaten anywhere', and scrambled eggs, are 'attentively served' in a large, elegant room with fine antiques. The bedrooms have TV and an eclectic selection of books; bathrooms have 'lashings of fast-running hot water'. The rooms in the basement might be 'a bit dark'. Two cats: Ginny, a handsome marmalade, is friendly; Ben (aged 17) is more standoffish. Restaurants of all kinds are nearby. (*AP Wiltshire, and others*)

Open All year, except Christmas.
Rooms 3 double.
Facilities Sitting room, breakfast room (baroque background music). Unsuitable for ♿.
Location In New Town, 5 mins' walk from centre. Parking. Bus-stop nearby.
Restrictions No smoking. Preferably no children under 15. No dogs.
Credit cards Diners, MasterCard, Visa.
Terms B&B: single £55, double £90.

Windmill House
Coltbridge Gardens
Edinburgh EH12 6AQ

Tel/Fax 0131-346 0024
Website www.windmillhouse.co.uk

Eulogies, both British and American, came this year for this 'delightful' B&B: 'Truly superb: excellent hospitality, service and accommodation.' The 'gracious hosts', Vivien and Mike Scott, 'sure go the extra mile to make your visit memorable'. In one case this 'included early breakfast, late arrivals, and detailed directions to my place of work'. The large Georgian-style house is in a beautiful wooded valley overlooking the Water of Leith, with views of the Pentlands, but Princes Street is only a mile away. The 'glorious sitting room' has an open fire. In cool weather a fire burns in the room where breakfast is served (in fine weather it can be taken on a terrace). 'The spacious bedrooms are handsomely furnished, yet warm and inviting.' They have a sitting area, TV and video, complimentary sherry, nuts, tea and coffee. The suite is in an old windmill, and there is also a self-catering cottage. (*Valerie Juneman, Trini Lye and Bob Hanley*)

Open All year, except Christmas/New Year.
Rooms 1 suite in old windmill, 3 double. Also self-catering cottage. No telephone.
Facilities Drawing room, breakfast room. Terrace. No background music. 2-acre garden, riverside walks. Unsuitable for ♿.

Location 1 mile from centre. From Murrayfield Ave, turn into Coltbridge Ave, leading to Coltbridge Gdns. Go to end of road; fork left up drive, left through stone gate pillars. Bus from centre (8 mins' walk).
Restrictions No smoking. No dogs.
Credit card Visa.
Terms [2001] B&B: double £85–£100, suite £120–£140. Child in parents' room: £25. *V*

See also SHORTLIST

ELGIN Moray ***See SHORTLIST*** **Map 5:C2**

ERISKA Argyll and Bute — Map 5:D1

Isle of Eriska
Ledaig
by Oban PA37 1SD

Tel 01631-720371
Fax 01631-720531
Email office@eriska-hotel.co.uk
Website www.eriska-hotel.co.uk

'Ten out of ten! Everything perfect.' 'A marvellous hotel. Where else are you greeted on arrival by name by the proprietor who then asks about the health of your dog?' This Scots baronial mansion, built in 1884, is on a tiny private island linked to the mainland by a wrought iron bridge. Turned into a hotel by Robin and Sheena Buchanan-Smith 27 years ago, it is now run by their 'very charming' son Beppo. 'The owners and staff provide first-class service, food and facilities. The views are fantastic.' The smell of wood smoke from blazing log fires pervades the panelled public rooms, which are comfortable, rather than smart, furnished with old-fashioned chintzes, leather chairs, standard lamps. There is a collection of malt whiskies in the library, and a piano, which visitors may play, in the bay-windowed drawing room. Each bedroom is named for a Hebridean island: some are large and light, with a huge bathroom, but others are small. Breakfasts are praised, as are the 'memorable' dinners – 'I can still taste the pork and crackling with Bramley apple sauce'. The menu is shown to guests during afternoon tea (which is free), and Robert MacPherson's elaborate 'classic Scottish' cooking is elegantly served with good crystal and silver. Other dishes: king scallops, lobster and langoustine poached in a lemongrass-scented broth, with saffron and coriander noodles; roasted brill with chargrilled vegetables and wild rocket; Glayva soufflé with a coffee-bean anglaise. Male guests are asked to wear jacket and tie at dinner. There is family accommodation, and high tea for children under ten. Wildlife abounds, including otters, seals, herons and deer; badgers come to the library door for their supper of bread and milk. Sporting facilities include a leisure centre with a 17-metre swimming pool, an all-weather tennis court, and a 'challenging' nine-hole golf course. Prospective guests are asked to pay a non-returnable deposit of £50 per person. Oban, Mull, Iona and Inverary can easily be visited from here. (*Peter and Pam Barratt, David Jervois; also Michael and Maureen Heath*)

Open All year, except Jan.
Rooms 16 double, 1 single. 2 on ground floor.
Facilities Hall, lounge, drawing room, bar/library, dining room; leisure centre: swimming pool, gym, sauna, games room. No background music. 300-acre island: tennis, croquet, golf, water sports, riding, clay- pigeon shooting. Wedding facilities.
Location 12 miles N of Oban. At A828, north of Benderloch, follow signs to Isle of Eriska. Train: Connel Ferry, 6 miles.
Restrictions No smoking in dining room. No children under 5 in swimming pool, under 15 in gym, under 10 at dinner. No dogs in public rooms.
Credit cards MasterCard, Visa.
Terms [2001] (*Min. advance reservation 2 nights*) B&B: single £175, double £225–£270. Set dinner £38.50. Weekly rates. Off-season breaks. Christmas package.

EVIE Orkney — Map 5:A3

Woodwick House NEW/BUDGET
Evie KW17 2PQ

Tel 01856-751330
Fax 01856-751383
Email woodwickhouse@appleonline.net
Website www.orknet.co.uk/woodwick

'The atmosphere is welcoming, unassuming and tranquil. Guests are treated as individuals. Bedrooms are simply but effectively decorated, in keeping with the style of the house. Management are courteous, never obtrusive, always prepared to find time to chat.' Set in some of Orkney's only woods, this small guest house, run by Ann Herdman and Gloria Wright, stands in an overgrown garden with bluebells, a rookery, and a small stream running down to Woodwick Bay, where seals are sometimes seen. The lounges have open peat fires; one has TV, videos and books, another has a baby grand piano which guests may play. The bedrooms are a bit basic for some visitors – no telephone or TV ('our emphasis is on peace,' writes Ms Herdman), not all have private facilities, and the plumbing can be noisy. 'Imaginative and excellent' dinners on a set menu include local specialities, eg, oysters, freshly caught lobster, North Ronaldsay lamb, Woodwick raspberries, 'and the chef will prepare guests' favourite dishes: bread-and-butter pudding is very popular'. Fresh herbs and organic produce are used; special diets are catered for. Breakfast includes home-made marmalade. Notices and leaflets proclaim the house's affiliation with the Dandelion Trust (see also *Hazelwood House*, Loddiswell, England). Concerts, poetry readings and musical recitals are held once a month, and there is sometimes a spontaneous *ceilidh*. Orkney's two main towns, Stromness and Kirkwall, are 20 minutes' drive away. The Tingwall ferry just down the river makes regular trips to other islands. The RSPB at Birsay, and Loch Harray (good fishing), are nearby. (*Kay and Martin Slingsby*)

Open All year.
Rooms 7 double, 1 single. 2 with bath, 2 with shower. 2 on ground floor. No telephone/radio/TV.
Facilities Lounge, TV lounge, dining room; room (with piano) for entertainments. No background music. 12-acre grounds on bay: fishing, birdwatching; beach 2 miles. Wedding facilities.
Location From A965 turn on to A966 to Evie. After 7 miles, right at *Woodwick House* sign; 1st left; house down track among trees. Kirkwall–Tingwall ferry; taxi/bus.
Restriction No smoking: restaurant, bedrooms.
Credit cards MasterCard, Visa.
Terms [2001] B&B £27–£46. Lunches available. Set dinner £22. Christmas, New Year packages.

FORRES Moray *See SHORTLIST* Map 5:C2

FORSS Highland Map 5:B2

Forss Country House *Tel* 01847-861201
Forss, by Thurso KW14 7XY *Fax* 01847-861301
Email jamie@forsshouse.freeserve.co.uk
Website www.forsscountryhouse.co.uk

'I recommend this hotel unreservedly,' says a visitor this year to James and Jacqueline MacGregor's Grade II listed house by the river Forss. The quite austere building, dating from 1810, has tall chimneys, and 'it is beautiful, with comfortable rooms, and a charming staff'. There are open fires in the panelled lounge and bar, and the dining room is smart and light, with a green decor and a carved Adam-style fireplace. 'The food was superb, with perfectly cooked vegetables and always a hot pudding; service was first rate.' Chef Catriona MacLean's four-course menu offers, eg, tomato bruschetta with basil and garlic; carrot and orange soup; wild Forss salmon pan-fried in oatmeal; hot ginger sponge pudding with lemon sauce. Snacks are available to residents as an alternative. Breakfast is served in a conservatory overlooking the garden. The bedrooms and bathrooms are commended for comfort and spaciousness. Some rooms are in 'sportsmen's lodges' in the large wooded grounds, where there are 'lovely walks', a waterfall, a mill, a ruined kirk on a rocky beach, and plenty of wildlife (seabirds, buzzards, foxes and otters). Many of *Forss House*'s guests are there for the fishing (salmon and trout); ghillies and tuition are available, and there are a drying room, freezing facilities, etc. Children are welcomed; cots, high chairs, baby-listening and an early supper are provided. Dounreay nuclear plant is two miles away. (*Val Ferguson*)

Open 6 Jan–23 Dec.
Rooms 1 suite, 9 double. 1 equipped for ♿. 5 in lodges in the grounds.
Facilities Reception, lounge, cocktail bar, restaurant, conservatory. No background music. 25-acre grounds: river, rookery, woodlands. Beaches, fishing, walking, birdwatching, seals nearby. Wedding facilities.
Location 5 miles W of Thurso on A836. Train: Thurso. Air: Wick.
Restrictions No smoking in restaurant. Dogs in selected bedrooms, not in public rooms.

Credit cards Amex, MasterCard, Visa.
Terms B&B: £45–£57.50; D,B&B £67.50–£80. Set dinner £22.50. Fishing packages.

FORT WILLIAM Highland — Map 5:C1

Ashburn House BUDGET
4 Achintore Road
Fort William PH33 6RQ

Tel 01397-706000
Fax 01397-702024
Email ashburn.house@tinyworld.co.uk
Website www.scotland2000.com/ashburn

A bay-windowed Victorian house with a castellated tower, close to Loch Linnhe, looking across to the Ardgour hills. The hosts, Allan and Sandra Henderson, are 'knowledgeable and friendly', says a visitor this year. They pamper their visitors with complimentary tea on arrival and the servicing of bedrooms at night. The double rooms have a six-foot bed which guests – particularly Americans – love. Two bedrooms are on the ground floor; the others are reached by a barley-twist pine staircase. The large conservatory lounge has beautiful loch views and a supply of games (chess, dominoes, etc). The 'spectacular breakfast', in a room that also looks over the loch, includes fruit, yogurt, creamy porridge, a Highland grill, and freshly baked scones. The house has a musical theme: it is filled with musical instruments; menus are decorated with quavers; soft traditional Highland music is played in the breakfast room much of the day. A good selection of eating places can be found nearby, also Ben Nevis and the West Highland Museum (with Jacobite artefacts). The Hendersons can arrange private tours of the Highlands, Inverness and Skye. (*SW, and others*)

Open 1 Mar–end Nov.
Rooms 4 double, 3 single. 2 on ground floor. No telephone
Facilities Conservatory/lounge, breakfast room (soft traditional Highland music). ¾-acre garden: stream. Fishing nearby.
Location 10 mins' walk from centre. 450 yards after entering 30 mph zone (A82 south). Train, bus stations nearby. Private parking.
Restrictions No smoking. Guide dogs only.
Credit cards Amex, MasterCard, Visa.
Terms B&B £30–£45. Reductions for weekly stays.

The Grange
Grange Road
Fort William
PH33 6JF

Tel 01397-705516
Fax 01397-701595
Email jcampbell@grangefortwilliam.com
Website www.grangefortwilliam.com

'Superb in every way,' says a new report on this white-painted, bay-windowed late Victorian house, which a few years ago won the Scottish Tourist Board's 'Best B&B in Scotland' award. It stands above sloping grounds with statuary, looking down to Loch Linnhe. The town centre is a short walk away. The 'most courteous hosts', Joan and John Campbell, 'take great trouble over little details, eg, the times of the Skye ferry'. Breakfast, ordered the night before from an extensive menu, is served on 'beautiful glass-topped tables' and it includes fruit compote, Mallaig kippers and haggis. Only four bedrooms, all different, each described in detail in the brochure. All are supplied with fresh flowers and sherry; they look over the garden or the loch. The Terrace Room (the best) has its own terrace leading on to the gardens, and a king-size antique bed. The Garden Room, with its French oak furniture and Victorian-style bathroom, is the most peaceful; Rob Roy, with a colonial-style bed and a spacious bathroom, is named in honour of Jessica Lange, who stayed here during the filming of *Rob Roy*. There is 'a cheerful log fire in the cosy lounge', and hand-crafted walking sticks are for sale – 'a bargain at £3'. No dinners, but *Crannog*, 'fantastic fish in a casual, friendly ambience', is recommended. Or you could try *Inverlochy Castle* (see below) five miles away. (*Barbara M Wooldridge*)

Open Mar–Nov.
Rooms 4 double. 1 on ground floor. No telephone.
Facilities Lounge, breakfast room (classical background music). ¾-acre garden. Sea loch 100 yds. Unsuitable for ♿.
Location 10 mins' walk from centre. From High St take A82 towards Glasgow. Left into Ashburn La; *Grange* at top on left. Parking. Station ½ mile.
Restrictions No smoking. No children under 12. Guide dogs only.
Credit cards MasterCard, Visa (to guarantee booking, not for payment).
Terms B&B £38–£48. Special breaks in late Oct.

Inverlochy Castle
Torlundy
Fort William PH33 6SN

Tel 01397-702177
Fax 01397-702953
Email info@inverlochy.co.uk
Website www.inverlochy.co.uk

César award in 1984

Amid the magnificent scenery of the foothills of Ben Nevis, this baronial pile was built by Lord Abinger in 1863, near the site of a 13th-century castle. It is now one of the most expensive hotels in Great Britain (Relais & Châteaux), owned by an overseas businessman. It mostly continues to win praise: 'A happy hotel.' 'What is impressive in an establishment of this grandeur, is the kindness of the service.' One couple, though, felt that 'attention to detail had slipped'. Michael Leonard, the 'exemplary' managing director, has presided for 25 years, but there have been recent changes among senior staff. The exterior may look austere, but inside all is traditional opulence: a Great Hall with Venetian chandeliers and cherubs among clouds on a frescoed ceiling; a high-ceilinged billiard room with a marble fireplace. The 'bright and beautifully furnished' bedrooms in the main house look over the lovely gardens. 'For a fraction of the price' you can stay in the *Factor's House* annexe (its rooms are not serviced at night), and use the hotel's facilities. Matthew Gray, former *sous-chef*, now runs the *Michelin*-starred restaurant. His menus include, eg, tian of tomato and crab with crispy garlic shavings; fillet of beef with mustard and herb crust

and Madeira sauce with foie gras; tower of chocolate with strawberry mousse and a vanilla froth. The room-service breakfast, and the Scottish breakfast in the restaurant, are both thought 'excellent'. Children are welcomed. Many sporting activities are available (see below), and a falconry display can be arranged. (*Conrad and Marilyn Dehn, PH, and others*)

Open All year, except mid-Jan–mid-Feb.
Rooms 1 suite, 15 double, 1 single. 5 in *Factor's House*.
Facilities Great Hall (pianist at weekends), drawing room, billiard room, restaurant; function facilities. 24-hour room service. 500-acre estate: gardens, tennis, loch, fishing, birdwatching. Golf, skiing nearby. Chauffeur-driven limousines for hire. Unsuitable for ♿. Wedding facilities.
Location On A82, 3 miles NE of Fort William, just past golf club. Follow signs to hotel; ignore signs to Inverlochy village/castle ruins.
Restrictions Smoking banned in restaurant, discouraged in bedrooms. Dogs at management's discretion.
Credit cards Amex, MasterCard, Visa.
Terms [2001] B&B: single £180–£255, double £250–£380, suite £390–£480. Set lunch £25–£30, dinner £45–£50. Christmas, New Year, winter packages.

GLASGOW — Map 5:D2

Malmaison
278 West George Street
G2 4LL

Tel 0141-572 1000
Fax 0141-572 1002
Email glasgow@malmaison.com
Website www.malmaison.com

Of the *Malmaison* group of smart, sophisticated city hotels (there are others in Edinburgh, Manchester, Newcastle and Leeds), this is perhaps the most attractive. Once a Greek Orthodox church, it was built in the early 19th century; an extension was added in 1997. It has a magnificent Art Nouveau central staircase. 'The staff were all very welcoming (much more so than in another *Malmaison* we visited),' says a visitor in 2001. 'Our decent-sized room had a good bathroom, and all the goodies one associates with *Malmaison* [stylish decor using bold colours and stripes, CD-player, minibar, huge bed, decent shower]. It looked over Strathclyde Police HQ, but we were not disturbed.' Some suites are on two levels. 'Breakfast was good. So much interesting food on the buffet table that we didn't even think about cooked dishes.' It is served in the cheerful atrium, open to the glass roof of the first floor, and doubles as the Italian-style *Café Mal*, serving pasta, pizzas, grills and salads during the day. The brasserie/bar in the dark vaulted basement serves informal meals, 'competently cooked', eg, citrus-cured salmon with fennel remoulade; roast lamb niçoise with tapenade; espresso ice cream. For keep-fit enthusiasts there is the Gymtonic. 'With its excellent location, this is a good base for exploring Glasgow and its marvellous galleries and museums.' (*Sara Price*)

Open All year.
Rooms 8 suites, 64 double. Some on ground floor. 4 adapted for ♿.
Facilities Lift. Café/breakfast room, bar/brasserie; fitness room; meeting room. Background jazz/contemporary music in public areas all day.
Location Central (rooms double-glazed). Corner of West George and Pitt

streets, opposite police station. NCP parking nearby.
Restrictions No smoking in 18 bedrooms. Guide dogs only.
Credit cards All major cards accepted.
Terms [2001] Room: single/double £110, suite £150–£165. Breakfast £8.75–£10.75. Set lunch £11.95, dinner £14.95. Full alc £25–£30. 2-day weekend breaks. Christmas package.

One Devonshire Gardens
1–3 Devonshire Gardens
Glasgow G12 0UX

Tel 0141-339 2001
Fax 0141-337 1663
Email onedevonshire@btconnect.com
Website www.one-devonshire-gardens.com

'This is somewhere special,' write visitors in 2001, confirming that recent changes have not dimmed the attraction of this sophisticated and luxurious place, founded by the wizard hotelier, Ken McCulloch. The new owners, Residence International (a Scottish time-share company), have installed a new manager, Tracey Patterson, added 14 extra rooms (in the former *Devonshire Hotel* nearby), and expanded the restaurant, which has been taken over by Gordon Ramsay Restaurants, and renamed *Amaryllis*. This has caused much media excitement, partly because of Ramsay's pugnacious comments about other Scottish restaurateurs, and partly because he has employed, as manager of *Amaryllis*, Fiona Nairn, the ex-wife of one of his targets, the celebrity chef Nick Nairn. The head chef, David Dempsey, previously *sous-chef* in Ramsay's eponymous Chelsea restaurant, and a Glasgow native, aims to retain the restaurant's *Michelin* star with his elaborate dishes, eg, mosaic of sautéed foie gras, confit chicken pressed with a salad of green beans; fillet of line-caught sea bass with artichokes and baby fennel, red wine sauce; lavender crème brûlée. The decor remains sumptuous, in the hotel's 'dark, distinctive style'. Individually styled bedrooms have bold colours, heavy fabrics, lights with dimmer switches, fruit, magazines, a CD-player. Beds are large; most bathrooms have a deep marble bath, but some have a power shower. 'Our spacious suite was very comfortable; room service was good and prompt. Staff were helpful. In the restaurant, perhaps a little dated, but very fine, the starter of scallops on crunchy vegetables was a perfect balance of textures and flavours; medium-rare roast saddle of Scottish lamb was the best I have ever eaten. The waiter was happy to discuss the food when asked. The *sommelier* was equally knowledgeable, and the wines were excellent.' The hotel is in a tree-lined Victorian terrace, at a busy traffic crossing, but windows are double-glazed, and light sleepers can ask for a rear-facing room. (*Stephen and Pauline Glover*)

Open All year.
Rooms 4 suites, 37 double.
Facilities 2 drawing rooms, bar, restaurant; private dining room, boardroom; patio garden. No background music. Unsuitable for ♿.
Location 2 miles from centre at intersection of Great Western and Hyndland roads. Back rooms quietest. On-street parking in front.
Restriction No dogs in public rooms.
Credit cards All major cards accepted.
Terms Room: single £125–£145, double £160–£275, suite £195–£345. Breakfast £10.50–£14.50. Set lunch £18, dinner £25. Full alc £75.

The Town House
4 Hughenden Terrace
Glasgow G12 9XR

Tel 0141-357 0862
Fax 0141-339 9605
Email hospitality@thetownhouseglasgow.com
Website www.thetownhouseglasgow.com

In a conservation area in Glasgow's West End, Michael Ferguson's B&B is a handsome double-fronted late Victorian sandstone house. 'The setting is quiet; parking is easy.' Inside are deep cornices, high celings and elaborately carved architraves; but the style is unpretentious. A report this year: 'We enjoyed the large bedroom, the simple but comfortable furniture. The really friendly drawing room feels like your own space, and allows you to chat or not with other guests as you choose.' It has a fire and a large book collection; alcoholic drinks can be served here, or in the bedrooms. The staff are 'helpful, and concerned for guests' comfort, without being fussy'. The 'excellent' cooked breakfasts include kippers, smokies and smoked salmon (but one visitor found the coffee 'stewed'). Fruit, sweets and shortbread in the bedroom are replenished daily. Shower rooms are on the small side, and sometimes awkwardly placed, and the water pressure may be weak. Bedrooms at the top are small. Snack meals and packed lunches are available. Guests have access to the sports and social facilities of the adjacent Western Lawn Tennis and Hillhead sports clubs. The restaurants and shops in Byres Road, the Botanic Gardens and the university are all within ten to 15 minutes' walk. (*Nigel Fletcher, and others*)

Important: There is another hotel called *Town House* in Glasgow, in Royal Crescent; make sure the taxi driver knows where to take you.

Open All year.
Rooms 2 family, 8 double. All with shower. 1 on ground floor.
Facilities Lounge, breakfast room (Celtic music). Small garden. Access to adjacent sports clubs (visitors' fee £2–£4). Unsuitable for ♿.
Location 1½ miles W of centre. Leave A82 at Hyndland Rd, 1st right into Hughenden Rd, right at mini-roundabout. Street parking. Underground and Bus 59 to centre.
Restrictions No smoking: breakfast room, bedrooms. No dogs.
Credit cards MasterCard, Visa.
Terms B&B £36–£60. Child in parents' room: under 5, £5; 6–12, £8.

See also SHORTLIST

GLEN CANNICH Highland — Map 5:C2

Mullardoch House
Glen Cannich
by Beauly IV4 7LX

Tel/Fax 01456-415460
Email andy@mullhouse1.demon.co.uk
Website www.mullhouse1.demon.co.uk

'The best hotel we stayed at in Scotland.' 'Absolutely excellent.' Praise is almost universal for Andy Johnston's handsome white hunting lodge situated in the heart of the Highlands, with lovely views across Loch Sealbhanach to the Affric mountains. A burn runs through the garden. Even one dissenter (a failure to put right a room allocation error quickly enough left him with the impression that 'single bookings are not welcome in high season') acknowledged the house to be 'elegant and beautifully maintained, and the food excellent'. More typical was: 'It is remote, quiet and entirely peaceful. The standard of comfort was high, the staff were young, friendly and efficient, and the food was superb. Who could object to pan-fried scallops, home-made soup, fillet of beef, and butterscotch pudding after a long day's climbing in the mountains?' Michael Jenkins's 'modern Scottish' menu might also include seafood wontons; cauliflower and cumin soup; seared duck breast with sweet potato mash; lemon posset. 'Breakfast is similarly good.' The approach is by an eight-mile drive up a single-track road through beautiful Glen Cannich. Wildlife abounds, and you might see a stag appear out of the mist on any nearby hill. There are log fires, flowered fabrics and old furniture in the public rooms; spacious bedrooms have stunning views, bathrooms have a long bath. Plenty of sporting activities are available: walking of all degrees of difficulty, from strolls along the river to several Munros; fishing in the hotel's beats or on local estates; boating on ten-mile-long Loch Mullardoch. Nearby castles include Brodie, Cawdor, Urquhart. (*Bob Cocker, John and Hilary Maddicott, and others*)

Open All year.
Rooms 1 suite, 5 double.
Facilities Large hall, lounge, bar, dining room. No background music. 2-acre grounds: lawns, wooded walks. Shooting, stalking, fishing arranged; golf nearby. Unsuitable for ♿. Wedding facilities.
Location A831 from Beauly, then unclassified road for 8 miles through Glen Cannich. Transport to and from Inverness airport/station can be arranged.
Restrictions No smoking: restaurant, bedrooms. No dogs in public rooms.
Credit cards MasterCard, Visa.
Terms B&B £48–£66; D,B&B £75–£93. Set dinner £27.

GLEN LYON Perth and Kinross — Map 5:D2

Invervar Lodge NEW
Glen Lyon
by Aberfeldy PH15 2PL

Tel 01887-877206
Fax 01887-877223
Email invervar.lodge@btinternet.com
Website www.btinternet.com/~invervar.lodge/

A former Victorian hunting lodge, in a 'spectacularly beautiful' glen. It is now run as a guest house, where Christopher and Sonja Seiler provide 'high-quality continental hospitality', according to the nominator. 'He comes from a family of Swiss hoteliers and has all the characteristics you'd expect, being welcoming without being overwhelming. No pseudo country house atmosphere, no servility; lots of service, attention to detail. You get up when you like; breakfast and dinner were when we wanted them. When we asked for non-feather pillows, a non-feather duvet was also provided. The house is very calm: no music, TV only if you want it (not in the bedrooms).' Both the residents' lounge and dining room have an open fire. 'The furnishings are very attractive. It's hard not to relax. After dinner you stroll out to look at the deer.' The Seilers now serve no meat, and we would welcome reports on their 'international vegetarian gourmet cuisine'. A sample no-choice menu includes wild mushroom pâté; aubergine and feta cheese parcel; caramelised pear tart. Meals are taken at a large communal table, and guests bring their own wine. 'Superb walking from the door', and 13 Munros are nearby. Alternative therapies (shiatsu and reflexology, etc) are offered; 'but they do not obtrude'. (*Benjamin Twist*)

Open All year, except Christmas, possibly New Year.
Rooms 4 double. No telephone/TV, etc.
Facilities Lounge, dining room. 1-acre garden: pond. Swedish massage, shiatsu, aromatherapy, reflexology, stress relief tuition available. River Lyon 300 yds. Unsuitable for ♿.
Location N of Stirling. 5 miles NW of Fortingall into Glen Lyon. Bus from Aberfeldy.
Restrictions No smoking: dining room, bedrooms. Dogs by arrangement.
Credit cards MasterCard, Visa.
Terms [2001] B&B: £33–£39, single supplement. Set dinner £22.50–£24.50.

GLENELG Highland — Map 5:C1

Glenelg Inn
Glenelg Bay
by Kyle of Lochalsh
IV40 8JR

Tel 01599-522273
Fax 01599-522283
Email christophermain@glenelg-inn.com
Website www.glenelg-inn.com

'A spectacular drive through the mountains' leads to this 'charming old inn' (Johnson and Boswell visited in 1773). It is now the lively centre of village life, in a 'superb setting' on Glenelg Bay, the haunt of the legendary local hero, Fionn MacCumhail. The bedrooms look across the Sound of Sleat to the mountains of Skye. Owned and run by the 'exuberant' Christopher Main, the inn has received mixed reports this year. Most visitors enjoyed their stay: 'We were warmly received; our charming cottage-style bedroom was small but spotlessly clean. Our bathroom had good fluffy towels.' 'Very good value.' But one couple complained of noise, from other bedrooms through thin walls, and from late-night gatherings below. 'And meals were not relaxing because of the constant to-and-fro between the kitchen at one end of the dining room and the pub at the other.' Reports on the food vary from 'disappointing', 'good, if the chef was in the kitchen', to 'very good'. The four-course dinners might include scallop, monkfish and prawn puff pastry tart; local sole with a herb crust. Service is 'enthusiastic', but 'a bit chaotic' at breakfast; this – 'very good, when it came' – offers fruit salad, porridge, kippers, and 'the best sausages I've tasted in years'. The bar, large and panelled, is full of local fishermen and farmers; traditional music is played, and occasional *ceilidhs* are held. The large morning room (residents' lounge) has an open fire, deer heads and old furniture. Mr Main's wife, Rebecca, has created a big, attractive garden with tables for drinks and meals. Her large oil paintings (landscapes and seascapes) hang in the house. Glenelg is the nearest place on the mainland to Skye; a little ferry takes cars across in summer. There's plenty of wildlife; several castles are nearby, also Gavin Maxwell's Sandaig. (Good Pub Guide, *Val Ferguson, HJM Tucker, Gill and Dave Crawshaw, and others*)

Open All year ('more or less').
Rooms 6 double. 1 on ground floor. No telephone/TV.
Facilities Morning room, pub (traditional background music all day; *ceilidhs* 2 or 3 times a month), dining room. 2-acre grounds: garden down to sea, sailing, fishing. Unsuitable for ♿. Small wedding facilities.
Location Seafront of village on Sound of Sleat. Parking.
Restrictions No smoking in dining room. No dogs in public rooms, except pub.
Credit cards Diners, MasterCard, Visa.
Terms D,B&B £72–£92. Bar meals. Set lunch £15, dinner £25.

GULLANE East Lothian — Map 5:D3

Greywalls
Muirfield, Gullane EH31 2EG

Tel 01620-842144
Fax 01620-842241
Email hotel@greywalls.co.uk
Website www.greywalls.co.uk

With its elegant crescent shape and warm honey-coloured stone, this is one of the loveliest examples of Sir Edwin Lutyens's domestic architecture. It was built in 1901 for a keen golfer, who wanted to be 'within a mashie niblick shot of the 18th green of Muirfield golf club'; many guests are American golfers. The 'really beautiful' garden was designed by Gertrude Jekyll. The house has been in the family of the present owners since 1924. It was opened as a luxury hotel in 1948 by Colonel John Weaver, and has been run by his son and daughter-in-law, Giles and Ros Weaver, since 1977 (now with Sue Prime as manager). It has a panelled library, an 'inviting' sun porch, and a lounge with an open fire. A sheltered terrace opens on to a large rose garden. Service is 'most attentive', and the owners seek to maintain the atmosphere of a private country house. The best bedrooms, furnished with antiques, have views of the links, the Firth of Forth, or the Lammermuir Hills. One room, in the garden, is called the King's Loo, recalling its purpose when Edward VII was a visitor. In the formal restaurant, decorated in green, men are asked to wear a jacket and tie at dinner (you must reserve your table). Modern British dishes cooked by the chef, Simon Burns, include potato and leek risotto with rabbit salad; puréed red pepper and lentil soup with truffle essence; halibut fillet with langoustine tails roasted with wild garlic; vanilla mousse with brandy and Agen prunes. Two tortoises 'amble round the garden'. Sandy beaches, castles and stately homes are nearby. More reports, please.

Open Mid-Apr–mid-Oct.
Rooms 19 double, 4 single. 5 in grounds. 2 on ground floor.
Facilities Sitting rooms, library, bar, restaurant. No background music. 4-acre grounds: walled garden, croquet, tennis, putting. Golf course adjacent; sea, safe bathing, 10 mins' walk.
Location Signposted off A198 (Gullane High St). Train: Drem; taxi.
Restrictions No smoking in restaurant. No dogs in public rooms.
Credit cards All major cards accepted.
Terms B&B: single £115, double £225. Set lunch £20, dinner £40. Spring and autumn breaks. *V*

INVERNESS Highland — Map 5:C2

Dunain Park
Inverness IV3 8JN

Tel 01463-230512
Fax 01463-224532
Email dunainparkhotel@btinternet.com
Website www.dunainparkhotel.co.uk

César award in 2001

'Difficult to praise too highly.' 'A great find.' 'A beautiful house; a lovely garden; large and comfortable lounges. We had a spacious, exceptionally comfortable, suite. Not in-your-face luxury but quiet hospitality.' 'Achieves the rare combinations of absolute attention to detail with utter lack of pretension.' Just some of this year's 'whole-hearted endorsements' for this 'great hotel'. There was near-unanimous praise for the owners, Edward and Ann Nicoll, their manager, Alexandra Campbell, and staff: 'most warm and welcoming', providing 'five-star service'. The Italianate 19th-century mansion stands in large wooded grounds overlooking the river Ness and the Caledonian Canal. It has a 'homely feel': leather settees, armchairs, log fires, family photographs in the lounges – but the lighting is 'too discreet for needlework or reading', one visitor said. Some bedrooms are in the main house; spacious suites are in a new wing. A small (very warm) swimming pool and sauna are in a log cabin in the grounds. Ann Nicoll now shares the cooking with Justin Sharp. One dissenter found the food 'disappointing', but most called it 'superb', 'wonderful'. Choice is varied; portions are large. There is a separate steak menu, and a *carte* with choices like beef Wellington; bacon-wrapped loin of venison stuffed with haggis; always a vegetarian dish. 'The dessert buffet is a meal on its own.' Children have their own menu. Over 200 malt whiskies are stocked. Breakfasts are copious, with 'good thick toast of the old-fashioned sort', and jams made from home-grown raspberries and strawberries. Good walking and climbing nearby, 20 golf courses, and plenty to see: Loch Ness, Cawdor Castle and Culloden battlefield. (*James L Clarke, Colin Pearson, Iain and Grace Macniven, RJ Hancock, John Partington, Jean and George Dundas, and others*)

Open All year.
Rooms 8 suites (1 with access for ♿), 5 double; two 2-bedroomed cottages in grounds.
Facilities 2 lounges, restaurant; drying room. No background music. 6-acre grounds: croquet, covered swimming pool, sauna. Fishing, shooting, golf, tennis, winter sports nearby.
Location 1 mile S of Inverness. Turn left off A82 after Craig Dunain hospital. Station, 2½ miles; then taxi.
Restrictions No smoking: restaurant, some bedrooms. 'Well-behaved children welcomed.' Dogs by arrangement, not in public rooms.
Credit cards All major cards accepted.
Terms [2001] B&B £49–£99; D,B&B £69–£124. Full alc £35. Low-season rates. 3-day breaks. Christmas/New Year/Easter packages.

See also SHORTLIST

IONA Argyll and Bute — Map 5:D1

Argyll Hotel NEW/BUDGET
Isle of Iona PA76 6SJ

Tel 01681-700334
Fax 01681-700510
Email reception@argyllhoteliona.co.uk
Website www.argyllhoteliona.co.uk

On the 'magical, mystical' little island where John Smith, former leader of the Labour Party, lies buried, this 'small, simple hotel' is the best place to stay, says our inspector. 'It is one of the taller buildings in this tiny village, part of a row of two-storey houses within a minute's walk from the small jetty where the ferry from Mull docks. Reception was very welcoming. We neither expected nor got bag-carrying – we brought our luggage on trolleys supplied at the pier. Our bedroom was small, but had good storage, pleasant watercolours, a collection of elderly but interesting paperback books, and a small but well-planned bathroom. The dining room, though not glamorous, has well-spaced tables, proper tablecloths, friendly, quick service. Dinners were good, if not special: huge fillet steaks, excellent ice cream, good, reasonably priced wines. Breakfast had the usual choice of help-yourself cereals, muesli and juices. Juices, good kippers, butter and marmalade in dishes, very good crisp toast.' Snacks, light lunches and afternoon teas are served. Many ingredients are organically home-grown. The new owner/chefs, Daniel Morgan and Claire Bachellerie, recently redecorated much of the 19th-century building. The dining room, the two lounges (each with a fireplace) and the plant-filled sun lounge all look over the Sound of Iona to the hills of Mull. Children are welcomed; dogs 'are happily accommodated, but the local crofters insist that they are exercised on a lead'. The 11th-century abbey is a quarter of a mile away. Car-free Iona has cliffs, beaches, an 18-hole golf course kept trim by sheep and cattle; boat trips to Staffa and Fingal's Cave can be arranged.

Open Apr–Oct.
Rooms 9 double (8 with facilities *en suite*), 6 single. No telephone/TV.
Facilities 2 lounges, sun lounge with TV, restaurant; small conference room. No background music. Small garden. On sea shore. Unsuitable for ♿.
Location By pier in the only village street. No cars on Iona. Hotel will help with travel arrangements.
Restrictions No smoking in restaurant, some lounges. No dogs in restaurant.
Credit cards MasterCard, Visa.
Terms [2001] B&B £18–£48; D,B&B £31–£65. Full alc £22. Child in parents' room: under 3, £5; 5–15: D,B&B £15; in own room: 50% of adult rate. 1-night bookings sometimes refused. *V*

> The 'Budget' label by a hotel's name indicates an establishment where dinner, bed and breakfast cost around £50 per person, or B&B about £30 and an evening meal about £20. These are only a rough guide, and do not always apply to single accommodation, nor do they necessarily apply in high season.

ISLE ORNSAY Highland Map 5:C1

The Duisdale
Isle Ornsay, Sleat
Isle of Skye IV43 8QW

Tel 01471-833202
Fax 01471-833404
Email marie@duisdalehotel.demon.co.uk
Website www.duisdale.com

'From the minute we arrived we felt at home,' say visitors to Marie Campbell's 19th-century hunting lodge. 'We were treated like special friends.' The setting 'is lovely' – above the Sound of Sleat, in large grounds with woods and wildlife, and the beach is a five-minute walk away The decor is 'traditional and tasteful'. There are antiques and good fabrics throughout, log fires in the lounges, lovely views from many bedrooms (four have a carved oak four-poster bed). Some rooms are small, but still comfortable. There is a cottage in the garden, good for a family. Mrs Campbell and her young staff are 'friendly and professional', and the food is 'exceptional'. 'Terrific dinners' of five courses include, eg, smoked haddock and chive soup; local grilled lobster with sorrel butter; roast loin of hill lamb with rosemary jus; Highland cheeses; hot chocolate soufflé with Drambuie cream. Many herbs and vegetables are home-grown. There's a wide choice at breakfast (eggs Benedict, smoked salmon, wild mushrooms, haddock kedgeree, etc), and the 'lightest of scones', fresh-baked each morning by Mrs Campbell, 'are a talking point among the guests'. Children are made welcome, and will enjoy the dovecote, the lambs and chickens on the farm, and the seals and otters on the beach nearby. Very popular for weddings. (*Rina and Jack Doherty, Colin Pearson*)

Open Mar–end Oct.
Rooms 4 suites, 12 double, 3 single, 2 rooms in garden cottage. No TV.
Facilities Lounge, library, conservatory/TV room, dining room. No background music. 25-acre grounds: gardens, croquet, putting, forest walks. Sea 500 yds. Unsuitable for ♿. Wedding facilities.
Location Near Armadale ferry and Skye Bridge.
Restrictions No smoking: restaurant, bedrooms. No children under 6 at dinner. No dogs.
Credit cards Amex, MasterCard, Visa.
Terms [2001] B&B: single £65–£85, double £80–£130, family £100–£140; D,B&B from £89 per person. Set dinner £24; full alc £32. 3-day breaks. *V*

KELSO Scottish Borders Map 5:E3

Ednam House
Bridge Street
Kelso TD5 7HT

Tel 01573-224168
Fax 01573-226319
Email ednamhouse@excite.co.uk
Website www.ednamhouse.com

A 'magnificent Georgian mansion' (1761), in a 'superb setting' on the river Tweed. Its gardens face open country, but it is near the centre of this small Borders town. The Brooks family have owned and run it since 1928, and now the fourth generation, represented by Ralph and Anne Brooks, 'have brought a new zest to the place'. It has evoked mixed feelings this year: 'Lovely in every way,' writes one visitor.

'The reception rooms are beautifully decorated and furnished,' said another (they are old-fashioned, with patterned wallpaper, elaborate plasterwork and carved wood). Some bedrooms have been refurbished: 'Ours had a tasteful decor, enormous bed, very comfortable mattress, a large bathroom with top-quality fixtures, a power shower, white fluffy towels, bathrobes, lovely toiletries, lashings of hot water.' But the bedrooms in the extension are thought less attractive, and some walls are thin. 'The long, steep staircase to the dining room might be off-putting to some', but the room itself is large, with views over the river, and attractively candlelit at night. 'Service is friendly, by long-serving staff, and the five-course menu is imaginative – one evening it included delicious ostrich.' Other visitors called the cooking 'solid Scottish'. You can take fewer courses at a reduced price. During the morning, there is free coffee in the lounge. One visitor wrote of the 'slightly impersonal atmosphere of a large hotel', but another found the staff attentive, 'and the owners arranged salmon-casting lessons for us at short notice'. The 'laid-back' ambience is liked; *Ednam House* is popular with fishermen and golfers, and dogs are welcomed. Excursions are arranged, to Bamburgh Castle, Holy Island, etc. (*Janice Carrera, Mr and Mrs GA Lilley, and others*)

Open 16 Jan–24 Dec.
Rooms 22 double, 8 single. Suite in cottage planned for autumn 2001.
Facilities 3 lounges, 2 bars, restaurant, TV room. No background music. 3-acre grounds. Unsuitable for ♿.
Location Central, near river Tweed. Parking. Helipad.
Restrictions No smoking: bedrooms, some public areas. No dogs in restaurant.
Credit cards MasterCard, Visa.
Terms [2001] B&B: single £58–£63, double £84–£117; D,B&B: single £83, double £157. Packed lunch available. Set lunch £13, dinner £22. Golf breaks.

KENTALLEN Highland — Map 5:D1

Ardsheal House
Kentallen of Appin
PA38 4BX

Tel 01631-740227
Fax 01631-740342
Email info@ardsheal.co.uk
Website www.ardsheal.co.uk

'What a find! We really were made to feel like guests in a private house.' It is the family home of Neil and Philippa Sutherland, and is furnished with family antiques and portraits; earlier it belonged to the Stewarts of Appin. It stands in a huge estate, one of the oldest natural woodlands in Scotland, on a hill with 'breathtaking' views over Loch Linnhe to the mountains of Morvern. Nearby is the scene of the Appin murder, the inspiration for Robert Louis Stevenson's *Kidnapped*. 'Our stay owed much of its success to the remarkable standards of care and attention from the proprietors. Neil Sutherland, a kilted Highlander, is an accomplished host, with all the restraint and wisdom of Jeeves.' His wife produces 'outstanding' food, aided by a couple from the Philippines. The four-course menus, which always include a soup, have no choice, but vegetarians and special diets are catered for with advance warning. The style of cooking is described as 'British dinner party', eg, gateau of smoked salmon and 'being piped in to dinner was a lovely touch'. Breakfasts include freshly squeezed orange juice and good porridge. The bedrooms vary in size; the best look over the loch. 'From our splendid room, the sunsets over the water and the mountains were more exotic than a whole gallery of pictures.' (*RJ Hancock, John and Yvonne Perry*)

Open Feb–Nov; occasional closures during this period. Lunch not served.
Rooms 1 family, 6 double, 1 single. No TV.
Facilities Hall with seating, 2 sitting rooms, dining room (occasional Scottish background music during dinner), billiard room. 11-acre garden in 800-acre estate: riding, fishing, boating. Sea loch with pebble beach ½ mile. Unsuitable for ♿.
Location 17 miles SW of Fort William, on A828, 5 miles S of Ballachulish bridge. Train to Fort William or bus to Ballachulish.
Restrictions No smoking: dining room, some bedrooms. Dogs by arrangement, not in dining room.
Credit cards Amex, MasterCard, Visa.
Terms B&B £45. Set dinner £25.

KILCHRENAN Argyll and Bute — Map 5:D1

Ardanaiseig
Kilchrenan
by Taynuilt PA35 1HE

Tel 01866-833333
Fax 01866-833222
Email ardanaiseig@clara.net
Website www.ardanaiseig-hotel.com

Romantically situated on the banks of Loch Awe, this grand mansion stands in magnificent, rambling gardens at the end of a three-mile road. Built in the Scottish baronial manner for Colonel Archibald Campbell in 1834, it later became a sedate luxury hotel. This changed when the bearded antiquarian and naturalist, Bennie Gray, bought it on a whim, adding it to his empire of art workshops which includes Gray's Antiques Market, Oxford Street, London. It is now 'a bit off the wall, but in a rather delightful way'. 'Wonderful', 'memorable', guests have written. The decor is bold, if 'slightly eccentric', with antiquities and some audacious colour schemes in the large bedrooms. In a small classical Greek-style amphitheatre by the water, some 'rather way-out' performances of song and dance, many based on the Celtic myths, are held. In the much-admired restaurant, overlooking the lake, chef Gary Goldie serves French-influenced dishes, eg, ravioli of smoked haddock, Meaux mustard sauce and crispy leek; herb-crusted saddle of lamb with shallot purée; prune and Armagnac soufflé with Armagnac anglaise. Coffee, with home-made petits fours, is served by a wood fire in the drawing room. An old steam launch takes guests on Loch Awe, where the hotel owns an island. Dougal, Hector and William Wallace, the Highland cattle, graze in a pasture. 'They love being fed, and having their hair combed,' says the manager, Robert Francis. An 'autumn gold' package entices guests to visit when the trees are at their most beautiful. More reports, please.

Open Mar–3 Jan.
Rooms 16 double. Some on ground floor. Self-catering cottage ¼ mile.
Facilities Drawing room, library/bar, snooker/games room, restaurant

(occasional Celtic background music). 250-acre grounds on loch: gardens, open-air theatre, tennis, croquet, safe bathing, fishing. Unsuitable for ♿. Wedding facilities.
Location From A85, 1 mile E of Taynuilt, take B845 to Kilchrenan. Left at single track by *Kilchrenan Inn*. Continue for 3 miles.
Restrictions No smoking in public rooms, except library. No dogs in public rooms.
Credit cards All major cards accepted.
Terms [2001] B&B: £39–£125; D,B&B £59–£148. Full alc £54.50. Spring/autumn reductions. Christmas package.

Taychreggan
Kilchrenan
by Taynuilt PA35 1HQ

Tel 01866-833211 and 833366
Fax 01866-833244
Email info@taychregganhotel.co.uk
Website www.taychregganhotel.co.uk

In a 'truly tranquil setting' in large, wooded grounds on the banks of Loch Awe, this 300-year-old stone drovers' inn is now a smart hotel. The owner, Annie Paul, has sold a majority share to North American Country Inns (see also *Hunstrete House*, Hunstrete, England). But the manager (for the past five years), Alastair Stevenson, remains. One reporter in 2000 wrote of a poorly maintained bedroom, but a regular *Guide* correspondent, visiting in 2001, was impressed: 'The site is wonderful. Furnishings are comfortable, everything well kept, though our room in a new wing was a bit soulless. Dinner had delicious starters (first-rate soups), main courses a bit complicated, good veg, excellent house wines, terrific cheeses. Service was assiduous without being pushy.' Chef Jerome Prodanu's five-course dinner (modern Scottish cooking) is taken at candlelit antique tables overlooking the loch. Bar lunches are served, alfresco in fine weather, and there is a large array of malt whiskies. Many guests have come for the fishing. The view down the loch 'is magical', and there is 'fantastic scenery' all around. The buildings are arranged around a flowery cobbled courtyard, and furnished in country house style: flagstone floors, good fabrics and rugs, modern art. The bedrooms (best ones are in the old house) are lavishly draped and well equipped; some have a four-poster bed. The drive up the north side of the loch is recommended. Lots to do locally: fishing and boating; walking and picnicking in the forests; historic houses and castles to visit; 13 Munros within an hour's drive. (*Anne Laurence, and others*)

Open All year.
Rooms 1 suite, 18 double. Some have TV.
Facilities 3 lounges, lounge bar, restaurant; jazz/classical background music; snooker room; function rooms. 25-acre grounds on loch: boats, water sports, fishing (ghillie available). Riding, deer-stalking, walking, climbing, golf nearby. Unsuitable for ♿. Wedding facilities.
Location 22 miles SE of Oban. 1 mile E of Taynuilt, turn off A85 on to B845;

follow signs to lochside. Hotel at end of 7-mile single track. Train/bus: Taynuilt; hotel will meet.
Restrictions No smoking: restaurant, most bedrooms. No children under 14. Dogs by arrangement, not in public rooms.
Credit cards Amex, MasterCard, Visa.
Terms B&B: single £65–£105, double £90–£130, suite £215 per person. Set lunch £16.50, dinner £35. Christmas, New Year breaks. *V*

KILLIECRANKIE Perth and Kinross — Map 5:D2

Killiecrankie Hotel NEW
Killiecrankie
by Pitlochry PH16 5LG

Tel 01796-473220
Fax 01796-472451
Email enquiries@killiecrankiehotel.co.uk
Website www.killiecrankiehotel.co.uk

'It is the owners' warmth and care for their guests' welfare that makes this such a welcoming place.' 'Almost like staying in somebody's home.' 'Very good value for money.' Praise came again this year for Colin and Carole Anderson, who have presided since 1988 at their white Victorian former manse. It fell from the *Guide* last year when they put it on the market, but they did not sell, and plan to stay a few more years. The setting is beautiful, at the entrance to the Pass of Killiecrankie, overlooking the river Garry. The bedrooms are 'plain and comfortable, with a Scandinavian feel'. Bathrooms 'have everything you might require'. The little residents' lounge 'is tiny and stuffed with sofas', but there is a 'lovely garden where you can sit during the long summer evenings', and plenty of wildlife – roe deer, red squirrels, birds, etc – in the grounds and beyond. The bar does a flourishing meal trade, and the cooking of Mark Easton in the restaurant is greatly admired: eg, warm pigeon breast salad with bacon, prunes and a Drambuie and orange dressing; grilled sea bass with saffron and roast vegetable couscous; dark chocolate fondant with white chocolate and orange sauce. 'The food is attractively presented without being fussy.' 'Puddings are heavenly.' The wine list has a good selection of half bottles. Breakfast includes black pudding, 'the best scrambled eggs ever', freshly baked croissants. 'The staff, including Australian girls, are friendly and well trained.' Children and dogs are welcomed. A lovely riverside walk starts opposite. Across the river is an RSPB reserve, and the drive through the beeches to the Queen's View of Loch Tummel is recommended, especially in October. Glamis, Scone and Blair castles are nearby. (*Mrs MH Box, John and Sandy Chute; also* Good Pub Guide)

Open All year, except Jan.
Rooms 1 suite, 7 double, 2 single.
Facilities Lounge, bar, restaurant. No background music. 4-acre grounds. Fishing on river Garry ¼ mile; golf nearby. Unsuitable for ♿.
Location 3 miles NW of Pitlochry, off A9. Train/bus: Pitlochry; taxi.
Restrictions No smoking: restaurant, bedrooms. No children under 5 at dinner.
Credit cards MasterCard, Visa.
Terms D,B&B: single £69–£89, double £138–£178. Bar meals. Set dinner £32.50. Reductions for 3 nights or more. Wine-tasting weekends. Christmas package. 1-night bookings sometimes refused.

KINGUSSIE Highland — Map 5:C2

The Cross
Tweed Mill Brae
Kingussie PH21 1TC

Tel 01540-661166
Fax 01540-661080
Email relax@thecross.co.uk
Website www.thecross.co.uk

By the river Gynack, in wooded grounds with native trees, wild flowers, and plenty of wildlife (including red squirrels, a few roe deer), stands Tony and Ruth Hadley's simply but stylishly converted 19th-century stone-built tweed mill. The modest building provides plain but pleasant bedrooms. 'We love it,' says one visitor this year. 'The largest and most comfortable room of our entire trip, with a very well-equipped bathroom,' adds another. There is a chess set in the upstairs sitting room, and modern and local art hangs on the walls. The skilful 'Scottish eclectic' cooking of Ruth Hadley and Becca Henderson is served in a room with rough stone walls and heavy beams. The five-course menu could be: prawn and smoked salmon parcel; pea and mint soup; poached hake on a bed of green lentils; pan-fried fillet of venison, or duck breast oriental; chocolate fondant, crème caramel or cheese. There is no choice until the main course. Portions are large. Continental breakfasts include bowls of fresh raspberries, cherries, peaches, cereals, fresh croissants and home-made jams. A nice touch comes with the bill – guests are presented with all the menus they had, and the names of the wines. Tony Hadley is friendly and 'very helpful with advice and the loan of maps – there is some lovely countryside around to explore'. Local activities include skiing at Aviemore, water sports at Loch Insh, pony-trekking and gliding. The Gynack varies from a gentle stream in summer to a raging torrent in spring when the snow melts. (*Barbara M Wooldridge, HJM Tucker*)

Open 1 Mar–1 Dec. Restaurant closed midday and Tues.
Rooms 9 double. TV, tea-making facilities, on request.
Facilities Ramp. 2 lounges (1 with TV), restaurant. No background music. 4-acre grounds: river (no fishing). Golf, walking, climbing nearby. Only restaurant suitable for ♿.
Location 350 yds up Ardbroilach Rd from traffic lights at town centre. Left at sign down private road. Train/coach to Kingussie; taxi, 'or we collect'.
Restrictions No smoking: restaurant, bedrooms. No children under 8. No dogs.
Credit cards MasterCard, Visa.
Terms Double room: B&B £155; D,B&B £230. Set dinner £37.50. Guests staying 1 night only are expected to dine in. Wine weekends Nov.

KIRKCUDBRIGHT Dumfries and Galloway — Map 5:E2

Gladstone House BUDGET
48 High Street
Kirkcudbright DG6 4JX

Tel/Fax 01557-331734
Email sue@gladstonehouse.freeserve.co.uk

Susan and James Westbrook's 'welcoming B&B' is an imposing Georgian house, once the home of a well-to-do 17th-century merchant, in a central but quiet street. Of the three guest bedrooms, the best is a double whose window seats overlook the impressive architecture of the high street and the maze of gardens running to the river. The bathrooms have a power shower and plenty of towels. One bedroom is small; some walls are thin. The snug residents' lounge is smoke-free and muzak-free, and supplied with board games. Breakfast has plenty of choice, including scrambled eggs and smoked salmon, and haggis. The Westbrooks also run a coffee business, so many types of coffee are on offer. Tea is served in the garden in summer. Susan Westbrook is 'very friendly and a mine of local information'. There are restaurants nearby. Once a thriving port, this attractive town (its name is pronounced Kurcoobrie) is now much favoured by artists: the hotel is in a conservation district. It makes a good base for visiting the Burns trail; Broughton House, a National Trust for Scotland property, is just down the road. Good walking and golf are nearby. More reports, please.

Open All year, except Christmas/New Year.
Rooms 3 double. No telephone.
Facilities Lounge, breakfast room. No background music. ⅓-acre garden. Harbour 5 mins' walk. Unsuitable for ♿.
Location Centre of town, behind MacLellan's Castle, two doors away from Tolbooth. Street parking. Train: Dumfries; then bus/taxi.
Restrictions No smoking. No children under 14. No dogs.
Credit cards MasterCard, Visa.
Terms B&B double £60.65.

Selkirk Arms NEW
High Street
Kirkcudbright DG6 4JG

Tel 01557-330402
Fax 01557-331639
Email reception@selkirkarmshotel.co.uk
Website www.selkirkarmshotel.co.uk

In centre of charming old town: Mr and Mrs Morris's 200-year-old inn (Best Western), once frequented by Robert Burns, and featured as The MacClennan Arms *in Dorothy Sayers'* The Five Red Herrings. *'A bustling place, with exceptionally friendly young staff, ambrosial food [local smoked salmon, scallops, game, cheeses] in bar and restaurant,' says nominator. 16 bedrooms (1 suitable for ♿), 'not fancy', but good-sized, with good bathroom; quietest ones face garden. Lounge, 3 bars. No background music. Closed Christmas. No smoking: restaurant, bedrooms. No dogs in public rooms. All major credit cards accepted. B&B: single £62, double £90, triple £105. Set dinner (2–3 courses) £19.95–£23 [2001].*

LOCHINVER Highland — Map 5:B1

The Albannach
Baddidarroch
Lochinver IV27 4LP

Tel 01571-844407
Fax 01571-844285
Email the.albannach@virginnet.co.uk

The emphasis in this award-winning small hotel, perched high above Lochinver's busy fishing harbour, is 'firmly on food and a genuinely Scottish atmosphere without kitsch', say the 'young, enthusiastic' owner/chefs, Colin Craig and Lesley Crosfield. Their 19th-century house stands in a walled garden, looking across the bay to the Assynt mountains. The public rooms and all but one bedroom enjoy the view. 'The ambience and the cooking are superb,' said an admirer. The five-course no-choice set dinner (special dietary needs are catered for) is served beside a fire in the panelled and candlelit restaurant. Locally caught fish, organic vegetables grown by two Assynt crofters, and free-range local beef and lamb are cooked in a contemporary way, eg, carpaccio of highland beef; roast red pepper soufflé; baked fillet of halibut on marsh samphire; aniseed parfait. Bread and oatcakes are home-baked. Colin Craig 'keeps a good cellar and is happy to give advice'. No bar: drinks and coffee are taken in the panelled 'snug' with its central fireplace, or in a conservatory. 'We have long operated a draconian no-smoking policy,' write the owners, 'though it has been said that the terrace is a fine spot for a post-prandial puff (umbrellas provided).' Plenty of local information. (*BMW*)

Open 15 Mar–30 Nov, possibly Christmas, New Year. Occasionally closed Mon.
Rooms 5 double. 1 in byre, with private patio, 5 yds. No TV.
Facilities Ramp. Snug, conservatory, dining room. No background music. ½-acre garden, 12 acres wild croftland. Sea loch at foot of drive; sandy beaches 2 miles.
Location At foot of hill, ½ mile from village. Right over old stone bridge, signposted Baddidarroch; after ½ mile, cross cattle grid; turn left.
Restrictions No smoking. No children under 12. No dogs.
Credit cards MasterCard, Visa.
Terms D,B&B £82.50–£117. Set dinner £36.

Inver Lodge
Iolaire Road
Lochinver IV27 4LU

Tel 01571-844496
Fax 01571-844395
Email stay@inverlodge.com
Website www.inverlodge.com

'A luxurious hotel in a wonderful position,' writes an appreciative visitor to Anne and Edmund Vestey's modern cliff-top building. It stands in superb highland scenery above Lochinver's harbour, looking across to the Western Isles. 'The views are stunning': surrounding is the spectacular beauty of the mountains of Assynt; below is the sea loch. The external walls of the 'rather barrack-like' construction have been painted this year, 'to soften the architecture'. Inside, the public rooms are spacious, with a traditional decor: patterned carpets, stags' heads, an open fire in the lounge. The spacious bedrooms 'are restful', with clear colours, period furniture, a large bed, fruit renewed daily, fresh flowers, good views. 'Our sophisticated bathroom was tiled in dark green.' The manager, Nicholas Gorton, 'runs the place with great efficiency'; 'the staff are friendly', housekeeping 'is impeccable'. The main caveat in the past has been the food, described by some guests as 'mundane', with 'tiny portions (not for walkers and fishermen)'; we'd be grateful for reports on the 'modern Scottish' cooking of the new chef, Peter Woods. Local lobster, lamb, venison and beef are served in the restaurant, where 'tables are impeccably set; staff are pleasant', picture windows look over the loch, and seals can often be seen. 'Breakfasts are good' and include porridge, fruit, yogurt, smoked haddock, salmon kedgeree. Fishing and stalking can be arranged. (*Val Ferguson, and others*)

Open Apr–Nov.
Rooms 20 double.
Facilities 2 lounges, bar, restaurant; sauna, solarium; gift shop. No background music. 1-acre garden. Sea ½ mile; loch/river trout fishing, birdwatching, walking, stalking nearby. Unsuitable for ♿. Wedding facilities.
Location A837 from Ullapool. Hotel ½ mile from village, above Lochinver Bay. Bus from Inverness, Ullapool, Lairg.
Restrictions No smoking in restaurant. No children under 10 in restaurant at night. No dogs in public rooms.
Credit cards All major cards accepted.
Terms B&B £65–£80; D,B&B £90–£125. Set dinner £30. Discount packages on application. *V*

LOCHRANZA North Ayrshire — Map 5:D1

Apple Lodge BUDGET
Lochranza
Isle of Arran KA27 8HJ

Tel/Fax 01770-830229
Email applelodge@easicom.com

César award in 2000

Once the village manse, this small guest house is close to the sea and a mile from the Kintyre ferry. The 'welcoming hosts' are much admired (Jeannie Boyd cooks; her husband, John, manages), and the meals are 'delicious and attractively served'. *Apple Lodge* offers 'excellent value for money', say *Guide* readers. 'Difficult to fault,' one wrote. 'The silence is deafening.' The bedrooms are warm and comfortable; three are in the main house; a self-contained cottage suite, attached to the house, costs only £5 extra per person. Guests are consulted in advance about the set dinner – no dish is repeated during a stay – which is served at separate tables with candles, crystal and freshly cut flowers. A typical menu includes gateau of locally smoked chicken and avocado with a citrus dressing; chargrilled tuna with ginger and spring onion; terrine of three crushed fruits with a kiwi sauce. No licence; bring your own wine. The lounge has an open fire and board games. Eagles fly over the house; the resident red deer are often only feet away; otters and basking sharks are sometimes seen, and the sun sets romantically over the ruins of Lochranza Castle. There is excellent hill-walking from the doorstep, and a golf course close by. Brodick Castle and gardens are worth a visit. More reports, please.

Open All year, except Christmas, New Year.
Rooms 1 self-contained cottage suite, 3 double. No telephone (payphone available).
Facilities Lounge, 2 dining rooms (light classical background music, if requested, during dinner). ¼-acre garden. Sea loch 200 yds: rocky beach, fishing, sailing. Golf nearby. Unsuitable for ♿.
Location N side of island, on A841, ½ mile past village sign, opposite golf course. Bus from ferry.
Restrictions No smoking: dining room, bedrooms. No children under 12. No dogs.
Credit cards None accepted.

Terms [2001] B&B £30–£35; D,B&B £48–£53. Set dinner £19. 1-night bookings refused in advance in high season.

LYBSTER Highland — Map 5:B2

Portland Arms
Lybster KW3 6BS

Tel 01593-721721
Fax 01593-721722
Email portland.arms@btconnect.com
Website www.portlandarms.co.uk

One of the *Guide*'s most northerly entries, this handsome old granite coaching inn on the A99 is just a mile from the sea, south of Wick. Owned by Jim and Jo Sutherland, it is energetically managed by Mark Stevens with an 'extremely friendly' staff. Newly refurbished, with coordinating colours and a bold use of pattern ('someone has a real eye for fabrics'), the bedrooms are spacious 'and immaculate'. The 'lovely, comfortable' lounge has a peat and log fire. An Aga has been installed for the chef, Meg Sibbald. She provides dishes like spicy fish-cakes with red pepper and chilli dressing; roast collops of venison with skirlie and juniper red wine sauce; also a wide range of snacks, home-made soups and puddings (eg, oaty fruit crumble) and jokily named delights for the young ('dinosaurs for dinner'; 'jiggly jelly'). Toys, books, videos, etc, are supplied for children. Bar lunches are served. Breakfast is 'very good'. Weddings, conferences and family gatherings are catered for. The hotel is set back from the main road, but there is some traffic noise. Nearby is the dramatic Caithness coast with its wildlife and heritage centres; the Orkney Islands are within reach for a day-trip. Aga demonstration breaks are held. (Good Pub Guide*, and others*)

Open All year except 1–3 Jan.
Rooms 4 family, 13 double, 5 single. Some on ground floor.
Facilities Lounge, 2 bars, restaurant; function/wedding facilities; 'gentle traditional' background music throughout. Small garden. Sea, fishing, rock beach 1 mile; golf, deer-stalking, grouse shooting, pony-trekking nearby.
Location On A99, 13 miles SW of Wick, 3 miles N of Latheron. Car park.
Restrictions No smoking: restaurant, bedrooms. No dogs.
Credit cards All major cards accepted.
Terms [2001] B&B: single £45–£55, double £68–£75, suite £75–£85. Full alc £22.50. Christmas package.

MARYCULTER Aberdeenshire *See SHORTLIST* — Map 5:C3

MELROSE Scottish Borders *See SHORTLIST* — Map 5:E3

****

Traveller's tale Guest house in Sussex. The young woman in charge was very pleasant and the food was good, but the dear little baby 'singing' and banging a spoon on her chair all through breakfast we could have done without. The baby was the owner's.

****

MOFFAT Dumfries and Galloway Map 5:E2

Beechwood Country House
Harthope Place
Moffat DG10 9HX

Tel 01683-220210
Fax 01683-220889
Email info@beechwoodhousehotel.co.uk
Website www.beechwoodhousehotel.co.uk

'Set up a quiet track five minutes' walk from town, this is the perfect place to stay. It is friendly and personal; the proprietors are delightful.' 'Jeff and Lynda Rogers work hard to ensure the high standard of service – he got up to make us breakfast 45 minutes before the normal time, so we could get an early start.' Two favourable reports this year on this handsome old house, set amid beech trees in large grounds overlooking the Annan valley. The lounges (one for smokers) 'with high ceilings and lots of easy chairs', and the dining room, are spacious. And while some bedrooms are small, 'beds are comfortable, and the bathrooms provide every imaginable extra'. One dissenting report complained of an 'uncoordinated room, with an out-of-date bathroom', 'amateurish service', loud background music during dinner, and 'disappointing food'. But other visitors enjoyed the cooking of the new chef, Alan Mitchell. The menu changes only once a week, but 'longer-stay guests are asked for their preferences, and given special dishes'. 'Delicious appetisers' precede the five-course dinner, which has main courses like monkfish tails wrapped in smoked bacon with mussels and a saffron sauce; sautéed ribbons of Angus beef in a Pommery mustard sauce. At breakfast, 'grapefruit comes in an artistic arrangement with orange segments', and oatcakes and preserves are home-made. Moffat, just off the M74 and well placed for a stop on the way north or south, is a frequent winner of the 'Scotland in Bloom' award. At least 12 stately homes are within an hour's drive. Edinburgh and Glasgow are 53 and 54 miles away respectively. (*Margaret Box, WK Wood, and others*)

Open 17 Feb–31 Dec.
Rooms 7 double.
Facilities Lounge, lounge bar, conservatory, restaurant (background opera in kitchen during meals). 1-acre garden. Fishing in river Annan, 300 yds; golf, tennis, riding, pony-trekking, rough shooting nearby. Unsuitable for ♿. Wedding facilities.
Location ½ mile from town centre. Turn right off High St at church. Parking. Train: Lockerbie; then bus.
Restrictions No smoking: restaurant, lounge. No dogs in restaurant.
Credit cards Amex, MasterCard, Visa.
Terms B&B: single £58, double £83; D,B&B: single £72.50, double £125. Set lunch £15.50, dinner £26. Reduced rates for children. Winter discounts. Christmas package. *V*

Moffat House
High Street
Moffat DG10 9HL

Tel 01683-220039
Fax 01683-221288
Email moffat@talk21.com
Website www.moffathouse.co.uk

Handsome John Adam house (Best Western) with fine staircase; a hotel since 1950, well modernised but retaining period charm. In main square of town in Annan valley. Traditional/modern cooking in Hopetoun's Restaurant *(classical background music); lounge/bar with light meals, log fire; conservatories. 3-acre grounds. No smoking: restaurant, bedrooms. No dogs in public rooms. Amex, MasterCard, Visa accepted. Wedding/function facilities. Golf packages in conjunction with local club. 21 bedrooms, 2 with 4-poster, some suitable for ♿. B&B: single £50–£65, double £70–£94. Set lunch/dinner £24. More reports, please.*

See also SHORTLIST

MUIR OF ORD Highland **Map 5:C2**

The Dower House
Highfield
Muir of Ord IV6 7XN

Tel/Fax 01463-870090
Email ghg@thedowerhouse.co.uk
Website www.thedowerhouse.co.uk

'Our third visit. Everything as good as ever. There is a fairy-tale quality about it. Our bedroom was luxurious. Dinner was well balanced and delicious.' Robyn and Mena Aitchison cater for both individual guests and house parties in their dower house in large grounds between the rivers Beauly and Conon. The building is 'charming', in *cottage-orné* style, with an abundance of antiques, flowery wallpaper, old carved furniture. The small lounge has a bar concealed in a cupboard, potted plants and many books. Some bedrooms and bathrooms are small, but the best rooms have a large, comfortable bed, and a big bathroom with a freestanding Victorian bath, fluffy towels and 'every conceivable extra'. Three rooms are in a gatehouse. One small boy enjoyed playing the pump organ at the foot of his little bed in his suite's (fortunately soundproof) sitting room. Guests are expected to dine in. Robyn Aitchison's three-course, no-choice dinner is 'modern British', eg, grilled red gurnard with rosemary dressing; fillet of beef with roast butter squash; hot pineapple with rum sauce. Home-made chocolates accompany after-dinner coffee. Generous breakfasts include local heather honey. Over 20 varieties of songbird, and also red kites, have been spotted in the grounds. Close by is some of Scotland's most spectacular scenery, with 'wonderful walking'; also castles, gardens, beaches, distilleries, etc. 'If total peace is what you want, this is the place for you.' (*Val Ferguson*)

Open All year, except Christmas, 2 weeks Nov.
Rooms 2 suites, 4 double. 3 in lodge (also let as self-catering unit).
Facilities Lounge, dining room. No background music. 5-acre grounds: small formal garden, swings, tree house. Walking, fishing, golf, beaches nearby. Unsuitable for ♿.
Location 15 miles NW of Inverness. 1 mile N of Muir of Ord, on A862 to Dingwall; left at double bend sign; through maroon gates.
Restrictions No smoking: dining room, bedrooms. No dogs in public rooms.
Credit cards MasterCard, Visa.
Terms B&B £45–£105. Set lunch £21.00, dinner £35.

NAIRN Highland **Map 5:C2**

Clifton House
Viewfield Street
Nairn IV12 4HW

Tel 01667-453119
Fax 01667-452836
Email macintyre@clifton-hotel.co.uk
Website www.clifton-hotel.co.uk

César award in 1987

'Top marks' again for this rose-covered Victorian stone villa, 'eccentric, but truly comfortable'. 'The care we received was exceptional,' says a visitor in 2001, 'though two French farces were being rehearsed during our stay. No farcical elements in the service, kindness and generosity at this glorious, rambling hotel. The food was faultless.' For 70 years this has been the family home of the kilted owner, J Gordon Macintyre, who presides with an enthusiastic staff. It is crammed with antiques, pictures and theatrical memorabilia, and filled with flowers. In winter, concerts and recitals are held. The drawing room has an open fire and hand-blocked Pugin wallpaper identical to that used in the robing room of the Palace of Westminster in 1849. Stylish bedrooms, of varying sizes and shapes, have antique furniture; some have silk-covered walls, and mirrors to create an illusion of space; one is 'a grand chamber hung with damask round a great four-poster'. 'We chose the delightful top-floor eyrie so we could enjoy the wintry views of the Moray Firth and snowy mountains beyond.' The dining rooms are theatrical in style – the larger one serves as a theatre in winter. Mr Macintyre still cooks, though his son, Charles, is the principal chef, using local or home-grown ingredients on the daily-changing menu. The first two courses, written in French, are well-executed Gallic dishes, eg, foie de volaille au cognac; saumon au beurre blanc. Then come British puddings like chocolate mousse; sherry trifle; then Scottish cheeses. 'The wine list must be the best in Scotland.' Breakfast, served 'without time limit', has fresh juices, good coffee, over 20 different teas, porridge, muesli, oatcakes, free-range eggs, kippers. Snack lunches and picnics are available. Nairn, a pretty grey stone town spread along a park by the shore, is a good centre for sightseeing: Brodie and Cawdor castles, Culloden, Loch Ness, etc. Mr Macintyre, 'both host and guide', is a fount of knowledge about the area. (*David Sulkin*)

Open Mid-Jan–mid-Dec.
Rooms 8 double, 4 single. All with bath (no shower). No telephone/TV.
Facilities Sitting room, 2 drawing rooms, TV room/library, 2 dining rooms (classical background music during dinner); concerts, recitals Sept–Apr. 1-acre garden. Beach, golf, tennis, public swimming pool, fishing, shooting, riding nearby. Unsuitable for ♿. Wedding facilities.
Location Turn E at roundabout on A96 in town centre. Parking. Near train/bus stations.
Restrictions No smoking in 1 dining room. No dogs in dining rooms.
Credit cards All major cards accepted.
Terms B&B: single £60, double £95–£107; D,B&B £85 per person. Full alc £31. Special rates for guests attending performances. *V*

Give the *Guide* positive support. Don't leave feedback to others.

NEWTON STEWART Dumfries and Galloway — Map 5:E1

Kirroughtree House
Newton Stewart DG8 6AN

Tel 01671-402141
Fax 01671-402425
Email info@kirroughtreehouse.co.uk
Website www.kirroughtreehouse.co.uk

Built as a private house in 1719, and later much visited by Robert Burns, this impressive white country mansion, long a hotel, has been owned by the McMillan family since 1992. It stands amid green lawns and shrubs in large grounds adjacent to the Galloway Forest Park. It is managed 'very professionally', says a correspondent, by Jim Stirling. Its oak-panelled lounge, hung with oil paintings, has French windows leading out to the garden. A wooden 'modesty staircase' (with small panels to prevent a glimpse of a lady's ankles) leads to spacious bedrooms. Many have good views. 'Mine, in a tower, was warm and comfortable, with an adjoining sitting room.' The 'excellent chef', Ian Bennett, offers plenty of choice on the four-course menus which can include chicken velouté; millefeuille of scallops and foie gras; supreme of brill with herb risotto, aubergine caviar, braised leeks and mussel and saffron sauce; hot chocolate fondant with chocolate sauce and Armagnac ice cream. Tables are set with white linen, crystal and bone china; men are asked to wear a jacket and tie in the evening. Nearby are many wonderful gardens, and the delightful town of Kirkcudbright. Golf packages can be arranged on the nearby Cally course. More reports, please.

Open Mid-Feb–3 Jan.
Rooms 2 suites, 13 double, 2 single.
Facilities 2 lounges, restaurant. No background music. 8-acre grounds: gardens, tennis, croquet, pitch 'n' putt. Golf, fishing, shooting, stalking, hill-walking nearby. Unsuitable for ♿.
Location 1½ miles NE of Newton Stewart. From A75, take A712 to New Galloway. Hotel driveway 300 yds on left. Bus from Stranraer and Dumfries.
Restrictions No smoking: restaurant, 1 lounge. No children under 10. No dogs in public rooms.
Credit cards Amex, MasterCard, Visa.
Terms B&B £67.50–£100; D,B&B £75–£120. Alc lunch £27.50; set Sun lunch £15, dinner £35. Golfing, gardens breaks, etc. Christmas, New Year packages. 1-night bookings sometimes refused.

OBAN Argyll and Bute — Map 5:D1

Maridon House NEW/BUDGET
Dunuaran Road
Oban PA34 4NE

Tel/Fax 01631-562670
Email maridonhse@aol.com
Website www.west-scotland-tourism.com/maridon-house

At S end of Oban bay, conveniently set 200 yards behind pier where island ferries leave: B&B, 'quiet and friendly, simple but comfortable', in trim old house recently refurbished and painted blue. Run by owner, Mrs Fiona Hall. Small lounge. Dogs welcomed. 8 good bedrooms (1 on ground floor), good bathrooms; cooked breakfasts praised. No smoking. Unsuitable for ♿. Fine view of islands from hill behind; town centre 10 minutes' walk. Occasional closures for owner's holidays. MasterCard, Visa accepted. B&B £16–£20.

See also SHORTLIST

OLDMELDRUM Aberdeenshire *See SHORTLIST* Map 5:C3

ONICH Highland Map 5:C1

Cuilcheanna House BUDGET *Tel* 01855-821226
Onich, by Fort William PH33 6SD *Email* relax@cuilcheanna.freeserve.co.uk

A neat white country guest house in a secluded setting in small grounds, a field away from Loch Linnhe. It has 'wonderful views' across to the hills of Mull. The bedrooms are well furnished, and some have loch views. The owners, Russell and Linda Scott, are 'warm, hospitable hosts', says the nominator. 'We encourage our guests to feel at home in a relaxed atmosphere,' they write, and they describe their food as 'modern home cooking, with peasant and foreign influences'. Linda Scott's four-course no-choice dinner menu, served by candlelight at 7.30, might feature feta frittata; fillet of Mallaig cod with red kidney bean sauce and leek and bacon mash; amaretti semi-freddo with coffee sauce; Scottish farmhouse cheeses. 'The lounge, comfortable but a little small, has log fires, books and TV.' Local wildlife includes roe deer, red squirrels, seals and otters; woodpeckers frequent the garden. Fort William and Glencoe are within easy reach. So is Corran ferry, making day-trips possible to Morvern, the Isle of Mull and the lovely Ardnamurchan peninsula. Autumn breaks (when the colours are particularly beautiful) are offered; wine and food weekends are held. (*SM*)

Open Easter–end Oct.
Rooms 7 double. No telephone/TV.
Facilities Lounge with TV, dining room. No background music. Small garden. Near Loch Linnhe: shingle beach. Unsuitable for ♿.
Location 10 miles SW of Fort William (infrequent buses); off A82 (signposted).
Restrictions No smoking. No children under 12. No dogs in public rooms.
Credit cards MasterCard, Visa.
Terms B&B £29.50–£44.50; D,B&B £50–£65. Autumn breaks. Stays of more than 1 night sometimes encouraged bank holidays, etc.

PEAT INN Fife Map 5:D3

The Peat Inn NEW *Tel* 01334-840206
Peat Inn, by Cupar *Fax* 01334-840530
KY15 5LH *Email* reception@thepeatinn.co.uk
Website www.thepeatinn.co.uk

David Wilson has been bringing inventive *haute cuisine* to the East Neuk of Fife for 30 years in this former village inn, restored to the *Guide* this year by an enthusiastic inspection report. It stands at a crossroads near St Andrews, and is much patronised by locals and visiting golfers. Mr Wilson's artist wife, Patricia, is responsible for the decor, and the francophile couple have created 'a distinct feeling of France'. In 1987, they added *The Residence*, a long, low chalet-style building with eight suites (most are split-level). 'This is a restaurant-with-rooms but, unusually for such places, it has a comfortable sitting room, by the corridor that leads to the bedrooms.' Just as well, as the bar, though 'bright and welcoming, with a roaring fire', can be crowded before dinner. 'The bedrooms are attractive, if slightly aged, with well-matched colours, frills and drapes, nice pictures, efficient heating.' Their sitting rooms overlook the neat garden through large windows. Beds are large; bathrooms are small, but have fluffy white towels and bathrobes, plenty of shelf space. The restaurant, in three dining rooms (two are 'Jacobean'), has good paintings, 'sublimely comfortable upholstered chairs'. 'The food was exceptional, simplicity and sophistication combined; service was faultless. David Wilson transforms the best local ingredients into memorable dishes. Turbot with herbs and shallots, and fillet of beef with potato cake, were cooked to perfection; tempting puddings included a refreshing lemon parfait; trio of caramel ice cream. The formidable wine list is renowned as one of the best in Scotland, though there is little under £20.' Breakfast, brought punctually to the suite, included 'large glasses of freshly squeezed orange juice; perfectly timed boiled eggs'. Inchcolm Abbey, Falkland Palace, Kellie Castle, and a host of pretty fishing villages are nearby.

Open Tues–Sat all year, except Christmas, New Year.
Rooms 8 suites. 1 on ground floor with access for ♿. All in annexe.
Facilities Ramp. Reception lounge, lounge, restaurant. No background music. ½-acre garden.
Location At crossroads of B940 and B941, 6 miles SW of St Andrews.
Restrictions No smoking in restaurant. No dogs in public rooms.
Credit cards Amex, MasterCard, Visa.
Terms B&B: suite £145–£155 (single rate £95). Set lunch £19.50, dinner £30; full alc £40. 3 nights D,B&B for the price of 2, Nov–end Apr.

PEEBLES Scottish Borders — Map 5:E2

Castle Venlaw
Edinburgh Road
Peebles EH45 8QG

Tel 01721-720384
Fax 01721-724066
Email enquiries@venlaw.co.uk
Website www.venlaw.co.uk

Turreted 18th-century mansion, in large wooded grounds on slopes of the Moorfoot hills just off A702, 2 miles NE of Peebles. Welcoming owners, John and Shirley Sloggie; friendly staff. 13 bedrooms, most are 'well-furnished if slightly lacking personal style'; some are large. Families welcomed: tower suite has children's 'den' with bunk beds, games, books. Lounge, library bar (background CDs), restaurant. Good traditional dinners (special grill menu) and bar meals, 'but table d'hôte menu changes only weekly'. Good breakfasts. Fishing in river Tweed, 1 mile. Unsuitable for ♿. No smoking in restaurant. No dogs in public rooms. MasterCard, Visa accepted. B&B £55–£85; D,B&B £55–£95. Set dinner £23. *V*

Cringletie House NEW
Peebles
EH45 8PL

Tel 01721-730233
Fax 01721-730244
Email enquiries@cringletie.com
Website www.cringletie.com

Turreted pink stone Scots baronial mansion, managed by Kellie Bradford, recently extensively refurbished at vast expense. In 28-acre estate (formal gardens and rolling hills) in lovely Borders countryside, 2 miles N of Peebles on A703. 'Highly recommended' by young readers this year. 'Excellent service from friendly staff; superb food'('modern Scottish'). Ramps; lounge, library, conservatory, bar, dining room (no smoking); classical background music at lunch and dinner. Lavish decor: painted ceilings, antiques, leather sofas. Tennis, putting, croquet, walled kitchen garden. 14 golf courses within 30 mins' drive; fishing on river Tweed. No dogs in public rooms. Amex, MasterCard, Visa accepted. 14 bedrooms, 2 on ground floor. B&B £55–£90; D,B&B £80–£110. Set lunch £15.95, dinner £32.90.

See also SHORTLIST

PENNYGHAEL Argyll and Bute — Map 5:D1

Pennyghael Hotel
Isle of Mull PA70 6HB

Tel 01681-704288
Fax 01681-704205

In a tiny village on the shores of Loch Scridain, a deep inlet on the west coast of Mull, stands this small white 17th-century farmhouse. The exterior is plain, and the decor might not be to everyone's taste, but the owners, Tony and Sandra Read, consider the location as one of their main attractions ('we have one of the best views in the UK'). Guests on their third visit concur: 'The views over Loch Scridain to Ben More and Iona are magical, whatever the season. Sometimes one is lucky enough to see an otter close by. The hosts are friendly, the atmosphere is welcoming. The rooms are comfortable and well appointed, and the food is imaginative, and beautifully presented.' Sandra Read's 'Scottish traditional home cooking', using local ingredients and served by candlelight, features, eg, warm salad of pan-seared scallops; slow-roasted crispy duckling à l'orange; brown sugar raspberry meringues with home-made vanilla parfait ice cream. The lounge/bar has a good supply of malt whiskies; the dining room has an open fire and views of Ben More (Mull's highest peak) and Iona. In the morning, fruit salad precedes a traditional Scottish breakfast. There are some spacious self-catering cottages, suitable for families – children under 12 are not allowed in the hotel. The rocky shoreline is home to a huge variety of wildlife: otters, golden eagles, buzzards, red deer, and perhaps a pine marten. The island also has a great variety of wild flowers. Buses are infrequent; a car is essential if you want to tour. (*Eileen and Peter Davis, and others*)

Open Hotel Mar–Oct, cottages all year. Lunch not served.
Rooms 6 double. 2 on ground floor, with ramp. Also 3 self-catering cottages.

Facilities Lounge/bar, dining room. No background music. 1-acre grounds on sea loch (shingle beach).
Location On A849 to Iona, beside Loch Scridain. Ferry from Oban.
Restrictions No smoking in dining room. Children under 12 in self-catering cottages only. No dogs in public rooms.
Credit cards MasterCard, Visa.
Terms B&B £35–£49. Set dinner £24. Reductions for 3 or more nights.

PITLOCHRY Perth and Kinross *See SHORTLIST* Map 5:D2

PLOCKTON Highland Map 5:C1

The Haven
Plockton IV52 8TW

Tel 01599-544223 and 544334
Fax 01599-544467
Website www.smoothhound.co.uk/hotels/thehaven

Built around 1900, this converted merchants' house stands near the harbour in a picturesque National Trust village of white cottages, clusters of small boats and views of steep blue hills ringing the opposite shore of Loch Carron (it was the setting for BBC's *Hamish Macbeth*). The owners, Annan and Jill Dryburgh, 'maintain high standards', say *Guide* correspondents. They offer 'good value', and 'the staff are very friendly'. The bedrooms, including large singles, are 'bright and pretty', with good views. There are two suites; the one at the top of the house up a steep flight of stairs 'was surprising in its spaciousness' with two bedrooms, a sitting room and a bathroom with 'lovely fluffy towels'. The modern Scottish cooking, with a choice of five or six dishes for each course, in the large dining room graced by a pipe organ, has been popular with locals, but this year there is a new chef, so we would appreciate reports. There is 'a good range and quality of half-bottle wines'. 'Enjoyable breakfasts – eggs, bacon, etc cooked to perfection, and memorable porridge.' There are log fires in the lounges for winter, a conservatory for summer. Nearby are Glenelg, and Sandaig where Gavin Maxwell lived. You may see otters on the banks of the loch. (*Pam and Peter Barratt*)

Open 1 Feb–20 Dec. Restaurant closed midday.
Rooms 2 suites, 12 double, 1 single.
Facilities 2 lounges, conservatory, cocktail bar, dining room; Scottish background music evenings. 1¼-acre grounds. Loch 30 yds; boating, fishing, sea trips, etc. Unsuitable for ♿.
Location In village, 5 miles N of Kyle of Lochalsh. Private parking.
Restrictions No smoking: dining room, 1 lounge. No children under 7. No dogs in public rooms.
Credit cards MasterCard, Visa.
Terms B&B £37–£41; D,B&B £55–£75. Mini-breaks.

****

Traveller's tale Hotel in Wales. The room was minuscule, cluttered and unheated. The double bed was right next to the wall and window. I had to crawl across from the other side to get in. No side table for glass, book, etc. The, walls were paper-thin and the noise from the jazz trio in the bar below was loud.

****

PORT APPIN Argyll and Bute Map 5:D1

The Airds Hotel
Port Appin PA38 4DF

Tel 01631-730236
Fax 01631-730535
Email airds@airds-hotel.com
Website www.airds-hotel.com

César award in 1994

'There is no hotel so nice – we never tire of its qualities of peace and kindly attention.' This small building overlooking Loch Linnhe inspires devotees, who 'feel lucky to find such a place in such a wild and beautiful setting'. 'The epitome of luxury and relaxation, it has become our favourite hotel in Scotland.' Once a ferry inn, it is now a sybaritic Relais & Châteaux member, owned by Betty and Eric Allen for many years. Their son, Graeme, is manager, and co-chef with Steve McCallum. They have a *Michelin* star and 'the quality of the food remains high without being pretentious; service is pleasant but unobtrusive'. There are 'wonderful tasty soups, succulent venison, divine puddings'; four courses might include ravioli of lobster and langoustine with samphire, herbs and lobster sauce; fillet of turbot on a pea purée; vanilla panna cotta with poached berries and raspberry sauce. The wine list is 'one of the most judiciously chosen in Scotland'. There is a colourful little garden in front of the hotel. The bedrooms and bathrooms are chic and pretty; some, at the top, are small. 'The suite was beautifully decorated and warm, and the bathroom big enough to contain a family of five.' The drawing rooms are 'inviting', with chintzes, patterned carpets, pictures of Scottish scenes, open fires and flowers. The little conservatory, in front, is 'a delightful place for pre-dinner drinks, always accompanied by delicious nibbles'. A short walk leads to Port Appin and a boat-trip to Lismore; seals can sometimes be seen playing in the loch. (*Jean and George Dundas, Val Ferguson, Mr and Mrs JE Rednall*)

Open All year, except Christmas, 6–26 Jan.
Rooms 1 suite, 11 double. 2 on ground floor. Also 4 double (budget) in *Linnhe House* 60 yds.
Facilities Lounge, conservatory, restaurant. No background music. 1-acre garden. Near loch: shingle beach, bathing, fishing, boating; pony-trekking, forest walks nearby. Unsuitable for ♿.
Location 2 miles off A828, 25 miles from Fort William (N) and Oban (S). Parking.
Restrictions No smoking: restaurant, bedrooms. No dogs in public rooms.
Credit cards MasterCard, Visa.
Terms D,B&B £105–£165. Set dinner £50. 3-day New Year package.

Hotels will often try to persuade you to stay for two nights at the weekend. Resist this pressure if you want to stay only one night.

PORT CHARLOTTE Argyll and Bute Map 5:D1

Port Charlotte Hotel NEW
Main Street
Port Charlotte
Isle of IslayPA48 7TUPA48 7TU

Tel 01496-850360
Fax 01496-850361
Email carl@portcharlottehot.demon.co.uk
Website www.milford.co.uk/go/portcharlotte

Port Charlotte is a conservation village on the southernmost of the Inner Hebrides, and this recently restored Victorian hotel stands on the west shore of Loch Indaal. It is 'exceptional', say the nominators: 'Welcoming, comfortable, with amazing views. The food was interesting and excellent, as were the whiskies. The locals in the bar were unusually friendly, and we discovered that one of them was responsible for the cows that provided the beef (rather mysteriously, this appeared on the Seafood Lunch menu).' Islay lamb, game, oysters, scallops and crab also feature on the daily-changing *à la carte* menus – the chef, Alan Bell, prepares them in 'modern Scottish' style. Vegetarians are catered for. Open fires warm the bar and the residents' lounge. Almost all the bedrooms look over the sea; they have antiques, and oriental rugs on bare floorboards. Islay is a birdwatcher's paradise. Its climate is 'variable, but mild, owing to its position astride the Gulf Stream', say the resident owners, Carl and Jan Reavey. 'Its varied land and seascapes range from spectacular cliffs to magnificent, often deserted, beaches where otters play and seals bask in the sun.' (*Dr Lesley Kay and Dr Nick Booth*)

Open All year, except Christmas Day.
Rooms 8 double, 2 single. 2 on ground floor.
Facilities Residents' lounge, public bar, restaurant; traditional Scottish music sometimes; conservatory. Small garden. Beach opposite.
Location Centre of village on W shore of Loch Indaal, 7 miles N of Rinns Point.
Restrictions No smoking: restaurant, bedrooms. No dogs in public rooms, except conservatory.
Credit cards MasterCard, Visa.
Terms [2001] B&B: single £55–£59, double £60–£90. Full alc £31. 3 nights for the price of 2 Oct–Mar.

PORTREE Highland Map 5:C1

Viewfield House
Portree
Isle of Skye
IV51 9EU

Tel 01478-612217
Fax 01478-613517
Email info@viewfieldhouse.com
Website www.viewfieldhouse.com

César award in 1993

Standing in large wooded grounds on the outskirts of Skye's main town, this baronial pile is the family home – since the 18th century – of Hugh Macdonald, who runs it as a guest house with his Californian wife, Linda. Little has changed since before 1914, save the plumbing, and last year's newfangled addition of telephones in bedrooms – a rare concession to the modern world. It is thought 'splendidly eccentric'; stags' horns, stuffed eagles and fading family portraits are among its adornments, and the hall is a repository of imperial mementos: Persian carpets, Burmese gongs, Benares brass, and bric-a-brac of the Raj. Visitors enjoy the 'good food and warm friendliness' provided by the 'charming owners'. The bedrooms are well furnished; most are large, with a large bathroom (no shampoos, etc), and a view of the loch; one on the nursery floor is small, with a minute bathroom. An open fire burns in the 'gorgeous sitting room'. No hotel-style reception and facilities, and no formal bar, but drinks are served at any time on request. A gong announces dinner, served with heavy old family silver and crystal in the candlelit dining room with its antique wallpaper. There is no choice in the five-course dinners ('traditional British with the occasional US touch'), but vegetarian dishes and a fish option for the main course are always available. Fillets of venison with hawthorn sauce, or cod with leeks and ginger might follow twice-cooked smoked salmon and dill soufflé, or creamy dahl soup. Helpings are large, with up to five different vegetables. Puddings include almond shortcake with spiced apples; then come Scottish cheeses. For after-dinner entertainment there is 'good conversation'. Breakfasts 'are good, with high-quality local produce'. Laundry facilities for guests are now available. (*C and MD*)

Open Mid-Apr–mid-Oct.
Rooms 10 double, 2 single, 10 with private facilities. 1 on ground floor suitable for ♿. No TV.
Facilities Drawing room, morning/TV room, dining room. No background music. 20-acre grounds: croquet, swings, woodland walks, garden centre. Sea fishing 200 yds, river fishing 2 miles.
Location S side of Portree, 10 mins' walk from centre. Take A87 towards Broadford; turn right just after BP station on left. Bus from Portree passes entrance.
Restrictions No smoking: dining room, bedrooms. No dogs in public rooms.
Credit cards MasterCard, Visa.
Terms B&B £35–£47.50. Set dinner £20. Packed lunches available. 3/5-day rates. 1-night group bookings sometimes refused. *V*

ST ANDREWS Fife *See SHORTLIST* — Map 5:D3

ST MARGARET'S HOPE Orkney — Map 5:A3

The Creel Inn — *Tel* 01856-831311
Front Road — *Email* alan@thecreel.freeserve.co.uk
St Margaret's Hope KW17 2SL — *Website* www.thecreel.co.uk

Alan and Joyce Craigie's restaurant-with-rooms, revamped this year (redecorated throughout; new breakfast room). On seafront of main village of South Ronaldsay, 20 mins' drive S of Orkney's capital, Kirkwall. 'Lovely food; comfortable, if simple, accommodation'; good views across bay. Alan Craigie, 'an excellent and talented chef', cooks with 'Orcadian influence', especially seafood and local meat, eg, crab and mussel bisque; North Ronaldsay lamb terrine; salmon, wolf-fish and sea bream stew. Good breakfasts (porridge, local kippers). Small lounge, 2 dining rooms. Open Apr–Oct. Unsuitable for ♿. No smoking:

restaurant, bedrooms. Guide dogs only. MasterCard, Visa accepted. 4 bedrooms (1 in annexe). B&B: single £40–£50, double £55–£70. Set dinner £30. More reports, please.

SCARISTA Western Isles **Map 5:B1**

Scarista House NEW
Scarista
Isle of Harris HS3 3HX

Tel 01859-550238
Fax 01859-550277
Email timandpatricia@scaristahouse.com
Website www.scaristahouse.com

A welcome return to the *Guide* for this remote small guest house: 'The location is one of the most beautiful in Britain, with its prospect of the huge beach and the Atlantic beyond. We have stayed regularly for some 20 years, most recently with our small daughter in one of the comfortable cottages on a terrace behind the main house. The new owners, Tim and Patricia Martin, combine professional management with friendliness, and many members of staff are old hands. The food is excellent in a straightforward way, and the wine list is interesting and fairly priced.' Local ingredients are used in the menus (eg, prawn and squat lobster bisque; scallops and lemon sole in wine, butter and basil). Organic bread is home-baked; jams, marmalade, ice creams and yogurt are home-made. The Martins and their co-owner, Neil King, have completely redecorated the listed Georgian manse. 'The bedrooms are not large,' they write, 'but all have sea views. We have tried to choose furniture and fabrics that reflect the period of the house, and there are antiques, paintings and books in every room.' A drawing room and library, both with a fire, are available to guests. No TV; plenty of classical CDs. Wildlife abounds on Harris; fishing can be arranged, and close to the house is a 'spectacular' nine-hole golf course where Nick Faldo has played. (*Brian and Lesley Knox*)

Open All year, except Christmas, occasionally in winter.
Rooms 5 double. 2 in annexe. Also 2 self-catering cottages. No TV.
Facilities Drawing room, library, dining room. No background music. 1-acre garden. Sandy beach 200 yds. Golf, fishing nearby. Unsuitable for ♿.
Location 15 miles SW of Tarbert on A859. Bus from Tarbert.
Restriction No smoking: dining room, bedrooms.
Credit cards MasterCard, Visa.
Terms B&B £65–£80. Set dinner £32. 3 nights for the price of 2 in winter.

SCOURIE Highland **Map 5:B2**

Eddrachilles NEW
Badcall Bay
Scourie IV27 4TH

Tel 01971-502080
Fax 01971-502477
Email enq@eddrachilles.com
Website www.eddrachilles.com

'We have stayed here 19 years in succession. It may not be everyone's cup of tea, but we find it unsurpassed for a combination of price, quality and efficiency. The views are spectacular.' 'There are not many hotels in this remote and beautiful part of Scotland, and good hotels are even harder to find, but you need look no further than this.'

Two reports on this 200-year-old building return it to the *Guide*. Owned and run for many years by Mr and Mrs Alistair Wood, it stands in a large estate, overlooking beautiful island-studded Badcall Bay: The interior is 'mainly modern, and spotless', and the owners and staff are 'very friendly'. Mr Wood is 'always at hand when needed, but is never obtrusive', and 'every guest is greeted by name'. 'There is a large and comfortable lounge attached to an attractive sunroom; the dining room, in the oldest part of the house, has a stone-flagged floor, and lots of character.' Mrs Wood's three-course menus change daily, and the 'beautifully cooked food, faultlessly served' can include salmon fish-cakes; roast topside of beef; apple crumble and custard. There is always a vegetarian choice. The bedrooms are 'not over-large, but well designed and well equipped'. A good base for exploring this area of 'breathtaking beauty, with its lovely beaches, lochs and mountains, and abundant wildlife'. The magnificent cliffs of the Handa Island bird sanctuary are nearby. (*Roger Hughes, AJ Gillingwater*)

Note: As we went to press we learned that the hotel was on the market.

Open 21 Mar–21 Oct.
Rooms 11 double, some on ground floor.
Facilities 2 lounges, lounge bar (classical background music at night), bar, restaurant. 320-acre grounds. Sea 100 yds. Membership of local angling club arranged. Unsuitable for ♿.
Location On A894 2 miles S of Scourie, signposted and visible from main road.
Restrictions No smoking in restaurant. No children under 3. No dogs.
Credit cards MasterCard, Visa.
Terms B&B £40–£61; D,B&B £50–£73. Set dinner £13.20; full alc £29.50. Reductions for 3 or more nights.

SHIELDAIG Highland — Map 5:C1

Tigh an Eilean — *Tel* 01520-755251
Shieldaig — *Fax* 01520-755321
Loch Torridon IV54 8XN — *Email* tighaneileanhotel@shieldaig.fsnet.co.uk

'Our favourite hotel in Scotland, still as perfect as ever.' 'Excellent, in a charming spot.' 'Terrific. Scores highly for value for money.' In their old inn on the shores of Loch Torridon, Christopher and Cathryn Field offer 'high standards of food, comfort and service', say their many admirers. The group of old slated buildings stands by the sea in an enchanting fishing village' amid the 'dazzlingly beautiful, wild countryside' of Wester Ross. It looks across the shore to Shieldaig island, a National Trust sanctuary for ancient pines, and there is 'good rock pool exploration' on the shore at low tide. Bedrooms are 'tastefully furnished'; the two lounges (one has a wood-burning stove) are 'cosy and pretty'; there is a library/bar with many books on the area. Christopher Field and the new head chef, Alasdair Robertson, produce 'Scottish/classical French' cooking using home-grown herbs and local ingredients. The emphasis is on fish and shellfish (delivered each day from the jetty), eg, scallops in a vine tomato filo basket; crab thermidor; warm chocolate tart with whisky cream. The three-course menu changes each night, and the wine list 'contains some real bargains'. Good bar snacks are served (eg, seafood stew) – this is the village pub; in fine weather, visitors sit on benches admiring the view. The copious breakfasts include 'excellent porridge'. Children are flexibly catered for, and 'well-behaved dogs' are welcomed. Guests may look at the stars through a ten-inch astronomical telescope; the hotel owns some kayaks; small boats can be hired in the village; fishing can be arranged; there is good walking and climbing, and a nine-hole golf course at Lochcarron. (*Anne P Heaton, Mr and Mrs Tom Miller, William Goodhart; also* Good Pub Guide)

Open Early Apr–end Oct.
Rooms 8 double, 3 single. No telephone/TV.
Facilities Lounge, lounge with TV and wood-burning stove, bar/library, village bar (separate entrance), dining room; drying room. No background music. Small front courtyard, small rear garden. Fishing, swimming, hill-walking, golf nearby. Unsuitable for ♿.
Location Centre of quiet village off A896. Parking opposite. Train: Strathcarron; bus connects with lunchtime train, or they will meet.
Restrictions No smoking: dining room, 1 lounge. No dogs in public rooms.
Credit cards MasterCard, Visa.
Terms [2001] B&B £49.50–£55; D,B&B £76.50–£82. Bar meals. Set dinner £27. Child in parents' room: under 8, free; 8–13, 50% of adult rate. Reductions for 3 or more nights.

SKIRLING Scottish Borders — Map 5:E2

Skirling House
Skirling, Biggar ML12 6HD

Tel 01899-860274
Fax 01899-860255
Email enquiry@skirlinghouse.com
Website www.skirlinghouse.com

'The finest small hotel we know in Britain – not to say anywhere.' Praise again for Bob and Isobel Hunter's ever-popular Wolsey Lodge, on the green of a tiny village amid lovely Borders scenery. It was built in 1908 as the summer home of the Scottish art connoisseur, Lord Carmichael, and is a fine example of the Arts and Crafts movement, with decorative carvings, remarkable wrought iron sculptures of animals, and in the drawing room, a 16th-century carved wood Florentine ceiling. Bob Hunter is in charge of the guests and the cooking – he is 'a magician in the kitchen', one regular wrote. His wife, who has a full-time job as an equities banker in Edinburgh, helps and serves dinner in the evenings. 'They are bright and charming people, with whom it is a pleasure to discuss almost anything.' The house is elegantly furnished; bedrooms and beds are large; bathrooms are spacious. The four-course no-choice dinners, served at 8 pm (usually at separate tables), are always enjoyed. The cooking is 'modern Scottish, with influences from the US and Asia', eg, venison carpaccio; honey-roast quail; regional cheeses; chocolate fondant with malt ice cream. There is an 'excellent wine list'. You can take drinks in the garden; afternoon tea with fruit cake, and after-dinner coffee, are served beside a fire in the lounge. 'Breakfasts are wonderful; in addition to ordinary fare, there is always a special – Finnan haddock, scrambled eggs with smoked salmon and chives, French toast with apples and blood pudding – plus extras like potato scones, fantastic fruit compotes and home-made fruit muffins.' Two black Labradors and two 'beautiful cats' are much in evidence, and the owners' chickens supply fresh eggs. A good base for exploring the Borders, also New Lanark, Neidpath Castle, Traquair House, and Peebles. (*Robert Freidus*)

Open Mar–after New Year. Closed 1 week Nov.
Rooms 4 double. 1 on ground floor. Also 2 cottages (normally self-catering).
Facilities Drawing room, study, library, dining room, conservatory. No background music. 5½-acre garden adjoining 100-acre farm: tennis, croquet. Fishing on river Tweed.
Location Opposite green in lower part of village on A72, 2 miles E of Biggar. Local buses.
Restrictions No smoking. Dogs by arrangement, not in public rooms.
Credit cards MasterCard, Visa.
Terms B&B £35–£45. Set dinner £22. *V*

SPEAN BRIDGE Highland — Map 5:C1

Old Pines
Spean Bridge
by Fort William
PH34 4EG

Tel 01397-712324
Fax 01397-712433
Email goodhotel@oldpines.co.uk
Website www.oldpines.co.uk

Standing among Scots pines in large grounds above a Highland village is this informally run restaurant-with-rooms run by Bill and Sukie Barber (they like to be known by their first names). Converted in 1990 from their family home, which was built some 20 years ago in Scandinavian style, it has fine views across to Aonach Mor and Ben Nevis. Children are welcomed (the Barbers have five of their eight children still at home); they take high tea in the kitchen with the hosts' children (although older children can eat in the restaurant, minimum charge £17.50) and play together among the ducks, geese and assorted resident animals. There are toys, play areas, snooker, table tennis, etc. There was high praise again this year (but some criticism, too). 'A most enjoyable stay. Laid-back, but highly efficient. First-class food and service.' 'Magnificent meals, much enjoyed in the dinner-party setting of shared tables. The atmosphere was unique, and so relaxed it hardly felt like a hotel – might not be some people's style.' And indeed it wasn't. 'We found the atmosphere rather intense, with the feeling that you were intruding in someone's family home,' said one report. One family were unhappy that they had not been warned about the no-choice communal eating, and found the arrangements 'too chaotic' for true child-friendliness. The dinner menu, served at '7.30-ish', is displayed at teatime, so that alternatives can be requested. The food is generally praised: this was a *Good Food Guide* restaurant of the year in 2000, and Sukie Barber is a Master Chef of Great Britain. Five-course dinners include, eg, Mallaig fish soup with garlic mayonnaise; salad of prawns and smoked mussels; roast lamb with kidney and a barley, leek and herb risotto; lemon and raspberry posset. For breakfast there is freshly squeezed orange juice, home-smoked bacon and salmon, scrambled eggs from the Barbers' hens. Bread, preserves, pasta and ice creams are home-made; locally grown organic fruit and vegetables are used. The bedrooms have a smart, 'modern rustic' decor, but some walls are thin. As it is all on one level, the house is suitable for wheelchair visitors. The half-board rate includes early morning tea, and afternoon tea with scones and cakes. (*Mr and Mrs Tom Mills, Mrs EJ Gleason, and others*)

Open All year except Christmas, last week Nov–1st week Dec. Restaurant closed Mon, and Sun night to non-residents.
Rooms 1 family suite, 6 double, 1 single. All on ground floor. 5 suitable for ♿. No telephone.
Facilities Ramp. 3 sitting rooms, restaurant; children's playroom. No background music. 30-acre grounds: children's play areas. Free loch fishing 2 miles, sea 10 miles. Wedding facilities.
Location 1 mile N of Spean Bridge. Turn off A82 on to B8004 by Commando Memorial; 300 yds on right. Train: Fort William; then bus or they will meet.
Restrictions No smoking. Children 'encouraged into playroom' after 7 pm. No dogs in house.
Credit cards MasterCard, Visa.
Terms D,B&B: single £65–£80, double £130–£160, family £185–£240. Full alc lunch £21.50; set dinner £24.50–£30. Child in parents' room: £7.50 plus food. 3/7-night rates. Winter packages. *V*

STRATHYRE Stirling — Map 5:D2

Creagan House
Strathyre FK18 8ND

Tel 01877-384638
Fax 01877-384319
Email eatandstay@creaganhouse.co.uk
Website www.creaganhouse.co.uk

Warm praise continues for Gordon and Cherry Gunn's restaurant-with-rooms in a sheltered valley at the head of Loch Lubnaig: 'A friendly welcome (met at the door by Cherry) in relaxing surroundings.' 'Every dinner was delicious' (*Michelin Bib Gourmand*). The 17th-century farmhouse is full of character: the old parlour and the small drawing room are filled with ornately carved antique pieces of Scottish furniture, and miscellaneous objects and souvenirs. The dining room is a 1970s 'baronial-style' addition, with a steep vaulted ceiling, a highly polished oak floor, trestle tables. A vast fireplace, flanked by stone lions and adorned with swords and flags, occupies one end of the room, which is warmed by a vigorous gas log fire. The bedrooms are cottagey, with dark oak beams and furniture (one has a four-poster bed). 'Ours had a two-seater sofa, much appreciated – so many hotels furnish a double room with only one chair.' Gordon Gunn's cooking is 'adventurous, and of a high standard – wonderful smokie in a pokie'; other dishes: saffron scallops with angel hair spaghetti; loin of venison on wild mushroom risotto with truffle, juniper and Madeira sauce. The plentiful vegetables (many are organically grown) are 'perfectly cooked'. 'Very good' breakfasts, 'served at almost any time', include 'supper porridge', 'unbeatable black pudding', home-made jams and preserves, sometimes kidneys. Visitors' dogs are welcomed (their owners are asked to make a donation to Guide Dogs for the Blind).

Plenty of activities are available (see below); local sights include Scone Palace, Stirling Castle, Drummond Castle gardens, the Scottish Antiques and Arts Centre at Doune. (*MC and AM Allwood, Gill and Dave Crawshaw*)

Open All year, except 20 Jan–2 Mar, 1 week Oct. Restaurant closed midday, except for pre-arranged groups.
Rooms 5 double. 1 on ground floor. TV on request. No telephone.
Facilities Lounge, restaurant; writing/private dining room. No background music. 1-acre grounds: stream; access to Queen Elizabeth Forest Park. Golf, fishing, shooting, climbing, cycling, water sports nearby.
Location ¼ mile N of village, set back from A84 (some traffic noise).
Restrictions No smoking: restaurant, bedrooms. No dogs in public rooms.
Credit cards Amex, MasterCard, Visa.
Terms B&B: single £52.50, double £85. Set dinner £25.50. 10% reduction for 3 or more days. Christmas package. *V*

STRONTIAN Highland — Map 5:C1

Kilcamb Lodge
Strontian
PH36 4HY

Tel 01967-402257
Fax 01967-402041
Email kilcamblodge@aol.com
Website www.kilcamblodge.co.uk

César award in 1997

'Good food, a perfect setting by the loch, a cosy room beautifully furnished, *really* deluxe, and all for less than half the price we paid at a more "hallowed", but less satisfying, hotel.' A visitor this year pays tribute to Peter and Anne Blakeway's stone house, Georgian with Victorian additions, on the edge of a small village on Loch Sunart. It is reached by a steep drive off a scenic road through Glen Tarbert, after a short ride on the Corran ferry. Many guests have been coming for years, and the atmosphere is bright, breezy, with laughter in the bar'. In the 'spectacularly beautiful' surrounding countryside there is much wildlife: red deer, squirrels, otters, seals, pine martens, hawks, golden eagles. Inside are open fires, fresh flowers, decorative plates. The 'well-appointed' bedrooms are priced according to size and aspect; the best ones are spacious, with handsome fabrics, a window seat and a loch view. 'Housekeeping is very good, service is unobtrusive; Peter Blakeway is an affable host.' His father, Gordon, grows organic fruit, vegetables and herbs, and catches fish for the kitchen. Visitors like the pricing structure: on top of the room rate, you pay for breakfast and dinner according to what you consume. Some would like more daily change on the menu, but the meals are generally enjoyed. The chef, Neil Mellis, cooks modern dishes, using local beef, lamb and venison. Smoked salmon layered with Lochaber smoked cheese with a lemon and caper dressing is 'an old favourite'; spinach and Parmesan tart is 'a perfect starter or light main course'. The Gordon girls – free-range chickens – provide fresh eggs, and breakfast has freshly squeezed fruit juices, newly baked croissants, a good selection of cereals. Stricker, the black Labrador, 'will lead the way on walks'. A day-trip to Mull or Skye is possible, or an outing in *Kilcamb*'s fishing boat. (*Pat Darby, JCP Cole, PH*)